Get the eBook FREE!

(PDF, ePub, Kindle, and liveBook all included)

We believe that once you buy a book from us, you should be able to read it in any format we have available. To get electronic versions of this book at no additional cost to you, purchase and then register this book at the Manning website.

Go to https://www.manning.com/freebook and follow the instructions to complete your pBook registration.

That's it!
Thanks from Manning!

Data Science Bookcamp

Data Science Bookcamp

FIVE PYTHON PROJECTS

LEONARD APELTSIN

MANNING

SHELTER ISLAND

For online information and ordering of this and other Manning books, please visit www.manning.com. The publisher offers discounts on this book when ordered in quantity. For more information, please contact

    Special Sales Department
    Manning Publications Co.
    20 Baldwin Road
    PO Box 761
    Shelter Island, NY 11964
    Email: orders@manning.com

Development editor:	Elesha Hyde
Technical development editors:	Arthur Zubarev and Alvin Raj
Review editors:	Ivan Martinović and Adriana Sabo
Production editor:	Deirdre S. Hiam
Copy editor:	Tiffany Taylor
Proofreader:	Katie Tennant
Technical proofreader:	Raffaella Ventaglio
Typesetter:	Dennis Dalinnik
Cover designer:	Marija Tudor

Manning Publications Co.
20 Baldwin Road
PO Box 761
Shelter Island, NY 11964

ISBN: 9781617296253
Printed in the United States of America

To my teacher, Alexander Vishnevsky,
who taught me how to think

brief contents

contents

preface

Another promising candidate had failed their data science interview, and I began to wonder why. The year was 2018, and I was struggling to expand the data science team at my startup. I had interviewed dozens of seemingly qualified candidates, only to reject them all. The latest rejected applicant was an economics PhD from a top-notch school. Recently, the applicant had transitioned into data science after completing a 10-week bootcamp. I asked the applicant to discuss an analytics problem that was very relevant to our company. They immediately brought up a trendy algorithm that was not applicable to the situation. When I tried to debate the algorithm's incompatibilities, the candidate was at a loss. They didn't know how the algorithm actually worked or the appropriate circumstances under which to use it. These details hadn't been taught to them at the bootcamp.

After the rejected candidate departed, I began to reflect on my own data science education. How different it had been! Back in 2006, data science was not yet a coveted career choice, and DS bootcamps did not yet exist. In those days, I was a poor grad student struggling to pay the rent in pricey San Francisco. My graduate research required me to analyze millions of genetic links to diseases. I realized that my skills were transferable to other areas of analysis, and thus my data science consultancy was born.

Unbeknownst to my graduate advisor, I began to solicit analytics work from random Bay Area companies. That freelance work helped pay the bills, so I could not be too choosy about the data-driven assignments I tackled. Thus, I would sign up for a variety of data science tasks, ranging from simple statistical analyses to complex predictive modeling. Sometimes I would find myself overwhelmed by a seemingly intractable data problem, but in the end, I'd persevere. My struggles taught me the nuances of diverse analytics techniques and how to best combine them to reach elegant solutions. More importantly, I learned how common techniques can fail and how to surmount these failure points to deliver impactful results. As my skill set grew, my data science career began to flourish. Eventually, I became a leader in the field.

Would I have achieved the same level of success through rote memorization at a 10-week bootcamp? Probably not. Many bootcamps prioritize the study of standalone algorithms over more cohesive problem-solving skills. Furthermore, the hype over an algorithm's strengths tends to be emphasized over its weaknesses. Consequently, students are sometimes ill prepared to handle data science in real-world settings. That insight inspired me to write this book.

I decided to replicate my own data science education by exposing you, my readers, to a set of increasingly challenging analytics problems. Additionally, I chose to arm you with tools and techniques required to handle these problems effectively. My aim is to holistically help you cultivate your analytic problem-solving skills. This way, when you interview for that junior data science position, you will be much more likely to get the job.

acknowledgments

Writing this book was very hard. I definitely could not have done it alone. Fortunately, my family and friends provided their support during this arduous journey. First and foremost, I thank my mother, Irina Apeltsin. She kept me motivated during those difficult days when the task before me seemed insurmountable. Additionally, I thank my grandmother, Vera Fisher, whose pragmatic advice kept me on track as I plowed through the material for my book.

Furthermore, I'd like to thank my childhood friend Vadim Stolnik. Vadim is a brilliant graphic designer who helped me with the book's myriad illustrations. Also, I want to acknowledge my friend and colleague Emmanuel Yera, who had my back during my initial writing efforts. Moreover, I must mention my dear dance partner Alexandria Law, who kept my spirits up during my struggles and also helped pick out this book's cover.

Next, I thank my editor at Manning, Elesha Hyde. Over the course of the past three years, you've worked tirelessly to ensure that I deliver something truly of value to my readers. I will forever be grateful for your patience, optimism, and ceaseless commitment to quality. You've pushed me to become a better writer, and my readers will ultimately benefit from these efforts. Additionally, I'd like to acknowledge my technical development editor Arthur Zubarov and my technical proofreader Rafaella Ventaglio. Your inputs helped me craft a better, cleaner book. I also thank Deirdre Hiam, my project editor; Tiffany Taylor, my copyeditior; Katie Tennant, my proofreader; and everyone else at Manning who had a hand in this book.

To all the reviewers—Adam Scheller, Adriaan Beiertz, Alan Bogusiewicz, Amaresh Rajasekharan, Ayon Roy, Bill Mitchell, Bob Quintus, David Jacobs, Diego Casella, Duncan McRae, Elias Rangel, Frank L Quintana, Grzegorz Bernas, Jason Hales, Jean-François Morin, Jeff Smith, Jim Amrhein, Joe Justesen, John Kasiewicz, Maxim Kupfer, Michael Johnson, Michał Ambroziewicz, Raffaella Ventaglio, Ravi Sajnani, Robert Diana, Simone Sguazza, Sriram Macharla, and Stuart Woodward—thank you. Your suggestions helped make this a better book.

about this book

Open-ended problem-solving abilities are essential for a data science career. Unfortunately, these abilities cannot be acquired simply by reading. To become a problem solver, you must persistently solve difficult problems. With this in mind, I've structured my book around case studies: open-ended problems modeled on real-world situations. The case studies range from online advertisement analysis to tracking disease outbreaks using news data. Upon completing these case studies, you will be well suited to begin a career in data science.

Who should read this book

This book's intended reader is an educated novice who is interested in transitioning to a data science career. When I imagine a typical reader, I picture a fourth-year college student studying economics who wishes to explore a broader range of analytics opportunities, or a chemistry major already out of school who is searching for a more data-centric career path. Or perhaps the reader is a successful frontend web developer with a very limited mathematics background who would like to give data science a shot. None of my potential readers have ever taken a data science class, leaving them inexperienced when it comes to diverse data analysis. The purpose of this book is to eliminate that skill deficiency.

My readers are required to know the bare-bones basics of Python programming. Self-taught beginning Python should be sufficient to explore the exercises in the book. Your mathematical knowledge is not expected to extend beyond basic high-school trigonometry.

How this book is organized

This book contains five case studies of progressing difficulty. Each case study begins with a detailed problem statement, which you will need to resolve. The problem statement is followed by two to five sections that introduce the data science skills required to solve the problem. These skill sections cover fundamental libraries, as well as mathematical and algorithmic techniques. Each final case study section describes the solution to the problem.

Case study 1 pertains to basic probability theory:

- Section 1 discusses how to compute probabilities using straightforward Python.
- Section 2 introduces the concept of probability distributions. It also introduces the Matplotlib visualization library, which can be used to visualize the distributions.
- Section 3 discusses how to estimate probabilities using randomized simulations. The NumPy numerical computing library is introduced to facilitate efficient simulation execution.
- Section 4 contains the case study solution.

Case study 2 extends beyond probability into statistics:

- Section 5 introduces simple statistical measures of centrality and dispersion. It also introduces the SciPy scientific computing library, which contains a useful statistics module.
- Section 6 dives deep into the central limit theorem, which can be used to make statistical predictions.
- Section 7 discusses various statistical inference techniques, which can be used to distinguish interesting data patterns from random noise. Additionally, this section illustrates the dangers of incorrect inference usage and how these dangers can be best avoided.
- Section 8 introduces the Pandas library, which can be utilized to preprocess tabular data before statistical analysis.
- Section 9 contains the case study solution.

Case study 3 focuses on the unsupervised clustering of geographic data:

- Section 10 illustrates how measures of centrality can be used to cluster data into groups. The scikit-learn library is also introduced to facilitate efficient clustering.
- Section 11 focuses on geographic data extraction and visualization. Extraction from text is carried out with the GeoNamesCache library, while visualization is achieved using the Cartopy map-plotting library.
- Section 12 contains the case study solution.

Case study 4 focuses on natural language processing using large-scale numeric computations:

- Section 13 illustrates how to efficiently compute similarities between texts using matrix multiplication. NumPy's built-in matrix optimizations are used extensively for this purpose.
- Section 14 shows how to utilize dimension reduction for more efficient matrix analysis. Mathematical theory is discussed in conjunction with scikit-learn's dimension-reduction methods.
- Section 15 applies natural language processing techniques to a very large text dataset. The section discusses how to best explore and cluster that text data.
- Section 16 shows how to extract text from online data using the Beautiful Soup HTML-parsing library.
- Section 17 contains the case study solution.

Case study 5 completes the book with a discussion of network theory and supervised machine learning:

- Section 18 introduces basic network theory in conjunction with the NetworkX graph analysis library.
- Section 19 shows how to utilize network flow to find clusters in network data. Probabilistic simulations and matrix multiplications are used to achieve effective clustering.
- Section 20 introduces a simple supervised machine learning algorithm based on network theory. Common machine learning evaluation techniques are also illustrated using scikit-learn.
- Section 21 discusses additional machine learning techniques, which rely on memory-efficient linear classifiers.
- Section 22 dives into the flaws of previously introduced supervised learning methodologies. The flaws are subsequently circumvented using nonlinear decision tree classifiers.
- Section 23 contains the case study solution.

Each section of the book builds on the algorithms and libraries introduced in previous sections. Hence, you are encouraged to go through this book cover to cover to minimize confusion. But if you are already familiar with a subset of the material in the book, feel free to skip that familiar material. Finally, I strongly recommend that you tackle each case study problem on your own before reading the solution. Independently trying to solve each problem will maximize the value of this book.

About the code

This book contains many examples of source code, both in numbered listings and inline with normal text. In both cases, the source code is formatted in a `fixed-width` font `like this` to separate it from ordinary text. The source code in the listings is structured in modular chunks, with written explanations that precede each modular bit of code. That code presentation style is well suited for display in a Jupyter notebook since notebooks bridge functional code samples with written explanations. Consequently, the source code for each case study is available for download in a Jupyter notebook at www.manning.com/books/data-science-bookcamp. These notebooks combine code listings with summarized explanations from the book. Per usual notebook style, interdependencies exist between separate notebook cells. Thus, it's recommended that you run the code samples in the exact order they appear in the notebook: otherwise you risk encountering a dependency-driven error.

about the author

LEONARD APELTSIN is the head of data science at Anomaly. His team applies advanced analytics to uncover healthcare fraud, waste, and abuse. Prior to Anomaly, Leonard led the machine learning development efforts at Primer AI, a startup that specializes in natural language processing. As a founding member, Leonard helped grow the Primer AI team from 4 to nearly 100 employees. Before venturing into startups, Leonard worked in academia, uncovering hidden patterns in genetically linked diseases. His discoveries have been published in the subsidiaries of the journals *Science* and *Nature*. Leonard holds BS degrees in biology and computer science from Carnegie Mellon University and a PhD in bioinformatics from The University of California, San Francisco.

about the cover illustration

The figure on the cover of *Data Science Bookcamp* is captioned "Habitante du Tyrol," or resident of Tyrol. The illustration is taken from a collection of dress costumes from various countries by Jacques Grasset de Saint-Sauveur (1757–1810), titled *Costumes de Différents Pays,* published in France in 1797. Each illustration is finely drawn and colored by hand. The rich variety of Grasset de Saint-Sauveur's collection reminds us vividly of how culturally apart the world's towns and regions were just 200 years ago. Isolated from each other, people spoke different dialects and languages. On the streets or in the countryside, it was easy to identify where they lived and what their trade or station in life was just by their dress.

The way we dress has changed since then and the diversity by region, so rich at the time, has faded away. It is now hard to tell apart the inhabitants of different continents, let alone different towns, regions, or countries. Perhaps we have traded cultural diversity for a more varied personal life—certainly for a more varied and fast-paced technological life.

At a time when it is hard to tell one computer book from another, Manning celebrates the inventiveness and initiative of the computer business with book covers based on the rich diversity of regional life of two centuries ago, brought back to life by Grasset de Saint-Sauveur's pictures.

Finding the winning strategy in a card game

Problem statement

Would you like to win a bit of money? Let's wager on a card game for minor stakes. In front of you is a shuffled deck of cards. All 52 cards lie face down. Half the cards are red, and half are black. I will proceed to flip over the cards one by one. If the last card I flip over is red, you'll win a dollar. Otherwise, you'll lose a dollar.

Here's the twist: you can ask me to halt the game at any time. Once you say "Halt," I will flip over the next card and end the game. That next card will serve as the final card. You will win a dollar if it's red, as shown in figure CS1.1.

We can play the game as many times as you like. The deck will be reshuffled every time. After each round, we'll exchange money. What is your best approach to winning this game?

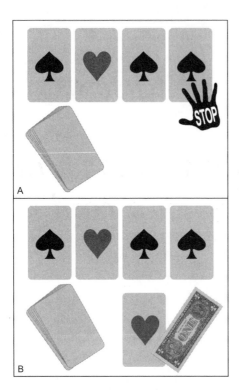

Figure CS1.1   The card-flipping game. We start with a shuffled deck. I repeatedly flip over the top card from the deck. (A) I have just flipped the fourth card. You instruct me to stop. (B) I flip over the fifth and final card. The final card is red. You win a dollar.

Overview

To address the problem at hand, we will need to know how to

1   Compute the probabilities of observable events using sample space analysis.
2   Plot the probabilities of events across a range of interval values.
3   Simulate random processes, such as coin flips and card shuffling, using Python.
4   Evaluate our confidence in decisions drawn from simulations using confidence interval analysis.

Computing probabilities using Python

Few things in life are certain; most things are driven by chance. Whenever we cheer for our favorite sports team, or purchase a lottery ticket, or make an investment in the stock market, we hope for some particular outcome, but that outcome cannot ever be guaranteed. Randomness permeates our day-to-day experiences. Fortunately, that randomness can still be mitigated and controlled. We know that some unpredictable events occur more rarely than others and that certain decisions carry less uncertainty than other much-riskier choices. Driving to work in a car is safer than riding a motorcycle. Investing part of your savings in a retirement account is safer than betting it all on a single hand of blackjack. We can intrinsically sense these trade-offs in certainty because even the most unpredictable systems still show some predictable behaviors. These behaviors have been rigorously studied using *probability theory*. Probability theory is an inherently complex branch of math. However, aspects of the theory can be understood without knowing the mathematical

3

underpinnings. In fact, difficult probability problems can be solved in Python without needing to know a single math equation. Such an equation-free approach to probability requires a baseline understanding of what mathematicians call a *sample space*.

1.1 *Sample space analysis: An equation-free approach for measuring uncertainty in outcomes*

Certain actions have measurable outcomes. A *sample space* is the set of all the possible outcomes an action could produce. Let's take the simple action of flipping a coin. The coin will land on either heads or tails. Thus, the coin flip will produce one of two measurable outcomes: *heads* or *tails*. By storing these outcomes in a Python set, we can create a sample space of coin flips.

Listing 1.1   Creating a sample space of coin flips

```
sample_space = {'Heads', 'Tails'}
```
⊲—— Storing elements in curly brackets creates a Python set. A Python set is a collection of unique, unordered elements.

Suppose we choose an element of `sample_space` at random. What fraction of the time will the chosen element equal `Heads`? Well, our sample space holds two possible elements. Each element occupies an equal fraction of the space within the set. Therefore, we expect `Heads` to be selected with a frequency of 1/2. That frequency is formally defined as the *probability* of an outcome. All outcomes within `sample_space` share an identical probability, which is equal to `1 / len(sample_space)`.

Listing 1.2   Computing the probability of heads

```
probability_heads = 1 / len(sample_space)
print(f'Probability of choosing heads is {probability_heads}')

Probability of choosing heads is 0.5
```

The probability of choosing `Heads` equals 0.5. This relates directly to the action of flipping a coin. We'll assume the coin is unbiased, which means the coin is equally likely to fall on either heads or tails. Thus, a coin flip is conceptually equivalent to choosing a random element from `sample_space`. The probability of the coin landing on heads is therefore 0.5; the probability of it landing on tails is also equal to 0.5.

We've assigned probabilities to our two measurable outcomes. However, there are additional questions we could ask. What is the probability that the coin lands on either heads or tails? Or, more exotically, what is the probability that the coin will spin forever in the air, landing on neither heads nor tails? To find rigorous answers, we need to define the concept of an *event*. An event is the subset of those elements within `sample_space` that satisfy some *event condition* (as shown in figure 1.1). An event condition is a simple Boolean function whose input is a single `sample_space` element. The function returns `True` only if the element satisfies our condition constraints.

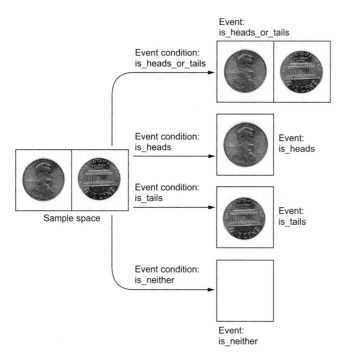

Figure 1.1   Four event conditions applied to a sample space. The sample space contains two outcomes: heads and tails. Arrows represent the event conditions. Every event condition is a yes-or-no function. Each function filters out those outcomes that do not satisfy its terms. The remaining outcomes form an event. Each event contains a subset of the outcomes found in the sample space. Four events are possible: heads, tails, heads or tails, and neither heads nor tails.

Let's define two event conditions: one where the coin lands on either heads or tails, and another where the coin lands on neither heads nor tails.

Listing 1.3   Defining event conditions

```
def is_heads_or_tails(outcome):  return outcome in {'Heads', 'Tails'}
def is_neither(outcome): return not is_heads_or_tails(outcome)
```

Also, for the sake of completeness, let's define event conditions for the two basic events in which the coin satisfies exactly one of our two potential outcomes.

Listing 1.4   Defining additional event conditions

```
def is_heads(outcome): return outcome == 'Heads'
def is_tails(outcome): return outcome == 'Tails'
```

We can pass event conditions into a generalized `get_matching_event` function. That function is defined in listing 1.5. Its inputs are an event condition and a generic sample space. The function iterates through the generic sample space and returns the set of outcomes where `event_condition(outcome)` is True.

Listing 1.5 Defining an event-detection function

```
def get_matching_event(event_condition, sample_space):
    return set([outcome for outcome in sample_space
                if event_condition(outcome)])
```

Let's execute `get_matching_event` on our four event conditions. Then we'll output the four extracted events.

Listing 1.6 Detecting events using event conditions

```
event_conditions = [is_heads_or_tails, is_heads, is_tails, is_neither]

for event_condition in event_conditions:
    print(f"Event Condition: {event_condition.__name__}")      ◁──┐  Prints the
    event = get_matching_event(event_condition, sample_space)       name of an
    print(f'Event: {event}\n')                                      event_condition
                                                                    function

Event Condition: is_heads_or_tails
Event: {'Tails', 'Heads'}

Event Condition: is_heads
Event: {'Heads'}

Event Condition: is_tails
Event: {'Tails'}

Event Condition: is_neither
Event: set()
```

We've successfully extracted four events from `sample_space`. What is the probability of each event occurring? Earlier, we showed that the probability of a single-element outcome for a fair coin is `1 / len(sample_space)`. This property can be generalized to include multi-element events. The probability of an event is equal to `len(event) / len(sample_space)`, but only if all outcomes are known to occur with equal likelihood. In other words, the probability of a multi-element event for a fair coin is equal to the event size divided by the sample space size. We now use event size to compute the four event probabilities.

Listing 1.7 Computing event probabilities

```
def compute_probability(event_condition, generic_sample_space):
    event = get_matching_event(event_condition, generic_sample_space)   ◁──┐
    return len(event) / len(generic_sample_space)
   ▷
```

Probability is equal to event size divided by sample space size.

The compute_probability function extracts the event associated with an inputted event condition to compute its probability.

```
for event_condition in event_conditions:
    prob = compute_probability(event_condition, sample_space)
    name = event_condition.__name__
    print(f"Probability of event arising from '{name}' is {prob}")
```

```
Probability of event arising from 'is_heads_or_tails' is 1.0
Probability of event arising from 'is_heads' is 0.5
Probability of event arising from 'is_tails' is 0.5
Probability of event arising from 'is_neither' is 0.0
```

The executed code outputs a diverse range of event probabilities, the smallest of which is 0.0 and the largest of which is 1.0. These values represent the lower and upper bounds of probability; no probability can ever fall below 0.0 or rise above 1.0.

1.1.1 *Analyzing a biased coin*

We computed probabilities for an unbiased coin. What would happen if that coin was biased? Suppose, for instance, that a coin is four times more likely to land on heads relative to tails. How do we compute the likelihoods of outcomes that are not weighted in an equal manner? Well, we can construct a weighted sample space represented by a Python dictionary. Each outcome is treated as a key whose value maps to the associated weight. In our example, Heads is weighted four times as heavily as Tails, so we map Tails to 1 and Heads to 4.

Listing 1.8   Representing a weighted sample space

```
weighted_sample_space = {'Heads': 4, 'Tails': 1}
```

Our new sample space is stored in a dictionary. This allows us to redefine the size of the sample space as the sum of all dictionary weights. Within weighted_sample_space, that sum will equal 5.

Listing 1.9   Checking the weighted sample space size

```
sample_space_size = sum(weighted_sample_space.values())
assert sample_space_size == 5
```

We can redefine event size in a similar manner. Each event is a set of outcomes, and those outcomes map to weights. Summing over the weights yields the event size. Thus, the size of the event satisfying the is_heads_or_tails event condition is also 5.

Listing 1.10   Checking the weighted event size

```
event = get_matching_event(is_heads_or_tails, weighted_sample_space)    ◄─┐
event_size = sum(weighted_sample_space[outcome] for outcome in event)
assert event_size == 5
```

As a reminder, this function iterates over each outcome in
the inputted sample space. Thus, it will work as expected on our
dictionary input. This is because Python iterates over dictionary keys,
not key-value pairs as in many other popular programming languages.

Our generalized definitions of sample space size and event size permit us to create a compute_event_probability function. The function takes as input a generic_sample_ space variable that can be either a weighted dictionary or an unweighted set.

Listing 1.11   Defining a generalized event probability function

```
def compute_event_probability(event_condition, generic_sample_space):
    event = get_matching_event(event_condition, generic_sample_space)
    if type(generic_sample_space) == type(set()):          ◁──┐
        return len(event) / len(generic_sample_space)           Checks whether
                                                                 generic_event_space
    event_size = sum(generic_sample_space[outcome]               is a set
                  for outcome in event)
    return event_size / sum(generic_sample_space.values())
```

We can now output all the event probabilities for the biased coin without needing to redefine our four event condition functions.

Listing 1.12   Computing weighted event probabilities

```
for event_condition in event_conditions:
    prob = compute_event_probability(event_condition, weighted_sample_space)
    name = event_condition.__name__
    print(f"Probability of event arising from '{name}' is {prob}")

Probability of event arising from 'is_heads' is 0.8
Probability of event arising from 'is_tails' is 0.2
Probability of event arising from 'is_heads_or_tails' is 1.0
Probability of event arising from 'is_neither' is 0.0
```

With just a few lines of code, we have constructed a tool for solving many problems in probability. Let's apply this tool to problems more complex than a simple coin flip.

1.2   Computing nontrivial probabilities

We'll now solve several example problems using compute_event_probability.

1.2.1   Problem 1: Analyzing a family with four children

Suppose a family has four children. What is the probability that exactly two of the children are boys? We'll assume that each child is equally likely to be either a boy or a girl. Thus we can construct an unweighted sample space where each outcome represents one possible sequence of four children, as shown in figure 1.2.

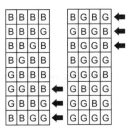

Figure 1.2   The sample space for four sibling children. Each row in the sample space contains 1 of 16 possible outcomes. Every outcome represents a unique combination of four children. The sex of each child is indicated by a letter: B for boy and G for girl. Outcomes with two boys are marked by an arrow. There are six such arrows; thus, the probability of two boys equals 6 / 16.

Listing 1.13 Computing the sample space of children

```
possible_children = ['Boy', 'Girl']
sample_space = set()
for child1 in possible_children:
    for child2 in possible_children:
        for child3 in possible_children:
            for child4 in possible_children:
                outcome = (child1, child2, child3, child4)
                sample_space.add(outcome)
```

> Each possible sequence of four children is represented by a four-element tuple.

We ran four nested for loops to explore the sequence of four births. This is not an efficient use of code. We can more easily generate our sample space using Python's built-in `itertools.product` function, which returns all pairwise combinations of all elements across all input lists. Next, we input four instances of the possible_children list into `itertools.product`. The product function then iterates over all four instances of the list, computing all the combinations of list elements. The final output equals our sample space.

Listing 1.14 Computing the sample space using `product`

> The * operator unpacks multiple arguments stored within a list. These arguments are then passed into a specified function. Thus, calling product(*(4 * [possible_children])) is equivalent to calling product(possible_children, possible_children, possible_children, possible_children).

```
from itertools import product
all_combinations = product(*(4 * [possible_children]))
assert set(all_combinations) == sample_space
```

> Note that after running this line, all_combinations will be empty. This is because product returns a Python iterator, which can be iterated over only once. For us, this isn't an issue. We are about to compute the sample space even more efficiently, and all_combinations will not be use in future code.

We can make our code even more efficient by executing set(product(possible_children, repeat=4)). In general, running product(possible_children, repeat=n) returns an iterable over all possible combinations of n children.

Listing 1.15 Passing `repeat` **into** `product`

```
sample_space_efficient = set(product(possible_children, repeat=4))
assert sample_space == sample_space_efficient
```

Let's calculate the fraction of sample_space that is composed of families with two boys. We define a has_two_boys event condition and then pass that condition into compute_event_probability.

Listing 1.16 Computing the probability of two boys

```
def has_two_boys(outcome): return len([child for child in outcome
                                        if child == 'Boy']) == 2
```

```
prob = compute_event_probability(has_two_boys, sample_space)
print(f"Probability of 2 boys is {prob}")
```

```
Probability of 2 boys is 0.375
```

The probability of exactly two boys being born in a family of four children is 0.375. By implication, we expect 37.5% of families with four children to contain an equal number of boys and girls. Of course, the actual observed percentage of families with two boys will vary due to random chance.

1.2.2   *Problem 2: Analyzing multiple die rolls*

Suppose we're shown a fair six-sided die whose faces are numbered from 1 to 6. The die is rolled six times. What is the probability that these six die rolls add up to 21?

We begin by defining the possible values of any single roll. These are integers that range from 1 to 6.

Listing 1.17   Defining all possible rolls of a six-sided die

```
possible_rolls = list(range(1, 7))
print(possible_rolls)
```

```
[1, 2, 3, 4, 5, 6]
```

Next, we create the sample space for six consecutive rolls using the product function.

Listing 1.18   Sample space for six consecutive die rolls

```
sample_space = set(product(possible_rolls, repeat=6))
```

Finally, we define a has_sum_of_21 event condition that we'll subsequently pass into compute_event_probability.

Listing 1.19   Computing the probability of a die-roll sum

```
def has_sum_of_21(outcome): return sum(outcome) == 21
```

> Conceptually, rolling a single die six times is equivalent to rolling six dice simultaneously.

```
prob = compute_event_probability(has_sum_of_21, sample_space)
print(f"6 rolls sum to 21 with a probability of {prob}")
```

```
6 rolls sum to 21 with a probability of 0.09284979423868313
```

The six die rolls will sum to 21 more than 9% of the time. Note that our analysis can be coded more concisely using a lambda expression. *Lambda expressions* are one-line anonymous functions that do not require a name. In this book, we use lambda expressions to pass short functions into other functions.

Listing 1.20 Computing the probability using a lambda expression

```
prob = compute_event_probability(lambda x: sum(x) == 21, sample_space)
assert prob == compute_event_probability(has_sum_of_21, sample_space)
```

Lambda expressions allow us to define short functions in a single line of code. Coding lambda x: is functionally equivalent to coding func(x):. Thus, lambda x: sum(x) == 21 is functionally equivalent to has_sum_of_21.

1.2.3 *Problem 3: Computing die-roll probabilities using weighted sample spaces*

We've just computed the likelihood of six die rolls summing to 21. Now, let's recompute that probability using a weighted sample space. We need to convert our unweighted sample space set into a weighted sample space dictionary; this will require us to identify all possible die-roll sums. Then we must count the number of times each sum appears across all possible die-roll combinations. These combinations are already stored in our computed `sample_space` set. By mapping the die-roll sums to their occurrence counts, we will produce a `weighted_sample_space` result.

Listing 1.21 Mapping die-roll sums to occurrence counts

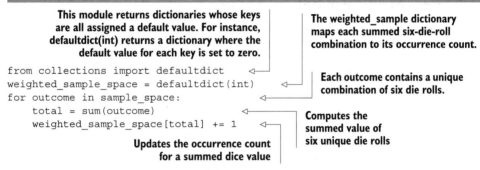

This module returns dictionaries whose keys are all assigned a default value. For instance, defaultdict(int) returns a dictionary where the default value for each key is set to zero.

The weighted_sample dictionary maps each summed six-die-roll combination to its occurrence count.

```
from collections import defaultdict
weighted_sample_space = defaultdict(int)
for outcome in sample_space:
    total = sum(outcome)
    weighted_sample_space[total] += 1
```

Each outcome contains a unique combination of six die rolls.

Computes the summed value of six unique die rolls

Updates the occurrence count for a summed dice value

Before we recompute our probability, let's briefly explore the properties of `weighted_sample_space`. Not all weights in the sample space are equal—some of the weights are much smaller than others. For instance, there is only one way for the rolls to sum to 6: we must roll precisely six 1s to achieve that dice-sum combination. Hence, we expect `weighted_sample_space[6]` to equal 1. We expect `weighted_sample_space[36]` to also equal 1, since we must roll six 6s to achieve a sum of 36.

Listing 1.22 Checking very rare die-roll combinations

```
assert weighted_sample_space[6] == 1
assert weighted_sample_space[36] == 1
```

Meanwhile, the value of `weighted_sample_space[21]` is noticeably higher.

Listing 1.23   Checking a more common die-roll combination

```
num_combinations = weighted_sample_space[21]
print(f"There are {num_combinations } ways for 6 die rolls to sum to 21")

There are 4332 ways for 6 die rolls to sum to 21
```

As the output shows, there are 4,332 ways for six die rolls to sum to 21. For example, we could roll four 4s, followed by a 3 and then a 2. Or we could roll three 4s followed by a 5, a 3, and a 1. Thousands of other combinations are possible. This is why a sum of 21 is much more probable than a sum of 6.

Listing 1.24   Exploring different ways of summing to 21

```
assert sum([4, 4, 4, 4, 3, 2]) == 21
assert sum([4, 4, 4, 5, 3, 1]) == 21
```

Note that the observed count of 4,332 is equal to the length of an unweighted event whose die rolls add up to 21. Also, the sum of values in `weighted_sample` is equal to the length of `sample_space`. Hence, a direct link exists between unweighted and weighted event probability computation.

Listing 1.25   Comparing weighted events and regular events

```
event = get_matching_event(lambda x: sum(x) == 21, sample_space)
assert weighted_sample_space[21] == len(event)
assert sum(weighted_sample_space.values()) == len(sample_space)
```

Let's now recompute the probability using the `weighted_sample_space` dictionary. The final probability of rolling a 21 should remain unchanged.

Listing 1.26   Computing the weighted event probability of die rolls

```
prob = compute_event_probability(lambda x: x == 21,
                                 weighted_sample_space)
assert prob == compute_event_probability(has_sum_of_21, sample_space)
print(f"6 rolls sum to 21 with a probability of {prob}")

6 rolls sum to 21 with a probability of 0.09284979423868313
```

What is the benefit of using a weighted sample space over an unweighted one? Less memory usage! As we see next, the unweighted `sample_space` set has on the order of 150 times more elements than the weighted sample space dictionary.

Listing 1.27   Comparing weighted to unweighted event space size

```
print('Number of Elements in Unweighted Sample Space:')
print(len(sample_space))
print('Number of Elements in Weighted Sample Space:')
print(len(weighted_sample_space))
```

```
Number of Elements in Unweighted Sample Space:
46656
Number of Elements in Weighted Sample Space:
31
```

1.3 Computing probabilities over interval ranges

So far, we've only analyzed event conditions that satisfy some single value. Now we'll analyze event conditions that span intervals of values. An *interval* is the set of all the numbers between and including two boundary cutoffs. Let's define an is_in_interval function that checks whether a number falls within a specified interval. We'll control the interval boundaries by passing a minimum and a maximum parameter.

Listing 1.28 Defining an interval function

> Defines a closed interval in which the min/max boundaries are included. However, it's also possible to define open intervals when needed. In open intervals, at least one of the boundaries is excluded.

```
def is_in_interval(number, minimum, maximum):
    return minimum <= number <= maximum        ⟵
```

Given the is_in_interval function, we can compute the probability that an event's associated value falls within some numeric range. For instance, let's compute the likelihood that our six consecutive die rolls sum to a value between 10 and 21 (inclusive).

Listing 1.29 Computing the probability over an interval

```
prob = compute_event_probability(lambda x: is_in_interval(x, 10, 21),   ⟵
                                 weighted_sample_space)
print(f"Probability of interval is {prob}")
```

> Lambda function that takes some input x and returns True if x falls in an interval between 10 and 21. This one-line lambda function serves as our event condition.

```
Probability of interval is 0.5446244855967078
```

The six die rolls will fall into that interval range more than 54% of the time. Thus, if a roll sum of 13 or 20 comes up, we should not be surprised.

1.3.1 Evaluating extremes using interval analysis

Interval analysis is critical to solving a whole class of very important problems in probability and statistics. One such problem involves the evaluation of extremes: the problem boils down to whether observed data is too extreme to be believable.

Data seems extreme when it is too unusual to have occurred by random chance. For instance, suppose we observe 10 flips of an allegedly fair coin, and that coin lands on heads 8 out of 10 times. Is this a sensible result for a fair coin? Or is our coin secretly biased toward landing on heads? To find out, we must answer the following question: what is the probability that 10 fair coin flips lead to an extreme number of heads? We'll define an extreme head count as eight heads or more. Thus, we can describe the problem as follows: what is the probability that 10 fair coin flips produce from 8 to 10 heads?

We'll find our answer by computing an interval probability. However, first we need the sample space for every possible sequence of 10 flipped coins. Let's generate a weighted sample space. As previously discussed, this is more efficient than using a non-weighted representation.

The following code creates a `weighted_sample_space` dictionary. Its keys equal the total number of observable heads, ranging from 0 through 10. These head counts map to values. Each value holds the number of coin-flip combinations that contain the associated head count. We thus expect `weighted_sample_space[10]` to equal 1, since there is just one possible way to flip a coin 10 times and get 10 heads. Meanwhile, we expect `weighted_sample_space[9]` to equal 10, since a single tail among 9 heads can occur across 10 different positions.

Listing 1.30 Computing the sample space for 10 coin flips

For reusability, we define a general function that returns a weighted sample space for num_flips coin flips. The num_flips parameter is preset to 10 coin flips.

```python
def generate_coin_sample_space(num_flips=10):      ◁────────────────
    weighted_sample_space = defaultdict(int)
    for coin_flips in product(['Heads', 'Tails'], repeat=num_flips):
        heads_count = len([outcome for outcome in coin_flips      ◁──────
                         if outcome == 'Heads'])
        weighted_sample_space[heads_count] += 1          Number of heads in a
                                                         unique sequence of
    return weighted_sample_space                         num_flips coin flips

weighted_sample_space = generate_coin_sample_space()
assert weighted_sample_space[10] == 1
assert weighted_sample_space[9] == 10
```

Our weighted sample space is ready. We now compute the probability of observing an interval from 8 to 10 heads.

Listing 1.31 Computing an extreme head-count probability

```python
prob = compute_event_probability(lambda x: is_in_interval(x, 8, 10),
                                 weighted_sample_space)
print(f"Probability of observing more than 7 heads is {prob}")

Probability of observing more than 7 heads is 0.0546875
```

Ten fair coin flips produce more than seven heads approximately 5% of the time. Our observed head count does not commonly occur. Does this mean the coin is biased? Not necessarily. We haven't yet considered extreme tail counts. If we had observed eight tails and not eight heads, we would have still been suspicious of the coin. Our computed interval did not take this extreme into account—instead, we treated eight or more tails as just another normal possibility. To evaluate the fairness of our coin, we must include the likelihood of observing eight tails or more. This is equivalent to observing two heads or fewer.

Let's formulate the problem as follows: what is the probability that 10 fair coin flips produce either 0 to 2 heads or 8 to 10 heads? Or, stated more concisely, what is the probability that the coin flips do *not* produce from 3 to 7 heads? That probability is computed here.

Listing 1.32 Computing an extreme interval probability

```
prob = compute_event_probability(lambda x: not is_in_interval(x, 3, 7),
                                 weighted_sample_space)
print(f"Probability of observing more than 7 heads or 7 tails is {prob}")

Probability of observing more than 7 heads or 7 tails is 0.109375
```

Ten fair coin flips produce at least eight identical results approximately 10% of the time. That probability is low but still within the realm of plausibility. Without additional evidence, it's difficult to decide whether the coin is truly biased. So, let's collect that evidence. Suppose we flip the coin 10 additional times, and 8 more heads come up. This brings us to 16 heads out of 20 coin flips total. Our confidence in the fairness of the coin has been reduced, but by how much? We can find out by measuring the change in probability. Let's find the probability of 20 fair coin flips *not* producing from 5 to 15 heads.

Listing 1.33 Analyzing extreme head counts for 20 fair coin flips

```
weighted_sample_space_20_flips = generate_coin_sample_space(num_flips=20)
prob = compute_event_probability(lambda x: not is_in_interval(x, 5, 15),
                                 weighted_sample_space_20_flips)
print(f"Probability of observing more than 15 heads or 15 tails is {prob}")

Probability of observing more than 15 heads or 15 tails is 0.01181793212890625
```

The updated probability has dropped from approximately 0.1 to approximately 0.01. Thus, the added evidence has caused a tenfold decrease in our confidence in the coin's fairness. Despite this probability drop, the ratio of heads to tails has remained constant at 4 to 1. Both our original and updated experiments produced 80% heads and 20% tails. This leads to an interesting question: why does the probability of observing an extreme result decrease as the coin is flipped more times? We can find out through detailed mathematical analysis. However, a much more intuitive solution is to just visualize the distribution of head counts across our two sample space dictionaries. The visualization would effectively be a plot of keys (head counts) versus values (combination counts) present in each dictionary. We can carry out this plot using Matplotlib, Python's most popular visualization library. In the subsequent section, we discuss Matplotlib usage and its application to probability theory.

Summary

- A *sample space* is the set of all the possible outcomes an action can produce.
- An *event* is a subset of the sample space containing just those outcomes that satisfy some *event condition*. An event condition is a Boolean function that takes as input an outcome and returns either `True` or `False`.
- The *probability* of an event equals the fraction of event outcomes over all the possible outcomes in the entire sample space.
- Probabilities can be computed over *numeric intervals*. An interval is defined as the set of all the numbers sandwiched between two boundary values.
- Interval probabilities are useful for determining whether an observation appears extreme.

Plotting probabilities using Matplotlib

2

This section covers

- Creating simple plots using Matplotlib
- Labeling plotted data
- What is a probability distribution?
- Plotting and comparing multiple probability distributions

Data plots are among the most valuable tools in any data scientist's arsenal. Without good visualizations, we are effectively crippled in our ability to glean insights from our data. Fortunately, we have at our disposal the external Python Matplotlib library, which is fully optimized for outputting high-caliber plots and data visualizations. In this section, we use Matplotlib to better comprehend the coin-flip probabilities that we computed in section 1.

2.1 Basic Matplotlib plots

Let's begin by installing the Matplotlib library.

> **NOTE** Call `pip install matplotlib` from the command line terminal to install the Matplotlib library.

Once installation is complete, import `matplotlib.pyplot`, which is the library's main plot-generation module. According to convention, the module is commonly imported using the shortened alias `plt`.

Listing 2.1   Importing Matplotlib

```
import matplotlib.pyplot as plt
```

We will now plot some data using `plt.plot`. That method takes as input two iterables: x and y. Calling `plt.plot(x, y)` prepares a 2D plot of x versus y; displaying the plot requires a subsequent call to `plt.show()`. Let's assign our x to equal integers 0 through 10 and our y values to equal double the values of x. The following code visualizes that linear relationship (figure 2.1).

Listing 2.2   Plotting a linear relationship

```
x = range(0, 10)
y = [2 * value for value in x]
plt.plot(x, y)
plt.show()
```

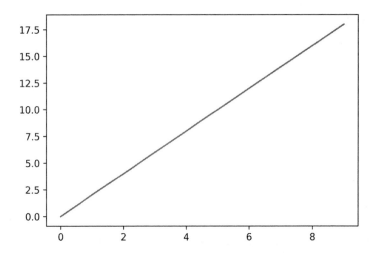

Figure 2.1   A Matplotlib plot of x versus 2x. The x variable represents integers 0 through 10.

WARNING   The axes in the linear plot are not evenly spaced, so the slope of the plotted line appears less steep than it actually is. We can equalize both axes by calling `plt.axis('equal')`. However, this will lead to an awkward visualization containing too much empty space. Throughout this book, we rely on Matplotlib's automated axes adjustments while also carefully observing the adjusted lengths.

The visualization is complete. Within it, our 10 y-axis points have been connected using smooth line segments. If we prefer to visualize the 10 points individually, we can do so using the `plt.scatter` method (figure 2.2).

Listing 2.3   Plotting individual data points

```
plt.scatter(x, y)
plt.show()
```

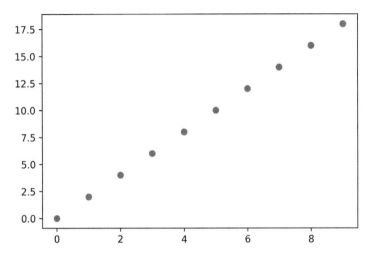

Figure 2.2   A Matplotlib scatter plot of x versus 2 * x. The x variable represents integers 0 through 10. The individual integers are visible as scattered points in the plot.

Suppose we want to emphasize the interval where x begins at 2 and ends at 6. We do this by shading the area under the plotted curve over the specified interval, using the `plt.fill_between` method. The method takes as input both x and y and also a where parameter, which defines the interval coverage. The input of the where parameter is a list of Boolean values in which an element is True if the x value at the corresponding index falls within the interval we specified. In the following code, we set the where parameter to equal `[is_in_interval(value, 2, 6) for value in x]`. We also execute `plt.plot(x,y)` to juxtapose the shaded interval with the smoothly connected line (figure 2.3).

Listing 2.4   Shading an interval beneath a connected plot

```
plt.plot(x, y)
where = [is_in_interval(value, 2, 6) for value in x]
plt.fill_between(x, y, where=where)
plt.show()
```

So far, we have reviewed three visualization methods: `plt.plot`, `plt.scatter`, and `plt.fill_between`. Let's execute all three methods in a single plot (figure 2.4). Doing

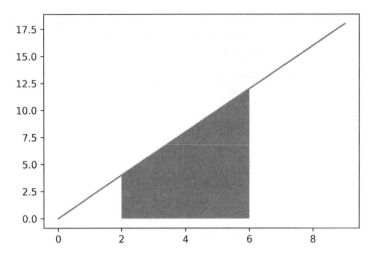

Figure 2.3 A connected plot with a shaded interval. The interval covers all values between 2 and 6.

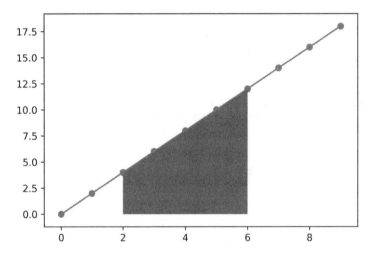

Figure 2.4 A connected plot and a scatter plot combined with a shaded interval. The individual integers in the plot appear as points marking a smooth, indivisible line.

so highlights an interval beneath a continuous line while also exposing individual coordinates.

Listing 2.5 Exposing individual coordinates within a continuous plot

```
plt.scatter(x, y)
plt.plot(x, y)
plt.fill_between(x, y, where=where)
plt.show()
```

No data plot is ever truly complete without descriptive x-axis and y-axis labels. Such labels can be set using the `plt.xlabel` and `plt.ylabel` methods (figure 2.5).

Listing 2.6   Adding axis labels

```
plt.plot(x, y)
plt.xlabel('Values between zero and ten')
plt.ylabel('Twice the values of x')
plt.show()
```

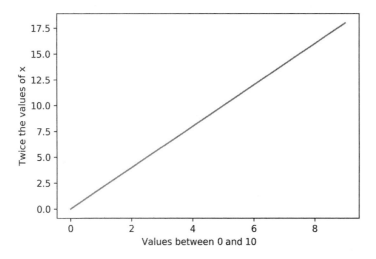

Figure 2.5   A Matplotlib plot with x-axis and y-axis labels

Common Matplotlib methods
- `plt.plot(x, y)`—Plots the elements of x versus the elements of y. The plotted points are connected using smooth line segments.
- `plt.scatter(x, y)`—Plots the elements of x versus the elements of y. The plotted points are visualized individually and are not connected by any lines.
- `plt.fill_between(x, y, where=booleans)`—Highlights a subset of the area beneath a plotted curve. The curve is obtained by plotting x versus y. The `where` parameter defines all highlighted intervals; it takes a list of Booleans that correspond to elements of x. Each Boolean is `True` if its corresponding x value is located within a highlighted interval.
- `plt.xlabel(label)`—Sets the x label of the plotted curve to equal `label`.
- `plt.ylabel(label)`—Sets the y label of the plotted curve to equal `label`.

2.2   *Plotting coin-flip probabilities*

We now have tools to visualize the relationship between a coin-flip count and the probability of heads. In section 1, we examined the probability of seeing 80% or more heads across a series of coin flips. That probability decreased as the coin-flip count went up, and we wanted to know why. We'll soon find out by plotting head counts versus their associated coin-flip combination counts. These values were already computed in our section 1 analysis. The keys in the `weighted_sample_space` dictionary contain all possible head counts across 10 flipped coins. These head counts map to combination counts. Meanwhile, the `weighted_sample_space_20_flips` dictionary contains the head-count mappings for 20 flipped coins.

Our aim is to compare the plotted data from both these dictionaries. We begin by plotting the elements of `weighted_sample_space`: we plot its keys on the x-axis versus the associated values on the y-axis. The x-axis corresponds to `'Head-count'`, and the y-axis corresponds to `'Number of coin-flip combinations with x heads'`. We use a scatter plot to visualize key-to-value relationships directly without connecting any plotted points (figure 2.6).

Listing 2.7   Plotting the coin-flip weighted sample space

```
x_10_flips = list(weighted_sample_space.keys())
y_10_flips = [weighted_sample_space[key] for key in x_10_flips]
plt.scatter(x_10_flips, y_10_flips)
plt.xlabel('Head-count')
plt.ylabel('Number of coin-flip combinations with x heads')
plt.show()
```

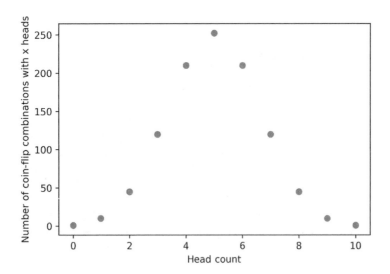

Figure 2.6   A scatter plot representation of the sample space for 10 flipped coins. The symmetric plot is centered around a peak at 5 of 10 counted heads.

The visualized sample space takes on a symmetric shape. The symmetry is set around a peak head count of 5. Therefore, head-count combinations closer to 5 occur more frequently than those that are further from 5. As we learned in the previous section, such frequencies correspond to probabilities. Thus, a head count is more probable if its value is closer to 5. Let's emphasize this by plotting the probabilities directly on the y-axis (figure 2.7). The probability plot will allow us to replace our lengthy y-axis label with a more concisely stated `'Probability'`. We can compute the y-axis probabilities by taking our existing combination counts and dividing them by the total sample space size.

Listing 2.8 Plotting the coin-flip probabilities

```python
sample_space_size = sum(weighted_sample_space.values())
prob_x_10_flips = [value / sample_space_size for value in y_10_flips]
plt.scatter(x_10_flips, prob_x_10_flips)
plt.xlabel('Head-count')
plt.ylabel('Probability')
plt.show()
```

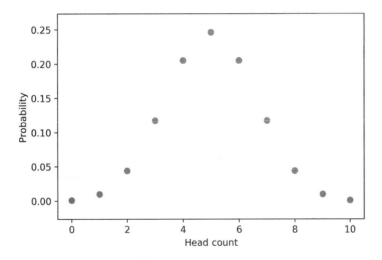

Figure 2.7 A scatter plot mapping head counts to their probability of occurrence. Probabilities can be inferred by looking directly at the plot.

Our plot permits us to visually estimate the probability of any head count. Thus, just by glancing at the plot, we can determine that the probability of observing five heads is approximately 0.25. This mapping between x-values and probabilities is referred to as a *probability distribution*. Probability distributions exhibit certain mathematically consistent properties that make them useful for likelihood analysis. For instance, consider the x-values of any probability distribution: they correspond to all the possible values of a random variable r. The probability that r falls within some interval is equal to the area beneath the probability curve over the span of that interval. Therefore, the total area beneath a probability distribution always equals 1.0. This holds for any distribution, including our head-count plot. Listing 2.9 confirms this by executing sum(prob_ x_10_flips).

> **NOTE** We can compute the area beneath each head-count probability p by using a vertical rectangle. The height of the rectangle is p. The width of the rectangle is 1.0, since all consecutive head counts on the x-axis are spaced one unit apart. Hence, the area of the rectangle is p * 1.0, which equals p. Consequently, the total area beneath the distribution equals sum([p for p in prob_x_10_flips]). In section 3, we'll do a deeper dive into how rectangles can be used to determine the area.

Listing 2.9   Confirming that all probabilities sum to 1.0

```
assert sum(prob_x_10_flips) == 1.0
```

The area beneath the head-count interval of 8 through 10 is equal to the probability of observing eight heads or more. Let's visualize that area using the plt.fill_ between method. We also utilize plt.plot and plt.scatter to display individual head counts encompassing the shaded interval (figure 2.8).

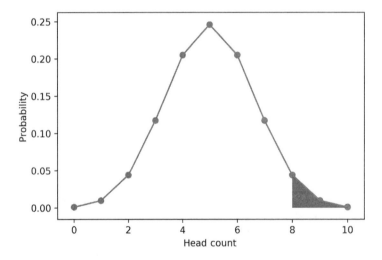

Figure 2.8   Overlaid smooth plot and scatter plot representations of the coin-flip probability distribution. A shaded interval covers head counts 8 through 10. The shaded area equals the probability of observing eight or more heads.

Listing 2.10   Shading the interval under a probability curve

```
plt.plot(x_10_flips, prob_x_10_flips)
plt.scatter(x_10_flips, prob_x_10_flips)
where = [is_in_interval(value, 8, 10) for value in x_10_flips]
```

```
plt.fill_between(x_10_flips, prob_x_10_flips, where=where)
plt.xlabel('Head-count')
plt.ylabel('Probability')
plt.show()
```

NOTE We've purposefully smoothed the shaded interval to make a visually appealing plot. However, the true interval area is not smooth: it is composed of discrete, rectangular blocks, which resemble steps. The steps are discrete because the head counts are indivisible integers. If we wish to visualize the actual step-shaped area, we can pass a `ds="steps-mid"` parameter into `plt.plot` and a `step="mid"` parameter into `plt.fill_between`.

Now, let's also shade the interval demarcating the probability of observing eight tails or more. The following code highlights the extremes along both tail ends of our probability distribution (figure 2.9).

Listing 2.11 Shading the interval under the extremes of a probability curve

```
plt.plot(x_10_flips, prob_x_10_flips)
plt.scatter(x_10_flips, prob_x_10_flips)
where = [not is_in_interval(value, 3, 7) for value in x_10_flips]
plt.fill_between(x_10_flips, prob_x_10_flips, where=where)
plt.xlabel('Head-count')
plt.ylabel('Probability')
plt.show()
```

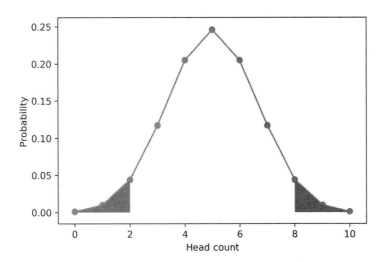

Figure 2.9 Overlaid smooth plot and scatter plot representations of the coin-flip probability distribution. Two shaded intervals span an extreme number of heads and tails. The intervals are symmetric, visually implying that their probabilities are equal.

The two symmetrically shaded intervals cover the right and left tail ends of the coin-flip curve. Based on our previous analysis, we know that the probability of observing more than seven heads or tails is approximately 10%. Therefore, each of the symmetrically shaded tail segments should cover approximately 5% of the total area under the curve.

2.2.1 *Comparing multiple coin-flip probability distributions*

Plotting the 10-coin-flip distribution makes it easier to visually comprehend the associated interval probabilities. Let's extend our plot to also encompass the distribution for 20 flipped coins. We'll plot both distributions on a single figure, although first we must compute the x-axis head counts and y-axis probabilities for the 20-coin-flip distribution.

Listing 2.12 Computing probabilities for a 20-coin-flip distribution

```
x_20_flips = list(weighted_sample_space_20_flips.keys())
y_20_flips = [weighted_sample_space_20_flips[key] for key in x_20_flips]
sample_space_size = sum(weighted_sample_space_20_flips.values())
prob_x_20_flips = [value / sample_space_size for value in y_20_flips]
```

Now we are ready to visualize the two distributions simultaneously (figure 2.10). We do this by executing `plt.plot` and `plt.scatter` on both probability distributions. We also pass a few style-related parameters into these method calls. One of the parameters is `color`: to distinguish the second distribution, we set its color to `black` by passing `color='black'`. Alternatively, we can avoid typing out the entire color name by passing `'k'`, Matplotlib's single-character code for black. We can make the second distribution

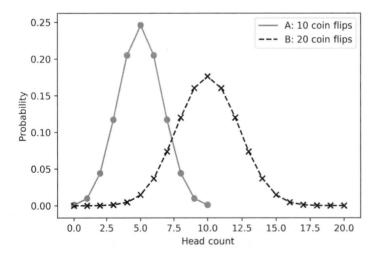

Figure 2.10   The probability distributions for 10 coin flips (A) and 20 coin flips (B). The 20-coin-flip distribution is marked by dashed lines and x-shaped scattered points.

stand out in other ways: passing `linestyle=='--'` into `plt.plot` ensures that the distribution points are connected using dashed lines instead of regular lines. We can also distinguish the individual points using x-shaped markers rather than filled circles by passing `marker='x'` into `plt.scatter`. Finally, we add a legend to our figure by passing a `label` parameter into each of our two `plt.plot` calls and executing the `plt.legend()` method to display the legend. Within the legend, the 10-coin-flip distribution and the 20-coin-flip distribution are labeled A and B, respectively.

Listing 2.13 Plotting two simultaneous distributions

```
plt.plot(x_10_flips, prob_x_10_flips, label='A: 10 coin-flips')
plt.scatter(x_10_flips, prob_x_10_flips)
plt.plot(x_20_flips, prob_x_20_flips, color='black', linestyle='--',
         label='B: 20 coin-flips')
plt.scatter(x_20_flips, prob_x_20_flips, color='k', marker='x')
plt.xlabel('Head-count')
plt.ylabel('Probability')
plt.legend()
plt.show()
```

Common Matplotlib style parameters

- `color`—Determines the color of the plotted output. This setting can be a color name or a single-character code. Both `color='black'` and `color='k'` generate a black plot, and both `color='red'` and `color='r'` generate a red plot.
- `linestyle`—Determines the style of the plotted line that connects the data points. Its default value equals `'-'`. Inputting `linestyle='-'` generates a connected line, `linestyle='--'` generates a dashed line, `linestyle=':'` generates a dotted line, and `linestyle='.'` generates a line composed of alternating dots and dashes.
- `marker`—Determines the style of markers assigned to individually plotted points. Its default value equals `'o'`. Inputting `marker='o'` generates a circular marker, `marker='x'` generates an x-shaped marker, `marker='s'` generates a square-shaped marker, and `marker='p'` generates a pentagon-shaped marker.
- `label`—Maps a label to the specified color and style. This mapping appears in the legend of the plot. A subsequent call to `plt.legend()` is required to make the legend visible.

We've visualized our two distributions. Next, we highlight our interval of interest (80% heads or tails) across each of the two curves (figure 2.11). Note that the area beneath the tail ends of distribution B is very small; we remove the scatter points to highlight the tail-end intervals more clearly. We also replace the line style of distribution B with the more transparent `linestyle=':'`.

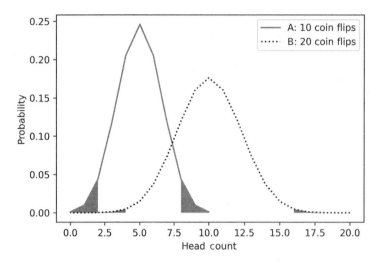

Figure 2.11   The probability distributions for 10 coin flips (A) and 20 coin flips (B). Shaded intervals beneath both distributions represent an extreme number of heads and tails. The shaded interval beneath B occupies one-tenth the area of the shaded interval beneath A.

Listing 2.14   Highlighting intervals beneath two plotted distributions

```
plt.plot(x_10_flips, prob_x_10_flips, label='A: 10 coin-flips')
plt.plot(x_20_flips, prob_x_20_flips, color='k', linestyle=':',
         label='B: 20 coin-flips')

where_10 = [not is_in_interval(value, 3, 7) for value in x_10_flips]
plt.fill_between(x_10_flips, prob_x_10_flips, where=where_10)
where_20 = [not is_in_interval(value, 5, 15) for value in x_20_flips]
plt.fill_between(x_20_flips, prob_x_20_flips, where=where_20)

plt.xlabel('Head-Count')
plt.ylabel('Probability')
plt.legend()
plt.show()
```

The shaded area beneath the tail ends of distribution B is much lower than the shaded interval beneath distribution A. This is because distribution A has fatter, more elevated tail ends that cover a thicker area quantity. Thickness in the tails accounts for differences in interval probabilities.

The visualization is informative, but only if we highlight the interval areas beneath both curves. Without the calls to plt.fill_between, we cannot answer the question we posed earlier: why does the probability of observing 80% or more heads decrease as the fair coin is flipped more times? The answer is hard to extrapolate because the two distributions show little overlap, making it difficult to do a direct visual comparison. Perhaps we can improve the plot by aligning the distribution peaks. Distribution

A is centered at 5 head counts (out of 10 coin flips), and distribution B is centered at 10 head counts (out of 20 coin flips). If we convert the head counts into frequencies (by dividing by the total coin flips), then both distribution peaks should align at a frequency of 0.5. The conversion should also align our head-count intervals of 8-to-10 and 16-to-20 so that they both lie on the interval 0.8-to-1.0. Let's execute this conversion and regenerate the plot (figure 2.12).

Listing 2.15 Converting head counts into frequencies

```
x_10_frequencies = [head_count /10 for head_count in x_10_flips]
x_20_frequencies = [head_count /20 for head_count in x_20_flips]

plt.plot(x_10_frequencies, prob_x_10_flips, label='A: 10 coin-flips')
plt.plot(x_20_frequencies, prob_x_20_flips, color='k', linestyle=':',
    label='B: 20 coin-flips')
plt.legend()

plt.xlabel('Head-Frequency')
plt.ylabel('Probability')
plt.show()
```

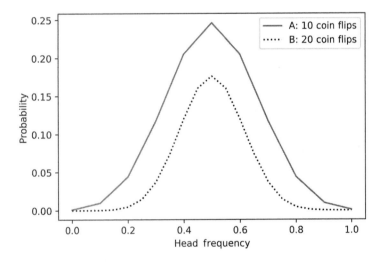

Figure 2.12   The head-count frequencies for 10 coin flips (A) and 20 coin flips (B) plotted against their probabilities. Both y-axis peaks align at a frequency of 0.5. The area of A fully covers the area of B because the total area of each plot no longer sums to 1.0.

As expected, the two peaks now both align at the head frequency of 0.5. However, our division by the head counts has reduced the areas beneath the two curves by tenfold and twentyfold, respectively. The total area beneath each curve no longer equals 1.0. This is a problem: as we've discussed, the total area under a curve must sum to 1.0 if we wish to infer an interval probability. However, we can fix the area sums if we multiply the y-axis values of curves A and B by 10 and 20. The adjusted y-values will no longer refer to probabilities, so we'll have to name them something else. The appropriate term to use is *relative likelihood*, which mathematically refers to a y-axis value within a curve whose total area is 1.0. We therefore name our new y-axis variables `relative_likelihood_10` and `relative_likelihood_20`.

Listing 2.16   Computing relative likelihoods of frequencies

```
relative_likelihood_10 = [10 * prob for prob in prob_x_10_flips]
relative_likelihood_20 = [20 * prob for prob in prob_x_20_flips]
```

The conversion is complete. It's time to plot our two new curves while also highlighting the intervals associated with our `where_10` and `where_20` Boolean arrays (figure 2.13).

Listing 2.17   Plotting aligned relative likelihood curves

```
plt.plot(x_10_frequencies, relative_likelihood_10, label='A: 10 coin-flips')
plt.plot(x_20_frequencies, relative_likelihood_20, color='k',
         linestyle=':', label='B: 20 coin-flips')

plt.fill_between(x_10_frequencies, relative_likelihood_10, where=where_10)
plt.fill_between(x_20_frequencies, relative_likelihood_20, where=where_20)

plt.legend()
plt.xlabel('Head-Frequency')
plt.ylabel('Relative Likelihood')
plt.show()
```

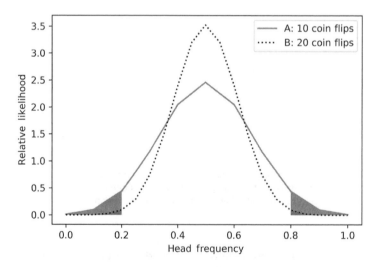

Figure 2.13   The head-count frequencies for 10 coin flips (A) and 20 coin flips (B) plotted against their relative likelihoods. Shaded intervals beneath both plots represent an extreme number of heads and tails. The areas of these intervals correspond to probabilities because the total area of each plot sums to 1.0.

Within the plot, curve A resembles a short yet wide-shouldered bodybuilder, while curve B could be compared to a taller and thinner individual. Since curve A is wider, its area over more extreme head-frequency intervals is larger. Hence, observed recordings of such frequencies are more likely to occur when the coin-flip count is 10 and not 20. Meanwhile, the thinner, more vertical curve B covers more area around the central frequency of 0.5.

If we flip more than 20 coins, how will this influence our frequency distribution? According to probability theory, each additional coin flip will cause the frequency curve to grow even taller and thinner (figure 2.14). The curve will transform like a stretched rubber band that's being pulled vertically upward: it will lose thickness in exchange for vertical length. As the total number of coin flips extends into the millions and billions, the curve will completely lose its girth, becoming a single very long vertical peak whose center lies at a frequency of 0.5. Beyond that frequency, the nonexistent area beneath the vertical line will approach zero. It follows that the area beneath the peak will approach 1.0 because our total area must always equal 1.0. The area of 1.0 corresponds to a probability of 1.0. Thus, as the number of coin flips approaches infinity, the frequency of heads will come to equal the actual probability of heads with absolute certainty.

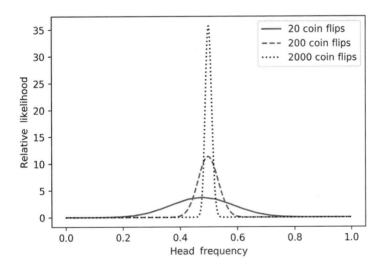

Figure 2.14 Hypothetical head-count frequencies plotted over an increasing number of coin flips. All y-axis peaks align at a frequency of 0.5. The peaks grow higher and more narrow as the coin-flip count goes up. At 2,000 coin flips, the constricted area of the peak is centered almost entirely at 0.5. With infinite coin flips, the resulting peak should stretch into a single, vertical line that's perfectly positioned at 0.5.

The relationship between infinite coin flips and absolute certainty is guaranteed by a fundamental theorem in probability theory: *the law of large numbers.* According to that law, the frequency of an observation becomes virtually indistinguishable from the probability of that observation when the number of observations grows high. Therefore, with enough coin flips, our frequency of heads will equal the actual probability of heads, which is 0.5. Beyond mere coin flips, we can apply the law to more complex phenomena, such as card games. If we run enough card game simulations, then our frequency of a win will equal the actual probability of a win.

In the subsequent section, we will show how the law of large numbers can be combined with random simulations to approximate complex probabilities. Eventually, we will execute simulations to find the probabilities of randomly drawn cards. However, as the law of large numbers indicates, these simulations must be run on a large, computationally expensive scale. Therefore, efficient simulation implementation requires us to familiarize ourselves with the NumPy numeric computation library. That library is discussed in section 3.

Summary

- By plotting every possible numeric observation versus its probability, we generate a probability distribution. The total area beneath a probability distribution sums to 1.0. The area beneath a specific interval of the distribution equals the probability of observing some value within that interval.
- The y-axis values of a probability distribution do not necessarily need to equal probabilities, as long as the plotted area sums to 1.0.
- The probability distribution of a fair coin-flip sequence resembles a symmetric curve. Its x-axis head counts can be converted into frequencies. During that conversion, we can maintain an area of 1.0 by converting y-axis probabilities into relative likelihoods. The peak of the converted curve is centered at a frequency of 0.5. If the coin-flip count is increased, then the peak will also rise as the curve becomes more narrow on its sides.
- According to the *law of large numbers*, the frequency of any observation will approach the probability of that observation as the observation count grows large. Thus, a fair-coin distribution becomes dominated by its central frequency of 0.5 as the coin-flip count goes up.

Running random simulations in NumPy

This section covers

- Basic usage of the NumPy library
- Simulating random observations using NumPy
- Visualizing simulated data
- Estimating unknown probabilities from simulated observations

NumPy, which stands for Numerical Python, is the engine that powers Pythonic data science. Python, despite its many virtues, is simply not suited for large-scale numeric analysis. Hence, data scientists must rely on the external NumPy library to efficiently manipulate and store numeric data. NumPy is an incredibly powerful tool for processing large collections of raw numbers. Thus, many of Python's external data processing libraries are NumPy compatible. One such library is Matplotlib, which we introduced in the previous section. Other NumPy-driven libraries are discussed in later portions of the book. This section focuses on randomized numerical simulations. We will use NumPy to analyze billions of random data points; these random observations will allow us to learn hidden probabilities.

3.1   *Simulating random coin flips and die rolls using NumPy*

NumPy should already be installed in your working environment as one of the Matplotlib requirements. Let's import NumPy as np based on common NumPy usage convention.

> **NOTE** NumPy can also be installed independently of Matplotlib by calling pip install numpy from the command line terminal.

Listing 3.1   Importing NumPy

```
import numpy as np
```

Now that NumPy is imported, we can carry out random simulations using the np.random module. That module is useful for generating random values and simulating random processes. For instance, calling np.random.randint(1, 7) produces a random integer between 1 and 6. The method chooses from the six possible integers with equal likelihood, thus simulating a single roll of a standard die.

Listing 3.2   Simulating a randomly rolled die

```
die_roll = np.random.randint(1, 7)
assert 1 <= die_roll <= 6
```

The generated die_roll value is random, and its assigned value will vary among the readers of this book. The inconsistency could make it difficult to perfectly re-create certain random simulations in this section. We need a way of ensuring that all our random outputs can be reproduced at home. Conveniently, consistency can easily be maintained by calling np.random.seed(0); this method call makes sequences of randomly chosen values reproducible. After the call, we can directly guarantee that our first three dice rolls will land on values 5, 6, and 1.

Listing 3.3   Seeding reproducible random die rolls

```
np.random.seed(0)
die_rolls = [np.random.randint(1, 7) for _ in range(3)]
assert die_rolls == [5, 6, 1]
```

Adjusting the inputted x into np.random.randint(0, x) allows us to simulate any number of discrete outcomes. For instance, setting x to 52 will simulate a randomly drawn card. Alternatively, setting x to 2 will simulate a single flip of an unbiased coin. Let's generate that coin flip by calling np.random.randint(0, 2); this method call returns a random value equal to either 0 or 1. We assume that 0 stands for tails and 1 stands for heads.

Listing 3.4 Simulating one fair coin flip

```
np.random.seed(0)
coin_flip = np.random.randint(0, 2)
print(f"Coin landed on {'heads' if coin_flip == 1 else 'tails'}")
```

```
Coin landed on tails
```

Next, we simulate a sequence of 10 coin flips and then compute the observed frequency of heads.

Listing 3.5 Simulating 10 fair coin flips

```
np.random.seed(0)
def frequency_heads(coin_flip_sequence):
    total_heads = len([head for head in coin_flip_sequence if head == 1])    ◁───┐
    return total_heads / len(coin_flip_sequence)

coin_flips = [np.random.randint(0, 2) for _ in range(10)]
freq_heads = frequency_heads(coin_flips)
print(f"Frequency of Heads is {freq_heads}")
```

> **Note that we can compute the head count more efficiently by running sum(coin_flip_sequence).**

```
Frequency of Heads is 0.8
```

The observed frequency is 0.8, which is quite disproportionate to the actual probability of heads. However, as we have learned, 10 coin flips will produce such extreme frequencies approximately 10% of the time. More coin flips are required to estimate the actual probability.

Let's see what happens when we flip the coin 1,000 times. After each flip, we record the total frequency of heads observed in the sequence. Once the coin flips are completed, we visualize our output by plotting the coin-flip count versus the frequency count (figure 3.1). Our plot also includes a horizontal line along the actual probability of 0.5. We generate that line by calling `plt.axhline(0.5, color='k')`.

Listing 3.6 Plotting simulated fair coin-flip frequencies

```
np.random.seed(0)
coin_flips = []
frequencies = []
for _ in range(1000):
    coin_flips.append(np.random.randint(0, 2))
    frequencies.append(frequency_heads(coin_flips))

plt.plot(list(range(1000)), frequencies)
plt.axhline(0.5, color='k')
plt.xlabel('Number of Coin Flips')
plt.ylabel('Head-Frequency')
plt.show()
```

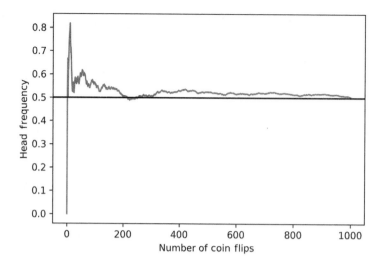

Figure 3.1   The number of fair coin flips plotted against the observed head-count frequency. The frequency fluctuates wildly before stabilizing at around 0.5.

The probability of heads slowly converges to 0.5. Thus, the law of large numbers appears to hold up.

3.1.1   Analyzing biased coin flips

We've simulated a sequence of unbiased coin flips, but what if we wish to simulate a coin that falls on heads 70% of the time? Well, we can generate that biased output by calling np.random.binomial(1, 0.7). The binomial method name refers to the generic coin-flip distribution, which mathematicians call the *binomial distribution*. The method takes as input two parameters: the number of coin flips and the probability of the desired coin-flip outcome. The method executes the specified number of biased coin flips and then counts the instances when the desired outcome was observed. When the number of coin flips is set to 1, the method returns a binary value of 0 or 1. In our case, a value of 1 represents our desired observation of heads.

Listing 3.7   Simulating biased coin flips

```
np.random.seed(0)
print("Let's flip the biased coin once.")
coin_flip = np.random.binomial(1, 0.7)
print(f"Biased coin landed on {'heads' if coin_flip == 1 else 'tails'}.")

print("\nLet's flip the biased coin 10 times.")
number_coin_flips = 10
head_count = np.random.binomial(number_coin_flips, .7)
print((f"{head_count} heads were observed out of "
       f"{number_coin_flips} biased coin flips"))
```

```
Let's flip the biased coin once.
Biased coin landed on heads.

Let's flip the biased coin 10 times.
6 heads were observed out of 10 biased coin flips
```

Let's generate a sequence of 1,000 biased coin flips. We then check if the frequency converges to 0.7.

Listing 3.8   Computing coin-flip-frequency convergence

```
np.random.seed(0)
head_count = np.random.binomial(1000, 0.7)
frequency = head_count / 1000
print(f"Frequency of Heads is {frequency}")


Frequency of Heads is 0.697
```

The frequency of heads approximates 0.7 but is not actually equal to 0.7. In fact, the frequency value is 0.003 units smaller than the true probability of heads. Suppose we recompute the frequency of 1,000 coin flips five more times. Will all the frequencies be lower than 0.7? Will certain frequencies hit the exact value of 0.7? We'll find out by executing `np.random.binomial(1000, 0.7)` over five looped iterations.

Listing 3.9   Recomputing coin-flip-frequency convergence

```
np.random.seed(0)
assert np.random.binomial(1000, 0.7) / 1000 == 0.697     ◁──┐
for i in range(1, 6):
    head_count = np.random.binomial(1000, 0.7)
    frequency = head_count / 1000
    print(f"Frequency at iteration {i} is {frequency}")
    if frequency == 0.7:
        print("Frequency equals the probability!\n")


Frequency at iteration 1 is 0.69
Frequency at iteration 2 is 0.7
Frequency equals the probability!

Frequency at iteration 3 is 0.707
Frequency at iteration 4 is 0.702
Frequency at iteration 5 is 0.699
```

> **As a reminder, we seeded our random number generator to maintain consistent output. Thus, our first pseudorandom sampling will return the previously observed frequency of 0.697. We'll skip over this result to generate five fresh frequencies.**

Just one of the five iterations produced a measurement that equaled the real probability. Twice the measured frequency was slightly too low, and twice it was slightly too high. The observed frequency appears to fluctuate over every sampling of 1,000 coin flips. It seems that even though the law of large numbers allows us to approximate the actual probability, some uncertainty still remains. Data science is somewhat messy, and we cannot always be certain of the conclusions we draw from our data. Nevertheless, our uncertainty can be measured and contained using what mathematicians call a *confidence interval.*

3.2 Computing confidence intervals using histograms and NumPy arrays

Suppose we're handed a biased coin whose bias we don't know. We flip the coin 1,000 times and observe a frequency of 0.709. We know the frequency approximates the actual probability, but by how much? More precisely, what are the chances of the actual probability falling within an interval close to 0.709 (such as an interval between 0.7 and 0.71)? To find out, we must do additional sampling.

We've previously sampled our coin over five iterations of 1,000 coin flips each. The sampling produced some fluctuations in the frequency. Let's explore these fluctuations by increasing our frequency count from 5 to 500. We can execute this supplementary sampling by running [np.random.binomial(1000, 0.7) for _ in range(500)].

Listing 3.10   Computing frequencies with 500 flips per sample

```
np.random.seed(0)
head_count_list = [np.random.binomial(1000, 0.7) for _ in range(500)]
```

However, we can more efficiently sample over 500 iterations by running np.random.binomial(coin_flip_count, 0.7, size=500). The optional size parameter allows us to execute np.random.binomial(coin_flip_count, 0.7) 500 times while using NumPy's internal optimizations.

Listing 3.11   Optimizing the coin-flip-frequency computation

```
np.random.seed(0)
head_count_array = np.random.binomial(1000, 0.7, 500)
```

The output is not a Python list but a NumPy array data structure. As previously noted, NumPy arrays can more efficiently store numeric data. The actual numeric quantities stored in both head_count_array and head_count_list remain the same. We prove this by converting the array into a list using the head_count_array.tolist() method.

Listing 3.12   Converting a NumPy array to a Python list

```
assert head_count_array.tolist() == head_count_list
```

Conversely, we can also convert our Python list into a value-equivalent NumPy array by calling np.array(head_count_list). The equality between the converted array and head_count_array can be confirmed using the np.array_equal method.

Listing 3.13   Converting a Python list to a NumPy array

```
new_array = np.array(head_count_list)
assert np.array_equal(new_array, head_count_array) == True
```

Why should we prefer to use a NumPy array over a standard Python list? Well, besides the aforementioned memory optimizations and analysis speed-ups, NumPy makes it easier to implement clean code. For instance, NumPy offers more straightforward multiplication and division. Dividing a NumPy array directly by x creates a new array whose elements are all divided by x. Thus, executing `head_count_array / 1000` will automatically transform our head counts into frequencies. By contrast, frequency calculation across `head_count_list` requires that we either iterate over all elements in the list or use Python's convoluted `map` function.

Listing 3.14   Computing frequencies using NumPy

```
frequency_array = head_count_array / 1000
assert frequency_array.tolist() == [head_count / 1000
                                    for head_count in head_count_list]
assert frequency_array.tolist() == list(map(lambda x: x / 1000,
                                            head_count_list))
```

Useful NumPy methods for running random simulations
- `np.random.randint(x, y)`—Returns a random integer between x and y-1, inclusive.
- `np.random.binomial(1, p)`—Returns a single random value equal to 0 or 1. The probability that the value equals 1 is p.
- `np.random.binomial(x, p)`—Runs x instances of `np.random.binomial(1, p)` and returns the summed result. The returned value represents the number of nonzero observations across x samples.
- `np.random.binomial(x, p, size=y)`—Returns an array of y elements. Each array element is equal to a random output of `np.random.binomial(x, p)`.
- `np.random.binomial(x, p, size=y) / x`—Returns an array of y elements. Each element represents the frequency of nonzero observations across x samples.

We've converted our head-count array into a frequency array using a simple division operation. Let's explore the contents of `frequency_array` in greater detail. We start by outputting the first 20 sampled frequencies using the same : index-slicing delimiter utilized by Python lists. Note that unlike a printed list, the NumPy array does not contain commas in its output.

Listing 3.15   Printing a NumPy frequency array

```
print(frequency_array[:20])

[ 0.697  0.69   0.7    0.707  0.702  0.699  0.723  0.67   0.702  0.713
  0.721  0.689  0.711  0.697  0.717  0.691  0.731  0.697  0.722  0.728]
```

The sampled frequencies fluctuate from 0.69 to approximately 0.731. Of course, an additional 480 frequencies remain in `frequency_array`. Let's extract the minimum and maximum array values by calling the `frequency_array.min()` and `frequency_array.max()` methods.

Listing 3.16   Finding the largest and smallest frequency values

```
min_freq = frequency_array.min()
max_freq = frequency_array.max()
print(f"Minimum frequency observed: {min_freq}")
print(f"Maximum frequency observed: {max_freq}")
print(f"Difference across frequency range: {max_freq - min_freq}")

Minimum frequency observed: 0.656
Maximum frequency observed: 0.733
Difference across frequency range: 0.07699999999999996
```

Somewhere in the frequency range of 0.656 to 0.733 lies the true probability of heads. That interval span is noticeably large, with a more than 7% difference between the largest and smallest sampled values. Perhaps we can narrow the frequency range by plotting all unique frequencies against their occurrence counts (figure 3.2).

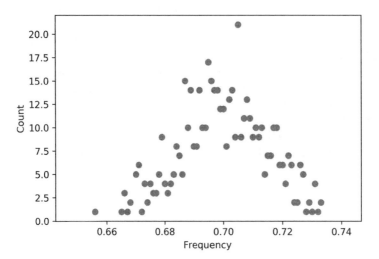

Figure 3.2   A scatter plot of 500 head-count frequencies plotted against the frequency counts. The frequencies are centered around 0.7. Certain proximate frequencies appear as overlapping dots in the plot.

Listing 3.17   Plotting measured frequencies

```
frequency_counts = defaultdict(int)
for frequency in frequency_array:
    frequency_counts[frequency] += 1

frequencies = list(frequency_counts.keys())
counts = [frequency_counts[freq] for freq in frequencies]
```

```
plt.scatter(frequencies, counts)
plt.xlabel('Frequency')
plt.ylabel('Count')
plt.show()
```

The visualization is informative: frequencies close to 0.7 occur more commonly than other, more distant values. However, our plot is also flawed, since nearly identical frequencies appear as overlapping dots in the chart. We should group these proximate frequencies together instead of treating them as individual points.

3.2.1 Binning similar points in histogram plots

Let's try a more nuanced visualization by binning together frequencies that are in close proximity to each other. We subdivide our frequency range into N equally spaced bins and then place all frequency values into one of those bins. By definition, the values in any given bin are at most $1/N$ units apart. Then we count the total values in each bin and visualize the counts using a plot.

The bin-based plot we just described is called a *histogram*. We can generate histograms in Matplotlib by calling `plt.hist`. The method takes as input the sequence of values to be binned and an optional `bins` parameter, which specifies the total number of bins. Thus, calling `plt.hist(frequency_array, bins=77)` will split our data across 77 bins, each covering a width of .01 units. Alternatively, we can pass in `bins=auto`, and Matplotlib will select an appropriate bin width using a common optimization technique (the details of which are beyond the scope of this book). Let's plot a histogram while optimizing bin width by calling `plt.hist(frequency_array, bins='auto')` (figure 3.3).

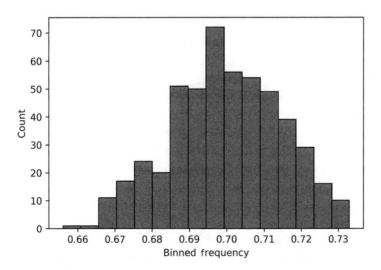

Figure 3.3 A histogram of 500 binned frequencies plotted against the number of elements in each bin. The bin with the most elements is centered around a frequency of 0.7.

NOTE   In listing 3.18, we also include an `edgecolor='black'` parameter. This helps us visually distinguish the boundaries between bins by coloring the bin edges black.

Listing 3.18   Plotting a frequency histogram using `plt.hist`

```
plt.hist(frequency_array, bins='auto', edgecolor='black')
plt.xlabel('Binned Frequency')
plt.ylabel('Count')
plt.show()
```

In our plotted histogram, the bin with the highest frequency count falls between 0.69 and 0.70. This bin rises noticeably higher than the dozen or so other bins. We can obtain a more precise bin count using `counts`, which is a NumPy array returned by `plt.hist`. The array holds the y-axis frequency counts for each binned group. Let's call `plt.hist` to return `counts` and subsequently access `counts.size` to find the total number of binned groups.

Listing 3.19   Counting bins in a plotted histogram

```
counts, _, _ = plt.hist(frequency_array, bins='auto',
                        edgecolor='black')

print(f"Number of Bins: {counts.size}")
```

⟵ **counts is one of three variables returned by plt.hist. The other variables are discussed later in this section.**

```
Number of Bins: 16
```

There are 16 bins in the histogram. How wide is each bin? We can find out by dividing the total frequency range by 16. Alternatively, we can use the `bin_edges` array, which is the second variable returned by `plt.hist`. This array holds the x-axis positions of the vertical bin edges in the plot. Thus, the difference between any two consecutive edge positions equals the bin width.

Listing 3.20   Finding the width of bins in a histogram

```
counts, bin_edges, _ = plt.hist(frequency_array, bins='auto',
                                edgecolor='black')

bin_width = bin_edges[1] - bin_edges[0]
assert bin_width == (max_freq - min_freq) / counts.size
print(f"Bin width: {bin_width}")
```

```
Bin width: 0.004812499999999997
```

NOTE   The size of `bin_edges` is always one greater than the size of the `counts`. Why is that the case? Imagine if we had only one rectangular bin: it would be bounded by two vertical lines. Adding an additional bin would also increase the boundary size by 1. If we extrapolate that logic to N bins, then we'd expect to see $N + 1$ boundary lines.

The bin_edges array can be used in tandem with counts to output the element count and coverage range for any specified bin. Let's define an output_bin_coverage function that prints the count and coverage for any bin at position i.

Listing 3.21 Getting a bin's frequency and size

```
def output_bin_coverage(i):              A bin at position i contains
    count = int(counts[i])               counts[i] frequencies.
    range_start, range_end = bin_edges[i], bin_edges[i+1]
    range_string = f"{range_start} - {range_end}"
    print((f"The bin for frequency range {range_string} contains "
           f"{count} element{'' if count == 1 else 's'}"))

output_bin_coverage(0)                    A bin at position i covers a
output_bin_coverage(5)                    frequency range of bin_edges[i]
                                          through bin_edges[i+1].
```

```
The bin for frequency range 0.656 - 0.6608125 contains 1 element
The bin for frequency range 0.6800625 - 0.684875 contains 20 elements
```

Now, let's compute the count and frequency range for the highest peak in our histogram. For this, we need the index of counts.max(). Conveniently, NumPy arrays have a built-in argmax method, which returns the index of the maximum value in an array.

Listing 3.22 Finding the index of an array's maximum value

```
assert counts[counts.argmax()] == counts.max()
```

Thus, calling output_bin_coverage(counts.argmax()) should provide us with the output we've requested.

Listing 3.23 Using argmax to return a histogram's peak

```
output_bin_coverage(counts.argmax())
```

```
The bin for frequency range 0.6945 - 0.6993125 contains 72 elements
```

3.2.2 Deriving probabilities from histograms

The most-occupied bin in the histogram contains 72 elements and covers a frequency range of approximately 0.694 to 0.699. How can we determine whether the actual probability of heads falls within that range (without knowing the answer in advance)? One option is to calculate the likelihood that a randomly measured frequency falls within 0.694 to 0.699. If that likelihood were 1.0, then 100% of measured frequencies would be covered by the range. These measured frequencies would occasionally include the actual probability of heads, so we would be 100% confident that our true probability lay somewhere between 0.694 and 0.699. Even if the likelihood were lower, at 95%, we would still be fairly confident that the range enclosed our true probability value.

How should we calculate the likelihood? Earlier, we showed that the likelihood of an interval equals its area under a curve, but only when the total plotted area sums to 1.0. The area under our histogram is greater than 1.0 and thus must be modified by passing `density=True` into `plt.hist`. The passed parameter maintains the histogram's shape while forcing its area's sum to equal 1.0.

Listing 3.24   Plotting a histogram's relative likelihoods

```
likelihoods, bin_edges, _ = plt.hist(frequency_array, bins='auto',
                                      edgecolor='black', density=True)
plt.xlabel('Binned Frequency')
plt.ylabel('Relative Likelihood')
plt.show()
```

The binned counts have now been replaced by relative likelihoods, which are stored in the `likelihoods` array (figure 3.4). As we've discussed, *relative likelihood* is a term applied to the y-values of a plot whose area sums to 1.0. Of course, the area beneath our histogram now sums to 1.0. We can prove this by summing the rectangular area of each bin, which equals the bin's vertical likelihood value multiplied by `bin_width`. Hence, the area beneath the histogram is equal to the summed likelihoods multiplied by `bin_width`. Consequently, calling `likelihoods.sum() * bin_width` should return an area of 1.0.

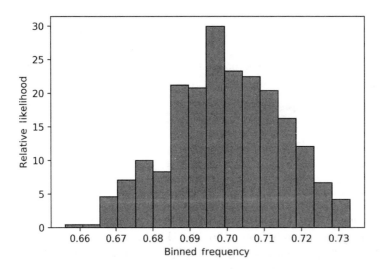

Figure 3.4   A histogram of 500 binned frequencies plotted against their associated relative likelihoods. The area of the histogram sums to 1.0. That area can be computed by summing over the rectangular areas of each bin.

NOTE   The total area equals the summed rectangle areas in the histogram. In figure 3.4, the length of the longest rectangles is quite large, so we visually estimate that the total area is greater than 1.0.

Listing 3.25 Computing the total area under a histogram

```
assert likelihoods.sum() * bin_width == 1.0
```

The histogram's total area sums to 1.0. Thus, the area beneath the histogram's peak now equals the probability of a randomly sampled frequency falling within the 0.694 to 0.699 interval range. Let's compute this value by calculating the area of the bin positioned at `likelihoods.argmax()`.

Listing 3.26 Computing the probability of the peak frequencies

```
index = likelihoods.argmax()
area = likelihoods[index] * bin_width
range_start, range_end = bin_edges[index], bin_edges[index+1]
range_string = f"{range_start} - {range_end}"
print(f"Sampled frequency falls within interval {range_string} with
        probability {area}")
```

```
Sampled frequency falls within interval 0.6945 - 0.6993125 with probability
    0.144
```

The probability is approximately 14%. That value is low, but we can increase it by expanding our interval range beyond one bin. We stretch the range to cover neighboring bins at indices `likelihoods.argmax() - 1` and `likelihoods.argmax() + 1`.

> **NOTE** As a reminder, Python's indexing notation is inclusive of the start index and exclusive of the end index. Hence, we set the end index to equal `likelihoods.argmax() + 2` to include `likelihoods.argmax() + 1`.

Listing 3.27 Increasing the probability of a frequency range

```
peak_index = likelihoods.argmax()
start_index, end_index = (peak_index - 1, peak_index + 2)
area = likelihoods[start_index: end_index + 1].sum() * bin_width
range_start, range_end = bin_edges[start_index], bin_edges[end_index]
range_string = f"{range_start} - {range_end}"
print(f"Sampled frequency falls within interval {range_string} with
        probability {area}")
```

```
Sampled frequency falls within interval 0.6896875 - 0.704125 with probability
    0.464
```

The three bins cover a frequency range of approximately 0.689 to 0.704. Their associated probability is 0.464. Thus, the three bins represent what statisticians call a 46.4% *confidence interval*, which means we are 46.4% confident that our true probability falls within the three-bin range. That confidence percentage is too low. Statisticians prefer a confidence interval of 95% or more. We reach that confidence interval by iteratively expanding our leftmost bin and rightmost bin until the interval area stretches past 0.95.

Listing 3.28   Computing a high confidence interval

```
def compute_high_confidence_interval(likelihoods, bin_width):
    peak_index = likelihoods.argmax()
    area = likelihoods[peak_index] * bin_width
    start_index, end_index = peak_index, peak_index + 1
    while area < 0.95:
        if start_index > 0:
            start_index -= 1
        if end_index < likelihoods.size - 1:
            end_index += 1

        area = likelihoods[start_index: end_index + 1].sum() * bin_width

    range_start, range_end = bin_edges[start_index], bin_edges[end_index]
    range_string = f"{range_start:.6f} - {range_end:.6f}"
    print((f"The frequency range {range_string} represents a "
           f"{100 * area:.2f}% confidence interval"))
    return start_index, end_index

compute_high_confidence_interval(likelihoods, bin_width)
```

```
The frequency range 0.670438 - 0.723375 represents a 95.40% confidence interval
```

The frequency range of roughly 0.670 to 0.723 represents a 95.4% confidence interval. Thus, a sampled sequence of 1,000 biased coin flips should fall within that range 95.4% of the time. We're fairly confident that the true probability lies somewhere between 0.670 and 0.723. However, we still cannot tell for sure whether the true probability is closer to 0.67 or 0.72. We need to somehow narrow that range to obtain a more informative probability estimation.

3.2.3   *Shrinking the range of a high confidence interval*

How can we taper down our range while maintaining a 95% confidence interval? Perhaps we should try elevating the frequency count from 500 to something noticeably larger. Previously, we've sampled 500 frequencies, where each frequency represented 1,000 biased coin flips. Instead, let's sample 100,000 frequencies while keeping the coin-flip count constant at 1,000.

Listing 3.29   Sampling 100,000 frequencies

```
np.random.seed(0)
head_count_array = np.random.binomial(1000, 0.7, 100000)
frequency_array = head_count_array / 1000
assert frequency_array.size == 100000
```

We will recompute the histogram on the updated frequency_array, which now holds 200-fold more frequency elements. Then we visualize that histogram while also searching for a high confidence interval. Let's incorporate the confidence interval into our visualization by coloring the histogram bars in its range (figure 3.5). The histogram

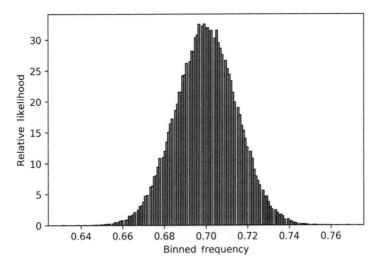

Figure 3.5 A histogram of 100,000 binned frequencies plotted against their associated relative likelihoods. Highlighted bars delineate the 95% confidence interval, which represents 95% of the histogram's area. That interval covers a frequency range of roughly 0.670–0.727.

bars can be visually modified by relying on `patches`, which is the third variable returned by `plt.hist`. The graphical details of each bin at index `i` are accessible through `patches[i]`. If we wish to color the *i*th bin yellow, we can simply call `patches[i].set_facecolor('yellow')`. In this manner, we can highlight all the specified histogram bars that fall within the updated interval range.

Listing 3.30 Coloring histogram bars over an interval

```
likelihoods, bin_edges, patches = plt.hist(frequency_array, bins='auto',
                                            edgecolor='black', density=True)
bin_width = bin_edges[1] - bin_edges[0]
start_index, end_index = compute_high_confidence_interval(likelihoods,
                                                          bin_width)

for i in range(start_index, end_index):
    patches[i].set_facecolor('yellow')
plt.xlabel('Binned Frequency')
plt.ylabel('Relative Likelihood')

plt.show()

The frequency range 0.670429 - 0.727857 represents a 95.42% confidence interval
```

The recomputed histogram resembles a symmetric bell-shaped curve. Many of its bars have been highlighted using the `set_facecolor` method. The highlighted bars represent a 95% confidence interval. The interval covers a frequency range of roughly

0.670 to 0.727. This new frequency range is nearly identical to the one we saw before: increasing the frequency sample size did not reduce the range. Perhaps we should also increase the number of coin flips per frequency sample from 1,000 to 50,000 (figure 3.6). We keep the frequency sample size steady at 100,000, thus leading to 5 billion flipped coins.

Listing 3.31   Sampling 5 billion flipped coins

```
np.random.seed(0)
head_count_array = np.random.binomial(50000, 0.7, 100000)
frequency_array = head_count_array / 50000

likelihoods, bin_edges, patches = plt.hist(frequency_array, bins='auto',
                                    edgecolor='black', density=True)
bin_width = bin_edges[1] - bin_edges[0]
start_index, end_index = compute_high_confidence_interval(likelihoods,
                                    bin_width)

for i in range(start_index, end_index):
    patches[i].set_facecolor('yellow')
plt.xlabel('Binned Frequency')
plt.ylabel('Relative Likelihood')

plt.show()
```

```
The frequency range 0.695769 - 0.703708 represents a 95.06% confidence interval
```

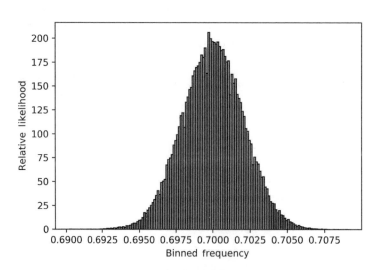

Figure 3.6   A histogram of 100,000 binned frequencies plotted against their associated relative likelihoods. Highlighted bars delineate the 95% confidence interval, which represents 95% of the histogram's area. That interval covers a frequency range of roughly 0.695–0.703.

The new 95.06% confidence interval covers a frequency range of roughly 0.695 to 0.703. If we round the range to two decimal places, it equals 0.70 to 0.70. We are thus exceedingly confident that our true probability is approximately 0.70. By increasing the coin flips per sample, we've successfully narrowed the range of our 95% confidence interval.

On a separate note, our updated histogram once again resembles a bell-shaped curve. That curve is referred to as either the *Gaussian distribution* or the *normal distribution*. The normal distribution is incredibly important to probability theory and statistics due to the *central limit theorem*. According to this theorem, sampled frequency distributions take the shape of a normal distribution when the number of samples is large. Furthermore, the theorem predicts a narrowing of likely frequencies as the size of each frequency sample increases. This is perfectly consistent with our observations, which are summarized here:

1 Initially, we sampled 1,000 coin flips 500 times.
2 Each sequence of 1,000 coin flips was converted to a frequency.
3 We plotted the histogram of 500 frequencies representing 50,000 total coin flips.
4 The histogram shape was not symmetric. It peaked at approximately 0.7.
5 We increased the frequency count from 500 to 100,000.
6 We plotted the histogram of 100,000 frequencies representing 1 million total coin flips.
7 The new histogram's shape resembled a normal curve. It continued peaking at 0.7.
8 We summed the rectangular area of bins around the peak. We stopped once the added bins covered 95% of the area under the histogram.
9 These bins represented a frequency range of approximately 0.670–0.723.
10 We increased the coin flips per sample from 1,000 to 50,000.
11 We plotted the histogram of 100,000 frequencies representing 5 billion total coin flips.
12 The updated histogram's shape continued to resemble a normal curve.
13 We recomputed the range covering 95% of the histogram's area.
14 The range width shrank to approximately 0.695–0.703.
15 Thus, when we increased our per-frequency flip count, the range of likely frequencies began to narrow at around 0.7.

3.2.4 Computing histograms in NumPy

Calling the `plt.hist` method automatically generates a histogram plot. Can we obtain the histogram likelihoods and bin edges without creating a plot? Yes, because `plt.hist` uses NumPy's non-visual `np.histogram` function. This function takes as input all parameters that don't relate to histogram visualization, such as `frequency_arrays`, `bins='auto'`, and `density=True`. It then returns two variables not associated with plot manipulation: `likelihoods` and `bin_edges`. Therefore, we can run `compute_high_confidence_interval` while bypassing visualization simply by calling `np.histogram`.

Listing 3.32 Computing a histogram using `np.histogram`

```
np.random.seed(0)

likelihoods, bin_edges = np.histogram(frequency_array, bins='auto',
                                      density=True)
bin_width = bin_edges[1] - bin_edges[0]
compute_high_confidence_interval(likelihoods, bin_width)
```

> We no longer store the start and end index variables returned by this function since there is no longer a need to highlight an interval range in a histogram plot.

```
The frequency range 0.695769 - 0.703708 represents a 95.06% confidence interval
```

Useful histogram functions

- `plt.hist(data, bins=10)`—Plots a histogram in which the elements of data are distributed across 10 equally spaced bins.
- `plt.hist(data, bins='auto')`—Plots a histogram whose bin count is determined automatically, based on the data distribution. `auto` is the default setting of `_bins`.
- `plt.hist(data, edges='black')`—In the plotted histogram, the edges of each bin are marked by black vertical lines.
- `counts, _, _ = plt.hist(data)`—The `counts` array is the first of the three variables returned by `plt.hist`. It holds the count of elements contained in each bin. These counts appear on the y-axis of the histogram plot.
- `_, bin_edges, _ = plt.hist(data)`—The `bin_edges` array is the second of the three variables returned by `plt.hist`. It holds the x-axis positions of the vertical bin edges in the plot. Subtracting `bin_edges[i]` from `bin_edges[i + 1]` returns the width of every bin. Multiplying the width by `counts[i]` returns the area of the rectangular bin at position `i`.
- `likelihoods, _, _ = plt.hist(data, density=True)`—The binned counts are transformed into likelihoods so that the area beneath the histogram sums to 1.0. Thus, the histogram is transformed into a probability distribution. Multiplying the bin width by `likelihoods[i]` returns the probability of a random outcome falling within a range of `bin_edges[i]` - `bin_edges[i +1]`.
- `_, _, patches = plt.hist(data)`—The `patches` list is the third of the three variables returned by `plt.hist`. The graphical settings of each bin at index `i` are stored in `patches[i]`. Calling `patches[i].set_facecolor('yellow')` changes the color of the histogram bin at position `i`.
- `likelihoods, bin_edges = np.histogram(data, density=True)`—Returns the histogram likelihoods and bin edges without actually plotting the results.

3.3 *Using confidence intervals to analyze a biased deck of cards*

Suppose you're shown a biased 52-card deck. Each card is either red or black, but the color counts aren't equal. How many red cards are present in the deck? You could find out by counting all the red cards one by one, but that would be too easy. Let's add a constraint to make the problem more interesting. You are only allowed to see the first card in the deck! If you wish to see a new card, you must first reshuffle. You're permitted to reshuffle as many times as you like and to view the top card after each shuffle.

Given these constraints, we must solve the problem using random sampling. Let's begin by modeling a 52-card deck with an unknown number of red cards. That red count is an integer between 0 and 52, which we can generate using np.random.randint. We'll keep the value of our random red_card_count value hidden until we've found a solution using sampling.

Listing 3.33   Generating a random red card count

```
np.random.seed(0)
total_cards = 52
red_card_count = np.random.randint(0, total_cards + 1)
```

Now let's compute black_card_count by using the constraint that red_card_count and black_card_count must sum to 52 cards total. We also maintain bias by ensuring that the two counts are not equal.

Listing 3.34   Generating a black card count

```
black_card_count = total_cards - red_card_count
assert black_card_count != red_card_count
```

During the modeling phase, we'll shuffle the deck and flip over the first card. What is the probability the card will be red? Well, a red card represents one of two possible outcomes: red or black. These outcomes can be characterized by the sample space {'red_card', 'black_card'}, but only when the two outcomes are equally likely. However, in our biased deck, the outcomes are weighted by red_card_count and black_card_count. A weighted sample space dict is therefore required, in which the dictionary values equal the count variables. We label the associated keys 'red_card' and 'black_card'. Passing weighted_sample_space into compute_event_probability will allow us to compute the probability of drawing a red card.

Listing 3.35   Computing card probabilities using a sample space

```
weighted_sample_space = {'red_card': red_card_count,
                         'black_card': black_card_count}
prob_red = compute_event_probability(lambda x: x == 'red_card',
                         weighted_sample_space)
```

As a reminder, the `compute_event_probability` function divides the `red_card_count` variable by the sum of `red_card_count` and `black_card_count` to compute the probability. Furthermore, the sum of `red_card_count` and `black_card_count` is equal to `total_cards`. Therefore, the probability of drawing a red card is equal to `red_card_count` divided by `total_cards`. Let's verify that.

Listing 3.36   Computing card probabilities using division

```
assert prob_red == red_card_count / total_cards
```

How should we utilize `prob_red` to model a flipped-over first card? Well, the card flip will produce one of two possible outputs: red or black. These two outcomes can be modeled as coin flips in which heads and tails are replaced by colors. Therefore, we can model the flipped card using the binomial distribution. Calling `np.random.binomial(1, prob_red)` returns 1 if the first card is red and 0 otherwise.

Listing 3.37   Simulating a random card

```
np.random.seed(0)
color = 'red' if np.random.binomial(1, prob_red) else 'black'
print(f"The first card in the shuffled deck is {color}")

The first card in the shuffled deck is red
```

We shuffle the deck 10 times and flip over the first card after each shuffle.

Listing 3.38   Simulating 10 random cards

```
np.random.seed(0)
red_count = np.random.binomial(10, prob_red)
print(f"In {red_count} of out 10 shuffles, a red card came up first.")

In 8 of out 10 shuffles, a red card came up first.
```

A red card appeared at the top of the deck in 8 out of 10 random shuffles. Does this mean that 80% of the cards are red? Of course not. We've previously shown how such outcomes are common when the sampling size is low. Instead of shuffling the deck 10 times, let's shuffle it 50,000 times. Then we compute the frequency and then redo the shuffling procedure another 100,000 times. We execute these steps by calling `np.random.binomial(50000, prob_red, 100000)` and dividing by 50,000. The resulting frequency array can be transformed into a histogram that will allow us to compute a 95% confidence interval for flipping over a red card. We compute the confidence interval by expanding the range of bins around the histogram's peak until that range covers 95% of the histogram's area.

Listing 3.39 Computing card probability confidence intervals

Converts 100,000 red counts into 100,000 frequencies

Counts the observed red cards out of 50,000 shuffles; repeats 100,000 times

```
np.random.seed(0)
red_card_count_array = np.random.binomial(50000, prob_red, 100000)
frequency_array = red_card_count_array / 50000

likelihoods, bin_edges = np.histogram(frequency_array, bins='auto',
                                      density=True)
bin_width = bin_edges[1] - bin_edges[0]
start_index, end_index = compute_high_confidence_interval(likelihoods,
                                      bin_width)

The frequency range 0.842865 - 0.849139 represents a 95.16% confidence interval
```

Computes the frequency histogram

Computes the 95% confidence interval for the histogram

We are very confident that prob_red lies between 0.842865 and 0.849139. We also know that prob_red equals red_card_count / total_cards, and therefore red_card_count equals prob_red * total_cards. Thus, we are highly confident that red_card_count lies between 0.842865 * total_cards and 0.849139 * total_cards. Let's compute the likely range of red_card_count. We round the end points of the range to the nearest integers because red_card_count corresponds to an integer value.

Listing 3.40 Estimating the red card count

```
range_start = round(0.842771 * total_cards)
range_end = round(0.849139 * total_cards)
print(f"The number of red cards in the deck is between {range_start} and
    {range_end}")

The number of red cards in the deck is between 44 and 44
```

We are very confident that there are 44 red cards in the deck. Let's check if our solution is correct.

Listing 3.41 Validating the red card count

```
if red_card_count == 44:
    print('We are correct! There are 44 red cards in the deck')
else:
    print('Oops! Our sampling estimation was wrong.')

We are correct! There are 44 red cards in the deck
```

There are indeed 44 red cards in the deck. We were able to determine this without manually counting all the cards. Our use of random card-shuffle sampling and confidence interval calculations proved sufficient to uncover the solution.

3.4 *Using permutations to shuffle cards*

Card shuffling requires us to randomly reorder the elements of a card deck. That random reordering can be carried out using the `np.random.shuffle` method. The function takes as input an ordered array or list and shuffles its elements in place. The following code randomly shuffles a deck of cards containing two red cards (represented by 1s) and two black cards (represented by 0s).

Listing 3.42 Shuffling a four-card deck

```
np.random.seed(0)
card_deck = [1, 1, 0, 0]
np.random.shuffle(card_deck)
print(card_deck)
```

```
[0, 0, 1, 1]
```

The shuffle method has rearranged the elements in `card_deck`. If we prefer to carry out the shuffle while retaining a copy of the original unshuffled deck, we can do so using `np.random.permutation`. The method returns a NumPy array containing a random ordering of cards. Meanwhile, the elements of the original inputted deck remain unchanged.

Listing 3.43 Returning a copy of the shuffled deck

```
np.random.seed(0)
unshuffled_deck = [1, 1, 0, 0]
shuffled_deck = np.random.permutation(unshuffled_deck)
assert unshuffled_deck == [1, 1, 0, 0]
print(shuffled_deck)
```

```
[0 0 1 1]
```

The random ordering of elements returned by `np.random.permutation` is mathematically called a *permutation*. Random permutations vary from the original ordering most of the time. On rare occasions, they may equal the original, unshuffled permutation. What is the probability that a shuffled permutation will exactly equal `unshuffled_deck`?

We can of course find out through sampling. However, the four-element deck is small enough to be analyzed using sample spaces. Composing the sample space requires us to cycle through all possible permutations of the deck. We can do so using the `iter-tools.permutations` function. Calling `itertools.permutations(unshuffled_deck)` will return an iterable over every possible permutation of the deck. Let's use the function to output the first three permutations. Note that these permutations are printed as Python tuples, not as arrays or lists. Tuples, unlike arrays or lists, cannot be modified in place: they are represented using parentheses.

Listing 3.44 Iterating over card permutations

```
import itertools
for permutation in list(itertools.permutations(unshuffled_deck))[:3]:
    print(permutation)


(1, 1, 0, 0)
(1, 1, 0, 0)
(1, 0, 1, 0)
```

The first two generated permutations are identical to each other. Why is that the case? Well, the first permutation is just the original `unshuffled_deck` with no rearranged elements. Meanwhile, the second permutation was generated by swapping the third and fourth elements of the first permutation. However, both those elements were zeros, so the swap did not impact the list. We can confirm that the swap actually took place by examining the first three permutations of `[0, 1, 2, 3]`.

Listing 3.45 Monitoring permutation swaps

```
for permutation in list(itertools.permutations([0, 1, 2, 3]))[:3]:
    print(permutation)


(0, 1, 2, 3)
(0, 1, 3, 2)
(0, 2, 1, 3)
```

Certain permutations of the four-card deck occur more than once. Thus, we can hypothesize that certain permutations might occur more frequently than others. Let's check this hypothesis by storing the permutation counts in a `weighted_sample_space` dictionary.

Listing 3.46 Computing permutation counts

```
weighted_sample_space = defaultdict(int)
for permutation in itertools.permutations(unshuffled_deck):
    weighted_sample_space[permutation] += 1

for permutation, count in weighted_sample_space.items():
    print(f"Permutation {permutation} occurs {count} times")


Permutation (1, 1, 0, 0) occurs 4 times
Permutation (1, 0, 1, 0) occurs 4 times
Permutation (1, 0, 0, 1) occurs 4 times
Permutation (0, 1, 1, 0) occurs 4 times
Permutation (0, 1, 0, 1) occurs 4 times
Permutation (0, 0, 1, 1) occurs 4 times
```

All the permutations occur with equal frequency. Consequently, all card arrangements are equally likely, and a weighted sample space is not required. An unweighted sample space equal to set(itertools.permutations(unshuffled_deck)) should sufficiently resolve the problem.

Listing 3.47   Computing permutation probabilities

Defines a lambda function that takes as input some x and returns True if x equals our unshuffled deck. This one-line lambda function serves as our event condition.

The unweighted sample space equals the set of all the unique permutations of the deck.

```
sample_space = set(itertools.permutations(unshuffled_deck))
event_condition = lambda x: list(x) == unshuffled_deck
prob = compute_event_probability(event_condition, sample_space)
assert prob == 1 / len(sample_space)
print(f"Probability that a shuffle does not alter the deck is {prob}")


Probability that a shuffle does not alter the deck is 0.16666666666666666
```

Computes the probability of observing an event that satisfies our event condition

Suppose we are handed a generic unshuffled_deck of size N containing $N/2$ red cards. Mathematically, it can be shown that all the color permutations of the deck will occur with equal likelihood. Thus, we can compute probabilities directly using the deck's unweighted sample space. Unfortunately, creating this sample space is not feasible for a 52-card deck since the number of possible permutations is astronomically large: 8.06×10^{67}, which is larger than the number of atoms on Earth. If we attempted to compute a 52-card sample space, our program would run for many days before eventually running out of memory. However, such a sample space can easily be computed for a smaller 10-card deck.

Listing 3.48   Computing a 10-card sample space

```
red_cards = 5 * [1]
black_cards = 5 * [0]
unshuffled_deck = red_cards + black_cards
sample_space = set(itertools.permutations(unshuffled_deck))
print(f"Sample space for a 10-card deck contains {len(sample_space)}
        elements")


Sample space for a 10-card deck contains 252 elements
```

We have been tasked with finding the best strategy for drawing a red card. The 10-card sample_space set could prove useful in these efforts: the set allows us to compute the probabilities of various competing strategies directly. We can thus rank our strategies based on their 10-card deck performance and then apply the top-ranking strategies to a 52-card deck.

Summary

- The `np.random.binomial` method can simulate random coin flips. The method gets its name from the *binomial distribution*, which is a generic distribution that captures coin-flip probabilities.

- When a coin is flipped repeatedly, its frequency of heads converges toward the actual probability of heads. However, the final frequency may differ slightly from the actual probability.

- We can visualize the variability of recorded coin-flip frequencies by plotting a *histogram*. A histogram shows binned counts of observed numeric values. The counts can be transformed into relative likelihoods so that the area beneath the histogram sums to 1.0. Effectively, the transformed histogram becomes a probability distribution. The area around the distribution's peak represents a *confidence interval*. A confidence interval is the likelihood that an unknown probability falls within a certain frequency range. Generally, we prefer a confidence interval that is at 95% or higher.

- The shape of a frequency histogram resembles a bell-shaped curve when the number of sampled frequencies is high. That curve is referred to as either the *Gaussian distribution* or the *normal distribution*. According to the *central limit theorem*, the 95% confidence interval associated with the bell curve becomes narrower as the size of each frequency sample increases.

- Simulated card shuffles can be carried out using the `np.random.permutation` method. This method returns a random permutation of the inputted deck of cards. The *permutation* represents a random ordering of card elements. We can iterate over every possible permutation by calling `itertools.permutations`. Iterating over all the permutations for a 52-card deck is computationally impossible. However, we can easily capture all the permutations of a smaller 10-card deck. These permutations can be used to compute the small deck's sample space.

Case study 1 solution

This section covers

- Card game simulations
- Probabilistic strategy optimization
- Confidence intervals

Our aim is to play a card game in which the cards are iteratively flipped until we tell the dealer to stop. Then one additional card is flipped. If that card is red, we win a dollar; otherwise, we lose a dollar. Our goal is to discover a strategy that best predicts a red card in the deck. We will do so by

1. Developing multiple strategies for predicting red cards in a randomly shuffled deck.
2. Applying each strategy across multiple simulations to compute its probability of success within a high confidence interval. If these computations prove to be intractable, we will instead focus on those strategies that perform best across a 10-card sample space.
3. Returning the simplest strategy associated with the highest probability of success.

WARNING Spoiler alert! The solution to case study 1 is about to be revealed. I strongly encourage you to try to solve the problem prior to reading the solution. The original problem statement is available for reference at the beginning of the case study.

4.1 Predicting red cards in a shuffled deck

We start by creating a deck holding 26 red cards and 26 black cards. Black cards are represented by 0s, and red cards are represented by 1s.

Listing 4.1 Modeling a 52-card deck

```
red_cards = 26 * [1]
black_cards = 26 * [0]
unshuffled_deck = red_cards + black_cards
```

We proceed to shuffle the deck.

Listing 4.2 Shuffling a 52-card deck

```
np.random.seed(1)
shuffled_deck = np.random.permutation(unshuffled_deck)
```

Now we iteratively flip over the cards in the deck, stopping when the next card is more likely to be red. Then we flip over the next card. We win if that card is red.

How do we decide when we should stop? One simple strategy is to terminate the game when the number of red cards remaining in the deck is greater than the number of black cards remaining in the deck. Let's execute that strategy on the shuffled deck.

Listing 4.3 Coding a card game strategy

Subtracts the total cards seen thus far from 52. This total equals i + 1, since i is initially set to zero. Alternatively, we can run enumerate(shuffled_deck[:-1], 1) so that i is initially set to 1.

```
remaining_red_cards = 26
for i, card in enumerate(shuffled_deck[:-1]):
    remaining_red_cards -= card
    remaining_total_cards = 52 - i - 1       ◄────
    if remaining_red_cards / remaining_total_cards > 0.5:
        break

print(f"Stopping the game at index {i}.")
final_card = shuffled_deck[i + 1]
color = 'red' if final_card else 0
print(f"The next card in the deck is {'red' if final_card else 'black'}.")
print(f"We have {'won' if final_card else 'lost'}!")
```

```
Stopping the game at index 1.
The next card in the deck is red.
We have won!
```

The strategy yielded a win on our very first try. Our strategy halts when the fraction of remaining red cards is greater than half of the remaining total cards. We can generalize that fraction to equal a `min_red_fraction` parameter, thus halting when the red card ratio is greater than the inputted parameter value. This generalized strategy is implemented next with `min_red_fraction` preset to 0.5.

Listing 4.4   Generalizing the card game strategy

```
np.random.seed(0)
total_cards = 52
total_red_cards = 26                                              Shuffles the
def execute_strategy(min_fraction_red=0.5, shuffled_deck=None,    unshuffled
                     return_index=False):                        deck if no
    if shuffled_deck is None:                                     input deck
        shuffled_deck = np.random.permutation(unshuffled_deck)  ◁─┘ is provided

    remaining_red_cards = total_red_cards

    for i, card in enumerate(shuffled_deck[:-1]):
        remaining_red_cards -= card
        fraction_red_cards = remaining_red_cards / (total_cards - i - 1)
        if fraction_red_cards > min_fraction_red:
            break

    return (i+1, shuffled_deck[i+1]) if return_index else shuffled_deck[i+1]  ◁─┐
```
                                                    Optionally returns the card
                                                index along with the final card

4.1.1   *Estimating the probability of strategy success*

Let's apply our basic strategy to a series of 1,000 random shuffles.

Listing 4.5   Running the strategy over 1,000 shuffles

```
observations = np.array([execute_strategy() for _ in range(1000)])
```

The total fraction of 1s in observations corresponds to the observed fraction of red cards and therefore to the fraction of wins. We can compute this fraction by summing the 1s in `observations` and dividing by the array size. As an aside, that computation can also be carried out by calling `observations.mean()`.

Listing 4.6   Computing the frequency of wins

```
frequency_wins = observations.sum() / 1000
assert frequency_wins == observations.mean()
print(f"The frequency of wins is {frequency_wins}")

The frequency of wins is 0.511
```

We've won 51.1% of the total games! Our strategy appears to be working: 511 wins and 489 losses will net us a total profit of $22.

Listing 4.7 Computing total profit

```
dollars_won = frequency_wins * 1000
dollars_lost = (1 - frequency_wins) * 1000
total_profit = dollars_won - dollars_lost
print(f"Total profit is ${total_profit:.2f}")

Total profit is $22.00
```

The strategy worked well for a sample size of 1,000 shuffles. We now plot the strategy's win-frequency convergence over a series of sample sizes ranging from 1 through 10,000 (figure 4.1).

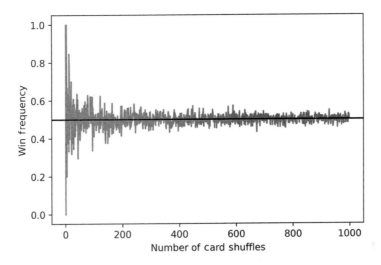

Figure 4.1 The number of played games plotted against the observed win-count frequency. The frequencies fluctuate around a value of 0.5. We cannot tell if the probability of winning is above or below 0.5.

Listing 4.8 Plotting simulated frequencies of wins

```
np.random.seed(0)                                Returns the frequency of wins for
def repeat_game(number_repeats):   ◁─────        a specified number of games
    observations = np.array([execute_strategy()
                             for _ in range(number_repeats)])
    return observations.mean()

frequencies = []
for i in range(1, 1000):
    frequencies.append(repeat_game(i))
```

```
plt.plot(list(range(1, 1000)), frequencies)
plt.axhline(0.5, color='k')
plt.xlabel('Number of Card Shuffles')
plt.ylabel('Win-Frequency')
plt.show()
print(f"The win-frequency for 10,000 shuffles is {frequencies[-1]}")

The win-frequency for 10,000 shuffles is 0.5035035035035035
```

The strategy yields a win frequency of over 50% when 10,000 card shuffles are sampled. However, the strategy also fluctuates above and below 50% throughout the entire sampling process. How confident are we that the probability of a win is actually greater than 0.5? We can find out using confidence interval analysis (figure 4.2). We compute the confidence interval by sampling 10,000 card shuffles 300 times, for a total of 3 million shuffles. Shuffling an array is a computationally expensive procedure, so listing 4.9 takes approximately 40 seconds to run.

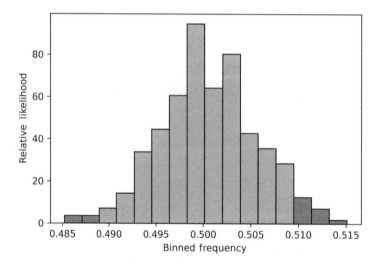

Figure 4.2 **A histogram of 300 binned frequencies plotted against their associated relative likelihoods. Highlighted bars delineate the 95% confidence interval. That interval covers a frequency range of roughly 0.488–0.508.**

Listing 4.9   Computing the confidence interval for 3 million shuffles

```
np.random.seed(0)
frequency_array = np.array([repeat_game(10000) for _ in range(300)])

likelihoods, bin_edges, patches = plt.hist(frequency_array, bins='auto',
                                            edgecolor='black', density=True)
bin_width = bin_edges[1] - bin_edges[0]
```

```
start_index, end_index = compute_high_confidence_interval(likelihoods,
    bin_width)
```

As a reminder, we defined the compute_high_confidence_interval function in section 3.

```
for i in range(start_index, end_index):
    patches[i].set_facecolor('yellow')
plt.xlabel('Binned Frequency')
plt.ylabel('Relative Likelihood')

plt.show()
```

```
The frequency range 0.488938 - 0.509494 represents a 97.00% confidence
    interval
```

We are quite confident that the actual probability lies somewhere between 0.488 and 0.509. However, we still don't know whether that probability is above 0.5 or below 0.5. This is a problem: even a minor misinterpretation of the true probability could cause us to lose money.

Imagine that the true probability is 0.5001. If we apply our strategy to 1 billion shuffles, we should expect to win \$200,000. Now suppose we were wrong, and the actual probability is 0.4999. In this scenario, we will lose \$200,000. A tiny error over the fourth decimal space could cost us hundreds of thousands of dollars.

We must be absolutely certain that the true probability lies above 0.5. Thus, we must narrow the 95% confidence interval by increasing the sample size at the expense of running time. The following code samples 50,000 shuffles over 3,000 iterations. It takes approximately an hour to run.

WARNING The following code will take an hour to run.

Listing 4.10 Computing the confidence interval for 150 million shuffles

```
np.random.seed(0)

frequency_array = np.array([repeat_game(50000) for _ in range(3000)])
likelihoods, bin_edges = np.histogram(frequency_array, bins='auto',
                                      density=True)
bin_width = bin_edges[1] - bin_edges[0]
compute_high_confidence_interval(likelihoods, bin_width)
```

```
The frequency range 0.495601 - 0.504345 represents a 96.03% confidence
    interval
```

We've executed our sampling. Unfortunately, the new confidence interval still does not discern whether the true probability lies above 0.5. So what should we do? Increasing the number of samples is not computationally feasible (unless we're willing to let the simulation run for a couple of days). Perhaps increasing min_red_fraction from 0.5 to 0.75 will yield an improvement. Let's update our strategy and go for a long walk as our simulation takes another hour to run.

WARNING The following code will take an hour to run.

Listing 4.11   Computing the confidence interval for an updated strategy

```
np.random.seed(0)
def repeat_game(number_repeats, min_red_fraction):
    observations = np.array([execute_strategy(min_red_fraction)
                             for _ in range(number_repeats)])
    return observations.mean()

frequency_array = np.array([repeat_game(50000, 0.75) for _ in range(3000)])
likelihoods, bin_edges = np.histogram(frequency_array, bins='auto',
                                      density=True)
bin_width = bin_edges[1] - bin_edges[0]
compute_high_confidence_interval(likelihoods, bin_width)

The frequency range 0.495535 - 0.504344 represents a 96.43% confidence
    interval
```

Nope! The span of our confidence interval remains unresolved since it still covers both profitable and unprofitable probabilities.

Perhaps we can gain more insight by applying our strategies to a 10-card deck. That deck's sample space can be explored in its entirety, thus letting us compute the exact probability of a win.

4.2   *Optimizing strategies using the sample space for a 10-card deck*

The following code computes the sample space for a 10-card deck. Then it applies our basic strategy to that sample space. The final output is the probability that the strategy will yield a win.

Listing 4.12   Applying a basic strategy to a 10-card deck

```
total_cards = 10                              As a reminder, itertools was
total_red_cards = int(total_cards / 2)        previously imported in section 3.
total_black_cards = total_red_cards
unshuffled_deck = [1] * total_red_cards + [0] * total_black_cards
sample_space = set(itertools.permutations(unshuffled_deck))   ◁
win_condition = lambda x: execute_strategy(shuffled_deck=np.array(x))
prob_win = compute_event_probability(win_condition, sample_space)   ◁
print(f"Probability of a win is {prob_win}")
                                                     We defined the
Probability of a win is 0.5                    compute_event_probability
                                                  function in section 1.
Event condition where our
basic strategy yields a win
```

Surprisingly, our basic strategy yields a win only 50% of the time. This is no better than selecting the first card at random! Maybe our min_red_fraction parameter was insufficiently low. We can find out by sampling all the two-decimal min_red_fraction values between 0.50 and 1.0. The following code computes the win probabilities over a range of min_red_fraction values and returns the minimum and maximum probabilities.

Listing 4.13 Applying multiple strategies to a 10-card deck

```
def scan_strategies():
    fractions = [value / 100 for value in range(50, 100)]
    probabilities = []
    for frac in fractions:
        win_condition = lambda x: execute_strategy(frac,
                                             shuffled_deck=np.array(x))
        probabilities.append(compute_event_probability(win_condition,
                                                   sample_space))

    return probabilities

probabilities = scan_strategies()
print(f"Lowest probability of win is {min(probabilities)}")
print(f"Highest probability of win is {max(probabilities)}")

Lowest probability of win is 0.5
Highest probability of win is 0.5
```

Both the lowest and highest probabilities are equal to 0.5! None of our strategies have outperformed a random card choice. Perhaps adjusting the deck size will yield some improvement. Let's analyze the sample spaces of decks containing two, four, six, and eight cards. We apply all strategies to each sample space and return their probabilities of winning. Then we search for a probability that isn't equal to 0.5.

Listing 4.14 Applying multiple strategies to multiple decks

```
for total_cards in [2, 4, 6, 8]:
    total_red_cards = int(total_cards / 2)
    total_black_cards = total_red_cards
    unshuffled_deck = [1] * total_red_cards + [0] * total_black_cards

    sample_space = set(itertools.permutations(unshuffled_deck))
    probabilities = scan_strategies()
    if all(prob == 0.5 for prob in probabilities):
        print(f"No winning strategy found for deck of size {total_cards}")
    else:
        print(f"Winning strategy found for deck of size {total_cards}")

No winning strategy found for deck of size 2
No winning strategy found for deck of size 4
No winning strategy found for deck of size 6
No winning strategy found for deck of size 8
```

All of the strategies yield a probability of 0.5 across the small decks. Each time we increase the deck size, we add two additional cards to the deck, but this fails to improve performance. A strategy that fails on a 2-card deck continues to fail on a 4-card deck, and a strategy that fails on an 8-card deck continues to fail on a 10-card deck. We can extrapolate this logic even further. A strategy that fails on a 10-card deck will probably fail on a 12-card deck, and thus on a 14-card deck and a 16-card deck.

Eventually, it will fail on a 52-card deck. Qualitatively, this inductive argument makes sense. Mathematically, it can be proven to be true. Right now, we don't need to concern ourselves with the math. What's important is that our instincts have been proven wrong. Our strategies don't work on a 10-card deck, and we have little reason to believe they will work on a 52-card deck. Why do the strategies fail?

Intuitively, our initial strategy made sense: if there are more red cards than black cards in the deck, then we are more likely to pick a red card from the deck. However, we failed to take into account those scenarios when the red cards never outnumber the black cards. For instance, suppose the first 26 cards are red and the remainder are black. In these circumstances, our strategies will fail to halt, and we will lose. Also, let's consider a shuffled deck where the first 25 cards are red, the next 26 cards are black, and the final card is red. Here, our strategy will fail to halt, but we will still win. It seems each strategy can lead to one of four scenarios:

- Strategy halts and the next card is red. We win.
- Strategy halts and the next card is black. We lose.
- Strategy doesn't halt and the final card is red. We win.
- Strategy doesn't halt and the final card is black. We lose.

Let's sample how frequently the four scenarios occur across 50,000 card shuffles. We record these frequencies over our range of two-digit `min_red_fraction` values. We then plot each `min_red_fraction` value against the occurrence rates observed from the four scenarios (figure 4.3).

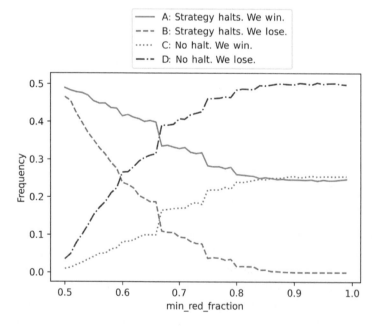

Figure 4.3   **The `min_red_fraction` parameter is plotted against the sampled frequencies for all four possible scenarios. Scenario A initially has a frequency of roughly 0.49, but eventually it drops to 0.25. Scenario C has a frequency of roughly 0.01, but eventually it increases to 0.25. The frequency sums for A and C remain at approximately 0.5, thus reflecting a 50% chance of winning the game.**

Listing 4.15 Plotting strategy outcomes across a 52-card deck

This list contains all instances of losses.

Scenario where our strategy halts and we win

This list contains all instances of wins.

```
np.random.seed(0)
total_cards = 52
total_red_cards = 26
unshuffled_deck = red_cards + black_cards

def repeat_game_detailed(number_repeats, min_red_fraction):

    observations = [execute_strategy(min_red_fraction, return_index=True)
                        for _ in range(num_repeats)]
    successes = [index for index, card, in observations if card == 1]
    halt_success = len([index for index in successes if index != 51])
    no_halt_success = len(successes) - halt_success

    failures = [index for index, card, in observations if card == 0]
    halt_failure = len([index for index in failures if index != 51])
    no_halt_failure = len(failures) - halt_failure
    result = [halt_success, halt_failure, no_halt_success, no_halt_failure]
    return [r / number_repeats for r in result]

fractions = [value / 100 for value in range(50, 100)]
num_repeats = 50000
result_types = [[], [], [], []]

for fraction in fractions:
    result = repeat_game_detailed(num_repeats, fraction)
    for i in range(4):
        result_types[i].append(result[i])

plt.plot(fractions, result_types[0],
        label='A) Strategy Halts. We Win.')
plt.plot(fractions, result_types[1], linestyle='--',
        label='B) Strategy Halts. We Lose.')
plt.plot(fractions, result_types[2], linestyle=':',
        label='C) No Halt. We Win.')
plt.plot(fractions, result_types[3], linestyle='-.',
        label='D) No Halt. We Lose.')
plt.xlabel('min_red_fraction')
plt.ylabel('Frequency')
plt.legend(bbox_to_anchor=(1.0, 0.5))
plt.show()
```

We execute a strategy across num_repeats simulations.

Scenario where our strategy doesn't halt and we win

We return the observed frequencies for all four scenarios.

We scan the scenario frequencies across multiple strategies.

Scenario where our strategy doesn't halt and we lose

Scenario where our strategy halts and we lose

The bbox_to_anchor parameter is used to position the legend above the plot to avoid overlap with the four plotted curves.

Let's examine the plot at the min_red_fraction value of 0.5. Here, scenario A (*Strategy Halts. We Win.*) is the most common outcome, with a frequency of approximately 0.49. Meanwhile, a halt leads to a loss approximately 46% of the time (strategy B). So why do we maintain a 50% chance of winning the game? Well, in 1% of the cases, our strategy fails to halt, but we still win (scenario C). The strategy's weakness is counter-balanced by random chance.

Within the plot, as the min_red_fraction goes up, the frequency of scenario A goes down. The more conservative we are, the less likely we are to stop the game prematurely and yield a win. Meanwhile, the success rate of scenario C increases. The more conservative we are, the higher the likelihood of reaching the final card and winning by chance.

As `min_red_fraction` increases, both scenario A and scenario C converge to a frequency of 0.25. Thus the probability of a win remains at 50%. Sometimes our strategy halts, and we do win. Other times, the strategy halts, and we still lose. Any advantage that each strategy offers is automatically wiped out by these losses. However, we occasionally get lucky: our strategy fails to halt, yet we win the game. These lucky wins amend our losses, and our probability of winning stays the same. No matter what we do, our likelihood of winning remains fifty-fifty. Therefore, the optimal strategy we can offer is to pick the first card in the shuffled deck.

Listing 4.16 The optimal winning strategy

```
def optimal_strategy(shuffled_deck):
    return shuffled_deck[0]
```

Summary

- Probabilities can be counterintuitive. Innately, we assumed that our planned card game strategy would perform better than random. However, this proved not to be the case. We must be careful when dealing with random processes. It's best to rigorously test all our intuitive assumptions prior to wagering on any future outcome.
- Sometimes, even large-scale simulations fail to find a probability within the required level of precision. However, by simplifying our problem, we can utilize sample spaces to yield insights. Sample spaces allow us to test our intuition. If our intuitive solution fails on a toy version of the problem, it is also likely to fail on the actual version of the problem.

Assessing online ad clicks for significance

Problem statement

Fred is a loyal friend, and he needs your help. Fred just launched a burger bistro in the city of Brisbane. The bistro is open for business, but business is slow. Fred wants to entice new customers to come and try his tasty burgers. To do this, Fred will run an online advertising campaign directed at Brisbane residents. Every weekday, between 11:00 a.m. and 1:00 p.m., Fred will purchase 3,000 ads aimed at hungry locals. Every ad will be viewed by a single Brisbane resident. The text of every ad will read, "Hungry? Try the Best Burger in Brisbane. Come to Fred's." Clicking the text will take potential customers to Fred's site. Each displayed ad will cost our friend one cent, but Fred believes the investment will be worth it.

Fred is getting ready to execute his ad campaign. However, he runs into a problem. Fred previews his ad, and its text is blue. Fred believes that blue is a boring color. He feels that other colors could yield more clicks. Fortunately, Fred's advertising software allows him to choose from 30 different colors. Is there a text color that will bring more clicks than blue? Fred decides to find out.

Fred instigates an experiment. Every weekday for a month, Fred purchases 3,000 online ads. The text of every ad is assigned to one of 30 possible colors. The advertisements are distributed evenly by color. Thus, 100 ads with the same color are viewed by 100 people every day. For example, 100 people view a blue ad, and another 100 people view a green ad. These numbers add up to 3,000 views that are distributed across the 30 colors. Fred's advertising software automatically tracks all daily views. It also records the daily clicks associated with each of the 30 colors. The software stores this data in a table. That table holds the clicks per day and views per day for every specified color. Each table row maps a color to the views and clicks for all analyzed days.

Fred has carried out his experiment. He obtained ad-click data for all 20 weekdays of the month. That data is organized by color. Now, Fred wants to know if there is a color that draws significantly more ad clicks than blue. Unfortunately, Fred doesn't know how to properly interpret the results. He's not sure which clicks are meaningful and which clicks have occurred purely randomly. Fred is brilliant at broiling burgers but has no training in data analysis. This is why Fred has turned to you for help. Fred asks you to analyze his table and to compare the counts of daily clicks. He's searching for a color that draws significantly more ad clicks than blue. Are you willing to help Fred? If so, he's promised you free burgers for a year!

Dataset description

Fred's ad-click data is stored in the file colored_ad_click_table.csv. The .csv file extension is an acronym for *comma-separated values*. Our .csv file is a table stored as text. The table columns are separated by commas. The first line in the file contains the comma-separated labels for the columns. The first 99 characters of that line are *Color, Click Count: Day 1, View Count: Day 1, Click Count: Day 2, View Count: Day 2, Click Count: Day 3,*.

Let's briefly clarify the column labels:

- Column 1: *Color*
  - Each row in the column corresponds to one of 30 possible text colors.
- Column 2: *Click Count: Day 1*
  - The column tallies the times each colored ad was clicked on day 1 of Fred's experiment.
- Column 3: *View Count: Day 1*
  - The column tallies the times each ad was viewed on day 1 of Fred's experiment.
  - According to Fred, all daily views are expected to equal 100.
- The remaining 38 columns contain the clicks per day and views per day for the other 19 days of the experiment.

Overview

To address the problem at hand, we need to know how to do the following:

- Measure the centrality and dispersion of sampled data.
- Interpret the significance of two diverging means through p-value calculation.
- Minimize mistakes associated with misleading p-value measurements.
- Load and manipulate data stored in tables using Python.

Basic probability and statistical analysis using SciPy

This section covers

- Analyzing binomials using the SciPy library
- Defining dataset centrality
- Defining dataset dispersion
- Computing the centrality and dispersion of probability distributions

Statistics is a branch of mathematics dealing with the collection and interpretation of numeric data. It is the precursor of all modern data science. The term *statistic* originally signified "the science of the state" because statistical methods were first developed to analyze the data of state governments. Since ancient times, government agencies have gathered data pertaining to their populace. That data would be used to levy taxes and organize large military campaigns. Hence, critical state decisions depended on the quality of data. Poor record keeping could lead to potentially disastrous results. That is why state bureaucrats were very concerned by any random fluctuations in their records. Probability theory eventually tamed these fluctuations, making the randomness interpretable. Ever since then, statistics and probability theory have been closely intertwined.

Statistics and probability theory are closely related, but in some ways, they are very different. Probability theory studies random processes over a potentially infinite number of measurements. It is not bound by real-world limitations. This allows us to model the behavior of a coin by imagining millions of coin flips. In real life, flipping a coin millions of times is a pointlessly time-consuming endeavor. Surely we can sacrifice some data instead of flipping coins all day and night. Statisticians acknowledge these constraints placed on us by the data-gathering process. Real-world data collection is costly and time consuming. Every data point carries a price. We cannot survey a country's population without employing government officials. We cannot test our online ads without paying for every ad that's clicked. Thus, the size of our final dataset usually depends on the size of our initial budget. If the budget is constrained, then the data will also be constrained. This trade-off between data and resourcing lies at the heart of modern statistics. Statistics help us understand exactly how much data is sufficient to draw insights and make impactful decisions. The purpose of statistics is to find meaning in data even when that data is limited in size.

Statistics is highly mathematical and usually taught using math equations. Nevertheless, direct exposure to equations is not a prerequisite for statistical understanding. In fact, many data scientists do not write formulas when running statistical analyses. Instead, they use Python libraries such as SciPy, which handle all the complex math calculations. However, proper library usage still requires an intuitive understanding of statistical procedures. In this section, we cultivate our understanding of statistics by applying probability theory to real-world problems.

5.1 *Exploring the relationships between data and probability using SciPy*

SciPy, which is short for *Scientific Python*, provides many useful methods for scientific analysis. The SciPy library includes an entire module for addressing problems in probability and statistics: `scipy.stats`. Let's install the library and import the `stats` module.

NOTE Call `pip install scipy` from the command line terminal to install the SciPy library.

> **Listing 5.1 Importing the `stats` module from SciPy**

```
from scipy import stats
```

The `stats` module is very useful for assessing the randomness of data. For example, in section 1, we computed the probability of a fair coin producing at least 16 heads after 20 flips. Our calculations required us to examine all possible combinations of 20 flipped coins. Then we computed the probability of observing 16 or more heads or 16 or more tails to measure the randomness of our observations. SciPy allows us to measure this probability directly using the `stats.binom_test` method. The method is named after the binomial distribution, which governs how a flipped coin might fall.

The method requires three parameters: the number of heads, the total number of coin flips, and the probability of a coin landing on heads. Let's apply the binomial test to 16 heads observed from 20 coin flips. Our output should equal the previously computed value of approximately 0.011.

> **NOTE** SciPy and standard Python handle low-value decimal points differently. In section 1, when we computed the probability, the final value was rounded to 17 significant digits. SciPy, on the other hand, returns a value containing 18 significant digits. Thus, for consistency's sake, we round our SciPy output to 17 digits.

Listing 5.2 Analyzing extreme head counts using SciPy

```
num_heads = 16
num_flips = 20
prob_head = 0.5
prob = stats.binom_test(num_heads, num_flips, prob_head)
print(f"Probability of observing more than 15 heads or 15 tails is {prob:.17f}")
```

```
Probability of observing more than 15 heads or 15 tails is 0.01181793212890625
```

It's worth emphasizing that `stats.binom_test` did not compute the probability of observing 16 heads. Rather, it returned the probability of seeing a coin-flip sequence where 16 or more coins fell on the same face. If we want the probability of seeing exactly 16 heads, then we must utilize the `stats.binom.pmf` method. That method represents the *probability mass function* of the binomial distribution. A probability mass function maps inputted integer values to their probability of occurrence. Thus, calling `stats.binom.pmf(num_heads, num_flips, prob_heads)` returns the likelihood of a coin yielding `num_heads` number of heads. Under current settings, this equals the probability of a fair coin falling on heads 16 out of 20 times.

Listing 5.3 Computing an exact probability using `stats.binom.pmf`

```
prob_16_heads = stats.binom.pmf(num_heads, num_flips, prob_head)
print(f"The probability of seeing {num_heads} of {num_flips} heads is
    {prob_16_heads}")
```

```
The probability of seeing 16 of 20 heads is 0.004620552062988271
```

We've used `stats.binom.pmf` to find the probability of seeing exactly 16 heads. However, that method is also able to compute multiple probabilities simultaneously. Multiple head-count probabilities can be processed by passing in a list of head-count values. For instance, passing `[4, 16]` returns a two-element NumPy array containing the probabilities of seeing 4 heads and 16 heads, respectively. Conceptually, the probability of seeing 4 heads and 16 tails equals the probability of seeing 4 tails and 16 heads. Thus, executing `stats.binom.pmf([4, 16], num_flips, prob_head)` should return a two-element array whose elements are equal. Let's confirm.

Listing 5.4   Computing an array of probabilities using `stats.binom.pmf`

```
probabilities = stats.binom.pmf([4, 16], num_flips, prob_head)
assert probabilities.tolist() == [prob_16_heads] * 2
```

List-passing allows us to compute probabilities across intervals. For example, if we pass `range(21)` into `stats.binom.pmf`, then the outputted array will contain all probabilities across the interval of every possible head count. As we learned in section 1, the sum of these probabilities should equal 1.0.

> **NOTE** Summing low-value decimals is computationally tricky. Over the course of the summation, tiny errors accumulate. Due to these errors, our final summed probability will marginally diverge from 1.0 unless we round it to 14 significant digits. We do this rounding in the next listing.

Listing 5.5   Computing an interval probability using `stats.binom.pmf`

```
interval_all_counts = range(21)
probabilities = stats.binom.pmf(interval_all_counts, num_flips, prob_head)
total_prob = probabilities.sum()
print(f"Total sum of probabilities equals {total_prob:.14f}")

Total sum of probabilities equals 1.00000000000000
```

Also, as discussed in section 2, plotting `interval_all_counts` versus `probabilities` reveals the shape of our 20-coin-flip distribution. Thus, we can generate the distribution plot without having to iterate through possible coin-flip combinations (figure 5.1).

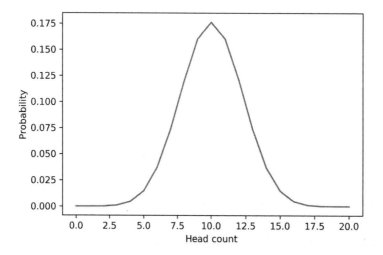

Figure 5.1   The probability distribution for 20 coin flips, generated using SciPy

Listing 5.6 Plotting a 20-coin-flip binomial distribution

```
import matplotlib.pyplot as plt
plt.plot(interval_all_counts, probabilities)
plt.xlabel('Head-count')
plt.ylabel('Probability')
plt.show()
```

In section 2, our ability to visualize the binomial was limited by the total number of coin-flip combinations that we needed to compute. This is no longer the case. The `stats.binom.pmf` method lets us display any distribution associated with an arbitrary coin-flip count. Let's use our newfound freedom to simultaneously plot the distributions for 20, 80, 140, and 200 coin flips (figure 5.2).

Listing 5.7 Plotting five different binomial distributions

```
flip_counts = [20, 80, 140, 200]
linestyles = ['-', '--', '-.', ':']
colors = ['b', 'g', 'r', 'k']

for num_flips, linestyle, color in zip(flip_counts, linestyles, colors):
    x_values = range(num_flips + 1)
    y_values = stats.binom.pmf(x_values, num_flips, 0.5)
    plt.plot(x_values, y_values, linestyle=linestyle, color=color,
             label=f'{num_flips} coin-flips')
plt.legend()
plt.xlabel('Head-count')
plt.ylabel('Probability')
plt.show()
```

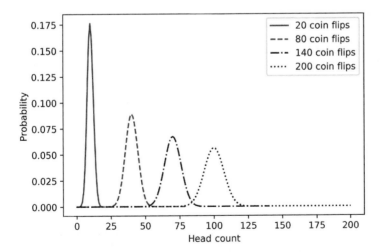

Figure 5.2 Multiple binomial probability distributions across 20, 80, 140, and 200 coin flips. The distribution centers shift right as the coin-flip count goes up. Also, every distribution becomes more dispersed around its center as the coin-flip count increases.

Within the plot, the central peak of each binomial appears to shift rightward as the coin-flip count goes up. Also, the 20-coin-flip distribution is noticeably thinner than the 200-coin-flip distribution. In other words, the plotted distributions grow more dispersed around their central positions as these central positions move to the right.

Such shifts in centrality and dispersion are commonly encountered in data analysis. We previously observed dispersion shifts in section 3, where we used randomly sampled data to visualize several histogram distributions. Subsequently, we observed that the plotted histogram thickness was dependent on our sample size. At the time, our observations were purely qualitative since we lacked a metric for comparing the thickness of two plots. However, simply noting that one plot appears thicker than another is insufficient. Likewise, stating that one plot is more rightward than another is also insufficient. We need to quantify our distribution differences. We must assign specific numbers to centrality and dispersion to discern how these numbers change from plot to plot. Doing so requires that we familiarize ourselves with the concepts of *variance* and *mean*.

5.2   *Mean as a measure of centrality*

Suppose we wish to study our local temperature over the first week of summer. When summer comes around, we glance at the thermometer outside our window. At noon, the temperature is exactly 80 degrees. We repeat our noon measurements over the next six days. Our measurements are 80, 77, 73, 61, 74, 79, and 81 degrees. Let's store these measurements in a NumPy array.

Listing 5.8   Storing recorded temperatures in a NumPy array

```
import numpy as np
measurements = np.array([80, 77, 73, 61, 74, 79, 81])
```

We'll now attempt to summarize our measurements using a single central value. First, we sort the measurements in place by calling `measurements.sort()`. Then, we plot the sorted temperatures in order to evaluate their centrality (figure 5.3).

Listing 5.9   Plotting the recorded temperatures

```
measurements.sort()
number_of_days = measurements.size
plt.plot(range(number_of_days), measurements)
plt.scatter(range(number_of_days), measurements)
plt.ylabel('Temperature')
plt.show()
```

Based on the plot, a central temperature exists somewhere between 60 degrees and 80 degrees. Therefore, we can naively estimate the center as approximately 70 degrees. Let's quantify our estimate as the midpoint between the lowest value and the highest value in the plot. We compute that midpoint by taking half the difference between the minimum and maximum temperatures and adding it to the minimum temperature.

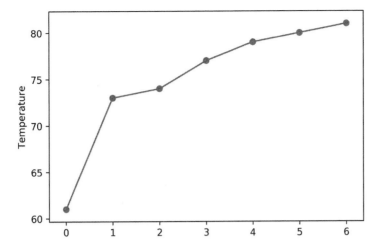

Figure 5.3 A plot containing seven sorted temperatures. A central temperature exists somewhere between 60 and 80 degrees.

(We can also obtain the same value by summing the minimum and maximum directly and dividing that sum by 2.)

Listing 5.10 Finding the midpoint temperature

```
difference = measurements.max() - measurements.min()
midpoint = measurements.min() + difference / 2
assert midpoint == (measurements.max() + measurements.min()) / 2
print(f"The midpoint temperature is {midpoint} degrees")
```

```
The midpoint temperature is 71.0 degrees
```

The midpoint temperature is 71 degrees. Let's mark that midpoint on our plot using a horizontal line. We draw the horizontal line by calling `plt.axhline(midpoint)` (figure 5.4).

Listing 5.11 Plotting the midpoint temperature

```
plt.plot(range(number_of_days), measurements)
plt.scatter(range(number_of_days), measurements)
plt.axhline(midpoint, color='k', linestyle='--')
plt.ylabel('Temperature')
plt.show()
```

Our plotted midpoint seems a little low: six of our seven measurements are higher than the midpoint. Intuitively, our central value should split the measurements more evenly—the number of temperatures above and below the center should be approximately equal. We can achieve this equality by choosing the middle element in our sorted seven-element array. The middle element, which statisticians call the *median*,

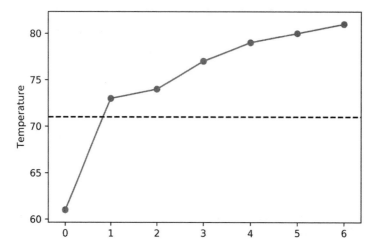

Figure 5.4   A plot containing seven sorted temperatures. A temperature of 71 degrees marks the midpoint between the highest and lowest temperatures. That midpoint seems low: six of seven temperatures are above the midpoint value.

will split our measurements into two equal parts. Three measurements will appear below the median, and three measurements will appear above it. 3 is also the index in the measurements array where the median is present. Let's add the median to our plot (figure 5.5).

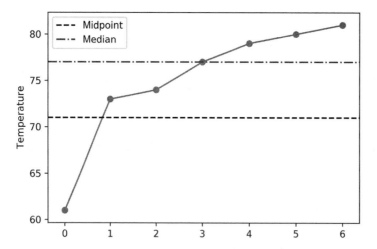

Figure 5.5   A plot containing seven sorted temperatures. A median of 77 degrees splits the temperatures in half. The median appears slightly off balance: it is closer to the three upper temperatures than to the three lower temperatures.

Listing 5.12   Plotting the median temperature

```
median = measurements[3]
print(f"The median temperature is {median} degrees")
plt.plot(range(number_of_days), measurements)
plt.scatter(range(number_of_days), measurements)
plt.axhline(midpoint, color='k', linestyle='--', label='midpoint')
plt.axhline(median, color='g', linestyle='-.', label='median')
plt.legend()
plt.ylabel('Temperature')
plt.show()
```

```
The median temperature is 77 degrees
```

Our median of 77 degrees splits the temperatures in half. However, the split is not well balanced since the median is closer to the upper three temperatures in the plot. In particular, the median is noticeably far from our minimum measure of 61 degrees. Perhaps we can balance the split by penalizing the median for being too far from the minimum. We'll implement this penalty using the *squared distance*, which is simply the square of the difference between two values. The squared distance grows quadratically as the two values are pushed further apart. Thus, if we penalize our central value based on its distance to 61, the squared distance penalty will grow noticeably larger as it drifts away from 61 degrees (figure 5.6).

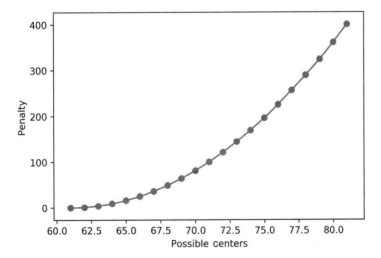

Figure 5.6   A plot of possible centers penalized based on their squared distances relative to the minimum temperature of 61 degrees. Not surprisingly, the minimum penalty occurs at 61 degrees. Unfortunately, the penalty doesn't take into account the distance to the remaining six recorded temperatures.

Listing 5.13   Penalizing centers using the squared distance from the minimum

```
def squared_distance(value1, value2):
    return (value1 - value2) ** 2                    Uses the range of values between
                                                     the minimum and maximum measured
                                                     temperatures as our set of possible centers
possible_centers = range(measurements.min(), measurements.max() + 1)  ◁
penalties = [squared_distance(center, 61) for center in possible_centers]
plt.plot(possible_centers, penalties)
plt.scatter(possible_centers, penalties)
plt.xlabel('Possible Centers')
plt.ylabel('Penalty')
plt.show()
```

Our plot displays the penalty across a range of possible centers based on their distance to our minimum. As the centers shift toward 61, the penalty drops, but their distance to the remaining six measurements increases. Thus, we ought to penalize each potential center based on its squared distance to all seven measurements. We'll do so by defining a sum of squared distances function, which will add up the squared distances between some value and the measurement array. That function will serve as our new penalty. Plotting the possible centers against their penalties will allow us to find the center whose penalty is minimized (figure 5.7).

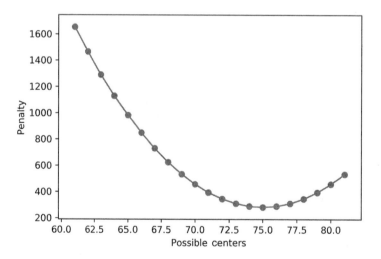

Figure 5.7   A plot of possible centers penalized based on the sum of their squared distances relative to all recorded temperatures. The minimum penalty occurs at 75 degrees.

Listing 5.14   Penalizing centers using the total sum of squared distances

```
def sum_of_squared_distances(value, measurements):
    return sum(squared_distance(value, m) for m in measurements)
```

```
penalties = [sum_of_squared_distances(center, measurements)
             for center in possible_centers]
plt.plot(possible_centers, penalties)
plt.scatter(possible_centers, penalties)
plt.xlabel('Possible Centers')
plt.ylabel('Penalty')
plt.show()
```

Based on our plot, the temperature of 75 degrees incurs the lowest penalty. We'll informally refer to this temperature value as our "least-penalized center." Let's demarcate it using a horizontal line on our temperature plot (figure 5.8).

Listing 5.15 Plotting the least-penalized temperature

```
least_penalized = 75
assert least_penalized == possible_centers[np.argmin(penalties)]

plt.plot(range(number_of_days), measurements)
plt.scatter(range(number_of_days), measurements)
plt.axhline(midpoint, color='k', linestyle='--', label='midpoint')
plt.axhline(median, color='g', linestyle='-.', label='median')
plt.axhline(least_penalized, color='r', linestyle='-',
            label='least penalized center')
plt.legend()
plt.ylabel('Temperature')
plt.show()
```

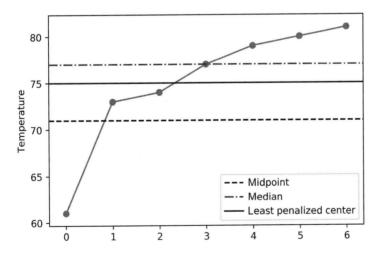

Figure 5.8 A plot containing seven sorted temperatures. The least-penalized center of 75 degrees splits the temperatures in a balanced manner.

The least-penalized center splits the measured temperatures fairly evenly: four measurements appear above it, and three measurements appear below it. Thus, this center maintains a balanced data split while providing a closer distance to the coldest recorded temperature relative to the median.

The least-penalized center is a good measure of centrality. It minimizes all the penalties incurred for being too far from any given point, which leads to balanced distances between the center and every data point. Unfortunately, our computation of that center was very inefficient. Scanning all possible penalties is not a scalable solution. Is there a more efficient way to compute the center? Yes! Mathematicians have shown that the sum-of-squared-distances error is always minimized by the *average* value of a dataset. Thus, we can compute the least-penalized center directly. We simply need to sum all the elements in measurements and then divide that sum by the array size.

Listing 5.16   Computing the least-penalized center using an average value

```
assert measurements.sum() / measurements.size == least_penalized
```

A summed array of values divided by array size is formally called the *arithmetic mean*. Informally, the value is referred to as the *mean* or the average of the array. The mean can be computed by calling the mean method of a NumPy array. We can also compute the mean by calling the np.mean and np.average methods.

Listing 5.17   Computing the mean using NumPy

```
mean = measurements.mean()
assert mean == least_penalized
assert mean == np.mean(measurements)
assert mean == np.average(measurements)
```

The np.average method differs from the np.mean method because it takes as input an optional weights parameter. The weights parameter is a list of numeric weights that capture the importance of the measurements relative to each other. When all the weights are equal, the output of np.average is no different from np.mean. However, adjusting the weights leads to a difference in the outputs.

Listing 5.18   Passing weights into np.average

```
equal_weights = [1] * 7
assert mean == np.average(measurements, weights=equal_weights)

unequal_weights = [100] + [1] * 6
assert mean != np.average(measurements, weights=unequal_weights)
```

The weights parameter is useful for computing the mean across duplicate measurements. Suppose we analyze 10 temperature measurements where 75 degrees appears 9 times and 77 degrees appears just once. The full list of measurements is represented by 9 * [75] + [77]. We can compute the mean by calling np.mean on that list. We can also compute the mean by calling np.average([75, 77], weights=[9, 1]); both computations are equal.

Listing 5.19   Computing the weighted mean of duplicate values

```
weighted_mean = np.average([75, 77], weights=[9, 1])
print(f"The mean is {weighted_mean}")
assert weighted_mean == np.mean(9 * [75] + [77]) == weighted_mean
```

```
The mean is 75.2
```

Computing the weighted mean serves as a shortcut for computing the regular mean when duplicates are present. In the computation, the relative ratio of unique measurement counts is represented by the ratio of the weights. Thus, even if we convert our absolute counts of 9 and 1 into relative weights of 900 and 100, the final value of weighted_mean should remain the same. This is also true if the weights are converted into relative probabilities of 0.9 and 0.1.

Listing 5.20   Computing the weighted mean of relative weights

```
assert weighted_mean == np.average([75, 77], weights=[900, 100])
assert weighted_mean == np.average([75, 77], weights=[0.9, 0.1])
```

We can treat probabilities as weights. Consequently, this allows us to compute the mean of any probability distribution.

5.2.1   *Finding the mean of a probability distribution*

At this point in the book, we are intimately familiar with the 20-coin-flip binomial distribution. The distribution's peak is symmetrically centered at 10 heads. How does that peak compare to the distribution's mean? Let's find out. We compute the mean by passing a probabilities array into the weights parameter of np.average. Then we plot the mean as a vertical line that cuts across the distribution (figure 5.9).

Listing 5.21   Computing the mean of a binomial distribution

```
num_flips = 20
interval_all_counts = range(num_flips + 1)
probabilities = stats.binom.pmf(interval_all_counts, 20, prob_head)
mean_binomial = np.average(interval_all_counts, weights=probabilities)
print(f"The mean of the binomial is {mean_binomial:.2f} heads")
plt.plot(interval_all_counts, probabilities)
plt.axvline(mean_binomial, color='k', linestyle='--')   ◁──┐ The axvline method
plt.xlabel('Head-count')                                     │ plots a vertical line
plt.ylabel('Probability')                                    │ at a specified x
plt.show()                                                    │ coordinate.
```

```
The mean of the binomial is 10.00 heads
```

The mean of the binomial is 10 heads. It cuts across the distribution's central peak and perfectly captures the binomial's centrality. For this reason, SciPy allows us to obtain the mean of any binomial simply by calling stats.binom.mean. The stats.binom.mean

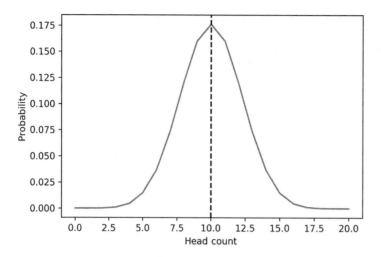

Figure 5.9   A 20-coin-flip binomial distribution bisected by its mean. The mean is positioned directly in the distribution's center.

method takes as input two parameters: the number of coin flips and the probability of heads.

Listing 5.22   Computing the binomial mean using SciPy

```
assert stats.binom.mean(num_flips, 0.5) == 10
```

Using the `stats.binom.mean` method, we can rigorously analyze the relationship between binomial centrality and coin-flip count. Let's plot the binomial mean across a range of coin-flip counts from 0 through 500 (figure 5.10).

Listing 5.23   Plotting multiple binomial means

```
means = [stats.binom.mean(num_flips, 0.5) for num_flips in range(500)]
plt.plot(range(500), means)
plt.xlabel('Coin Flips')
plt.ylabel('Mean')
plt.show()
```

The coin-flip count and mean share a linear relationship in which the mean is equal to half the coin-flip count. With this in mind, let's consider the mean of the single coin-flip binomial distribution (commonly called the *Bernoulli distribution*). The Bernoulli distribution has a coin-flip count of 1, so its mean is equal to 0.5. Not surprisingly, the probability of a fair coin landing on heads is equal to the Bernoulli mean.

Listing 5.24   Predicting the mean of a Bernoulli distribution

```
num_flips = 1
assert stats.binom.mean(num_flips, 0.5) == 0.5
```

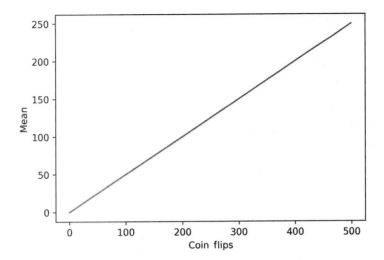

Figure 5.10 Coin-flip count plotted against binomial mean. The relationship is linear. The mean of each binomial is equal to half its coin-flip count.

We can use the observed linear relationship to predict the mean of a 1,000-coin-flip distribution. We expect that mean to equal 500 and be positioned in the distribution's center. Let's confirm that this is the case (figure 5.11).

Listing 5.25   Predicting the mean of a 1,000-coin-flip distribution

```
num_flips = 1000
assert stats.binom.mean(num_flips, 0.5) == 500

interval_all_counts = range(num_flips)
probabilities = stats.binom.pmf(interval_all_counts, num_flips, 0.5)
plt.axvline(500, color='k', linestyle='--')
plt.plot(interval_all_counts, probabilities)
plt.xlabel('Head-count')
plt.ylabel('Probability')
plt.show()
```

A distribution's mean serves as an excellent measure of centrality. Let's now explore the use of variance as a measure of dispersion.

5.3   *Variance as a measure of dispersion*

Dispersion is the scattering of data points around some central value. A smaller dispersion indicates more predictable data. A larger dispersion indicates greater data fluctuations. Consider a scenario where we measure summer temperatures in California and Kentucky. We gather three measurements for each state, at random locations. California is a huge state, with very diverse climates, so we expect to see fluctuations in our measurements. Our measured California temperatures are 52, 77, and 96 degrees.

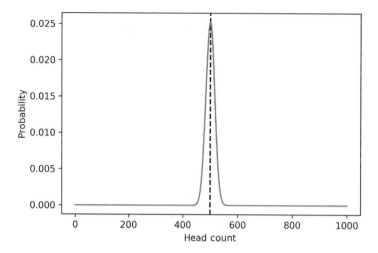

Figure 5.11   A 1,000-coin-flip binomial distribution bisected by its mean. The mean is positioned directly in the distribution's center.

Our measured Kentucky temperatures are 71, 75, and 79 degrees. We store these measured temperatures and compute their means.

Listing 5.26   Measuring the means of multiple temperature arrays

```
california = np.array([52, 77, 96])
kentucky = np.array([71, 75, 79])

print(f"Mean California temperature is {california.mean()}")
print(f"Mean Kentucky temperature is {california.mean()}")

Mean California temperature is 75.0
Mean Kentucky temperature is 75.0
```

The means of the two measurement arrays both equal 75. California and Kentucky appear to share the same central temperature value. Despite this, the two measurement arrays are far from equal. The California temperatures are much more dispersed and unpredictable: they range from 52 to 96 degrees. Meanwhile, the stable Kentucky temperatures range from the low 70s to high 70s. They are more closely centered around the mean. We visualize this difference in dispersion by plotting the two measurement arrays (figure 5.12). Additionally, we demarcate the mean by plotting a horizontal line.

Listing 5.27   Visualizing the difference in dispersion

```
plt.plot(range(3), california, color='b', label='California')
plt.scatter(range(3), california, color='b')
plt.plot(range(3), kentucky, color='r', linestyle='-.', label='Kentucky')
plt.scatter(range(3), kentucky, color='r')
```

```
plt.axhline(75, color='k', linestyle='--', label='Mean')
plt.legend()
plt.show()
```

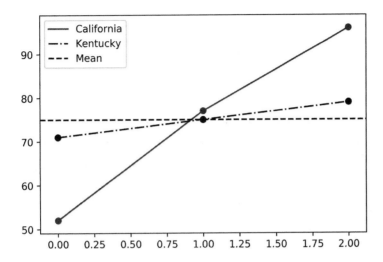

Figure 5.12 A plot of sorted temperatures for California and Kentucky. Temperatures in both states share a mean of 75 degrees. The California temperatures are more dispersed around that mean.

Within the plot, the three Kentucky temperatures nearly overlap with the flat mean. Meanwhile, the majority of California temperatures are noticeably more distant from the mean. We can quantify these observations if we penalize the California measurements for being too distant from their center. Previously, we computed such penalties using the sum-of-squared-distances function. Now we'll compute the sum of squared distances between the California measurements and their mean. Statisticians refer to the sum of squared distances from the mean as simply the *sum of squares*. We define a sum_of_squares function and then apply it to our California temperatures.

Listing 5.28 Computing California's sum of squares

```
def sum_of_squares(data):
    mean = np.mean(data)
    return sum(squared_distance(value, mean) for value in data)

california_sum_squares = sum_of_squares(california)
print(f"California's sum of squares is {california_sum_squares}")

California's sum of squares is 974.0
```

California's sum of squares is 974. We expect Kentucky's sum of squares to be noticeably lower. Let's confirm.

Listing 5.29   Computing Kentucky's sum of squares

```
kentucky_sum_squares = sum_of_squares(kentucky)
print(f"Kentucky's sum of squares is {kentucky_sum_squares}")
```

```
Kentucky's sum of squares is 32.0
```

Kentucky's sum of squares is 32. Thus, we see a thirtyfold difference between our California results and our Kentucky calculations. This isn't surprising, because the Kentucky data points are much less dispersed. The sum of squares helps measure that dispersion—however, the measurement is not perfect. Suppose we duplicate the temperatures in the California array by recording each temperature twice. The level of dispersion will remain the same even though the sum of squares will double.

Listing 5.30   Computing sum of squares after array duplication

```
california_duplicated = np.array(california.tolist() * 2)
duplicated_sum_squares = sum_of_squares(california_duplicated)
print(f"Duplicated California sum of squares is {duplicated_sum_squares}")
assert duplicated_sum_squares == 2 * california_sum_squares
```

```
Duplicated California sum of squares is 1948.0
```

The sum of squares is not a good measure of dispersion because it's influenced by the size of the inputted array. Fortunately, that influence is easy to eliminate if we divide the sum of squares by the array size. Dividing california_sum_squares by california.size produces a value equal to duplicated_sum_squares / california_duplicated.size.

Listing 5.31   Dividing sum of squares by array size

```
value1 = california_sum_squares / california.size
value2 = duplicated_sum_squares / california_duplicated.size
assert value1 == value2
```

Dividing the sum of squares by the number of measurements produces what statisticians call the *variance*. Conceptually, the variance is equal to the average squared distance from the mean.

Listing 5.32   Computing the variance from mean squared distance

```
def variance(data):
    mean = np.mean(data)
    return np.mean([squared_distance(value, mean) for value in data])

assert variance(california) == california_sum_squares / california.size
```

The variances for the california and california_duplicated arrays are equal since their levels of dispersion are identical.

Listing 5.33 Computing the variance after array duplication

```
assert variance(california) == variance(california_duplicated)
```

Meanwhile, the variances for the California and Kentucky arrays retain their thirty-fold ratio caused by a difference in dispersion.

Listing 5.34 Comparing the variances of California and Kentucky

```
california_variance = variance(california)
kentucky_variance = variance(kentucky)
print(f"California Variance is {california_variance}")
print(f"Kentucky Variance is {kentucky_variance}")

California Variance is 324.6666666666667
Kentucky Variance is 10.666666666666666
```

Variance is a good measure of dispersion. It can be computed by calling np.var on a Python list or NumPy array. The variance of a NumPy array can also be computed using the array's built-in var method.

Listing 5.35 Computing the variance using NumPy

```
assert california_variance == california.var()
assert california_variance == np.var(california)
```

Variance is dependent on the mean. If we compute a weighted mean, then we must also compute a weighted variance. Computing the weighted variance is easy: as stated earlier, the variance is simply the average of all the squared distances from the mean, so the weighted variance is the weighted average of all the squared distances from the weighted mean. Let's define a weighted_variance function that takes as input two parameters: a data list and weights. It then computes the weighted mean and uses the np.average method to compute the weighted average of the squared distances from that mean.

Listing 5.36 Computing the weighted variance using np.average

```
def weighted_variance(data, weights):
    mean = np.average(data, weights=weights)
    squared_distances = [squared_distance(value, mean) for value in data]
    return np.average(squared_distances, weights=weights)

assert weighted_variance([75, 77], [9, 1]) == np.var(9 * [75] + [77])    ◁──┐
```
weighted_variance lets us treat duplicated elements as weights.

The weighted_variance function can take as its input an array of probabilities. This allows us to compute the variance of any probability distribution.

5.3.1   *Finding the variance of a probability distribution*

Let's compute the variance of the binomial distribution associated with 20 fair coin flips. We run the computation by assigning a probabilities array to the weights parameter of weighted_variance.

Listing 5.37   Computing the variance of a binomial distribution

```
interval_all_counts = range(21)
probabilities = stats.binom.pmf(interval_all_counts, 20, prob_head)
variance_binomial = weighted_variance(interval_all_counts, probabilities)
print(f"The variance of the binomial is {variance_binomial:.2f} heads")

The variance of the binomial is 5.00 heads
```

The binomial's variance is 5, which is equal to half of the binomial's mean. That variance can be computed more directly using SciPy's stats.binom.var method.

Listing 5.38   Computing the binomial variance using SciPy

```
assert stats.binom.var(20, prob_head) == 5.0
assert stats.binom.var(20, prob_head) == stats.binom.mean(20, prob_head) / 2
```

Using the stats.binom.var method, we can rigorously analyze the relationship between binomial dispersion and coin-flip count. Let's plot the binomial variance across a range of coin-flip counts from 0 to 500 (figure 5.13).

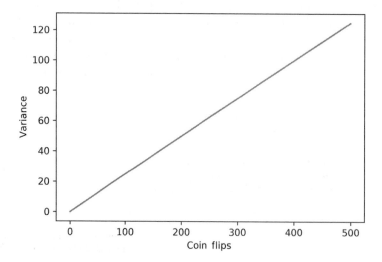

Figure 5.13   Coin-flip count plotted against binomial variance. The relationship is linear. The variance of each binomial is equal to one-fourth of its coin-flip count.

Listing 5.39 Plotting multiple binomial variances

```
variances = [stats.binom.var(num_flips, prob_head)
              for num_flips in range(500)]
plt.plot(range(500), variances)
plt.xlabel('Coin Flips')
plt.ylabel('Variance')
plt.show()
```

The binomial's variance, like its mean, is linearly related to the coin-flip count. The variance is equal to one-fourth of the coin-flip count. Thus, the Bernoulli distribution has a variance of 0.25 because its coin-flip count is 1. By this logic, we can expect a variance of 250 for a 1,000-coin-flip distribution.

Listing 5.40 Predicting binomial variances

```
assert stats.binom.var(1, 0.5) == 0.25
assert stats.binom.var(1000, 0.5) == 250
```

Common SciPy methods for binomial analysis

- `stats.binom.mean(num_flips, prob_heads)`—Returns the mean of a binomial where the flip count equals `num_flips` and the probability of heads equals `prob_heads`.
- `stats.binom.var(num_flips, prob_heads)`—Returns the variance of a binomial where the flip count equals `num_flips` and probability of heads equals `prob_heads`.
- `stats.binom.pmf(head_count_int, num_flips, prob_heads)`—Returns the probability of observing `head_count_int` heads out of `num_flips` coin flips. A single coin flip's probability of heads is set to `prob_heads`.
- `stats.binom.pmf(head_count_array, num_flips, prob_heads)`—Returns an array of binomial probabilities. These are obtained by executing `stats.binom.pmf(e, num_flips, prob_head)` on each element e of `head_count_array`.
- `stats.binom_test(head_count_int, num_flips, prob_heads)`—Returns the probability of `num_flips` coin flips generating at least `head_count_int` heads or `tail_count_int` tails. A single coin flip's probability of heads is set to `prob_heads`.

The variance is a powerful measure of data dispersion. However, statisticians often use an alternative measure, which they call the *standard deviation*. The standard deviation is equal to the square root of the variance. It can be computed by calling `np.std`. Squaring the output of `np.std` naturally returns the variance.

Listing 5.41   Computing the standard deviation

```
data = [1, 2, 3]
standard_deviation = np.std(data)
assert standard_deviation ** 2 == np.var(data)
```

We sometimes use standard deviation instead of variance to track units more easily. All measurements have units. For example, our temperatures were in units of degrees Fahrenheit. When we squared the distances of the temperature to their mean, we also squared their units; therefore, our variance was in units of degrees Fahrenheit squared. Such squared units are very tricky to conceptualize. Taking the square root converts the units back to degrees Fahrenheit: a standard deviation in units of degrees Fahrenheit is more easily interpretable than the variance.

The mean and standard deviation are incredibly useful values. They allow us to do the following:

- *Compare numeric datasets.* Suppose we're given two arrays of recorded temperatures for two consecutive summers. We can quantify the differences between these summer records using mean and standard deviation.
- *Compare probability distributions.* Suppose two climate research labs publish probability distributions. Each distribution captures all temperature probabilities across a standard summer day. We can summarize the differences between the two distributions by comparing their means and standard deviations.
- *Compare a numeric dataset to a probability distribution.* Suppose a well-known probability distribution captures a decade's worth of temperature probabilities. However, recently recorded summer temperatures appear to contradict these probability outputs. Is this a sign of climate change or simply a random anomaly? We can find out by juxtaposing the centrality and dispersion for the distribution and the temperature dataset.

The third use case underlies much of statistics. In the subsequent sections, we learn how to compare datasets to distribution likelihoods. Many of our comparisons focus on the normal distribution, which commonly arises in data analysis. Conveniently, that distribution's bell-shaped curve is a direct function of mean and standard deviation. We'll soon use SciPy, along with these two parameters, to better grasp the normal curve's significance.

Summary

- A *probability mass function* maps inputted integer values to their probability of occurrence.
- The probability mass function for the binomial distribution can be generated by calling `stats.binom.pmf`.
- *Mean* is a good measure of a dataset's centrality. It minimizes the *sum of squares* relative to the dataset. We can compute an unweighted mean by summing the

dataset values and dividing by the dataset size. We can also compute a weighted mean by inputting a `weights` array into `np.average`. The weighted mean of the binomial distribution increases linearly with the coin-flip count.

- *Variance* is a good measure of a dataset's dispersion. It equals the average squared distance of the data point from the mean. The weighted variance of the binomial distribution increases linearly with the coin-flip count.

- The *standard deviation* is an alternative measure of dispersion. It equals the square root of the variance. The standard deviation maintains the units used in a dataset.

Making predictions using the central limit theorem and SciPy

This section covers

- Analyzing the normal curve using the SciPy library
- Predicting mean and variance using the central limit theorem
- Predicting population properties using the central limit theorem

The *normal distribution* is a bell-shaped curve that we introduced in section 3. The curve arises naturally from random data sampling due to the central limit theorem. Previously, we noted how, according to that theorem, repeatedly sampled frequencies take the shape of a normal curve. Furthermore, the theorem predicts a narrowing of that curve as the size of each frequency sample goes up. In other words, the distribution's standard deviation should decrease as the sampling size increases.

The central limit theorem lies at the heart of all classic statistics. In this section, we probe the theorem in great detail using the computational power of SciPy. Eventually, we learn how to use the theorem to make predictions from limited data.

6.1 *Manipulating the normal distribution using SciPy*

In section 3, we showed how random coin-flip sampling produces a normal curve. Let's generate a normal distribution by plotting a histogram of coin-flip samples. Our input into the histogram will contain 100,000 head-count frequencies. Computing the frequencies will require us to sample a series of coin flips 100,000 times. Each sample will contain an array of 0s and 1s representing 10,000 flipped coins. We'll refer to the array length as our sample size. If we use the sample size to divide the sum of values in the sample, we will compute the observed head-count frequency. Conceptually, this frequency is equal to simply taking the sample's mean.

The following code computes the head-count frequency of a single random sample and confirms its relationship to the mean. Note that every data point in the sample is drawn from the Bernoulli distribution.

Listing 6.1 Computing head-count frequencies from the mean

```
np.random.seed(0)
sample_size = 10000
sample = np.array([np.random.binomial(1, 0.5) for _ in range(sample_size)])
head_count = sample.sum()
head_count_frequency = head_count / sample_size
assert head_count_frequency == sample.mean()
```

The head-count frequency is identical to the sample mean.

Of course, we can compute all 100,000 head-count frequencies in a single line of code, as discussed in section 3.

Listing 6.2 Computing 100,000 head-count frequencies

```
np.random.seed(0)
frequencies = np.random.binomial(sample_size, 0.5, 100000) / sample_size
```

Each sampled frequency equals the mean of 10,000 randomly flipped coins. Therefore, we rename our frequencies variable sample_means. We then visualize our sample_means data as a histogram (figure 6.1).

Listing 6.3 Visualizing sample means in a histogram

```
sample_means = frequencies
likelihoods, bin_edges, _ = plt.hist(sample_means, bins='auto',
                                      edgecolor='black', density=True)
plt.xlabel('Binned Sample Mean')
plt.ylabel('Relative Likelihood')
plt.show()
```

The histogram is shaped like a normal distribution. Let's calculate the distribution's mean and standard deviation.

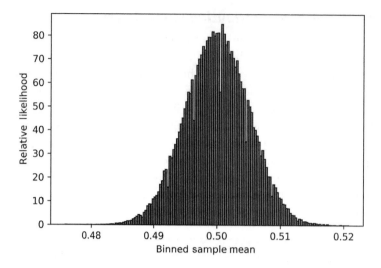

Figure 6.1   **A histogram of 100,000 sampled means plotted against their relative likelihoods. The histogram resembles a bell-shaped normal distribution.**

Listing 6.4   Computing the mean and standard deviation of a histogram

```
mean_normal = np.average(bin_edges[:-1], weights=likelihoods)
var_normal = weighted_variance(bin_edges[:-1], likelihoods)
std_normal = var_normal ** 0.5
print(f"Mean is approximately {mean_normal:.2f}")
print(f"Standard deviation is approximately {std_normal:.3f}")

Mean is approximately 0.50
Standard deviation is approximately 0.005
```

The distribution's mean is approximately 0.5, and its standard deviation is approximately 0.005. In a normal distribution, these values can be computed directly from the distribution's peak. We just need the peak's x-value and y-value coordinates. The x-value equals the distribution's mean, and the standard deviation is equal to the inverse of the y-value multiplied by $(2\pi)^{1/2}$. These properties are derived from the mathematical analysis of the normal curve. Let's recompute the mean and standard deviation using just the coordinates of the peak.

Listing 6.5   Computing mean and standard deviation from peak coordinates

```
import math
peak_x_value = bin_edges[likelihoods.argmax()]
print(f"Mean is approximately {peak_x_value:.2f}")
peak_y_value = likelihoods.max()
std_from_peak = (peak_y_value * (2* math.pi) ** 0.5) ** -1
print(f"Standard deviation is approximately {std_from_peak:.3f}")

Mean is approximately 0.50
Standard deviation is approximately 0.005
```

Additionally, we can compute the mean and standard deviation simply by calling `stats.norm.fit(sample_means)`. This SciPy method returns the two parameters required to re-create the normal distribution formed by our data.

Listing 6.6 Computing mean and standard deviation using `stats.norm.fit`

```
fitted_mean, fitted_std = stats.norm.fit(sample_means)
print(f"Mean is approximately {fitted_mean:.2f}")
print(f"Standard deviation is approximately {fitted_std:.3f}")

Mean is approximately 0.50
Standard deviation is approximately 0.005
```

The computed mean and standard deviation can be used to reproduce our normal curve. We can regenerate the curve by calling `stats.norm.pdf(bin_edges, fitted_mean, fitted_std)`. SciPy's `stats.norm.pdf` method represents the *probability density function* of a normal distribution. A probability density function is like a probability mass function but with one key difference: it does not return probabilities. Instead, it returns relative likelihoods. As discussed in section 2, relative likelihoods are the y-axis values of a curve whose total area equals 1.0. Unlike probabilities, these likelihoods can equal values that are greater than 1.0. Despite this, the total area beneath a plotted likelihood interval still equals the probability of observing a random value within that interval.

Let's compute the relative likelihoods using `stats.norm.pdf`. Then we plot the likelihoods together with the sampled coin-flip histogram (figure 6.2).

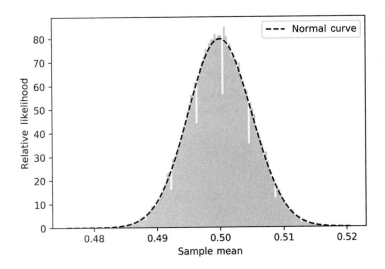

Figure 6.2 A histogram overlaid with a normal probability density function. The parameters defining the plotted normal curve were computed using SciPy. The plotted normal curve fits nicely over the histogram.

Listing 6.7   Computing normal likelihoods using `stats.norm.pdf`

```
normal_likelihoods = stats.norm.pdf(bin_edges, fitted_mean, fitted_std)
plt.plot(bin_edges, normal_likelihoods, color='k', linestyle='--',
        label='Normal Curve')
plt.hist(sample_means, bins='auto', alpha=0.2, color='r', density=True)
plt.legend()
plt.xlabel('Sample Mean')
plt.ylabel('Relative Likelihood')
plt.show()
```

The alpha parameter is used to make the histogram more transparent to better contrast the histogram with the plotted likelihood curve.

The plotted curve fits well over the histogram. The curve's peak sits at an x-axis position of 0.5 and rises to a y-axis position of approximately 80. As a reminder, the peak's x and y coordinates are a direct function of `fitted_mean` and `fitted_std`. To emphasize this important relationship, let's do a simple exercise: we'll shift the peak 0.01 units to the right while also doubling the peak's height (figure 6.3). How do we execute the shift? Well, the peak's axis is equal to the mean, so we adjust the input mean to `fitted_mean + 0.01`. Also, the peak's height is inversely proportional to the standard deviation. Therefore, inputting `fitted_std / 2` should double the height of the peak.

Listing 6.8   Manipulating a normal curve's peak coordinates

```
adjusted_likelihoods = stats.norm.pdf(bin_edges, fitted_mean + 0.01,
                                      fitted_std / 2)
plt.plot(bin_edges, adjusted_likelihoods, color='k', linestyle='--')
plt.hist(sample_means, bins='auto', alpha=0.2, color='r', density=True)
plt.xlabel('Sample Mean')
plt.ylabel('Relative Likelihood')
plt.show()
```

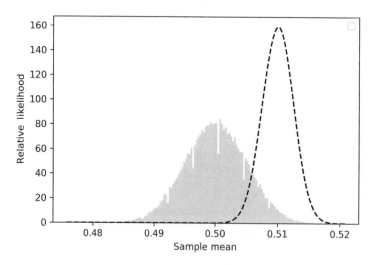

Figure 6.3   A modified normal curve whose center is .01 units to the right of the histogram. The peak of the curve is twice the height of the histogram's peak. These modifications were achieved by manipulating the histogram's mean and standard deviation.

6.1.1   *Comparing two sampled normal curves*

SciPy allows us to explore and adjust the shape of the normal distribution based on the inputted parameters. Also, the values of these input parameters depend on how we sample random data. Let's quadruple the coin-flip sample size to 40,000 and plot the resulting distribution changes. The following code compares the plotted shapes of the old and updated normal distributions, which we label A and B, respectively (figure 6.4).

Listing 6.9   Plotting two curves with different samples sizes

```
np.random.seed(0)
new_sample_size = 40000
new_head_counts = np.random.binomial(new_sample_size, 0.5, 100000)
new_mean, new_std = stats.norm.fit(new_head_counts / new_sample_size)
new_likelihoods = stats.norm.pdf(bin_edges, new_mean, new_std)
plt.plot(bin_edges, normal_likelihoods, color='k', linestyle='--',
         label='A: Sample Size 10K')
plt.plot(bin_edges, new_likelihoods, color='b', label='B: Sample Size 40K')
plt.legend()
plt.xlabel('Sample Mean')
plt.ylabel('Relative Likelihood')
plt.show()
```

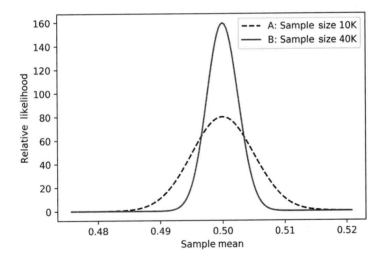

Figure 6.4   Two normal distributions generated using coin-flip data. Distribution A was derived using a sample size of 10,000 coin flips per sample. Distribution B was derived using a sample size of 40,000 coin flips per sample. Both distributions are centered around a mean value of 0.5. However, distribution B is much more narrowly dispersed around its center, and the peak of distribution B is twice as high as the peak of distribution A. Given the relationship between peak height and variance, we can infer that the variance of distribution B is one-fourth the variance of distribution A.

Both normal distributions are centered around the sample mean value of 0.5. However, the distribution with the larger sample size is more narrowly centered around its peak. This is consistent with what we saw in section 3. In that section, we observed that as the sample size increases, the peak location stays constant while the area around the peak contracts in width. The narrowing of the peak leads to a drop in the confidence interval range. A confidence interval represents the likely value range covering the true probability of heads. Previously, we used confidence intervals to estimate the probability of heads from the x-axis head-count frequencies. Now our x-axis represents the sample means, where every sample mean is identical to a head-count frequency. Thus, we can use our sample means to find the probability of heads. Also, as a reminder, all coin samples were drawn from the Bernoulli distribution. We've recently shown that the mean of the Bernoulli distribution equals the probability of heads, so (not surprisingly) each sample's mean serves as an estimate of the true Bernoulli mean. We can interpret the confidence interval as a likely value range covering the true Bernoulli mean.

Let's calculate the 95% confidence interval for the true Bernoulli mean using normal distribution B. Previously, we manually computed the 95% confidence interval by exploring the curve area around the peak. However, SciPy allows us to automatically extract that range by calling `stats.norm.interval(0.95, mean, std)`. The method returns an interval that covers 95% of the area beneath the normal distribution defined by `mean` and `std`.

Listing 6.10 Computing a confidence interval using SciPy

```
mean, std = new_mean, new_std
start, end = stats.norm.interval(0.95, mean, std)
print(f"The true mean of the sampled binomial distribution is between
    {start:.3f} and {end:.3f}")
```

```
The true mean of the sampled binomial distribution is between 0.495 and 0.505
```

We are 95% confident that the true mean of our sampled Bernoulli distribution is between 0.495 and 0.505. In fact, that mean is equal to exactly 0.5. We can confirm this using SciPy.

Listing 6.11 Confirming the Bernoulli mean

```
assert stats.binom.mean(1, 0.5) == 0.5
```

Let's now attempt to estimate the variance of the Bernoulli distribution based on the plotted normal curves. At first glance, this seems like a difficult task. Although the means of the two plotted distributions remain constant at 0.5, their variances shift noticeably. The relative shift in variance can be estimated by comparing peaks. The peak of distribution B is twice as high as the peak of distribution A. This height is inversely proportional to the standard deviation, so the standard deviation of distribution B is

> **Common SciPy methods for normal curve analysis**
> - `stats.norm.fit(data)`—Returns the mean and standard deviation required to fit a normal curve to `data`.
> - `stats.norm.pdf(observation, mean, std)`—Returns the likelihood mapped to a single value of a normal curve defined by mean `mean` and standard deviation `std`.
> - `stats.norm.pdf(observation_array, mean, std)`—Returns an array of normal likelihoods. These are obtained by executing `stats.norm.pdf(e, mean, std)` on each element `e` of `observation_array`.
> - `stats.norm.interval(x_percent, mean, std)`—Returns the `x_percent` confidence interval defined by mean `mean` and standard deviation `std`.

half the standard deviation of distribution A. Since the standard deviation is the square root of the variance, we can infer that the variance of distribution B is one-fourth the variance of distribution A. Thus, increasing the sample size fourfold from 10,000 to 40,000 leads to a fourfold decrease in the variance.

Listing 6.12   Assessing shift in variance after increased sampling

```
variance_ratio = (new_std ** 2) / (fitted_std ** 2)
print(f"The ratio of variances is approximately {variance_ratio:.2f}")
```

```
The ratio of variances is approximately 0.25
```

It appears that variance is inversely proportional to sample size. If so, a fourfold decrease in sample size from 10,000 to 2,500 should generate a fourfold increase in the variance. Let's generate some head counts using a sample size of 2,500 and confirm if this is the case.

Listing 6.13   Assessing shift in variance after decreased sampling

```
np.random.seed(0)
reduced_sample_size = 2500
head_counts = np.random.binomial(reduced_sample_size, 0.5, 100000)
_, std = stats.norm.fit(head_counts / reduced_sample_size)
variance_ratio = (std ** 2) / (fitted_std ** 2)
print(f"The ratio of variances is approximately {variance_ratio:.1f}")
```

```
The ratio of variances is approximately 4.0
```

Yes! A fourfold decrease in the sample size leads to a fourfold increase in the variance. Thus, if we decrease the sample size from 10,000 to 1, we can expect a 10,000-fold increase in the variance. That variance for a sample size of 1 should be equal to `(fitted_std ** 2) * 10000`.

Listing 6.14   Predicting variance for a sample size of 1

```
estimated_variance = (fitted_std ** 2) * 10000
print(f"Estimated variance for a sample size of 1 is
    {estimated_variance:.2f}")
```

```
Estimated variance for a sample size of 1 is 0.25
```

Our estimated variance for a sample size of 1 is 0.25. However, if the sample size were 1, then our `sample_means` array would simply be a sequence of randomly recorded 1s and 0s. By definition, that array would represent the output of the Bernoulli distribution, so running `sample_means.var` would approximate the variance of the Bernoulli distribution. Thus our estimated variance for a sample size of 1 equals the variance of the Bernoulli distribution. In fact, the Bernoulli variance does equal 0.25.

Listing 6.15   Confirming the predicted variance for a sample size of 1

```
assert stats.binom.var(1, 0.5) == 0.25
```

We have just used the normal distribution to compute the variance and mean of the Bernoulli distribution from which we sampled. Let's review the chain of steps that led to our results:

1. We sampled random 1s and 0s from the Bernoulli distribution.
2. Each sequence of `sample_size` 1s and 0s was grouped into a single sample.
3. We computed a mean for every sample.
4. The sample means produced a normal curve. We found its mean and standard deviation.
5. The mean of the normal curve equaled the mean of the Bernoulli distribution.
6. The variance of the normal curve multiplied by the sample size equaled the variance of the Bernoulli distribution.

What if we had sampled from some other non-Bernoulli distribution? Would we still be able to estimate the mean and variance through random sampling? Yes, we would! According to the central limit theorem, sampling mean values from almost any distribution will produce a normal curve. This includes distributions such as the following:

- The *Poisson distribution* (`stats.poisson.pmf`). Commonly used to model
  - Number of customers who visit a store per hour
  - Number of clicks on an online ad per second
- The *Gamma distribution* (`scipy.stats.gamma.pdf`). Commonly used to model
  - Monthly rainfall in a region
  - Banking loan defaults based on loan size

- The *log-normal* distribution (`scipy.stats.lognorm.pdf`). Commonly used to model
  - Fluctuating stock prices
  - Incubation periods of infectious diseases
- Countless distributions occurring in nature that haven't yet been assigned a name

WARNING   Under edge-case circumstances, sampling does not produce a normal curve. This is occasionally true of the Pareto distribution, which is used to model income inequality.

Once we've sampled a normal curve, we can use it to analyze the underlying distribution. The mean of the normal curve approximates the mean of the underlying distribution. Also, the variance of the normal curve multiplied by the sample size approximates the variance of the underlying distribution.

NOTE   In other words, if we sample from a distribution with variance var, we obtain a normal curve with variance `sample_size / var`. As the sample size approaches infinity, the variance of the normal curve approaches zero. At zero variance, the normal curve collapses into a single vertical line positioned at the mean. This property can be used to derive the law of large numbers, which we introduced in section 2.

The relationship between a normal distribution produced by sampling and the properties of the underlying distribution serves as a foundation for all statistics. Using that relationship, we can use the normal curve to estimate both the mean and variance of almost any distribution through random sampling.

6.2 Determining the mean and variance of a population through random sampling

Suppose we are tasked with finding the average age of people living in a town. The town's population is exactly 50,000 people. The following code simulates the ages of the townsfolk using the `np.random.randint` method.

Listing 6.16   Generating a random population

```
np.random.seed(0)
population_ages = np.random.randint(1, 85, size=50000)
```

How do we compute the average age of the residents? One cumbersome approach would be to take a census of every resident in the town. We could record all 50,000 ages and then compute their mean. That exact mean would cover the entire population, which is why it's called the *population mean*. Furthermore, the variance of an entire population is referred to as the *population variance*. Let's quickly compute the population mean and population variance of our simulated town.

Listing 6.17 Computing the population mean and variance

```
population_mean = population_ages.mean()
population_variance = population_ages.var()
```

Computing the population mean is easy when we have simulated data. However, obtaining that data in real life would be incredibly time consuming. We would have to interview all 50,000 people. Without more resources, interviewing the whole town would be borderline impossible.

A simpler approach would be to interview 10 randomly chosen people in the town. We'd record the ages from this random sample and then compute the sample mean. Let's simulate the sampling process by drawing 10 random ages from the `np.random`. `choice` method. Executing `np.random.choice(age, size=sample_size)` returns an array of 10 randomly sampled ages. After sampling is complete, we will compute the mean of the resulting 10-element array.

Listing 6.18 Simulating 10 interviewed people

```
np.random.seed(0)
sample_size = 10
sample = np.random.choice(population_ages, size=sample_size)
sample_mean = sample.mean()
```

Of course, our sample mean is likely to be noisy and inexact. We can measure that noise by finding the percent difference between `sample_mean` and `population_mean`.

Listing 6.19 Comparing the sample mean to the population mean

```
percent_diff = lambda v1, v2: 100 * abs(v1 - v2) / v2
percent_diff_means = percent_diff(sample_mean, population_mean)
print(f"There is a {percent_diff_means:.2f} percent difference between
        means.")
```

```
There is a 27.59 percent difference between means
```

There is approximately a 27% difference between the sample mean and the population mean. Clearly, our sample is insufficient to estimate the mean—we need to gather more samples. Perhaps we should increase our sampling to cover 1,000 residents of the town. This seems like a reasonable objective that is preferable to surveying all 50,000 residents. Unfortunately, interviewing 1,000 people will still be very time consuming: even if we assume an idealistic interview rate of 2 people per minute, it will take us eight hours to reach our interview goal. Conceivably, we can optimize our time by parallelizing the interview process. We can post an ad in the local paper asking for 100 volunteers: each volunteer will survey 10 random people to sample their ages and then send us a computed sample mean. Thus we will receive 100 sample means representing 1,000 interviews total.

NOTE Each volunteer will send us a sample mean. Conceivably, the volunteers could send the full data instead. However, the sample means are preferable, for the following reasons. First, the means don't require as much memory storage as the full data. Second, the means can be plotted as a histogram to check the quality of our sample size. If that histogram does not approximate a normal curve, then additional samples will be required.

Let's simulate our surveying process.

Listing 6.20   Computing sample means across 1,000 people

```
np.random.seed(0)
sample_means = [np.random.choice(population_ages, size=sample_size).mean()
                for _ in range(100)]
```

According to the central limit theorem, a histogram of sample means should resemble the normal distribution. Furthermore, the mean of the normal distribution should approximate the population mean. We can confirm that this is the case by fitting the sample means to a normal distribution (figure 6.5).

Listing 6.21   Fitting sample means to a normal curve

```
likelihoods, bin_edges, _  = plt.hist(sample_means, bins='auto', alpha=0.2,
                                      color='r', density=True)
mean, std = stats.norm.fit(sample_means)
normal_likelihoods = stats.norm.pdf(bin_edges, mean, std)
plt.plot(bin_edges, normal_likelihoods, color='k', linestyle='--')
plt.xlabel('Sample Mean')
plt.ylabel('Relative Likelihood')
plt.show()
```

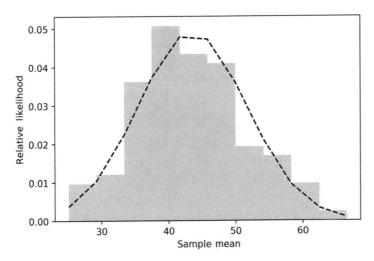

Figure 6.5   A histogram computed from 100 age samples. The histogram is overlaid with its associated normal distribution. The normal distribution's mean and standard deviation parameters were derived from the plotted histogram data.

Our histogram is not very smooth because we've only processed 100 data points. However, the histogram's shape still approximates a normal distribution. We print that distribution's mean and compare it to the population mean.

Listing 6.22   Comparing the normal mean to the population mean

```
print(f"Actual population mean is approximately {population_mean:.2f}")
percent_diff_means = percent_diff(mean, population_mean)
print(f"There is a {percent_diff_means:.2f}% difference between means.")

Actual population mean is approximately 42.53
There is a 2.17% difference between means.
```

Our estimated mean of the ages is roughly 43. The actual population mean is roughly 42.5. There is an approximately 2% difference between the estimated mean and the actual mean. Thus our result, while not perfect, is still a very good approximation of the actual average age within the town.

Now, we briefly turn our attention to the standard deviation computed from the normal distribution. Squaring the standard deviation produces the distribution's variance. According to the central limit theorem, we can use that variance to estimate the variance of ages in the town. We simply need to multiply the computed variance by the sample size.

Listing 6.23   Estimating the population variance

```
normal_variance = std ** 2
estimated_variance = normal_variance * sample_size
```

Let's compare the estimated variance to the population variance.

Listing 6.24   Comparing the estimated variance to the population variance

```
print(f"Estimated variance is approximately {estimated_variance:.2f}")
print(f"Actual population variance is approximately
    {population_variance:.2f}")
percent_diff_var = percent_diff(estimated_variance, population_variance)
print(f"There is a {percent_diff_var:.2f} percent difference between
    variances.")

Estimated variance is approximately 576.73
Actual population variance is approximately 584.33
There is a 1.30 percent difference between variances.
```

There is approximately a 1.3% difference between the estimated variance and the population variance. We've thus approximated the town's variance to a relatively accurate degree while sampling only 2% of the people living in the town. Our estimates may not be 100% perfect. However, the amount of time we saved more than makes up for that minuscule drop in accuracy.

So far, we've only used the central limit theorem to estimate the population mean and variance. However, the power of the theorem goes beyond the mere estimation of distribution parameters. We can use the central limit theorem to make predictions about people.

6.3   *Making predictions using the mean and variance*

Let's now consider a new scenario in which we analyze a fifth-grade classroom. Mrs. Mann is a brilliant fifth-grade teacher. She has spent 25 years inspiring a love of learning in her students. Her classroom holds 20 students. Thus, over the years, she has taught 500 students total.

> **NOTE**   We are assuming that each year, Mrs. Mann teaches exactly 20 students. Of course, in real life, classroom size might fluctuate from year to year.

Her students frequently outperform other fifth graders in the state. That performance is measured using scholastic assessment exams, which are administered to all fifth graders every year. These exams are graded from 0 to 100. All grades can be accessed by querying the state assessment database. However, due to poor database design, the queryable exam records do not specify the year when each exam was taken.

Imagine we're tasked with addressing the following question: Has Mrs. Mann ever taught a class that collectively aced the assessment exam? More specifically, has she ever taught a class of 20 students whose mean assessment grade was above 89%?

To answer that question, assume that we've queried the state database. We've obtained grades for all of Mrs. Mann's past students. Of course, a lack of temporal information prevents us from grouping the grades by year. Thus, we cannot simply scan the records for a yearly mean above 89%. However, we can still compute the mean and variance across the 500 total grades. Let's suppose the mean is equal to 84 and the variance is equal to 25. We'll refer to these values as the population mean and population variance, since they cover the entire population of students who've ever been taught by Mrs. Mann.

Listing 6.25   Population mean and variance of recorded grades

```
population_mean = 84
population_variance = 25
```

Let's model the yearly test results of Mrs. Mann's class as a collection of 20 grades randomly drawn from a distribution with mean population_mean and variance population_variance. This model is simplistic. It makes several extreme assumptions, such as these:

- Performance of each student in the class does not depend on any other student.
  In real life, this assumption doesn't always hold. For instance, disruptive students can negatively impact the performance of others.

- Exams are equally difficult every year.

  In real life, standardized exams can be adjusted by government officials.

- Local economic factors are negligible.

  In real life, fluctuating economies impact school district budgets and as well as student home environments. These external factors can affect the quality of grades.

Our simplifications might impact prediction accuracy. However, given our limited data, we have little choice in the matter. Statisticians are frequently forced to make such compromises to address otherwise intractable problems. Most of the time, their simplified predictions still reasonably reflect real-world behaviors.

Given our simple model, we can sample a random batch of 20 grades. What is the probability that the grades will have a mean of at least 90? This probability can easily be computed using the central limit theorem. According to the theorem, the likelihood distribution of mean grades will resemble a normal curve. The mean of the normal curve will equal population_mean. The variance of the normal curve will equal population_variance divided by our sample size of 20 students. Taking the square root of that variance produces the standard deviation of the curve, which statisticians call the *standard error of the mean* (SEM). By definition, the SEM equals the population standard deviation divided by the square root of the sample size. We compute the curve parameters and plot the normal curve next (figure 6.6).

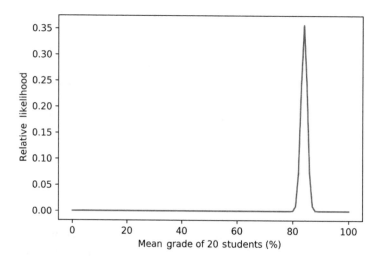

Figure 6.6   A normal distribution derived from the population mean and the standard error from the mean (SEM). The SEM is equal to the standard deviation divided by the square root of the sample size. The area beneath the plotted curve can be used to calculate probabilities.

Listing 6.26 Plotting a normal curve using the mean and SEM

```
mean = population_mean
population_std = population_variance ** 0.5
sem = population_std / (20 ** 0.5)
grade_range = range(101)
normal_likelihoods = stats.norm.pdf(grade_range, mean, sem)
plt.plot(grade_range, normal_likelihoods)
plt.xlabel('Mean Grade of 20 Students (%)')
plt.ylabel('Relative Likelihood')
plt.show()
```

> **The population standard deviation equals the square root of the population variance.**

> **The SEM equals population_std divided by the square root of the sample size. Alternatively, we can compute the SEM by running (population_variance / 20) ** 0.5.**

The area beneath the plotted curve approaches zero at values higher than 89%. That area is also equal to the probability of a given observation. Therefore, the probability of observing a mean grade that's at or above 90% is incredibly low. Still, to be sure, we need to compute the actual probability. Thus, we need to somehow accurately measure the area under the normal distribution.

6.3.1 Computing the area beneath a normal curve

In section 3, we computed areas under histograms. Determining these areas proved easy. All histograms, by definition, are made up of small rectangular units: we could sum the areas of rectangles composing a specified interval, and the total sum equaled the interval's area. Unfortunately, our smooth normal curve does not decompose into rectangles. So how do we find its area? One simple solution is to subdivide the normal curve into small, trapezoidal units. This ancient technique is referred to as the *trapezoidal rule*. A trapezoid is a four-sided polygon with two parallel sides; the trapezoid's area is equal to the sum of these parallel sides multiplied by half the distance between them. Summing over multiple consecutive trapezoid areas approximates the area over an interval, as shown in figure 6.7.

The trapezoidal rule is very easy to execute in just a few lines of code. Alternatively, we can utilize NumPy's `np.trapz` method to take the area of an inputted array. Let's apply the trapezoidal rule to our normal distribution. We want to test how well the rule approximates the total area covered by `normal_likelihoods`. Ideally, that area will approximate 1.0.

Listing 6.27 Approximating the area using the trapezoidal rule

> **The area of each trapezoid equals the sum of two consecutive likelihoods divided by 2. The x-coordinate distance between the trapezoid sides is 1, so it doesn't factor into our calculations.**

```
total_area = np.sum([normal_likelihoods[i: i + 2].sum() / 2
                     for i in range(normal_likelihoods.size - 1)])

assert total_area == np.trapz(normal_likelihoods)
print(f"Estimated area under the curve is {total_area}")

Estimated area under the curve is 1.0000000000384808
```

> **Note that NumPy executes the trapezoidal rule in a mathematically more efficient manner.**

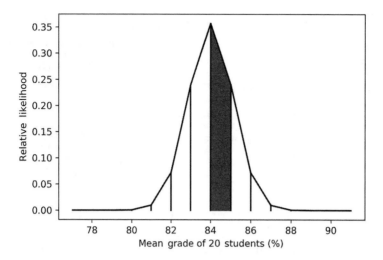

Figure 6.7 **A normal distribution subdivided into trapezoidal regions. The lower-left corner of each trapezoid is located at an x coordinate of i. The parallel sides of each trapezoid are defined by `stats.norm.pdf(i)` and `stats.norm.pdf(i + 1)`. These parallel sides are 1 unit apart. The area of the trapezoid at position 84 has been shaded in. That area is equal to `(stats.norm.pdf(84) + stats.norm.pdf(85)) / 2`. Summing trapezoid areas across an interval range approximates the total area over that interval.**

The estimated area is very close to 1.0, but it's not exactly equal to 1.0. In fact, it is slightly greater than 1.0. If we're willing to tolerate this minor imprecision, then our trapezoidal rule output is acceptable. Otherwise, we need a precise solution for the area of a normal distribution. That precision is provided by SciPy. We can access a mathematically exact solution using the `stats.norm.sf` method. This method represents the *survival function* of the normal curve. The survival function equals the distribution's area over an interval that's greater than some x. In other words, the survival function is the exact solution to the area approximated by `np.trapz(normal_likelihoods[x:])`. Thus, we can expect `stats.norm.sf(0, mean, sem)` to equal 1.0.

Listing 6.28   Computing the total area using SciPy

```
assert stats.norm.sf(0, mean, sem) == 1.0
```

Theoretically, the lower-bound x-value of a normal curve stretches into negative infinity. Therefore, this actual area is microscopically smaller than 1.0. However, the difference is so negligible that SciPy is unable to detect it. For our intents and purposes, we can treat the precise area as 1.0.

Similarly, we expect `stats.norm.sf(mean, mean, sem)` to equal 0.5, since the mean perfectly splits the normal curve into two equal halves (figure 6.8). Thus, the interval of values beyond the mean covers half the area of the normal curve. Meanwhile, we

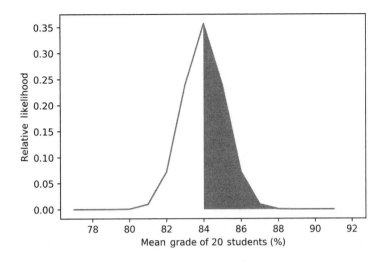

Figure 6.8 We've highlighted the area denoted by `stats.norm.sf(mean,
mean, sem)`. That area covers an interval of values greater than or equal to
the mean. The shaded area equals half the total area of the curve. Its exact
value is 0.5.

expect `np.trapz(normal_likelihoods[mean:])` to approximate but not fully equal
0.5. Let's confirm.

Listing 6.29 Inputting the mean into the survival function

```
assert stats.norm.sf(mean, mean, sem) == 0.5
estimated_area = np.trapz(normal_likelihoods[mean:])
print(f"Estimated area beyond the mean is {estimated_area}")

Estimated area beyond the mean is 0.5000000000192404
```

Common methods for measuring curve area
- `numpy.trapz(array)`—Executes the trapezoidal rule to estimate the area of
  `array`. The x-coordinate difference between the array elements is set to 1.
- `numpy.trapz(array, dx=dx)`—Executes the trapezoidal rule to estimate the
  area of `array`. The x-coordinate difference between the array elements is set
  to `dx`.
- `stats.norm.sf(x_value, mean, std)`—Returns the area beneath a normal curve, covering an interval that's greater than or equal to `x_value`. The
  mean and standard deviation of the normal curve are set to `mean` and `std`,
  respectively.
- `stats.norm.sf(x_array, mean, std)`—Returns an array of areas. These
  are obtained by executing `stats.norm.sf(e, mean, std)` on each element `e`
  of `x_array`.

Now, let's execute stats.norm.sf(90, mean, sem). This returns the area over an interval of values lying beyond 90%. The area represents the likelihood of 20 students jointly acing an exam.

> **Listing 6.30   Computing the probability of a good collective grade**

```
area  = stats.norm.sf(90, mean, sem)
print(f"Probability of 20 students acing the exam is {area}")

Probability of 20 students acing the exam is 4.012555633463782e-08
```

As expected, the probability is low.

6.3.2   Interpreting the computed probability

The probability of all the students acing the exam is approximately 1 in 25 million. The exam is held just once a year, so it would take about 25 million years for a random arrangement of students to achieve that level of performance. Meanwhile, Mrs. Mann has been teaching for only 25 years. This represents a million-fold difference in magnitude. What are the odds of her presiding over a classroom with an average grade of at least 90%? Practically zero. We can conclude that such a classroom never existed!

> **NOTE**   The actual odds can be computed by running 1 - stats.binom.pmf(0, 25, stats.norm.sf(90, mean, sem)). Can you figure out why?

Of course, we could be wrong. Perhaps a group of very talented fifth graders randomly wound up in the same classroom. This is highly unlikely, but nonetheless, it's possible. Also, our simple calculations didn't factor in changes to the exam. What if the exam gets easier every year? This would invalidate our treatment of the grades as a randomly drawn sample.

It seems our final conclusion is imperfect. We did the best we could, given what we knew, but some uncertainty remains. To eliminate that uncertainty, we'd need the missing dates for the graded exams. Unfortunately, that data was not provided. Quite commonly, statisticians are forced to make consequential decisions from limited records. Consider the following two scenarios:

- A coffee farm ships 500 tons of coffee beans per year in 5-pound bags. On average, 1% of the beans are moldy, with a standard deviation of 0.2%. The FDA permits a maximum of 3% moldy beans per bag. Does there exist a bag that violates the FDA's requirements?

  We can apply the central limit theorem if we assume that mold growth is independent of time. However, mold could grow more rapidly in the humid summer months. Regrettably, we lack the records to confirm.

- A seaside town is building a seawall to defend against tsunamis. According to historical data, the average tsunami height is 23 feet, with a standard deviation of 4 feet. The planned wall height is 33 feet. Is that height sufficient to protect the town?

It's tempting to assume that the tsunami average height will remain unchanged from year to year. However, certain studies indicate that climate change is causing sea levels to rise. Climate change might lead to more powerful tsunamis in the future. Regrettably, the scientific data is not conclusive enough to know for sure.

In both scenarios, we must make important decisions by relying on statistical techniques. These techniques depend on certain assumptions that might not hold. Consequently, we must exercise great caution when we draw conclusions from incomplete information. In the coming section, we continue to explore both the risks and advantages of making decisions based on limited data.

Summary

- A normal distribution's mean and standard deviation are determined by the position of its peak. The mean is equal to the x coordinate of the peak. Meanwhile, the standard deviation is equal to the inverse of the y coordinate multiplied by $(2\pi)^{1/2}$.
- A probability density function maps inputted float values to their likelihood weights. Taking the area underneath that curve produces a probability.
- Repeatedly sampling the mean from almost any distribution produces a normal curve. The mean of the normal curve approximates the mean of the underlying distribution. Also, the variance of the normal curve multiplied by the sample size approximates the variance of the underlying distribution.
- The *standard error of the mean* (SEM) equals the population standard deviation divided by the square root of the sample size. Consequently, dividing the population variance by the sample size and subsequently taking the square root also generates the SEM. The SEM, coupled with the population mean, allows us to compute the probability of observing certain sample combinations.
- The *trapezoidal rule* allows us to estimate the area under a curve by decomposing that curve into trapezoidal units. Then we simply sum over the areas of each trapezoid.
- A *survival function* measures a distribution's area over an interval that's greater than some x.
- We must cautiously consider our assumptions while making inferences from limited data.

Statistical
hypothesis testing

This section covers

- Comparing sample means to population means
- Comparing means of two distinct samples
- What is statistical significance?
- Common statistical errors and how to avoid them

Many ordinary people are forced to make hard choices every day. This is especially true of jurors in the American justice system. Jurors preside over a defendant's fate during a trial. They consider the evidence and then decide between two competing hypotheses:

- The defendant is innocent.
- The defendant is guilty.

The two hypotheses are not weighted equally: the defendant is presumed to be innocent until proven guilty. Thus, the jurors assume that the innocence hypothesis is true. They can only reject the innocence hypothesis if the prosecution's evidence is convincing. Yet the evidence is rarely 100% conclusive, and some doubt of the defendant's guilt remains. That doubt is factored into the legal process. The jury is instructed to accept the innocence hypothesis if there is "reasonable doubt" of the defendant's guilt. They can only reject the innocence hypothesis if the defendant appears guilty "beyond a reasonable doubt."

Reasonable doubt is an abstract concept that's hard to define precisely. Nonetheless, we can distinguish between reasonable and unreasonable doubt across a range of real-world scenarios. Consider the following two trial cases:

- DNA evidence links the defendant directly to the crime. There is a 1 in a billion chance that the DNA does not belong to the defendant.
- Blood-type evidence links the defendant directly to the crime. There is a 1 in 15 chance that the blood does not belong to the defendant.

In the first scenario, the jury cannot be 100% certain of the defendant's guilt. There is a 1 in a billion chance that an innocent defendant is on trial. Such circumstances, however, are incredibly unlikely. It's not reasonable to assume that this is the case. Thus, the jury should reject the innocence hypothesis.

Meanwhile, in the second scenario, the doubt is much more prevalent: 1 in 15 people share the same blood type as the defendant. It's reasonable to assume that someone else could have been present at the crime scene. While the jurors might doubt the defendant's innocence, they will also reasonably doubt the defendant's guilt. Thus, the jurors can't reject the innocence hypothesis unless additional proof of guilt is offered.

In our two scenarios, the jurors are carrying out a *statistical hypothesis test*. Such tests allow statisticians to choose between two competing hypotheses, both of which arise from uncertain data. One of the hypotheses is accepted or rejected based on a measured level of doubt. In this section, we explore several well-known statistical hypothesis testing techniques. We begin with a simple test to measure whether a sample mean noticeably deviates from an existing population.

7.1 Assessing the divergence between sample mean and population mean

In section 6, we used statistics to analyze a single fifth-grade classroom. Now, let's imagine a scenario where we analyze every fifth-grade classroom in North Dakota. One spring day, all fifth graders in the state are given the same assessment exam. The exam grades are fed into North Dakota's assessment database, and the population mean and variance are computed across all grades in the state. According to the records, the population mean is 80, and the population variance is 100. Let's quickly store these values for later use.

Listing 7.1 Population mean and variance of North Dakota grades

```
population_mean = 80
population_variance = 100
```

Next, suppose we travel to South Dakota and encounter a fifth-grade class whose mean exam grade equals 84%. This 18-student class has outperformed North Dakota's population by 4 percentage points. Are fifth graders in South Dakota better educated than their North Dakota counterparts? If so, North Dakota should incorporate South Dakotan teaching methods into the curriculum. The curriculum adjustment would be costly, but the payoff to the students would be worth it. Of course, it's also possible that the observed exam difference is a mere statistical fluke. Which is it? We'll try to find out using hypothesis testing.

We face two rival possibilities. First, it's possible that the overall student population is identical across the neighboring states. In other words, a typical South Dakota classroom is no different from a typical North Dakota classroom. Under such circumstances, South Dakota's population mean and variance values would be indistinguishable from those of its neighbor. Statisticians refer to this hypothetical parameter equivalency as the *null hypothesis*. If the null hypothesis is true, then our high-performing South Dakota classroom is simply an outlier and doesn't represent the actual mean.

Alternatively, it's feasible that the classroom's high performance is representative of South Dakota's general population. Thus the state's mean and variance values would differ from North Dakota's population parameters. Statisticians call this the *alternative hypothesis*. If the alternative hypothesis is true, we'll update North Dakota's fifth-grade curriculum. However, the alternative hypothesis is only true when the null hypothesis is false (and vice versa). Therefore, to justify the curriculum overhaul, we must first show that the null hypothesis is unlikely to be true. We can measure this likelihood using the central limit theorem.

Let's temporarily assume that the null hypothesis is true and both Dakotas share the same population mean and variance. Consequently, we can model our 18-student classroom as a random sample taken from a normal distribution. That distribution's mean will equal `population_mean`, and its standard deviation will equal the standard error of the mean (SEM), defined as `(population_variance / 18) ** 0.5`.

Listing 7.2 Normal curve parameters if the null hypothesis is true

```
mean = population_mean
sem = (population_variance / 18) ** 0.5
```

If the null hypothesis is true, the probability of encountering an average exam grade of at least 84% is equal to `stats.norm.sf(84 mean, sem)`. Let's check that probability.

Listing 7.3 Finding the probability of a high-performance grade

```
prob_high_grade = stats.norm.sf(84, mean, sem)
print(f"Probability of an average grade >= 84 is {prob_high_grade}")

Probability of an average grade >= 84 is 0.044843010885182284
```

Under the null hypothesis, a random South Dakotan classroom will obtain an average grade of at least 84% with a probability of 0.044. This probability is low, and hence the

4% grade difference with the population mean appears extreme. But is it actually extreme? In section 1, we asked a similar question when we examined the likelihood of observing 8 heads out of 10 coin flips. In our coin analysis, we summed the probability of overperformance with the probability of underperformance. In other words, we summed the probability of observing eight or more heads with the probability of observing two heads or fewer. Here, our dilemma is identical. Analyzing exam overperformance is insufficient to evaluate extremeness; we must also consider the likelihood of an equally extreme underperformance. Therefore, we need to compute the probability of observing a sample mean that is at least four percentage points below the population mean of 80%.

We will now compute the probability of observing an exam average that's less than or equal to 76%. The calculation can be carried out with SciPy's `stats.norm.cdf` method, which computes the *cumulative distribution function* of the normal curve. A cumulative distribution function is the direct opposite of the survival function, as seen in figure 7.1. Applying `stats.norm.cdf` to x returns the area under a normal curve that ranges from negative infinity to x.

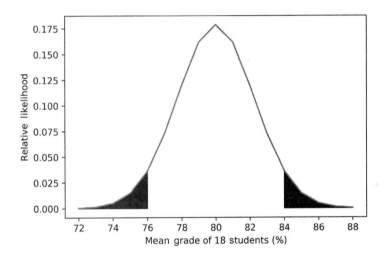

Figure 7.1 Two areas are highlighted beneath a normal curve. The leftmost area covers all x-values that are less than or equal to 76%. We can compute that area using the cumulative distribution function. To execute the function, we simply need to call `stats.norm.cdf(76, mean, sem)`. Meanwhile, the rightmost area covers all x-values that are at least 84%. We can compute that area using the survival function. To execute the function, we call `stats.norm.sf(84, mean, sem)`.

We now use `stats.norm.cdf` to find the probability of observing an unusually low average grade.

```
prob_low_grade = stats.norm.cdf(76, mean, sem)
print(f"Probability of an average grade <= 76 is {prob_low_grade}")
```

```
Probability of an average grade <= 76 is 0.044843010885182284
```

It appears that `prob_low_grade` is equal to `prob_high_grade`. This equality arises from the symmetric shape of the normal curve. The cumulative distribution and the survival function are mirror images that are reflected across the mean. Thus, `stats.norm.sf(mean + x, mean, sem)` always equals `stats.norm.cdf(mean - x, mean, sem)` for any input x. Next, we visualize both functions to confirm their reflection across a vertically plotted mean (figure 7.2).

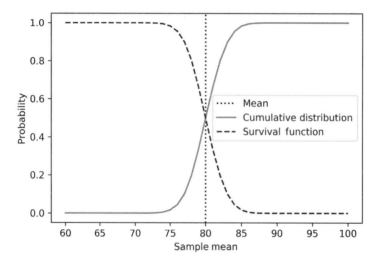

Figure 7.2   A cumulative distribution function of a normal distribution plotted together with the survival function. The cumulative distribution function and the survival function are mirror images. They are reflected across the normal curve's mean, which is plotted as a vertical line.

```
for x in range(-100, 100):
    sf_value = stats.norm.sf(mean + x, mean,   sem)
    assert sf_value == stats.norm.cdf(mean - x, mean, sem)

plt.axvline(mean, color='k', label='Mean', linestyle=':')
x_values = range(60, 101)
plt.plot(x_values, stats.norm.cdf(x_values, mean, sem),
        label='Cumulative Distribution')
plt.plot(x_values, stats.norm.sf(x_values, mean, sem),
        label='Survival Function', linestyle='--', color='r')
```

```
plt.xlabel('Sample Mean')
plt.ylabel('Probability')
plt.legend()
plt.show()
```

Now we are ready to sum `prob_high_grade` and `prob_low_grade`. Due to symmetry, that sum equals 2 * `prob_high_grade`. Conceptually, the sum represents the probability of observing an extreme deviation from the population mean when the null hypothesis is true. Statisticians refer to this null-hypothesis-driven probability as the *p-value*. Let's print the p-value arising from our data.

Listing 7.6   Computing the null-hypothesis-driven p-value

```
p_value = prob_low_grade + prob_high_grade
assert p_value == 2 * prob_high_grade
print(f"The p-value is {p_value}")
```

```
The p-value is 0.08968602177036457
```

Under the null hypothesis, there is approximately a 9% chance of observing the grade extreme at random. It's therefore plausible that the null hypothesis is true and the extreme test average is just a random fluctuation. We haven't definitively proved this, but our calculations raise serious doubts about restructuring North Dakota's fifth-grade curriculum. What if the average of the South Dakotan class had equaled 85%, not 84%? Let's check if that slight grade shift would have influenced our p-value.

Listing 7.7   Computing the p-value for an adjusted sample mean

```
def compute_p_value(observed_mean, population_mean, sem):
    mean_diff = abs(population_mean - observed_mean)
    prob_high = stats.norm.sf(population_mean + mean_diff, population_mean, sem)
    return 2 * prob_high

new_p_value = compute_p_value(85, mean, sem)
print(f"The updated p-value is {new_p_value}")
```

```
The updated p-value is 0.03389485352468927
```

A tiny increase in the average grade has caused a threefold decrease in the p-value. Now, under the null hypothesis, there's only a 3.3% chance of observing an average test grade that's at least as extreme as 85%. This likelihood is low, and we might therefore be tempted to reject the null hypothesis. Should we accept the alternative hypothesis and invest our time and money in revamping North Dakota's school system?

This is not an easy question to answer. Generally, statisticians tend to reject the null hypothesis if the p-value is less than or equal to 0.05. The threshold of 0.05 is called the *significance level,* and p-values below that threshold are deemed to be *statistically significant.* However, 0.05 is just an arbitrary cutoff intended to heuristically uncover interesting data, not to make critical decisions. The threshold was first introduced in 1935 by famed statistician Ronald Fisher; later, Fisher said that the significance level should not remain static and should be manually adjusted based on the nature of the analysis. Regrettably, by then it was too late: the 0.05 cutoff had been adopted as our standard measure of significance. Today, most statisticians agree that a p-value below 0.05 implies an interesting signal in the data, so a p-value of 0.033 is sufficient to temporarily reject the null hypothesis and get one's data published in a scientific journal. Unfortunately, the threshold of 0.05 doesn't actually arise from the laws of mathematics and statistics: it's an ad hoc value chosen by the academic community as a requirement for research publication. As a consequence, many research journals are flooded with *type I errors*. A type I error is defined as an erroneous rejection of the null hypothesis. Such errors occur when random data fluctuations are interpreted as genuine deviations from the population mean. Scientific articles containing type I errors falsely assert a difference between means where none exists.

How do we limit type I errors? Well, some scientists believe that a threshold of 0.05 is unreasonably high and that we should only reject the null hypothesis if the p-value is much lower. But there is currently no consensus on whether using a lower threshold is appropriate, since doing so would lead to an increase in *type II errors*, in which we wrongly reject the alternative hypothesis. When scientists commit a type II error, they fail to notice a legitimate discovery.

Selecting an optimal significance level is difficult. Nevertheless, let's temporarily set the significance level to a very stringent value of 0.001. What would be the minimum grade average that would fall below this threshold? Let's find out. We loop through all grade averages above 80%, computing the p-value as we go. We stop when we encounter a p-value that's less than or equal to 0.001.

Listing 7.8 Scanning for a stringent p-value result

```python
for grade in range(80, 100):
    p_value = compute_p_value(grade, mean, sem)
    if p_value < 0.001:
        break

print(f"An average grade of {grade} leads to a p-value of {p_value}")

An average grade of 88 leads to a p-value of 0.0006885138966450773
```

Given the new threshold, we would require an average grade of at least 88% to reject the null hypothesis. Thus, an average grade of 87% would not be considered statistically significant, even though it's noticeably higher than the population mean. Our lowering of the cutoff has inevitably exposed us to an increased risk of type II errors. Consequently, in this book, we maintain the commonly accepted p-value cutoff of 0.05. But we also proceed with excessive caution to avoid erroneously rejecting the null hypothesis. In particular, we do our best to minimize the most common cause of type I errors and the topic of the next subsection: data dredging.

7.2 Data dredging: Coming to false conclusions through oversampling

Sometimes, statistics students utilize the p-value incorrectly. Consider the following simple scenario. Two roommates pour out a bag of candy. The bag contains multiple candy pieces in five different colors. There are more blue candies in the bag than any other individual color. The first roommate assumes that blue is the dominant color in any candy bag. The second roommate disagrees: she computes the p-value based on the null hypothesis that all colors occur with equal likelihood. That p-value is greater than 0.05. However, the first roommate refuses to back down. He opens another bag of candy. The p-value is recomputed from the contents of that bag. This time, the p-value is equal to 0.05. The first roommate claims victory: he asserts that given the low p-value, the null hypothesis is probably false. Yet he is wrong.

The first roommate fundamentally misconstrued the meaning of the p-value. He wrongly assumed it represents the probability of the null hypothesis being true. In fact, the p-value represents the probability of observing deviations if the null hypothesis is true. The difference between the definitions is subtle but very important: the first definition implies that the null hypothesis is likely to be false if the p-value is low; but the second definition guarantees that we'll eventually observe a low p-value by repeatedly counting candies, even when the null hypothesis is true. Furthermore, the frequency of low p-value observations will equal the p-value itself. Hence, if we open 100 bags of candy, we should expect to observe a p-value of 0.05 approximately five times. By taking random measurements repeatedly, we will eventually obtain a statistically significant result, even if no statistical significance exists!

Running the same experiment too many times increases our risk of type I errors. Let's explore this notion in the context of our fifth-grade exam analysis. Suppose that North Dakota's statewide test performance does not diverge from the exam results in the other 49 states. More precisely, we'll assume that the national mean and variance equal North Dakota's `population_mean` and `population_variance` exam-grade results. Thus, the null hypothesis is true for all the states in the United States.

Furthermore, let's assume we don't yet know that the null hypothesis is always true. The only things we know for sure are North Dakota's population mean and variance. We set out on a road trip in search of a state whose grade distribution differs from North Dakota's distribution. Unfortunately, our search is bound to be futile because no such state exists.

Our first stop is Montana. There, we choose a random fifth-grade classroom of 18 students. We then compute the classroom's average grade. Since the null hypothesis is secretly true, we can simulate the value of that average grade by sampling from a normal distribution defined by `mean` and `sem`. Let's simulate the exam performance of the class by calling `np.random.normal(mean, sem)`. The method call samples from a normal distribution defined by the inputted variables.

```
np.random.seed(0)
random_average_grade = np.random.normal(mean, sem)
print(f"Average grade equals {random_average_grade:.2f}")
```

```
Average grade equals 84.16
```

The average exam grade in the class equals approximately 84.16. We can determine if that average is statistically significant by checking if its p-value is less than or equal to 0.05.

```
if compute_p_value(random_average_grade, mean, sem) <= 0.05:
    print("The observed result is statistically significant")
else:
    print("The observed result is not statistically significant")
```

```
The observed result is not statistically significant
```

The average grade is not statistically significant. We will continue our journey and visit a single 18-student classroom in each of the remaining 48 states, computing the grade average for each classroom. The p-value will also be computed. Once we discover a statistically significant p-value, our journey will end.

The following code simulates our travels. It iterates through the remaining 48 states, randomly drawing a grade average for each state. Once a statistically significant grade average is discovered, the iteration loop will stop.

```
np.random.seed(0)
for i in range(1, 49):
    print(f"We visited state {i + 1}")
    random_average_grade = np.random.normal(mean, sem)
    p_value = compute_p_value(random_average_grade, mean, sem)
    if p_value <= 0.05:
        print("We found a statistically significant result.")
        print(f"The average grade was {random_average_grade:.2f}")
        print(f"The p-value was {p_value}")
        break

if i == 48:
    print("We visited every state and found no significant results.")
```

```
We visited state 2
We visited state 3
We visited state 4
We visited state 5
We found a statistically significant result.
The average grade was 85.28
The p-value was 0.025032993883401307
```

The fifth state that we visit produces a statistically significant result! A classroom in the state has a grade average of 85.28. The associated p-value of 0.025 falls below our 0.05 cutoff. It appears we can reject the null hypothesis! However, this conclusion is erroneous since the null hypothesis is true. What went wrong? Well, as stated earlier, the frequency of low p-value observations will equal the p-value itself. Therefore, we expect to encounter a p-value of 0.025 approximately 2.5% of the time, even if the null hypothesis is true. Since we are traveling across 49 states, and 2.5% of 49 is 1.225, we should expect to visit approximately one state with a random p-value of roughly 0.025.

Our quest to find a statistically significant result was doomed from the start because we have misused statistics. We have indulged in the cardinal statistical sin of *data dredging*, also known as *data fishing* or *p-hacking*. In data dredging, experiments are repeated over and over until a statistically significant result is found. Then the statistically significant result is presented to others, while the remaining failed experiments are discarded. Data dredging is the most common cause of type I errors in scientific publications. Sadly, sometimes researchers formulate a hypothesis and repeat an experiment until the particular false hypothesis is validated as true. For instance, a researcher might hypothesize that certain candies cause cancer in mice. The researcher proceeds to feed a specific candy brand to a group of mice, but no cancer link is found. The researcher then switches the brand of candy and runs the experiment again. And again. And again. Years later, a brand of candy linked to cancer is finally found. Of course, the actual experiment outcome is borderline fraudulent. No real statistical link exists between cancer and candy—the researcher has simply run the experiment too many times, until a low p-value was randomly measured.

Avoiding data dredging is not difficult: we must simply choose in advance a finite number of experiments to run. Then we set our significance level to 0.05 divided by the planned experiment count. This simple technique is known as the *Bonferroni correction*. Let's repeat our analysis of US exam performance using the Bonferroni correction. The analysis requires us to visit 49 states to evaluate 49 classrooms, so our significance level should be set to 0.05 / 49.

Listing 7.12 Using the Bonferroni correction to adjust significance

```
num_planned_experiments = 49
significance_level = .05 / num_planned_experiments
```

We rerun our analysis, which will terminate if we encounter a p-value that's less than or equal to significance_level.

Listing 7.13 Rerunning an analysis using an adjusted significance level

```
np.random.seed(0)
for i in range(49):
    random_average_grade = np.random.normal(mean, sem)
    p_value = compute_p_value(random_average_grade, mean, sem)
```

```
    if p_value <= significance_level:
        print("We found a statistically significant result.")
        print(f"The average grade was {random_average_grade:.2f}")
        print(f"The p-value was {p_value}")
        break

if i == 48:
    print("We visited every state and found no significant results.")
```

```
We visited every state and found no significant results.
```

We've visited 49 states and found no statistically significant deviations from North Dakota's population mean and variance. The Bonferroni correction has allowed us to avoid a type I error.

As a final word of caution, the Bonferroni correction only works if we divide 0.05 by the number of planned experiments. It is not effective if we divide by the count of completed experiments. For instance, if we plan to run 1,000 experiments, but the p-value of our very first experiment equals 0.025, we should not alter our significance level to 0.05 / 1. Similarly, if the p-value of the second completed experiment equals 0.025, we should maintain a significance level of 0.05 / 1000 rather than adjust it to 0.05 / 2. Otherwise, we risk wrongly biasing our conclusions toward our first few experimental outcomes. All experiments must be treated equally for us to draw a fair, correct conclusion.

The Bonferroni correction is a useful technique for more accurate hypothesis testing. It can be applied to all kinds of statistical hypothesis tests beyond just simple tests that exploit both population mean and variance. This is fortunate because statistical tests vary in their levels of complexity. In the next subsection, we explore a more complicated test that does not depend on knowing the population variance.

7.3 *Bootstrapping with replacement: Testing a hypothesis when the population variance is unknown*

We are easily able to compute a p-value using the population mean and variance. Regrettably, in many real-life circumstances, the population variance is not known. Consider the following scenario, in which we own a very large aquarium. It holds 20 tropical fish of lengths varying from 2 cm to nearly 120 cm. The average fish length equals 27 cm. We represent these fish lengths using the fish_lengths array.

Listing 7.14 Defining lengths of fish in an aquarium

```
fish_lengths = np.array([46.7, 17.1, 2.0, 19.2, 7.9, 15.0, 43.4,
                         8.8, 47.8, 19.5, 2.9, 53.0, 23.5, 118.5,
                         3.8, 2.9, 53.9, 23.9, 2.0, 28.2])
assert fish_lengths.mean() == 27
```

Does our aquarium accurately capture the distributed lengths of real tropical fish? We would like to find out. A trusted source informs us that the population mean length of wild tropical fish equals 37 cm. There is a sizable 10 cm difference between the population mean and our sample mean. That difference feels significant, but feelings have no place in rigorous statistics. We must determine if the difference is statistically significant in order to draw a valid conclusion.

Thus far, we have measured statistical significance using our `compute_p_value` function. However, we cannot apply this function to our fish data since we don't know the population variance! Without the population variance, we cannot compute the SEM, which is a variable required to run `compute_p_value`. How do we find the standard error of the mean when the population variance is not known?

At first glance, it appears we have no way of finding the SEM. We could naively treat our sample variance as an estimate of the population variance by executing `fish_lengths.var()`. Unfortunately, small samples are prone to random variance fluctuations, so any such estimate is highly unreliable. Thus, we are stuck. We face a seemingly impenetrable problem and must rely on a seemingly impossible solution: *bootstrapping with replacement*. The term *bootstrapping* originates from the phrase "pull yourself up by your bootstraps." The phrase refers to lifting yourself into the air by pulling on the laces of your boots. Of course, doing so is impossible. In bootstrapping with replacement, we'll attempt something equally impossible by computing a p-value directly from our limited data! Despite this seemingly ludicrous solution, we will be successful in our efforts.

We begin the bootstrapping procedure by removing a random fish from the aquarium. The length of the selected fish is measured for later use.

Listing 7.15   Sampling a random fish from the aquarium

```
np.random.seed(0)
random_fish_length = np.random.choice(fish_lengths, size=1)[0]
sampled_fish_lengths = [random_fish_length]
```

Now we place the chosen fish back into the aquarium. This replacement step is where bootstrapping with replacement gets its name. After we return the fish, we reach into the aquarium again and choose another fish at random. There is a 1 in 20 chance that we'll select the same fish as before, which is perfectly acceptable. We record the length of the chosen fish and place it back into the water. Then we repeat the procedure 18 more times until 20 random fish lengths have been measured.

Listing 7.16   Sampling 20 random fish with repetition

```
np.random.seed(0)
for _ in range(20):
    random_fish_length = np.random.choice(fish_lengths, size=1)[0]
    sampled_fish_lengths.append(random_fish_length)
```

The `sampled_fish_lengths` list contains 20 measurements, all taken from the 20-element `fish_lengths` array. However, the elements of `fish_lengths` and `sampled_fish_lengths` are not identical. Due to random sampling, the mean values of the array and the list are likely to differ.

Listing 7.17   Comparing the sample mean to the aquarium mean

```
sample_mean = np.mean(sampled_fish_lengths)
print(f"Mean of sampled fish lengths is {sample_mean:.2f} cm")
```

```
Mean of sampled fish lengths is 26.03 cm
```

The mean of the sampled fish lengths is 26.03 cm. It deviates from our original mean by 0.97 cm. Thus, sampling with replacement has introduced some variance into our observations. If we sample another 20 measurements from the aquarium, we can expect the subsequent sample mean to also deviate from 27 cm. Let's confirm by repeating our sampling using a single line of code: np.random.choice(fish_lengths, size=20, replace=True). Setting the replace parameter to True ensures that we sample with replacement from the fish_lengths array.

Listing 7.18   Sampling with replacement using NumPy

As a side note, the replace parameter is currently set to True by default within the function.

```
np.random.seed(0)
new_sampled_fish_lengths = np.random.choice(fish_lengths, size=20,
                                            replace=True)   ◁
new_sample_mean = new_sampled_fish_lengths.mean()
print(f"Mean of the new sampled fish lengths is {new_sample_mean:.2f} cm")
```

```
Mean of the new sampled fish lengths is 26.16 cm
```

The new sample mean equals 26.16 cm. Our mean values will fluctuate when we sample with replacement: fluctuation implies randomness, and thus our mean values are randomly distributed. Let's explore the shape of this random distribution by repeating our sampling process 150,000 times. During iteration, we compute the mean of 20 random fish; then we plot a histogram of the 150,000 sampled means (figure 7.3).

Listing 7.19   Plotting the distribution of 150,000 sampled means

```
np.random.seed(0)
sample_means = [np.random.choice(fish_lengths,
                                 size=20,
                                 replace=True).mean()
                for _ in range(150000)]
likelihoods, bin_edges, _ = plt.hist(sample_means, bins='auto',
                                     edgecolor='black', density=True)
plt.xlabel('Binned Sample Mean')
plt.ylabel('Relative Likelihood')
plt.show()
```

The histogram we've generated is not a normal curve. The shape is not symmetric: its left side rises more steeply than its right side. Mathematicians refer to this asymmetry as a *skew*. We can confirm the skew in our histogram by calling stats.skew(sample_means). The stats.skew method returns a nonzero value when the inputted data is asymmetric.

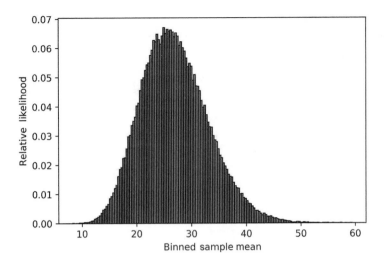

Figure 7.3 A histogram of sample means computed using sampling with replacement. The histogram is not bell shaped; it's asymmetric.

Listing 7.20 Computing the skew of an asymmetric distribution

```
assert abs(stats.skew(sample_means)) > 0.4
```

No data is ever perfectly symmetric, and the skew is rarely 0.0, even if the data is sampled from a normal curve. However, normal data tends to have a skew that is exceedingly close to 0.0. Any data with a skew whose absolute value is greater than 0.04 is very unlikely to come from a normal distribution.

Our asymmetric histogram cannot be modeled using a normal distribution. Nevertheless, the histogram represents a continuous probability distribution. Like all continuous distributions, the histogram can be mapped to a probability density function, a cumulative distribution function, and a survival function. Knowing the function outputs would be useful. For instance, the survival function would give us the probability of observing a sample mean that's greater than our population mean. We could obtain the function outputs by manually writing code that computes the curve area using the bin_edges and likelihoods arrays.

Alternatively, we can just use SciPy, which provides us with a method for obtaining all three functions from the histogram. That method is stats.rv_histogram, which takes as input a tuple defined by the bin_edges and likelihoods arrays. Calling stats.rv_histogram((likelihoods, bin_edges)) returns a random_variable SciPy object containing pdf, cdf, and sf methods, just like stats.norm. The random_variable .pdf method outputs the probability density for the histogram. Likewise, the random_variable.cdf and random_variable.sf methods output the cumulative distribution function and the survival function, respectively.

The following code computes the `random_variable` object arising from the histogram. Then we plot the probability density function by calling `random_variable.pdf` `(bin_edges)` (figure 7.4).

Listing 7.21   Fitting data to a generic distribution using SciPy

```
random_variable = stats.rv_histogram((likelihoods, bin_edges))
plt.plot(bin_edges, random_variable.pdf(bin_edges))
plt.hist(sample_means, bins='auto', alpha=0.1, color='r', density=True)
plt.xlabel('Sample Mean')
plt.ylabel('Relative Likelihood')
plt.show()
```

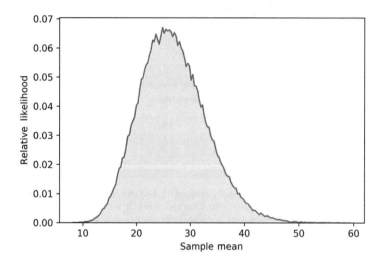

Figure 7.4   An asymmetric histogram overlaid with its probability density function. We used SciPy to learn the probability density function from the histogram.

As expected, the probability density function perfectly resembles the histogram shape. Let's now plot both the cumulative distribution function and the survival function associated with `random_variable`. We should anticipate that the two plotted functions will not be symmetric around the mean. To check for this asymmetry, we plot the distribution's mean using a vertical line. We obtain that mean by calling `random_variable.mean()` (figure 7.5).

Listing 7.22   Plotting the mean and interval areas for a generic distribution

```
rv_mean = random_variable.mean()
print(f"Mean of the distribution is approximately {rv_mean:.2f} cm")

plt.axvline(random_variable.mean(), color='k', label='Mean', linestyle=':')
plt.plot(bin_edges, random_variable.cdf(bin_edges),
         label='Cumulative Distribution')
```

```
plt.plot(bin_edges, random_variable.sf(bin_edges),
        label='Survival', linestyle='--', color='r')
plt.xlabel('Sample Mean')
plt.ylabel('Probability')
plt.legend()
plt.show()
```

```
Mean of the distribution is approximately 27.00 cm
```

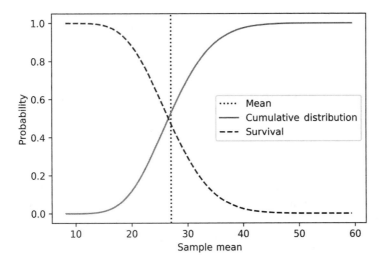

Figure 7.5 A cumulative distribution function of an asymmetric distribution plotted together with the survival function. The two functions no longer symmetrically reflect across the mean as they did in our normal-curve analysis. Therefore, we can no longer compute the p-value simply by doubling the survival function output.

The mean of the distribution is approximately 27 cm, which is also the mean length of the fish in our aquarium. A random fish sample is likely to produce a value that is close to the aquarium's mean. However, sampling with replacement sometimes produces a value greater than 37 cm or less than 17 cm. The probabilities of observing these extremes can be computed from our two plotted functions. Let's examine these two functions in more detail.

Based on our plot, the cumulative distribution function and the survival function are not mirror images. Nor do they intersect directly at the mean, as they did in our normal-curve analysis. Our distribution doesn't behave like a symmetric normal curve, which leads to certain consequences. Using the symmetric curve, we could compute the p-value by doubling the survival function. In our asymmetric distribution, the survival function by itself is insufficient for computing tail-end probabilities. Fortunately, we can use both the survival function and the cumulative distribution function to uncover probabilities of extreme observations. Using these probabilities, we can evaluate the statistical significance.

We can measure significance by answering this question: what is the probability that 20 sampled (with replacement) fish produce a mean as extreme as the population mean? As a reminder, the population mean is 37 cm, which is 10 cm greater than our distribution mean. Therefore, *extremeness* is defined as a sampled output that's at least 10 cm away from `rv_mean`. Based on our previous discussions, the problem can be broken down into computing two distinct values. First we must compute the probability of observing a sample mean that's at least 37 cm, and then we must compute the probability of observing a sample mean that's less than or equal to 17 cm. The former probability equals `random_variable.sf(37)`, while the latter equals `random_variable.cdf(17)`. Summing these two values will provide us with our answer.

> **Listing 7.23   Computing the probability of an extreme sample mean**

```
prob_extreme= random_variable.sf(37) + random_variable.cdf(17)
print("Probability of observing an extreme sample mean is approximately "
    f"{prob_extreme:.2f}")
```

```
Probability of observing an extreme sample mean is approximately 0.10
```

The probability of observing an extreme value from our sampling is approximately 0.10. In other words, one-tenth of random aquarium samplings will produce a mean that's at least as extreme as the population mean. Our population mean is not as far from the aquarium mean as we thought. In fact, a mean discrepancy of 10 cm or more will appear in 10% of sampled fish outputs. Thus, the difference between our sample mean of 27 cm and our population mean of 37 cm is not statistically significant.

By now, all this should seem familiar. The `prob_extreme` value is just the p-value in disguise. When the null hypothesis is true, the difference between the sample mean and population mean will be at least 10 cm in 10% of sampled cases. This p-value of 0.1 is greater than our cutoff of 0.05. So, we cannot reject the null hypothesis. There is no statistically significant difference between our sample mean and population mean.

We've computed a p-value in a roundabout way. Some readers may be suspicious of our methods—after all, sampling from our limited collection of 20 fish seems like a strange way to draw statistical insights. Nevertheless, the described technique is legitimate. Bootstrapping with replacement is a reliable procedure for extracting the p-value, especially when dealing with limited data.

Useful methods for bootstrapping with replacement

- `rv = stats.rv_histogram((likelihoods, bin_edges))`—Creates a random variable object `rv` based on the histogram output of `likelihoods`, `bin_edges = np.hist(data)`.
- `p_value = rv.sf(head_extreme) + random_variable.cdf(tail_extreme)`—Computes a p-value from a random variable object based on the survival output and the cumulative distribution output of the head extreme and tail extreme, respectively.

- `z = np.random.choice(x, size=y, replace=True)`—Samples `y` elements from array `x` with replacement. The samples are stored in array `z`. In bootstrapping with replacement, `y == x.size`.

The bootstrapping technique has been rigorously studied for more than four decades. Statisticians have uncovered multiple variations of this technique for accurate p-value computation. We've just reviewed one such variation; now we will briefly introduce another. It has been shown that sampling with replacement approximates a dataset's SEM. Basically, the standard deviation of the sampled distribution is equal to the SEM when the null hypothesis is true. Thus, if the null hypothesis is true, our missing SEM is equal to `random_variable.std`. This gives us yet another way of finding the p-value. We simply need to execute `compute_p_value(27, 37, random_variable.std)`; that computed p-value should equal approximately 0.1. Let's confirm.

Listing 7.24 Using bootstrapping to estimate the SEM

```
estimated_sem = random_variable.std()
p_value = compute_p_value(27, 37, estimated_sem)
print(f"P-value computed from estimated SEM is approximately {p_value:.2f}")

P-value computed from estimated SEM is approximately 0.10
```

As expected, the computed p-value is approximately 0.1. We've shown how bootstrapping with replacement provides us with two divergent approaches for computing the p-value. The first approach requires us to do the following:

1 Sample with replacement from the data. Repeat tens of thousands of times to obtain a list of sample means.
2 Generate a histogram from the sample means.
3 Convert the histogram to a distribution using the `stats.rv_histogram` method.
4 Take the area beneath the left and right extremes of the distribution curve using the survival function and the cumulative distribution function.

Meanwhile, the second approach appears to be slightly simpler:

1 Sample with replacement from the data. Repeat tens of thousands of times to obtain a list of sample means.
2 Compute the standard deviation of the means to approximate the SEM.
3 Use the estimated SEM to carry out basic hypothesis testing using our `compute_p_value` function.

Let's briefly discuss a third approach, which is even easier to implement. This approach does not require a histogram, nor does it rely on a custom `compute_value_function`. Instead, the technique uses the law of large numbers introduced in section 2. According to that law, the frequency of observed events approximates the probability of event occurrence if the sample count is sufficiently large. Thus, we can estimate the p-value simply by computing the frequency of extreme observations. Let's quickly apply this technique to `sample_means` by counting means that do not fall between 17 cm and 37 cm. We will divide the count by `len(sample_means)` in order to compute the p-value.

Listing 7.25   Computing the p-value from direct counts

```
number_extreme_values = 0
for sample_mean in sample_means:
    if not 17 < sample_mean < 37:
        number_extreme_values += 1

p_value = number_extreme_values / len(sample_means)
print(f"P-value is approximately {p_value:.2f}")

P-value is approximately 0.10
```

Bootstrapping with replacement is a simple but powerful technique for making inferences from limited data. However, the technique still presupposes the knowledge of a population mean. Unfortunately, in real-life situations, the population mean is rarely known. For instance, in this case study, we are required to analyze an online ad-click table that does not include a population mean. This missing information will not stop us: in the next subsection, we learn how to compare collected samples when both the population mean and the population variance are unknown.

7.4   *Permutation testing: Comparing means of samples when the population parameters are unknown*

Sometimes, in statistics, we need to compare two distinct sample means while the population parameters remain unknown. Let's explore one such scenario.

Suppose our neighbor also owns an aquarium. Her aquarium contains 10 fish whose average length is 46 cm. We represent these new fish lengths using the `new_fish_lengths` array.

Listing 7.26   Defining lengths of fish in a new aquarium

```
new_fish_lengths = np.array([51, 46.5, 51.6, 47, 54.4, 40.5, 43, 43.1,
                             35.9, 47.0])
assert new_fish_lengths.mean() == 46
```

We want to compare the contents of our neighbor's aquarium with our own. We begin by measuring the difference between `new_fish_lengths.mean()` and `fish_lengths.mean()`.

Listing 7.27   Computing the difference between two sample means

```
mean_diff = abs(new_fish_lengths.mean() - fish_lengths.mean())
print(f"There is a {mean_diff:.2f} cm difference between the two means")

There is a 19.00 cm difference between the two means
```

There is a 19 cm difference between the two aquarium means. That difference is substantial, but is it statistically significant? We want to find out. However, all our previous analyses have relied on a population mean. Currently, we have two sample means but no population mean. This makes it difficult to evaluate the null hypothesis, which assumes that fish from both aquariums share a population mean. This presumed shared value is now unknown. What should we do?

We need to reframe the null hypothesis so that it doesn't directly depend on the population mean. If the null hypothesis is true, then the 20 fish in the first aquarium and the 10 fish in the second aquarium are all drawn from the same population. Under the hypothesis, it doesn't really matter which 20 fish wind up in aquarium A and which 10 fish wind up in aquarium B. The arrangements of fish between the two aquariums will have little effect. Random rearrangements of the fish will cause the `mean_diff` variable to fluctuate, but that difference between means should fluctuate in a predictable manner.

Hence, we don't need to know the sample mean to evaluate the null hypothesis. Instead, we can focus on the random permutations of fish between the two aquariums. This will allow us to carry out a *permutation test*, where `mean_diff` is used to compute statistical significance. Like bootstrapping with replacement, the permutation test relies on random sampling of data.

We begin the permutation test by placing all 30 fish into a single aquarium. The unification of our fish can be modeled using the `np.hstack` method. The method takes as input a list of NumPy arrays, which are then merged together into a single NumPy array.

Listing 7.28 Merging two arrays using `np.hstack`

```
total_fish_lengths = np.hstack([fish_lengths, new_fish_lengths])
assert total_fish_lengths.size == 30
```

Once the fish are grouped together, we allow them to swim in random directions. This fully randomizes the positions of the fish in the aquarium. We use the `np.random .shuffle` method to shuffle the positions of the fish.

Listing 7.29 Shuffling the positions of merged fish

```
np.random.seed(0)
np.random.shuffle(total_fish_lengths)
```

Next, we choose 20 of our randomly shuffled fish. These 20 fish will be moved to a separate aquarium. The other 10 fish will remain. Once more, we'll have 20 fish in aquarium A and 10 fish in aquarium B. However, the mean lengths of the fish in each aquarium will probably differ from `fish_lengths.mean()` and `new_fish_lengths.mean()`, so the difference between mean fish lengths will also change. Let's confirm.

Listing 7.30   Computing the difference between two random sample means

```
random_20_fish_lengths = total_fish_lengths[:20]
random_10_fish_lengths = total_fish_lengths[20:]
mean_diff = random_20_fish_lengths.mean() - random_10_fish_lengths.mean()
print(f"The new difference between mean fish lengths is {mean_diff:.2f}")
```

```
The new difference between mean fish lengths is 14.33
```

The sampled difference between fish lengths is no longer 19 cm: now it is 14.33 cm. As expected, `mean_diff` is a fluctuating random variable, so we can find its distribution through random sampling. Next, we repeat our fish-shuffling procedure 30,000 times to obtain a histogram of `mean_diff` values (figure 7.6).

Listing 7.31   Plotting the fluctuating difference between means

```
np.random.seed(0)
mean_diffs = []
for _ in range(30000):
    np.random.shuffle(total_fish_lengths)
    mean_diff = total_fish_lengths[:20].mean() -
    total_fish_lengths[20:].mean()
    mean_diffs.append(mean_diff)

likelihoods, bin_edges, _ = plt.hist(mean_diffs, bins='auto',
                                     edgecolor='black', density=True)
plt.xlabel('Binned Mean Difference')
plt.ylabel('Relative Likelihood')
plt.show()
```

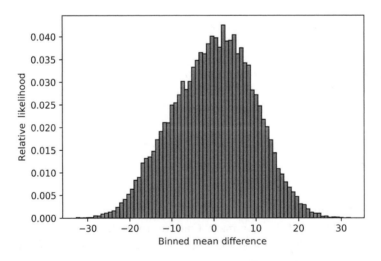

Figure 7.6   A histogram of sample mean differences computed using random rearrangements of samples into two distinct groups

Next, we fit the histogram to a random variable using the `stats.rv_histogram` method.

> **Listing 7.32   Fitting the histogram to a random variable**

```
random_variable = stats.rv_histogram((likelihoods, bin_edges))
```

Finally, we use the `random_variable` object to carry out hypothesis testing. We want to know the probability of observing an extreme value when the null hypothesis is true. We define extremeness as a difference between means whose absolute value is at least 19 cm. Thus, our p-value will equal `random_variable.cdf(-19)` + `random_variable.sf(19)`.

> **Listing 7.33   Computing the permutation p-value**

```
p_value = random_variable.sf(19) + random_variable.cdf(-19)
print(f"P-value is approximately {p_value:.2f}")

P-value is approximately 0.04
```

The p-value is approximately 0.04, which falls below our significance threshold of 0.05. Hence, the mean difference between fish lengths is statistically significant. The fish in the two aquariums do not originate from a shared distribution.

As an aside, we can simplify our permutation test by using the law of large numbers. We simply need to compute the frequency of extreme recorded samples, just as we did with bootstrapping with replacement. Let's use this alternative method to recompute our p-value of approximately 0.04.

> **Listing 7.34   Computing the permutation p-value from direct counts**

```
number_extreme_values = 0.0
for min_diff in mean_diffs:
    if not -19 < min_diff < 19:
        number_extreme_values += 1

p_value = number_extreme_values / len(mean_diffs)
print(f"P-value is approximately {p_value:.2f}")

P-value is approximately 0.04
```

The permutation test allows us to statistically compare differences between two lists of collected samples. The nature of these samples isn't important; they could be fish lengths, or they could be ad-click counts. Hence, the permutation test could be very useful when we compare our recorded ad-click counts to uncover optimal ad colors during the case study resolution.

Summary

- Statistical hypothesis testing requires us to choose between two competing hypotheses. According to the *null hypothesis,* a pair of populations are identical. According to the *alternative hypothesis,* the pair of populations are not identical.

- To evaluate the null hypothesis, we must compute a *p-value.* The p-value equals the probability of observing our data when the null hypothesis is true. The null hypothesis is rejected if the p-value is lower than a specified *significance level* threshold. Typically, the significance level is set to 0.05.

- If we reject the null hypothesis, and the null hypothesis is true, we commit a *type I error.* If we fail to reject the null hypothesis and the alternative hypothesis is true, we commit a type II error.

- *Data dredging* increases our risk of type I errors. In data dredging, an experiment is repeated until the p-value falls below the significance level. We can minimize data dredging by carrying out a *Bonferroni correction,* in which the significance level is divided by the experiment count.

- We can compare a sample mean to a population mean and variance by relying on the central limit theorem. The population variance is needed to compute the SEM. If we're not provided with the population variance, we can estimate the SEM using *bootstrapping with replacement.*

- We can compare the means of two distinct samples by running a *permutation test.*

Analyzing tables using Pandas

This section covers

- Storing 2D tables using the Pandas library
- Summarizing 2D table content
- Manipulating row and column content
- Visualizing tables using the Seaborn library

The ad-click data for case study 2 is saved in a two-dimensional table. Data tables are commonly used to store information. The tables may be stored in different formats: some tables are saved as spreadsheets in Excel, and others are text-based CSV files in which the columns are separated by commas. The formatting of a table isn't important. What is important is its structure. All tables have structural features in common: every table contains horizontal rows and vertical columns, and quite often, column headers also hold explicit column names.

8.1　Storing tables using basic Python

Let's define a sample table in Python. The table stores measurements for various species of fish, in centimeters. Our measurement table contains three columns: Fish, Length, and Width. The Fish column stores a labeled species of fish, and the Length and Width columns specify the length and width of each fish species. We represent this table as a dictionary. The column names serve as dictionary keys, and these keys map to lists of column values.

Listing 8.1　Storing a table using Python data structures

```python
fish_measures = {'Fish': ['Angelfish', 'Zebrafish', 'Killifish', 'Swordtail'],
                 'Length':[15.2, 6.5, 9, 6],
                 'Width': [7.7, 2.1, 4.5, 2]}
```

Suppose we want to know the length of a zebrafish. To obtain the length, we must first access the index of the 'Zebrafish' element in fish_measures['Fish']. Then we need to check that index in fish_measures['Length']. The process is slightly convoluted, as illustrated in the following code.

Listing 8.2　Accessing table columns using a dictionary

```python
zebrafish_index = fish_measures['Fish'].index('Zebrafish')
zebrafish_length = fish_measures['Length'][zebrafish_index]
print(f"The length of a zebrafish is {zebrafish_length:.2f} cm")

The length of a zebrafish is 6.50 cm
```

Our dictionary representation is functional but also difficult to use. A better solution is provided by the Pandas library, which is designed for table manipulation.

8.2　Exploring tables using Pandas

Let's install the Pandas library. Once Pandas is installed, we will import it as pd using common Pandas usage convention.

NOTE　Call pip install pandas from the command line terminal to install the Pandas library.

Listing 8.3　Importing the Pandas library

```python
import pandas as pd
```

We now load our fish_measures tables into Pandas by calling pd.DataFrame(fish_measures). That method call returns a Pandas DataFrame object. The term *data frame* is a common synonym for *table* in statistical software jargon. Basically, the DataFrame object will convert our dictionary into a two-dimensional table. According to convention, Pandas DataFrame objects are assigned to a variable df. Here, we execute df = pd.DataFrame(fish_measures) and then print the contents of df.

Listing 8.4 Loading a table into Pandas

```
df = pd.DataFrame(fish_measures)
print(df)
```

```
        Fish  Length  Width
0  Angelfish    15.2    7.7
1  Zebrafish     6.5    2.1
2  Killifish     9.0    4.5
3  Swordtail     6.0    2.0
```

The alignments between table rows and columns are clearly visible in the printed output. Our table is small and therefore easy to display. However, for larger tables, we might prefer to print only the first few rows. Calling `print(df.head(x))` prints just the first x rows in a table. Let's print the first two rows by calling `print(df.head(2))`.

Listing 8.5 Accessing the first two rows of a table

```
print(df.head(2))
```

```
        Fish  Length  Width
0  Angelfish    15.2    7.7
1  Zebrafish     6.5    2.1
```

A better way to summarize a larger Pandas table is to execute `pd.describe()`. By default, this method generates statistics for all numeric columns in the table. The statistical output includes minimum and maximum column values as well as the mean and standard deviation. When we print `pd.describe()`, we should expect to see information for the numeric `Length` and `Width` columns but not for the string-based `Fish` column.

Listing 8.6 Summarizing the numeric columns

```
print(df.describe())
```

```
          Length      Width
count   4.000000   4.000000
mean    9.175000   4.075000
std     4.225616   2.678775
min     6.000000   2.000000
25%     6.375000   2.075000
50%     7.750000   3.300000
75%    10.550000   5.300000
max    15.200000   7.700000
```

Outputs of the Pandas describe method
- count—The number of elements in each column.
- mean—The mean of the elements in each column.
- std—The standard deviation of the elements in each column.

(continued)
- min—The minimum value in each column.
- 25%—25% of the column elements fall below this value.
- 50%—50% of the column elements fall below this value. The value is identical to the median.
- 75%—75% of the column elements fall below this value.
- max—The maximum value in each column.

According to the summary, the mean of Length is 9.175 cm and the mean of Width is 4.075 cm. Additional statistical information is also included in the output. Sometimes that other information is not very useful—if all we care about is the mean, we can omit the other outputs by calling df.mean().

Listing 8.7   Computing the column mean

```
print(df.mean())

Length    9.175
Width     4.075
dtype: float64
```

The df.describe() method is intended to run on numeric columns. However, we can force it to process strings by calling df.describe(include=[np.object]). Setting the include parameter to [np.object] instructs Pandas to search for table columns built on top of NumPy string arrays. Since we cannot run statistical analysis on strings, the resulting output does not contain statistical information. Instead, the description counts the total number of unique strings and the frequency with which the most common string occurs. The most frequent string is also included. Our Fish column contains four unique strings, and each string is mentioned only once. Therefore, we expect the most frequent string to be chosen at random with a frequency of 1.

Listing 8.8   Summarizing the string columns

```
print(df.describe(include=[np.object]))
```

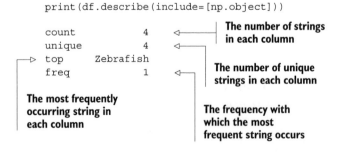

```
count              4
unique             4
top        Zebrafish
freq               1
```

The number of strings in each column

The number of unique strings in each column

The most frequently occurring string in each column

The frequency with which the most frequent string occurs

Pandas summarization methods
- `df.head()`—Returns the first five rows in data frame `df`
- `df.head(x)`—Returns the first `x` rows in data frame `df`
- `df.describe()`—Returns statistics relating to numeric columns in `df`
- `df.describe(include=[np.object])`—Returns statistics relating to string columns in `df`
- `df.mean()`—Returns the mean of all numeric columns in `df`

As mentioned, the `Fish` column is built on top of a NumPy string array. In fact, the entire data frame is built on top of a two-dimensional NumPy array. Pandas stores all the data in NumPy for quick manipulation. We can retrieve the underlying NumPy array by accessing `df.values`.

Listing 8.9 Retrieving the table as a 2D NumPy array

```
print(df.values)
assert type(df.values) == np.ndarray

[['Angelfish' 15.2 7.7]
 ['Zebrafish' 6.5 2.1]
 ['Killifish' 9.0 4.5]
 ['Swordtail' 6.0 2.0]]
```

8.3 Retrieving table columns

Let's turn our attention to retrieving individual columns, which can be accessed using their column names. We can output all the column names by calling `print(df .columns)`.

Listing 8.10 Accessing all column names

```
print(df.columns)

Index(['Fish', 'Length', 'Width'], dtype='object')
```

Now let's print all of the data stored in the `Fish` column by accessing `df.Fish`.

Listing 8.11 Accessing an individual column

```
print(df.Fish)

0    Angelfish
1    Zebrafish
2    Killifish
3    Swordtail
Name: Fish, dtype: object
```

Note that the printed output is not a NumPy array. Rather, `df.Fish` is a Pandas object that represents a one-dimensional array. To print a NumPy array, we must run `print (df.Fish.values)`.

Listing 8.12   Retrieving a column as a NumPy array

```
print(df.Fish.values)
assert type(df.Fish.values) == np.ndarray

['Angelfish' 'Zebrafish' 'Killifish' 'Swordtail']
```

We've accessed the Fish column using df.Fish. We can also access Fish using a dictionary-style bracket representation by printing df['Fish'].

Listing 8.13   Accessing a column using brackets

```
print(df['Fish'])

0    Angelfish
1    Zebrafish
2    Killifish
3    Swordtail
Name: Fish, dtype: object
```

The bracket representation allows us to retrieve multiple columns by running df[name_list], where name_list is a list of column names. Suppose we want to retrieve both the Fish column and the Length column. Running df[['Fish', 'Length']] returns a truncated table containing only those two columns.

Listing 8.14   Accessing multiple columns using brackets

```
print(df[['Fish', 'Length']])

        Fish  Length
0  Angelfish    15.2
1  Zebrafish     6.5
2  Killifish     9.0
3  Swordtail     6.0
```

We can analyze data stored in df a variety of ways. We can, for instance, sort our rows based on a value of a single column. Calling df.sort_values('Length') returns a new table whose rows are sorted based on length.

Listing 8.15   Sorting rows by column value

```
print(df.sort_values('Length'))

        Fish  Length  Width
3  Swordtail     6.0    2.0
1  Zebrafish     6.5    2.1
2  Killifish     9.0    4.5
0  Angelfish    15.2    7.7
```

Furthermore, we can use values in columns to filter out unwanted rows. For example, calling df[df.Width >= 3] returns a table whose rows contain a width of at least 3 cm.

Listing 8.16 Filtering rows by column value

```
print(df[df.Width >= 3])
```

```
        Fish  Length  Width
0  Angelfish    15.2    7.7
2  Killifish     9.0    4.5
```

> **Pandas column-retrieval methods**
> - `df.columns`—Returns the column names in data frame `df`
> - `df.x`—Returns column `x`
> - `df[x]`—Returns column `x`
> - `df[[x,y]]`—Returns columns `x` and `y`
> - `df.x.values`—Returns column `x` as a NumPy array
> - `df.sort_values(x)`—Returns a data frame sorted by the values in column `x`
> - `df[df.x > y]`—Returns a data frame filtered by the values in column `x` that are `> y`

8.4 Retrieving table rows

Now let's turn our attention to retrieving rows in `df`. Unlike columns, our rows do not have preassigned label values. To compensate, Pandas assigns a special index to each row. These indices appear on the leftmost side of the printed table. Based on the printed output, the index for the `Angelfish` row is 0 and the index for the `Swordtail` row is 3. We can access these rows by calling `df.loc[[0, 3]]`. As a general rule, executing `df.loc[[index_list]]` locates all the rows whose indices appear in `index_list`. Let's now locate the rows that align with the `Swordtail` and `Angelfish` indices.

Listing 8.17 Accessing rows by index

```
print(df.loc[[0, 3]])
```

```
        Fish  Length  Width
0  Angelfish    15.2    7.7
3  Swordtail     6.0    2.0
```

Suppose we wish to retrieve rows using species names and not numeric indices. More precisely, we want to retrieve those rows whose `Fish` column contains either `'Angelfish'` or `'Swordtail'`. In Pandas, that retrieval process is a bit tricky: we need to execute `df[booleans]`, where `booleans` is a list of Booleans that are `True` if they match a row of interest. Basically, the indices of `True` values must correspond to rows that match either `'Angelfish'` or `'Whitefish'`. How do we obtain the `booleans` list? One naive approach is to iterate over `df.Fish`, returning `True` if a column value appears in `['Angelfish', 'Swordtail']`. Let's run the naive approach next.

Listing 8.18   Accessing rows by column value

```
booleans = [name in ['Angelfish', 'Swordtail']
            for name in df.Fish]
print(df[booleans])

        Fish  Length  Width
0  Angelfish    15.2    7.7
3  Swordtail     6.0    2.0
```

We can more concisely locate rows of interest using the isin method. Calling df.Fish.isin(['Angelfish', Swordtail']) returns an analogue of our previously computed booleans list. Thus, we can retrieve all the rows in a single line of code by running df[df.Fish.isin(['Angelfish', 'Swordtail'])].

Listing 8.19   Accessing rows by column value using `isin`

```
print(df[df.Fish.isin(['Angelfish', 'Swordtail'])])

        Fish  Length  Width
0  Angelfish    15.2    7.7
3  Swordtail     6.0    2.0
```

The df table stores two measurements across four species of fish. We can easily access measurements in the columns; unfortunately, accessing rows by species is harder since the row indices don't equal the species names. Let's remedy the situation by replacing the row indices with species. We swap numbers for species names using the df.set_index method. Calling df.set_index('Fish', inplace=True) sets our indices to equal the species in the Fish column. The inplace=True parameter modifies the indices internally rather than returning a modified copy of df.

Listing 8.20   Swapping row indices for column values

```
df.set_index('Fish', inplace=True)
print(df)

      Fish  Length  Width
Angelfish    15.2    7.7
Zebrafish     6.5    2.1
Killifish     9.0    4.5
Swordtail     6.0    2.0
```

The leftmost index column is no longer numeric: the numbers have been replaced with species names. We can now access the Angelfish and Swordtail columns by running df.loc[['Angelfish', 'Swordtail'].

Listing 8.21 Accessing rows by string index

```
print(df.loc[['Angelfish', 'Swordtail']])
```

```
      Fish  Length  Width
Angelfish    15.2    7.7
Swordtail     6.0    2.0
```

Pandas row-retrieval methods
- `df.loc[[x, y]]`—Returns the rows located at indices x and y
- `df[booleans]`—Returns the rows where `booleans[i]` is `True` for column i
- `df[name in array for name in df.x]`—Returns rows where column name x is present in `array`
- `df[df.x.isin(array)])`—Returns rows where column name x is present in `array`
- `df.set_index('x', inplace=True)`—Swaps numeric row indices for the column values in column x

8.5 *Modifying table rows and columns*

Currently, each table row contains the length and width of a specified fish. What will happen if we swap our rows and columns? We can find out by running `df.T`. The `T` stands for *transpose*: in a transpose operation, the elements of a table are flipped around its diagonal so that the rows and columns are switched. Let's transpose our table and print the results.

Listing 8.22 Swapping rows and columns

```
df_transposed = df.T
print(df_transposed)
```

```
Fish    Angelfish  Zebrafish  Killifish  Swordtail
Length       15.2        6.5        9.0        6.0
Width         7.7        2.1        4.5        2.0
```

We've modified the table: each column now refers to an individual species of fish, and each row refers to a particular measurement type. The first row holds length, and the second row holds width. Thus, calling `print(df_transposed.Swordtail)` will print the swordtail's length and width.

Listing 8.23 Printing a transposed column

```
print(df_transposed.Swordtail)
```

```
Length    6.0
Width     2.0
Name: Swordtail, dtype: float64
```

Let's modify our table by adding clownfish measurements to df_transposed. The length and width of a clownfish are 10.6 cm and 3.7 cm, respectively. We add these measurements by running df_transposed['Clownfish'] = [10.6, 3.7].

Listing 8.24   Adding a new column

```
df_transposed['Clownfish'] = [10.6, 3.7]
print(df_transposed)

Fish    Angelfish  Zebrafish  Killifish  Swordtail  Clownfish
Length       15.2        6.5        9.0        6.0       10.6
Width         7.7        2.1        4.5        2.0        3.7
```

Alternatively, we can assign new columns using the df_transposed.assign method. The method lets us add multiple columns by passing in more than one column name. For instance, calling df_transposed.assign(Clownfish2=[10.6, 3.7], Clownfish3=[10.6, 3.7]) returns a table with two new columns; *Clownfish2* and *Clownfish3*. Note that the assign method never adds new columns directly to a table—instead, it returns a copy of the table containing the new data.

Listing 8.25   Adding multiple new columns

```
df_new = df_transposed.assign(Clownfish2=[10.6, 3.7], Clownfish3=[10.6, 3.7])
assert 'Clownfish2' not in df_transposed.columns
assert 'Clownfish2' in df_new.columns
print(df_new)

Fish    Angelfish  Zebrafish  Killifish  Swordtail  Clownfish  Clownfish2  \
Length       15.2        6.5        9.0        6.0       10.6        10.6
Width         7.7        2.1        4.5        2.0        3.7         3.7

Fish    Clownfish3
Length        10.6
Width          3.7
```

Our newly added columns are redundant. We delete these columns by calling df_new.drop(columns=['Clownfish2', 'Clownfish3'], inplace=True). The df_new .drop method drops all specified columns from a table.

Listing 8.26   Deleting multiple columns

```
df_new.drop(columns=['Clownfish2', 'Clownfish3'], inplace=True)
print(df_new)

Fish    Angelfish  Zebrafish  Killifish  Swordtail  Clownfish
Length       15.2        6.5        9.0        6.0       10.6
Width         7.7        2.1        4.5        2.0        3.7
```

We now utilize the stored measurements to compute the surface area of each fish. We can treat every fish as an ellipse with an area of math.pi * length * width / 4. To find each area, we must iterate over the values in every column. Iterating over columns in a data frame is just like iterating over elements in a dictionary: we simply execute df_new.items(). Doing so returns an iterable of tuples containing column names and column values. Let's iterate over the columns in df_new to get the area of every fish.

Listing 8.27   Iterating over column values

```
areas = []
for fish_species, (length, width) in df_new.items():
    area = math.pi * length * width / 4
    print(f"Area of {fish_species} is {area}")
    areas.append(area)


Area of Angelfish is 91.92300104403735
Area of Zebrafish is 10.720684930375171
Area of Killifish is 31.808625617596654
Area of Swordtail is 9.42477796076938
Area of Clownfish is 30.80331596844792
```

Let's add the computed areas to our table. We can augment a new Area row by executing df_new.loc['Area'] = areas. Then we need to run df_new.reindex() to update the row indices with the added Area name.

Listing 8.28   Adding a new row

```
df_new.loc['Area'] = areas
df_new.reindex()
print(df_new)


Fish    Angelfish  Zebrafish  Killifish  Swordtail  Clownfish
Length  15.200000   6.500000   9.000000   6.000000  10.600000
Width    7.700000   2.100000   4.500000   2.000000   3.700000
Area    91.923001  10.720685  31.808626   9.424778  30.803316
```

Our updated table contains three rows and five columns. We can confirm by accessing df_new.shape.

Listing 8.29   Checking the table shape

```
row_count, column_count = df_new.shape
print(f"Our table contains {row_count} rows and {column_count} columns")


Our table contains 3 rows and 5 columns
```

Modifying data frames in Pandas

- df.T—Returns a transposed data frame, where rows and columns are swapped.
- df[x] = array—Creates a new column x. df.x maps to values in array.

> *(continued)*
> - `df.assign(x=array)`—Returns a data frame containing all the elements of `df` and a new column x. `df.x` maps to values in `array`.
> - `df.assign(x=array, y=array2)`—Returns a data frame containing two new columns, x and y.
> - `df.drop(columns=[x, y])`—Returns a data frame in which columns x and y have been deleted.
> - `df.drop(columns=[x, y], inplace=True)`—Deletes columns x and y in place, thus modifying `df`.
> - `df.loc[x] = array`—Adds a new row at index x. We need to run `df.reindex()` for that row to be accessible.

8.6   *Saving and loading table data*

We've finished making changes to the table. Let's store the table for later use. Calling `df_new.to_csv('Fish_measurements.csv')` saves the table to a CSV file in which the columns are delimited by commas.

Listing 8.30   Saving a table to a CSV file

```
df_new.to_csv('Fish_measurements.csv')
with open('Fish_measurements.csv') as f:
    print(f.read())

,Angelfish,Zebrafish,Killifish,Swordtail,Clownfish
Length,15.2,6.5,9.0,6.0,10.6
Width,7.7,2.1,4.5,2.0,3.7
Area,91.92300104403735,10.720684930375171,31.808625617596654,9.42477796076938
    ,30.80331596844792
```

The CSV file can be loaded into Pandas using the `pd.read_csv` method. Calling `pd.read_csv('Fish_measurements.csv', index_col=0)` returns a data frame containing all our table information. The optional `index_col` parameter specifies which column holds the row index names. If no column is specified, numeric row indices are automatically assigned.

Listing 8.31   Loading a table from a CSV file

```
df = pd.read_csv('Fish_measurements.csv', index_col=0)
print(df)
print("\nRow index names when column is assigned:")
print(df.index.values)

df_no_assign = pd.read_csv('Fish_measurements.csv')
print("\nRow index names when no column is assigned:")
print(df_no_assign.index.values)
```

```
         Angelfish  Zebrafish   Killifish  Swordtail  Clownfish
Length   15.200000   6.500000    9.000000   6.000000  10.600000
Width     7.700000   2.100000    4.500000   2.000000   3.700000
Area     91.923001  10.720685   31.808626   9.424778  30.803316
```

```
Row index names when column is assigned:
['Length' 'Width' 'Area']
```

```
Row index names when no column is assigned:
[0 1 2]
```

Using pd.csv, we can load the case study ad-click table into Pandas. Then we'll be able to efficiently analyze that table.

Saving and loading data frames in Pandas
- pd.DataFrame(dictionary)—Converts the data in dictionary to a data frame.
- pd.read_csv(filename)—Converts a CSV file to a data frame.
- pd.read_csv(filename, index_col=i)—Converts a CSV file to a data frame. The *i*th column provides row index names.
- df.to_csv(filename)—Saves the contents of df to a CSV file.

8.7 *Visualizing tables using Seaborn*

We can view the contents of a Pandas table using a simple print command. However, some numeric tables are too large to be viewed as printed output. Such tables are more easily displayed using heatmaps. A *heatmap* is a graphical representation of a table in which numeric cells are colored by value; the color shades shift continuously depending on the value size. The end result is a bird's-eye view of value differences in the table.

The easiest way to create a heatmap is to use the external Seaborn library. Seaborn is a visualization library built on top of Matplotlib and is closely integrated with Pandas data frames. Let's install the library and then import Seaborn as sns.

NOTE Call pip install seaborn from the command line terminal to install the Seaborn library.

Listing 8.32 Importing the Seaborn library

```
import seaborn as sns
```

Now we visualize our data frame as a heatmap by calling sns.heatmap(df) (figure 8.1).

Listing 8.33 Visualizing a heatmap using Seaborn

```
sns.heatmap(df)
plt.show()
```

We've plotted a heatmap of fish measurements. The displayed colors correspond with measurement values. The mappings between color shades and values are shown in a legend

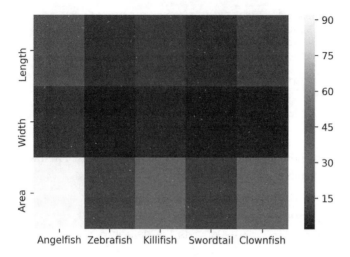

Figure 8.1   A heatmap of fish measurements. Its color legend specifies the mapping between measurements and colors. Darker colors correspond to lower measurement values. Lighter colors correspond to higher measurement values.

to the right of the plot. Lighter colors map to higher measurement values. Thus, we can immediately tell that the area of an angelfish is the largest measurement in the plot.

We can alter the color palette in the heatmap plot by passing in a `cmap` parameter. The following code executes `sns.heatmap(df, cmap='YlGnBu')` to create a heatmap where the color shades transition from yellow to green and then to blue (figure 8.2).

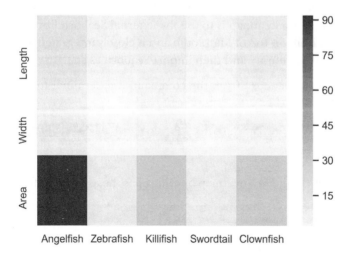

Figure 8.2   A heatmap of fish measurements. Darker colors correspond to higher measurement values. Lighter colors correspond to lower measurement values.

Listing 8.34   Adjusting heatmap colors

```
sns.heatmap(df, cmap='YlGnBu')
plt.show()
```

In the updated heatmap, the color tones have flipped: now darker colors correspond to higher measurements. We can confirm this by annotating the plot with the actual measurement values. We annotate the heatmap by passing `anot=True` into the `sns.heatmap` method (figure 8.3).

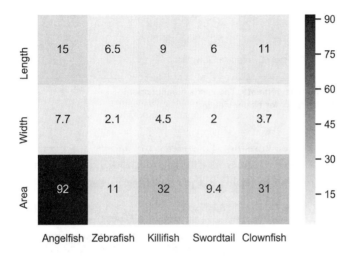

Figure 8.3   A heatmap of fish measurements. The actual measurement values are included in the plot.

Listing 8.35   Annotating the heatmap

```
sns.heatmap(df, cmap='YlGnBu', annot=True)
plt.show()
```

As mentioned previously, the Seaborn library is built on top of Matplotlib. Consequently, we can use Matplotlib commands to modify the elements of the heatmap. For example, calling `plt.yticks(rotation=0)` rotates the y-axis measurement labels, which makes them easier to read (figure 8.4).

Listing 8.36   Rotating heatmap labels using Matplotlib

```
sns.heatmap(df, cmap='YlGnBu', annot=True)
plt.yticks(rotation=0)
plt.show()
```

Finally, we should note that the `sns.heatmap` method can also process 2D lists and arrays. Thus, running `sns.heatmap(df.values)` also creates a heatmap plot, but the

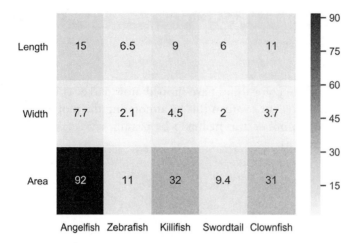

Figure 8.4   A heatmap of fish measurements. The y-axis measurement labels have been rotated horizontally for easier viewing.

y-axis and x-axis labels will be missing. To specify the labels, we need to pass the `xticklabels` and `yticklabels` parameters into the method. The following code uses our table's array representation to replicate the contents of figure 8.4.

Listing 8.37   Visualizing a heatmap from a NumPy array

```
sns.heatmap(df.values,                          As a reminder, df.values returns a 2D
            cmap='YlGnBu', annot=True,          NumPy array underlying the data frame.
            xticklabels=df.columns,
            yticklabels=df.index)               The x-axis fish labels are manually
plt.yticks(rotation=0)                          set to equal the column names.
plt.show()
                                                The y-axis measurement labels are
                                                manually set to equal the row indices.
```

Seaborn heatmap visualization commands

- `sns.heatmap(array)`—Generates a heatmap from the contents of the 2D array.
- `sns.heatmap(array, xticklabels=x, yticklabels=y)`—Generates a heatmap from the contents of the 2D `array`. The x-labels and y-labels are set to equal `x` and `y`, respectively.
- `sns.heatmap(df)`—Generates a heatmap from the contents of the data frame `df`. The x-labels and y-labels are automatically set to equal `df.columns` and `df.index`, respectively.
- `sns.heatmap(df, cmap=m)`—Generates a heatmap where the color scheme is specified by `m`.
- `sns.heatmap(df, annot=True)`—Generates a heatmap where the annotated values are included in the plot.

Summary

- 2D table structures can easily be processed using Pandas. We can load the data into Pandas using dictionaries or external files.
- Pandas stores each table in a data frame built on top of a NumPy array.
- Columns in a data frame have a name; we can use these names to access the columns. Meanwhile, the rows in a data frame are assigned numeric indices by default; we can use these indices to access the rows. It is also possible to swap the numeric row indices for string names.
- We can summarize the contents of a data frame using the `describe` method. The method returns valuable statistics such as the mean and standard deviation.
- We can visualize the contents of a data frame using a colored *heatmap*.

Case study 2 solution

This section covers

- Measuring statistical significance
- Permutation testing
- Manipulating tables using Pandas

We've been asked to analyze the online ad-click data collected by our buddy Fred. His advertising data table monitors ad clicks across 30 different colors. Our aim is to discover an ad color that generates significantly more clicks than blue. We will do so by following these steps:

1. Load and clean our advertising data using Pandas.
2. Run a permutation test between blue and the other recorded colors.
3. Check the computed p-values for statistical significance using a properly determined significance level.

WARNING Spoiler alert! The solution to case study 2 is about to be revealed. I strongly encourage you to try to solve the problem before reading the solution. The original problem statement is available for reference at the beginning of the case study.

9.1 *Processing the ad-click table in Pandas*

Let's begin by loading our ad-click table into Pandas. Then we check the number of rows and columns in the table.

Listing 9.1 Loading the ad-click table into Pandas

```
df = pd.read_csv('colored_ad_click_table.csv')
num_rows, num_cols = df.shape
print(f"Table contains {num_rows} rows and {num_cols} columns")
```

```
Table contains 30 rows and 41 columns
```

Our table contains 30 rows and 41 columns. The rows should correspond to clicks per day and views per day associated with individual colors. Let's confirm by checking the column names.

Listing 9.2 Checking the column names

```
print(df.columns)
```

```
Index(['Color', 'Click Count: Day 1', 'View Count: Day 1',
       'Click Count: Day 2', 'View Count: Day 2', 'Click Count: Day 3',
       'View Count: Day 3', 'Click Count: Day 4', 'View Count: Day 4',
       'Click Count: Day 5', 'View Count: Day 5', 'Click Count: Day 6',
       'View Count: Day 6', 'Click Count: Day 7', 'View Count: Day 7',
       'Click Count: Day 8', 'View Count: Day 8', 'Click Count: Day 9',
       'View Count: Day 9', 'Click Count: Day 10', 'View Count: Day 10',
       'Click Count: Day 11', 'View Count: Day 11', 'Click Count: Day 12',
       'View Count: Day 12', 'Click Count: Day 13', 'View Count: Day 13',
       'Click Count: Day 14', 'View Count: Day 14', 'Click Count: Day 15',
       'View Count: Day 15', 'Click Count: Day 16', 'View Count: Day 16',
       'Click Count: Day 17', 'View Count: Day 17', 'Click Count: Day 18',
       'View Count: Day 18', 'Click Count: Day 19', 'View Count: Day 19',
       'Click Count: Day 20', 'View Count: Day 20'],
      dtype='object')
```

The columns are consistent with our expectations: the first column contains all of the analyzed colors, and the remaining 40 columns hold the click counts and view counts for each day of the experiment. As a sanity check, let's examine the quality of the data stored in our table. We start by outputting the analyzed color names.

Listing 9.3 Checking the color names

```
print(df.Color.values)
```

```
['Pink' 'Gray' 'Sapphire' 'Purple' 'Coral' 'Olive' 'Navy' 'Maroon' 'Teal'
 'Cyan' 'Orange' 'Black' 'Tan' 'Red' 'Blue' 'Brown' 'Turquoise' 'Indigo'
 'Gold' 'Jade' 'Ultramarine' 'Yellow' 'Viridian' 'Violet' 'Green'
 'Aquamarine' 'Magenta' 'Silver' 'Bronze' 'Lime']
```

30 common colors are present in the *Color* column. The first letter of every color name is capitalized. Thus, we can confirm that the color blue is present by executing `assert 'Blue' in df.Color`.

Listing 9.4   Checking for blue

```
assert 'Blue' in df.Color.values
```

The string-based *Color* column looks good. Let's turn our attention to the remaining 40 numeric columns. Outputting all 40 columns would lead to an overwhelming amount of data. Instead, we'll examine columns for the first day of the experiment: `Click Count: Day 1` and `View Count: Day 1`. We select these two columns and use `describe()` to summarize their contents.

Listing 9.5   Summarizing day 1 of the experiment

```
selected_columns = ['Color', 'Click Count: Day 1', 'View Count: Day 1']
print(df[selected_columns].describe())


       Click Count: Day 1  View Count: Day 1
count          30.000000               30.0
mean           23.533333              100.0
std             7.454382                0.0
min            12.000000              100.0
25%            19.250000              100.0
50%            24.000000              100.0
75%            26.750000              100.0
max            49.000000              100.0
```

The values in the `Click Count: Day 1` column range from 12 to 49 clicks. Meanwhile, the minimum and maximum values in `View Count: Day 1` are both equal to 100 views. Therefore, all the values in that column are equal to 100 views. This behavior is expected. We were specifically informed that each color receives 100 daily views. Let's confirm that all the daily views equal 100.

Listing 9.6   Confirming equivalent daily views

```
view_columns = [column for column in df.columns if 'View' in column]
assert np.all(df[view_columns].values == 100)   ◁─┐  Efficient NumPy code to ensure that
                                                   │  values in a NumPy array equal 100
```

All view counts equal 100. Therefore, all 20 `View Count` columns are redundant. We can delete them from our table.

Listing 9.7   Deleting view counts from the table

```
df.drop(columns=view_columns, inplace=True)
print(df.columns)
```

```
Index(['Color', 'Click Count: Day 1', 'Click Count: Day 2',
       'Click Count: Day 3', 'Click Count: Day 4', 'Click Count: Day 5',
       'Click Count: Day 6', 'Click Count: Day 7', 'Click Count: Day 8',
       'Click Count: Day 9', 'Click Count: Day 10', 'Click Count: Day 11',
       'Click Count: Day 12', 'Click Count: Day 13', 'Click Count: Day 14',
       'Click Count: Day 15', 'Click Count: Day 16', 'Click Count: Day 17',
       'Click Count: Day 18', 'Click Count: Day 19', 'Click Count: Day 20'],
      dtype='object')
```

The redundant columns have been removed. Only the color and click-count data remain. Our 20 `Click Count` columns correspond to the number of clicks per 100 daily views, so we can treat these counts as percentages. Effectively, the color in each row is mapped to the percentage of daily ad clicks. Let's summarize the percentage of daily ad clicks for blue ads. To generate that summary, we index each row by color and then call `df.T.Blue.describe()`.

Listing 9.8 Summarizing daily blue-click statistics

```
df.set_index('Color', inplace=True)
print(df.T.Blue.describe())


count    20.000000
mean     28.350000
std       5.499043
min      18.000000
25%      25.750000
50%      27.500000
75%      30.250000
max      42.000000
Name: Blue, dtype: float64
```

The daily click percentages for blue range from 18% to 42%. The mean percent of clicks is 28.35%: on average, 28.35% of blue ads receive a click per view. This average click rate is pretty good. How does it compare to the other 29 colors? We are ready to find out.

9.2 *Computing p-values from differences in means*

Let's start by filtering the data. We delete blue, leaving behind the other 29 colors. Then we transpose our table to access colors by column name.

Listing 9.9 Creating a no-blue table

```
df_not_blue = df.T.drop(columns='Blue')
print(df_not_blue.head(2))


Color               Pink  Gray  Sapphire  Purple  Coral  Olive  Navy  Maroon  \
Click Count: Day 1    21    27        30      26     26     26    38      21
Click Count: Day 2    20    27        32      21     24     19    29      29
```

Color		Teal	Cyan	...	Ultramarine	Yellow	Viridian	Violet	\
Click Count: Day 1		25	24	...	49	14	27	15	
Click Count: Day 2		25	22	...	41	24	23	22	

Color	Green	Aquamarine	Magenta	Silver	Bronze	Lime
Click Count: Day 1	14	24	18	26	19	20
Click Count: Day 2	25	28	21	24	19	19

```
[2 rows x 29 columns]
```

Our `df_not_blue` table contains the percent clicks for 29 colors. We would like to compare these percentages to our blue percentages. More precisely, we want to know if there exists a color whose mean click rate is statistically different from the mean click rate of blue. How do we compare these means? The sample mean for every color is easily obtainable, but we do not have a population mean. Thus, our best option is to run a permutation test. To run the test, we need to define a reusable permutation test function. The function will take as input two NumPy arrays and return a p-value as its output.

Listing 9.10   Defining a permutation test function

```python
def permutation_test(data_array_a, data_array_b):
    data_mean_a = data_array_a.mean()
    data_mean_b = data_array_b.mean()
    extreme_mean_diff = abs(data_mean_a - data_mean_b)        ⟵┤ Observed difference
    total_data = np.hstack([data_array_a, data_array_b])        │ between sample means
    number_extreme_values = 0.0
    for _ in range(30000):
        np.random.shuffle(total_data)
        sample_a = total_data[:data_array_a.size]
        sample_b = total_data[data_array_a.size:]
        if abs(sample_a.mean() - sample_b.mean()) >= extreme_mean_diff:   ⟵┐
            number_extreme_values += 1                              The difference between
                                                                   resampled means is
    p_value = number_extreme_values / 30000                          extremely large.
    return p_value
```

We'll run a permutation test between blue and the other 29 colors. Then we'll sort these colors based on their p-value results. Our outputs are visualized as a heatmap (figure 9.1), to better emphasize the differences between p-values.

Listing 9.11   Running a permutation test across colors

Efficient Python code to sort a dictionary and return two lists: a list of sorted values and a list of associated keys. Each sorted p-value at position i aligns with the color in sorted_colors[i].

```python
np.random.seed(0)
blue_clicks = df.T.Blue.values
color_to_p_value = {}
for color, color_clicks in df_not_blue.items():
    p_value = permutation_test(blue_clicks, color_clicks)
    color_to_p_value[color] = p_value

sorted_colors, sorted_p_values = zip(*sorted(color_to_p_value.items(),    ⟵
                                     key=lambda x: x[1]))
```

```
plt.figure(figsize=(3, 10))
sns.heatmap([[p_value] for p_value in sorted_p_values],
            cmap='YlGnBu', annot=True, xticklabels=['p-value'],
            yticklabels=sorted_colors)
plt.show()
```

Adjusts the width and height of the plotted heatmap to 3 inches and 10 inches, respectively. These adjustments improve the quality of our heatmap visualization.

The sns.heatmap method takes as its input a 2D table. Thus, we transform our 1D list of p-values into a 2D table containing 29 rows and 1 column.

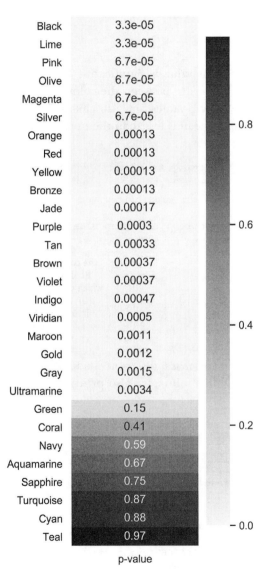

Figure 9.1 A heatmap of p-value/color pairs returned by the permutation test: 21 of the colors map to a p-value lower than 0.05.

The majority of colors generate a p-value that is noticeably lower than 0.05. Black has the lowest p-value: its ad-click percentages must deviate significantly from blue. But from a design perspective, black is not a very clickable color. Text links usually are not black, because black links are hard to distinguish from regular text. Something suspicious is going on here: what exactly is the difference between recorded clicks for black and blue? We can check by printing `df_not_blue.Black.mean()`.

Listing 9.12   Finding the mean click rate of black

```
mean_black = df_not_blue.Black.mean()
print(f"Mean click-rate of black is {mean_black}")
```

```
Mean click-rate of black is 21.6
```

The mean click rate of black is 21.6. This value is significantly lower than the blue mean of 28.35. Hence, the statistical difference between the colors is caused by fewer people clicking black. Perhaps other low p-values are also caused by inferior click rates. Let's filter out those colors whose mean is less than the mean of blue and then print the remaining colors.

Listing 9.13   Filtering colors with inferior click rates

```
remaining_colors = df[df.T.mean().values > blue_clicks.mean()].index   ◁
size = remaining_colors.size
print(f"{size} colors have on average more clicks than Blue.")
print("These colors are:")
print(remaining_colors.values)
```

```
5 colors have on average more clicks than Blue.
These colors are:
['Sapphire' 'Navy' 'Teal' 'Ultramarine' 'Aquamarine']
```

> Efficient one-line code to filter the colors. First, the code creates a Boolean array. The array specifies which colors contain a mean greater than blue. The Boolean array is fed into df for filtering. The indices of the filtered result specify the remaining color names.

Only five colors remain. Each of these colors is a different shade of blue. Let's print the sorted p-values for the five remaining colors; we also print the mean clicks for easier analysis.

Listing 9.14   Printing the five remaining colors

```
for color, p_value in sorted(color_to_p_value.items(), key=lambda x: x[1]):
    if color in remaining_colors:
        mean = df_not_blue[color].mean()
        print(f"{color} has a p-value of {p_value} and a mean of {mean}")
```

```
Ultramarine has a p-value of 0.0034 and a mean of 34.2
Navy has a p-value of 0.5911666666666666 and a mean of 29.3
Aquamarine has a p-value of 0.6654666666666667 and a mean of 29.2
Sapphire has a p-value of 0.7457666666666667 and a mean of 28.9
Teal has a p-value of 0.9745 and a mean of 28.45
```

9.3 *Determining statistical significance*

Four of the colors have large p-values. Only one color has a p-value that's small. That color is ultramarine: a special shade of blue. Its mean of 34.2 is greater than blue's mean of 28.35. Ultramarine's p-value is 0.0034. Is that p-value statistically significant? Well, it's more than 10 times lower than the standard significance level of 0.05. However, that significance level does not take into account our comparisons between blue and 29 other colors. Each comparison is an experiment testing whether a color differs from blue. If we run enough experiments, then we are guaranteed to encounter a low p-value sooner or later. The best way to correct for this is to execute a Bonferroni correction—otherwise, we will fall victim to p-value hacking. To carry out a Bonferroni correction, we lower the significance level to 0.05 / 29.

Listing 9.15   Applying the Bonferroni correction

```
significance_level = 0.05 / 29
print(f"Adjusted significance level is {significance_level}")
if color_to_p_value['Ultramarine'] <= significance_level:
    print("Our p-value is statistically significant")
else:
    print("Our p-value is not statistically significant")

Adjusted significance level is 0.001724137931034483
Our p-value is not statistically significant
```

Our p-value is not statistically significant—Fred carried out too many experiments for us to draw a meaningful conclusion. Not all of these experiments were necessary. There is no valid reason to expect that black, brown, or gray would outperform blue. Perhaps if Fred had disregarded some of these colors, our analysis would have been more fruitful. Conceivably, if Fred had simply compared blue to the other five variants of blue, we might have obtained a statistically significant result. Let's explore the hypothetical situation where Fred instigates five experiments and ultramarine's p-value remains unchanged.

Listing 9.16   Exploring a hypothetical significance level

```
hypothetical_sig_level = 0.05 / 5
print(f"Hypothetical significance level is {hypothetical_sig_level}")
if color_to_p_value['Ultramarine'] <= hypothetical_sig_level:
    print("Our hypothetical p-value would have been statistically significant")
else:
    print("Our hypothetical p-value would not have been statistically
          significant")

Hypothetical significance level is 0.01
Our hypothetical p-value would have been statistically significant
```

Under these hypothetical conditions, our results would be statistically significant. Sadly, we can't use the hypothetical conditions to lower our significance level. We have no guarantee that rerunning the experiments would reproduce a p-value of 0.0034. P-values fluctuate, and superfluous experiments increase the chance of untrustworthy fluctuations. Given Fred's high experiment count, we simply cannot draw a statistically significant conclusion.

However, all is not lost. Ultramarine still represents a promising substitute for blue. Should Fred carry out that substitution? Perhaps. Let's consider our two alternative scenarios. In the first scenario, the null hypothesis is true. If that's the case, then both blue and ultramarine share the same population mean. Under these circumstances, swapping ultramarine for blue will not affect the ad click rate. In the second scenario, the higher ultramarine click rate is actually statistically significant. If that's the case, then swapping ultramarine for blue will yield more ad clicks. Therefore, Fred has everything to gain and nothing to lose by setting all his ads to ultramarine.

From a logical standpoint, Fred should definitely swap blue for ultramarine. But if he carries out the swap, some uncertainty will remain; Fred will never know if ultramarine truly returns more clicks than blue. What if Fred's curiosity gets the best of him? If he really wants an answer, his only choice is to run another experiment. In that experiment, half the displayed ads would be blue and the other displayed ads would be ultramarine. Fred's software would exhibit the advertisements while recording all the clicks and views. Then we could recompute the p-value and compare it to the appropriate significance level, which would remain at 0.05. The Bonferroni correction would not be necessary because only a single experiment would be run. After the p-value comparison, Fred would finally know whether ultramarine outperforms blue.

9.4   *41 shades of blue: A real-life cautionary tale*

Fred assumed that analyzing every single color would yield more impactful results, but he was wrong. More data isn't necessarily better: sometimes more data leads to more uncertainty.

Fred is not a statistician. He can be forgiven for failing to comprehend the consequences of overanalysis. The same cannot be said of certain quantitative experts operating in business today. Take, for example, a notorious incident that occurred at a well-known corporation. The corporation needed to select a color for the web links on its site. The chief designer chose a visually appealing shade of blue, but a top-level executive distrusted this decision. Why did the designer choose this shade of blue and not another?

The executive came from a quantitative background and insisted that link color should be selected scientifically via a massive analytic test that would supposedly determine the perfect shade of blue. 41 shades of blue were assigned to company web links completely at random, and millions of clicks were recorded. Eventually, the "optimal" shade of blue was selected based on maximum clicks per view.

The executive proceeded to make the methodology public. Worldwide, statisticians cringed. The executive's decisions revealed an ignorance of basic statistics, and that ignorance embarrassed both the executive and the company.

Summary

- More data isn't always better. Running a pointless surplus of analytic tests increases the chance of anomalous results.

- It's worth taking the time to think about a problem before running an analysis. If Fred had carefully considered the 31 colors, he would have realized that it was pointless to test them all. Many colors make ugly links. Colors like black are very unlikely to yield more clicks than blue. Filtering the color set would have led to a more informative test.

- Even though Fred's experiment was flawed, we still managed to extract a useful insight. Ultramarine might prove to be a reasonable substitute for blue, though more testing is required. Occasionally, data scientists are presented with flawed data, but good insights may still be possible.

Tracking disease outbreaks using news headlines

Problem statement

Congratulations! You have just been hired by the American Institute of Health. The Institute monitors disease epidemics in both foreign and domestic lands. A critical component of the monitoring process is analyzing published news data. Each day, the Institute receives hundreds of news headlines describing disease outbreaks in various locations. The news headlines are too numerous to be analyzed by hand.

Your first assignment is as follows: You will process the daily quota of news headlines and extract locations that are mentioned You will then cluster the headlines based on their geographic distribution. Finally, you will review the largest clusters within and outside the United States. Any interesting findings should be reported to your immediate superior.

Dataset description

The file headlines.txt contains the hundreds of headlines that you must analyze. Each headline appears on a separate line in the file.

Overview

To address the problem at hand, we need to know how to do the following:

- Cluster datasets using multiple techniques and distance measures.
- Measure distances between locations on a spherical globe.
- Visualize locations on a map.
- Extract location coordinates from headline text.

Clustering data into groups

This section covers

- Clustering data by centrality
- Clustering data by density
- Trade-offs between clustering algorithms
- Executing clustering using the scikit-learn library
- Iterating over clusters using Pandas

Clustering is the process of organizing data points into conceptually meaningful groups. What makes a given group "conceptually meaningful"? There is no easy answer to that question. The usefulness of any clustered output is dependent on the task we've been assigned.

Imagine that we're asked to cluster a collection of pet photos. Do we cluster fish and lizards in one group and fluffy pets (such as hamsters, cats, and dogs) in another? Or should hamsters, cats, and dogs be assigned three separate clusters of their own? If so, perhaps we should consider clustering pets by breed. Thus, Chihuahuas and Great Danes fall into diverging clusters. Differentiating between dog breeds will not be easy. However, we can easily distinguish between Chihuahuas and Great Danes based on breed size. Maybe we should compromise: we'll cluster on both fluffiness and size, thus bypassing the distinction between the Cairn Terrier and the similar-looking Norwich Terrier.

Is the compromise worth it? It depends on our data science task. Suppose we work for a pet food company, and our aim is to estimate demand for dog food, cat food, and lizard food. Under these conditions, we must distinguish between fluffy dogs, fluffy cats, and scaly lizards. However, we won't need to resolve differences between separate dog breeds. Alternatively, imagine an analyst at a vet's office who's trying to group pet patients by their breed. This second task requires a much more granular level of group resolution.

Different situations require different clustering techniques. As data scientists, we must choose the correct clustering solution. Over the course of our careers, we will cluster thousands (if not tens of thousands) of datasets using a variety of clustering techniques. The most commonly used algorithms rely on some notion of centrality to distinguish between clusters.

10.1   *Using centrality to discover clusters*

In section 5, we learned how the centrality of data can be represented using the mean. Later, in section 7, we computed the mean length of a single group of fish. Eventually, we compared two separate sets of fish by analyzing the difference between their means. We utilized that difference to determine whether all the fish belonged to the same group. Intuitively, all data points in a single group should cluster around one central value. Meanwhile, the measurements in two divergent groups should cluster around two different means. Thus, we can utilize centrality to distinguish between two divergent groups. Let's explore this notion in concrete detail.

Suppose we take a field trip to a lively local pub and see two dartboards hanging side by side. Each of the dartboards is covered in darts, and darts also protrude from the walls. The tipsy players in the pub aim for the bull's-eye of one board or the other. Frequently, they miss, which leads to the observed scattering of darts centered around the two bull's-eyes.

Let's simulate the scattering numerically. We'll treat each bull's-eye location as a 2D coordinate. Darts are randomly flung at that coordinate. Consequently, the 2D positions of the darts are randomly distributed. The most appropriate distribution for modeling dart positions is the normal distribution, for the following reasons:

- A typical dart thrower aims at the bull's-eye, not at the edge of the dartboard. Thus, each dart is more likely to strike close to the center of the board. This behavior is consistent with random normal samples, in which values closer to the mean occur more frequently than other, more distant values.
- We expect the darts to strike the board symmetrically relative to the center. Darts will strike 3 inches left of center and 3 inches right of center with equal frequency. This symmetry is captured by the bell-shaped normal curve.

Suppose the first bull's-eye is located at coordinate [0, 0]. A dart is thrown at that coordinate. We'll model the x and y positions of the dart using two normal distributions. These distributions share a mean of 0, and we also assume that they share a variance of 2. The following code generates the random coordinates of the dart.

Listing 10.1 Modeling dart coordinates using two normal distributions

```
import numpy as np
np.random.seed(0)
mean = 0
variance = 2
x = np.random.normal(mean, variance ** 0.5)
y = np.random.normal(mean, variance ** 0.5)
print(f"The x coordinate of a randomly thrown dart is {x:.2f}")
print(f"The y coordinate of a randomly thrown dart is {y:.2f}")


The x coordinate of a randomly thrown dart is 2.49
The y coordinate of a randomly thrown dart is 0.57
```

NOTE We can more efficiently model dart positions using the np.random
.multivariate_normal method. This method selects a single random point
from a *multivariate normal distribution*. The multivariate normal curve is simply
a normal curve that is extended to more than one dimension. Our 2D multivariate normal distribution will resemble a round hill whose summit is positioned at [0, 0].

Let's simulate 5,000 random darts tossed at the bull's-eye positioned at [0, 0]. We also
simulate 5,000 random darts tossed at a second bull's-eye, positioned at [0, 6]. Then
we generate a scatter plot of all the random dart coordinates (figure 10.1).

Listing 10.2 Simulating randomly thrown darts

```
import matplotlib.pyplot as plt
np.random.seed(1)
bulls_eye1 = [0, 0]
bulls_eye2 = [6, 0]
bulls_eyes = [bulls_eye1, bulls_eye2]
x_coordinates, y_coordinates = [], []
for bulls_eye in bulls_eyes:
    for _ in range(5000):
        x = np.random.normal(bulls_eye[0], variance ** 0.5)
        y = np.random.normal(bulls_eye[1], variance ** 0.5)
        x_coordinates.append(x)
        y_coordinates.append(y)

plt.scatter(x_coordinates, y_coordinates)
plt.show()
```

NOTE Listing 10.2 includes a nested five-line for loop beginning with for _
in range(5000). It's possible to use NumPy to execute this loop in just one
line of code: running x_coordinates, y_coordinates = np.random.multi-
variate_normal(bulls_eye, np.diag(2 * [variance]), 5000).T returns
5,000 x and y coordinates sampled from the multivariate normal distribution.

Two overlapping dart groups appear in the plot. The two groups represent 10,000
darts. Half the darts were aimed at the bull's-eye on the left, and the rest were aimed

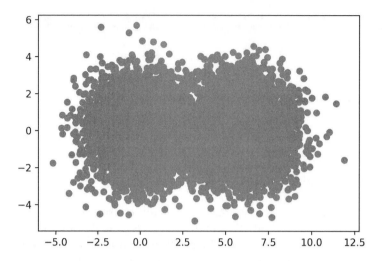

Figure 10.1   A simulation of darts randomly scattered around two bull's-eye targets

toward the right. Each dart has an intended target, which we can estimate by looking at the plot. Darts closer to [0, 0] were probably aimed at the bull's-eye on the left. We'll incorporate this assumption into our dart plot.

Let's assign each dart to its nearest bull's-eye. We start by defining a nearest_ bulls_eye function that takes as input a dart list holding a dart's x and y positions. The function returns the index of the bull's-eye that is most proximate to dart. We measure dart proximity using *Euclidean distance*, which is the standard straight-line distance between two points.

> **NOTE**   Euclidean distance arises from the Pythagorean theorem. Suppose we examine a dart at position [x_dart, y_dart] relative to a bull's-eye at position [x_bull, y_bull]. According to the Pythagorean theorem, $distance^2 = (x\_dart - x\_bull)^2 + (y\_dart - y\_bull)^2$. We can solve for distance using a custom Euclidean function. Alternatively, we can use the scipy.spatial .distance.euclidean function provided by SciPy.

The following code defines nearest_bulls_eye and applies it to darts [0, 1] and [6, 1].

Listing 10.3   Assigning darts to the nearest bull's-eye

```
from scipy.spatial.distance import euclidean
def nearest_bulls_eye(dart):
    distances = [euclidean(dart, bulls_e) for bulls_e in bulls_eyes]
    return np.argmin(distances)

darts = [[0,1], [6, 1]]
for dart in darts:
```

Obtains the Euclidean distance between the dart and each bull's-eye using the euclidean function imported from SciPy

Returns the index matching the shortest bull's-eye distance in the array

```
    index = nearest_bulls_eye(dart)
    print(f"The dart at position {dart} is closest to bulls-eye {index}")
```

```
The dart at position [0, 1] is closest to bulls-eye 0
The dart at position [6, 1] is closest to bulls-eye 1
```

Now we apply `nearest_bulls_eye` to all our computed dart coordinates. Each dart point is plotted using one of two colors to distinguish between the two bull's-eye assignments (figure 10.2).

Listing 10.4 Coloring darts based on the nearest bull's-eye

Selects the darts most proximate to bulls_eyes[bs_index]

Helper function that plots the colored elements of an inputted darts list. Each dart in darts serves as input for nearest_bulls_eye.

```
def color_by_cluster(darts):
    nearest_bulls_eyes = [nearest_bulls_eye(dart) for dart in darts]
    for bs_index in range(len(bulls_eyes)):
        selected_darts = [darts[i] for i in range(len(darts))
                          if bs_index == nearest_bulls_eyes[i]]
        x_coordinates, y_coordinates = np.array(selected_darts).T
        plt.scatter(x_coordinates, y_coordinates,
                    color=['g', 'k'][bs_index])
    plt.show()

darts = [[x_coordinates[i], y_coordinates[i]]
         for i in range(len(x_coordinates))]
color_by_cluster(darts)
```

Separates the x and y coordinates of each dart by transposing an array of selected darts. As discussed in section 8, the transpose swaps the row and column positions within a 2D data structure.

Combines the separate coordinates of each dart into a single list of x and y coordinates.

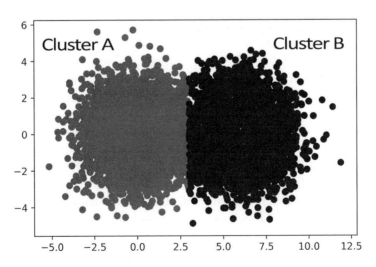

Figure 10.2 Darts colored based on proximity to the nearest bull's-eye. Cluster A represents all points closest to the left bull's-eye, and cluster B represents all points closest to the right bull's-eye.

The colored darts split sensibly into two even clusters. How would we identify such clusters if no central coordinates were provided? Well, one primitive strategy is to simply guess the location of the bull's-eyes. We can pick two random darts and hope these darts are somehow relatively close to each of the bull's-eyes, although the likelihood of that happening is incredibly low. In most cases, coloring darts based on two randomly chosen centers will not yield good results (figure 10.3).

Listing 10.5   Assigning darts to randomly chosen centers

```python
bulls_eyes = np.array(darts[:2])
color_by_cluster(darts)
```
◁—— **Randomly selects the first two darts to be our representative bull's-eyes**

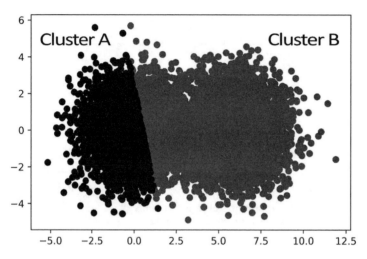

Figure 10.3   Darts colored based on proximity to randomly selected centers. Cluster B is stretched too far to the left.

Our indiscriminately chosen centers feel wrong qualitatively. For instance, cluster B on the right seems to be stretching way too far to the left. The arbitrary center we've assigned doesn't appear to match its actual bull's-eye point. But there's a way to remedy our error: we can compute the mean coordinates of all the points in the stretched right clustered group and then utilize these coordinates to adjust our estimation of the group's center. After assigning the cluster's mean coordinates to the bull's-eye, we can reapply our distance-based grouping technique to adjust the rightmost cluster's boundaries. In fact, for maximum effectiveness, we will also reset the leftmost cluster's center to its mean prior to rerunning our centrality-based clustering (figure 10.4).

> **NOTE**   When we compute the mean of a 1D array, we return a single value. We are now extending that definition to encompass multiple dimensions. When we compute the mean of a 2D array, we return the mean of all x coordinates and also the mean of all y coordinates. The final output is a 2D array containing means across the x-axis and y-axis.

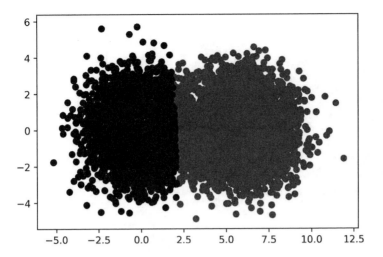

Figure 10.4 **Darts colored based on proximity to recomputed centers. The two clusters now appear to be more even.**

Listing 10.6 Assigning darts to centers based on means

```
def update_bulls_eyes(darts):
    updated_bulls_eyes = []
    nearest_bulls_eyes = [nearest_bulls_eye(dart) for dart in darts]
    for bs_index in range(len(bulls_eyes)):
        selected_darts = [darts[i] for i in range(len(darts))
                          if bs_index == nearest_bulls_eyes[i]]
        x_coordinates, y_coordinates = np.array(selected_darts).T
        mean_center = [np.mean(x_coordinates), np.mean(y_coordinates)]    ◁
        updated_bulls_eyes.append(mean_center)

    return updated_bulls_eyes


bulls_eyes = update_bulls_eyes(darts)
color_by_cluster(darts)
```

Takes the mean of the x and y coordinates for all the darts assigned to a given bull's-eye. These average coordinates are then used to update our estimated bull's-eye position. We can more efficiently run this calculation by executing np.mean(selected_darts, axis=0).

The results are already looking better, although they're not quite as effective as they could be. The cluster's centers still appear a little off. Let's remedy the results by repeating the mean-based centrality adjustment over 10 additional iterations (figure 10.5).

Listing 10.7 Adjusting bull's-eye positions over 10 iterations

```
for i in range(10):
    bulls_eyes = update_bulls_eyes(darts)

color_by_cluster(darts)
```

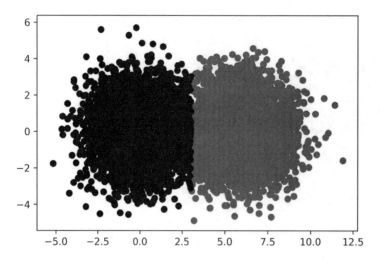

Figure 10.5   Darts colored based on proximity to iteratively recomputed centers

The two sets of darts are now perfectly clustered! We have essentially replicated the *K-means* clustering algorithm, which organizes data using centrality.

10.2   K-means: A clustering algorithm for grouping data into K central groups

The K-means algorithm assumes that inputted data points swirl around *K* different centers. Each central coordinate is like a hidden bull's-eye surrounded by scattered data points. The purpose of the algorithm is to uncover these hidden central coordinates.

We initialize K-means by first selecting *K*, which is the number of central coordinates we will search for. In our dartboard analysis, *K* was set to 2, although generally *K* can equal any whole number. The algorithm chooses *K* data points at random. These data points are treated as though they are true centers. Then the algorithm iterates by updating the chosen central locations, which data scientists call *centroids*. During a single iteration, every data point is assigned to its closest center, leading to the formation of *K* groups. Next, the center of each group is updated. The new center equals the mean of the group's coordinates. If we repeat the process long enough, the group means will converge to *K* representative centers (figure 10.6). The convergence is mathematically guaranteed. However, we cannot know in advance the number of iterations required for the convergence to take place. A common trick is to halt the iterations when none of the newly computed centers deviate significantly from their predecessors.

K-means is not without its limitations. The algorithm is predicated on our knowledge of *K*: the number of clusters to look for. Frequently, such knowledge is not available. Also, while K-means commonly finds reasonable centers, it's not mathematically

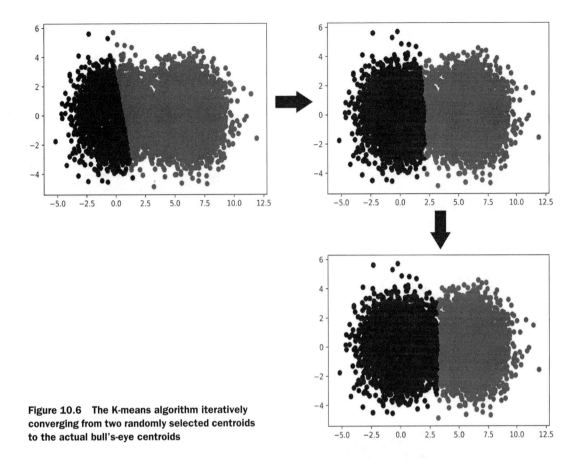

Figure 10.6　The K-means algorithm iteratively converging from two randomly selected centroids to the actual bull's-eye centroids

guaranteed to find the best possible centers in the data. Occasionally, K-means returns unintuitive or suboptimal groups due to poor selection of random centroids at the initialization step of the algorithm. Finally, K-means presupposes that the clusters in the data actually swirl around *K* central locations. But as we learn later in the section, this supposition does not always hold.

10.2.1　K-means clustering using scikit-learn

The K-means algorithm runs in a reasonable time if it is implemented efficiently. A speedy implementation of the algorithm is available through the external scikit-learn library. Scikit-learn is an extremely popular machine learning toolkit built on top of NumPy and SciPy. It features a variety of core classification, regression, and clustering algorithms—including, of course, K-means. Let's install the library. Then we import scikit-learn's `KMeans` clustering class.

> **NOTE**　Call `pip install scikit-learn` from the command line terminal to install the scikit-learn library.

```
from sklearn.cluster import KMeans
```

Applying `KMeans` to our `darts` data is easy. First, we need to run `KMeans(n_clus-ters=2)`, which will create a `cluster_model` object capable of finding two bull's-eye centers. Then, we can execute K-means by running `cluster_model.fit_predict(darts)`. That method call will return an `assigned_bulls_eyes` array that stores the bull's-eye index of each dart.

```
cluster_model = KMeans(n_clusters=2)                    ◁
assigned_bulls_eyes = cluster_model.fit_predict(darts)  ◁

print("Bull's-eye assignments:")
print(assigned_bulls_eyes)

Bull's-eye assignments:
[0 0 0 ... 1 1 1]
```

Optimizes two centers using the K-means algorithm and returns the assigned cluster for each dart

Creates a cluster_model object in which the number of centers is set to 2

Let's color our darts based on their clustering assignments to verify the results (figure 10.7).

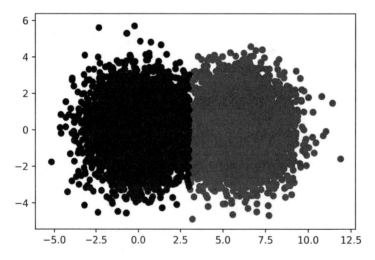

Figure 10.7   The K-means clustering results returned by scikit-learn are consistent with our expectations.

```
for bs_index in range(len(bulls_eyes)):
    selected_darts = [darts[i] for i in range(len(darts))
                      if bs_index == assigned_bulls_eyes[i]]
```

```
    x_coordinates, y_coordinates = np.array(selected_darts).T
    plt.scatter(x_coordinates, y_coordinates,
                color=['g', 'k'][bs_index])
plt.show()
```

Our clustering model has located the centroids in the data. Now we can reuse these centroids to analyze new data points that the model has not seen before. Executing `cluster_model.predict([x, y])` assigns a centroid to a data point defined by x and y. We use the `predict` method to cluster two new data points.

Listing 10.11 Using `cluster_model` to cluster new data

```
new_darts = [[500, 500], [-500, -500]]
new_bulls_eye_assignments = cluster_model.predict(new_darts)
for i, dart in enumerate(new_darts):
    bulls_eye_index = new_bulls_eye_assignments[i]
    print(f"Dart at {dart} is closest to bull's-eye {bulls_eye_index}")
```

```
Dart at [500, 500] is closest to bull's-eye 0
Dart at [-500, -500] is closest to bull's-eye 1
```

10.2.2 *Selecting the optimal K using the elbow method*

K-means relies on an inputted *K*. This can be a serious hindrance when the number of authentic clusters in the data isn't known in advance. We can, however, estimate an appropriate value for *K* using a technique known as the *elbow method*.

The elbow method depends on a calculated value called *inertia*, which is the sum of the squared distances between each point and its closest K-means center. If *K* is 1, then the inertia equals the sum of all squared distances to the dataset's mean. This value, as discussed in section 5, is directly proportional to the variance. Variance, in turn, is a measure of dispersion. Thus, if *K* is 1, the inertia is an estimate of dispersion. This property holds true even if *K* is greater than 1. Basically, inertia estimates total dispersion around our *K* computed means.

By estimating dispersion, we can determine whether our *K* value is too high or too low. For example, imagine that we set *K* to 1. Potentially, many of our data points will be positioned too far from one center. Our dispersion will be large, and our inertia will be large. As we increase *K* toward a more sensible number, the additional centers will cause the inertia to decrease. Eventually, if we go overboard and set *K* equal to the total number of points, each data point will fall into its own private cluster. Dispersion will be eliminated, and inertia will drop to zero (figure 10.8).

Some inertia values are too large. Others are too low. Somewhere in between might lie a value that's just right. How do we find it?

Let's work out a solution. We begin by plotting the inertia of our dartboard dataset over a large range of *K* values (figure 10.9). Inertia is automatically computed for each scikit-learn `KMeans` object. We can access this stored value through the model's `inertia_` attribute.

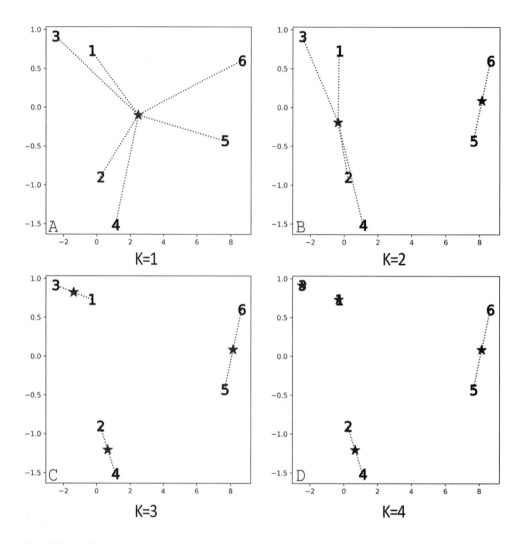

Figure 10.8   Six points, numbered 1 through 6, are plotted in 2D space. The centers, marked by stars, are computed across various values of *K*. A line is drawn from every point to its nearest center. Inertia is computed by summing the squared lengths of the six lines. (A) *K* = 1. All six lines stretch out from a single center. The inertia is quite large. (B) *K* = 2. Points 5 and 6 are very close to a second center. The inertia is reduced. (C) *K* = 3. Points 1 and 3 are substantially closer to a newly formed center. Points 2 and 4 are also substantially closer to a newly formed center. The inertia has radically decreased. (D) *K* = 4. Points 1 and 3 now overlap with their centers. Their contribution to the inertia has shifted from a very low value to zero. The distances between the remaining four points and their associated centers remain unchanged. Thus, increasing *K* from 3 to 4 caused a very small decrease in inertia.

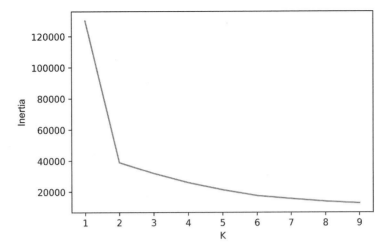

Figure 10.9   An inertia plot for a dartboard simulation containing two bull's-eye targets. The plot resembles an arm bent at the elbow. The elbow points directly to a *K* of 2.

Listing 10.12   Plotting the K-means inertia

```
k_values = range(1, 10)
inertia_values = [KMeans(k).fit(darts).inertia_
                  for k in k_values]

plt.plot(k_values, inertia_values)
plt.xlabel('K')
plt.ylabel('Inertia')
plt.show()
```

The generated plot resembles an arm bent at the elbow, and the elbow points at a *K* value of 2. As we already know, this *K* accurately captures the two centers we have pre-programmed into the dataset.

Will the approach still hold if the number of present centers is increased? We can find out by adding an additional bull's-eye to our dart-throwing simulation. After we increase the cluster count to 3, we regenerate our inertia plot (figure 10.10).

Listing 10.13   Plotting inertia for a 3-dartboard simulation

```
new_bulls_eye = [12, 0]
for _ in range(5000):
    x = np.random.normal(new_bulls_eye[0], variance ** 0.5)
    y = np.random.normal(new_bulls_eye[1], variance ** 0.5)
    darts.append([x, y])

inertia_values = [KMeans(k).fit(darts).inertia_
                  for k in k_values]
```

```
plt.plot(k_values, inertia_values)
plt.xlabel('K')
plt.ylabel('Inertia')
plt.show()
```

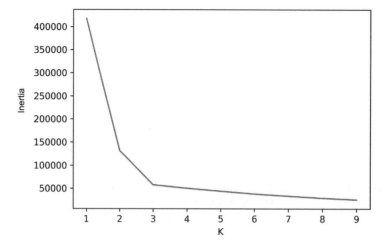

Figure 10.10 **An inertia plot for a dartboard simulation containing three bull's-eye targets. The plot resembles an arm bent at the elbow. The lowermost portion of the elbow points to a *K* of 3.**

Adding a third center leads to a new elbow whose lowermost inclination points to a *K* value of 3. Essentially, our elbow plot traces the dispersion captured by each incremental *K*. A rapid decrease in inertia between consecutive *K* values implies that scattered data points have been assigned to a tighter cluster. The reduction in inertia incrementally loses its impact as the inertia curve flattens out. This transition from a vertical drop to a gentler angle leads to the presence of an elbow shape in our plot. We can use the position of the elbow to select a proper *K* in the K-means algorithm.

The elbow method selection criterion is a useful heuristic, but it is not guaranteed to work in every case. Under certain conditions, the elbow levels off slowly over multiple *K* values, making it difficult to choose a single valid cluster count.

NOTE There exist more powerful *K*-selection methodologies, such as the *silhouette score*, which captures the distance of each point to neighboring clusters. A thorough discussion of the silhouette score is beyond the scope of this book. However, you're encouraged to explore the score on your own, using the `sklearn.metrics.silhouette_score` method.

The elbow method isn't perfect, but it performs reasonably well if the data is centered on *K* distinct means. Of course, this assumes that our data clusters differ due to centrality. However, in many instances, data clusters differ due to the density of the data

---

K-means clustering methods

- `k_means_model = KMeans(n_clusters=K)`—Creates a K-means model to search for *K* different centroids. We need to fit these centroids to inputted data.
- `clusters = k_means_model.fit_predict(data)`—Executes K-means on inputted data using an initialized `KMeans` object. The returned `clusters` array contains cluster IDs ranging from 0 to *K*. The cluster ID of `data[i]` is equal to `clusters[i]`.
- `clusters = KMeans(n_clusters=K).fit_predict(data)`—Executes K-means in a single line of code, and returns the resulting clusters.
- `new_clusters = k_means_model.predict(new_data)`—Finds the nearest centroids to previously unseen data using the existing centroids in a data-optimized `KMeans` object.
- `inertia = k_means_model.inertia_`—Returns the inertia associated with a data-optimized `KMeans` object.
- `inertia = KMeans(n_clusters=K).fit(data).inertia_`—Executes K-means in a single line of code, and returns the resulting inertia.

---

points in space. Let's explore the concept of density-driven clusters, which are not dependent on centrality.

10.3 *Using density to discover clusters*

Suppose an astronomer discovers a new planet at the far-flung edge of the solar system. The planet, much like Saturn, has multiple rings spinning in constant orbits around its center. Each ring is formed from thousands of rocks. We'll model these rocks as individual points defined by x and y coordinates. Let's generate three rock rings composed of many rocks, using scikit-learn's `make_circles` function (figure 10.11).

Listing 10.14   Simulating rings around a planet

```
from sklearn.datasets import make_circles

x_coordinates = []
y_coordinates = []
for factor in [.3, .6, 0.99]:
    rock_ring, _ = make_circles(n_samples=800, factor=factor,
                                noise=.03, random_state=1)
    for rock in rock_ring:
        x_coordinates.append(rock[0])
        y_coordinates.append(rock[1])

plt.scatter(x_coordinates, y_coordinates)
plt.show()
```

The make_circles function creates two concentric circles in 2D. The scale of the smaller circle's radius relative to the larger circle is determined by the factor parameter.

Three ring groups are clearly present in the plot. Let's search for these three clusters using K-means by setting *K* to 3 (figure 10.12).

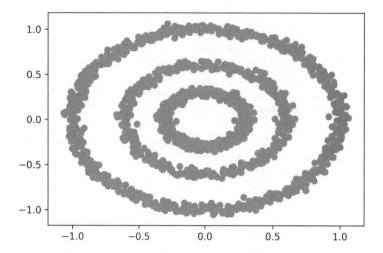

Figure 10.11   A simulation of three rock rings positioned around a central point

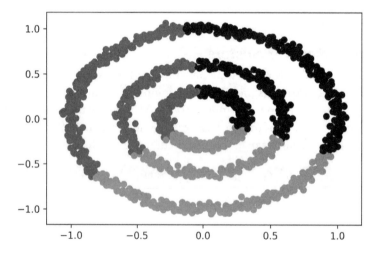

Figure 10.12   K-means clustering fails to properly identify the three distinct rock rings.

Listing 10.15   Using K-means to cluster rings

```
rocks = [[x_coordinates[i], y_coordinates[i]]
         for i in range(len(x_coordinates))]
rock_clusters = KMeans(3).fit_predict(rocks)

colors = [['g', 'y', 'k'][cluster] for cluster in  rock_clusters]
plt.scatter(x_coordinates, y_coordinates, color=colors)
plt.show()
```

The output is an utter failure! K-means dissects the data into three symmetric segments, and each segment spans multiple rings. The solution doesn't align with our intuitive expectation that each ring should fall into its own distinct group. What went wrong? Well, K-means assumed that the three clusters were defined by three unique centers, but the actual rings spin around a single central point. The difference between clusters is driven not by centrality, but by density. Each ring is constructed from a dense collection of points, with empty areas of sparsely populated space serving as the boundaries between rings.

We need to design an algorithm that clusters data in dense regions of space. Doing so requires that we define whether a given region is dense or sparse. One simple definition of *density* is as follows: a point is in a dense region only if it's located within a distance X of Y other points. We'll refer to X and Y as epsilon and min_points, respectively. The following code sets epsilon to 0.1 and min_points to 10. Thus, our rocks are present in a dense region of space if they're within a 0.1 radius of at least 10 other rocks.

Listing 10.16 Specifying density parameters

```
epsilon = 0.1
min_points = 10
```

Let's analyze the density of the first rock in our rocks list. We begin by searching for all other rocks within epsilon units of rocks[0]. We store the indices of these neighboring rocks in a neighbor_indices list.

Listing 10.17 Finding the neighbors of rocks[0]

```
neighbor_indices = [i for i, rock in enumerate(rocks[1:])
                    if euclidean(rocks[0], rock) <= epsilon]
```

Now we compare the number of neighbors to min_points to determine whether rocks[0] lies in a dense region of space.

Listing 10.18 Checking the density of rocks[0]

```
num_neighbors = len(neighbor_indices)
print(f"The rock at index 0 has {num_neighbors} neighbors.")

if num_neighbors >= min_points:
    print("It lies in a dense region.")
else:
    print("It does not lie in a dense region.")
```

```
The rock at index 0 has 40 neighbors.
It lies in a dense region.
```

The rock at index 0 lies in a dense region of space. Do the neighbors of rocks[0] also share that dense region of space? This is a tricky question to answer. After all, it's possible that every neighbor has fewer than `min_points` neighbors of its own. Under our rigorous density definition, we wouldn't consider these neighbors to be dense points. However, this would lead to a ludicrous situation in which the dense region is composed of just a single point: `rocks[0]`. We can avoid such absurd outcomes by updating our density definition. Let's formally define *density* as follows:

- If a point is located within `epsilon` distance of `min_points` neighbors, then that point is in a dense region of space.
- Every neighbor of a point in a dense region of space also clusters in that space.

Based on our updated definition, we can combine `rocks[0]` and its neighbors into a single dense cluster.

Listing 10.19   Creating a dense cluster

```
dense_region_indices = [0] + neighbor_indices
dense_region_cluster = [rocks[i] for i in dense_region_indices]
dense_cluster_size = len(dense_region_cluster)
print(f"We found a dense cluster containing {dense_cluster_size} rocks")
```

```
We found a dense cluster containing 41 rocks
```

The rock at index 0 and its neighbors form a single 41-element dense cluster. Do any neighbors of the neighbors belong to a dense region of space? If so, then by our updated definition, these rocks also belong to the dense cluster. Thus, by analyzing additional neighboring points, we can expand the size of `dense_region_cluster`.

Listing 10.20   Expanding a dense cluster

> **Converts dense_region_indices into a set. This allows us to update the set with additional indices without worrying about duplicates.**

```
dense_region_indices = set(dense_region_indices)        ⟵──────────┘
for index in neighbor_indices:
    point = rocks[index]
    neighbors_of_neighbors = [i for i, rock in enumerate(rocks)
                              if euclidean(point, rock) <= epsilon]
    if len(neighbors_of_neighbors) >= min_points:
        dense_region_indices.update(neighbors_of_neighbors)

dense_region_cluster = [rocks[i] for i in dense_region_indices]
dense_cluster_size = len(dense_region_cluster)
print(f"We expanded our cluster to include {dense_cluster_size} rocks")
```

```
We expanded our cluster to include 781 rocks
```

We've iterated over neighbors of neighbors and expanded our dense cluster nearly twentyfold. Why stop there? We can expand our cluster even further by analyzing the density of newly encountered neighbors. Iteratively repeating our analysis will increase the breadth of our cluster boundary. Eventually, the boundary will spread to completely encompass one of our rock rings. Then, with no new neighbors to absorb, we can repeat the iterative analysis on a `rocks` element that has not been analyzed thus far. The repetition will lead to the clustering of additional dense rings.

The procedure just described is known as DBSCAN. The DBSCAN algorithm organizes data based on its spatial distribution.

10.4 DBSCAN: A clustering algorithm for grouping data based on spatial density

DBSCAN is an acronym that stands for *density-based spatial clustering of applications with noise*. This is a ridiculously long name for what essentially is a very simple technique:

1. Select a random `point` coordinate from a `data` list.
2. Obtain all neighbors within `epsilon` distance of that `point`.
3. If fewer than `min_points` neighbors are discovered, repeat step 1 using a different random point. Otherwise, group `point` and its neighbors into a single cluster.
4. Iteratively repeat steps 2 and 3 across all newly discovered neighbors. All neighboring dense points are merged into the cluster. Iterations terminate after the cluster stops expanding.
5. After extracting the entire cluster, repeat steps 1-4 on all data points whose density hasn't yet been analyzed.

The DBSCAN procedure can be programmed in less than 20 lines of code. However, any basic implementation will run very slowly on our `rocks` list. Programming a fast implementation requires some very nuanced optimizations that improve neighbor traversal speed and are beyond the scope of this book. Fortunately, there's no need for us to rebuild the algorithm from scratch: scikit-learn provides a speedy `DBSCAN` class, which we can import from `sklearn.cluster`. Let's import and initialize the class by assigning `epsilon` and `min_points` using the eps and min_samples parameters. Then we utilize `DBSCAN` to cluster our three rings (figure 10.13).

Listing 10.21   Using `DBSCAN` to cluster rings

Creates a cluster_model object to carry out density clustering. An epsilon value of 0.1 is passed in using the eps parameter. A min_points value of 10 is passed in using the min_samples parameter.

```
from sklearn.cluster import DBSCAN
cluster_model = DBSCAN(eps=epsilon, min_samples=min_points)
rock_clusters = cluster_model.fit_predict(rocks)
colors = [['g', 'y', 'k'][cluster] for cluster in rock_clusters]
plt.scatter(x_coordinates, y_coordinates, color=colors)
plt.show()
```

Clusters the rock rings based on density, and returns the assigned cluster for each rock

---

DBSCAN has successfully identified the three rock rings. The algorithm succeeded where K-means failed.

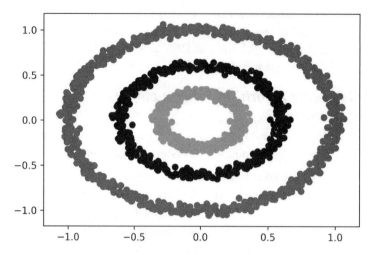

Figure 10.13   DBSCAN clustering accurately identifies the three distinct rock rings.

10.4.1 *Comparing DBSCAN and K-means*

DBSCAN is an advantageous algorithm for clustering data composed of curving and dense shapes. Also, unlike K-means, the algorithm doesn't require an approximation of the cluster count before execution. Additionally, DBSCAN can filter random outliers located in sparse regions of space. For example, if we add an outlier located beyond the boundary of the rings, DBSCAN will assign it a cluster ID of −1. The negative value indicates that the outlier cannot be clustered with the rest of the dataset.

> **NOTE** Unlike K-means, a fitted DBSCAN model cannot be reapplied to brand-new data. Instead, we need to combine new and old data and execute the clustering from scratch. This is because computed K-means centers can easily be compared to additional data points. However, the additional data points could influence the density distribution of previously seen data, which forces DBSCAN to recompute all clusters.

Listing 10.22   Finding outliers using DBSCAN

```
noisy_data = rocks + [[1000, -1000]]
clusters = DBSCAN(eps=epsilon,
                  min_samples=min_points).fit_predict(noisy_data)
assert clusters[-1] == -1
```

Another advantage of the DBSCAN technique is that it does not depend on the mean. Meanwhile, the K-means algorithm requires us to compute the mean coordinates of grouped points. As we discussed in section 5, these mean coordinates minimize the sum of squared distances to the center. The minimization property holds only if the squared distances are Euclidean. Thus, if our coordinates are not Euclidean, the mean is not very useful, and the K-means algorithm should not be applied. However, the Euclidean distance is not the only metric for gauging separation between points—infinite metrics exist for defining distance. We explore a few of them in the subsequent subsection. In the process, we learn how to integrate these metrics into our DBSCAN clustering output.

10.4.2 *Clustering based on non-Euclidean distance*

Suppose that we are visiting Manhattan and wish to know the walking distance from the Empire State Building to Columbus Circle. The Empire State Building is located at the intersection of 34th Street and Fifth Avenue. Meanwhile, Columbus Circle is located at the intersection of 57th Street and Eighth Avenue. The streets and avenues in Manhattan are always perpendicular to each other. This lets us represent Manhattan as a 2D coordinate system, where streets are positioned on the x-axis and avenues are positioned on the y-axis. Under this representation, the Empire State Building is located at coordinate (34, 5), and Columbus Circle is located at coordinate (57, 8). We can easily calculate a straight-line Euclidean distance between the two coordinate points. However, that final length would be impassable because towering steel buildings occupy the area outlined by every city block. A more correct solution is limited to a path across the perpendicular sidewalks that form the city's grid. Such a route requires us to walk 3 blocks between Fifth Avenue and Third Avenue and then 23 blocks between 34th Street and 57th Street, for a total distance of 26 blocks. Manhattan's average block length is 0.17 miles, so we can estimate the walking distance as 4.42 miles. Let's compute that walking distance directly using a generalized `manhattan_distance` function.

Listing 10.23   Computing the Manhattan distance

```
def manhattan_distance(point_a, point_b):
    num_blocks = np.sum(np.absolute(point_a - point_b))
    return 0.17 * num_blocks

x = np.array([34, 5])
y = np.array([57, 8])
distance = manhattan_distance(x, y)
```
⟵ **We can also generate this output by importing cityblock from scipy.spatial.distance and then running 0.17 * cityblock(x, y).**

```
print(f"Manhattan distance is {distance} miles")
```

```
Manhattan distance is 4.42 miles
```

Now, suppose we wish to cluster more than two Manhattan locations. We'll assume each cluster holds a point that is within a one-mile walk of three other clustered points. This assumption lets us apply DBSCAN clustering using scikit-learn's `DBSCAN` class. We set `eps` to 1 and `min_samples` to 3 during DBSCAN's initialization. Furthermore, we pass `metric= manhattan_distance` into the initialization method. The `metric` parameter swaps Euclidean distance for our custom distance metric, so the clustering distance correctly reflects the grid-based constraints within the city. The following code clusters Manhattan coordinates and plots them on a grid along with their cluster designations (figure 10.14).

Listing 10.24   Clustering using Manhattan distance

```
points = [[35, 5], [33, 6], [37, 4], [40, 7], [45, 5]]
clusters = DBSCAN(eps=1, min_samples=3,
                  metric=manhattan_distance).fit_predict(points)

for i, cluster in enumerate(clusters):
    point = points[i]
    if cluster == -1:
        print(f"Point at index {i} is an outlier")
        plt.scatter(point[0], point[1], marker='x', color='k')
    else:
        print(f"Point at index {i} is in cluster {cluster}")
        plt.scatter(point[0], point[1], color='g')

plt.grid(True, which='both', alpha=0.5)
plt.minorticks_on()

plt.show()
```

The manhattan_distance function is passed into DBSCAN through the metric parameter.

Outliers are plotted using x-shaped markers.

The grid method displays the rectangular grid across which we compute Manhattan distance.

```
Point at index 0 is in cluster 0
Point at index 1 is in cluster 0
Point at index 2 is in cluster 0
Point at index 3 is an outlier
Point at index 4 is an outlier
```

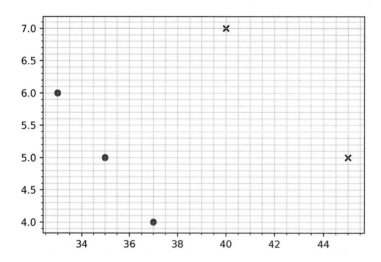

Figure 10.14   Five points in a rectangular grid have been clustered using the Manhattan distance. The three points in the lower-left corner of the grid fall within a single cluster. The remaining two points are outliers, marked by an x.

The first three locations fall within a single cluster, and the remaining points are outliers. Could we have detected that cluster using the K-means algorithm? Perhaps. After all, our Manhattan block coordinates can be averaged out, making them compatible with a K-means implementation. What if we swap Manhattan distance for a different metric where average coordinates are not so easily obtained? Let's define a nonlinear distance metric with the following properties: two points are 0 units apart if all their elements are negative, 2 units apart if all their elements are non-negative, and 10 units apart otherwise. Given this ridiculous measure of distance, can we compute the mean of any two arbitrary points? We can't, and K-means cannot be applied. A weakness of the algorithm is that it depends on the existence of an average distance. Unlike K-means, the DBSCAN algorithm does not require our distance function to be linearly divisible. Thus, we can easily run DBSCAN clustering using our ridiculous distance metric.

Listing 10.25 Clustering using a ridiculous measure of distance

```
def ridiculous_measure(point_a, point_b):
    is_negative_a = np.array(point_a) < 0          Returns a Boolean array
    is_negative_b = np.array(point_b) < 0          where is_negative_a[i] is
    if is_negative_a.all() and is_negative_b.all():   True if point_a[i] < 0
        return 0
    elif is_negative_a.any() or is_negative_b.any():     All elements of
        return 10                                        point_a and
    else:             All elements are                   point_b are
        return 2      non-negative.                       negative.

points = [[-1, -1], [-10, -10], [-1000, -13435], [3,5], [5,-7]]
                                                   A negative element
                                                   exists, but not all
                                                   elements are
                                                   negative.
clusters = DBSCAN(eps=.1, min_samples=2,
                  metric=ridiculous_measure).fit_predict(points)

for i, cluster in enumerate(clusters):
    point = points[i]
    if cluster == -1:
        print(f"{point} is an outlier")
    else:
        print(f"{point} falls in cluster {cluster}")


[-1, -1] falls in cluster 0
[-10, -10] falls in cluster 0
[-1000, -13435] falls in cluster 0
[3, 5] is an outlier
[5, -7] is an outlier
```

Running DBSCAN with our `ridiculous_measure` metric leads to the clustering of negative coordinates into a single group. All other coordinates are treated as outliers. These results are not conceptually practical, but the flexibility with regard to metric selection is much appreciated. We are not constrained in our metric choice! We could, for instance, set the metric to compute traversal distance based on the curvature of the Earth. Such a metric would be particularly useful for clustering geographic locations.

DBSCAN clustering methods

- `dbscan_model = DBSCAN(eps=epsilon, min_samples=min_points)`—Creates a DBSCAN model to cluster by density. A dense point is defined as having at least `min_points` neighbors within a distance of `epsilon`. The neighbors are considered to be part of the same cluster as the point.
- `clusters = dbscan_model.fit_predict(data)`—Executes DBSCAN on inputted data using an initialized `DBSCAN` object. The `clusters` array contains cluster IDs. The cluster ID of `data[i]` is equal to `clusters[i]`. Unclustered outlier points are assigned an ID of –1.
- `clusters = DBSCAN(eps=epsilon, min_samples=min_points).fit_predict(data)`—Executes DBSCAN in a single line of code, and returns the resulting clusters.
- `dbscan_model = DBSCAN(eps=epsilon, min_samples=min_points, metric=metric_function)`—Creates a DBSCAN model where the distance metric is defined by a custom metric function. The `metric_function` distance metric does not need to be Euclidean.

DBSCAN does have certain drawbacks. The algorithm is intended to detect clusters with similar point-density distributions. However, real-world data varies in density. For instance, pizza shops in Manhattan are distributed more densely than pizza shops in Orange County, California. Thus, we might have trouble choosing density parameters that will let us cluster shops in both locations. This highlights another limitation of the algorithm: DBSCAN requires meaningful values for the `eps` and `min_samples` parameters. In particular, varying `eps` inputs will greatly impact the quality of clustering. Unfortunately, there is no one reliable procedure for estimating the appropriate `eps`. While certain heuristics are occasionally mentioned in the literature, their benefit is minimal. Most of the time, we must rely on our gut-level understanding of the problem to assign practical inputs to the two DBSCAN parameters. For example, if we were to cluster a set of geographic locations, our `eps` and `min_samples` values would depend on whether the locations are spread out across the entire globe or whether they are constrained to a single geographic region. In each instance, our understanding of density and distance would vary. Generally speaking, if we are clustering random cities spread out across the Earth, we can set the `min_samples` and `eps` parameters to equal three cities and 250 miles, respectively. This assumes each cluster holds a city within 250 miles of at least three other clustered cities. For a more regional location distribution, a lower `eps` value is required.

10.5 Analyzing clusters using Pandas

So far, we have kept our data inputs and clustering outputs separate. For instance, in our rock ring analysis, the input data is in the `rocks` list and the clustering output is in a `rock_clusters` array. Tracking both the coordinates and the clusters requires us to map indices between the input list and the output array. Thus, if we wish to extract all the rocks in cluster 0, we must obtain all instances of `rocks[i]` where `rock_clusters[i] == 0`. This index analysis is convoluted. We can more intuitively analyze clustered rocks by combining the coordinates and the clusters together in a single Pandas table.

The following code creates a Pandas table with three columns: `X`, `Y`, and `Cluster`. Each *i*th row in the table holds the x coordinate, the y coordinate, and the cluster of the rock located at `rocks[i]`.

Listing 10.26   Storing clustered coordinates in a table

```python
import pandas as pd
x_coordinates, y_coordinates = np.array(rocks).T
df = pd.DataFrame({'X': x_coordinates, 'Y': y_coordinates,
                   'Cluster': rock_clusters})
```

Our Pandas table lets us easily access the rocks in any cluster. Let's plot the rocks that fall into cluster 0, using techniques described in section 8 (figure 10.15).

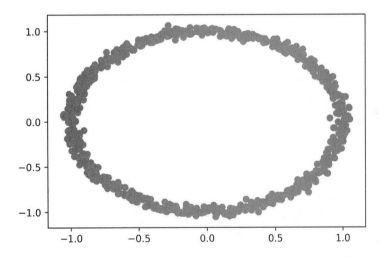

Figure 10.15   Rocks that fall into cluster 0

Listing 10.27   Plotting a single cluster using Pandas

```python
df_cluster = df[df.Cluster == 0]
plt.scatter(df_cluster.X, df_cluster.Y)
plt.show()
```

Select just those rows where the Cluster column equals 0

Plots the X and Y columns of the selected rows. Note that we can also execute the scatter plot by running df_cluster.plot.scatter(x='X', y='Y').

Pandas allows us to obtain a table containing elements from any single cluster. Alternatively, we might want to obtain multiple tables, where each table maps to a cluster ID. In Pandas, this is done by calling df.groupby('Cluster'). The groupby method will create three tables: one for each cluster. It will return an iterable over the mappings between cluster IDs and tables. Let's use the groupby method to iterate over our three clusters. We'll subsequently plot the rocks in cluster 1 and cluster 2, but not the rocks in cluster 0 (figure 10.16).

> **NOTE** Calling df.groupby('Cluster') returns more than just an iterable: it returns a DataFrameGroupBy object, which provides additional methods for cluster filtering and analysis.

Listing 10.28　Iterating over clusters using Pandas

```
for cluster_id, df_cluster in df.groupby('Cluster'):
    if cluster_id == 0:
        print(f"Skipping over cluster {cluster_id}")
        continue

    print(f"Plotting cluster {cluster_id}")
    plt.scatter(df_cluster.X, df_cluster.Y)

plt.show()
```

Each element of the iterable returned by df.groupby('Cluster') is a tuple. The first element of the tuple is the cluster ID obtained from df.Cluster. The second element is a table composed of all rows where df.Cluster equals the cluster ID.

```
Skipping over cluster 0
Plotting cluster 1
Plotting cluster 2
```

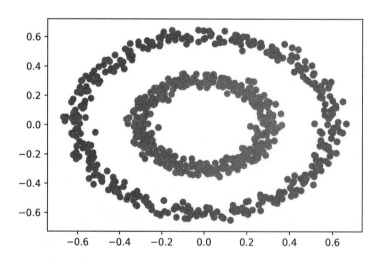

Figure 10.16　Rocks that fall into clusters 1 and 2

The Pandas groupby method lets us iteratively examine different clusters. This could prove useful in our case study 3 analysis.

Summary

- The *K-means* algorithm clusters inputted data by searching for *K centroids*. These centroids represent the mean coordinates of the discovered data groups. K-means is initialized by selecting *K* random centroids. Each data point is then clustered based on its nearest centroid, and the centroids are iteratively recomputed until they converge on stable locations.

- K-means is guaranteed to converge to a solution. However, that solution may not be optimal.

- K-means requires Euclidean distances to distinguish between points. The algorithm is not intended to cluster non-Euclidean coordinates.

- After executing K-means clustering, we can compute the *inertia* of the result. Inertia equals the sum of the squared distances between each data point and its closest center.

- Plotting the inertia across a range of *K* values generates an *elbow plot*. The elbow component in the elbow-shaped plot should point downward to a reasonable *K* value. Using the elbow plot, we can heuristically select a meaningful *K* input for K-means.

- The *DBSCAN* algorithm clusters data based on density. Density is defined using the `epsilon` and `min_points` parameters. If a point is located within `epsilon` distance of `min_points` neighbors, then that point is in a dense region of space. Every neighbor of a point in a dense region of space also clusters in that space. DBSCAN iteratively expands the boundaries of a dense region of space until a complete cluster is detected.

- Points in non-dense regions are not clustered by the DBSCAN algorithm. They are treated as outliers.

- DBSCAN is an advantageous algorithm for clustering data composed of curving and dense shapes.

- DBSCAN can cluster using arbitrary, non-Euclidean distances.

- There is no reliable heuristic for choosing appropriate `epsilon` and `min_points` parameters. However, if we wish to cluster global cities, we can set the two parameters to 250 miles and three cities, respectively.

- Storing clustered data in a Pandas table allows us to intuitively iterate over clusters with the `groupby` method.

Geographic location visualization and analysis

This section covers

- Computing the distance between geographic locations
- Plotting locations on a map using the Cartopy library
- Extracting geo-coordinates from location names
- Finding location names in text using regular expressions

People have relied on location information since before the dawn of recorded history. Cave dwellers once carved maps of hunting routes into mammoth tusks. Such maps evolved as civilizations flourished. The ancient Babylonians fully mapped the borders of their vast empire. Much later, in 3000 BC, Greek scholars improved cartography using mathematical innovations. The Greeks discovered that the Earth was round and accurately computed the planet's circumference. Greek mathematicians laid the groundwork for measuring distances across the Earth's curved surface. Such measurements required the creation of a geographic coordinate system: a rudimentary system based on latitude and longitude was introduced in 2000 BC.

Combining cartography with latitude and longitude helped revolutionize maritime navigation. Sailors could more freely travel the seas by checking their positions on a map. Roughly speaking, maritime navigation protocols followed these three steps:

1 *Data observation*—A sailor recorded a series of observations including wind direction, the position of the stars, and (after approximately AD 1300) the northward direction of a compass.

2 *Mathematical and algorithmic analysis of data*—A navigator analyzed all of the data to estimate the ship's position. Sometimes the analysis required trigonometric calculations. More commonly, the navigator consulted a series of rule-based measurement charts. By algorithmically adhering to the rules in the charts, the navigator could figure out the ship's coordinates.

3 *Visualizing and decision making*—The captain examined the computed location on a map relative to the expected destination. Then the captain would give orders to adjust the ship's orientation based on the visualized results.

This navigation paradigm perfectly encapsulates the standard data science process. As data scientists, we are offered raw observations. We algorithmically analyze that data. Then, we visualize the results to make critical decisions. Thus, data science and location analysis are linked. That link has only grown stronger through the centuries. Today, countless corporations analyze locations in ways the ancient Greeks could never have imagined. Hedge funds study satellite photos of farmlands to make bets on the global soybean market. Transport-service providers analyze vast traffic patterns to efficiently route fleets of cars. Epidemiologists process newspaper data to monitor the global spread of disease.

In this section, we explore a variety of techniques for analyzing and visualizing geographic locations. We begin with the simple task of calculating the distance between two geographic points.

11.1 The great-circle distance: A metric for computing the distance between two global points

What is the shortest travel distance between any pair of points on Earth? The distance cannot be a straight line since direct linear travel would require burrowing deep through the Earth's crust. A much more realistic path entails traveling along our spherical planet's curved surface. This direct path between two points along the surface of a sphere is called the *great-circle distance* (figure 11.1).

We can compute the great-circle distance given a sphere and two points on that sphere. Any point on the sphere's surface can be represented using *spherical coordinates* x and y, where x and y measure the angles of the point relative to the x-axis and y-axis (figure 11.2).

Let's define a basic `great_circle_distance` function that takes as input two pairs of spherical coordinates. For simplicity's sake, we will assume that the coordinates are present on a unit sphere with a radius of 1. This simplification allows us to define

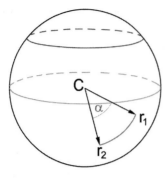

Figure 11.1 Visualizing the great-circle distance between two points on the surface of a sphere. These points are labeled r_1 and r_2. A curved arc designates the traveling distance between them. The arc length is equal to the radius of the sphere multiplied by α, where α is the angle between points relative to the sphere's center at **C**.

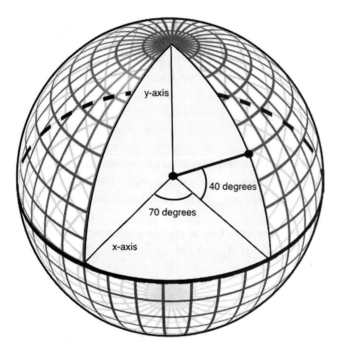

Figure 11.2 Representing a point on the surface of a sphere using spherical coordinates. The point is reached as we rotate 70 degrees away from the x-axis and 40 degrees toward the y-axis. Hence, its spherical coordinates are (70, 40).

great_circle_distance in just four lines of code. The function depends on a series of well-known trigonometric operations; a detailed derivation of these operations is beyond the scope of this book.

Listing 11.1   Defining a great-circle distance function

Imports three common trigonometric functions from Python's math module

Computes the angular difference between the two pairs of spherical coordinates

```
from math import cos, sin, asin

def great_circle_distance(x1, y1, x2, y2):
    delta_x, delta_y = x2 - x1, y2 - y1
```

```
haversin = sin(delta_x / 2) ** 2 + np.product([cos(x1), cos(x2),   ◁───────┐
                                               sin(delta_y / 2) ** 2])       │
return 2 * asin(haversin ** 0.5)                                            │
```

> **Executes a series of well-known trigonometric operations to obtain**
> **the great-circle distance on a unit sphere. The np.product function**
> **multiplies together three of the trigonometric values.**

Python's trigonometric functions assume that the input angle is in radians, where 0 degrees equal 0 radians and 180 degrees equal π radians. Let's calculate the great-circle distance between two points that lie 180 degrees apart relative to both the x-axis and the y-axis.

> **NOTE** Radians measure the length of a unit circle arc relative to an angle. The maximum arc length equals the unit-circle circumference of 2π. Traversing the circumference of a circle requires a 360-degree angle. Thus, 2π radians equal 360 degrees, and a single degree equals π / 180 radians.

Listing 11.2   Computing the great-circle distance

```
from math import pi
distance = great_circle_distance(0, 0, 0, pi)
print(f"The distance equals {distance} units")

The distance equals 3.141592653589793 units
```

The points are exactly π units apart, half the distance required to circumnavigate a unit circle. That value is the longest possible distance we can travel between two spherical points. This is akin to traveling between the North and South Poles of any planet. We'll confirm by analyzing the latitudes and longitudes of Earth's North Pole and South Pole. Terrestrial latitudes and longitudes are spherical coordinates measured in degrees. Let's begin by recording the known coordinates of each pole.

Listing 11.3   Defining the coordinates of Earth's poles

```
latitude_north, longitude_north = (90.0, 0)    ◁───────┐
latitude_south, longitude_south = (-90.0, 0)          │
```

> **Technically speaking, the North Pole and South Pole do not have an**
> **official longitude coordinate. However, we're mathematically**
> **justified in assigning a zero longitude to each pole.**

Latitudes and longitudes measure spherical coordinates in degrees, not radians. We'll thus convert to radians from degrees using the np.radians function. The function takes as input a list of degrees and returns a radian array. This result can subsequently be inputted into great_circle_distance.

Listing 11.4   Computing the great-circle distance between poles

```
to_radians =  np.radians([latitude_north, longitude_north,
                          latitude_south, longitude_south])
```

```
distance = great_circle_distance(*to_radians.tolist())
print(f"The unit-circle distance between poles equals {distance} units")

The unit-circle distance between poles equals 3.141592653589793 units
```

As a reminder, running func(*[arg1, arg2]) is a
Python shortcut for executing func(arg1, arg2).

As expected, the distance between poles on a unit sphere is π. Now, let's measure the distance between two poles here on Earth. The radius of Earth is not 1 hypothetical unit but rather 3956 actual miles, so we must multiply `distance` by 3956 to obtain a terrestrial measurement.

Listing 11.5   Computing the travel distance between Earth's poles

```
earth_distance = 3956 * distance
print(f"The distance between poles equals {earth_distance} miles")

The distance between poles equals 12428.14053760122 miles
```

The distance between the two poles is approximately 12,400 miles. We were able to compute it by converting the latitudes and longitudes to radians, calculating their unit-sphere distance, and then multiplying that value by the radius of Earth. We can now create a general `travel_distance` function to calculate the travel mileage between any two terrestrial points.

Listing 11.6   Defining a travel distance function

```
def travel_distance(lat1, lon1, lat2, lon2):
    to_radians = np.radians([lat1, lon1, lat2, lon2])
    return 3956 * great_circle_distance(*to_radians.tolist())

assert travel_distance(90, 0, -90, 0) == earth_distance
```

Our `travel_distance` function is a non-Euclidean metric for measuring distances between locations. As discussed in the previous section, we can pass such metrics into the DBSCAN clustering algorithm, so we can use `travel_distance` to cluster locations based on their spatial distributions. Then we can visually validate the clusters by plotting the locations on a map. This map plot can be executed using the external Cartopy visualization library.

11.2 *Plotting maps using Cartopy*

Visualizing geographic data is a common data science task. One external library used to map such data is Cartopy: a Matplotlib-compatible tool for generating maps in Python. Unfortunately, Cartopy can be a little tricky to install. Every other library in this book can be installed with the one-line `pip install` command. This calls the `pip` package-management system, which then connects to an external server of Python libraries. Pip subsequently installs the selected library along with all its Python dependencies, which represent additional library requirements.

NOTE For example, NumPy is a dependency of Matplotlib. Calling `pip install matplotlib` automatically installs NumPy on a local machine, if NumPy has not been installed already.

Pip works well when the dependencies are all written in Python. However, Cartopy has a dependency that's written in C++. The GEOS library is a geo-spatial engine that underlies Cartopy's visualizations. It cannot be installed using pip, so Cartopy also cannot be installed directly using pip. We're left with two options:

- Manually installing GEOS and Cartopy
- Installing the Cartopy library using the Conda package manager

Let's discuss the pros and cons of each approach.

NOTE For a deeper dive into Python dependencies, see Manning's "Managing Python Dependencies" liveVideo: www.manning.com/livevideo/talk-python-managing-python-dependencies.

11.2.1 *Manually installing GEOS and Cartopy*

The GEOS installation varies based on the operating system. On macOS, it can be installed by calling `brew install proj geos` from the command line; and on Linux, it can be installed by calling `apt-get` instead of `brew`. Additionally, Windows users can download and install the library from https://trac.osgeo.org/geos. Once GEOS is installed, Cartopy and its dependencies can be added with the following sequential pip commands:

1 `pip install --upgrade cython numpy pyshp six`
   This installs all Python dependencies except the Shapely shape-rendering library.

2 `pip install shapely --no-binary shapely`
   The Shapely library must be compiled from scratch so that it links to GEOS. The `no-binary` command ensures a fresh compilation.

3 `pip install cartopy`
   Now that the dependencies are ready, we call Cartopy using pip.

Manual installation can be cumbersome. Our alternative is to utilize the Conda package manager.

11.2.2 *Utilizing the Conda package manager*

Conda, like pip, is a package manager that can download and install external libraries. Unlike pip, Conda can easily handle non-Python dependencies. Also unlike pip, Conda does not come preinstalled on most machines: it must be downloaded and installed from https://docs.conda.io/en/latest/miniconda.html. Then we can easily install the Cartopy library by running `conda install -c conda-forge cartopy`.

Unfortunately, using Conda has some trade-offs. When Conda installs a new Python library, it does so in an isolated environment called a *virtual environment*. The virtual environment has its own version of Python, which is separated from the main version of Python that resides on a user's machine. Consequently, the Cartopy library is installed in the virtual environment but not the main environment. This can cause confusion when importing Cartopy, especially in a Jupyter notebook, because Jupyter points to the main environment by default. To add the Conda environment to Jupyter, we must run the following two commands:

1 `conda install -c anaconda ipykernel`
2 `python -m ipykernel install --user --name=base`

Doing so ensures that the Jupyter notebook can interact with a Conda environment called `base`, which is the default name of the environment created by Conda.

Now we can select the `base` environment from Jupyter's drop-down menu when creating a new notebook (figure 11.3). Then we'll be able to import Cartopy in the notebook.

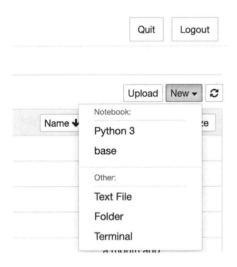

Figure 11.3   Selecting the environment when creating a new notebook. Conda's `base` environment can be selected from the drop-down menu. Choosing `base` allows us to import the installed Cartopy library.

NOTE   Conda's default virtual environment is called `base`. However, Conda allows us to create and track multiple environments. To create a new virtual environment called `new_env`, we need to execute `conda create -n new_env` from the command line. Then we can switch to the new environment by running `conda activate new_env`. Running `conda activate base` switches back to base, where Cartopy is installed. Additionally, the `conda deactivate` command switches to our machine's default Python settings. We can also check the current environment's name by running `conda info`.

Let's confirm installation by running `import cartopy` from within a Jupyter notebook.

Listing 11.7   Importing the Cartopy library

```
import cartopy
```

Cartopy installation can be confusing, but the confusion is worth it. Cartopy is the best, most commonly used map visualization tool for Python. Let's plot some maps.

11.2.3 *Visualizing maps*

A geographic map is a 2D representation of a 3D surface on a globe. Flattening the spherical globe is carried out using a process called *projection*. There are many different types of map projections: the simplest involves superimposing the globe on an unrolled cylinder, which yields a 2D map whose (x, y) coordinates perfectly correspond with longitude and latitude.

> **NOTE** In most other projections, the 2D grid coordinates don't equal the spherical coordinates. Hence, they require conversion from one coordinate system to another. We encounter this issue later in the section.

This technique is called the *equidistant cylindrical projection* or *plate carrée projection*. We utilize this standard projection in our plots by importing `PlateCarree` from `cartopy.crs`.

> **NOTE** The `cartopy.crs` module includes many other projection types. We can, for instance, import `Orthographic`: doing so returns an *orthographic projection* in which the Earth is represented from the perspective of a viewer in the outer reaches of the galaxy.

Listing 11.8 Importing the plate carrée projection

```
from cartopy.crs import PlateCarree
```

The `PlateCarree` class can be used in conjunction with Matplotlib to visualize the Earth. For instance, running `plt.axes(projection=PlateCarree()).coastlines()` plots the outlines of the Earth's seven continents. More precisely, `plt.axes(projection=PlateCarree())` initializes a custom Matplotlib axis capable of visualizing maps. Subsequently, the `coastlines` method call draws the coastline boundaries of the continents (figure 11.4).

Listing 11.9 Visualizing the Earth using Cartopy

```
plt.axes(projection=PlateCarree()).coastlines()
plt.show()
```

Our plotted map is a bit small. We can increase the map size using Matplotlib's `plt.figure` function. Calling `plt.figure(figsize=(width, height))` creates a figure that is `width` inches wide and `height` inches high. Listing 11.10 increases the figure size to 12 x 8 inches before generating the world map (figure 11.5).

> **NOTE** The actual dimensions of the figure in the book are not 12 x 8 inches due to image formatting.

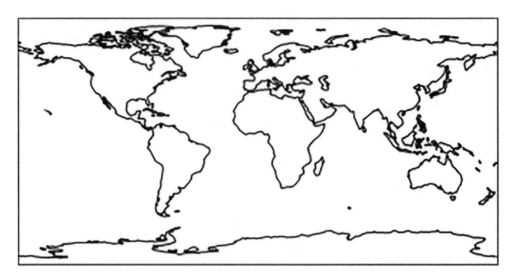

Figure 11.4   A standard map of the Earth on which the coastlines of the continents have been plotted

Listing 11.10   Visualizing a larger map of the Earth

```
plt.figure(figsize=(12, 8))
plt.axes(projection=PlateCarree()).coastlines()
plt.show()
```

Creates a larger figure that is 12 inches wide and 8 inches high

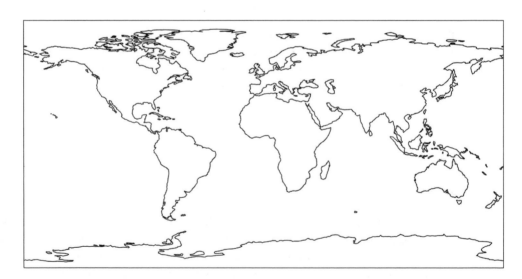

Figure 11.5   A standard map of the Earth on which the coastlines of the continents have been plotted. The map's size has been increased using Matplotlib's `plt.figure` function.

So far, our map looks sparse and uninviting. We can improve the quality by calling `plt.axes(projection=PlateCarree()).stock_img()`. The method call colors the map using topographic information: oceans are colored blue, and forested regions are colored green (figure 11.6).

Listing 11.11 Coloring a map of the Earth

```
fig = plt.figure(figsize=(12, 8))
plt.axes(projection=PlateCarree()).stock_img()
plt.show()
```

Figure 11.6 A standard map of the Earth that has been colored to display oceanographic and topographic details

Our colored map does not include the border lines demarcating coastal boundaries. Adding these boundaries will improve the map's quality. However, we are unable to add both color and boundaries in a single line of code. Instead, we need to execute the following three lines (figure 11.7):

1 `ax = plt.axes(projection=PlateCarree())`
   This line initializes a custom Matplotlib axis capable of visualizing maps. Per standard convention, the axis is assigned to the ax variable.
2 `ax.coastlines()`
   This line adds the coastlines to the plot.
3 `ax.stock_img()`
   This line adds the topographic colors to the plot.

Let's run these steps to generate a crisp, colorful map.

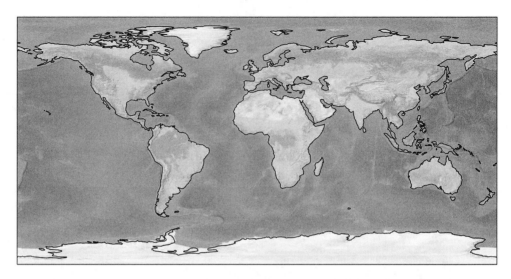

Figure 11.7   A standard map of the Earth that has been colored to display oceanographic and topographic details. Furthermore, plotted coastlines provide crisp details for the continental boundaries.

Listing 11.12   Plotting coastlines together with map colors

```
plt.figure(figsize=(12, 8))
ax = plt.axes(projection=PlateCarree())
ax.coastlines()
ax.stock_img()
plt.show()
```

Note that `ax.stock_img()` relies on a saved stock image of the Earth to color the map. This image renders poorly when a user zooms in on the map (which we'll do shortly). Alternatively, we can color the oceans and continents using the `ax.add_feature` method, which displays special Cartopy features stored in the `cartopy.feature` module. For example, calling `ax.add_feature(cartopy.feature.OCEAN)` colors all the oceans blue, and inputting `cartopy.feature.LAND` colors all land masses beige. Let's utilize these features to color the map (figure 11.8).

Listing 11.13   Adding colors with the `feature` module

```
plt.figure(figsize=(12, 8))
ax = plt.axes(projection=PlateCarree())
ax.coastlines()                         ◁———  We continue to display
ax.add_feature(cartopy.feature.OCEAN)          the coastlines to add
ax.add_feature(cartopy.feature.LAND)           crispness to the image.
plt.show()
```

Currently, national borders are missing from the plot. Cartopy treats these borders as a feature in the `feature` module. We can incorporate country borders by calling `ax.add_feature(cartopy.feature.BORDERS)` (figure 11.9).

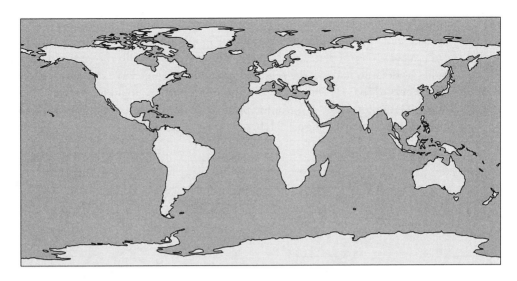

Figure 11.8 **A standard map of the Earth that has been colored using the `feature` module**

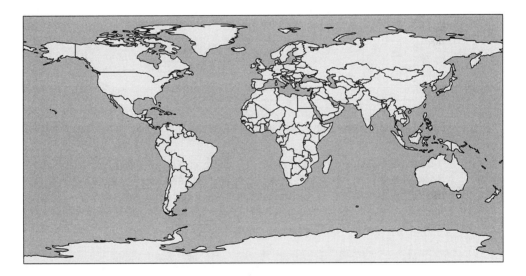

Figure 11.9 **A standard map of the Earth including national borderlines**

Listing 11.14 Adding national borders to the plot

```
plt.figure(figsize=(12, 8))
ax = plt.axes(projection=PlateCarree())
ax.coastlines()
ax.add_feature(cartopy.feature.BORDERS)
ax.add_feature(cartopy.feature.OCEAN)
ax.add_feature(cartopy.feature.LAND)
plt.show()
```

Suppose we are given a list of locations defined by pairs of latitudes and longitudes. We can plot these locations on a global map as a standard scatter plot by calling `ax.scatter(longitudes, latitudes)`. However, Matplotlib zooms in on the scattered points by default, making the mapped image incomplete. We can prevent this by calling `ax.set_global()`, which extends the plotted image to all four edges of the globe. Listing 11.15 plots some geographic points; for simplicity, we limit our map content to the coastal boundaries (figure 11.10).

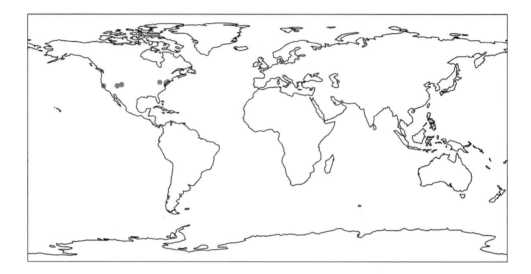

Figure 11.10   A standard map of the Earth with plotted latitude and longitude coordinates

NOTE   As previously mentioned, the plate carrée projection yields a 2D grid in which `longitudes` and `latitudes` can be plotted directly on the axes. For other projections, this is not the case: they require a transformation of `longitudes` and `latitudes` before the scatter plot is generated. Shortly, we discuss how to properly handle that transformation.

Listing 11.15   Plotting coordinates on a map

```
plt.figure(figsize=(12, 8))
coordinates = [(39.9526, -75.1652), (37.7749, -122.4194),
               (40.4406, -79.9959), (38.6807, -108.9769),
               (37.8716, -112.2727), (40.7831, -73.9712)]

latitudes, longitudes = np.array(coordinates).T
ax = plt.axes(projection=PlateCarree())
ax.scatter(longitudes, latitudes)
ax.set_global()
ax.coastlines()
plt.show()
```

The plotted points all fall within the borders of North America. We can simplify the map by zooming in on that continent. However, first we need to adjust the *map extent*, which is the geographic area shown on a map. The extent is determined by a rectangle whose corners are positioned on the minimum and maximum latitude and longitude coordinates on display. In Cartopy, these corners are defined by a four-element tuple of the form (`min_lon, max_lon, min_lat, max_lat`). Passing that list into `ax.set_extent` adjusts the boundaries of the map.

We now assign a common North American extent to a `north_america_extent` variable. Then we utilize the `ax.set_extent` method to zoom in on North America. We regenerate our scatter plot, this time adding color by passing `color='r'` into `ax.scatter`; we also utilize the `feature` module to color the map while adding national borders (figure 11.11).

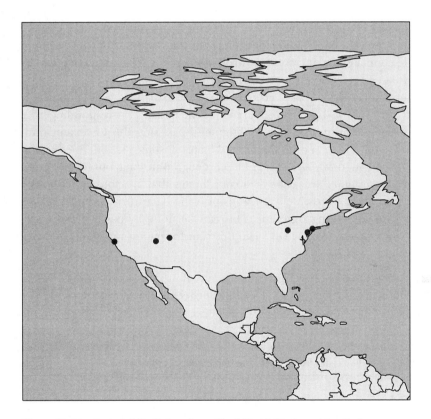

Figure 11.11 A map of North America with plotted latitude and longitude coordinates

Listing 11.16 Plotting North American coordinates

```
plt.figure(figsize=(12, 8))
ax = plt.axes(projection=PlateCarree())
```

```
north_america_extent = (-145, -50, 0, 90)
ax.set_extent(north_america_extent)
ax.scatter(longitudes, latitudes, color='r')

def add_map_features():
    ax.coastlines()
    ax.add_feature(cartopy.feature.BORDERS)
    ax.add_feature(cartopy.feature.OCEAN)
    ax.add_feature(cartopy.feature.LAND)

add_map_features()
plt.show()
```

The North American extent occurs between −145 and −50 degrees longitude and between 0 and 90 degrees latitude.

This function adds common features to a map. It is reused elsewhere in this section.

We successfully zoomed in on North America. Now we'll zoom in further, to the United States. Unfortunately, the plate carrée projection is insufficient for this purpose: that technique distorts the map if we zoom in too close on any country.

Instead, we will rely on the *Lambert conformal conic projection*. In this projection, a cone is placed on top of the spherical Earth. The cone's circular base covers the region we intend to map. Then, coordinates in the region are projected onto the surface of the cone. Finally, the cone is unrolled to create a 2D map. However, that map's 2D coordinates don't directly equal longitude and latitude.

Cartopy includes a `LambertConformal` class in the `csr` module. Executing `plt.axes(projection=LambertConformal())` yields axes corresponding to the Lambert conformal coordinate system. Subsequently, passing the US extent into `ax.set_extent` will zoom the map onto the United States. Listing 11.17 defines `us_extent` and passes it into the method. We'll also plot our geographic data, but first we need to transform `longitudes` and `latitudes` into coordinates that are compatible with `LambertConformal`: in other words, we must transform the data from `PlateCarree`-compatible coordinates to something different. This can be done by passing `transform=PlateCarree()` into `ax.scatter()`. Let's run this transformation to visualize our points on a US map (figure 11.12).

NOTE When this code is first run, Cartopy downloads and installs the Lambert conformal projection. Hence, an internet connection is required to execute the code for the very first time.

Listing 11.17 Plotting US coordinates

Transforms longitudes and latitudes from PlateCarree-compatible coordinates to ax.projection-compatible coordinates (where ax.projection equals LambertConformal).

Imports the Lambert conformal conic projection

```
from cartopy.crs import LambertConformal

plt.figure(figsize=(12, 8))
ax = plt.axes(projection=LambertConformal())
us_extent = (-120, -75, 20, 50)
ax.set_extent(us_extent)

ax.scatter(longitudes, latitudes, color='r',
           transform=PlateCarree(),
           s=100)
```

The ax axis corresponds with LambertConformal coordinates.

The US extent occurs between −120 and −75 degrees longitude and between 20 and 50 degrees latitude.

The s parameter specifies the plotted marker size. We increase that size for better visibility.

```
add_map_features()
plt.show()
```

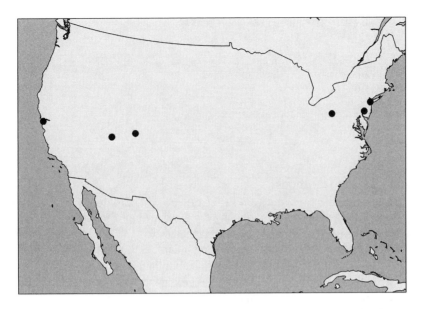

Figure 11.12   A Lambert conformal view of the United States with plotted latitude and longitude coordinates

Our map of the United States is looking a little sparse. Let's add state borders by calling `ax.add_feature(cartopy.feature.STATES)` (figure 11.13).

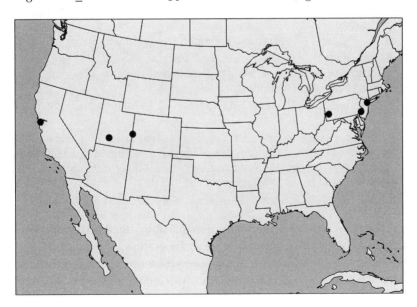

Figure 11.13   A Lambert conformal view of the United States including state borders

Listing 11.18   Plotting a US map including state borders

```
fig = plt.figure(figsize=(12, 8))
ax = plt.axes(projection=LambertConformal())
ax.set_extent(us_extent)

ax.scatter(longitudes, latitudes, color='r',
           transform=PlateCarree(),
           s=100)

ax.add_feature(cartopy.feature.STATES)
add_map_features()
plt.show()
```

Common Cartopy methods

- `ax = plt.axes(projection=PlateCarree())`—Creates a custom Matplotlib axis for generating a map using a plate carrée projection
- `ax = plt.axes(projection=LambertConformal())`—Creates a custom Matplotlib axis for generating a map using a Lambert conformal conic projection
- `ax.coastlines()`—Plots continental coastlines on a map
- `ax.add_feature(cartopy.feature.BORDERS)`—Plots national boundaries on a map
- `ax.add_feature(cartopy.feature.STATES)`— Plots US state boundaries on a map
- `ax.stock_img()`—Colors a plotted map using topographic information
- `ax.add_feature(cartopy.feature.OCEAN)`—Colors all the oceans blue on the map
- `ax.add_feature(cartopy.feature.LAND)`—Colors all the land masses beige on the map
- `ax.set_global()`—Extends the plotted image to all four edges of the globe
- `ax.set_extent(min_lon, max_lon, min_lat, max_lat)`—Adjusts the plotted map extent, which is the geographic area shown on a map, using minimum and maximum latitudes and longitudes
- `ax.scatter(longitudes, latitudes)`—Plots latitude and longitude coordinates on a map
- `ax.scatter(longitudes, latitudes, transform=PlateCarree())`—Plots latitude and longitude coordinates on a map while transforming the data from `PlateCarree`-compatible coordinates to something different (such as Lambert conformal conic coordinates)

Cartopy allows us to plot any location on a map. All we need is the location's latitude and longitude. Of course, we must know these geographic coordinates before plotting them on a map, so we need a mapping between location names and their geographic properties. That mapping is provided by the GeoNamesCache location-tracking library.

11.3 *Location tracking using GeoNamesCache*

The GeoNames database (http://geonames.org) is an excellent resource for obtaining geographic data. GeoNames contains over 11 million place names spanning all the countries in the world. In addition, GeoNames stores valuable information such as latitude and longitude. Thus, we can use the database to determine the precise geographic locations of cities and countries discovered in text.

How do we access the GeoNames data? Well, we could manually download the GeoNames data dump (http://download.geonames.org/export/dump), parse it, and then store the output data structure. That would take a lot of work. Fortunately, someone has already done the hard work for us by creating the GeoNamesCache library.

GeoNamesCache is designed to efficiently retrieve data about continents, countries, cities, and US counties and states. The library provides six easy-to-use methods to support access to location data: get_continents, get_countries, get_cities, get_countries_by_name, get_cities_by_name, and get_us_counties. Let's install the library and explore its usage in more detail. We begin by initializing a GeonamesCache location-tracking object.

> **NOTE** Call pip install geonamescache from the command line terminal to install the GeoNamesCache library.

Listing 11.19 Initializing a GeonamesCache **object**

```
from geonamescache import GeonamesCache
gc = GeonamesCache()
```

Let's use our gc object to explore the seven continents. We run gc.get_continents() to retrieve a dictionary of continent-related information. Then we investigate the dictionary's structure by printing out its keys.

Listing 11.20 Fetching all seven continents from GeoNamesCache

```
continents = gc.get_continents()
print(continents.keys())

dict_keys(['AF', 'AS', 'EU', 'NA', 'OC', 'SA', 'AN'])
```

The dictionary keys represent shorthand encoding of continent names in which *Africa* is transformed into 'AF' and *North America* is transformed into 'NA'. Let's check the values mapped to every key by passing in the code for *North America*.

> **NOTE** continents is a nested dictionary. Thus, the seven top-level keys map to content-specific dictionary structures. Listing 11.21 outputs the content-specific keys contained in the continents['NA'] dictionary.

Listing 11.21 Fetching North America from GeoNamesCache

```
north_america = continents['NA']
print(north_america.keys())

dict_keys(['lng', 'geonameId', 'timezone', 'bbox', 'toponymName',
'asciiName', 'astergdem', 'fcl', 'population', 'wikipediaURL',
'adminName5', 'srtm3', 'adminName4', 'adminName3', 'alternateNames',
'cc2', 'adminName2', 'name', 'fclName', 'fcodeName', 'adminName1',
'lat', 'fcode', 'continentCode'])
```

Many of the north_america data elements represent various naming schemes for the North American continent. Such information is not very useful.

Listing 11.22 Printing North America's naming schemes

```
for name_key in ['name', 'asciiName', 'toponymName']:
    print(north_america[name_key])

North America
North America
North America
```

However, other elements hold more value. For example, the 'lat' and 'lng' keys map to the latitude and longitude of the most central location in North America. Let's visualize this location on a map (figure 11.14).

Listing 11.23 Mapping North America's central coordinates

```
latitude = float(north_america['lat'])          ◁──────  The lat and lng
longitude = float(north_america['lng'])                  keys map to North
                                                         American's central
plt.figure(figsize=(12, 8))                              latitude and
ax = plt.axes(projection=PlateCarree())                  longitude.
ax.set_extent(north_america_extent)
ax.scatter([longitude], [latitude], s=200)
add_map_features()
plt.show()
```

11.3.1 Accessing country information

The ability to access continental data is useful, although our primary concern is analyzing cities and countries. We can analyze countries using the get_countries method. It returns a dictionary whose two-character keys encode the names of 252 different countries. As with the continents, the country codes capture the abbreviated country names. For example, the code for *Canada* is 'CA', and the code for *United States* is 'US'. Accessing gc.get_countries()['US'] returns a dictionary containing useful US data.

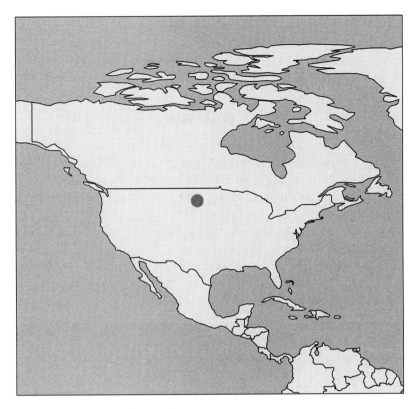

Figure 11.14   The central North American latitude and longitude plotted on a map of North America

Listing 11.24   Fetching US data from GeoNamesCache

```
countries = gc.get_countries()
num_countries = len(countries)
print(f"GeonamesCache holds data for {num_countries} countries.")

us_data = countries['US']
print("The following data pertains to the United States:")
print(us_data)

GeonamesCache holds data for 252 countries.
The following data pertains to the United States:
{'geonameid': 6252001,
'name': 'United States',
'iso': 'US',
'iso3': 'USA',
'isonumeric': 840,
'fips': 'US',
'continentcode': 'NA',          US continent
'capital': 'Washington',        code
'areakm2': 9629091,
```

US continent
code

Capital of the US

US area, in square
kilometers

```
'population': 310232863,          ◁——┐  US population
'tld': '.us',
'currencycode': 'USD',
'currencyname': 'Dollar',         ◁——┐  Currency of the US
'phone': '1',
'postalcoderegex': '^\\d{5}(-\\d{4})?$',    Common spoken
'languages': 'en-US,es-US,haw,fr',   ◁——┘  languages in the US
'neighbours': 'CA,MX,CU'}         ◁——┐  US neighboring territories
```

The outputted country data includes many useful elements, such as the country's capital, currency, area, spoken languages, and population. Regrettably, GeoNames-Cache fails to provide the central latitude and longitude associated with the country's area. However, as we shortly discover, a country's centrality can be estimated using city coordinates.

Additionally, there is valuable information in each country's `'neighbours'` element (the spelling is written in British English). The `'neighbours'` key maps to a comma-delimited string of country codes that signify neighboring territories. We can obtain more details about each neighbor by splitting the string and passing the codes into the `'countries'` dictionary.

Listing 11.25   Fetching neighboring countries

```
us_neighbors = us_data['neighbours']
for neighbor_code in us_neighbors.split(','):
    print(countries[neighbor_code]['name'])


Canada
Mexico
Cuba
```

According to GeoNamesCache, the immediate neighbors of the United States are Canada, Mexico, and Cuba. We can all agree on the first two locations, although whether Cuba is a neighbor remains questionable. Cuba does not directly border the United States. Also, if the Caribbean island nation is really a neighbor, why isn't Haiti included in that list? More importantly, how did Cuba get included in the first place? Well, GeoNames is a collaborative project run by a community of editors (like a location-focused Wikipedia). At some point, an editor decided that Cuba is a neighbor of the United States. Some might disagree with this decision, so it is important to remember that GeoNames is not a gold standard repository of location information. Instead, it is a tool for quickly accessing large quantities of location data. Some of that data may be imprecise, so please be cautious when using GeoNamesCache.

The get_countries method requires a country's two-character code. However, for most countries, we will not know the code. Fortunately, we can query all countries by name using the get_countries_by_names method, which returns a dictionary whose elements are country names rather than codes.

Listing 11.26 Fetching countries by name

```
result = gc.get_countries_by_names()['United States']
assert result == countries['US']
```

11.3.2 Accessing city information

Now, let's turn our attention to analyzing cities. The `get_cities` method returns a dictionary whose keys are unique IDs mapping back to city data. The following code outputs that data for a single city.

Listing 11.27 Fetching `cities` from GeoNamesCache

```
cities = gc.get_cities()
num_cities = len(cities)
print(f"GeoNamesCache holds data for {num_cities} total cities")
city_id = list(cities.keys())[0]
print(cities[city_id])
```

`cities` is a dictionary mapping a unique `city_id` to geographic information.

```
{'geonameid': 3041563,          ← Unique city ID
 'name': 'Andorra la Vella',    ← City name
 'latitude': 42.50779,          ← Latitude
 'longitude': 1.52109,          ← Longitude
 'countrycode': 'AD',           ← Code of the country where the city is found
 'population': 20430,           ← Population
 'timezone': 'Europe/Andorra'}  ← Time zone
```

The data for each city contains the city name, its latitude and longitude, its population, and the reference code for the country where that city is located. By utilizing the country code, we can create a new mapping between a country and all of its territorial cities. Let's isolate and count all US cities stored in GeoNamesCache.

> **NOTE** As we've discussed, GeoNames is not perfect. Certain US cities may be missing from the database. Over time, these cities will be added. Thus, the observed city count may increase with every library update.

Listing 11.28 Fetching US cities from GeoNamesCache

```
us_cities = [city for city in cities.values()
             if city['countrycode'] == 'US']
num_us_cities = len(us_cities)
print(f"GeoNamesCache holds data for {num_us_cities} US cities.")

GeoNamesCache holds data for 3248 US cities
```

GeoNamesCache contains information about more than 3,000 US cities. Each city's data dictionary contains a latitude and a longitude. Let's find the average US latitude and longitude, which will approximate the central coordinates of the United States.

Note that the approximation is not perfect. The calculated average does not take into account the curvature of the Earth and is inappropriately weighted by city location. A disproportionate number of US cities are located near the Atlantic Ocean, and thus the approximation is skewed toward the East. In the following code, we approximate and plot the US center while remaining fully aware that our approximation is not ideal (figure 11.15).

Listing 11.29   Approximating US central coordinates

```
center_lat = np.mean([city['latitude']
                        for city in us_cities])
center_lon = np.mean([city['longitude']
                        for city in us_cities])

fig = plt.figure(figsize=(12, 8))
ax = plt.axes(projection=LambertConformal())
ax.set_extent(us_extent)
ax.scatter([center_lon], [center_lat], transform=PlateCarree(), s=200)
ax.add_feature(cartopy.feature.STATES)
add_map_features()
plt.show()
```

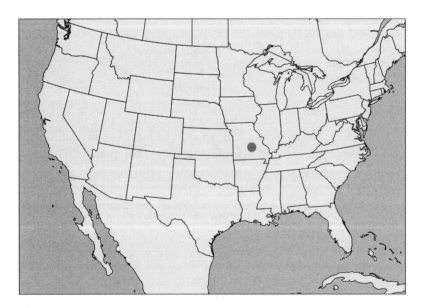

Figure 11.15   The central location of the United States is approximated by averaging the coordinates of every US city in GeoNamesCache. The approximation is slightly skewed toward the east.

The get_cities method is suitable for iterating over city information but not querying cities by name. To search by name, we must rely on get_cities_by_name. This method takes as an input a city name and returns a list of data outputs for all cities with that name.

Listing 11.30 Fetching cities by name

```
matched_cities_by_name = gc.get_cities_by_name('Philadelphia')
print(matched_cities_by_name)

[{'4560349': {'geonameid': 4560349, 'name': 'Philadelphia',
'latitude': 39.95233, 'longitude': -75.16379, 'countrycode': 'US',
'population': 1567442, 'timezone': 'America/New_York'}}]
```

The get_cities_by_name method may return more than one city because city names are not always unique. For example, GeoNamesCache contains six different instances of the city name San Francisco in five different countries. Calling gc.get_cities_ by_name('San Francisco') returns data for each of these San Francisco instances. Let's iterate over that data and print the country where each San Francisco is found.

Listing 11.31 Fetching multiple cities with a shared name

```
matched_cities_list = gc.get_cities_by_name('San Francisco')

for i, san_francisco in enumerate(matched_cities_list):
    city_info = list(san_francisco.values())[0]
    country_code = city_info['countrycode']
    country = countries[country_code]['name']
    print(f"The San Francisco at index {i} is located in {country}")

The San Francisco at index 0 is located in Argentina
The San Francisco at index 1 is located in Costa Rica
The San Francisco at index 2 is located in Philippines
The San Francisco at index 3 is located in Philippines
The San Francisco at index 4 is located in El Salvador
The San Francisco at index 5 is located in United States
```

Multiple cities commonly share an identical name, and choosing among such cities can be difficult. Suppose, for instance, that someone queries a search engine for the "weather in Athens." The search engine must then choose between Athens, Ohio and Athens, Greece. Additional context is required to correctly disambiguate between the locations. Is the user from Ohio? Are they planning a trip to Greece? Without that context, the search engine must guess. Usually, the safest guess is the city with the largest population. From a statistical standpoint, the more populous cities are more likely to be referenced in everyday conversation. Choosing the most-populated city isn't guaranteed to work all the time, but it's still better than making a completely random choice. Let's see what happens when we plot the most populated San Francisco location (figure 11.16).

Listing 11.32   Mapping the most populous San Francisco

```
best_sf = max(gc.get_cities_by_name('San Francisco'),
              key=lambda x: list(x.values())[0]['population'])
sf_data = list(best_sf.values())[0]
sf_lat = sf_data['latitude']
sf_lon = sf_data['longitude']

plt.figure(figsize=(12, 8))
ax = plt.axes(projection=LambertConformal())
ax.set_extent(us_extent)
ax.scatter(sf_lon, sf_lat, transform=PlateCarree(), s=200)
add_map_features()
ax.text(sf_lon + 1, sf_lat, ' San Francisco', fontsize=16,
        transform=PlateCarree())
plt.show()
```

The ax.text method allows us to write "San Francisco" at the specified longitude and latitude. We slightly shift the longitude to the right to avoid overlapping the scatter plot dot. Also, on this map, the state borders are not plotted to better display the written text.

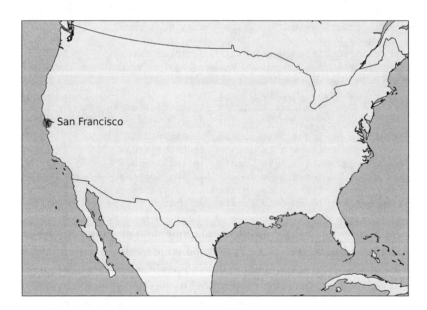

Figure 11.16   Among the six San Franciscos stored in GeoNamesCache, the city with the largest population is in California, as expected.

Selecting the San Francisco with the largest population returns the well-known Californian city rather than any of the lesser-known locations outside of the United States.

> **Common GeoNamesCache methods**
>
> - `gc = GeonamesCache()`—Initializes a `GeonamesCache` object
> - `gc.get_continents()`—Returns a dictionary mapping continent IDs to continent data
> - `gc.get_countries()`—Returns a dictionary mapping country IDs to country data
> - `gc.get_countries_by_names()`—Returns a dictionary mapping country names to country data
> - `gc.get_cities()`—Returns a dictionary mapping city IDs to city data
> - `gc.get_cities_by_name(city_name)`—Returns a list of cities that share the name `city_name`

11.3.3 *Limitations of the GeoNamesCache library*

GeoNamesCache is a useful tool, but it does have some significant flaws. First, the library's record of cities is far from complete. Certain sparsely populated locations in rural areas (whether the rural United States or rural China) are missing from the stored database records. Furthermore, the `get_cities_by_name` method maps only one version of a city's name to its geographic data. This poses a problem for cities like New York that have more than one commonly referenced name.

Listing 11.33 Fetching New York City from GeoNamesCache

```
for ny_name in ['New York', 'New York City']:
    if not gc.get_cities_by_name(ny_name):
        print(f"'{ny_name}' is not present in the GeoNamesCache database")
    else:
        print(f"'{ny_name}' is present in the GeoNamesCache database")

'New York' is not present in the GeoNamesCache database
'New York City' is present in the GeoNamesCache database
```

The single name-to-city mapping is particularly problematic due to the presence of diacritics in city names. *Diacritics* are accent marks that designate the proper pronunciation of non-English-sounding words. They are commonly found in city names: for example, Cañon City, Colorado; and Hagåtña, Guam.

Listing 11.34 Fetching accented cities from GeoNamesCache

```
print(gc.get_cities_by_name(u'Cañon City'))
print(gc.get_cities_by_name(u'Hagåtña'))

[{'5416005': {'geonameid': 5416005, 'name': 'Cañon City',
'latitude': 38.44098, 'longitude': -105.24245, 'countrycode': 'US',
'population': 16400, 'timezone': 'America/Denver'}}]
[{'4044012': {'geonameid': 4044012, 'name': 'Hagåtña',
'latitude': 13.47567, 'longitude': 144.74886, 'countrycode': 'GU',
'population': 1051, 'timezone': 'Pacific/Guam'}}]
```

How many of the cities stored in GeoNamesCache contain diacritics in their name? We can find out using the `unidecode` function from the external Unidecode library. The function strips all accent marks out of input text. By checking for differences between the input text and output text, we should be able to detect all city names containing accent marks.

NOTE Call `pip install Unidecode` from the command line terminal to install the Unidecode library.

Listing 11.35 Counting all accented cities in GeoNamesCache

```
from unidecode import unidecode
accented_names = [city['name'] for city in gc.get_cities().values()
                  if city['name'] != unidecode(city['name'])]
num_accented_cities = len(accented_names)

print(f"An example accented city name is '{accented_names[0]}'")
print(f"{num_accented_cities} cities have accented names")

An example accented city name is 'Khawr Fakkān'
4896 cities have accented names
```

Approximately 5,000 stored cities have diacritics in their names. These cities are commonly referenced without an accent in published text data. One way to ensure that we match all such cities is to create a dictionary of alternative city names; in it, the accent-free `unidecode` output maps back to the original accented names.

Listing 11.36 Stripping accents from alternative city names

```
alternative_names = {unidecode(name): name
                     for name in accented_names}
print(gc.get_cities_by_name(alternative_names['Hagatna']))

[{'4044012': {'geonameid': 4044012, 'name': 'Hagåtña',
'latitude': 13.47567, 'longitude': 144.74886, 'countrycode': 'GU',
 'population': 1051, 'timezone': 'Pacific/Guam'}}]
```

We can now match the stripped dictionary keys against all inputted text by passing the accented dictionary values into GeoNamesCache whenever a key match is found.

Listing 11.37 Finding accent-free city names in text

```
text = 'This sentence matches Hagatna'
for key, value in alternative_names.items():
    if key in text:
        print(gc.get_cities_by_name(value))
        break

[{'4044012': {'geonameid': 4044012, 'name': 'Hagåtña',
 'latitude': 13.47567, 'longitude': 144.74886, 'countrycode': 'GU',
  'population': 1051, 'timezone': 'Pacific/Guam'}}]
```

GeoNamesCache allows us to easily track locations along with their geographical coordinates. Using the library, we can also search for mentioned location names within any inputted text. However, finding names in text is not a trivial process. If we wish to match location names appropriately, we must learn proper Python text-matching techniques while also avoiding common pitfalls.

> **NOTE** The final subsection is intended for readers who are unfamiliar with basic string matching and regular expressions. If you are already familiar with these techniques, feel free to skip ahead.

11.4 Matching location names in text

In Python, we can easily determine whether one string is a substring of another or if the start of a string contains some predefined text.

Listing 11.38 Basic string matching

```
assert 'Boston' in 'Boston Marathon'
assert 'Boston Marathon'.startswith('Boston')
assert 'Boston Marathon'.endswith('Boston') == False
```

Unfortunately, Python's basic string syntax is quite limited. For example, there is no direct string method for executing a case-insensitive substring comparison. Furthermore, Python's string methods can't directly distinguish between sub-characters in a string and sub-phrases in a sentence. So if we wish to determine whether the phrase `'in a'` is present in a sentence, we cannot safely rely on basic matching. Otherwise, we run the risk of incorrectly matching character sequences such as `'sin apple'` or `'win attached'`.

Listing 11.39 Basic substring matching errors

```
assert 'in a' in 'sin apple'
assert 'in a' in 'win attached'
```

To overcome these limitations, we must rely on Python's built-in regular expression processing library, re. A *regular expression* (or *regex* for short) is a string-encoded pattern that can be compared against some text. Coded regex patterns range from simple string copies to incredibly complex formulations that very few people can decipher. In this subsection, we focus on simple regex composition and matching.

Most regex matching in Python can be executed with the re.search function. This function takes two inputs: a regex pattern and the text against which the pattern will be matched. It returns a Match object if a match is found or None otherwise. The Match object contains a start method and an end method; these methods return the start index and end index of the matched string in the text.

Listing 11.40   String matching using regexes

```
import re
regex = 'Boston'
random_text = 'Clown Patty'
match = re.search(regex, random_text)
assert match is None

matchable_text = 'Boston Marathon'
match = re.search(regex, matchable_text)
assert match is not None
start, end = match.start(), match.end()
matched_string = matchable_text[start: end]
assert matched_string == 'Boston'
```

Additionally, case-insensitive string matching is a breeze with re.search. We simply pass re.IGNORECASE as an added flags parameter.

Listing 11.41   Case-insensitive matching using regexes

```
for text in ['BOSTON', 'boston', 'BoSTOn']:
    assert re.search(regex, text, flags=re.IGNORECASE) is not None    ⟵
```
We can achieve the same result by passing flags=re.I into re.search.

Regexes also allow us to match exact words using word boundary detection. Adding the \b pattern to a regex string captures the start and end points of words (as defined by whitespaces and punctuation). However, because the backslash is a special character in the standard Python lexicon, we must take measures to ensure that the backslash is interpreted like a regular raw character. We do this by either adding another backslash to the backslash (a rather cumbersome approach) or preceding the string with an r literal. The latter solution ensures that the regex is treated as a raw string during analysis.

Listing 11.42   Word boundary matching using regexes

```
for regex in ['\\bin a\\b', r'\bin a\b']:
    for text in ['sin apple', 'win attached']:
        assert re.search(regex, text) is None

    text = 'Match in a string'
    assert re.search(regex, text) is not None
```

Now, let's carry out a more complicated match. We match against the sentence f'I visited {city} yesterday, where {city} represents one of three possible locations: Boston, Philadelphia, or San Francisco. The correct regex syntax for executing the match is r'I visited \b(Boston|Philadelphia|San Francisco)\b yesterday'.

NOTE The pipe | is an *Or* condition. It requires the regex to match from one of the three cities in our list. Furthermore, the parentheses limit the scope of the matched cities. Without them, the matched text range would stretch beyond 'San Francisco', all the way to 'San Francisco yesterday'.

Listing 11.43 Multicity matching using regexes

```
regex = r'I visited \b(Boston|Philadelphia|San Francisco)\b yesterday.'
assert re.search(regex, 'I visited Chicago yesterday.') is None

cities = ['Boston', 'Philadelphia', 'San Francisco']
for city in cities:
    assert re.search(regex, f'I visited {city} yesterday.') is not None
```

Finally, let's discuss how to run a regex search efficiently. Suppose we want to match a regex against 100 strings. For every match, re.search transforms the regex into a Python PatternObject. Each such transformation is computationally costly. We're better off executing the transformation only once using re.compile, which returns a compiled PatternObject. Then we can use the object's built-in search method while avoiding any additional compilation.

NOTE If we intend to use the compiled pattern for case-independent matching, we must pass flags=re.IGNORECASE into re.compile.

Listing 11.44 String matching using compiled regexes

```
compiled_re = re.compile(regex)
text = 'I visited Boston yesterday.'
for i in range(1000):
    assert compiled_re.search(text) is not None
```

> ### Common regex matching techniques
>
> - match = re.search(regex, text)—Returns a Match object if regex is present in text or None otherwise.
> - match = re.search(regex, text, flags=re.IGNORECASE)—Returns a Match object if regex is present in text or None otherwise. Matching is carried out independent of case.
> - match.start()—Returns the start index of a regex matched to an input text.
> - match.end()—Returns an end index of a regex matched to an input text.
> - compiled_regex = re.compile(regex)—Transforms the regex string into a compiled pattern-matching object.
> - match = compiled_regex.search(text)— Uses the compiled object's built-in search method to match a regex against text.
> - re.compile('Boston')—Compiles a regex to match the string 'Boston' against the text.

(continued)

- `re.compile('Boston', flags=re.IGNORECASE)`—Compiles a regex to match the string `'Boston'` against the text. The matching is independent of text case.
- `re.compile('\\bBoston\\b')`—Compiles a regex to match the word `'Boston'` against the text. Word boundaries are used to execute an exact word match.
- `re.compile(r'\bBoston\b')`—Compiles a regex to match the word `'Boston'` against the text. The inputted regex is treated as a raw string because of the `r` literal. Thus, we don't need to add additional backslashes to our `\b` word boundary delimiters.
- `re.compile(r'\b(Boston|Chicago)\b')`—Compiles a regex to match either the word `'Boston'` or the word `'Chicago'` to the text.

Regex matching allows us to find location names in text. Thus, the `re` module will prove invaluable for solving case study 3.

Summary

- The shortest travel distance between terrestrial points is along our planet's spherical surface. This *great-circle distance* can be computed using a series of well-known trigonometric operations.
- The latitude and longitude are *spherical coordinates*. These coordinates measure the angular position of a point on the surface of the Earth relative to the x-axis and y-axis.
- We can plot a latitude and longitude on a map using the Cartopy library. The library can visualize mapped data using multiple projection types. Our choice of projection is dependent on the plotted data. If the data spans the globe, we can use the standard *plate carrée*. If the data is confined to North America, we might consider using the *orthographic projection*. If the data points are located in the continental United States, we should use the *Lambert conformal conic projection*.
- We can obtain latitudes and longitudes from location names using the GeoNamesCache library. GeoNamesCache maps city names to latitudes and longitudes. It also maps country names to cities. Thus, given a country name, we can approximate its central coordinates by averaging the latitudes and longitudes of its cities. However, that approximation will not be perfect due to city bias and the curved shape of the Earth.
- Multiple cities commonly share an identical name. Thus, GeoNamesCache can map multiple coordinates to a single city name. Given only a city name without any other context, it is advisable to return the coordinates of the most populous city with that name.

- GeoNamesCache maps coordinates to accented versions of each city name. We can strip out these accents using the `unidecode` function from the external `Unidecode` library.
- *Regular expressions* can find location names in text. By combining GeoNames-Cache with Cartopy and regular expressions, we can plot locations mentioned in text.

Case study 3 solution

12

This section covers

- Extracting and visualizing locations
- Cleaning data
- Clustering locations

Our goal is to extract locations from disease-related headlines to uncover the largest active epidemics within and outside of the United States. We will do as follows:

1. Load the data.
2. Extract locations from the text using regular expressions and the GeoNamesCache library.
3. Check the location matches for errors.
4. Cluster the locations based on geographic distance.
5. Visualize the clusters on a map, and remove any errors.
6. Output representative locations from the largest clusters to draw interesting conclusions.

WARNING Spoiler alert! The solution to case study 3 is about to be revealed. I strongly encourage you to try to solve the problem before reading the solution. The original problem statement is available for reference at the beginning of the case study.

12.1　*Extracting locations from headline data*

We begin by loading the headline data.

Listing 12.1　Loading headline data

```
headline_file = open('headlines.txt','r')
headlines = [line.strip()
             for line in headline_file.readlines()]
num_headlines = len(headlines)
print(f"{num_headlines} headlines have been loaded")

650 headlines have been loaded
```

We have loaded 650 headlines. Now we need a mechanism for extracting city and country names from the headline text. One naive solution is to match the locations in GeoNamesCache against each and every headline. However, this approach will fail to match locations whose capitalization and accent marks diverge from the stored GeoNamesCache data. For more optimal matching, we should transform each location name into a case-independent and accent-independent regular expression. We can execute these transformations using a custom `name_to_regex` function. That function takes a location name as input and returns a compiled regular expression capable of identifying any location of our choosing.

Listing 12.2　Converting names to regexes

```
def name_to_regex(name):
    decoded_name = unidecode(name)
    if name != decoded_name:
        regex = fr'\b({name}|{decoded_name})\b'
    else:
        regex = fr'\b{name}\b'
    return re.compile(regex, flags=re.IGNORECASE)
```

Using `name_to_regex`, we can create a mapping between regular expressions and the original names in GeoNamesCache. Let's create two dictionaries, `country_to_name` and `city_to_name`, which map regular expressions to country names and city names, respectively.

Listing 12.3　Mapping names to regexes

```
countries = [country['name']
             for country in gc.get_countries().values()]
country_to_name = {name_to_regex(name): name
                   for name in countries}

cities = [city['name'] for city in gc.get_cities().values()]
city_to_name = {name_to_regex(name): name for name in cities}
```

Next, we use our mappings to define a function that looks for location names in text. The function takes as input both a headline and a location dictionary. It iterates over each regex key in the dictionary, returning the associated value if the regex pattern matches the headline.

Listing 12.4   Finding locations in text

```
def get_name_in_text(text, dictionary):
    for regex, name in sorted(dictionary.items(),
                          key=lambda x: x[1]):    ◁
        if regex.search(text):
            return name
    return None
```

> Iterating over dictionaries gives us a nondeterministic sequence of results. A change in sequence order could alter which locations are matched to the inputted text. This is especially true if multiple locations are present in the text. Sorting by location name ensures that function output does not change from run to run.

We utilize `get_name_in_text` to discover the cities and countries mentioned in the `headlines` list. Then we store the results in a Pandas table for easier analysis.

Listing 12.5   Finding locations in headlines

```
import pandas as pd

matched_countries = [get_name_in_text(headline, country_to_name)
                     for headline in headlines]
matched_cities = [get_name_in_text(headline, city_to_name)
                  for headline in headlines]
data = {'Headline': headlines, 'City': matched_cities,
        'Country': matched_countries}
df = pd.DataFrame(data)
```

Let's explore our location table. We start by summarizing the contents of `df` using the `describe` method.

Listing 12.6   Summarizing the location data

```
summary = df[['City', 'Country']].describe()
print(summary)

        City Country
count    619      15
unique   511      10
top       Of  Brazil
freq      45       3
```

NOTE   Multiple countries in the data share the top occurrence frequency of 3. Pandas does not have a deterministic method for selecting one top country over another. Depending on your local settings, a country other than Brazil could be returned as a top country, but it will still have a frequency of 3.

The table contains 619 mentions of cities representing 511 unique city names. It also contains just 15 countries representing 10 unique country names. The most frequently mentioned country is Brazil, which appears in three headlines.

The most frequently mentioned city is apparently "Of," Turkey. That doesn't seem right! The 45 instances of "Of" are more likely to match the preposition than the rarely referenced Turkish location. We will output some instances of "Of" to confirm the error.

Listing 12.7 Fetching cities named `"Of"`

```
of_cities = df[df.City == 'Of'][['City', 'Headline']]
ten_of_cities = of_cities.head(10)
print(ten_of_cities.to_string(index=False))          ◁──────  Converts df to a string in
                                                              which the row indices
City                                          Headline        have been removed. This
  Of              Case of Measles Reported in Vancouver       leads to more concise
  Of  Authorities are Worried about the Spread of Br...       printed output.
  Of  Authorities are Worried about the Spread of Ma...
  Of  Rochester authorities confirmed the spread of ...
  Of     Tokyo Encounters Severe Symptoms of Meningitis
  Of  Authorities are Worried about the Spread of In...
  Of             Spike of Pneumonia Cases in Springfield
  Of  The Spread of Measles in Spokane has been Conf...
  Of                     Outbreak of Zika in Panama City
  Of    Urbana Encounters Severe Symptoms of Meningitis
```

Yes, our matches to "Of" are definitely erroneous. We can fix the error by ensuring that all matches are capitalized. However, the observed bug is a symptom of a much bigger issue: in all the wrongly matched headlines, we matched to "Of" but not to the actual city name. This occurred because we didn't account for multiple matches in a headline. How frequently do headlines contain more than one match? Let's find out. We'll track the list of all matched cities in a headline using an additional `Cities` column.

Listing 12.8 Finding multicity headlines

```
                                          Returns a list of all unique
                                          cities in a headline
def get_cities_in_headline(headline):  ◁──┘
    cities_in_headline = set()               Makes sure the first letter of
    for regex, name in city_to_name.items():  the city name is capitalized
        match = regex.search(headline)
        if match:                                Adds a Cities column to
            if headline[match.start()].isupper():  ◁──┘  the table by using the
                cities_in_headline.add(name)         apply method, which applies
                                                      an inputted function to all
    return list(cities_in_headline)                   elements of a column to
                                                       create a brand new column
df['Cities'] = df['Headline'].apply(get_cities_in_headline)  ◁───────
df['Num_cities'] = df['Cities'].apply(len)
df_multiple_cities = df[df.Num_cities > 1]   ◁──  Filters out rows that do not
                                                  contain multiple city matches
Adds a column counting the
number of cities in a headline
```

```
num_rows, _ = df_multiple_cities.shape
print(f"{num_rows} headlines match multiple cities")
```

```
67 headlines match multiple cities
```
  ←—| **The city count may increase with data**
     updates to the GeoNamesCache library.

We find that 67 headlines contain more than one city, which represents approximately 10% of the data. Why do so many headlines match against multiple locations? Perhaps exploring some sample matches will yield an answer.

Listing 12.9 Sampling multicity headlines

```
ten_cities = df_multiple_cities[['Cities', 'Headline']].head(10)
print(ten_cities.to_string(index=False))
```

```
Cities                           Headline
[York, New York City]            Could Zika Reach New York City?
[Miami Beach, Miami]             First Case of Zika in Miami Beach
[San Juan, San]                  San Juan reports 1st U.S. Zika-related death
     amid outbreak
[Los Angeles, Los Ángeles]       New Los Angeles Hairstyle goes Viral
[Bay, Tampa]                     Tampa Bay Area Zika Case Count Climbs
[Ho Chi Minh City, Ho]           Zika cases in Vietnam's Ho Chi Minh City
     surge
[San, San Diego]                 Key Zika Findings in San Diego Institute
[H?t, Kuala Lumpur]              Kuala Lumpur is Hit By Zika Threat
[San, San Francisco]             Zika Virus Reaches San Francisco
[Salvador, San, San Salvador]    Zika worries in San Salvador
```

It appears that short, invalid city names are being matched to the headlines along with the longer, correct location names. For example, the city of 'San' is always returned along with more legitimate city names like 'San Francisco' and 'San Salvador'. How do we fix this error? One solution is to just return the longest city name whenever more than one matched city is found.

Listing 12.10 Selecting the longest city names

```
def get_longest_city(cities):
    if cities:
        return max(cities, key=len)
    return None

df['City'] = df['Cities'].apply(get_longest_city)
```

As a sanity check, we'll output rows that contain a short city name (four characters or fewer) to ensure that no erroneous short name is assigned to one of our headlines.

Listing 12.11 Printing the shortest city names

```
short_cities = df[df.City.str.len() <= 4][['City', 'Headline']]
print(short_cities.to_string(index=False))
```

```
City                                                        Headline
Lima                         Lima tries to address Zika Concerns
Pune                             Pune woman diagnosed with Zika
Rome    Authorities are Worried about the Spread of Ma...
Molo                        Molo Cholera Spread Causing Concern
Miri                                    Zika arrives in Miri
Nadi    More people in Nadi are infected with HIV ever...
Baud    Rumors about Tuberculosis Spreading in Baud ha...
Kobe                        Chikungunya re-emerges in Kobe
Waco                        More Zika patients reported in Waco
Erie                        Erie County sets Zika traps
Kent                          Kent is infested with Rabies
Reno    The Spread of Gonorrhea in Reno has been Confi...
Sibu                        Zika symptoms spotted in Sibu
Baku    The Spread of Herpes in Baku has been Confirmed
Bonn    Contaminated Meat Brings Trouble for Bonn Farmers
Jaen                        Zika Troubles come to Jaen
Yuma                        Zika seminars in Yuma County
Lyon                    Mad Cow Disease Detected in Lyon
Yiwu    Authorities are Worried about the Spread of He...
Suva    Suva authorities confirmed the spread of Rotav...
```

The results appear to be legitimate. Let's now shift our attention from cities to countries. Only 15 of the total headlines contain actual country information. The count is low enough for us to manually examine all of these headlines.

Listing 12.12 Fetching headlines with countries

```
df_countries = df[df.Country.notnull()][['City',
                                          'Country',
                                          'Headline']]
print(df_countries.to_string(index=False))
```

The df.Country.notnull() method returns a list of Booleans. Each Boolean equals True only if a country is present in the associated row.

```
           City      Country                                 Headline
          Recife       Brazil      Mystery Virus Spreads in Recife, Brazil
Ho Chi Minh City      Vietnam    Zika cases in Vietnam's Ho Chi Minh City surge
         Bangkok     Thailand              Thailand-Zika Virus in Bangkok
       Piracicaba       Brazil       Zika outbreak in Piracicaba, Brazil
           Klang     Malaysia          Zika surfaces in Klang, Malaysia
   Guatemala City    Guatemala   Rumors about Meningitis spreading in Guatemala...
      Belize City       Belize      Belize City under threat from Zika
        Campinas       Brazil            Student sick in Campinas, Brazil
      Mexico City       Mexico       Zika outbreak spreads to Mexico City
    Kota Kinabalu     Malaysia     New Zika Case in Kota Kinabalu, Malaysia
      Johor Bahru     Malaysia         Zika reaches Johor Bahru, Malaysia
        Hong Kong    Hong Kong           Norovirus Exposure in Hong Kong
      Panama City       Panama           Outbreak of Zika in Panama City
        Singapore    Singapore        Zika cases in Singapore reach 393
      Panama City       Panama      Panama City's first Zika related death
```

All of the country-bearing headlines also contain city information. Thus, we can assign a latitude and longitude without relying on the country's central coordinates. Consequently, we can disregard the country names from our analysis.

Listing 12.13   Dropping countries from the table

```
df.drop('Country', axis=1, inplace=True)
```

We are nearly ready to add latitudes and longitudes to our table. However, we first need to consider the rows where no locations were detected. Let's count the number of unmatched headlines and then print a subset of that data.

Listing 12.14   Exploring unmatched headlines

```
df_unmatched = df[df.City.isnull()]
num_unmatched = len(df_unmatched)
print(f"{num_unmatched} headlines contain no city matches.")
print(df_unmatched.head(10)[['Headline']].values)

39 headlines contain no city matches.
[['Louisiana Zika cases up to 26']
 ['Zika infects pregnant woman in Cebu']
 ['Spanish Flu Sighted in Antigua']
 ['Zika case reported in Oton']
 ['Hillsborough uses innovative trap against Zika 20 minutes ago']
 ['Maka City Experiences Influenza Outbreak']
 ['West Nile Virus Outbreak in Saint Johns']
 ['Malaria Exposure in Sussex']
 ['Greenwich Establishes Zika Task Force']
 ['Will West Nile Virus vaccine help Parsons?']]
```

Approximately 6% of the headlines do not match any cities. Some of these headlines mention legitimate cities, which GeoNamesCache failed to identify. How should we treat the missing cities? Well, given their low frequency, perhaps we should delete the missing mentions. The price for those deletions is a slight reduction in data quality, but that loss will not significantly impact our results because our coverage of matched cities is quite high.

Listing 12.15   Dropping unmatched headlines

```
df = df[~df.City.isnull()][['City', 'Headline']]
```

The ~ symbol reverses the Booleans in the list
returned by the df.City.isnull() method. Thus,
each reversed Boolean equals True only if
a city is present in the associated row.

12.2 *Visualizing and clustering the extracted location data*

All the rows in our table contain a city name. Now we can assign a latitude and longitude to each row. We utilize `get_cities_by_name` to return the coordinates of the most populated city bearing the extracted city name.

Listing 12.16 Assigning geographic coordinates to cities

```
latitudes, longitudes = [], []
for city_name in df.City.values:
    city = max(gc.get_cities_by_name(city_name),
            key=lambda x: list(x.values())[0]['population'])       ⊲─┐ Chooses the
    city = list(city.values())[0]     ⊲─┐                               matched city
    latitudes.append(city['latitude'])  │ Extracts city latitudes       with the largest
    longitudes.append(city['longitude']) │ and longitudes               population

df = df.assign(Latitude=latitudes, Longitude=longitudes)    ⊲─┐ Adds Latitude and
                                                                Longitude columns
                                                                to our table
```

With latitudes and longitudes assigned, we can attempt to cluster the data. Let's execute K-means across our set of 2D coordinates. We use the elbow method to choose a reasonable value for *K* (figure 12.1).

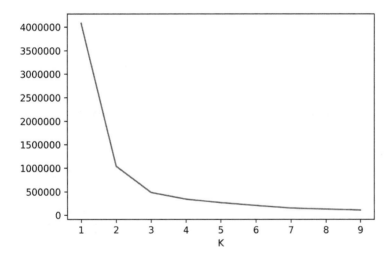

Figure 12.1 A geographic elbow curve points to a *K* of 3

Listing 12.17 Plotting a geographic elbow curve

```
coordinates = df[['Latitude', 'Longitude']].values
k_values = range(1, 10)
inertia_values = []
for k in k_values:
    inertia_values.append(KMeans(k).fit(coordinates).inertia_)
```

```
plt.plot(range(1, 10), inertia_values)
plt.xlabel('K')
plt.ylabel('Inertia')
plt.show()
```

The "elbow" in our elbow plot points to a *K* of 3. That *K* value is very low, limiting our scope to at most three different geographic territories. Still, we should maintain some faith in our analytic methodology. We cluster the locations into three groups and plot them on a map (figure 12.2).

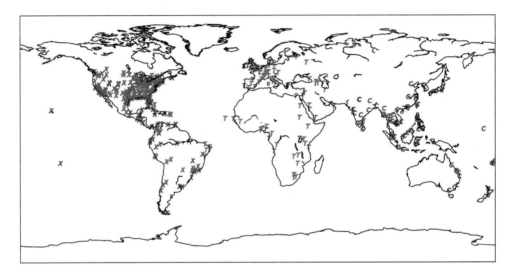

Figure 12.2   Mapped K-means city clusters. *K* is set to 3. The three clusters are spread thin across six continents.

Listing 12.18   Using K-means to cluster cities into three groups

```
def plot_clusters(clusters, longitudes, latitudes):
    plt.figure(figsize=(12, 10))
    ax = plt.axes(projection=PlateCarree())
    ax.coastlines()
    ax.scatter(longitudes, latitudes, c=clusters)
    ax.set_global()
    plt.show()
```

This function will be reused to plot clusters throughout the rest of our analysis.

```
df['Cluster'] = KMeans(3).fit_predict(coordinates)
plot_clusters(df.Cluster, df.Longitude, df.Latitude)
```

NOTE   The marker shapes in figures 12.1 through 12.5 have been manually adjusted to discriminate among clusters in the black-and-white print version of the book.

The results look pretty ridiculous. Our three clusters cover

- North and South America
- Africa and Europe
- Asia and Australia

These continental categories are too broad to be useful. Furthermore, all South American cities on the eastern coast awkwardly cluster with African and European locations (despite the fact that an entire ocean lies between them). These clusters are not helpful for understanding the data. Perhaps our K was too low after all. Let's disregard our elbow analysis and double the size of K to 6 (figure 12.3).

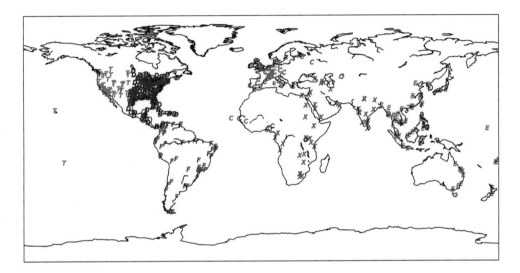

Figure 12.3 Mapped K-means city clusters. *K* is set to 6. Africa's clustered points are incorrectly split between the European and Asian continents.

Listing 12.19 Using K-means to cluster cities into six groups

```
df['Cluster'] = KMeans(6).fit_predict(coordinates)
plot_clusters(df.Cluster, df.Longitude, df.Latitude)
```

Increasing K improves clustering in North America and South America. South America now falls in its own separate cluster, and North America is split between two Western and Eastern cluster groups. However, on the other side of the Atlantic, the clustering quality remains low. Africa's geolocations are incorrectly split between Europe and Asia. K-mean's sense of centrality is unable to properly distinguish between Africa, Europe, and Asia. Perhaps the algorithm's reliance on Euclidean distance prevents it from capturing relationships between points distributed on our planet's curved surface.

As an alternate approach, we can attempt to execute DBSCAN clustering. The DBSCAN algorithm takes as input any distance metric of our choosing, allowing us to cluster on the great-circle distance between points. We start by coding a great-circle distance function whose inputs are a pair of NumPy arrays.

Listing 12.20   Defining a NumPy-based great-circle metric

```
def great_circle_distance(coord1, coord2, radius=3956):     ◁───┐  radius is preset to
    if np.array_equal(coord1, coord2):                          │  the radius of the
        return 0.0                                              │  Earth in miles.

    coord1, coord2 = np.radians(coord1), np.radians(coord2)
    delta_x, delta_y = coord2 - coord1
    haversin = sin(delta_x / 2) ** 2 + np.product([cos(coord1[0]),
                                                    cos(coord2[0]),
                                                    sin(delta_y / 2) ** 2])
    return  2 * radius * asin(haversin ** 0.5)
```

We've defined our distance metric and are nearly ready to run the DBSCAN algorithm. However, first we need to choose reasonable values for the eps and min_samples parameters. Let's assume the following: a global city cluster contains at least three cities that are on average no more than 250 miles apart. Based on these assumptions, we input values of 250 and 3 into eps and min_samples, respectively.

Listing 12.21   Using DBSCAN to cluster cities

```
metric = great_circle_distance
dbscan = DBSCAN(eps=250, min_samples=3, metric=metric)
df['Cluster'] = dbscan.fit_predict(coordinates)
```

DBSCAN assigns −1 to outlier data points that do not cluster. Let's remove these outliers from our table and then plot the remaining results (figure 12.4).

Listing 12.22   Plotting non-outlier DBSCAN clusters

```
df_no_outliers = df[df.Cluster > -1]
plot_clusters(df_no_outliers.Cluster, df_no_outliers.Longitude,
              df_no_outliers.Latitude)
```

DBSCAN has done a decent job generating discrete clusters in parts of South America, Asia, and southern Africa. The eastern United States, however, falls into a single overly dense cluster. Why is this the case? It is partially due to a certain narrative bias in Western media, which means American events are more likely to get coverage. This leads to a denser spread of mentioned locations. One way to overcome the geographic bias is to recluster US cities using a more rigorous epsilon parameter. Such a strategy seems sensible in the context of our problem statement, which asks for separate top clusters from American and globally grouped headlines. So, we'll cluster US locations

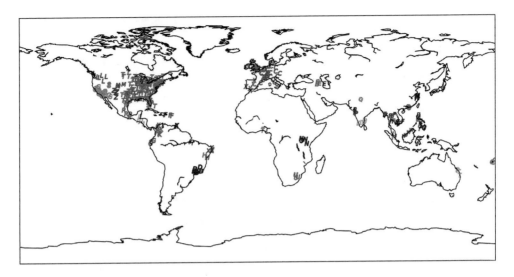

Figure 12.4 **Mapped DBSCAN city clusters computed using the great-circle distance metric**

independently from the rest of the world. To do so, we first assign country codes across each of our cities.

Listing 12.23 Assigning country codes to cities

```
def get_country_code(city_name):
    city = max(gc.get_cities_by_name(city_name),
            key=lambda x: list(x.values())[0]['population'])
    return list(city.values())[0]['countrycode']

df['Country_code'] = df.City.apply(get_country_code)
```

The country codes allow us to separate the data into two distinct `DataFrame` objects. The first object, `df_us`, holds the US locations. The second object, `df_not_us`, holds all the remaining global cities.

Listing 12.24 Separating US and global cities

```
df_us = df[df.Country_code == 'US']
df_not_us = df[df.Country_code != 'US']
```

We've separated US and non-US cities. Now we need to recluster the coordinates in the two separated tables. Reclustering `df_not_us` is unavoidable due to density changes caused by deleting all the US locations. However, we maintain eps of 250 while clustering that table. Meanwhile, we reduce eps for `df_us` by half (to 125) to acknowledge the tighter density of US locations. Finally, all outliers are deleted after we recluster.

Listing 12.25   Reclustering extracted cities

```
def re_cluster(input_df, eps):
    input_coord = input_df[['Latitude', 'Longitude']].values
    dbscan = DBSCAN(eps=eps, min_samples=3,
                    metric=great_circle_distance)
    clusters = dbscan.fit_predict(input_coord)
    input_df = input_df.assign(Cluster=clusters)
    return input_df[input_df.Cluster > -1]

df_not_us = re_cluster(df_not_us, 250)
df_us = re_cluster(df_us, 125)
```

12.3   *Extracting insights from location clusters*

Let's investigate the clustered data in the df_not_us table. We start by grouping the results using the Pandas groupby method.

Listing 12.26   Grouping cities by cluster

```
groups = df_not_us.groupby('Cluster')
num_groups = len(groups)
print(f"{num_groups} Non-US clusters have been detected")
```

```
31 Non-US clusters have been detected
```

31 global clusters have been detected. Let's sort these groups by size and count the headlines in the largest cluster.

Listing 12.27   Finding the largest cluster

```
sorted_groups = sorted(groups, key=lambda x: len(x[1]),
                       reverse=True)
group_id, largest_group = sorted_groups[0]
group_size = len(largest_group)
print(f"Largest cluster contains {group_size} headlines")
```

```
Largest cluster contains 51 headlines
```

The largest cluster contains 51 total headlines. Reading all these headlines individually will be a time-consuming process. We can save time by outputting just those headlines that represent the most central locations in the cluster. Centrality can be captured by calculating the average latitude and longitude of a group. Then we can compute the distance between every location and the average coordinates. Lower distances indicate higher centrality.

> **NOTE**   As we discussed in section 11, the average latitude and longitude merely approximate the center since they do not consider the curvature of the Earth.

Next, we define a compute_centrality function that assigns a Distance_to_center column to an inputted group.

Listing 12.28 Computing cluster centrality

```
def compute_centrality(group):
    group_coords = group[['Latitude', 'Longitude']].values
    center = group_coords.mean(axis=0)
    distance_to_center = [great_circle_distance(center, coord)
                          for coord in group_coords]
    group['Distance_to_center'] = distance_to_center
```

We can now sort all headlines by centrality. Let's print the five most central headlines in our largest cluster.

Listing 12.29 Finding the central headlines in the largest cluster

```
def sort_by_centrality(group):
    compute_centrality(group)
    return group.sort_values(by=['Distance_to_center'], ascending=True)

largest_group = sort_by_centrality(largest_group)
for headline in largest_group.Headline.values[:5]:
    print(headline)
```

```
Mad Cow Disease Disastrous to Brussels
Scientists in Paris to look for answers
More Livestock in Fontainebleau are infected with Mad Cow Disease
Mad Cow Disease Hits Rotterdam
Contaminated Meat Brings Trouble for Bonn Farmers
```

The central headlines in `largest_group` focus on an outbreak of mad cow disease in various European cities. We can confirm that the cluster's locale is centered in Europe by outputting the top countries associated with cities in the cluster.

Listing 12.30 Finding the top three countries in the largest cluster

```
from collections import Counter
def top_countries(group):
    countries = [gc.get_countries()[country_code]['name']
                 for country_code in group.Country_code.values]
    return Counter(countries).most_common(3)   ◁──┐   The Counter class tracks the
                                                      most-repeated elements in a
                                                      list, along with their counts.
print(top_countries(largest_group))
```

```
[('United Kingdom', 19), ('France', 7), ('Germany', 6)]
```

The most frequently mentioned cities in `largest_group` are located in the United Kingdom, France, and Germany. The majority of locations in `largest_group` are definitely in Europe.

Let's repeat this analysis across the four next-largest global clusters. The following code helps determine whether any other disease epidemics are currently threatening the globe.

Listing 12.31   Summarizing content in the largest clusters

```
for _, group in sorted_groups[1:5]:
    sorted_group = sort_by_centrality(group)
    print(top_countries(sorted_group))
    for headline in sorted_group.Headline.values[:5]:
        print(headline)
    print('\n')
```

```
[('Philippines', 16)]
Zika afflicts patient in Calamba
Hepatitis E re-emerges in Santa Rosa
More Zika patients reported in Indang
Batangas Tourism Takes a Hit as Virus Spreads
Spreading Zika reaches Bacoor


[('El Salvador', 3), ('Honduras', 2), ('Nicaragua', 2)]
Zika arrives in Tegucigalpa
Santa Barbara tests new cure for Hepatitis C
Zika Reported in Ilopango
More Zika cases in Soyapango
Zika worries in San Salvador


[('Thailand', 5), ('Cambodia', 3), ('Vietnam', 2)]
More Zika patients reported in Chanthaburi
Thailand-Zika Virus in Bangkok
Zika case reported in Phetchabun
Zika arrives in Udon Thani
More Zika patients reported in Kampong Speu


[('Canada', 10)]
Rumors about Pneumonia spreading in Ottawa have been refuted
More people in Toronto are infected with Hepatitis E every year
St. Catharines Patient in Critical Condition after Contracting Dengue
Varicella has Arrived in Milton
Rabies Exposure in Hamilton
```

Oh no! Zika is spreading through the Philippines! There are also Zika outbreaks in Southeast Asia and in Central America. The Canadian cluster, however, contains a mix of random disease headlines, which implies that no dominant outbreak is occurring in that northern territory.

Let's turn our attention to the US clusters. We start by visualizing the clusters on a map of the United States (figure 12.5).

Listing 12.32   Plotting US DBSCAN clusters

```
plt.figure(figsize=(12, 10))
ax = plt.axes(projection=LambertConformal())
ax.set_extent(us_extent)
```

```
ax.scatter(df_us.Longitude, df_us.Latitude, c=df_us.Cluster,
           transform=PlateCarree())
ax.coastlines()
ax.add_feature(cartopy.feature.STATES)
plt.show()
```

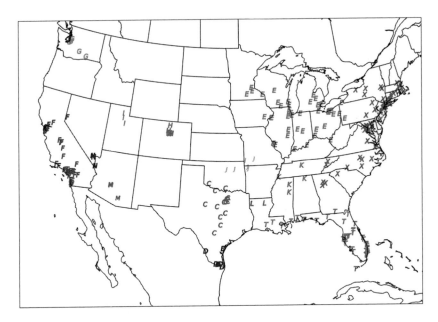

Figure 12.5   Mapped DBSCAN location clusters within the boundaries of the United States

The visualized map yields reasonable outputs. The eastern states no longer fall into a single dense cluster. We'll analyze the top five US clusters by printing their centrality-sorted headlines.

Listing 12.33   Summarizing content within the largest US clusters

```
us_groups = df_us.groupby('Cluster')
us_sorted_groups = sorted(us_groups, key=lambda x: len(x[1]),
                          reverse=True)
for _, group in us_sorted_groups[:5]:
    sorted_group = sort_by_centrality(group)
    for headline in sorted_group.Headline.values[:5]:
        print(headline)
    print('\n')
```

```
Schools in Bridgeton Closed Due to Mumps Outbreak
Philadelphia experts track pandemic
Vineland authorities confirmed the spread of Chlamydia
Baltimore plans for Zika virus
Will Swine Flu vaccine help Annapolis?
```

```
Bradenton Experiences Zika Troubles
Tampa Bay Area Zika Case Count Climbs
Zika Strikes St. Petersburg
New Zika Case Confirmed in Sarasota County
Zika spreads to Plant City


Rhinovirus Hits Bakersfield
Schools in Tulare Closed Due to Mumps Outbreak
New medicine wipes out West Nile Virus in Ventura
Hollywood Outbreak Film Premieres
Zika symptoms spotted in Hollywood


How to Avoid Hepatitis E in South Bend
Hepatitis E Hits Hammond
Chicago's First Zika Case Confirmed
Rumors about Hepatitis C spreading in Darien have been refuted
Rumors about Rotavirus Spreading in Joliet have been Refuted


More Zika patients reported in Fort Worth
Outbreak of Zika in Stephenville
Zika symptoms spotted in Arlington
Dallas man comes down with case of Zika
Zika spreads to Lewisville
```

The Zika epidemic has hit both Florida and Texas! This is very troubling. However, no discernible disease patterns are present in the other top clusters. Currently, the spreading Zika outbreak is confined to the southern United States. We will immediately report this to our superiors so they can take appropriate action. As we prepare to present our findings, let's plot one final image, which will appear on the front page of our report (figure 12.6). This image summarizes the menacing scope of the spreading Zika epidemic: it displays all US and global clusters where Zika is mentioned in more than 50% of article headlines.

Listing 12.34   Plotting Zika clusters

```python
def count_zika_mentions(headlines):          ◁───────       Counts the number of
    zika_regex = re.compile(r'\bzika\b',     ◁──────┐       times Zika is mentioned
                        flags=re.IGNORECASE)         │      in a list of headlines
    zika_count = 0
    for headline in headlines:                              Regex that matches an
        if zika_regex.search(headline):                     instance of the word "Zika"
            zika_count += 1                                  in a headline. The match is
                                                             case insensitive.
    return zika_count

fig = plt.figure(figsize=(15, 15))
ax = plt.axes(projection=PlateCarree())
```

```
for _, group in sorted_groups + us_sorted_groups:          ⟵─  Iterates over both US
    headlines = group.Headline.values                          and global clusters
    zika_count = count_zika_mentions(headlines)
    if float(zika_count) / len(headlines) > 0.5:           ⟵─  Plots clusters where Zika
        ax.scatter(group.Longitude, group.Latitude)            is mentioned in more than
                                                                50% of article headlines
ax.coastlines()
ax.set_global()
plt.show()
```

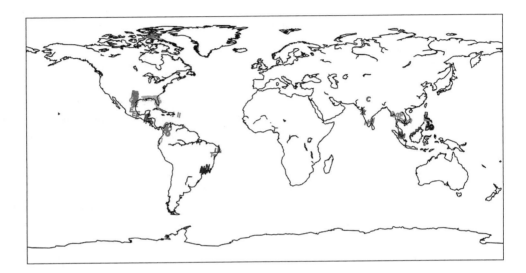

Figure 12.6 Mapped DBSCAN location clusters where Zika is mentioned in more than 50% of article headlines

We have successfully clustered our headlines by location and plotted those clusters where the word *Zika* is dominant. This relationship between our clusters and their textual content leads to an interesting question: is it possible to cluster the headlines based on text similarity rather than geographic distance? In other words, can we group our headlines by text overlap so that all the references to Zika automatically appear in a single cluster? Yes, we can! In the subsequent case study, we learn how to measure similarity between texts to group documents by topic.

Summary

- Data science tools can fail in unexpected ways. When we ran GeoNamesCache on our news headlines, the library incorrectly matched short city names (such as "Of" and "San") to the inputted text. Through data exploration, we were able to account for these mistakes. If, instead, we had blindly clustered the locations, our final output would have been junky. We must diligently explore our data prior to serious analysis.

- Sometimes, problematic data points are present in an otherwise good dataset. In our case, less than 6% of headlines incorrectly lacked a city assignment. Correcting for these headlines would have been difficult. Instead, we chose to delete the headlines from the dataset. Occasionally, it's okay to delete problematic examples if their impact on the dataset is minimal. However, we should weigh the pros and cons of the deletion before making a final decision.

- The elbow method heuristically picks K for K-means clustering. Heuristic tools are not guaranteed to work correctly every time. In our analysis, an elbow plot returned a K of 3. Obviously, this value was too low. Thus, we intervened and attempted to choose a different K. If we had indiscriminately trusted the elbow output, our final clustering would have been worthless.

- Common sense should dictate our analysis of clustering outputs. Earlier, we examined a K-means output where K equaled 6. We observed the clustering of Central African and European cities. This result was clearly wrong—Europe and Central Africa are very different locations. So, we transitioned to a different clustering approach. When common sense dictates that the clustering is wrong, we should try an alternate approach.

- Sometimes it's acceptable to break a dataset into parts and analyze each part individually. In our initial DBSCAN analysis, the algorithm failed to correctly cluster US cities. Most eastern US cities fell into a single cluster. We could have abandoned our DBSCAN approach. Instead, we clustered the US cities separately, using more appropriate parameters. Analyzing the dataset in two separate parts led to better clustering results.

Using online job postings to improve your data science resume

Problem statement

We're ready to expand our data science career. Six months from now, we'll apply for a new job. In preparation, we begin to draft our resume. The early draft is rough and incomplete. It doesn't yet cover our career goals or education. None-theless, the resume covers the first four case studies in this book, including this one, which we'll complete before seeking new employment.

Our resume draft is far from perfect. It's possible that certain vital data science skills are not yet represented. If so, what are those missing skills? We decide to find out analytically. After all, we are data scientists! We fill in gaps in knowledge using rigorous analysis, so why shouldn't we apply that rigorous analysis to ourselves?

First we need some data. We go online and visit a popular job-search site. The website offers millions of searchable job listings, posted by understaffed employers. A built-in search engine allows us to filter the jobs by keyword, such as *analyst* or *data scientist*. Additionally, the search engine can match jobs to uploaded documents. This feature is intended to search postings based on resume content. Unfortunately, our resume is still a work in progress. So instead, we search on the table of contents of this book! We copy and paste the first 15 listed sections of the table of contents into a text file.

Next, we upload the file to the job-search site. Material from the first four case studies is compared against millions of job listings, and thousands of job postings are returned. Some of these postings may be more relevant than others; we can't vouch for the search engine's overall quality, but the data is appreciated. We download the HTML from every posting.

Our goal is to extract common data science skills from the downloaded data. We'll then compare these skills to our resume to determine which skills are missing. To reach our goal, we'll proceed like this:

1 Parse out all the text from the downloaded HTML files.
2 Explore the parsed output to learn how job skills are commonly described in online postings. Perhaps specific HTML tags are more commonly used to underscore job skills.
3 Try to filter out any irrelevant job postings from our dataset. The search engine isn't perfect. Perhaps some irrelevant postings were erroneously downloaded. We can evaluate relevance by comparing the postings with our resume and the table of contents.
4 Cluster the job skills within the relevant postings, and visualize the clusters.
5 Compare the clustered skills to our resume content. We'll then make plans to update our resume with any missing data science skills.

Dataset description

Our rough draft of the resume is stored in the file resume.txt. The full text of that draft is as follows:

```
Experience

1. Developed probability simulations using NumPy
2. Assessed online ad clicks for statistical significance using permutation
     testing
3. Analyzed disease outbreaks using common clustering algorithms

Additional Skills

1. Data visualization using Matplotlib
2. Statistical analysis using SciPy
3. Processing structured tables using Pandas
4. Executing K-means clustering and DBSCAN clustering using scikit-learn
5. Extracting locations from text using GeoNamesCache
6. Location analysis and visualization using GeoNamesCache and Cartopy
7. Dimensionality reduction with PCA and SVD using scikit-learn
8. NLP analysis and text topic detection using scikit-learn
```

We'll learn skills 7 and 8 in the subsequent sections of this case study.

Our preliminary draft is short and incomplete. To compensate for any missing material, we also use the partial table of contents of this book, which is stored in the file table_of_contents.txt. It covers the first 15 sections of the book, as well as all the top-level subsection headers. The table of contents file has been utilized to search for thousands of relevant job postings that were downloaded and stored in a job_postings directory. Each file in the directory is an HTML file associated with an individual posting. These files can be viewed locally in your web browser.

Overview

To address the problem at hand, we need to know how to do the following:

- Measure similarity between texts
- Efficiently cluster large text datasets
- Visually display multiple text clusters
- Parse HTML files for text content

Measuring text similarities

This section covers

- What is natural language processing?
- Comparing texts based on word overlap
- Comparing texts using one-dimensional arrays called vectors
- Comparing texts using two-dimensional arrays called matrices
- Efficient matrix computation using NumPy

Rapid text analysis can save lives. Let's consider a real-world incident when US soldiers stormed a terrorist compound. In the compound, they discovered a computer containing terabytes of archived data. The data included documents, text messages, and emails pertaining to terrorist activities. The documents were too numerous to be read by any single human being. Fortunately, the soldiers were equipped with special software that could perform very fast text analysis. The software allowed the soldiers to process all of the text data without even having to leave the compound. The onsite analysis immediately revealed an active terrorist plot in a nearby neighborhood. The soldiers instantly responded to the plot and prevented a terrorist attack.

This swift defensive response would not have been possible without *natural language processing* (NLP) techniques. NLP is a branch of data science that focuses on speedy text analysis. Typically, NLP is applied to very large text datasets. NLP use cases are numerous and diverse and include the following:

- Corporate monitoring of social media posts to measure the public's sentiment toward a company's brand
- Analyzing transcribed call center conversations to monitor common customer complaints
- Matching people on dating sites based on written descriptions of shared interests
- Processing written doctors' notes to ensure proper patient diagnosis

These use cases depend on fast analysis. Delayed signal extraction could be costly. Unfortunately, the direct handling of text is an inherently slow process. Most computational techniques are optimized for numbers, not text. Consequently, NLP methods depend on a conversion from pure text to a numeric representation. Once all words and sentences have been replaced with numbers, the data can be analyzed very rapidly.

In this section, we focus on a basic NLP problem: measuring the similarity between two texts. We will quickly discover a feasible solution that is not computationally efficient. We will then explore a series of numerical techniques for rapidly computing text similarities. These computations will require us to transform our input texts into 2D numeric tables for full efficiency.

13.1   *Simple text comparison*

Many NLP tasks depend on the analysis of similarities and differences between texts. Suppose we want to compare three simple texts:

- `text1`—*She sells seashells by the seashore.*
- `text2`—*"Seashells! The seashells are on sale! By the seashore."*
- `text3`—*She sells 3 seashells to John, who lives by the lake.*

Our goal is to determine whether `text1` is more similar to `text2` or to `text3`. We start by assigning the texts to three variables.

Listing 13.1   **Assigning texts to variables**

```
text1 = 'She sells seashells by the seashore.'
text2 = '"Seashells! The seashells are on sale! By the seashore."'
text3 = 'She sells 3 seashells to John, who lives by the lake.'
```

Now we need to quantify the differences between texts. One basic approach is to simply count the words shared between each pair of texts. This requires us to split each text into a list of words. Text splitting in Python can be carried out using the built-in string `split` method.

NOTE The process of splitting text into individual words is commonly called *tokenization.*

Listing 13.2   Splitting texts into words

```
words_lists = [text.split() for text in [text1, text2, text3]]
words1, words2, words3 = words_lists

for i, words in enumerate(words_lists, 1):
    print(f"Words in text {i}")
    print(f"{words}\n")

Words in text 1
['She', 'sells', 'seashells', 'by', 'the', 'seashore.']

Words in text 2
['"Seashells!', 'The', 'seashells', 'are', 'on', 'sale!', 'By', 'the',
    'seashore."']

Words in text 3
['She', 'sells', '3', 'seashells', 'to', 'John,', 'who', 'lives', 'by',
    'the', 'lake.']
```

Even though we've split the texts, an accurate word comparison is not immediately possible for the following reasons:

- *Capitalization inconsistency*—The words *she* and *seashells* are capitalized in some texts but not others, making a direct comparison difficult.
- *Punctuation inconsistency*—For example, an exclamation point and a quotation mark are attached to *seashells* in text2 but not in the other texts.

We can eliminate the capitalization inconsistency by calling the built-in `lower` string method, which converts a string to lowercase. Furthermore, we can strip out punctuation from a word string by calling `word.replace(punctuation, ' ')`, where punctuation is set to `'!'` or `'"'`. Let's use these built-in string methods to eliminate all inconsistencies. We define a `simplify_text` function, which converts text to lowercase and removes all common punctuation.

Listing 13.3   Removing case sensitivity and punctuation

```
def simplify_text(text):
    for punctuation in ['.', ',', '!', '?', '"']:      ◁──  Strips out common
        text = text.replace(punctuation, '')                 punctuation from a
                                                             string and converts
    return text.lower()                                      the string to
                                                             lowercase
for i, words in enumerate(words_lists, 1):
    for j, word in enumerate(words):
        words[j] = simplify_text(word)

    print(f"Words in text {i}")
    print(f"{words}\n")
```

As a reminder, our immediate goal is to

1 Count all unique words in `text1` that are also present in `text2`.
2 Count all unique words in `text1` that are also present in `text3`.
3 Use the counts to determine whether `text2` or `text3` is more similar to `text1`.

Currently, we're just interested in comparing unique words. Therefore, duplicate words (like *seashore*, which appears twice in `text2`) will only be counted once. Thus, we can eliminate all duplicate words by converting each word list into a set.

Listing 13.4 Converting word lists to sets

```
words_sets = [set(words) for words in words_lists]
for i, unique_words in enumerate(words_sets, 1):
    print(f"Unique Words in text {i}")
    print(f"{unique_words}\n")

Unique Words in text 1
{'sells', 'seashells', 'by', 'seashore', 'the', 'she'}

Unique Words in text 2
{'by', 'on', 'are', 'sale', 'seashore', 'the', 'seashells'}

Unique Words in text 3
{'to', 'sells', 'seashells', 'lake', 'by', 'lives', 'the', 'john', '3',
 'who', 'she'}
```

Given two Python sets `set_a` and `set_b`, we can extract all overlapping elements by running `set_a & set_b`. Let's use the `&` operator to count overlapping words between text pairs (`text1`, `text2`) and (`text1`, `text3`).

NOTE Formally, the set of overlapping elements is called the *intersection* of two sets.

Listing 13.5 Extracting overlapping words between two texts

```
words_set1 = words_sets[0]
for i, words_set in enumerate(words_sets[1:], 2):
    shared_words = words_set1 & words_set
    print(f"Texts 1 and {i} share these {len(shared_words)} words:")
    print(f"{shared_words}\n")

Texts 1 and 2 share these 4 words:
{'seashore', 'by', 'the', 'seashells'}

Texts 1 and 3 share these 5 words:
{'sells', 'by', 'she', 'the', 'seashells'}
```

Texts 1 and 2 share four words, while texts 1 and 3 share five words. Does this mean `text1` is more similar to `text3` than to `text2`? Not necessarily. While texts 1 and 3 share five overlapping words, they also contain diverging words that appear in one text but not the other. Let's count all the diverging words between text pairs (text1, text2) and (text1, text3). We use the ^ operator to extract diverging elements between each pair of word sets.

Listing 13.6 Extracting diverging words between two texts

```
for i, words_set in enumerate(words_sets[1:], 2):
    diverging_words = words_set1 ^ words_set
    print(f"Texts 1 and {i} don't share these {len(diverging_words)} words:")
    print(f"{diverging_words}\n")

Texts 1 and 2 don't share these 5 words:
{'are', 'sells', 'sale', 'on', 'she'}

Texts 1 and 3 don't share these 7 words:
{'to', 'lake', 'lives', 'seashore', 'john', '3', 'who'}
```

Texts 1 and 3 contain two more diverging words than texts 1 and 2. Thus, texts 1 and 3 show significant word overlap and also significant divergence. To combine their overlap and divergence into a single similarity score, we must first combine all overlapping and diverging words between the texts. This aggregation, which is called a *union*, will contain all the unique words across the two texts. Given two Python sets set_a and set_b, we can compute their union by running set_a | set_b.

The differences between word divergence, intersection, and union are illustrated in figure 13.1. Here, the unique words in texts 1 and 2 are displayed in three rectangular boxes. The leftmost box and the rightmost box represent the diverging words between texts 1 and 2, respectively. Meanwhile, the middle box contains all the shared words at the intersection of texts 1 and 2. Together, the three boxes represent the union of all words in the two texts.

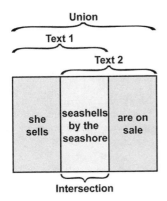

Figure 13.1 A visualized representation of the union, intersection, and divergence between two texts.

Common Python set operations

- set_a & set_b—Returns all overlapping elements between set_a and set_b
- set_a ^ set_b—Returns all diverging elements between set_a and set_b
- set_a | set_b—Returns the union of all elements between set_a and set_b
- set_a - set_b—Returns all elements in set_a that are not in set_b

---

Let's utilize the | operator to count the total unique words across text pairs (text1, text2) and (text1, text3).

Listing 13.7   Extracting the union of words between two texts

```
for i, words_set in enumerate(words_sets[1:], 2):
    total_words = words_set1 | words_set
    print(f"Together, texts 1 and {i} contain {len(total_words)} "
          f"unique words. These words are:\n {total_words}\n")
```

```
Together, texts 1 and 2 contain 9 unique words. These words are:
 {'sells', 'seashells', 'by', 'on', 'are', 'sale', 'seashore', 'the', 'she'}

Together, texts 1 and 3 contain 12 unique words. These words are:
 {'sells', 'lake', 'by', 'john', 'the', 'she', 'to', 'lives', 'seashore',
    '3', 'who', 'seashells'}
```

Together, text1 and text3 contain 12 unique words. Five of these words overlap, and seven diverge. Accordingly, both overlap and divergence represent complementary percentages of the total unique word count across texts. Let's output these percentages for text pairs (text1, text2) and (text1, text3).

Listing 13.8   Extracting the percentage of shared words between two texts

```
for i, words_set in enumerate(words_sets[1:], 2):
    shared_words = words_set1 & words_set
    diverging_words = words_set1 ^ words_set          Percent of total words
    total_words = words_set1 | words_set                 shared with text 1
    assert len(total_words) == len(shared_words) + len(diverging_words)
    percent_shared = 100 * len(shared_words) / len(total_words)      ◁──┘
    percent_diverging = 100 * len(diverging_words) / len(total_words)

    print(f"Together, texts 1 and {i} contain {len(total_words)} "
          f"unique words. \n{percent_shared:.2f}% of these words are "
          f"shared. \n{percent_diverging:.2f}% of these words diverge.\n")
```

Percent of total words that diverge from text 1 ──▷

```
Together, texts 1 and 2 contain 9 unique words.
44.44% of these words are shared.
55.56% of these words diverge.

Together, texts 1 and 3 contain 12 unique words.
41.67% of these words are shared.
58.33% of these words diverge.
```

Texts 1 and 3 share 41.67% of total words. The remaining 58.33% of words diverge. Meanwhile, texts 1 and 2 share 44.44% of total words. That percentage is higher, and thus we can infer that `text1` is more similar to `text2` than to `text3`.

We've essentially developed a simple metric for assessing similarities between texts. The metric works as follows:

1 Given two texts, extract a list of words from each text.
2 Count the unique words that are shared between the texts.
3 Divide the shared word count by the total unique words across both texts. Our output is a fraction of the total words shared between texts.

This similarity metric is referred to as the *Jaccard similarity*, or the *Jaccard index*.

The Jaccard similarity between texts 1 and 2 is illustrated in figure 13.2, where the texts are represented as two circles. The left circle corresponds to text 1, and the right circle corresponds to text 2. Each circle contains the words in its corresponding text. The two circles intersect, and their intersection contains all words that are shared between the texts. The Jaccard similarity equals the fraction of total words that are present in the intersection. Four of the nine words in the diagram appear in the intersection. Therefore, the Jaccard similarity is equal to 4 / 9.

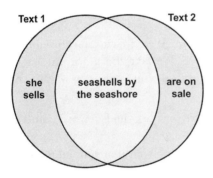

Figure 13.2 A visualized representation of the Jaccard similarity between two texts

13.1.1 *Exploring the Jaccard similarity*

The Jaccard similarity is a reasonable measure of text resemblance for the following reasons:

- The similarity takes into account both text overlap and text divergence.
- The fractional similarity is always between 0 and 1. The fraction is easy to interpret: 0 indicates that no words are shared, 0.5 indicates that half the words are shared, and 1 indicates that all the words are shared.
- The similarity is simple to implement.

Let's define a function to compute the Jaccard similarity.

Listing 13.9   Computing the Jaccard similarity

```
def jaccard_similarity(text_a, text_b):
    word_set_a, word_set_b = [set(simplify_text(text).split())
                              for text in [text_a, text_b]]
    num_shared = len(word_set_a & word_set_b)
    num_total = len(word_set_a | word_set_b)
    return num_shared / num_total

for text in [text2, text3]:
    similarity = jaccard_similarity(text1, text)
    print(f"The Jaccard similarity between '{text1}' and '{text}' "
          f"equals {similarity:.4f}." "\n")
```

```
The Jaccard similarity between 'She sells seashells by the seashore.' and
'"Seashells! The seashells are on sale! By the seashore."' equals 0.4444.

The Jaccard similarity between 'She sells seashells by the seashore.' and
'She sells 3 seashells to John, who lives by the lake.' equals 0.4167.
```

Our implementation of the Jaccard similarity is functional but not very efficient. The function executes two set-comparison operations: word_set_a & word_set_b and word_set_a | word_set_b. These operations compare and contrast all words between two sets. In Python, such comparisons are computationally costlier than streamlined numerical analysis.

How do we make the function more efficient? Well, we can start by eliminating the union computation word_set_a | word_set_b. We take the union in order to count the unique words between the sets, but there's a simpler way to obtain that count. Consider the following:

1 Adding len(word_set_a) and len(word_set_b) yields a word count where the shared words are counted twice.

2 Subtracting len(word_set_a & word_set_b) from that sum eliminates the double count. The final result equals len(word_set_a | word_set_b).

We can replace the union computation with len(word_set_a) + len(word_set_b) - num_shared, thus making our function more efficient. Let's modify the function while ensuring that our Jaccard output remains the same.

Listing 13.10   Efficiently computing the Jaccard similarity

```
def jaccard_similarity_efficient(text_a, text_b):
    word_set_a, word_set_b = [set(simplify_text(text).split())
                              for text in [text_a, text_b]]
    num_shared = len(word_set_a & word_set_b)
    num_total = len(word_set_a) + len(word_set_b) - num_shared   ◁──
    return num_shared / num_total

for text in [text2, text3]:
    similarity = jaccard_similarity_efficient(text1, text)
    assert similarity == jaccard_similarity(text1, text)
```

> **Unlike our previous jaccard_similarity function, here we compute num_total without executing any set-comparison operations.**

We've improved our Jaccard function. Unfortunately, the function still won't scale: it might run efficiently on hundreds of sentences but not on thousands of multisentence documents. The inefficiency is caused by our remaining set comparison, word_set_a & word_set_b. The operation is too slow to execute across thousands of complicated texts. Perhaps we can speed up the computation by somehow running it using NumPy. However, NumPy is intended to process numbers, not words, so we cannot use the library unless we replace all words with numeric values.

13.1.2 *Replacing words with numeric values*

Can we swap out words for numbers? Yes! We simply need to iterate over all words in all texts and assign each unique *i*th word a value of i. The mapping between words and their numeric values can be stored in a Python dictionary. We'll refer to this dictionary as our *vocabulary*. Let's build a vocabulary that covers all the words in our three texts. We'll also create a complementary value_to_word dictionary, which maps the numeric values back to words.

> **NOTE** Essentially, we're numbering all the words in the union of the texts. We iteratively choose a word and assign it a number, starting with zero. However, the order in which we choose the words is not important—we might as well reach blindly into a bag of words and pull the words out by random. That is why this technique is commonly referred to as the *bag-of-words* technique.

Listing 13.11 Assigning words to numbers in a vocabulary

```
words_set1, words_set2, words_set3 = words_sets
total_words = words_set1 | words_set2 | words_set3
vocabulary = {word : i for i, word in enumerate(total_words)}
value_to_word = {value: word for word, value in vocabulary.items()}
print(f"Our vocabulary contains {len(vocabulary)} words. "
      f"This vocabulary is:\n{vocabulary}")

Our vocabulary contains 15 words. This vocabulary is:
{'sells': 0, 'seashells': 1, 'to': 2, 'lake': 3, 'who': 4, 'by': 5,
 'on': 6, 'lives': 7, 'are': 8, 'sale': 9, 'seashore': 10, 'john': 11,
 '3': 12, 'the': 13, 'she': 14}
```

> **NOTE** The order of the words in the total_words variable in listing 13.11 may vary based on the installed version of Python. That order change will slightly alter certain figures used to display the texts later in this section. Setting total_words to equal ['sells', 'seashells', 'to', 'lake', 'who', 'by', 'on', 'lives', 'are', 'sale', 'seashore', 'john', '3', 'the', 'she'] will ensure consistency in the outputs.

Given our vocabulary, we can convert any text into a one-dimensional array of numbers. Mathematically, a 1D numeric array is called a *vector*. Hence, the process of converting text into a vector is called *text vectorization*.

NOTE Array dimensionality is different from data dimensionality. A data point has d dimensions if d coordinates are required to spatially represent that point. Meanwhile, an array has d dimensions if d values are required to describe the array's shape. Imagine that we have recorded five data points, each with three coordinates. Our data is three-dimensional because it can be plotted in 3D space. Additionally, we can store the data in a table containing five rows and three columns. That table has a two-element shape of (5, 3) and is therefore two-dimensional. Thus, we store our 3D data in a 2D array.

The simplest way to vectorize text is to create a vector of binary elements. Each index of that vector corresponds to a word in the vocabulary. Hence, the vector size equals the vocabulary size, even if some vocabulary words are missing from the associated text. If the word at index i is missing from the text, the *i*th vector element is set to 0. Otherwise, it is set to 1. Consequently, each vocabulary index in the vector maps to either 0 or 1.

For example, in vocabulary, the word *john* maps to a value of 11. Also, the word *john* is not present in text1. Thus, the vectorized representation of text1 has a 0 at index 11. Meanwhile, the word *john* is present in text3. Consequently, the vectorized representation of text3 has a 1 at index 11 (figure 13.3). In this manner, we can convert any text into a binary vector of 0s and 1s.

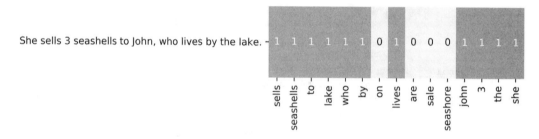

Figure 13.3   Text3 is converted into a binary vector. Each index in the vector corresponds to a word in the vocabulary. For example, index 0 corresponds to *sells*. This word is present in our text, so the first element of the vector is set to 1. Meanwhile, the words *on*, *are*, *sale*, and *seashore* are not present in the text. Their corresponding elements are thus set to 0 in the vector.

Let's use binary vectorization to convert all texts into NumPy arrays. We'll store the computed vectors in a 2D vectors list, which can be treated like a table. The table's rows will map to texts, and its columns will map to the vocabulary. Figure 13.4 visualizes the table as a heatmap using techniques discussed in section 8.

NOTE As discussed in section 8, heatmaps are best visualized using the Seaborn library.

Listing 13.12 Transforming words into binary vectors

```
import matplotlib.pyplot as plt
import numpy as np
import seaborn as sns

vectors = []
for i, words_set in enumerate(words_sets, 1):
    vector = np.array([0] * len(vocabulary))
    for word in words_set:
        vector[vocabulary[word]] = 1
    vectors.append(vector)

sns.heatmap(vectors, annot=True,   cmap='YlGnBu',
            xticklabels=vocabulary.keys(),
yticklabels=['Text 1', 'Text 2', 'Text 3'])
plt.yticks(rotation=0)
plt.show()
```

Generates an array of 0s. We can also generate this array by running np.zeros(len(vocabulary)).

As of Python 3.6, the dictionary keys method returns dictionary keys based on their order of insertion. In vocabulary, the order of insertion is equivalent to the word index.

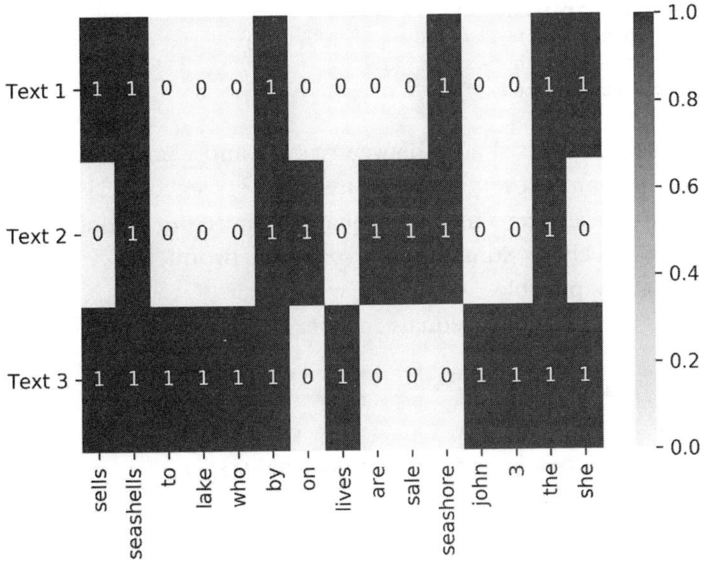

Figure 13.4   A table of vectorized texts. Rows correspond to labeled texts. Columns correspond to labeled words. Binary table elements are either 0 or 1. A nonzero value indicates the presence of a specified word in the specified text. Glancing at the table, we can immediately tell which words are shared across which texts.

Using our table, we can easily tell which words are shared between which texts. Take, for example, the word *sells*, which is tracked in the first column of the table. In that column, *sells* is assigned a 1 in the first and third rows of the table. These rows correspond to text1 and text3. Hence, we know that *sells* is shared between text1 and text3. More formally, the word is shared between the texts because vectors[0][0] == 1 and vectors[2][0] == 1. Furthermore, since both elements equal 1, their product must also equal 1. Consequently, the texts share a word in column i if the product of vectors[0][i] and vectors[2][i] is equal to 1.

Our binary vector representation allows us to extract shared words numerically. Suppose we wish to know whether the word in column i is present both in text1 and text2. If the associated vectors are labeled vector1 and vector2, then the word is present in both texts if vector1[i] * vector2[i] == 1. Here, we use pairwise vector multiplication to find all words shared by text1 and text2.

Listing 13.13   Finding shared words using vector arithmetic

```
vector1, vector2 = vectors[:2]
for i in range(len(vocabulary)):
    if vector1[i] * vector2[i]:
        shared_word = value_to_word[i]
        print(f"'{shared_word}' is present in both texts 1 and 2")

'seashells' is present in both texts 1 and 2
'by' is present in both texts 1 and 2
'seashore' is present in both texts 1 and 2
'the' is present in both texts 1 and 2
```

We've outputted all four words shared between text1 and text2. That shared word count is equal to the sum of every nonzero instance of vector1[i] * vector2[i]. Meanwhile, the sum of every zero instance equals 0. Therefore, we can compute the shared word count merely by summing the pairwise product of vector1[i] and vector2[i] across every possible i. In other words, sum(vector1[i] * vector2[i] for i in range(len(vocabulary))) equals len(words_set1 & words_set2).

Listing 13.14   Counting shared words using vector arithmetic

```
shared_word_count = sum(vector1[i] * vector2[i]
                        for i in range(len(vocabulary)))
assert shared_word_count == len(words_set1 & words_set2)
```

The sum of the pairwise products across all vector indices is called the *dot product*. Given two NumPy arrays vector_a and vector_b, we can compute their dot product by running vector_a.dot(vector_b). We can also compute the dot product using the @ operator by running vector_a @ vector_b. In our example, that dot product equals the number of shared words between texts 1 and 2, which of course also equals their intersection size. Thus, running vector1 @ vector2 produces a value that is equal to len(words_set1 & words_set2).

Listing 13.15   Computing a vector dot product using NumPy

```
assert vector1.dot(vector2) == shared_word_count
assert vector1 @ vector2 == shared_word_count
```

The dot product of vector1 and vector2 equals the shared word count between text1 and text2. Suppose that, instead, we take the dot product of vector1 with itself. That output should equal the number of words that text1 shares with text1. Stated more concisely, vector1 @ vector1 should equal the number of unique words in text1, which is also equal to len(words_set1). Let's confirm.

Listing 13.16 Counting total words using vector arithmetic

```
assert vector1 @ vector1 == len(words_set1)
assert vector2 @ vector2 == len(words_set2)
```

We are able to compute both shared word count and total unique word count using vector dot products. Essentially, we can compute the Jaccard similarity using only vector operations. This vectorized implementation of Jaccard is called the *Tanimoto similarity*.

Useful NumPy vector operations
- vector_a.dot(vector_b)—Returns the dot product between vector_a and vector_b. Equivalent to running sum(vector_a[i] * vector_b[i] for i in range(vector_a.size)).
- vector_b @ vector_b—Returns the dot product between vector_a and vector_b using the @ operator.
- binary_text_vector_a @ binary_text_vector_b—Returns the number of shared words between text_a and text_b.
- binary_text_vector_a @ binary_text_vector_a—Returns the number of unique words in text_a.

Let's define a tanimoto_similarity function. The function takes as input two vectors, vector_a and vector_b. Its output is equal to jaccard_similarity(text_a, text_b).

Listing 13.17 Computing text similarity using vector arithmetic

```
def tanimoto_similarity(vector_a, vector_b):
    num_shared = vector_a @ vector_b
    num_total = vector_a @ vector_a + vector_b @ vector_b - num_shared
    return num_shared / num_total

for i, text in enumerate([text2, text3], 1):
    similarity = tanimoto_similarity(vector1, vectors[i])
    assert similarity == jaccard_similarity(text1, text)
```

Our tanimoto_similarity function was intended to compare binary vectors. What would happen if we inputted two arrays with values other than 0 or 1? Technically, the function should return a similarity, but would that similarity make sense? For instance, vectors [5, 3] and [5, 2] are nearly identical. We expect their similarity to be nearly equal to 1. Let's test our expectations by inputting the vectors into `tanimoto_similarity`.

```
non_binary_vector1 = np.array([5, 3])
non_binary_vector2 = np.array([5, 2])
similarity = tanimoto_similarity(non_binary_vector1, non_binary_vector2)
print(f"The similarity of 2 non-binary vectors is {similarity}")

The similarity of 2 non-binary vectors is 0.96875
```

The outputted value is nearly equal to 1. Thus, `tanimoto_similarity` has successfully measured the similarity between two nearly identical vectors. The function can analyze non-binary inputs. This means we can use non-binary techniques to vectorize our texts before comparing their contents.

There are benefits to vectorizing texts in a non-binary way. Let's discuss these benefits in more detail.

13.2 *Vectorizing texts using word counts*

Binary vectorization captures the presence and absence of words in a text, but it doesn't capture word counts. This is unfortunate since word counts can provide a differentiating signal between texts. For example, suppose we're contrasting two texts: A and B. Text A mentions *Duck* 61 times and *Goose* twice. Text B mentions *Goose* 71 times and *Duck* only once. Based on the counts, we can infer that the two texts are rather different relative to the discussion of ducks and geese. That difference is not captured by binary vectorization, which assigns a 1 to the *Duck* index and *Goose* index of both texts. What if we replace all binary values with actual word counts? For instance, we can assign values of 61 and 2 to the *Duck* and *Goose* indices of vector A, while assigning 1 and 71 to the corresponding indices of vector B.

These assignments will produce vectors of word counts. A vector of word counts is commonly referred to as a *term-frequency vector*, or a *TF vector* for short. Let's compute the TF vectors of A and B using a two-element vocabulary {'duck': 0, 'goose': 1}. As a reminder, each word in the vocabulary maps to a vector index. Given the vocabulary, we can convert the texts into TF vectors [61, 2] and [1, 71]. Then we print the Tanimoto similarity of the two vectors.

```
similarity = tanimoto_similarity(np.array([61, 2]), np.array([1, 71]))
print(f"The similarity between texts is approximately {similarity:.3f}")

The similarity between texts is approximately 0.024
```

The TF vector similarity between the texts is very low. Let's compare it to the binary-vector similarity of the two texts. Each text has a binary-vector representation of [1, 1], and thus the binary similarity should equal 1.

Listing 13.20 Assessing identical vector similarity

```
assert tanimoto_similarity(np.array([1, 1]), np.array([1, 1])) == 1
```

Replacing binary values with word counts can greatly impact our similarity output. What will happen if we vectorize `text1`, `text2`, and `text3` based on their word counts? Let's find out. We start by computing TF vectors for each of the three texts using the word lists stored in `words_lists`. These vectors are visualized in figure 13.5 using a heatmap.

Listing 13.21 Computing TF vectors from word lists

```
tf_vectors = []
for i, words_list in enumerate(words_lists, 1):
    tf_vector = np.array([0] * len(vocabulary))
    for word in words_list:
        word_index = vocabulary[word]
        tf_vector[word_index] += 1          ◁─┐  Updates the word
                                              │  count using the word's
    tf_vectors.append(tf_vector)             │  vocabulary index
```

```
sns.heatmap(tf_vectors, cmap='YlGnBu', annot=True,
            xticklabels=vocabulary.keys(),
 yticklabels=['Text 1', 'Text 2', 'Text 3'])
plt.yticks(rotation=0)
plt.show()
```

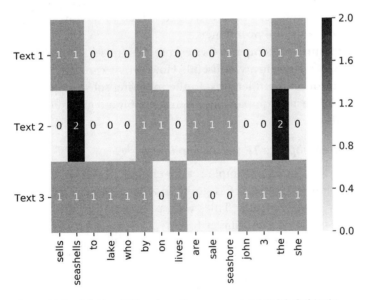

Figure 13.5 A table of TF vectors. Rows correspond to labeled texts. Columns correspond to labeled words. Each value indicates the count of a specified word in the specified text. Two words in the table are mentioned twice; all other words are mentioned no more than once.

The TF vectors of texts 1 and 3 are identical to previously seen binary vector outputs. However, the TF vector of text 2 is no longer binary since two words are mentioned more than once. How will this affect the similarity between `text1` and `text2`? Let's find out. The following code computes the TF vector similarity between `text1` and the other two texts. It also outputs the original binary vector similarity for comparison. Based on our observations, the similarity between `text1` and `text2` should shift, while the similarity between `text1` and `text3` should remain the same.

Listing 13.22   Comparing metrics of vector similarity

```
tf_vector1 = tf_vectors[0]
binary_vector1 = vectors[0]

for i, tf_vector in enumerate(tf_vectors[1:], 2):
    similarity = tanimoto_similarity(tf_vector1, tf_vector)
    old_similarity = tanimoto_similarity(binary_vector1, vectors[i - 1])
    print(f"The recomputed Tanimoto similarity between texts 1 and {i} is"
          f" {similarity:.4f}.")
    print(f"Previously, that similarity equaled {old_similarity:.4f} " "\n")
```

```
The recomputed Tanimoto similarity between texts 1 and 2 is 0.4615.
Previously, that similarity equaled 0.4444

The recomputed Tanimoto similarity between texts 1 and 3 is 0.4167.
Previously, that similarity equaled 0.4167
```

As expected, the similarity between `text1` and `text3` has stayed the same, while the similarity between `text1` and `text2` has increased. Thus, TF vectorization has made the affinity of the two texts more pronounced.

TF vectors yield improved comparisons because they're sensitive to count differences between texts. This sensitivity is useful. However, it can also be detrimental when comparing texts of different lengths. In the following subsection, we examine a flaw associated with TF vector comparison. Then we apply a technique called *normalization* to eliminate this flaw.

13.2.1   *Using normalization to improve TF vector similarity*

Imagine that you are testing a very simple search engine. The search engine takes a query and compares it to document titles stored in a database. The query's TF vector is compared to every vectorized title. Titles with a nonzero Tanimoto similarity are returned and ranked based on their similarity score.

Suppose you run a query for "Pepperoni Pizza" and the following two titles are returned:

- *Title A*—"Pepperoni Pizza! Pepperoni Pizza! Pepperoni Pizza!"
- *Title B*—"Pepperoni"

NOTE   These titles are purposefully oversimplified for easier visualization. Most real document titles are more complicated.

Which of our two titles best matches the query? Most data scientists would agree that title A is a better match than title B. Both title A and the query mention *pepperoni pizza*. Meanwhile, title B mentions only *pepperoni*. There is no indication that the associated document actually discusses pizza in any context.

Let's check whether title A ranks higher than title B relative to the query. We start by constructing TF vectors from a two-element vocabulary {pepperoni: 0, pizza: 1}.

Listing 13.23 Simple search engine vectorization

```
query_vector = np.array([1, 1])
title_a_vector = np.array([3, 3])
title_b_vector = np.array([1, 0])
```

We now compare the query to the titles and sort the titles based on the Tanimoto similarity.

Listing 13.24 Ranking titles by query similarity

```
titles = ["A: Pepperoni Pizza! Pepperoni Pizza! Pepperoni Pizza!",
          "B: Pepperoni"]
title_vectors = [title_a_vector, title_b_vector]
similarities = [tanimoto_similarity(query_vector, title_vector)
                for title_vector in title_vectors]

for index in sorted(range(len(titles)), key=lambda i: similarities[i],
                    reverse=True):
    title = titles[index]
    similarity = similarities[index]
    print(f"'{title}' has a query similarity of {similarity:.4f}")

'B: Pepperoni' has a query similarity of 0.5000
'A: Pepperoni Pizza! Pepperoni Pizza! Pepperoni Pizza!' has a query
    similarity of 0.4286
```

Unfortunately, title A outranks title B. This discrepancy in rankings is caused by text size. Title A has three times as many words as the query, while title B and the query differ by just a single word. Superficially, this difference can be used to distinguish texts by size. However, in our search engine, the size signal leads to faulty rankings. We need to subdue the influence of text size on ranked results. One naive approach is to just divide title_a_vector by 3. The division yields an output that is equal to query_vector. Therefore, running tanimoto_similarity(query_vector, title_a_vector / 3) should return a similarity of 1.

Listing 13.25 Eliminating size differences through division

```
assert np.array_equal(query_vector, title_a_vector / 3)
assert tanimoto_similarity(query_vector,
                           title_a_vector / 3) == 1
```

Using simple division, we can manipulate `title_a_vector` to equal `query_vector`. Such manipulation is not possible for `title_b_vector`. Why is this the case? To illustrate the answer, we need to plot all three vectors in 2D space.

How can we visualize our vectors? Well, from a mathematical standpoint, all vectors are geometric objects. Mathematicians treat every vector v as a line stretching from the origin to the numerical coordinates in v. Essentially, our three vectors are merely 2D line segments rising from the origin. We can visualize the segments in a 2D plot where the x-axis represents mentions of *pepperoni* and the y-axis represents mentions of *pizza* (figure 13.6).

Listing 13.26   Plotting TF vectors in 2D space

```
plt.plot([0, query_vector[0]], [0, query_vector[1]], c='k',
        linewidth=3, label='Query Vector')
plt.plot([0, title_a_vector[0]], [0, title_a_vector[1]], c='b',
        linestyle='--', label='Title A Vector')
plt.plot([0, title_b_vector[0]], [0, title_b_vector[1]], c='g',
        linewidth=2, linestyle='-.', label='Title B Vector')
plt.xlabel('Pepperoni')
plt.ylabel('Pizza')
plt.legend()
plt.show()
```

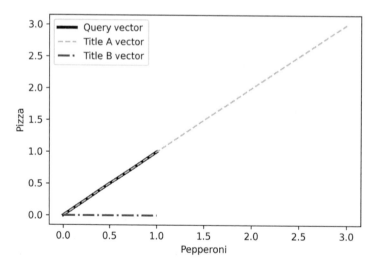

Figure 13.6   Three TF vectors have been plotted as lines in 2D space. Each vector stretches from the origin to its two-dimensional coordinates. The query vector and the title A vector both face in the same direction. The angle between these vectors is zero. However, one of the lines is three times as long as the other. Adjusting the segment lengths will force the two vectors to be identical.

In our plot, `title_a_vector` and `query_vector` point in the same direction. The only difference between the two lines is that `title_a_vector` is three times as long. Shrinking `title_a_vector` will force the two lines to be identical. Meanwhile, `title_b_vector` and `query_vector` point in different directions. We cannot make these vectors overlap. Shrinking or lengthening `title_b_vector` will not yield alignment with the other two line segments.

We've gained some insight by representing our vectors as line segments. These segments have geometric lengths. Hence, every vector has a geometric length, which is called the *magnitude*. The magnitude is also called the *Euclidean norm* or the *L2 norm*. All vectors have a magnitude, even those that can't be plotted in two dimensions. For instance, in figure 13.7, we illustrate the magnitude of a 3D vector associated with *Pepperoni Pizza Pie*.

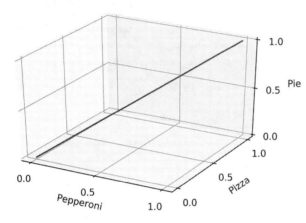

Figure 13.7 **The plotted TF vector representation of the three-word title *Pepperoni Pizza Pie*. This 3D vector stretches from the origin to its coordinates of (1, 1, 1). According to the Pythagorean theorem, the length of the plotted 3D segment is equal to** `(1 + 1 + 1) ** 0.5`. **That length is referred to as the *magnitude* of the vector.**

Measuring the magnitude allows us to account for differences in geometric lengths. There are several ways to compute the magnitude in Python. Given vector v, we can measure the magnitude naively by measuring the Euclidean distance between v and the origin. We can also find the magnitude using NumPy by running `np.linalg.norm(v)`. Finally, we can compute the magnitude using the Pythagorean theorem (figure 13.8).

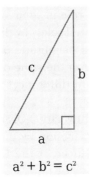

$$a^2 + b^2 = c^2$$

Figure 13.8 **Using the Pythagorean theorem to compute the magnitude of a vector. Generally, a two-dimensional vector [a, b] can be represented by a right triangle. The perpendicular segments of the triangle have lengths a and b. Meanwhile, the length of the triangle's hypotenuse is equal to c. According to the Pythagorean theorem,** `c * c == a * a + b * b`. **Hence, the vector's magnitude is equal to** `sum([value * value for value in vector]) ** 0.5`. **This formula extends beyond 2D to any arbitrary number of dimensions.**

According to the Pythagorean theorem, the squared distance of coordinate v to the origin is equal to sum([value * value for value in v]). This dovetails nicely with our earlier definition of the dot product. As a reminder, the dot product of two vectors v1 and v2 equals sum([value1 * value2 for value1, value2 in zip(v1, v2)]). Consequently, the dot product of v with itself equals sum([value * value for value in v]). Hence, the magnitude of v equals (v @ v) ** 0.5.

Let's output the magnitudes of our search engine vectors. Based on our observations, the magnitude of title_a_vector should equal three times the magnitude of query_vector.

Listing 13.27 Computing vector magnitude

```
from scipy.spatial.distance import euclidean          The magnitude equals the
from numpy.linalg import norm                          Euclidean distance between
                                                       the vector and the origin.
vector_names = ['Query Vector', 'Title A Vector', 'Title B Vector']
tf_search_vectors = [query_vector, title_a_vector, title_b_vector]
origin = np.array([0, 0])
for name, tf_vector in zip(vector_names, tf_search_vectors):
    magnitude = euclidean(tf_vector, origin)           ◁
    assert magnitude == norm(tf_vector)                ◁
    assert magnitude == (tf_vector @ tf_vector) ** 0.5  ◁
    print(f"{name}'s magnitude is approximately {magnitude:.4f}")

magnitude_ratio = norm(title_a_vector) / norm(query_vector)
print(f"\nVector A is {magnitude_ratio:.0f}x as long as Query Vector")
```

We can also compute the magnitude using the dot product.

```
Query Vector's magnitude is approximately 1.4142
Title A Vector's magnitude is approximately 4.2426
Title B Vector's magnitude is approximately 1.0000

Vector A is 3x as long as Query Vector
```

NumPy's norm function returns the magnitude.

As expected, there is a threefold difference between the magnitudes of query_vector and title_a_vector. Furthermore, the magnitudes of both vectors are greater than 1. Meanwhile, the magnitude of title_vector_b is equal to exactly 1. A vector with a magnitude of 1 is referred to as a *unit vector*. Unit vectors have many useful properties, which we discuss shortly. One benefit of unit vectors is that they are easy to compare: since unit vectors share an equal magnitude, it doesn't play a role in their similarity. Fundamentally, the difference between unit vectors is determined solely by direction.

Imagine if title_a_vector and query_vector both had a magnitude of 1. As a consequence, they'd share an equal length while also pointing in the same direction. In essence, the two vectors would be identical. The word count differences between our query and title A would no longer matter.

To illustrate this point, let's convert our TF vectors into unit vectors. Dividing any vector by its magnitude transforms that magnitude to 1. That division by the magnitude is called *normalization*, since the magnitude is also referenced as the L2 norm. Running v / norm(v) returns a *normalized vector* with a magnitude of 1.

We now normalize our vectors and generate a unit vector plot (figure 13.9). In the plot, two of the vectors should be identical.

Listing 13.28   Plotting normalized vectors

> The two normalized unit vectors are now identical. We use np.allclose to confirm, rather than np.array_equal, to compensate for minuscule floating-point errors that may occur during normalization.

```
unit_query_vector = query_vector / norm(query_vector)
unit_title_a_vector = title_a_vector / norm(title_a_vector)
assert np.allclose(unit_query_vector, unit_title_a_vector)      ◁
unit_title_b_vector = title_b_vector                        ◁

plt.plot([0, unit_query_vector[0]], [0, unit_query_vector[1]], c='k',
         linewidth=3, label='Normalized Query Vector')
plt.plot([0, unit_title_a_vector[0]], [0, unit_title_a_vector[1]], c='b',
         linestyle='--', label='Normalized Title A Vector')
plt.plot([0, unit_title_b_vector[0]], [0, unit_title_b_vector[1]], c='g',
         linewidth=2, linestyle='-.', label='Title B Vector')

plt.axis('equal')
plt.legend()
plt.show()
```

> This vector is already a unit vector. There is no need to normalize.

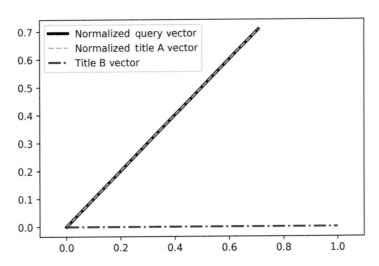

Figure 13.9   Our vectors have been normalized. All plotted vectors now have a magnitude of 1. The normalized query vector and normalized title A vector are identical in the plot.

The normalized query vector and the normalized title A vector are now indistinguishable. All differences arising from text size have been eliminated. Meanwhile, the location of the title B vector diverges from the query vector because the two segments point in different directions. If we rank our unit vectors based on their similarity to unit_query_vector, then unit_title_a_vector outranks unit_title_b_vector. As a consequence, title A outranks title B relative to the query.

Listing 13.29 Ranking titles by unit vector similarity

```
unit_title_vectors = [unit_title_a_vector, unit_title_b_vector]
similarities = [tanimoto_similarity(unit_query_vector, unit_title_vector)
                for unit_title_vector in unit_title_vectors]

for index in sorted(range(len(titles)), key=lambda i: similarities[i],
                    reverse=True):
    title = titles[index]
    similarity = similarities[index]
    print(f"'{title}' has a normalized query similarity of {similarity:.4f}")
```

```
'A: Pepperoni Pizza! Pepperoni Pizza! Pepperoni Pizza!' has a normalized
 query similarity of 1.0000
'B: Pepperoni' has a normalized query similarity of 0.5469
```

Common vector magnitude operations

- euclidean(vector, vector.size * [0])—Returns the vector's magnitude, which equals the Euclidean distance between vector and the origin
- norm(vector)—Returns the vector's magnitude using NumPy's norm function
- (vector @ vector) ** 0.5—Computes the vector's magnitude using the Pythagorean theorem
- vector / norm(vector)—Normalizes the vector so that its magnitude equals 1.0

Vector normalization has fixed a flaw in our search engine: the search engine is no longer overly sensitive to title length. In the process, we have inadvertently made our Tanimoto computation more efficient. Let's discuss why.

Suppose we measure the Tanimoto similarity of two unit vectors, u1 and u2. Logically, we can infer the following:

- The Tanimoto similarity equals u1 @ u2 / (u1 @ u1 + u2 @ u2 - u1 @ u2).
- u1 @ u1 equals norm(u1) ** 2. Based on our previous discussions, we know that u1 @ u1 equals the squared magnitude of u.
- u1 is a unit vector, so norm(u1) equals 1. Therefore, norm(u1) ** 2 equals 1. Thus u1 @ u1 equals 1.
- By that same logic, u2 @ u2 also equals 1.
- Hence, the Tanimoto similarity reduces to u1 @ u2 / (2 - u1 @ u2).

Taking the dot product of each vector with itself is no longer necessary. The only required vector computation is u1 @ u2.

Let's define a normalized_tanimoto function. The function takes as input two normalized vectors, u1 and u2, and computes their Tanimoto similarity directly from u1 @ u2. That result equals tanimoto_similarity(u1, u2).

Listing 13.30   Computing a unit vector Tanimoto similarity

```
def normalized_tanimoto(u1, u2):
    dot_product = u1 @ u2
    return dot_product / (2 - dot_product)

for unit_title_vector in unit_title_vectors[1:]:
    similarity = normalized_tanimoto(unit_query_vector, unit_title_vector)
    assert similarity == tanimoto_similarity(unit_query_vector,
                                             unit_title_vector)
```

The dot product of two unit vectors is a very special value. It can easily be converted into the angle between the vectors and also into the spatial distance between them. Why is this important? Well, common geometric metrics like vector angle and distance appear in all vector analysis libraries. Meanwhile, the Tanimoto similarity is used less frequently outside of NLP. It usually needs to be implemented from scratch, which can have serious real-world consequences. Imagine the following scenario. You're hired by a search engine company to improve all its pizza-related queries. You propose to use the normalized Tanimoto similarity as a metric of query relevance. However, your manager objects: they insist that, based on company policy, employees can only use relevance metrics that are already included in scikit-learn.

> **NOTE**   Sadly, this scenario is entirely realistic. Most organizations tend to validate their core metrics for both speed and quality. In large organizations, the validation process can take months. Thus, it's usually easier to rely on a prevalidated library than validate a brand-new metric.

The manager points you to the scikit-learn documentation that outlines the acceptable metric functions (http://mng.bz/9aM1). You see the scikit-learn metric names and functions displayed in the two-column table shown in figure 13.10. Multiple versions of a name can map to the same function. Four of the eight metrics refer to the Euclidean distance, and three refer to the Manhattan and Haversine (aka great circle) distances, which we introduced in section 11. Also, there's a reference to a metric called `'cosine'`, which we haven't yet discussed. There is no mention of a Tanimoto metric, so you can't use it to evaluate query relevance. What should you do?

The valid distance metrics, and the function they map to, are:

metric	Function
'cityblock'	metrics.pairwise.manhattan_distances
'cosine'	metrics.pairwise.cosine_distances
'euclidean'	metrics.pairwise.euclidean_distances
'haversine'	metrics.pairwise.haversine_distances
'l1'	metrics.pairwise.manhattan_distances
'l2'	metrics.pairwise.euclidean_distances
'manhattan'	metrics.pairwise.manhattan_distances
'nan_euclidean'	metrics.pairwise.nan_euclidean_distances

Figure 13.10   A screenshot of the scikit-learn document for valid distance metric implementations

Fortunately, math gives you a way out. If your vectors are normalized, their Tanimoto similarity can be substituted with the Euclidean and cosine metrics. This is because all three measures are very closely related to the normalized dot product. Let's examine why this is the case.

13.2.2 *Using unit vector dot products to convert between relevance metrics*

The unit vector dot product unites multiple types of comparison metrics. We've just seen how `tanimoto_similarity(u1, u2)` is a direct function of `u1 @ u2`. As it turns out, the Euclidean distance between unit vectors is also a function of `u1 @ u2`. It's not difficult to prove that `euclidean(u1, u2)` equals `(2 - 2* u1 @ u2) ** 0.5`. Additionally, the angle between linear unit vectors is likewise dependent on `u1 @ u2`. These relationships are illustrated in figure 13.11.

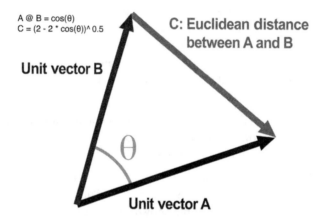

Figure 13.11   Two unit vectors, A and B. The angle between the vectors equals θ. The dot product of the vectors equals cosine(θ). C represents the Euclidean distance between the vectors, which equals $(2 - 2 * cosine(\theta))^{0.5}$.

Geometrically, the dot product of two unit vectors equals the cosine of the angle between them. Due to its equivalence with the cosine, the dot product of two unit vectors is commonly referred to as the *cosine similarity*. Given the cosine similarity `cs`, we can convert it to either Euclidean distance or the Tanimoto similarity by running `(2 - 2 * cs) ** 0.5` or `cs / (2 - cs)`, respectively.

> **NOTE** The cosine is a very important function in trigonometry. It maps an angle between lines to a value ranging from –1 to 1. If two lines point in an identical direction, then the angle between them is 0, and the cosine of the angle equals 1. If two lines point in opposite directions, then the angle between them is 180 degrees, and the cosine of that angle equals –1. Given a pair of vectors `v1` and `v2`, we can compute their cosine similarity by running

`(v1 / norm(v1)) @ (v2 / norm(v2))`. Then we can input that result into the inverse cosine function `np.arccos` to measure the angle between the vectors.

Listing 13.31 illustrates how easy it is to convert between the Tanimoto similarity, the cosine similarity, and the Euclidean distance. We compute the Tanimoto similarity between the query vector and each of our unit title vectors. The Tanimoto similarity is subsequently converted into the cosine similarity, and then the cosine similarity is converted into the Euclidean distance.

NOTE Additionally, we utilize the cosine similarity to compute the angle between the vectors. We do this to emphasize how the cosine metric reflects the angle between line segments.

Listing 13.31 Converting between unit vector metrics

```
unit_vector_names = ['Normalized Title A vector', 'Title B Vector']
u1 = unit_query_vector

for unit_vector_name, u2 in zip(unit_vector_names, unit_title_vectors):
    similarity = normalized_tanimoto(u1, u2)
    cosine_similarity  = 2 * similarity / (1 + similarity)     ◁──────┐
    assert cosine_similarity == u1 @ u2
    angle = np.arccos(cosine_similarity)
    euclidean_distance = (2 - 2 * cosine_similarity) ** 0.5
    assert round(euclidean_distance, 10) == round(euclidean(u1, u2), 10)
    measurements = {'Tanimoto similarity': similarity,
                    'cosine similarity': cosine_similarity,
                    'Euclidean distance': euclidean_distance,
                    'angle': np.degrees(angle)}

    print("We are comparing Normalized Query Vector and "
          f"{unit_vector_name}")
    for measurement_type, value in measurements.items():
        output = f"The {measurement_type} between vectors is {value:.4f}"
        if measurement_type == 'angle':
            output += ' degrees\n'

    print(output)
```

`normalized_tanimoto` is a function of `cosine_similarity`. Using basic algebra, we can invert the function to solve for `cosine_similarity`.

```
We are comparing Normalized Query Vector and Normalized Title A vector
The Tanimoto similarity between vectors is 1.0000
The cosine similarity between vectors is 1.0000
The Euclidean distance between vectors is 0.0000
The angle between vectors is 0.0000 degrees

We are comparing Normalized Query Vector and Title B Vector
The Tanimoto similarity between vectors is 0.5469
The cosine similarity between vectors is 0.7071
The Euclidean distance between vectors is 0.7654
The angle between vectors is 45.0000 degrees
```

The Tanimoto similarity between normalized vectors can be transformed into other metrics of similarity or distance. This is useful for the following reasons:

- Swapping the Tanimoto similarity for Euclidean distance allows us to carry out K-means clustering on text data. We discuss K-means clustering of texts in section 15.
- Swapping the Tanimoto similarity for cosine similarity simplifies our computational requirements. All our computations are reduced to basic dot product operations.

NOTE   NLP practitioners commonly use the cosine similarity instead of the Tanimoto similarity. Research shows that in the long term, the Tanimoto similarity is more accurate than the cosine similarity. However, in many practical applications, the two similarities are interchangeable.

Common unit vector comparison metrics
- `u1 @ u2`—The cosine of the angle between unit vectors `u1` and `u2`
- `(u1 @ u2) / (2 - u1 @ u2)`—The Tanimoto similarity between unit vectors `u1` and `u2`
- `(2 - 2 * u1 @ u2) ** 0.5`—The Euclidean distance between unit vectors `u1` and `u2`

Vector normalization allows us to swap between multiple comparison metrics. Other benefits of normalization include these:

- *Elimination of text length as a differentiating signal*—This lets us compare long and short texts with similar contents.
- *More efficient Tanimoto similarity computation*—Only a single dot product operation is required.
- *More efficient computation of the similarity between every pair of vectors*—This is called the *all-by-all* similarity.

The last benefit has not yet been discussed. However, we will shortly learn that a table of cross-text similarities can be elegantly computed using *matrix multiplication*. In mathematics, matrix multiplication generalizes the dot product from one-dimensional vectors to two-dimensional arrays. The generalized dot product leads to the efficient computation of similarities across all pairs of texts.

13.3   *Matrix multiplication for efficient similarity calculation*

When analyzing our *seashell*-centric texts, we compared each text pair individually. What if, instead, we visualized all pairwise similarities in a table? The rows and columns would correspond to individual texts, while the elements would correspond to Tanimoto similarities. The table would provide us with a bird's-eye view of all the relationships between texts. We would finally learn whether `text2` is more similar to `text1` or `text3`.

Let's generate a table of normalized Tanimoto similarities, using the process outlined in figure 13.12. We start by normalizing the TF vectors in our previously precomputed `tf_vectors` list. Then we iterate over every pair of vectors and compute their Tanimoto similarity. We store the similarities in a 2D `similarities` array, where `similarities[i][j]` equals the similarities between the *i*th text and the *j*th text. Finally, we visualize the `similarities` array using a heatmap (figure 13.13).

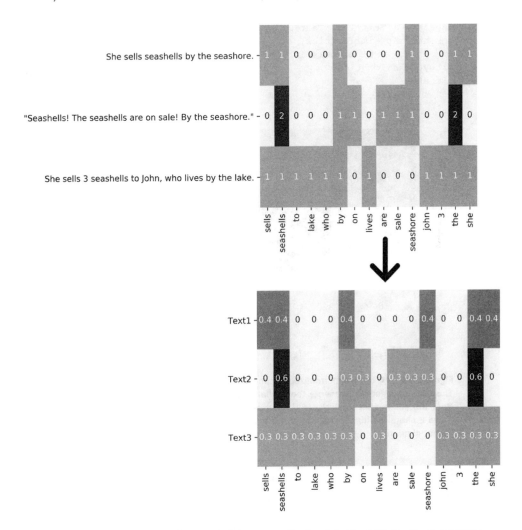

Figure 13.12 Transforming our three texts into a normalized matrix. The initial texts appear in the upper-left corner. These texts share a vocabulary of 15 unique words. We use the vocabulary to transform the texts into a matrix of word counts, which is in the upper-right corner. Its three rows correspond to the three texts, and its 15 columns track the occurrence count of every word in each text. We normalize these counts by dividing each row by its magnitude. The normalization produces the matrix in the lower-right corner. The dot product between any two rows in the normalized matrix equals the cosine similarity between the corresponding texts. Subsequently, running `cos / (2 - cos)` transforms the cosine similarity into the Tanimoto similarity.

Listing 13.32   Computing a table of normalized Tanimoto similarities

```
num_texts = len(tf_vectors)
similarities = np.array([[0.0] * num_texts for _ in range(num_texts)])
unit_vectors = np.array([vector / norm(vector) for vector in tf_vectors])
for i, vector_a in enumerate(unit_vectors):
    for j, vector_b in enumerate(unit_vectors):
        similarities[i][j] = normalized_tanimoto(vector_a, vector_b)

labels = ['Text 1', 'Text 2', 'Text 3']
sns.heatmap(similarities,  cmap='YlGnBu', annot=True,
        xticklabels=labels, yticklabels=labels)
plt.yticks(rotation=0)
plt.show()
```

> Creates a 2D array containing just zeros. We can more efficiently create this array by running np.zeros((num_texts, num_texts)). We fill this empty array with similarities between texts.

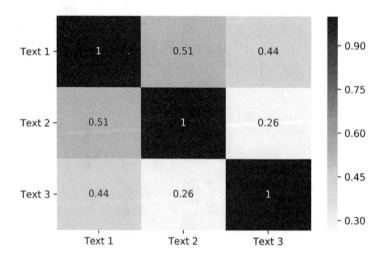

Figure 13.13   A table of normalized Tanimoto similarities across text pairs. The table's diagonal represents the similarity between each text and itself. Not surprisingly, that similarity is 1. Ignoring the diagonal, we see that texts 1 and 2 share the highest similarity. Meanwhile, texts 2 and 3 share the lowest similarity.

Looking at the table is informative. We can immediately tell which text pairs share the highest similarity. However, our table computation relied on inefficient code. The following computations are redundant and can be eliminated.

- The creation of an empty three-by-three array
- The nested for loop iteration across all pairwise vector combinations
- The individual computation of each pairwise vector similarity

We can purge our code of these operations using matrix multiplication. However, first we need to introduce basic matrix operations.

13.3.1 Basic matrix operations

Matrix operations power many subfields of data science, including NLP, network analysis, and machine learning. Therefore, knowing the basics of matrix manipulation is crucial for our data science careers. A *matrix* is the extension of a one-dimensional vector to two dimensions. In other words, a matrix is just a table of numbers. By that definition, `similarities` is a matrix, and so is `unit_vectors`. Most numeric tables discussed in this book are also naturally matrices.

> **NOTE** Every matrix is a numeric table, but not every numeric table is a matrix. All matrix rows must share an equal length. The same is true of all matrix columns. Thus, if a table contains both a five-element column and a seven-element column, it is not a matrix.

Since matrices are tables, they can be analyzed using Pandas. Conversely, numeric tables can be handled using 2D NumPy arrays. Both matrix representations are valid. In fact, Pandas DataFrames and NumPy arrays can sometimes be used interchangeably, because they share certain attributes. For instance, `matrix.shape` returns a count of rows and columns, regardless of whether `matrix` is a DataFrame or an array. Likewise, `matrix.T` transposes rows and columns, regardless of `matrix` type. Let's confirm.

Listing 13.33 Comparing Pandas and NumPy matrix attributes

```
import pandas as pd

matrices = [unit_vectors, pd.DataFrame(unit_vectors)]
matrix_types = ['2D NumPy array', 'Pandas DataFrame']

for matrix_type, matrix in zip(matrix_types, matrices):
    row_count, column_count = matrix.shape
    print(f"Our {matrix_type} contains "
        f"{row_count} rows and {column_count} columns")
    assert (column_count, row_count) == matrix.T.shape
```

Transposing the matrix flips the rows and columns.

```
Our 2D NumPy array contains 3 rows and 15 columns
Our Pandas DataFrame contains 3 rows and 15 columns
```

Pandas and NumPy table structures are similar. Nonetheless, there are certain benefits to storing matrices in 2D NumPy arrays. One immediate benefit is NumPy's integration of Python's built-in arithmetic operators: we can run basic arithmetic operations directly on NumPy arrays.

NUMPY MATRIX ARITHMETIC OPERATIONS

Occasionally in NLP we need to modify a matrix using basic arithmetic. Suppose, for instance, that we wish to compare a collection of documents based on both their bodies and titles. We hypothesize that title similarity is twice as important as body similarity since documents with similar titles are very likely to be thematically related. We thus decide to double the title similarity matrix to better weigh it relative to the body.

NOTE   This relative importance of title versus body is particularly true in news articles. Two articles that share a similar title are very likely to refer to the same news story, even if their bodies offer different perspectives on that story. A good heuristic for measuring news article similarity is to compute `2 * title_similarity + body_similarity`.

Doubling the values of a matrix is very easy to do in NumPy. For example, we can double our `similarities` matrix by running `2 * similarities`. We can also add `similarities` directly to itself by running `similarities + similarities`. Of course, the two arithmetic outputs will be equal. Meanwhile, running `similarities - similarities` will return a matrix of 0s. Furthermore, running `similarities - similarities - 1` will subtract 1 from each of the zeros.

NOTE   We are subtracting `similarities + 1` from `similarities` simply to show the arithmetic flexibility of NumPy. Normally, there's no valid reason to return this operation unless we really need a matrix of negative 1s.

Listing 13.34   NumPy array addition and subtraction

```
double_similarities = 2 * similarities
np.array_equal(double_similarities, similarities + similarities)
zero_matrix = similarities - similarities
negative_1_matrix = similarities - similarities - 1

for i in range(similarities.shape[0]):
    for j in range(similarities.shape[1]):
        assert double_similarities[i][j] == 2 * similarities[i][j]
        assert zero_matrix[i][j] == 0
        assert negative_1_matrix[i][j] == -1
```

In the same manner, we can multiply and divide NumPy arrays. Running `similarities / similarities` will divide each similarity by itself, thus returning a matrix of 1s. Meanwhile, running `similarities * similarities` will return a matrix of squared similarity values.

Listing 13.35   NumPy array multiplication and division

```
squared_similarities = similarities * similarities
assert np.array_equal(squared_similarities, similarities ** 2)
ones_matrix = similarities / similarities

for i in range(similarities.shape[0]):
    for j in range(similarities.shape[1]):
        assert squared_similarities[i][j] == similarities[i][j] ** 2
        assert ones_matrix[i][j] == 1
```

Matrix arithmetic lets us conveniently transition between similarity matrix types. For instance, we can convert our Tanimoto matrix into a cosine similarity matrix simply by running `2 * similarities / (1 + similarities)`. Thus, if we wish to compare the

Tanimoto similarity with the more popular cosine similarity, we can compute the second cosine matrix in just a single line of code.

Listing 13.36 Converting between matrix similarity-types

```
cosine_similarities  = 2 * similarities / (1 + similarities)
for i in range(similarities.shape[0]):
    for j in range(similarities.shape[1]):
        cosine_sim = unit_vectors[i] @ unit_vectors[j]
        assert round(cosine_similarities[i][j],
                     15) == round(cosine_sim, 15)
```

Confirms that the cosine similarity equals the actual vector dot product

Rounds the results because of floating-point errors

NumPy 2D arrays confer additional benefits over Pandas. Accessing rows and columns by index is much more straightforward in NumPy.

NUMPY MATRIX ROW AND COLUMN OPERATIONS

Given any 2D `matrix` array, we can access the row at index i by running `matrix[i]`. Likewise, we can access the column at index j by running `matrix[:,j]`. Let's use NumPy indexing to print the first row and column of both `unit_vectors` and `similarities`.

Listing 13.37 Accessing NumPy matrix rows and columns

```
for name, matrix in [('Similarities', similarities),
                     ('Unit Vectors', unit_vectors)]:
    print(f"Accessing rows and columns in the {name} Matrix.")
    row, column = matrix[0], matrix[:,0]
    print(f"Row at index 0 is:\n{row}")
    print(f"\nColumn at index 0 is:\n{column}\n")
```

```
Accessing rows and columns in the Similarities Matrix.
Row at index 0 is:
[1.         0.51442439 0.44452044]

Column at index 0 is:
[1.         0.51442439 0.44452044]

Accessing rows and columns in the Unit Vectors Matrix.
Row at index 0 is:
[0.40824829 0.40824829 0.         0.40824829 0.         0.
 0.         0.40824829 0.         0.         0.40824829 0.
 0.         0.         0.40824829]

Column at index 0 is:
[0.40824829 0.         0.30151134]
```

All printed rows and columns are one-dimensional NumPy arrays. Given two arrays, we can compute their dot product, but only if the array lengths are the same. In our output, both `similarities[0].size` and `unit_vectors[:,0].size` are equal to 3. Hence, we can take the dot product between the first row of `similarities` and the first column of `unit_vectors`. This particular row-to-column dot product is not useful in our text analysis, but it serves to illustrate our ability to easily compute the dot product between matrix rows and matrix columns. A little later, we will use that ability to compute text vector similarities with great efficiency.

Listing 13.38 Computing the dot product between a row and column

```
row = similarities[0]
column = unit_vectors[:,0]
dot_product = row @ column
print(f"The dot product between the row and column is: {dot_product:.4f}")

The dot product between the row and column is: 0.5423
```

In that same vein, we can take the dot product between every row in `similarities` and every column in `unit_vectors`. Let's print all possible dot product results.

Listing 13.39 Computing dot products between all rows and columns

```
num_rows = similarities.shape[0]
num_columns = unit_vectors.shape[1]
for i in range(num_rows):
    for j in range(num_columns):
        row = similarities[i]
        column = unit_vectors[:,j]
        dot_product = row @ column
        print(f"The dot product between row {i} column {j} is: "
              f"{dot_product:.4f}")

The dot product between row 0 column 0 is: 0.5423
The dot product between row 0 column 1 is: 0.8276
The dot product between row 0 column 2 is: 0.1340
The dot product between row 0 column 3 is: 0.6850
The dot product between row 0 column 4 is: 0.1427
The dot product between row 0 column 5 is: 0.1340
The dot product between row 0 column 6 is: 0.1427
The dot product between row 0 column 7 is: 0.5423
The dot product between row 0 column 8 is: 0.1340
The dot product between row 0 column 9 is: 0.1340
The dot product between row 0 column 10 is: 0.8276
The dot product between row 0 column 11 is: 0.1340
The dot product between row 0 column 12 is: 0.1340
The dot product between row 0 column 13 is: 0.1427
The dot product between row 0 column 14 is: 0.5509
The dot product between row 1 column 0 is: 0.2897
The dot product between row 1 column 1 is: 0.8444
The dot product between row 1 column 2 is: 0.0797
The dot product between row 1 column 3 is: 0.5671
The dot product between row 1 column 4 is: 0.2774
The dot product between row 1 column 5 is: 0.0797
The dot product between row 1 column 6 is: 0.2774
The dot product between row 1 column 7 is: 0.2897
The dot product between row 1 column 8 is: 0.0797
The dot product between row 1 column 9 is: 0.0797
The dot product between row 1 column 10 is: 0.8444
The dot product between row 1 column 11 is: 0.0797
```

```
The dot product between row 1 column 12 is: 0.0797
The dot product between row 1 column 13 is: 0.2774
The dot product between row 1 column 14 is: 0.4874
The dot product between row 2 column 0 is: 0.4830
The dot product between row 2 column 1 is: 0.6296
The dot product between row 2 column 2 is: 0.3015
The dot product between row 2 column 3 is: 0.5563
The dot product between row 2 column 4 is: 0.0733
The dot product between row 2 column 5 is: 0.3015
The dot product between row 2 column 6 is: 0.0733
The dot product between row 2 column 7 is: 0.4830
The dot product between row 2 column 8 is: 0.3015
The dot product between row 2 column 9 is: 0.3015
The dot product between row 2 column 10 is: 0.6296
The dot product between row 2 column 11 is: 0.3015
The dot product between row 2 column 12 is: 0.3015
The dot product between row 2 column 13 is: 0.0733
The dot product between row 2 column 14 is: 0.2548
```

We've generated 45 dot products: one for each row, column combination. Our printed outputs are excessive. These outputs can be stored more concisely in a table called dot_products, where dot_products[i][j] is equal to similarities[i] @ unit_vectors[:,j]. Of course, by definition, that table is a matrix.

Listing 13.40   Storing all-by-all dot products in a matrix

```
dot_products = np.zeros((num_rows, num_columns))      ◁──┐ Returns an empty
for i in range(num_rows):                                │ array of zeros
    for j in range(num_columns):
        dot_products[i][j] = similarities[i] @ unit_vectors[:,j]

print(dot_products)

[[0.54227624 0.82762755 0.13402795 0.6849519  0.14267565 0.13402795
  0.14267565 0.54227624 0.13402795 0.13402795 0.82762755 0.13402795
  0.13402795 0.14267565 0.55092394]
 [0.28970812 0.84440831 0.07969524 0.56705821 0.2773501  0.07969524
  0.2773501  0.28970812 0.07969524 0.07969524 0.84440831 0.07969524
  0.07969524 0.2773501  0.48736297]
 [0.48298605 0.62960397 0.30151134 0.55629501 0.07330896 0.30151134
  0.07330896 0.48298605 0.30151134 0.30151134 0.62960397 0.30151134
  0.30151134 0.07330896 0.25478367]]
```

The operation we've just executed is called a *matrix product*. It's a generalization of the vector dot product to two dimensions. Given two matrices, matrix_a and matrix_b, we can compute their product by calculating matrix_c, where matrix_c[i][j] is equal to matrix_a[i] @ matrix_b[:,j] (figure 13.14). Matrix products are crucial to many modern technological advancements. They power the ranking algorithms in massive search engines like Google, serve as the foundation for techniques used to train self-driving cars, and underlie much of modern NLP. The usefulness of matrix products will become apparent shortly, but first we must discuss matrix product operations in more detail.

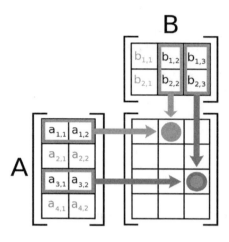

Figure 13.14 **Computing the matrix product of matrices A and B. The operation outputs a new matrix. Each element in the *i*th row and *j*th column of the output equals the dot product between the *i*th row of A and the *j*th column of B. For instance, the element in the first row and second column of the output equals $a_{1,1} * b_{1,2} + a_{1,2} * b_{2,2}$. Meanwhile, the element in the third row and third column of the output equals $a_{3,1} * b_{1,3} + a_{3,2} * b_{2,3}$.**

NUMPY MATRIX PRODUCTS

Naively, we can calculate `matrix_c` by running nested `for` loops across `matrix_a` and `matrix_b`. This technique is not efficient. Conveniently, NumPy's product operator `@` can be applied to 2D matrices as well as 1D arrays. If `matrix_a` and `matrix_b` are both NumPy arrays, then `matrix_c` equals `matrix_a @ matrix_b`. Thus, the matrix product of `similarities` and `unit_vectors` equals `similarities @ unit_vectors`. Let's confirm.

Listing 13.41 Computing a matrix product using NumPy

```
matrix_product = similarities @ unit_vectors
assert np.allclose(matrix_product, dot_products)
```

Asserts that all the elements of matrix_product are nearly identical to all the elements of dot_products. There are tiny differences in results due to floating-point errors.

What will happen if we flip our input matrices and run `unit_vectors @ similarities`? NumPy will throw an error! The computation takes the vector dot product between rows in `unit_vectors` and columns in `similarities`, but these rows and columns have different lengths. Therefore, the computation is not possible (figure 13.15).

Listing 13.42 Computing an erroneous matrix product

```
try:
    matrix_product = unit_vectors @ similarities
except:
    print("We can't compute the matrix product")

We can't compute the matrix product
```

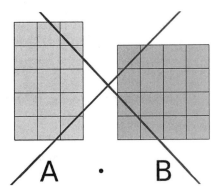

Figure 13.15 An erroneous effort to compute the matrix product of matrices A and B. Matrix A has three columns in each row, and matrix B has four rows in each column. We cannot take the dot product between a three-element row and a four-element column. Thus, running A @ B causes an error.

The matrix product is order dependent. The output of matrix_a @ matrix_b is not necessarily the same as matrix_b @ matrix_a. In words, we can distinguish between matrix_a @ matrix_b and matrix_b @ matrix_a as follows:

- matrix_a @ matrix_b is the product of matrix_a and matrix_b.
- matrix_b @ matrix_a is the product of matrix_b and matrix_a.

In mathematics, the words *product* and *multiplication* are often interchangeable. Thus, computing the matrix product is commonly called *matrix multiplication*. That name is so ubiquitous that NumPy includes an np.matmul function. The output of np.matmul (matrix_a, matrix_b) is identical to matrix_a @ matrix_b.

Listing 13.43 Running matrix multiplication using matmul

```
matrix_product = np.matmul(similarities, unit_vectors)
assert np.array_equal(matrix_product,
                      similarities @ unit_vectors)
```

Common NumPy matrix operations
- matrix.shape—Returns a tuple containing the row count and column count in the matrix.
- matrix.T—Returns a transposed matrix where rows and columns are swapped.
- matrix[i]—Returns the *i*th row in the matrix.
- matrix[:,j]—Returns the *j*th column in the matrix.
- k * matrix—Multiplies each element of the matrix by a constant k.
- matrix + k—Adds a constant k to each element of the matrix.
- matrix_a + matrix_b—Adds each element of matrix_a to matrix_b. Equivalent to running matrix_c[i][j] = matrix_a[i][j] + matrix_b[i][j] for every possible i and j.
- matrix_a * matrix_b—Multiplies each element of matrix_a with an element of matrix_b. Equivalent to running matrix_c[i][j] = matrix_a[i][j] * matrix_b[i][j] for every possible i and j.

(continued)

- `matrix_a @ matrix_b`—Returns the matrix product of `matrix_a` and `matrix_b`. Equivalent to running `matrix_c[i][j] = matrix_a[i] @ matrix_b[;,j]` for every possible `i` and `j`.
- `np.matmult(matrix_a, matrix_b)`—Returns the matrix product of `matrix_a` and `matrix_b`, without relying on the `@` operator.

NumPy lets us execute matrix multiplication without relying on nested `for` loops. This improvement is more than just cosmetic. Standard Python `for` loops are designed to run on generalized data lists; they are not optimized for numbers. Meanwhile, NumPy cleverly optimizes its array iterations. Consequently, matrix multiplication is noticeably faster when run in NumPy.

Let's compare the matrix product speed between NumPy and regular Python (figure 13.16). Listing 13.44 plots the product speed across matrices of variable sizes using both NumPy and Python `for` loops. Python's built-in `time` module is employed to time the matrix multiplications.

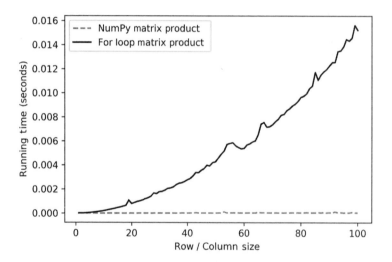

Figure 13.16   Matrix size plotted against product running times for NumPy and regular Python. NumPy is vastly faster than regular Python.

NOTE   Running times will fluctuate depending on the local state of the machine that is executing the code.

Listing 13.44   Comparing matrix product running times

```
import time

numpy_run_times = []
for_loop_run_times = []
```

```
matrix_sizes = range(1, 101)
for size in matrix_sizes:
    matrix = np.ones((size, size))      ◁─────

    start_time = time.time()      ◁─────
    matrix @ matrix
    numpy_run_times.append(time.time() - start_time)      ◁─┐

    start_time = time.time()
    for i in range(size):
        for j in range(size):
            matrix[i] @ matrix[:,j]

    for_loop_run_times.append(time.time() - start_time)      ◁─┐
plt.plot(matrix_sizes, numpy_run_times,
         label='NumPy Matrix Product', linestyle='--')
plt.plot(matrix_sizes, for_loop_run_times,
         label='For-Loop Matrix Product', color='k')
plt.xlabel('Row / Column Size')
plt.ylabel('Running Time (Seconds)')
plt.legend()
plt.show()
```

Creates a size-by-size matrix of ones, where size ranges from 1 to 100

Returns the current time in seconds

Stores the matrix product speed in NumPy

Stores the matrix product speed of a Python for loop

When it comes to matrix multiplication, NumPy greatly outperforms basic Python. NumPy matrix product code is more efficient to run and also to write. We will now use NumPy to compute our all-by-all text similarities with maximum efficiency.

13.3.2 *Computing all-by-all matrix similarities*

We've previously computed our text similarities by iterating over a `unit_vectors` matrix. This matrix holds the normalized TF vectors for our three seashell texts. What will happen if we multiply `unit_vectors` by `unit_vectors.T`? Well, `unit_vectors.T` is a transpose of `unit_vectors`. Therefore, each column i in the transpose equals row i in `unit_vectors`. Taking the dot product of `unit_vectors[i]` and `unit_vectors.T[:,i]` will return the cosine similarity between a unit vector and itself, as shown in figure 13.17. That similarity, of course, will equal 1. By this logic, `unit_vectors[i] @ unit_vectors[j].T` equals the cosine similarity between the *i*th and *j*th vectors. Consequently, `unit_vectors @ unit_vectors.T` returns a matrix of all-by-cosine similarities. The matrix should equal our previously computed `cosine_similarities` array. Let's confirm.

Listing 13.45 Obtaining cosines from a matrix product

```
cosine_matrix = unit_vectors @ unit_vectors.T
assert np.allclose(cosine_matrix, cosine_similarities)
```

Each element in `cosine_matrix` equals the cosine of the angle between two vectorized texts. That cosine can be transformed into a Tanimoto value, which generally

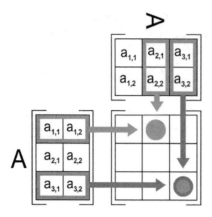

Figure 13.17   Computing the dot product between **A** and the transpose of **A**. The operation outputs a new matrix. Each element in the *i*th row and *j*th column of the output equals the dot product between the *i*th row of A and the *j*th column of A. Thus, the element in the third row and third column of the output equals the dot product of A[2] with itself. If matrix A is normalized, then that dot product will equal 1.0.

reflects word overlap and divergence between texts. Using NumPy arithmetic, we can convert `cosine_matrix` into a Tanimoto similarity matrix by running `cosine_matrix / (2 - cosine_matrix)`.

Listing 13.46   Converting cosines to a Tanimoto matrix

```
tanimoto_matrix = cosine_matrix / (2 - cosine_matrix)
assert np.allclose(tanimoto_matrix, similarities)
```

We've computed all the Tanimoto similarities in just two lines of code. We can also compute these similarities by inputting `unit_vectors` and `unit_vectors.T` directly into our `normalized_tanimoto` function. As a reminder, the function does the following:

1   Takes as input two NumPy arrays. Their dimensionality is not constrained.
2   Applies the `@` operator to the NumPy arrays. If the arrays are matrices, the operation returns a matrix product.
3   Uses arithmetic to modify the product. The arithmetic operations can be equally applied to both numbers and matrices.

Hence it's not surprising that `normalized_tanimoto(unit_vectors, unit_vectors.T)` returns an output equal to `tanimoto_matrix`.

Listing 13.47   Inputting matrices into `normalized_tanimoto`

```
output = normalized_tanimoto(unit_vectors, unit_vectors.T)
assert np.array_equal(output, tanimoto_matrix)
```

Given a matrix of normalized TF vectors, we can compute their all-by-all similarities in a single, efficient line of code.

> ### Common normalized matrix comparisons
>
> - `norm_matrix @ norm_matrix.T`—Returns a matrix of all-by-all cosine similarities
> - `norm_matrix @ norm_matrix.T / ( 2 - norm_matrix @ norm_matrix.T)`—
>   Returns a matrix of all-by-all Tanimoto similarities

13.4 *Computational limits of matrix multiplication*

Matrix multiplication speed is determined by the matrix size. NumPy may optimize for speed, but even NumPy has its limits. These limits become obvious when we compute real-world text matrix products. Issues arise from the matrix column count, which is dependent on vocabulary size. The total words in a vocabulary can spiral out of control when we begin to compare nontrivial texts.

Consider, for instance, the analysis of novels. The average novel contains roughly 5,000 to 10,000 unique words. *The Hobbit*, for example, contains 6,175 unique words. Meanwhile, *A Tale of Two Cities* contains 9,699 unique words. Some of the words overlap between the two novels; others do not. Together, the novels share a vocabulary size of 12,138 words. We can also throw a third novel into the mix. Adding *The Adventures of Tom Sawyer* expands the vocabulary size to 13,935 words. At this rate, adding 27 more novels will expand the vocabulary size to approximately 50,000 words.

Let's assume that 30 novels require a shared vocabulary containing 50,000 words. Furthermore, let's assume we take an all-by-all similarity across the 30 books. How much time is required to compute these similarities? Let's find out! We'll create a 30-book by 50,000-word `book_matrix`. All rows in the matrix will be normalized. Then we'll measure the running time of `normalized_tanimoto(book_matrix, book_matrix.T)`.

NOTE The purpose of our experiment is to test the impact of the matrix column count on running time. Here, the actual matrix contents don't matter. We thus oversimplify the situation by setting all word counts to 1. Consequently, the normalized values in each row equal `1 / 5000`. In a real-world setting, this would not be the case. Also, note that it's possible to optimize running time by tracking all zero-value matrix elements. Here, we don't consider the impact of zero values on matrix multiplication speed.

Listing 13.48 Timing an all-by-all comparison of 30 novels

```
vocabulary_size = 50000
normalized_vector = [1 / vocabulary_size] * vocabulary_size
book_count = 30

def measure_run_time(book_count):
    book_matrix = np.array([normalized_vector] * book_count)
    start_time = time.time()
    normalized_tanimoto(book_matrix, book_matrix.T)
    return time.time() - start_time
```

The function computes the running time on a book_count-by-50,000 matrix. The function is reused in the next two code listings.

```
run_time = measure_run_time(book_count)
print(f"It took {run_time:.4f} seconds to compute the similarities across a "
       f"{book_count}-book by {vocabulary_size}-word matrix")
```

```
It took 0.0051 seconds to compute the similarities across a 30-book by 50000-
    word matrix
```

The similarity matrix took approximately 5 milliseconds to compute. This is a reasonable running time. Will it stay reasonable as the number of analyzed books continues to increase? Let's check. We'll plot the running times across multiple book counts ranging from 30 to nearly 1,000 (figure 13.18). For consistency's sake, we'll keep the vocabulary size at 50,000.

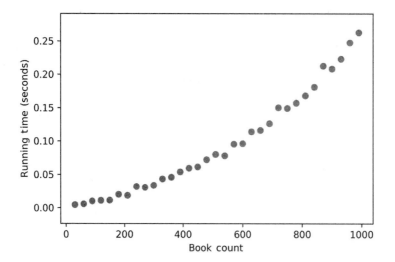

Figure 13.18   Book counts plotted against the running time of text comparisons. The running times increase quadratically.

Listing 13.49   Plotting book counts vs. running times

```
book_counts = range(30, 1000, 30)
run_times = [measure_run_time(book_count)
             for book_count in book_counts]
plt.scatter(book_counts, run_times)
plt.xlabel('Book Count')
plt.ylabel('Running Time (Seconds)')
plt.show()
```

We do not sample every single book count—the accumulated running time would be too slow.

Generates a scatter plot instead of a curve. Figure 13.18 fits the discrete points to a continuous parabolic curve.

The similarity running time rises quadratically with book count. At 1,000 books, the running time increases to approximately 0.27 seconds. This delay is tolerable. However, if we increase the book count even further, the delay is no longer acceptable. We can show this using simple math. Our plotted curve takes on a parabolic shape defined by y = n * (x ** 2). When x is approximately 1,000, y equals approximately

`0.27`. Thus, we can model our running times using the equation `y = (0.27 / (1000 **` `2)) * (x ** 2)`. Let's confirm by plotting equation outputs together with our precomputed measurements (figure 13.19). The two plots should mostly overlap.

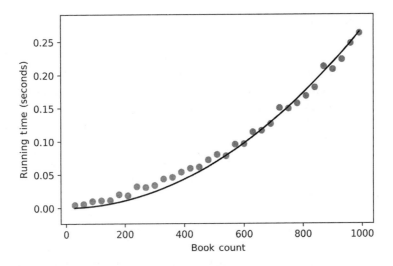

Figure 13.19 A quadratic curve plotted together with running times. The shape of the curve overlaps with the running time scatter plot.

Listing 13.50 Modeling running times using a quadratic curve

```
def y(x): return (0.27 / (1000 ** 2)) * (x ** 2)
plt.scatter(book_counts, run_times)
plt.plot(book_counts, y(np.array(book_counts)), c='k')
plt.xlabel('Book Count')
plt.ylabel('Running Time (Seconds)')
plt.show()
```

Our plotted equation overlaps with the measured times. Thus, we can use the equation to predict the speed of larger book comparisons. Let's see how long it will take to measure the similarity across 300,000 books.

> **NOTE** 300,000 may seem like an unusually large number. However, it reflects the 200,000 to 300,000 English-language novels that are published every year. If we wish to compare all the novels published in a year, we need to multiply matrices containing more than 200,000 rows.

Listing 13.51 Predicting the running time for 300,000 books

```
book_count = 300000
run_time = y(book_count) / 3600        Divides by 3600 to convert
                                       seconds into hours
print(f"It will take {run_time} hours to compute all-by-all similarities "
      f"from a {book_count}-book by {vocabulary_size}-word matrix")
```

```
It will take 6.75 hours to compute all-by-all similarities from a 300000-book
    by 50000-word matrix
```

It will take nearly 7 hours to compare 300,000 books. This delay in time is not acceptable, especially in industrial NLP systems, which are designed to process millions of texts in mere seconds. We need to somehow reduce the running time. One approach is to reduce the matrix size.

Our matrix is too large, partially because of column size. Each row contains 50,000 columns corresponding to 50,000 words. However, in a real-world setting, not all words are distributed equally. While some words are common across novels, other words may appear only once. For example, take the lengthy novel *Moby Dick*: 44% of the words in it are mentioned once and never used again. Some of the words are rarely mentioned in other novels. Removing them will lower the column size.

On the opposite end of the spectrum are common words that appear in every novel. Words like *the* do not provide a differentiating signal between texts. Removing common words will also reduce the column size.

It's possible to systematically reduce the dimensions of each matrix row from 50,000 to a more reasonable value. In the next section, we introduce a series of dimension-reduction techniques to shrink the shape of any inputted matrix. Reducing the dimensions of text matrices greatly lowers the running times of common NLP computations.

Summary

- We can compare texts using the *Jaccard similarity*. This similarity metric equals the fraction of total unique words that are shared between two texts.
- We can compute the Jaccard similarity by transforming our texts into binary vectors of 1s and 0s. Taking the *dot product* of two binary text vectors returns the shared word count between the texts. Meanwhile, the dot product of a text vector with itself returns the total count of words in the text. These values are sufficient to compute the Jaccard similarity.
- The *Tanimoto similarity* generalizes Jaccard to include non-binary vectors. This allows us to compare vectors of word counts, which are referred to as *TF vectors*.
- *TF vector similarity* is overly dependent on text size. We can eliminate this dependence using *normalization*. A vector can be normalized by first computing its *magnitude*, which is the vector's distance to the origin. Dividing a vector by its magnitude produces a normalized unit vector.
- The magnitude of a *unit vector* is 1. Furthermore, the Tanimoto similarity is partially dependent on vector magnitude. Thus, we can simplify the similarity function if it's run exclusively on unit vectors. Moreover, that unit vector similarity can be converted into other common metrics, such as *cosine similarity* and distance.
- We can efficiently compute all-by-all similarities using *matrix multiplication*. A *matrix* is just a 2D table of numbers. We can multiply two matrices by taking

pairwise dot products between every matrix row and matrix column. If we multiply a normalized matrix by its transpose, we produce a matrix of all-by-all cosine similarities. Using NumPy's matrix arithmetic, we transform these cosine similarities into Tanimoto similarities.

- Matrix multiplication is much faster in NumPy than in pure Python. However, even NumPy has its limits. Once a matrix gets too large, we need to find a way to reduce its size.

Dimension reduction of matrix data

14

This section covers

- Simplifying matrices with geometric rotations
- What is principal component analysis?
- Advanced matrix operations for reducing matrix size
- What is singular value decomposition?
- Dimension reduction using scikit-learn

Dimension reduction is a series of techniques for shrinking data while retaining its information content. These techniques permeate many of our everyday digital activities. Suppose, for instance, that you've just returned from a vacation in Belize. There are 10 vacation photos on your phone that you wish to message to a friend. Unfortunately, these photos are quite large, and your current wireless connection is slow. Each photo is 1,200 pixels tall and 1,200 pixels wide. It takes up 5.5 MB of memory and requires 15 seconds to transfer. Transferring all 10 photos will take 2.5 minutes. Fortunately, your messaging app offers you a better option: You can shrink each photo from 1,200 × 1,200 pixels to 600 × 480 pixels. This reduces the dimensions of each photo sixfold. By lowering the resolution, you'll sacrifice a little detail. However, the vacation photos will maintain most of their information—the lush jungles, blue seas, and shimmering sands will remain clearly

292

visible in the images. Therefore, the trade-off is worth it. Reducing the dimensionality by six will increase the transfer speed by six: it will take just 25 seconds to share the 10 photos with your friend.

There are, of course, more benefits to dimension reduction than just transfer speed. Consider, for instance, mapmaking, which can be treated as a dimension-reduction problem. Our Earth is a 3D sphere that can be accurately modeled as a globe. We can turn that globe into a map by projecting its 3D shape onto a 2D piece of paper. The paper map is easier to carry from place to place—unlike a globe, we can fold the map and put it in our pocket. Furthermore, the 2D map offers us additional advantages. Suppose we're asked to locate all the countries that border at least 10 other neighboring territories. Finding these dense border regions on a map is easy: we can glance at the 2D map to hone in on crowded country clusters. If we we use a globe, instead, the task becomes more challenging. We need to spin the globe across multiple perspectives because we can't see all the countries at once. In some ways, the globe's curvature acts as a layer of noise that interferes with our given task. Removing that curvature simplifies our effort, but at a price: the continent of Antarctica is essentially deleted from the map. Of course, there are no countries in Antarctica, so from the perspective of our task, that trade-off is worth it.

Our map analogy demonstrates the following advantages of dimensionally reduced data:

- More compact data is easier to transfer and store.
- Algorithmic tasks require less time when our data is smaller.
- Certain complex tasks, like cluster detection, can be simplified by removing unnecessary information.

The last two bullet points are very relevant to this case study. We want to cluster thousands of text documents by topic. The clustering will entail computing a matrix of all-by-all document similarities. As discussed in the previous section, this computation can be slow. Dimension reduction can speed up the process by reducing the number of data matrix columns. As a further bonus, dimensionally reduced text data has been shown to yield higher-quality topic clusters.

Let's dive deeper into the relationship between dimension reduction and data clustering. We start with a simple task in which we cluster 2D data in one dimension.

14.1 Clustering 2D data in one dimension

Dimension reduction has many uses, including more interpretable clustering. Consider a scenario in which we manage an online clothing store. When customers visit our website, they are asked to provide their height and weight. These measurements are added to a customer database. Two database columns are required to store each customer's measurements, and therefore the data is two-dimensional. The 2D measurements are used to offer customers appropriately sized clothing based on whatever inventory is available. Our inventory comes in three sizes: small, medium, and large. Given the measurement data for 180 customers, we would like to do the following:

- Group our customers into three distinct clusters based on size.
- Build an interpretable model to determine the clothing size category of each new customer using our computed clusters.
- Make our clustering simple enough for our nontechnical investors to comprehend.

The third point in particular limits our decisions. Our clustering can't rely on technical concepts, such as centroids or distances to the mean. Ideally, we'd be able to explain our model in a single figure. We can achieve this level of simplicity using dimension reduction. However, we first need to simulate the 2D measurement data for 180 customers. Let's start by simulating customer heights. Our heights range from 60 inches (5 ft) to 78 inches (6.5 ft). We fabricate these heights by calling `np.arange(60, 78, 0.1)`. This returns an array of heights between 60 and 78 inches, where each consecutive height increases by 0.1 inches.

Listing 14.1   Simulating a range of heights

```
import numpy as np
heights = np.arange(60, 78, 0.1)
```

Meanwhile, our simulated weights depend strongly on the height. A taller person is likely to weigh more than a shorter person. It has been shown that, on average, a person's weight in pounds equals approximately `4 * height - 130`. Of course, each individual person's weight fluctuates around this average value. We'll model these random fluctuations using a normal distribution with a standard deviation of 10 lb. Thus, given a `height` variable, we can model the weight as `4 * height - 130 + np.random.normal(scale=10)`. Next, we use this relationship to fabricate weights for each of our 180 heights.

Listing 14.2   Simulating weights using heights

```
np.random.seed(0)
random_fluctuations = np.random.normal(scale=10, size=heights.size)   ◁─── The scale parameter sets the standard deviation.
weights = 4 * heights - 130 + random_fluctuations
```

We can treat the heights and weights as two-dimensional coordinates in a measurements matrix. Let's store and plot these measured coordinates (figure 14.1).

Listing 14.3   Plotting 2D measurements

```
import matplotlib.pyplot as plt
measurements = np.array([heights, weights])
plt.scatter(measurements[0], measurements[1])
plt.xlabel('Height (in)')
plt.ylabel('Weight (lb)')
plt.show()
```

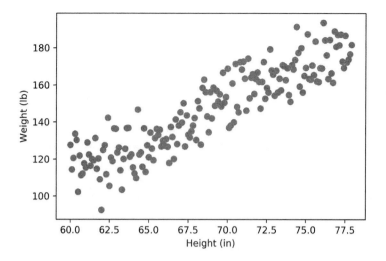

Figure 14.1 A plot of heights vs. weights. Their linear relationship is clearly visible.

The linear relationship between height and weight is clearly visible in the plot. Also, as expected, the height and weight axes are scaled differently. As a reminder, Matplotlib manipulates its 2D axes to make the final plot aesthetically pleasing. Normally, this is a good thing. However, we'll soon be rotating the plot to simplify our data. The rotation will shift the axes scaling, making the rotated data difficult to compare with the original data plot. Consequently, we should equalize our axes to obtain consistent visual output. Let's equalize the axes by calling `plt.axis('equal')` and then regenerate the plot (figure 14.2).

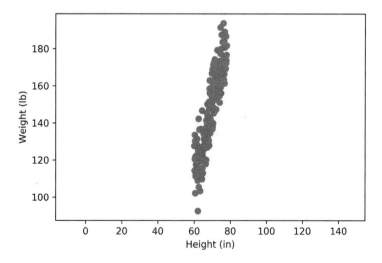

Figure 14.2 A plot of heights vs. weights with both axes scaled equally

Listing 14.4 Plotting 2D measurements using equally scaled axes

```
plt.scatter(measurements[0], measurements[1])
plt.xlabel('Height (in)')
plt.ylabel('Weight (lb)')
plt.axis('equal')
plt.show()
```

Our plot now forms a thin, cigar-like shape. We can cluster the cigar by size if we slice it into three equal parts. One way of obtaining the clusters is to utilize K-means. Of course, interpreting that output will require an understanding of the K-means algorithm. A less technical solution is to just tip the cigar on its side. If the cigar-shaped plot was positioned horizontally, we could separate it into three parts using two vertical slices, as shown in figure 14.3. The first slice would isolate 60 of the leftmost data points, and the second slice would isolate 60 of the rightmost customer points. These operations would segment our customers in a manner that's easy to explain, even to a nontechnical person.

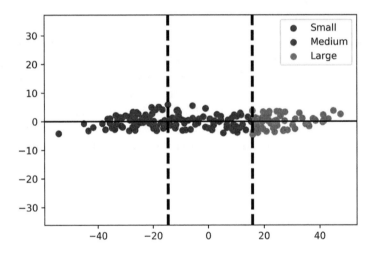

Figure 14.3 Our linear measurements, rotated horizontally so that they lie primarily on the x-axis. Two vertical cutoffs are sufficient to divide the data into three equal clusters: small, medium, and large. In the plot, the x-axis is sufficient for distinguishing between measurements. Thus, we can eliminate the y-axis with minimal information loss. Note that this figure was generated using listing 14.15.

> **NOTE** For the purposes of the exercise, we assume that small, medium, and large sizes are distributed equally. In the real-world clothing industry, this might not be the case.

If we rotate our data toward the x-axis, the horizontal x-values should be sufficient to distinguish between points. We can thus cluster the data without relying on the vertical y-values. Effectively, we'll be able to delete the y-values with minimal information loss. That deletion will reduce our data from two dimensions to one (figure 14.4).

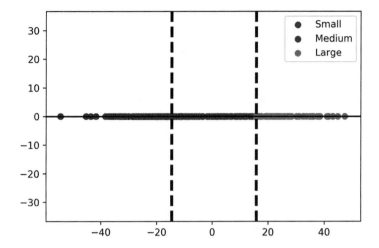

Figure 14.4   Our linear measurements, reduced to one dimension using horizontal rotation. The data points have been rotated toward the x-axis, and their y-value coordinates have been deleted. Nevertheless, the remaining x-values are sufficient to distinguish between points. Thus, our 1D output still allows us to split the data into three equal clusters.

We'll now attempt to cluster our 2D data by flipping the data on its side. This horizontal rotation will allow us to both cluster the data and reduce it to one dimension.

14.1.1 Reducing dimensions using rotation

To flip our data on its side, we must execute two separate steps:

1. Shift all of our data points so that they are centered on the origin of the plot, which is located at coordinates $(0, 0)$. This will make it easier to rotate the plot toward the x-axis.
2. Rotate the plotted data until the total distance of the data points to the x-axis is minimized.

Centering our data at the origin is trivial. The central point of every dataset is equal to its mean. Thus, we need to adjust our coordinates so that their x-value mean and y-value mean both equal zero. This can be done by subtracting the current mean from every coordinate; in other words, subtracting the mean height for `heights` and the mean weight from `weights` will produce a dataset that's centered at $(0, 0)$.

Let's shift our height and weight coordinates and store these changes in a `centered_data` array. Then we plot the shifted coordinates to verify that they are centered on the origin (figure 14.5).

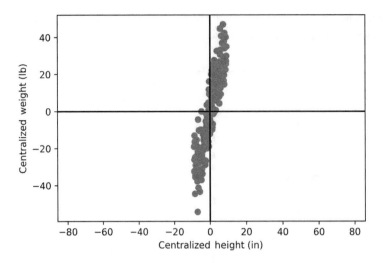

Figure 14.5   A plot of heights vs. weights, centered at the origin. The centered data can be rotated like a propeller.

Listing 14.5   Centering the measurements at the origin

```
centered_data = np.array([heights - heights.mean(),
                          weights - weights.mean()])
plt.scatter(centered_data[0], centered_data[1])
plt.axhline(0, c='black')          ⟵    Visualizes the x-axis
plt.axvline(0, c='black')               and y-axis to mark the
plt.xlabel('Centralized Height (in)')   location of the origin
plt.ylabel('Centralized Weight (lb)')
plt.axis('equal')
plt.show()
```

Our data is now perfectly centered at the origin. However, the orientation of the data is closer to the y-axis than the x-axis. Our goal is to adjust this orientation through rotation. We want to spin the plotted points around the origin until they overlap with the x-axis. Rotating a 2D plot around its center requires the use of a *rotation matrix*: a two-by-two array of the form `np.array([[cos(x), -sin(x)], [sin(x), cos(x)]])`, where x is the angle of rotation. The matrix product of this array and `centered_data` rotates the data by x radians. The rotation occurs in the counterclockwise direction. We can also rotate the data in the clockwise direction by inputting -x instead of x.

Let's utilize the rotation matrix to rotate `centered_data` clockwise by 90 degrees. Then we plot both the rotated data and the original `centered_data` array (figure 14.6).

Listing 14.6   Rotating `centered_data` by 90 degrees

```
from math import sin, cos
angle = np.radians(-90)                          ⟵    Converts the angle from
rotation_matrix = np.array([[cos(angle), -sin(angle)],    degrees to radians
                            [sin(angle), cos(angle)]])
```

```
rotated_data = rotation_matrix @ centered_data
plt.scatter(centered_data[0], centered_data[1], label='Original Data')
plt.scatter(rotated_data[0], rotated_data[1], c='y', label='Rotated Data')
plt.axhline(0, c='black')
plt.axvline(0, c='black')
plt.legend()
plt.axis('equal')
plt.show()
```

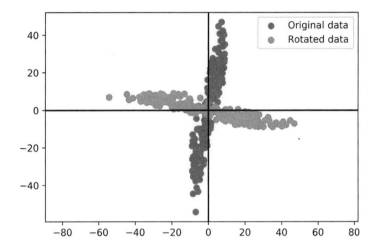

Figure 14.6 A plot of `centered_data` before and after a rotation. The data has been rotated 90 degrees about the origin. It is now positioned closer to the x-axis.

As expected, our `rotated_data` result is perpendicular to the `centered_data` plot. We have successfully rotated the plot by 90 degrees. Furthermore, our rotation has shifted the plot closer to the x-axis. We need a way to quantify this shift. Let's generate a penalty score that decreases as the data is rotated toward the x-axis.

We'll penalize all vertical y-axis values. Our penalty is based on the concept of squared distance, introduced in section 5. The penalty square equals the average squared y-value of `rotated_data`. Since y-values represent the distance to the x-axis, our penalty equals the average squared distance to the x-axis. When a rotated dataset moves closer to the x-axis, its average squared y-value decreases.

Given any `y_values` array, we can compute the penalty by running `sum([y ** 2 for y in y_values]) / y_values.size`. However, we can also compute the penalty by executing `y_values @ y_values / y.size`. The two results are identical, and the dot product computation is more efficient. Let's compare the penalty scores for `rotated_data` and `centered_data`.

Listing 14.7   Penalizing vertical y-values

```
data_labels = ['unrotated', 'rotated']
data_list = [centered_data, rotated_data]
for data_label, data in zip(data_labels, data_list):
    y_values = data[1]
    penalty = y_values @ y_values / y_values.size
    print(f"The penalty score for the {data_label} data is {penalty:.2f}")
```

```
The penalty score for the unrotated data is 519.82
The penalty score for the rotated data is 27.00
```

Rotating the data has reduced the penalty score by more than 20-fold. This reduction carries a statistical interpretation. We can link the penalty to the variance if we consider the following:

- Our penalty score equals the average squared y-value distance from 0 across a y_values array.
- y_values.mean() equals 0.
- Thus our penalty square equals the average squared y-value distance from the mean.
- The average square distance from the mean equals the variance.
- Our penalty score equals y_values.var().

We've inferred that the penalty score equals the y-axis variance. Consequently, our data rotation has reduced the y-axis variance by more than 20-fold. Let's confirm.

Listing 14.8   Equating penalties with y-axis variance

```
for data_label, data in zip(data_labels, data_list):
    y_var = data[1].var()
    penalty = data[1] @ data[1] / data[0].size
    assert round(y_var, 14) == round(penalty, 14)  ◁──┐
    print(f"The y-axis variance for the {data_label} data is {y_var:.2f}")
```

Rounds to take floating-point errors into account

```
The y-axis variance for the unrotated data is 519.82
The y-axis variance for the rotated data is 27.00
```

We can score rotations based on variance. Rotating the data toward the x-axis reduces the variance along the y-axis. How does this rotation influence the variance along the x-axis? Let's find out.

Listing 14.9   Measuring rotational x-axis variance

```
for data_label, data in zip(data_labels, data_list):
    x_var = data[0].var()
    print(f"The x-axis variance for the {data_label} data is {x_var:.2f}")
```

```
The x-axis variance for the unrotated data is 27.00
The x-axis variance for the rotated data is 519.82
```

The rotation has completely flipped the x-axis variance and the y-axis variance. However, the total sum of variance values has remained unchanged. Total variance is conserved even after the rotation. Let's verify this fact.

Listing 14.10 Confirming the conservation of total variance

```
total_variance = centered_data[0].var() + centered_data[1].var()
assert total_variance == rotated_data[0].var() + rotated_data[1].var()
```

Conservation of variance allows us to infer the following:

- x-axis variance and y-axis variance can be combined into a single percentage score, where x_values.var() / total_variance is equal to 1 - y_values.var() / total_variance.
- Rotating the data toward the x-axis leads to an increase in the x-axis variance and an equivalent decrease in the y-axis variance. Decreasing the vertical dispersion by p percent increases the horizontal dispersion by p percent.

The following code confirms these conclusions.

Listing 14.11 Exploring the percent coverage of axis variance

```
for data_label, data in zip(data_labels, data_list):
    percent_x_axis_var = 100 * data[0].var() / total_variance
    percent_y_axis_var = 100 * data[1].var() / total_variance
    print(f"In the {data_label} data, {percent_x_axis_var:.2f}% of the "
          "total variance is distributed across the x-axis")
    print(f"The remaining {percent_y_axis_var:.2f}% of the total "
          "variance is distributed across the y-axis\n")
```

```
In the unrotated data, 4.94% of the total variance is distributed across the
    x-axis
The remaining 95.06% of the total variance is distributed across the y-axis

In the rotated data, 95.06% of the total variance is distributed across the
    x-axis
The remaining 4.94% of the total variance is distributed across the y-axis
```

Rotating the data toward the x-axis has increased the x-axis variance by 90 percentage points. Simultaneously, the rotation has reduced the y-axis variance by these same 90 percentage points.

Let's rotate `centered_data` even further until its distance to the x-axis is minimized. Minimizing the distance to the x-axis is equivalent to

- Minimizing the percent of total variance covered by the y-axis. This minimizes vertical dispersion.
- Maximizing the percent of total variance covered by the x-axis. This maximizes horizontal dispersion.

We rotate `centered_data` toward the x-axis by maximizing horizontal dispersion. That dispersion is measured over all angles ranging from 1 degree to 180 degrees. We visualize these measurements in a plot (figure 14.7). Additionally, we extract the rotation angle that maximizes the percent of x-axis coverage. Our code prints out that angle and percentage while also marking the angle in our plot.

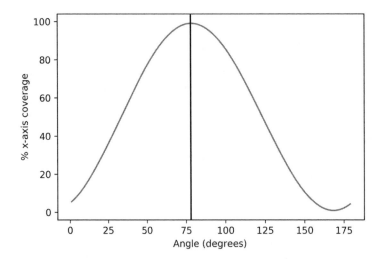

Figure 14.7 A plot of the rotation-angle vs. the percent of total variance covered by the x-axis. A vertical line marks the angle at which the x-axis variance is maximized. A rotation angle of 78.3 degrees shifts over 99% of the total variance to the x-axis. Rotating by that angle will allow us to dimensionally reduce our data.

Listing 14.12   Maximizing horizontal dispersion

Returns an array of angles ranging from 0 to 180, where each consecutive angle increases by 0.1 degrees

Rotates the data by input degrees. The data variable is preset to centered_data.

```
def rotate(angle, data=centered_data):
    angle = np.radians(-angle)
    rotation_matrix = np.array([[cos(angle), -sin(angle)],
                                [sin(angle), cos(angle)]])
    return rotation_matrix @ data

angles = np.arange(1, 180, 0.1)
x_variances = [(rotate(angle)[0].var()) for angle in angles]

percent_x_variances = 100 * np.array(x_variances) / total_variance
optimal_index = np.argmax(percent_x_variances)
optimal_angle = angles[optimal_index]
plt.plot(angles, percent_x_variances)
plt.axvline(optimal_angle, c='k')
plt.xlabel('Angle (degrees)')
```

Computes the x-axis variance for each rotation across every angle

Computes the angle of rotation resulting in the maximum variance

Plots a vertical line through optimal_ angle.

```
plt.ylabel('% x-axis coverage')
plt.show()

max_coverage = percent_x_variances[optimal_index]
max_x_var = x_variances[optimal_index]

print("The horizontal variance is maximized to approximately "
      f"{int(max_x_var)} after a {optimal_angle:.1f} degree rotation.")
print(f"That rotation distributes {max_coverage:.2f}% of the total "
      "variance onto the x-axis.")
```

```
The horizontal variance is maximized to approximately 541 after a 78.3 degree
    rotation.
That rotation distributes 99.08% of the total variance onto the x-axis.
```

Rotating `centered_data` by 78.3 degrees will maximize the horizontal dispersion. At that rotation angle, 99.08% of the total variance will be distributed across the x-axis. Thus, we can expect the rotated data to mostly lie along the 1D axis line. Let's confirm by running the rotation and then plotting the results (figure 14.8).

Listing 14.13 Plotting rotated data with high x-axis coverage

```
best_rotated_data = rotate(optimal_angle)
plt.scatter(best_rotated_data[0], best_rotated_data[1])
plt.axhline(0, c='black')
plt.axvline(0, c='black')
plt.axis('equal')
plt.show()
```

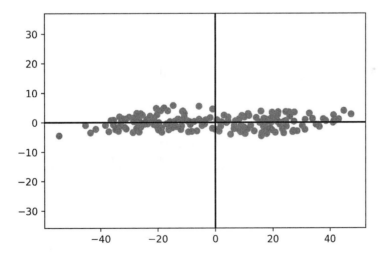

Figure 14.8 A plot of `centered_data` rotated by 78.3 degrees. This rotation maximizes variance along the x-axis and minimizes variance along the y-axis. Less than 1% of total variance lies along the y-axis. Thus, we can delete the y-coordinate with minimal information loss.

Most of the data lies close to the x-axis. The data's dispersion is maximized in that horizontal direction. Highly dispersed points are, by definition, highly separated. Separated points are easier to distinguish from each other. By contrast, the dispersion along our vertical y-axis has been minimized. Vertically, the data points are difficult to distinguish. Consequently, we can delete all y-axis coordinates with minimal information loss. That deletion should account for less than 1% of the total variance, so the remaining x-axis values will be sufficient to cluster our measurements.

Let's reduce `best_rotated_data` to 1D by disposing of the y-axis. Then we'll use the remaining 1D array to extract two clustering thresholds. The first threshold separates the small-sized customers from the medium-sized customers, and the second threshold separates the medium-sized customers from the large-sized customers. Together, the two thresholds separate our 180 customers into three equally sized clusters.

Listing 14.14   Reducing the rotated data to 1D for the purposes of clustering

```
x_values = best_rotated_data[0]
sorted_x_values = sorted(x_values)
cluster_size = int(x_values.size / 3)
small_cutoff = max(sorted_x_values[:cluster_size])
large_cutoff = min(sorted_x_values[-cluster_size:])
print(f"A 1D threshold of {small_cutoff:.2f} separates the small-sized "
      "and medium-sized customers.")
print(f"A 1D threshold of {large_cutoff:.2f} separates the medium-sized "
      "and large-sized customers.")
```

```
A 1D threshold of -14.61 separates the small-sized and medium-sized
    customers.
A 1D threshold of 15.80 separates the medium-sized and large-sized customers.
```

We can visualize our thresholds by utilizing them to vertically slice our `best_reduced_data` plot. The two slices split the plot into three segments, where each segment corresponds to a customer size. Next, we visualize the thresholds and the segments while coloring each segment (figure 14.9).

Listing 14.15   Plotting horizontal customer data separated into three segments

Takes as input a horizontally positioned customer dataset, segments the data using vertical thresholds, and plots each customer segment separately. This function is reused elsewhere in this section.

```
def plot_customer_segments(horizontal_2d_data):
    small, medium, large = [], [], []
    cluster_labels = ['Small', 'Medium', 'Large']
    for x_value, y_value in horizontal_2d_data.T:
        if x_value <= small_cutoff:
            small.append([x_value, y_value])
        elif small_cutoff < x_value < large_cutoff:
            medium.append([x_value, y_value])
        else:
            large.append([x_value, y_value])
```

1D x-value thresholds are utilized to segment the data.

```
for i, cluster in enumerate([small, medium, large]):          ⟵──┐ Each
    cluster_x_values, cluster_y_values = np.array(cluster).T        customer
    plt.scatter(cluster_x_values, cluster_y_values,                 segment is
                color=['g', 'b', 'y'][i],                           plotted
                label=cluster_labels[i])                            separately.

plt.axhline(0, c='black')
plt.axvline(large_cutoff, c='black', linewidth=3, linestyle='--')
plt.axvline(small_cutoff, c='black', linewidth=3, linestyle='--')
plt.axis('equal')
plt.legend()
plt.show()
```

```
plot_customer_segments(best_rotated_data)
```

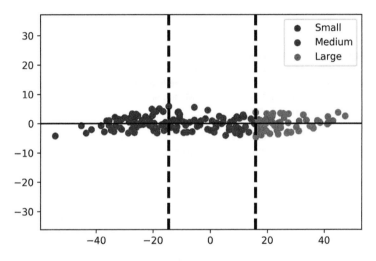

Figure 14.9   A horizontal plot of `centered_data`, segmented using two vertical thresholds. The segmentation splits the plot into three customer clusters: small, medium, and large. The one-dimensional x-axis is sufficient to extract these clusters.

Our 1D x_values array can sufficiently segment the customer data because it captures 99.08% of the data's variance. Consequently, we can use the array to reproduce 99.08% of our centered_data dataset (figure 14.10). We simply need to reintroduce the y-axis dimension by adding an array of zeros. Then we need to rotate the resulting array back to its original position. These steps are carried out next.

Listing 14.16   Reproducing 2D data from a 1D array

```
zero_y_values = np.zeros(x_values.size)          ⟵──┘ Returns a vector of zeros
reproduced_data = rotate(-optimal_angle, data=[x_values, zero_y_values])
```

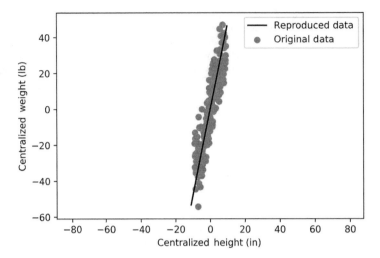

Figure 14.10   A plot of the reproduced data together with the original data points. Our `reproduced_data` **array forms a single line that cuts through our** `centered_data` **scatter plot. That line represents the linear direction in which data variance is maximized. 99.08% of the total variance is covered by the** `reproduced_data` **line.**

Let's plot `reproduced_data` together with our `centered_data` matrix to gauge the quality of the reproduction.

Listing 14.17   Plotting reproduced and original data

```
plt.plot(reproduced_data[0], reproduced_data[1], c='k',
         label='Reproduced Data')
plt.scatter(centered_data[0], centered_data[1], c='y',
            label='Original Data')
plt.axis('equal')
plt.legend()
plt.show()
```

The reproduced data forms a line that cuts directly through the middle of the `centered_data` scatter plot. The line represents the *first principal direction*, which is the linear direction in which the data's variance is maximized. Most 2D datasets contain two principal directions. The *second principal direction* is perpendicular to the first; it represents the remaining variance not covered by the first direction.

We can use the first principal direction to process the heights and weights of future customers. We'll assume that these customers originate from the same distribution that underlies our existing `measurements` data. If so, then their centralized heights and weights also lie along the first principal direction seen in figure 14.10. That alignment will eventually allow us to segment the new customer data using our existing thresholds.

Let's explore this scenario more concretely by simulating new customer measurements. Then we'll centralize and plot our measurement data (figure 14.11). We also plot a line representing the first principal direction—we expect the plotted measurements to align with that directional line.

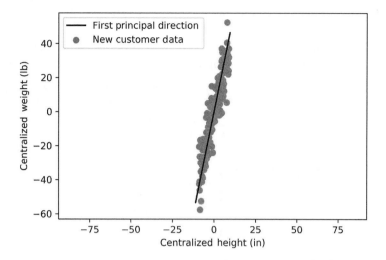

Figure 14.11 **A centralized plot containing new customer data together with the principal direction from our original customer dataset. The principal direction cuts directly through a previously unseen data plot. That direction's angle with the x-axis is known. Thus, we can confidently flip that data on its side for the purposes of clustering.**

NOTE The first principal direction intersects with the origin. Thus, we need to ensure that our new customer data also intersects with the origin, for alignment purposes. Consequently, we must centralize that data.

Listing 14.18 Simulating and plotting new customer data

> Separates all new heights by 0.11 inches to minimize overlap with previous heights

```
np.random.seed(1)
new_heights = np.arange(60, 78, .11)          ◁┘
random_fluctuations = np.random.normal(scale=10, size=new_heights.size)
new_weights =  4 * new_heights - 130 + random_fluctuations
new_centered_data = np.array([new_heights - heights.mean(),
                              new_weights - weights.mean()])     ◁────────
plt.scatter(new_centered_data[0], new_centered_data[1], c='y',
        label='New Customer Data')
plt.plot(reproduced_data[0], reproduced_data[1], c='k',
        label='First Principal Direction')
plt.xlabel('Centralized Height (in)')
plt.ylabel('Centralized Weight (lb)')
plt.axis('equal')
plt.legend()
plt.show()
```

> We assume that the new customer distribution is the same as the previously seen distribution. This allows us to utilize existing means for data centralization.

Our new customer data continues to lie along the first principal direction. That direction covers more than 99% of the data variance while also forming a 78.3-degree angle with the x-axis. Consequently, we can flip our new data on its side by rotating it 78.3 degrees. The resulting x-values cover more than 99% of the total variance. That high horizontal dispersion permits us to segment our customers without relying on y-value information. Our existing 1D segmentation thresholds should prove sufficient for that purpose.

Next, we position our new customer data horizontally and segment that data using our `plot_customer_segments` function (figure 14.12).

Listing 14.19   Rotating and segmenting our new customer data

```
new_horizontal_data = rotate(optimal_angle, data=new_centered_data)
plot_customer_segments(new_horizontal_data)
```

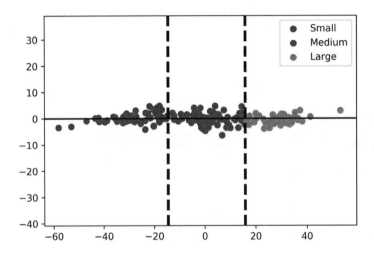

Figure 14.12   A horizontal plot of our new customer data. The data is segmented using two previously computed vertical thresholds. The segmentation splits the plot into three customer clusters: small, medium, and large. The one-dimensional x-axis is sufficient to extract these clusters.

We'll now briefly recap our observations. We can reduce any 2D array of customer measurements to one dimension by flipping the data on its side. The 1D horizontal x-values should be sufficient to cluster customers by size. Also, it's easier to flip the data when we know the principal direction along which the variance is maximized. Given the first principal direction, we dimensionally reduce customer data for easier clustering.

NOTE   As an added bonus, dimension reduction allows us to simplify our customer database. Rather than storing both height and weight, we can just store the horizontal x-value. Reducing database storage from 2D to one dimension will speed up customer lookups and lower our storage costs.

Thus far, we have extracted the first principal direction by rotating our data to maximize the variance. Unfortunately, this technique does not scale to higher dimensions. Imagine if we analyze a 1,000-dimensional dataset; checking every angle across 1,000 different axes is not computationally feasible. Fortunately, there's an easier way to extract all principal directions. We just need to apply a scalable algorithm known as *principal component analysis* (PCA).

We explore PCA in the next few subsections. It is simple to implement, but it can be tricky to understand. We thus explore the algorithm in parts. We begin by running scikit-learn's PCA implementation. We apply PCA to several datasets to achieve better clustering and visualization. Then we probe the weaknesses of the algorithm by deriving PCA from scratch. Finally, we eliminate these weaknesses.

14.2 Dimension reduction using PCA and scikit-learn

The PCA algorithm adjusts a dataset's axes so that most of the variance is spread across a small number of dimensions. Consequently, not every dimension is required to distinguish between the data points. Simplified data distinction leads to simplified clustering. Hence, it is fortunate that scikit-learn provides a principal component analysis class called `PCA`. Let's import `PCA` from `sklearn.decomposition`.

Listing 14.20 Importing `PCA` from scikit-learn

```
from sklearn.decomposition import PCA
```

Running `PCA()` initializes a `pca_model` object, which is structured similarly to the scikit-learn `cluster_model` objects utilized in section 10. In that section, we created models capable of clustering inputted arrays. Now, we create a PCA model capable of flipping our `measurements` array onto its side.

Listing 14.21 Initializing a `pca_model` object

```
pca_object = PCA()
```

Using `pca_model`, we can horizontally flip a 2D data matrix by running `pca_model.fit_transform(data)`. That method call assigns axes to the matrix columns and subsequently reorients these axes to maximize the variance. However, in our `measurements` array, the axes are stored in the matrix rows. Thus, we need to swap the rows and columns by taking the transpose of the matrix. Running `pca_model.fit_transform(measurements.T)` returns a `pca_transformed_data` matrix. The first matrix column represents the x-axis across which the variance is maximized, and the second column represents the y-axis across which the variance is minimized. The plot of these two columns should resemble a cigar lying on its side. Let's verify: we run the `fit_transform` method on `measurements.T` and then plot the columns of the result (figure 14.13). As a reminder, the *i*th column of a NumPy matrix M can be accessed by running `M[:,i]`.

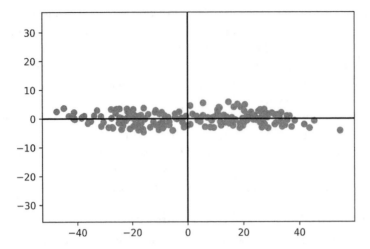

**Figure 14.13 Plotted output from scikit-learn's PCA implementation.
The plot is a mirror image of the horizontally positioned customer data from
figure 14.8. PCA has reoriented that data so its variance lies primarily along
the x-axis. Thus, the y-axis can be deleted with minimal information loss.**

Listing 14.22 Running PCA using scikit-learn

```
pca_transformed_data = pca_object.fit_transform(measurements.T)
plt.scatter(pca_transformed_data[:,0], pca_transformed_data[:,1])
plt.axhline(0, c='black')
plt.axvline(0, c='black')
plt.axis('equal')
plt.show()
```

Our plot is a mirror of figure 14.8, with the y-values reflected across the y-axis. Running PCA on a 2D dataset is guaranteed to tip over that data so it lies horizontally on the x-axis. However, the actual reflection of data is not restricted to one particular orientation.

> **NOTE** We can re-create our original horizontal plot by multiplying all y-values by −1. Consequently, running plot_customer_segments((pca_transformed_data * np.array([1, -1])).T) generates a plot of segmented customer sizes that's equivalent to figure 14.9.

Even though our plotted data is oriented differently, its x-axis variance coverage should remain consistent with our previous observations. We can confirm using the explained_variance_ratio_ attribute of pca_object. This attribute holds an array of fractional variances covered by each axis. Thus, 100 * pca_object.explained_variance_ratio_[0] should equal the previously observed x-axis coverage of approximately 99.08%. Let's verify.

Listing 14.23   Extracting variance from scikit-learn's PCA output
---

> The attribute is a NumPy array containing fractional coverage for each axis. Multiplying by 100 converts these fractions into percentages.

```
percent_variance_coverages = 100 * pca_object.explained_variance_ratio_   ◁──┘
x_axis_coverage, y_axis_coverage = percent_variance_coverages   ◁────┐
print(f"The x-axis of our PCA output covers {x_axis_coverage:.2f}% of "
      "the total variance")

The x-axis of our PCA output covers 99.08% of the total variance
```

> Each *i*th element of the array corresponds to the variance coverage of the *i*th axis.

Our `pca_object` has maximized the x-axis variance by uncovering the dataset's two principal directions. These directions are stored as vectors in the `pca.components` attribute (which is itself a matrix). As a reminder, vectors are linear segments that point in a certain direction from the origin. Also, the first principal direction is a line that rises from the origin. Consequently, we can represent the first principal direction as a vector called the *first principal component*. We can access the first principal component of our data by printing `pca_object.components[0]`. Next, we output that vector, as well as its magnitude.

Listing 14.24   Outputting the first principal component

```
first_pc = pca_object.components_[0]
magnitude = norm(first_pc)
print(f"Vector {first_pc} points in a direction that covers "
      f"{x_axis_coverage:.2f}% of the total variance.")
print(f"The vector has a magnitude of {magnitude}")

Vector [-0.20223994 -0.979336  ] points in a direction that covers 99.08%
of the total variance.
The vector has a magnitude of 1.0
```

The first principal component is a unit vector with a magnitude of 1.0. It stretches one whole unit length from the origin. Multiplying the vector by a number stretches the magnitude out further. If we stretch it far enough, we can capture the entire principal direction of our data. In other words, we can stretch the vector until it completely skewers the interior of our cigar-shaped plot, like a corn dog on a stick. The visualized result should be identical to figure 14.10.

> **NOTE**   If vector pc is a principal component, then -pc is also a principal component. The -pc vector represents the mirror image of pc. Both vectors lie along the first principal direction, even though they point away from each other. Hence, pc and -pc can be used interchangeably during the dimension reduction process.

Next, we generate that plot (figure 14.14). First, we stretch our `first_pc` vector until it extends 50 units in both the positive and negative directions from the origin. We

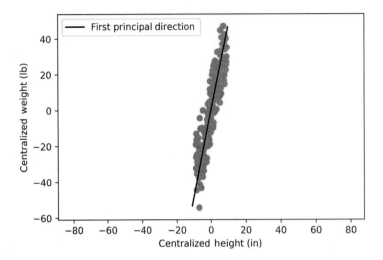

Figure 14.14   A centralized plot containing customer data together with the first principal direction. The direction has been plotted by stretching out the first principal component.

then plot the stretched segment along with our previously computed `centered_data` matrix. Later, we'll use the plotted segment to gain deeper insights into the workings of the PCA algorithm.

NOTE   We plot `centered_data` and not `measurements` because `centered_data` is centered at the origin. Our stretched-out vector is also centered at the origin. This makes the centered matrix and the vector visually comparable.

Listing 14.25   Stretching a unit vector to cover the first principal direction

```
def plot_stretched_vector(v, **kwargs):
    plt.plot([-50 * v[0], 50 * v[0]], [-50 * v[1], 50 * v[1]], **kwargs)

plt.plot(reproduced_data[0], reproduced_data[1], c='k',
         label='First Principal Direction')
plt.scatter(centered_data[0], centered_data[1], c='y')
plt.xlabel('Centralized Height (in)')
plt.ylabel('Centralized Weight (lb)')
plt.axis('equal')
plt.legend()
plt.show()
```

The function stretches out an inputted unit vector v. The stretched segment extends 50 units in both the positive and negative directions from the origin. Then the stretched segment is plotted. We reuse this function shortly.

We've used the first principal component to skewer our dataset along its first principal direction. In that same manner, we can stretch the other directional unit vector returned by the PCA algorithm. As stated earlier, most 2D datasets contain two principal directions. The second principal direction is perpendicular to the first, and its vectorized representation is called the *second principal component*. That component is stored in the second row of our computed `components` matrix.

Why should we care about the second principal component? After all, it points in a direction that covers less than 1% of data variance. Nonetheless, that component has its uses. Both the first and second principal components share a special relationship with our data's x- and y-axes. Visually uncovering that relationship will make PCA easier to understand. Hence, we now stretch and plot both of the components in the `components` matrix. Additionally, we plot `centered_data`, as well as both our axes. The final visualization will provide us with valuable insights (figure 14.15).

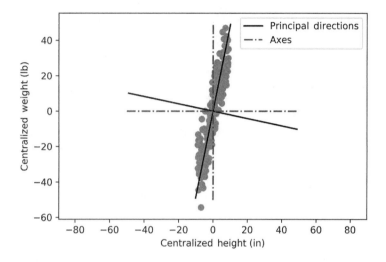

Figure 14.15 The first and second principal directions, plotted together with the customer data. These directions are perpendicular to each other. If we were to rotate the x- and y-axes by 78.3 degrees, they would align perfectly with the principal directions. Thus, swapping the axes with the principal directions reproduces the horizontal plot shown in figure 14.8.

Listing 14.26 Plotting principal directions, axes, and data information

```
principal_components = pca_object.components_
for i, pc in enumerate(principal_components):
    plot_stretched_vector(pc, c='k',
                          label='Principal Directions' if i == 0 else None)

for i, axis_vector in enumerate([np.array([0, 1]), np.array([1, 0])]):   ◁─┐
    plot_stretched_vector(axis_vector,  c='g', linestyle='-.',
                          label='Axes' if i == 0 else None)
                                                    Plots the x-axis and
plt.scatter(centered_data[0], centered_data[1], c='y')    y-axis by stretching out
plt.xlabel('Centralized Height (in)')               two unit vectors (one vertical
plt.ylabel('Centralized Weight (lb)')              and one horizontal) so that their
plt.axis('equal')                              magnitudes align with the stretched principal
plt.legend()                                  components. Consequently, the stretched axes and
plt.show()                            stretched principal components are rendered visually comparable.
```

According to the plot, the two principal directions are essentially rotated versions of the x- and y-axes. Imagine if we rotated our two axes counterclockwise by 78.3 degrees. After the rotation, the x-axis and y-axis would align with the two principal components. The variances covered by these axes would equal 99.02 and 0.08%, respectively. Hence, this axis swap would reproduce the horizontal plot in figure 14.8.

NOTE Tilting your head to the left while staring at figure 14.15 will help you picture this outcome.

The aforementioned axis swap is known as a *projection*. Swapping our two axes for the principal directions is referred to as a *projection onto the principal directions*. Using trigonometry, we can show that the projection of centered_data onto the principal directions is equal to the matrix product of centered_data and the two principal components. In other words, principal_components @ centered_data repositions the dataset's x and y coordinates relative to the principal directions. The final output should equal pca_transformed_data.T. Let's confirm with the code in listing 14.27.

NOTE More generally, the dot product between the *i*th principal component and a centered data point projects that data point onto the *i*th principal direction. Thus, running first_pc @ centered_data[i] projects the *i*th data point onto the first principal direction. The result equals the x-value obtained when the x-axis is swapped with the first principal direction (pca_transformed_data[i][0]). In this manner, we can project multiple data points onto multiple principal directions using matrix multiplication.

Listing 14.27 Swapping standard axes for principal directions using projection

```
projections = principal_components @ centered_data
assert np.allclose(pca_transformed_data.T, projections)
```

The reoriented output of PCA is dependent on projection. In general terms, the PCA algorithm works as follows:

1 Centralize the input data by subtracting the mean from each data point.
2 Compute the dataset's principal components. The computation details are discussed later in this section.
3 Take the matrix product between the centralized data and the principal components. This swaps the data's standard axes for its principal directions.

Generally, an *N*-dimensional dataset has *N* principal directions (one for each axis). The *k*th principal direction maximizes the variance not covered by the first $k-1$ directions. Thus, a 4D dataset has four principal directions: the first principal direction maximizes unidirectional dispersion, the second maximizes all unidirectional dispersion not covered by the first, and the final two cover all the remaining variance.

Here's where it gets interesting. Suppose we project a 4D dataset onto its four principal directions. The dataset's standard axes are thus swapped with its principal directions. Under the right circumstances, two of the new axes will cover a good chunk of the variance. Consequently, the remaining axes could be discarded, with minimal information loss. Disposing of the two axes would reduce the 4D dataset to two dimensions. We would then be able to visualize that data in a 2D scatter plot. Ideally, the 2D plot would maintain enough dispersion for us to correctly identify data clusters. Let's explore an actual scenario where we visualize 4D data in two dimensions.

> **Key terminology**
> - *First principal direction*—The linear direction in which data dispersion is maximized. Swapping the x-axis with the first principal direction reorients the dataset to maximize its spread horizontally. The reorientation can allow for more straightforward 1D clustering.
> - *Kth principal direction*—The linear direction that maximizes the variance not covered by the first $K - 1$ principal directions.
> - *Kth principal component*—A unit vector representation of the *Kth* principal direction. This vector can be utilized for directional projection.
> - *Projection*—Projecting data onto a principal direction is analogous to swapping a standard axis with that direction. We can project a dataset onto its top *K* principal directions by taking the matrix product of the centralized dataset with its top *K* principal components.

14.3 Clustering 4D data in two dimensions

Imagine we are botanists studying flowers in a blooming meadow. We randomly select 150 flowers. For every flower, we record the following measurements:

- The length of a colorful petal
- The width of the colorful petal
- The length of a green leaf supporting the petal
- The width of the green leaf supporting the petal

These 4D flower measurements already exist and can be accessed using scikit-learn. We can obtain the measurements by importing `load_iris` from `sklearn.datasets`. Calling `load_iris()['data']` returns a matrix containing 150 rows and 4 columns: each row corresponds to a flower, and each column corresponds to the leaf and petal measurements. Next, we load the data and print the measurements for a single flower. All recorded measurements are in centimeters.

Listing 14.28 Loading flower measurements from scikit-learn

```
from sklearn.datasets import load_iris
flower_data = load_iris()
flower_measurements = flower_data['data']
num_flowers, num_measurements = flower_measurements.shape
print(f"{num_flowers} flowers have been measured.")
```

```
print(f"{num_measurements} measurements were recorded for every flower.")
print("The first flower has the following measurements (in cm): "
      f"{flower_measurements[0]}")
```

```
150 flowers have been measured.
4 measurements were recorded for every flower.
The first flower has the following measurements (in cm): [5.1 3.5 1.4 0.2]
```

Given this matrix of flower measurements, our goals are as follows:

- We want to visualize our flower data in 2D space.
- We want to determine whether any clusters are present in the 2D visualization.
- We want to build a very simple model to distinguish between flower cluster types (assuming any clusters are found).

We start by visualizing the data. It is four-dimensional, but we want to plot it in 2D. Reducing the data to two dimensions requires that we project it onto its first and second principal directions. The remaining two directions can be discarded. Thus, our analysis only requires the first two principal components.

Using scikit-learn, we can limit PCA analysis to the top two principal components. We just need to run `PCA(n_components=2)` during the initialization of the `PCA` object. The initialized object will be capable of reducing input data to a two-dimensional projection. Next, we initialize a two-component `PCA` object and use `fit_transform` to reduce our flower measurements to 2D.

Listing 14.29   Reducing flower measurements to two dimensions

```
pca_object_2D = PCA(n_components=2)
transformed_data_2D = pca_object_2D.fit_transform(flower_measurements)
```

The computed `transformed_data_2D` matrix should be two-dimensional, containing just two columns. Let's confirm.

Listing 14.30   Checking the shape of a dimensionally reduced matrix

```
row_count, column_count = transformed_data_2D.shape
print(f"The matrix contains {row_count} rows, corresponding to "
      f"{row_count} recorded flowers.")
print(f"It also contains {column_count} columns, corresponding to "
      f"{column_count} dimensions.")
```

```
The matrix contains 150 rows, corresponding to 150 recorded flowers.
It also contains 2 columns, corresponding to 2 dimensions.
```

How much of the total data variance is covered by our outputted data matrix? We can find out using the `explained_variance_ratio_` attribute of `pca_object_2D`.

> **Listing 14.31 Measuring the variance coverage of a dimensionally reduced matrix**

```
def print_2D_variance_coverage(pca_object):
    percent_var_coverages = 100 * pca_object.explained_variance_ratio_
    x_axis_coverage, y_axis_coverage = percent_var_coverages
    total_coverage = x_axis_coverage + y_axis_coverage
    print(f"The x-axis covers {x_axis_coverage:.2f}% "
          "of the total variance")
    print(f"The y-axis covers {y_axis_coverage:.2f}% "
          "of the total variance")
    print(f"Together, the 2 axes cover {total_coverage:.2f}% "
          "of the total variance")

print_2D_variance_coverage(pca_object_2D)
```

Computes the variance coverage of the dimensionally reduced 2D dataset associated with pca_object. This function is reused elsewhere in the section.

```
The x-axis covers 92.46% of the total variance
The y-axis covers 5.31% of the total variance
Together, the 2 axes cover 97.77% of the total variance
```

Our dimensionally reduced matrix covers more than 97% of the total data variance. Thus, a scatter plot of `transformed_data_2D` should display most of the clustering patterns present in the dataset (figure 14.16).

> **Listing 14.32 Plotting flower data in 2D**

```
plt.scatter(transformed_data_2D[:,0], transformed_data_2D[:,1])
plt.show()
```

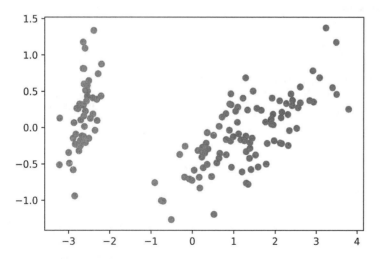

Figure 14.16 4D flower measurements plotted in 2D. The measurements were reduced to two dimensions using PCA. The reduced data covers more than 97% of the total variance. Our 2D plot is informative: two or three flower clusters are clearly visible.

Our flower data forms clusters when plotted in 2D. Based on the clustering, we can assume that two or three flower types are present. In fact, our measured data represents three unique species of flowers. This species information is stored in the `flower_data` dictionary. Next, we color our flower plot by species and verify that the colors fall in three distinct clusters (figure 14.17).

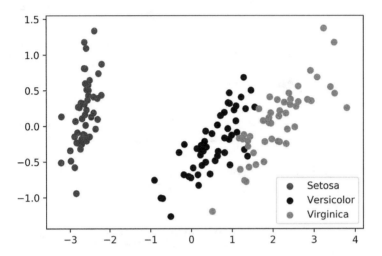

Figure 14.17   4D flower measurements plotted in 2D. Each plotted flower point is colored based on its species. The three species fall into three clusters. Thus, our 2D reduction correctly captures the signal required to distinguish between species.

Listing 14.33   Coloring plotted data by flower species

Plots dimensionally reduced flower data while coloring it by species. This function is reused elsewhere in the section.

Returns the names of the three flower species in our dataset

```
def visualize_flower_data(dim_reduced_data):
    species_names = flower_data['target_names']
    for i, species in enumerate(species_names):
        species_data = np.array([dim_reduced_data[j]
                                 for j in range(dim_reduced_data.shape[0])
                                 if flower_data['target'][j] == i]).T
        plt.scatter(species_data[0], species_data[1], label=species.title(),
                    color=['g', 'k', 'y'][i])
    plt.legend()
    plt.show()

visualize_flower_data(transformed_data_2D)
```

Plots each species using a unique color

Extracts just those coordinates associated with a particular species. For filtering purposes, we use flower_data[target], which maps to a list of species IDs. The IDs correspond to the three species names. If the *j*th flower corresponds to species_name[i], then its species ID equals *j*.

For the most part, the three species are spatially distinct. *Versicolor* and *Virgincia* share a bit of overlap, implying that they have similar petal properties. On the other hand, *Setosa* forms an entirely separate cluster. A vertical x-value threshold of −2 is sufficient to isolate *Setosa* from all other species. Hence, we can define a very simple *Setosa* detection function. The function takes as input a four-element array called `flower_sample`, which holds four petal measurements. The function will do the following:

1 Centralize the sample by subtracting the mean of `flower_measurements` from `flower_sample`. This mean is stored as an attribute in `pca_object_2D`. It is equal to `pca_object_2D.mean_`.

2 Project the centralized sample onto the first principal direction by taking its dot product with the first principal component. As a reminder, the first principal component is stored in `pca_object_2D.components_[0]`.

3 Check if the projected value is less than −2. If so, then the flower sample will be treated as a possible *Setosa* species.

NOTE Our *Setosa* detection function doesn't take into account any flower species beyond the three that we've recorded. However, the function should still sufficiently analyze new flowers in our meadow, where no additional species have been observed.

Next, we define the `detect_setosa` function and then analyze a flower sample with measurements (in cm) of `[4.8, 3.7, 1.2, 0.24]`.

Listing 14.34 Defining a Setosa detector based on dimensionally reduced data

```
def detect_setosa(flower_sample):
    centered_sample = flower_sample - pca_object_2D.mean_
    projection = pca_object_2D.components_[0] @ centered_sample
    if projection < -2:
        print("The sample could be a Setosa")
    else:
        print("The sample is not a Setosa")

new_flower_sample = np.array([4.8, 3.7, 1.2, 0.24])
detect_setosa(new_flower_sample)
```

```
The sample could be a Setosa
```

The flower sample could be a *Setosa* according to our simple threshold analysis, which was made possible by PCA. Various benefits of PCA include the following:

- Visualization of complex data.
- Simplified data classification and clustering.
- Simplified classification.
- Decreased memory usage. Reducing the data from four to two dimensions halves the number of bytes required to store the data.

- Faster computations. Reducing the data from four to two dimensions speeds up the computation time required to compute a similarity matrix fourfold.

So are we ready to use PCA to cluster our text data? Unfortunately, the answer is no. We must first discuss and address certain flaws that are inherent to the algorithm.

> **Common scikit-learn PCA methods**
> - `pca_object = PCA()`—Creates a `PCA` object capable of reorienting input data so that its axes align with its principal directions.
> - `pca_object = PCA(n_components=K)`—Creates a `PCA` object capable of reorienting input data so that *K* of its axes align with the top *K* principal directions. All other axes are ignored. This reduces data to *K* dimensions.
> - `pca_transformed_data = pca_object.fit_transform(data)`—Executes PCA on inputted data using an initialized `PCA` object. The `fit_transform` method assumes that the columns of the `data` matrix correspond to spatial axes. The axes are subsequently aligned with the data's principal direction. This result is stored in the `pca_transformed_data` matrix.
> - `pca_object.explained_variance_ratio_`—Returns the fractional variance coverage associated with each principal direction of a fitted `PCA` object. Each *i*th element corresponds to fractional variance coverage along the *i*th principal direction.
> - `pca_object.mean_`—Returns the mean of the input data, which has been fitted to the `PCA` object.
> - `pca_object.components_`—Returns the principal components of the input data, which have been fitted to the `PCA` object. Each *i*th row of the `components_` matrix corresponds to the *i*th principal component. Running `pca_object.components_[i] @ (data[j] - pca_object.mean_)` projects the *j*th data point onto the *i*th principal component. The projected output equals `pca_transformed_data[j][i]`.

14.3.1 Limitations of PCA

PCA does have some serious limitations. It is overly sensitive to units of measurement. For example, our flower measurements are all in centimeters, but we can imagine converting the first axis into millimeters by running `10 * flower_measurements[0]`. The information content of that axis should not change; however, its variance will shift. Let's convert the axis units to evaluate how the variance is affected.

Listing 14.35   Measuring the effect of unit change on axis variance

```
first_axis_var = flower_measurements[:,0].var()
print(f"The variance of the first axis is: {first_axis_var:.2f}")

flower_measurements[:,0] *= 10
first_axis_var = flower_measurements[:,0].var()
print("We've converted the measurements from cm to mm.\nThat variance "
      f"now equals {first_axis_var:.2f}")
```

```
The variance of the first axis is: 0.68
We've converted the measurements from cm to mm.
That variance now equals 68.11
```

Our variance has increased 100-fold. Now the first axis variance dominates our dataset. Consider the consequences of running PCA on these modified flower measurements: PCA will attempt to find the axis where variance is maximized. This, of course, will yield the first axis, where variance has increased from 0.68 to 68. Consequently, PCA will project all the data onto the first axis. Our reduced data will collapse to one dimension! We can prove this by refitting pca_object_2D to flower_measurements and then printing the variance coverage.

```
pca_object_2D.fit_transform(flower_measurements)      ◁——    Refits our PCA
print_2D_variance_coverage(pca_object_2D)                     object to the updated
                                                             flower_measurements
The x-axis covers 98.49% of the total variance               data
The y-axis covers 1.32% of the total variance
Together, the 2 axes cover 99.82% of the total variance
```

More than 98% of the variance now lies along a single axis. Previously, two dimensions were required to capture 97% of the data variance. Clearly, we've introduced an error into our data. How do we resolve it? One obvious solution is to ensure that all the axes share the same units of measurements. However, such a practical approach is not always possible. Sometimes the units of measurement are just not available. Other times, the axes correspond to different measurement types (such as length and weight), so the units are incompatible. What should we do?

Let's consider the root cause of our variance shift. We've made the values in flower_ measurements[:,0] larger, so their variance also grew larger. Differences in axis variance are caused by differences in value size. In the previous section, we were able to eliminate such differences in size using normalization. As a reminder, during normalization, a vector is divided by its magnitude. This produces a unit vector whose magnitude equals 1.0. Thus, if we normalize our axes, all the axes values will lie between 0 and 1. The dominance of the first axis will thus be eliminated. Let's normalize flower_ measurements and then reduce the normalized data to two dimensions. The resulting 2D variance coverage should once again approximate 97%.

```
for i in range(flower_measurements.shape[1]):
    flower_measurements[:,i] /= norm(flower_measurements[:,i])

transformed_data_2D = pca_object_2D.fit_transform(flower_measurements)
print_2D_variance_coverage(pca_object_2D)

The x-axis covers 94.00% of the total variance
The y-axis covers 3.67% of the total variance
Together, the 2 axes cover 97.67% of the total variance
```

Normalization has slightly modified our data. Now the first principal direction covers 94% of the total variance rather than 92.46%. Meanwhile, the second principal component covers 3.67% of total variance rather than 5.31%. Despite these changes, the total 2D variance coverage still sums to approximately 97%. We replot the PCA output to confirm that the 2D clustering patterns remain unchanged (figure 14.18).

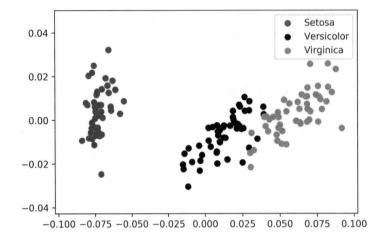

Figure 14.18   4D normalized flower measurements plotted in 2D. Each plotted flower point is colored based on its species. The three species fall into three clusters. Thus, our 2D reduction correctly captures the signal required to distinguish between species.

> **Listing 14.38   Plotting 2D PCA output after normalization**

```
visualize_flower_data(transformed_data_2D)
```

Our plot is slightly different from our previous observations. However, the three species of flowers continue to separate into three clusters, and *Setosa* remains spatially distinct from other species. Normalization has retained existing cluster separations while eliminating the error caused by unit differences.

Unfortunately, normalization does lead to unintended consequences. Our normalized axis values now lie between 0 and 1, so each axis mean is likewise between 0 and 1. All values lie less than 1 unit from their mean. This is a problem: PCA requires us to subtract the mean from each axis value to centralize our data. Then the centralized matrix is multiplied by the principal components to realign the axes. Regrettably, data centralization is not always achievable due to floating-point errors. It's computationally difficult to subtract similar values with 100% precision, so it is difficult to subtract the mean from a value that is very close to that mean. For example, suppose we analyze an array containing two data points, 1 + 1e-3 and 1 - 1e-3. The mean of the array is equal to 1. Subtracting 1 from the array should lead to a centralized mean of 0, but the actual mean will not equal 0 due to an error, illustrated next.

Listing 14.39 Illustrating errors caused by values proximate to their mean

```
data = np.array([1 + 1e-3, 1 - 1e-3])
mean = data.mean()
assert mean == 1
centralized_data = data - 2 * [mean]
assert centralized_data.mean() != 0      ◁——
print(f"Actual mean is equal to {centralized_data.mean()}")
```

> **The mean of the centralized data does not equal 0 as intended.**

```
Actual mean is equal to -5.551115123125783e-17
```

We cannot reliably centralize data that lies close to the mean. Hence, we can't reliably execute PCA on normalized data. What should we do?

A solution to our problem does exist. However, to derive it, we must dive deep into the guts of the PCA algorithm. We must learn how to compute the principal components from scratch without rotation. That computation process is a bit abstract, but it can be understood without studying advanced mathematics. Once we derive the PCA algorithm, we'll be able to modify it slightly. That minor modification will completely bypass data centralization. The modified algorithm, known as *singular value decomposition* (SVD), will allow us to efficiently cluster text data.

> **NOTE** If you're not interested in the SVD derivation, you can skip ahead to the final subsection. It describes SVD usage in scikit-learn.

14.4 *Computing principal components without rotation*

In this subsection, we learn how to extract the principal components from scratch. To better illustrate the extraction process, we'll visualize our component vectors. Of course, vectors are easier to plot when they are two-dimensional. Thus, we start by revisiting our customer measurements dataset whose principal components are 2D. As a reminder, we've computed the following outputs for this data:

- centralized_data—A centralized version of the measurements dataset. The mean of centralized_data is [0 0].
- first_pc—The first principal component of the measurements dataset. It is a two-element array.

As we've discussed, first_pc is a unit vector that points in the first principal direction. That direction maximizes the dispersion of the data. Earlier, we discovered the first principal direction by rotating our 2D dataset. The goal of that rotation was to either maximize the x-axis variance or minimize the y-axis variance. Previously, we computed axis variances using vector dot-product operations. However, we can measure axis variance more efficiently using matrix multiplication. More importantly, by storing all our variances in a matrix, we can extract our components without rotation. Let's consider the following:

- We've already shown that the variance of an `axis` array equals `axis @ axis / axis.size` (see listing 14.8).
- Thus, the variance of axis i in `centered_data` equals `centered_data[i] @ centered_data[i] / centered_data.shape[1]`.
- Consequently, running `centered_data @ centered_data.T / centered_data.shape[1]` will produce a matrix m, where `m[i][i]` equals the variance of axis i.

Essentially, we can compute all axis variances in a single matrix operation. We just need to multiply our matrix with its transpose while also dividing by data size. This produces a new matrix, called the *covariance matrix*. The diagonal of a covariance matrix stores the variance along each axis.

NOTE The non-diagonal elements of the covariance matrix have informative properties as well: they determine the direction of the linear slope between two axes. In `centered_data`, the slope between x and y is positive. Therefore, the non-diagonal elements in `centered_data @ centered_data.T` are also positive.

Next we compute the covariance matrix of `centered_data` and assign it to variable `cov_matrix`. Then we confirm that `cov_matrix[i][i]` equals the variance of the *i*th axis for every i.

Listing 14.40 Computing a covariance matrix

```
cov_matrix = centered_data @ centered_data.T / centered_data.shape[1]
print(f"Covariance matrix:\n {cov_matrix}")
for i in range(centered_data.shape[0]):
    variance = cov_matrix[i][i]
    assert round(variance, 10) == round(centered_data[i].var(), 10)    ◁──┐
```

```
Covariance matrix:                                          Rounds because of
 [[ 26.99916667 106.30456732]                              floating-point errors
 [106.30456732 519.8206294 ]]
```

The covariance matrix and the principal components share a very special (and useful) relationship: the normalized product of a covariance matrix and a principal component equals that principal component! Thus, normalizing `cov_matrix @ first_pc` produces a vector that's identical to `first_pc`. Let's illustrate this relationship by plotting `first_pc` and the normalized product of `cov_matrix` and `first_pc` (figure 14.19).

NOTE When taking the product of a matrix and a vector, we treat the vector as a single-column table. Thus, a vector with x elements is treated as a matrix with x rows and one column. Once the vector is reconfigured as a matrix, standard matrix multiplication is carried out. That multiplication produces another single-column matrix, which is equivalent to a vector. Consequently, the product of matrix M and vector v is equal to `np.array([row @ v for row in M])`.

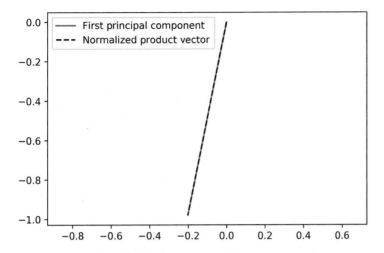

Figure 14.19 A plot of `first_pc` together with the normalized product of `cov_matrix` and `first_pc`. The two plotted vectors are identical. The product of the covariance matrix and the principal component points in the same direction as that principal component.

Listing 14.41 Exposing the relationship between `cov_matrix` and `first_pc`

```
def plot_vector(vector, **kwargs):
    plt.plot([0, vector[0]], [0, vector[1]], **kwargs)

plot_vector(first_pc, c='y', label='First Principal Component')
product_vector = cov_matrix @ first_pc
product_vector /= norm(product_vector)
plot_vector(product_vector, c='k', linestyle='--',
            label='Normalized Product Vector')

plt.legend()
plt.axis('equal')
plt.show()
```

This helper function plots a 2D vector as a line segment stretching from the origin.

The two plotted vectors are identical! The matrix-vector product of `cov_matrix` and `first_pc` points in the same direction as `first_pc`. Thus, by definition, `first_pc` is an *eigenvector* of `cov_matrix`. An eigenvector of a matrix satisfies the following special property: the product of the matrix and the eigenvector points in the same direction as the eigenvector. The direction will not shift, no matter how many times we take the product. So, `cov_matrix @ product_vector` points in the same direction as `product_vector`, and the angle between the vectors equals zero. Let's confirm.

Listing 14.42 Computing the angle between eigenvector products

```
product_vector2 = cov_matrix @ product_vector
product_vector2 /= norm(product_vector2)
```

```
cosine_similarity = product_vector @ product_vector2
angle = np.degrees(np.arccos(cosine_similarity))
print(f"The angle between vectors equals {angle:.2f} degrees")
```

```
The angle between vectors equals 0.00 degrees
```

Taking the arccosine of the cosine similarity returns the angle between vectors.

Both vectors are unit vectors. As discussed in section 13, the dot product of two unit vectors equals the cosine of their angle.

The product of a matrix and its eigenvector maintains the eigenvector's direction. However, in most cases, it alters the eigenvector's magnitude. For example, first_pc is an eigenvector with a magnitude of 1. Multiplying first_pc by the covariance matrix will increase that magnitude x-fold. Let's print the actual shift in magnitude by running norm(cov_matrix @ first_pc).

Listing 14.43   Measuring the shift in magnitude

```
new_magnitude = norm(cov_matrix @ first_pc)
print("Multiplication has stretched the first principal component by "
      f"approximately {new_magnitude:.1f} units.")
```

```
Multiplication has stretched the first principal component by
approximately 541.8 units
```

Multiplication has stretched first_pc by 541.8 units along the first principal direction. Thus, cov_matrix @ first_pc equals 541.8 * first_pc. Given any matrix m and its eigenvector eigen_vec, the product of m and eigen_vec always equals v * eigen_vec, where v is a numeric value formally called the *eigenvalue*. Our first_pc eigenvector has an eigenvalue of approximately 541. This value may seem familiar because we have seen it before: early in this section, we printed the maximized x-axis variance, which was approximately 541. Thus, our eigenvalue equals the variance along the first principal direction. We can confirm by calling (centered_data @ first_pc).var().

Listing 14.44   Comparing an eigenvalue to the variance

```
variance = (centered_data.T @ first_pc).var()
direction1_var = projections[0].var()
assert round(variance, 10) == round(direction1_var, 10)
print("The variance along the first principal direction is approximately"
      f" {variance:.1f}")
```

```
The variance along the first principal direction is approximately 541.8
```

Let's recap our observations:

- The first principal component is an eigenvector of the covariance matrix.
- The associated eigenvalue equals the variance along the first principal direction.

These observations are not coincidental. Mathematicians have proven the following:

- The principal components of a dataset are equal to the normalized eigenvectors of the dataset's covariance matrix.
- The variance along a principal direction is equal to the eigenvalue of the associated principal component.

Consequently, to uncover the first principal component, it is sufficient to do the following:

1 Compute the covariance matrix.
2 Find the eigenvector of the matrix with the largest eigenvalue. That eigenvector corresponds to the direction with the highest variance coverage.

We can extract the eigenvector with the largest eigenvalue using a straightforward algorithm called *power iteration.*

Key terminology

- *Covariance matrix*—`m @ m.T / m.shape[1]`, where `m` is a matrix with a mean of zero. The diagonal of the covariance matrix equals the variances along each axis of `m`.
- *Eigenvector*—A special type of vector associated with a matrix. If `m` is a matrix with eigenvector `eigen_vec`, then `m @ eigen_vec` points in the same direction as `eigen_vec`. Also, if `m` is a covariance matrix, `eigen_vec` is a principal component.
- *Eigenvalue*—A numeric value associated with an eigenvector. If `m` is a matrix with eigenvector `eigen_vec`, then `m @ eigen_vec` stretches the eigenvector by `eigenvalue` units. Therefore, the eigenvalue equals `norm(m @ eigen_vec) / norm(eigen_vec)`. The eigenvalue of a principal component equals the variance covered by that component.

14.4.1 Extracting eigenvectors using power iteration

Our goal is to obtain the eigenvectors of `cov_matrix`. The procedure for doing this is simple. We start by generating a random unit vector, `random_vector`.

Listing 14.45 Generating a random unit vector

```
np.random.seed(0)
random_vector = np.random.random(size=2)
random_vector /= norm(random_vector)
```

Next, we compute `cov_matrix @ random_vector`. This matrix-vector product both rotates and stretches our random vector. We normalize the new vector so that its magnitude is comparable to `random_vector` and then plot both the new vector and the random vector (figure 14.20). Our expectation is that the two vectors will point in different directions.

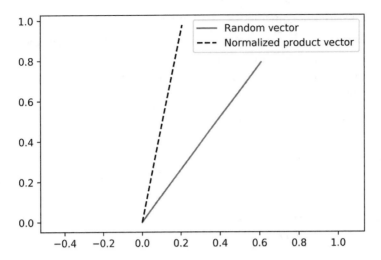

Figure 14.20   A plot of `random_vector` together with the normalized product of `cov_matrix` and `random_vector`. The two plotted vectors point in different directions.

Listing 14.46   Taking the product of `cov_matrix` and `random_vector`

```
product_vector = cov_matrix @ random_vector
product_vector /= norm(product_vector)

plt.plot([0, random_vector[0]], [0, random_vector[1]],
         label='Random Vector')
plt.plot([0, product_vector[0]], [0, product_vector[1]], linestyle='--',
         c='k', label='Normalized Product Vector')

plt.legend()
plt.axis('equal')
plt.show()
```

Our two vectors have nothing in common. Let's see what happens when we repeat the previous step by running `cov_matrix @ product_vector`. Next, we normalize and plot this additional vector along with the previously plotted `product_vector` (figure 14.21).

Listing 14.47   Taking the product of `cov_matrix` and `product_vector`

```
product_vector2 = cov_matrix @ product_vector
product_vector2 /= norm(product_vector2)

plt.plot([0, product_vector[0]], [0, product_vector[1]], linestyle='--',
         c='k', label='Normalized Product Vector')
plt.plot([0, product_vector2[0]], [0, product_vector2[1]], linestyle=':',
         c='r', label='Normalized Product Vector2')
plt.legend()
plt.axis('equal')
plt.show()
```

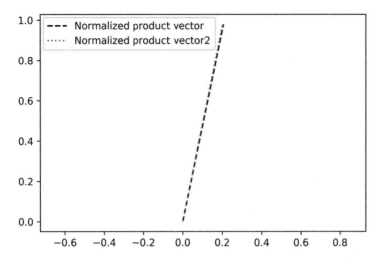

Figure 14.21 A plot of `product_vector` together with the normalized product of `cov_matrix` and `product_vector`. The two plotted vectors are identical. We've thus discovered an eigenvector of the covariance matrix.

Our product vectors point in an identical direction! Therefore, `product_vector` is an eigenvector of `cov_matrix`. Basically, we've carried out a *power iteration*, which is a simple algorithm for eigenvector detection. We were lucky in our usage of the algorithm: a single matrix multiplication was enough to uncover the eigenvector. More commonly, a few additional iterations are required.

Power iteration works as follows:

1 Generate a random unit vector.
2 Multiply the vector by our matrix, and normalize the result. Our unit vector is rotated.
3 Iteratively repeat the previous step until the unit vector gets "stuck"—it won't rotate anymore. By definition, it is now an eigenvector.

The power iteration is guaranteed to converge onto an eigenvector (if one exists). Generally, 10 iterations are more than sufficient to achieve convergence. The resulting eigenvector has the largest possible eigenvalue relative to the other eigenvectors of the matrix.

> **NOTE** Some matrices have eigenvectors with negative eigenvalues. In such circumstances, the power iteration returns the eigenvector with the largest absolute eigenvalue.

Let's define a `power_iteration` function that takes a matrix as input. It returns an eigenvector and an eigenvalue as output. We test the function by running `power_iteration(cov_matrix)`.

Listing 14.48   Implementing the power iteration algorithm

```
np.random.seed(0)
def power_iteration(matrix):
    random_vector = np.random.random(size=matrix.shape[0])
    random_vector = random_vector / norm(random_vector)
    old_rotated_vector = random_vector
    for _ in range(10):
        rotated_vector = matrix @ old_rotated_vector
        rotated_vector = rotated_vector / norm(rotated_vector)
        old_rotated_vector = rotated_vector

    eigenvector = rotated_vector
    eigenvalue = norm(matrix @ eigenvector)
    return eigenvector, eigenvalue

eigenvector, eigenvalue = power_iteration(cov_matrix)
print(f"The extracted eigenvector is {eigenvector}")
print(f"Its eigenvalue is approximately {eigenvalue: .1f}")

The extracted eigenvector is [0.20223994 0.979336  ]
Its eigenvalue is approximately  541.8
```

The `power_iteration` function has extracted an eigenvector with an eigenvalue of approximately 541. This corresponds to the variance along the first principal axis. Hence, our eigenvector equals the first principal component.

> **NOTE** You may have noticed that the extracted eigenvector in figure 14.21 stretches toward positive values in the plot. Meanwhile, the first principal component in figure 14.19 stretches toward negative values. As stated earlier, the principal component `pc` can be used interchangeably with `-pc` during PCA execution—projection onto principal directions will not be erroneously affected. The only noticeable effect will be a difference in reflection over the projected axes, as seen in figure 14.13.

Our function returns a single eigenvector with the largest eigenvalue. Consequently, `power_iteration(cov_matrix)` returns the principal component with the largest variance coverage. As stated earlier, the second principal component is also an eigenvector. Its eigenvalue corresponds to the variance along the second principal direction. Thus, that component is an eigenvector with the second largest eigenvalue. How do we find it? The solution requires just a few lines of code. That solution is not easy to understand without knowing higher mathematics, but we'll review its basic steps.

To extract the second eigenvector, we must eliminate all traces of the first eigenvector from `cov_matrix`. This process is known as *matrix deflation*. Once a matrix is deflated, its second-largest eigenvalue becomes its largest eigenvalue. To deflate `cov_matrix`, we must take the *outer product* of `eigenvector` with itself. That outer product is computed by taking the pairwise product of `eigenvector[i] * eigenvector[j]` for every possible value of i and j. The pairwise products are stored in a matrix M, where M[i][j] =

eigenvector[i] * eigenvector[j]. We can compute the outer product using two nested loops or using NumPy and running np.outer(eigenvector, eigenvector).

> **NOTE** Generally, the outer product is computed between two vectors v1 and v2. That outer product returns a matrix m where m[i][j] equals v1[i] * v2[j]. During matrix deflation, both v1 and v2 are equal to eigenvector.

Listing 14.49 Computing the outer product of an eigenvector with itself

```
outer_product = np.outer(eigenvector, eigenvector)
for i in range(eigenvector.size):
    for j in range(eigenvector.size):
        assert outer_product[i][j] == eigenvector[i] * eigenvector[j]
```

Given the outer product, we can deflate cov_matrix by running cov_matrix - eigenvalue * outer_product. That basic operation produces a matrix whose primary eigenvector is equal to the second principal component.

Listing 14.50 Deflating the covariance matrix

```
deflated_matrix = cov_matrix - eigenvalue * outer_product
```

Running product_iteration(deflated_matrix) returns an eigenvector that we'll call next_eigenvector. Based on our discussion, we know that the following should be true:

- next_eigenvector equals the second principal component.
- Thus, np.array([eigenvector, next_eigenvector]) equals a matrix of principal components that we call components.
- Executing components @ centered_data projects our dataset onto its principal directions.
- Plotting the projections should produce a horizontally positioned, cigar-shaped plot similar to the one in figure 14.8 or figure 14.13.

Next, we extract next_eigenvector and execute the aforementioned projections. We then plot the projections to confirm that our assumptions are true (figure 14.22).

Listing 14.51 Extracting the second principal component from the deflated matrix

```
np.random.seed(0)
next_eigenvector, _ = power_iteration(deflated_matrix)
components = np.array([eigenvector, next_eigenvector])
projections = components @ centered_data
plt.scatter(projections[0], projections[1])
plt.axhline(0, c='black')
plt.axvline(0, c='black')
plt.axis('equal')
plt.show()
```

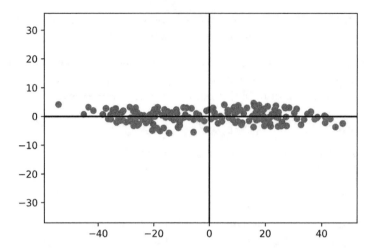

Figure 14.22   A plot of `centered_data` **projected onto its principal components, in which the components were computed using power iteration. The plot is identical to figure 14.13, which was generated using scikit-learn's PCA implementation.**

NumPy matrix deflation computations

- `np.outer(eigenvector, eigenvector)`—Computes the outer product of an eigenvector with itself. Returns a matrix `m` where `m[i][j]` equals `eigenvector[i] * eigenvector[j]`.
- `matrix -= eigenvalue * np.outer(eigenvector, eigenvector)`—Deflates a matrix by removing all traces of the eigenvector with the largest eigenvalue from the matrix. Running `power_iteration(matrix)` returns an eigenvector with the next largest eigenvalue.

We've basically developed an algorithm for extracting the top *K* principal components of a matrix whose rows all average to zero. Given any such `centered_matrix`, the algorithm is executed as follows:

1 Compute the covariance matrix of `centered_matrix` by running `centered_matrix @ centered_matrix.T`.

2 Run `power_iteration` on the covariance matrix. The function returns an eigenvector of the covariance matrix (`eigenvector`), corresponding to the largest possible eigenvalue (`eigenvalue`). This eigenvector equals the first principal component.

3 Deflate the matrix by subtracting `eigenvalue * np.outer(eigenvector, eigenvector)`. Running `power_iteration` on the deflated matrix extracts the next principal component.

4 Repeat the previous step $K - 2$ more times to extract the top K principal components.

Let's implement the algorithm by defining `find_top_principal_components`. The function extracts the top K principal components from a `centered_matrix` input.

Listing 14.52 Extracting the top *K* principal components

Makes a copy of the matrix so we can deflate that copy without modifying the original

Extracts the top K principal components from a matrix whose rows all average to zero. The value of K is preset to 2.

Principal components are simply the top eigenvectors of the covariance matrix (where eigenvector rank is determined by the eigenvalues). To emphasize this point, we define a separate function for extracting the top K eigenvectors of any matrix.

```python
def find_top_principal_components(centered_matrix, k=2):
    cov_matrix = centered_matrix @ centered_matrix.T
    cov_matrix /= centered_matrix[1].size
    return find_top_eigenvectors(cov_matrix, k=k)

def find_top_eigenvectors(matrix, k=2):
    matrix = matrix.copy()
    eigenvectors = []
    for _ in range(k):
        eigenvector, eigenvalue = power_iteration(matrix)
        eigenvectors.append(eigenvector)
        matrix -= eigenvalue * np.outer(eigenvector, eigenvector)

    return np.array(eigenvectors)
```

We defined a function for extracting the top K principal components of a dataset. The components allow us to project the dataset onto its top K principal directions. These directions maximize data dispersion along K axes. The remaining data axes can thus be disregarded, shrinking the coordinate column size to K. Consequently, we can reduce any dataset to K dimensions.

Basically, we're now able to run PCA from scratch without relying on scikit-learn. We can use PCA to reduce an N-dimensional dataset to K dimensions (where N is the column count of an input data matrix). To run the algorithm, we must execute the following steps:

1 Compute the mean along each of the axes in the dataset.
2 Subtract the mean from every axis, thus centering the dataset at the origin.
3 Extract the top K principal components of the centered dataset using the `find_top_principal_components` function.
4 Take the matrix product between the principal components and the centered dataset.

Let's implement these steps in a single function named `reduce_dimensions`. Why not name the function pca? Well, the first two steps of PCA require us to centralize our data. However, we'll soon learn that dimension reduction can be achieved without centralization. Thus, we pass an optional `centralize_data` parameter into our function.

We preset the parameter to True, guaranteeing that the function executes PCA under default conditions.

Listing 14.53   Defining a `reduce_dimensions` function

> The function takes as input a data matrix whose columns correspond to axes. This is consistent with the input orientation of scikit-learn's fit_transform method. The function then reduces the matrix from N columns to k columns.

```
def reduce_dimensions(data, k=2, centralize_data=True):
    data = data.T.copy()
    if centralize_data:
        for i in range(data.shape[0]):
            data[i] -= data[i].mean()

    principal_components = find_top_principal_components(data)
    return (principal_components @ data).T
```

> Data is transposed so that it remains consistent with the expected input into find_principal_components.

Optionally centralizes the data by subtracting its mean so the new mean equals 0

Let's test `reduce_dimensions` by applying it to our previously analyzed flower_measurements data. We reduce that data to 2D using our custom PCA implementation and then visualize the results (figure 14.23). Our plot should be consistent with the plot in figure 14.18.

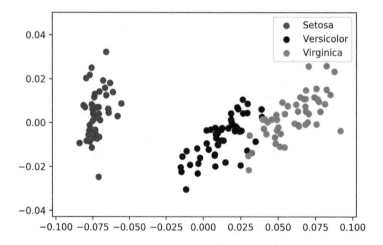

Figure 14.23   4D normalized flower measurements reduced to two dimensions using a custom PCA implementation. The plot is identical to the PCA output generated by scikit-learn.

Listing 14.54   Reducing flower data to 2D using a custom PCA implementation

```
np.random.seed(0)
dim_reduced_data = reduce_dimensions(flower_measurements)
visualize_flower_data(dim_reduced_data)
```

Our plot perfectly resembles scikit-learn's PCA output. We have reengineered scikit-learn's implementation, but with one big difference: in our function, centralization is optional. This will prove useful! As we've discussed, we can't reliably perform centralization on normalized data. Also, our flower dataset has been normalized to eliminate unit differences. Consequently, we cannot reliably run PCA on `flower_measurements`. One alternative is to bypass centralization by passing `centralize_data=False` into `reduce_dimensions`. This, of course, violates many assumptions of the PCA algorithm. However, the output could still be useful. What will happen if we reduce the dimensions of `flower_measurements` without centralization? Let's find out by setting `centralize_data` to `False` and plotting the results (figure 14.24).

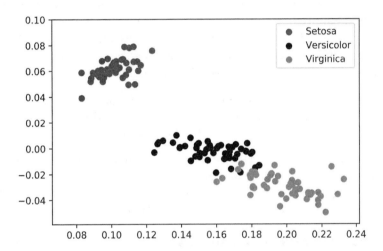

Figure 14.24 **4D normalized flower measurements reduced to two dimensions without centralization. Each plotted flower point is colored based on its species. The three species continue to fall into three clusters. However, the plot no longer resembles our PCA output.**

Listing 14.55 Running `reduce_dimensions` without centralization

As previously stated, the randomness of eigenvector extraction can influence 2D plot orientation. Here, we seed the algorithm to ensure that the orientation aligns with another plot, presented later (figure 14.25).

```
np.random.seed(3)
dim_reduced_data = reduce_dimensions(flower_measurements,
                                     centralize_data=False)
visualize_flower_data(dim_reduced_data)
```

In the output, the three species of flowers continue to separate into three clusters. Furthermore, *Setosa* remains spatially distinct from other species. However, there are changes in the plot. *Setosa* forms a tighter cluster than previously observed in the PCA results. This begs the question, is our latest plot as comprehensive as our PCA output? In other words, does it continue to represent 97% of the total data variance? We can check by measuring the variance of dim_reduced_data and dividing it by the total variance of flower_measurements.

Listing 14.56 Checking the variance of data reduced without centralization

```
variances = [sum(data[:,i].var() for i in range(data.shape[1]))
             for data in [dim_reduced_data, flower_measurements]]
dim_reduced_var, total_var = variances
percent_coverege = 100 * dim_reduced_var / total_var
print(f"Our plot covers {percent_coverege:.2f}% of the total variance")
```

```
Our plot covers 97.29% of the total variance
```

Our 2D variance coverage is maintained. Even though its value fluctuates slightly, the coverage remains at approximately 97%. We thus can reduce dimensionality without relying on centralization. However, centralization remains a defining feature of PCA, so our modified technique needs a different name. Officially, as mentioned earlier, the technique is called *singular value decomposition* (SVD).

WARNING Unlike PCA, SVD is not guaranteed to maximize the variance for each axis in the reduced output. However, in most real-world circumstances, SVD is able to dimensionally reduce data to a very practical degree.

The mathematical properties of SVD are complicated and lie beyond the scope of this book. Nonetheless, computer scientists can use these properties to execute SVD very efficiently, and these optimizations have been incorporated into scikit-learn. In the next subsection, we utilize scikit-learn's optimized SVD implementation.

14.5 *Efficient dimension reduction using SVD and scikit-learn*

Scikit-learn contains a dimension-reduction class called TruncatedSVD that is designed for optimal execution of SVD. Let's import TruncatedSVD from sklearn.decomposition.

Listing 14.57 Importing TruncatedSVD from scikit-learn

```
from sklearn.decomposition import TruncatedSVD
```

Applying TruncatedSVD to our flower_measurements data is easy. First, we need to run TruncatedSVD(n_components=2) to create an svd_object object capable of reducing data to two dimensions. Then, we can execute SVD by running svd_object.fit_predict(flower_measurements). That method call returns a two-dimensional svd_transformed_data matrix. Next, we apply TruncatedSVD and plot our results (figure 14.25). The plot should resemble our custom SVD output, shown in figure 14.24.

NOTE Unlike the PCA class, scikit-learn's TruncatedSVD implementation requires an n_components input. The default value for that parameter is preset to 2.

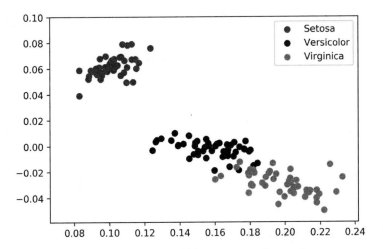

Figure 14.25　4D normalized flower measurements reduced to two dimensions using scikit-learn's SVD implementation. The output is identical to figure 14.24, which was generated using our custom SVD implementation.

Listing 14.58　Running SVD using scikit-learn

```
svd_object = TruncatedSVD(n_components=2)
svd_transformed_data = svd_object.fit_transform(flower_measurements)
visualize_flower_data(svd_transformed_data)
```

Not surprisingly, scikit-learn's results are identical to our custom SVD implementation. Scikit-learn's algorithm is faster and more memory efficient, but its output does not diverge from ours.

> **NOTE**　The outputs will not diverge when we reduce the number of dimensions. However, as the dimension count goes up, our implementation will become less precise because minor errors will creep into our eigenvector calculations. These minor errors will be magnified with each computed eigenvector. Scikit-learn, on the other hand, uses mathematical tricks to limit these errors.

We can further verify the overlap between outputs by comparing variance coverage. Our `svd_object` has an `explained_variance_ratio_` attribute that holds an array of the fractional variances covered by each reduced dimension. Summing over `100 *` `explained_variance_ratio_` should return the percent of total variance covered in the 2D plot. Based on our analysis, we expect that output to approximate 97.29%. Let's confirm.

Listing 14.59   Extracting variance from scikit-learn's SVD output

> The attribute is a NumPy array containing fractional coverage for each axis. Multiplying by 100 converts these fractions into percentages.

```
percent_variance_coverages = 100 * svd_object.explained_variance_ratio_     <─┐
x_axis_coverage, y_axis_coverage = percent_variance_coverages     <──────────┐│
total_2d_coverage = x_axis_coverage + y_axis_coverage
print(f"Our Scikit-Learn SVD output covers {total_2d_coverage:.2f}% of "
      "the total variance")

Our Scikit-Learn SVD output covers 97.29% of the total variance
```

> Each *i*th element of the array corresponds to the variance coverage of the *i*th axis.

Common scikit-learn SVD methods

- `svd_object = TruncatedSVD(n_components=K)`—Creates an SVD object capable of reducing input data to *K* dimensions.
- `svd_tranformed_data = svd_object.fit_transform(data)`—Executes SVD on inputted data using an initialized `TruncatedSVD` object. The `fit_transform` method assumes that the columns of the `data` matrix correspond to spatial axes. The dimensionally reduced results are stored in the `svd_transformed_data` matrix.
- `svd_object.explained_variance_ratio_`—Returns the fractional variance coverage associated with each dimensionally reduced axis of a fitted `TruncatedSVD` object.

Scikit-learn's optimized SVD implementation can decrease data from tens of thousands of dimensions to only a few hundred or a few dozen. The shrunken data can more efficiently be stored, transferred, and processed by predictive algorithms. Many real-world data tasks require SVD for data shrinkage before analysis. Applications range from image compression, to audio-noise removal, to natural language processing. NLP, in particular, is dependent on the algorithm due to the bloated nature of text data. As we discussed in the previous section, real-world documents form very large matrices whose column counts are way too high. We cannot multiply such matrices efficiently and therefore cannot compute text similarities. Fortunately, SVD makes these document matrices much more manageable. SVD allows us to shrink text-matrix column counts while retaining most of the variance, so we can compute large-scale text similarities in a timely manner. These text similarities can then be used to cluster the input documents.

In the subsequent section, we finally analyze large document datasets. We learn how to clean and cluster these datasets while also visualizing the clustering output. Our use of SVD will prove absolutely fundamental to this analysis.

Summary

- Reducing dataset dimensionality can simplify certain tasks, like clustering.

- We can reduce a 2D dataset to one dimension by rotating the data about the origin until the data points lie close to the x-axis. Doing so maximizes data spread along the x-axis, thus allowing us to delete the y-axis. However, the rotation requires us to first centralize the dataset so its mean coordinates lie at the origin.

- Rotating the data toward the x-axis is analogous to rotating the x-axis toward the *first principal direction*. The first principal direction is the linear direction in which data variance is maximized. The *second principal direction* is perpendicular to the first. In a 2D dataset, that direction represents the remaining variance not covered by the first principal direction.

- Dimensional reduction can be carried out using *principal component analysis* (PCA). PCA uncovers a dataset's principal directions and represents them as using unit vectors called *principal components*. The product of the centralized data matrix and the principal components swaps the data's standard axes with the principal directions. This axis swap is called a *projection*. When we project our data onto the principal directions, we maximize data dispersion along some axes and minimize it along others. Axes with minimized dispersion can be deleted.

- We can extract principal components by computing a *covariance matrix*: the matrix product of a centered dataset with itself, divided by the dataset size. The diagonal of that matrix represents the axes' variance values.

- Principal components are the *eigenvectors* of the covariance variance. Thus, by definition, the normalized product of the covariance matrix and each principal component is equal to that principal component.

- We can extract the top eigenvector of a matrix using the *power iteration* algorithm. Power iteration consists of repeated multiplication and normalization of a vector by a matrix. Applying power iteration to a covariance matrix returns the first principal component.

- By applying *matrix deflation*, we can eliminate all traces of an eigenvector. Deflating the covariance matrix and reapplying the power iteration returns the second principal component. Repeating that process iteratively returns all principal components.

- PCA is sensitive to units of measurement. Normalizing our input data reduces that sensitivity. However, as a consequence, the normalized data will be proximate to its mean. This is a problem because PCA requires us to subtract the mean from each axis value to centralize the data. Subtracting proximate values leads to floating-points errors.

- We can avoid these floating-point errors by refusing to centralize our data before running dimension reduction. The resulting output captures data variance to a sufficiently meaningful degree. This modified technique is called *singular value decomposition* (SVD).

NLP analysis
of large text datasets

This section covers

- Vectorizing texts using scikit-learn
- Dimensionally reducing vectorized text data
- Clustering large text datasets
- Visualizing text clusters
- Concurrently displaying multiple visualizations

Our previous discussions of natural language processing (NLP) techniques focused on toy examples and small datasets. In this section, we execute NLP on large collections of real-world texts. This type of analysis is seemingly straightforward, given the techniques presented thus far. For example, suppose we're doing market research across multiple online discussion forums. Each forum is composed of hundreds of users who discuss a specific topic, such as politics, fashion, technology, or cars. We want to automatically extract all the discussion topics based on the contents of the user conversations. These extracted topics will be used to plan a marketing campaign, which will target users based on their online interests.

How do we cluster user discussions into topics? One approach would be to do the following:

1 Convert all discussion texts into a matrix of word counts using techniques discussed in section 13.

2 Dimensionally reduce the word count matrix using singular value decomposition (SVD). This will allow us to efficiently complete all pairs of text similarities with matrix multiplication.

3 Utilize the matrix of text similarities to cluster the discussions into topics.

4 Explore the topic clusters to identify useful topics for our marketing campaign.

Of course, in real life, this simple analysis is not as straightforward as it seems. Unanswered questions still remain. How do we efficiently explore the topic clusters without reading all the clustered texts one at a time? Also, which of the clustering algorithms introduced in section 10 should we utilize to cluster the discussions?

Even at the level of pairwise text comparison, we face certain questions. How do we deal with common uninformative words such as *the*, *it*, and *they*? Should we penalize them? Ignore them? Filter them out entirely? What about other common, corpus-specific words such as the names of the websites that host the discussion forums?

All of these questions have answers that can best be understood by actually exploring an online forum dataset containing thousands of texts. Scikit-learn includes one such real-world dataset among its example data collections. In this section, we load, explore, and cluster this large dataset of online forums. Python's external data science libraries, such as scikit-learn and NumPy, will prove invaluable in this real-world analysis.

15.1 Loading online forum discussions using scikit-learn

Scikit-learn provides us with data from Usenet, which is a well-established online collection of discussion forums. These Usenet forums are called *newsgroups*. Each individual newsgroup focuses on some topic of discussion, which is briefly outlined in the newsgroup name. Users in a newsgroup converse by posting messages. These user posts are not limited in length, and hence some posts can be quite long. Both the diversity and the varying lengths of the posts will give us a chance to expand our NLP skills. For training purposes, the scikit-learn library provides access to over 10,000 posted messages. We can load these newsgroup posts by importing `fetch_20newsgroups` from `sklearn.datasets`. Calling `fetch_20newsgroups()` returns a newsgroups object that contains the textual data. Furthermore, optionally passing `remove=('headers', 'footers')` into the function call removes redundant information from the text. (That deleted metadata does not correspond to meaningful post content.) Listing 15.1 loads the newsgroup data while filtering redundant information.

> **WARNING** The newsgroups dataset is quite large. For this reason, it is not prepackaged with scikit-learn. Running `fetch_20newsgroups` forces scikit-learn to download and store the dataset on a local machine, so an internet connection is required when the dataset is first fetched. All subsequent calls to `fetch_20newsgroups` will load the dataset locally without requiring an internet connection.

Listing 15.1   Fetching the newsgroup dataset

```
from sklearn.datasets import fetch_20newsgroups
newsgroups = fetch_20newsgroups(remove=('headers', 'footers'))
```

The newsgroups object contains posts from 20 different newsgroups. As mentioned, each newsgroup's discussion theme is outlined in its name. We can view these newsgroup names by printing newsgroups.target_names.

Listing 15.2   Printing the names of all 20 newsgroups

```
print(newsgroups.target_names)
```

```
['alt.atheism', 'comp.graphics', 'comp.os.ms-windows.misc',
 'comp.sys.ibm.pc.hardware', 'comp.sys.mac.hardware', 'comp.windows.x',
 'misc.forsale', 'rec.autos', 'rec.motorcycles', 'rec.sport.baseball',
 'rec.sport.hockey', 'sci.crypt', 'sci.electronics', 'sci.med', 'sci.space',
 'soc.religion.christian', 'talk.politics.guns', 'talk.politics.mideast',
 'talk.politics.misc', 'talk.religion.misc']
```

The newsgroup categories vary greatly, from space exploration (*sci.space*) to cars (*rec.auto*) to electronics (*sci.electronics*). Some of the categories are very broad. For instance, politics (*talk.politics.misc*) can cover a wide range of political themes. Other categories are very narrow in scope: for example, *comp.sys.mac.hardware* focuses on Mac hardware, while *comp.sys.ibm.pc_hardware* focuses on PC hardware. Categorically, these two newsgroups are exceedingly similar: the only differentiator is whether the computer hardware belongs to a Mac or a PC. Sometimes categorical differences are subtle; boundaries between text topics are fluid and not necessarily etched in stone. We need to keep this in mind later in the section when we cluster the newsgroup posts.

Now, let's turn our attention to the actual newsgroup texts, which are stored as a list in the newsgroups.data attribute. For example, newsgroups.data[0] contains the text of the first stored newsgroup post. Let's output that post.

Listing 15.3   Printing the first newsgroup post

```
print(newsgroups.data[0])
```

```
I was wondering if anyone out there could enlighten me on this car I saw
the other day. It was a 2-door sports car, looked to be from the late 60s/
early 70s. It was called a Bricklin. The doors were really small.
In addition, the front bumper was separate from the rest of the body. This
is all I know. If anyone can tellme a model name, engine specs, years
of production, where this car is made, history, or whatever info you
have on this funky looking car, please e-mail.
```

The post is about a car. It probably was posted to the car discussion newsgroup, *rec.autos*. We can confirm by printing newsgroups.target_names[newsgroups.target[0]].

> **NOTE** newsgroups.target[i] returns the index of the newsgroup name associated with the *i*th document.

Listing 15.4 Printing the newsgroup name at index 0

```
origin = newsgroups.target_names[newsgroups.target[0]]
print(f"The post at index 0 first appeared in the '{origin}' group")

The post at index 0 first appeared in the 'rec.autos' group
```

As we predicted, our car-related post appeared in the car discussion group. The presence of a few keywords such as *car, bumper,* and *engine,* was sufficient to make this distinction. Of course, this is just one post out of many. Categorizing the remaining posts may not be so easy.

Let's dive deeper into our newsgroup dataset by printing out the dataset size.

Listing 15.5 Counting the number of newsgroup posts

```
dataset_size = len(newsgroups.data)
print(f"Our dataset contains {dataset_size} newsgroup posts")

Our dataset contains 11314 newsgroup posts
```

Our dataset contains over 11,000 posts. Our goal is to cluster these posts by topic, but carrying out text clustering on this scale requires computational efficiency. We need to efficiently compute newsgroup post similarities by representing our text data as a matrix. To do so, we need to transform each newsgroup post into a term-frequency (TF) vector. As discussed in section 13, a TF vector's indices map to word counts in a document. Previously, we computed these vectorized word counts using custom functions. Now we will compute them using scikit-learn.

15.2 Vectorizing documents using scikit-learn

Scikit-learn provides a built-in class for transforming input texts into TF vectors: CountVectorizer. Initializing CountVectorizer creates a vectorizer object capable of vectorizing our texts. Next, we import CountVectorizer from sklearn.feature_extraction.text and initialize the class.

Listing 15.6 Initializing a CountVectorizer object

```
from sklearn.feature_extraction.text import CountVectorizer
vectorizer = CountVectorizer()
```

We are now ready to vectorize the texts stored in the newsgroups.data list. All we need to do is run vectorizer.fit_transform(newsgroups.data). The method call returns the TF matrix corresponding to the vectorized newsgroup posts. As a reminder,

a TF matrix stores the counts of words (columns) across all texts (rows). Let's vectorize the posts and then print the resulting TF matrix.

Listing 15.7   Computing a TF matrix with scikit-learn

```
tf_matrix = vectorizer.fit_transform(newsgroups.data)
print(tf_matrix)

(0, 108644)    4
(0, 110106)    1
(0, 57577)     2
(0, 24398)     2
(0, 79534)     1
(0, 100942)    1
(0, 37154)     1
(0, 45141)     1
(0, 70570)     1
(0, 78701)     2
(0, 101084)    4
(0, 32499)     4
(0, 92157)     1
(0, 100827)    6
(0, 79461)     1
(0, 39275)     1
(0, 60326)     2
(0, 42332)     1
(0, 96432)     1
(0, 67137)     1
(0, 101732)    1
(0, 27703)     1
(0, 49871)     2
(0, 65338)     1
(0, 14106)     1
  :     :
(11313, 55901)    1
(11313, 93448)    1
(11313, 97535)    1
(11313, 93393)    1
(11313, 109366)   1
(11313, 102215)   1
(11313, 29148)    1
(11313, 26901)    1
(11313, 94401)    1
(11313, 89686)    1
(11313, 80827)    1
(11313, 72219)    1
(11313, 32984)    1
(11313, 82912)    1
(11313, 99934)    1
(11313, 96505)    1
(11313, 72102)    1
(11313, 32981)    1
(11313, 82692)    1
(11313, 101854)   1
```

```
(11313, 66399)    1
(11313, 63405)    1
(11313, 61366)    1
(11313, 7462)     1
(11313, 109600)     1
```

Our printed `tf_matrix` does not appear to be a NumPy array. What sort of data structure is it? We can check by printing `type(tf_matrix)`.

Listing 15.8 Checking the data type of `tf_matrix`

```
print(type(tf_matrix))

<class 'scipy.sparse.csr.csr_matrix'>
```

The matrix is a SciPy object called `csr_matrix`. *CSR* stands for *compressed sparse row*, which is a storage format for compressing matrices that are composed mostly of zeros. These mostly empty matrices are referred to as *sparse matrices*. They can be made smaller by storing only the nonzero elements. This compression leads to more efficient memory usage and faster computation. Large-scale text-based matrices are usually very sparse, since a single document normally contains just a small percentage of the total vocabulary. Thus, scikit-learn automatically converts the vectorized text to the CSR format. The conversion is carried out using a `csr_matrix` class imported from SciPy.

This interplay between various external data science libraries is useful but also a bit confusing. In particular, the differences between a NumPy array and a SciPy CSR matrix can be tricky for a newcomer to grasp. This is because arrays and CSR matrices share some, but not all, attributes. Also, arrays and CSR matrices are compatible with some, but not all, NumPy functions. To minimize confusion, we will convert `tf_matrix` into a 2D NumPy array. Most of our subsequent analyses will be carried out on that NumPy array. However, periodically, we will compare array usage with CSR matrix usage. Doing so will allow us to more fully comprehend the similarities and differences between the two matrix representations. Listing 15.9 converts `tf_matrix` to NumPy by running `tf_matrix.toarray()` and then prints the converted result.

> **WARNING** This conversion is very memory intensive, requiring almost 10 GB of memory. If your local machine has limited memory available, we suggest you execute this code in the cloud using Google Colaboratory (Colab), a free, cloud-based Jupyter Notebook environment with 12 GB freely available memory. Google provides a comprehensive introduction to using Colab that covers everything that you need to get started: https://colab.research.google.com/notebooks/welcome.ipynb.

Listing 15.9 Converting a CSR matrix to a NumPy array

```
tf_np_matrix = tf_matrix.toarray()
print(tf_np_matrix)
```

```
[[0 0 0 ... 0 0 0]
 [0 0 0 ... 0 0 0]
 [0 0 0 ... 0 0 0]
 ...
 [0 0 0 ... 0 0 0]
 [0 0 0 ... 0 0 0]
 [0 0 0 ... 0 0 0]]
```

The printed matrix is a 2D NumPy array. All previewed matrix elements are zeros, confirming that the matrix is rather sparse. Each matrix element corresponds to the count of a word in the post. The matrix rows represent the post, while the columns represent individual words. Thus, the total column count equals our dataset's vocabulary size. We access that count using the `shape` attribute. This attribute is shared by both the CSR matrix and the NumPy array. Let's use `tf_np_matrix.shape` to output the vocabulary size.

Listing 15.10   Checking the vocabulary size

```
assert tf_np_matrix.shape == tf_matrix.shape
num_posts, vocabulary_size = tf_np_matrix.shape
print(f"Our collection of {num_posts} newsgroup posts contain a total of "
      f"{vocabulary_size} unique words")
```

```
Our collection of 11314 newsgroup posts contain a total of 114751 unique
words
```

Our data contains 114751 unique words. However, most posts contain only a few dozen of these words. We can measure the unique word count of a post at index i by counting the number of nonzero elements in row `tf_np_matrix[i]`. The easiest way to count these nonzero elements is with NumPy. The library allows us to obtain all nonzero indices of the vector at `tf_np_matrix[i]`. We simply need to input the vector into the `np.flatnonzero` function. Next, we count and output the nonzero indices of the car post in `newsgroups.data[0]`.

Listing 15.11   Counting the unique words in the car post

This is equivalent to running np.nonzero(tf_vector)[0]. The np.nonzero function generalizes the computation of nonzero indices across an x-dimensional array. It returns a tuple of length x, where each *i*th tuple element represents the nonzero indices along the *i*th dimension. Hence, given a 1D tf_vector array, the np.nonzero function returns a tuple of the form (non_zero_indices).

```
import numpy as np
tf_vector = tf_np_matrix[0]
non_zero_indices = np.flatnonzero(tf_vector)          ◁─────────────────
num_unique_words = non_zero_indices.size
print(f"The newsgroup in row 0 contains {num_unique_words} unique words.")
print("The actual word counts map to the following column indices:\n")
print(non_zero_indices)
```

```
The newsgroup in row 0 contains 64 unique words.
The actual word-counts map to the following column indices:
```

```
[ 14106   15549   22088   23323   24398   27703   29357   30093   30629   32194
  32305   32499   37154   39275   42332   42333   43643   45089   45141   49871
  49881   50165   54442   55453   57577   58321   58842   60116   60326   64083
  65338   67137   67140   68931   69080   70570   72915   75280   78264   78701
  79055   79461   79534   82759   84398   87690   89161   92157   93304   95225
  96145   96432  100406  100827  100942  101084  101732  108644  109086  109254
 109294  110106  112936  113262]
```

The first newsgroup post contains 64 unique words. What are these words? To find out, we need a mapping between TF vector indices and word values. That mapping can be generated by calling `vectorizer.get_feature_names()`, which returns a list of words that we'll call words. Each index i corresponds to the *i*th word in the list. Thus, running `[words[i] for i in non_zero_indices]` will return all unique words in our post.

NOTE We can also obtain these words by calling `vectorizer.inverse_transform(tf_vector)`. The `inverse_transform` method returns all words associated with an inputted TF vector.

Listing 15.12 Printing the unique words in the car post

```
words = vectorizer.get_feature_names()
unique_words = [words[i] for i in non_zero_indices]
print(unique_words)
```

```
['60s', '70s', 'addition', 'all', 'anyone', 'be', 'body', 'bricklin',
'bumper', 'called', 'can', 'car', 'could', 'day', 'door', 'doors',
'early', 'engine', 'enlighten', 'from', 'front', 'funky', 'have',
'history', 'if', 'in', 'info', 'is', 'it', 'know', 'late', 'looked',
'looking', 'made', 'mail', 'me', 'model', 'name', 'of', 'on', 'or',
'other', 'out', 'please', 'production', 'really', 'rest', 'saw',
'separate', 'small', 'specs', 'sports', 'tellme', 'the', 'there',
'this', 'to', 'was', 'were', 'whatever', 'where', 'wondering', 'years',
'you']
```

We've printed all the words in `newsgroups.data[0]`. Of course, not all of these words have equal mention counts—some occur more frequently than others. Perhaps these frequent words are more relevant to the topic of cars. Listing 15.13 prints the 10 most frequent words in the post, along with their associated counts. We represent this output as a Pandas table for visualization purposes.

Extracting nonzero elements of 1D NumPy arrays

- `non_zero_indices = np.flatnonzero(np_vector)`—Returns the nonzero indices in a 1D NumPy array
- `non_zero_vector = np_vector[non_zero_indices]`—Selects the nonzero elements of a 1D NumPy array (assuming `non_zero_indices` corresponds to nonzero indices of that array)

Listing 15.13   Printing the most frequent words in the car post

```
import pandas as pd
data = {'Word': unique_words,
        'Count': tf_vector[non_zero_indices]}

df = pd.DataFrame(data).sort_values('Count', ascending=False)    ◁─┐
print(df[:10].to_string(index=False))
                                                            Sorts the Pandas table
Word   Count                                                based on counts, from
    the      6                                                 highest to lowest
   this      4
    was      4
    car      4
     if      2
     is      2
     it      2
   from      2
     on      2
 anyone      2
```

Four of the 64 words in the post are mentioned at least four times. One of these words is *car*, which is not surprising given that the post appeared in a car discussion group. The other three words, however, have nothing to do with cars: *the*, *this*, and *was* are among the most common words in the English language. They don't provide a differentiating signal between the car post and a post with a different theme—instead, the common words are a source of noise and increase the likelihood that two unrelated documents will cluster together. NLP practitioners refer to such noisy words as *stop words* because they are blocked from appearing in the vectorized results. Stop words are generally deleted from the text before vectorization. That is why the CountVectorizer class has a built-in stop-word deletion option. Running CountVectorizer(stop_words='english') initializes a vectorizer that is primed for stop-word deletion. The vectorizer ignores all of the most common English words in the text.

Next, we reinitialize a stop-word-aware vectorizer. Then we rerun fit_transform to recompute the TF matrix. The number of word columns in that matrix will be less than our previously computed vocabulary size of 114,751. We also regenerate our words list: this time, common stop words such as *the*, *this*, *of*, and *it* will be missing.

Listing 15.14   Removing stop words during vectorization

```
vectorizer = CountVectorizer(stop_words='english')         Checks to ensure that
tf_matrix = vectorizer.fit_transform(newsgroups.data)      our vocabulary size has
assert tf_matrix.shape[1] < 114751    ◁──┐                 gotten smaller

words = vectorizer.get_feature_names()                     Common stop
for common_word in ['the', 'this', 'was', 'if', 'it', 'on']:   ◁──  words have been
    assert common_word not in words                        filtered out.
```

All stop words have been deleted from the recomputed tf_matrix. Now we can regenerate the 10 most frequent words in newsgroups.data[0]. Note that in the process, we recompute tf_np_matrix, tf_vector, unique_words, non_zero_indices, and df.

WARNING   This regeneration is memory intensive, requiring 2.5 GB of memory.

Listing 15.15   Reprinting the top words after stop-word deletion

```python
tf_np_matrix = tf_matrix.toarray()
tf_vector = tf_np_matrix[0]
non_zero_indices = np.flatnonzero(tf_vector)
unique_words = [words[index] for index in non_zero_indices]
data = {'Word': unique_words,
        'Count': tf_vector[non_zero_indices]}

df = pd.DataFrame(data).sort_values('Count', ascending=False)
print(f"After stop-word deletion, {df.shape[0]} unique words remain.")
print("The 10 most frequent words are:\n")
print(df[:10].to_string(index=False))
```

```
After stop-word deletion, 34 unique words remain.
The 10 most frequent words are:

      Word  Count
       car      4
       60s      1
       saw      1
   looking      1
      mail      1
     model      1
production      1
    really      1
      rest      1
  separate      1
```

After stop-word filtering, 34 words remain. Among them, *car* is the only word that is mentioned more than once. The other 33 words share a mention count of 1 and are treated equally by the vectorizer. However, it's worth noting that not all words are equal in their relevancy. Some words are more relevant to a car discussion than others: for instance, the word *model* refers to a car model (although of course it could also refer to a supermodel or a machine learning model). Meanwhile, the word *really* is more general; it doesn't refer to anything car related. The word is so irrelevant and common that it could almost be a stop word. In fact, some NLP practitioners keep *really* on their stop-word list—but others don't. Unfortunately, there is no consensus about which words are always useless and which aren't. However, all practitioners agree that a word becomes less useful if it's mentioned in too many texts. Thus, *really* is less relevant than *model* because the former is mentioned in more posts. Therefore, when ranking words by relevance, we should use both post frequency and count. If two words share an equal count, we should rank them by post frequency, instead.

Let's rerank our 34 words based on both post frequency and count. Then we'll explore how these rankings can be used to improve text vectorization.

Common scikit-learn CountVectorizer methods

- `vectorizer = CountVectorizer()`—Initializes a `CountVectorizer` object capable of vectorizing input texts based on their TF counts.
- `vectorizer = CountVectorizer(stopwords='english')`—Initializes an object capable of vectorizing input texts while filtering for common English words like *this* and *the*.
- `tf_matrix = vectorizer.fit_transform(texts)`—Executes TF vectorization on a list of input texts using the initialized `vectorizer` object, and returns a CSR matrix of term frequency values. Each matrix row `i` corresponds to `texts[i]`. Each matrix column `j` corresponds to the term frequency of word `j`.
- `vocabulary_list = vectorizer.get_feature_names()`—Returns the vocabulary list associated with the columns of a computed TF matrix. Each column `j` of the matrix corresponds to `vocabulary_list[j]`.

15.3   *Ranking words by both post frequency and count*

Each of the 34 words in `df.Word` appears in a certain fraction of newsgroup posts. In NLP, this fraction is referred to as the *document frequency* of a word. We hypothesize that the document frequencies can improve our word rankings. As scientists, we will now attempt to validate this hypothesis by exploring how the document frequencies relate to word importance. Initially, we'll limit our exploration to a single document. Later, we will generalize our insights to the other documents in the dataset.

> **NOTE**   Such open-ended explorations are common to data science. We start by exploring a small slice of data. By probing that small sample, we can hone our intuition about grander patterns in the dataset. Then we can test that intuition on a larger scale.

We now begin our exploration. Our immediate goal is to compute 34 document frequencies, to try to improve our word relevancy rankings. We can compute these frequencies using a series of NumPy matrix manipulations. First, we want to select the columns of `tf_np_matrix` that correspond to the 34 nonzero indices in the `non_zero_indices` array. We can obtain this submatrix by running `tf_np_matrix[:,non_zero_indices]`.

Listing 15.16   Filtering matrix columns with `non_zero_indices`

```
sub_matrix = tf_np_matrix[:,non_zero_indices]
print("Our sub-matrix corresponds to the 34 words within post 0. "
      "The first row of the sub-matrix is:")
print(sub_matrix[0])
```

Accesses just those columns of the
matrix that hold nonzero values
in the first matrix row

```
Our sub-matrix corresponds to the 34 words within post 0. The first row of
 the sub-matrix is:
[1 1 1 1 1 1 4 1 1 1 1 1 1 1 1 1 1 1 1 1 1 1 1 1 1 1 1 1 1 1 1 1 1 1]
```

The first row of sub_matrix corresponds to the 34 word counts in df. Together, all the matrix rows correspond to counts across all posts. However, we are not currently interested in exact word counts: we just want to know whether each word is present or absent from each post. So, we need to convert our counts into binary values. Basically, we require a binary matrix where element (i, j) equals 1 if word j is present in post i, and 0 otherwise. We can binarize the submatrix by importing binarize from sklearn.preprocessing. Then, running binarize(sub_matrix) will produce the necessary results.

Listing 15.17   Converting word counts to binary values

```
from sklearn.preprocessing import binarize
binary_matrix = binarize(sub_matrix)        ◁─┐   The binarize function
print(binary_matrix)                              replaces all nonzero
                                                  elements with ones in any
                                                  x-dimensional array.
[[1 1 1 ... 1 1 1]
 [0 0 0 ... 0 0 0]
 [0 0 0 ... 0 1 0]
 ...
 [0 0 0 ... 0 0 0]
 [0 0 0 ... 0 0 0]
 [0 0 0 ... 0 0 0]]
```

Now we need to add together the rows of our binary submatrix. Doing so will produce a vector of integer counts. Each *i*th vector element will equal the number of unique posts in which word i is present. To sum the rows of a 2D array, we simply need to pass axis=0 into the sum method of the array. Running binary_matrix.sum(axis=0) returns a vector of unique post counts.

> **NOTE** A 2D NumPy array contains two axes: axis 0 corresponds to horizontal rows, and axis 1 corresponds to vertical columns. Thus, running binary_matrix.sum(axis=0) returns a vector of summed rows. Meanwhile, running binary_matrix.sum(axis=1) returns a vector of summed columns.

Listing 15.18   Summing matrix rows to obtain post counts

```
unique_post_mentions = binary_matrix.sum(axis=0)
print("This vector counts the unique posts in which each word is "
      f"mentioned:\n {unique_post_mentions}")            ◁─┐

This vector counts the unique posts in which each word is mentioned:
[  18   21  202  314    4   26  802  536  842  154   67  348  184   25
    7  368  469 3093  238  268  780  901  292   95 1493  407  354  158
  574   95   98    2  295 1174]
```

Generally, running multi_dim_array.sum(axis=i)
returns a vector of summed values across the
ith axis of a multidimensional array.

We should note that the previous three procedures can be combined into a single line of code by running `binarize(tf_np_matrix[:,non_zero_indices]).sum(axis=0)`. Furthermore, substituting NumPy's `tf_np_matrix` with SciPy's `tf_matrix` will still produce the same post mention counts.

Listing 15.19   Computing post mention counts in a single line of code

```
np_post_mentions = binarize(tf_np_matrix[:,non_zero_indices]).sum(axis=0)
csr_post_mentions = binarize(tf_matrix[:,non_zero_indices]).sum(axis=0)
print(f'NumPy matrix-generated counts:\n {np_post_mentions}\n')
print(f'CSR matrix-generated counts:\n {csr_post_mentions}')

NumPy matrix-generated counts:
[  18   21  202  314    4   26  802  536  842  154   67  348  184   25
    7  368  469 3093  238  268  780  901  292   95 1493  407  354  158
  574   95   98    2  295 1174]

CSR matrix-generated counts:
[[  18   21  202  314    4   26  802  536  842  154   67  348  184   25
     7  368  469 3093  238  268  780  901  292   95 1493  407  354  158
   574   95   98    2  295 1174]]                    ◄─────────────┐
```

The numbers in **np_post_mentions** and **csr_post_mentions** appear identical. However, **csr_post_mentions** contains an extra set of brackets because the aggregated sum of CSR matrix rows doesn't return a NumPy array; instead, it returns a special matrix object. In that object, the 1D vector is represented as a matrix with one row and n columns. To convert the matrix into a 1D NumPy array, we must run np.asarray(csr_post_mentions)[0].

Methods for aggregating matrix rows

- `vector_of_sums = np_matrix.sum(axis=0)`—Sums the rows of a NumPy matrix. If `np_matrix` is a TF matrix, then `vector_of_sums[i]` equals the total mention count of word i in the dataset.
- `vector_of_sums = binarize(np_matrix).sum(axis=0)`—Converts a NumPy matrix into a binary matrix and then sums its rows. If `np_matrix` is a TF matrix, then `vector_of_sums[i]` equals the total count of texts in which word i is mentioned.
- `matrix_1D = binarize(csr_matrix).sum(axis=0)`—Converts a CSR matrix to binary and then sums its rows. The returned result is a special one-dimensional matrix object—it is not a NumPy vector. `matrix_1D` can be converted into a NumPy vector by running `np.asarray(matrix_1D)[0]`.

Based on the printed vector of post mention counts, we know that some words appear in thousands of posts. Other words appear in fewer than a dozen posts. Let's transform these counts into document frequencies and align the frequencies with `df.Word`. Then we'll output all the words that are mentioned in at least 10% of newsgroup posts. These words are likely to appear across the board in a variety of posts; thus, we hypothesize that the printed words will not be specific to a particular topic. If the hypothesis is correct, these words will not be very relevant.

Listing 15.20 Printing the words with the highest document frequency

```
document_frequencies = unique_post_mentions / dataset_size
data = {'Word': unique_words,
        'Count': tf_vector[non_zero_indices],
        'Document Frequency': document_frequencies}

df = pd.DataFrame(data)
df_common_words = df[df['Document Frequency'] >= .1]
print(df_common_words.to_string(index=False))
```

We only choose words with a document frequency greater than 1/10.

```
  Word  Count  Document Frequency
  know      1            0.273378
 really      1            0.131960
  years      1            0.103765
```

As a reminder, the document frequency refers to all our posts. Meanwhile, the count refers to just the post at index 0.

Three of the 34 words have a document frequency greater than 0.1. As expected, these words are very general and not car specific. We thus can utilize document frequencies for ranking purposes. Let's rank our words by relevance in the following manner. First, we sort the words by count, from greatest to smallest. Then, all words with equal count are sorted by document frequency, from smallest to greatest. In Pandas, we can execute this dual-column sorting by running `df.sort_values(['Count', 'Document Frequency'], ascending=[False, True])`.

Listing 15.21 Ranking words by both count and document frequency

```
df_sorted = df.sort_values(['Count', 'Document Frequency'],
                           ascending=[False, True])
print(df_sorted[:10].to_string(index=False))
```

```
      Word  Count  Document Frequency
       car      4            0.047375
    tellme      1            0.000177
  bricklin      1            0.000354
     funky      1            0.000619
       60s      1            0.001591
       70s      1            0.001856
 enlighten      1            0.002210
    bumper      1            0.002298
     doors      1            0.005922
production      1            0.008397
```

Our sorting was successful. New car-related words, such as *bumper*, are now present in our list of top-ranked words. However, the actual sorting procedure was rather convoluted: it required us to sort two columns separately. Perhaps we can simplify the process by combining the word counts and document frequencies into a single score. How can we do this? One approach is to divide each word count by its associated document frequency. The resulting value will increase if either of the following is true:

- The word count goes up.
- The document frequency goes down.

Let's combine the word counts and the document frequencies into a single score. We start by computing 1 / document_frequencies. Doing so produces an array of *inverse document frequencies* (IDFs). Next, we multiply df.Count by the IDF array to compute the combined score. We then add both the IDF values and our combined scores to our Pandas table. Finally, we sort on the combined score and output the top results.

Listing 15.22 Combining counts and frequencies into a single score

```
inverse_document_frequencies = 1 / document_frequencies
df['IDF'] = inverse_document_frequencies
df['Combined'] = df.Count * inverse_document_frequencies
df_sorted = df.sort_values('Combined', ascending=False)
print(df_sorted[:10].to_string(index=False))
```

Word	Count	Document Frequency	IDF	Combined
tellme	1	0.000177	5657.000000	5657.000000
bricklin	1	0.000354	2828.500000	2828.500000
funky	1	0.000619	1616.285714	1616.285714
60s	1	0.001591	628.555556	628.555556
70s	1	0.001856	538.761905	538.761905
enlighten	1	0.002210	452.560000	452.560000
bumper	1	0.002298	435.153846	435.153846
doors	1	0.005922	168.865672	168.865672
specs	1	0.008397	119.094737	119.094737
production	1	0.008397	119.094737	119.094737

Our new ranking failed! The word *car* no longer appears at the top of the list. What happened? Well, let's take a look at our table. There is a problem with the IDF values: some of them are huge! The printed IDF values range from approximately 100 to over 5,000. Meanwhile, our word-count range is very small: from 1 to 4. Thus, when we multiply word counts by IDF values, the IDF dominates, and the counts have no impact on the final results. We need to somehow make our IDF values smaller. What should we do?

Data scientists are commonly confronted with numeric values that are too large. One way to shrink the values is to apply a logarithmic function. For instance, running np.log10(1000000) returns 6. Essentially, a value of 1,000,000 is replaced by the count of zeros in that value.

Listing 15.23 Shrinking a large value using its logarithm

```
assert np.log10(1000000) == 6
```

Let's recompute our ranking score by running df.Count * np.log10(df.IDF). The product of the counts and the shrunken IDF values should lead to a more reasonable ranking metric.

Listing 15.24 Adjusting the combined score using logarithms

```
df['Combined'] = df.Count * np.log10(df.IDF)
df_sorted = df.sort_values('Combined', ascending=False)
print(df_sorted[:10].to_string(index=False))
```

Word	Count	Document Frequency	IDF	Combined
car	4	0.047375	21.108209	5.297806
tellme	1	0.000177	5657.000000	3.752586
bricklin	1	0.000354	2828.500000	3.451556
funky	1	0.000619	1616.285714	3.208518
60s	1	0.001591	628.555556	2.798344
70s	1	0.001856	538.761905	2.731397
enlighten	1	0.002210	452.560000	2.655676
bumper	1	0.002298	435.153846	2.638643
doors	1	0.005922	168.865672	2.227541
specs	1	0.008397	119.094737	2.075893

Our adjusted ranking score has yielded good results. The word *car* is once again present at the top of the ranked list. Also, *bumper* still appears among the top 10 ranked words. Meanwhile, *really* is missing from the list.

Our effective score is called the *term frequency-inverse document frequency* (TFIDF). The TFIDF can be computed by taking the product of the TF (word count) and the log of the IDF.

> **NOTE** Mathematically, `np.log(1 / x)` is equal to `-np.log(x)`. Therefore, we can compute the TFIDF directly from the document frequencies. We simply need to run `df.Count * -np.log10(document_frequences)`. Also be aware that other, less common formulations of the TFIDF exist in the literature. For instance, when dealing with large documents, some NLP practitioners compute the TFIDF as `np.log(df.Count + 1) * -np.log10(document_frequences)`. This limits the influence of any very common word in a document.

The TFIDF is a simple but powerful metric for ranking words in a document. Of course, the metric is only relevant if that document is part of a larger document group. Otherwise, the computed TFIDF values all equal zero. The metric also loses its effectiveness when applied to small collections of similar tests. Nonetheless, for most real-world text datasets, the TFIDF produces good ranking results. And it has additional uses: it can be utilized to vectorize words in a document. The numeric content of `df.Combined` is essentially a vector produced by modifying the TF vector stored in `df.Count`. In this same manner, we can transform any TF vector into a TFIDF vector. We just need to multiply the TF vector by the log of inverse document frequencies.

Is there a benefit to transforming TF vectors into more complicated TFIDF vectors? Yes! In larger text datasets, TFIDF vectors provide a greater signal of textual similarity and divergence. For example, two texts that are both discussing cars are more likely to cluster together if their irrelevant vector elements are penalized. Thus, penalizing common words using the IDF improves the clustering of large text collections.

> **NOTE** This isn't necessarily true of smaller datasets, where the number of documents is low and the document frequency is high. Consequently, the IDF may be too small to meaningfully improve the clustering results.

We therefore stand to gain by transforming our TF matrix into a TFIDF matrix. We can easily execute this transformation using custom code. However, it's more convenient to compute the TFIDF matrix with scikit-learn's built-in `TfidfVectorizer` class.

15.3.1 *Computing TFIDF vectors with scikit-learn*

That `TfidfVectorizer` class is nearly identical to `CountVectorizer`, except that it takes IDF into account during the vectorization process. Next, we import `Tfidf-Vectorizer` from `sklearn.feature_extraction.text` and initialize the class by running `TfidfVectorizer(stop_words='english')`. The constructed `tfidf_vectorizer` object is parameterized to ignore all stop words. Subsequently, executing `tfidf_vectorizer.fit_transform(newsgroups.data)` returns a matrix of vectorized TFIDF values. The matrix shape is identical to `tf_matrix.shape`.

Listing 15.25   Computing a TFIDF matrix with scikit-learn

```
from sklearn.feature_extraction.text import TfidfVectorizer
tfidf_vectorizer = TfidfVectorizer(stop_words='english')
tfidf_matrix = tfidf_vectorizer.fit_transform(newsgroups.data)
assert tfidf_matrix.shape == tf_matrix.shape
```

Our `tfidf_vectorizer` has learned the same vocabulary as the simpler TF vectorizer. In fact, the indices of words in `tfidf_matrix` are identical to those of `tf_matrix`. We can confirm this by calling `tfidf_vectorizer.get_feature_names()`. The method call returns an ordered list of words identical to our previously computed `words` list.

Listing 15.26   Confirming the preservation of vectorized word indices

```
assert tfidf_vectorizer.get_feature_names() == words
```

Since word order is preserved, we should expect the nonzero indices of `tfidf_matrix[0]` to equal our previously computed `non_zero_indices` array. We'll confirm after converting `tfidf_matrix` from a CSR data structure to a NumPy array.

Listing 15.27   Confirming the preservation of nonzero indices

```
tfidf_np_matrix = tfidf_matrix.toarray()
tfidf_vector = tfidf_np_matrix[0]
tfidf_non_zero_indices = np.flatnonzero(tfidf_vector)
assert np.array_equal(tfidf_non_zero_indices,
                      non_zero_indices)
```

The nonzero indices of `tf_vector` and `tfidf_vector` are identical. We thus can add the TFIDF vector as a column in our existing `df` table. Adding a `TFIDF` column will allow us to compare scikit-learn's output with our manually computed score.

Listing 15.28   Adding a TFIDF vector to the existing Pandas table

```
df['TFIDF'] = tfidf_vector[non_zero_indices]
```

Sorting by df.TFIDF should produce a relevance ranking that is consistent with our previous observations. Let's verify that both df.TFIDF and df.Combined produce the same word rankings after sorting.

Listing 15.29   Sorting words by df.TFIDF

```
df_sorted_old = df.sort_values('Combined', ascending=False)
df_sorted_new = df.sort_values('TFIDF', ascending=False)
assert np.array_equal(df_sorted_old['Word'].values,
                      df_sorted_new['Word'].values)
print(df_sorted_new[:10].to_string(index=False))
```

Word	Count	Document Frequency	IDF	Combined	TFIDF
car	4	0.047375	21.108209	5.297806	0.459552
tellme	1	0.000177	5657.000000	3.752586	0.262118
bricklin	1	0.000354	2828.500000	3.451556	0.247619
funky	1	0.000619	1616.285714	3.208518	0.234280
60s	1	0.001591	628.555556	2.798344	0.209729
70s	1	0.001856	538.761905	2.731397	0.205568
enlighten	1	0.002210	452.560000	2.655676	0.200827
bumper	1	0.002298	435.153846	2.638643	0.199756
doors	1	0.005922	168.865672	2.227541	0.173540
specs	1	0.008397	119.094737	2.075893	0.163752

Our word rankings have remained unchanged. However, the values of the TFIDF and Combined columns are not identical. Our top 10 manually computed Combined values are all greater than 1, but all of scikit-learn's *TFIDF* values are less than 1. Why is this the case?

As it turns out, scikit-learn automatically normalizes its TFIDF vector results. The magnitude of df.TFIDF has been modified to equal 1. We can confirm by calling norm(df.TFIDF.values).

NOTE   To turn off normalization, we must pass norm=None into the vectorizer's initialization function. Running TfidfVectorizer(norm=None, stop_words='english') returns a vectorizer in which normalization has been deactivated.

Listing 15.30   Confirming that our TFIDF vector is normalized

```
from numpy.linalg import norm
assert norm(df.TFIDF.values) == 1
```

Why would scikit-learn automatically normalize the vectors? For our own benefit! As discussed in section 13, it's easier to compute text vector similarity when all vector magnitudes equal 1. Consequently, our normalized TFIDF matrix is primed for similarity analysis.

Common scikit-learn TfidfVectorizer methods

- `tfidf_vectorizer = TfidfVectorizer(stopwords='english')`—Initializes a `TfidfVectorizer` object capable of vectorizing input texts based on their TFIDF values. The object is preset to filter common English stop words.
- `tfidf_matrix = tfidf_vectorizer.fit_transform(texts)`—Executes TFIDF vectorization on a list of input texts using the initialized `vectorizer` object and returns a CSR matrix of normalized TFIDF values. Each row of the matrix is automatically normalized, for easier similarity computation.
- `vocabulary_list = tfidf_vectorizer.get_feature_names()`—Returns the vocabulary list associated with the columns of a computed TFIDF matrix. Each column j of the matrix corresponds to `vocabulary_list[j]`.

15.4 *Computing similarities across large document datasets*

Let's answer a simple question: which of our newsgroup posts is most similar to `newsgroups.post[0]`? We can get the answer by computing all the cosine similarities between `tfidf_np_matrix` and `tf_np_matrix[0]`. As discussed in section 13, these similarities can be obtained by taking the product of `tfidf_np_matrix` and `tfidf_matrix[0]`. The simple multiplication between the matrix and the vector is sufficient because all rows in the matrix have a magnitude of 1.

Listing 15.31   Computing similarities to a single newsgroup post

```
cosine_similarities = tfidf_np_matrix @ tfidf_np_matrix[0]
print(cosine_similarities)

[1.        0.00834093 0.04448717 ... 0.        0.00270615 0.01968562]
```

The matrix-vector product takes a few seconds to complete. Its output is a vector of cosine similarities: each *i*th index of the vector corresponds to the cosine similarity between `newsgroups.data[0]` and `newsgroups.data[i]`. From the printout, we can see that `cosine_similarities[0]` is equal to 1.0. This is not surprising since `newsgroups_data[0]` will have a perfect similarity with itself. What is the next-highest similarity in the vector? We can find out by calling `np.argsort(cosine_similarities)[-2]`. The `argsort` call sorts the array indices by their ascending values. So, the second-to-last index will correspond to the post with the second-highest similarity.

> **NOTE**   We are assuming that no other post exists with a perfect similarity of 1. Also, note that we can achieve the same result by calling `np.argmax(cosine_similarities[1:]) + 1`, although this approach only works for posts at index 0.

We now extract that index and print its corresponding similarity. We also print the corresponding text to confirm its overlap with the car post stored in `newsgroups.data[0]`.

> ### Listing 15.32 Finding the most similar newsgroup post

```
most_similar_index = np.argsort(cosine_similarities)[-2]
similarity = cosine_similarities[most_similar_index]
most_similar_post = newsgroups.data[most_similar_index]
print(f"The following post has a cosine similarity of {similarity:.2f} "
      "with newsgroups.data[0]:\n")
print(most_similar_post)
```

```
The following post has a cosine similarity of 0.64 with newsgroups.data[0]:

In article <1993Apr20.174246.14375@wam.umd.edu> lerxst@wam.umd.edu
(where's my
thing) writes:
>
>  I was wondering if anyone out there could enlighten me on this car I saw
> the other day. It was a 2-door sports car, looked to be from the late
> 60s/ early 70s. It was called a Bricklin. The doors were really small. In
addition,
> the front bumper was separate from the rest of the body. This is
> all I know. If anyone can tellme a model name, engine specs, years
> of production, where this car is made, history, or whatever info you
> have on this funky looking car, please e-mail.

Bricklins were manufactured in the 70s with engines from Ford. They are
rather odd looking with the encased front bumper. There aren't a lot of
them around, but Hemmings (Motor News) ususally has ten or so listed.
Basically, they are a performance Ford with new styling slapped on top.

>     ---- brought to you by your neighborhood Lerxst ----

Rush fan?
```

The printed text is a reply to the car post at index 0. The reply includes the original post, which is a question about a certain car brand. We see a detailed answer to the question near the very bottom of the reply. Due to textual overlap, both the original post and the reply are very similar to each other. Their cosine similarity is 0.64, which does not seem like a large number. However, in extensive text collections, a cosine similarity greater than 0.6 is a good indicator of overlapping content.

> **NOTE** As discussed in section 13, the cosine similarity can easily be converted into the Tanimoto similarity, which has a deeper theoretical basis for text overlap. We can convert `cosine_similarities` into Tanimoto similarities by running `cosine_similarities / (2 - cosine_similarities)`. However, that conversion will not change our final results. Choosing the top index of the Tanimoto array will still return the same posted reply. Thus, for simplicity's sake, we focus on the cosine similarity during our next few text-comparison examples.

Thus far, we've only analyzed the car post at index 0. Let's extend our analysis to another post. We'll pick a newsgroup post at random, choose its most similar neighbor, and then output both posts, along with their cosine similarity. To make this exercise more interesting, we'll first compute a matrix of all-by-all cosine similarities. We'll then use the matrix to select our random pair of similar posts.

> **NOTE** Why are we computing a matrix of all-by-all similarities? Mostly, it's to practice what we've learned in the previous section. However, having access to that matrix does confer certain benefits. Suppose we wish to increase our network of neighboring posts from 2 to 10. We also wish to include the neighbor of every neighbor (similar to our derivation of DBSCAN in section 10). Under such circumstances, it is much more efficient to compute all text similarities in advance.

How do we compute the matrix of all-by-all cosine similarities? The naive approach is to multiply `tfidf_np_matrix` with its transpose. However, for reasons discussed in section 13, this matrix multiplication is not computationally efficient. Our TFIDF matrix has over 100,000 columns. We need to reduce the matrix size before executing the multiplication. In the previous section, we learned how to reduce the column count using scikit-learn's `TruncatedSVD` class. The class is able to shrink a matrix to a specified number of columns. The reduced column count is determined by the n_components parameter. According to scikit-learn's documentation, an n_components value of 100 is recommended for processing text data.

> **NOTE** Scikit-learn's documentation occasionally provides useful parameters for common algorithm applications. For instance, take a look at the Truncated-SVD documentation at http://mng.bz/PXP9. According to that page, "Truncated SVD works on term count/tf-idf matrices as returned by the vectorizers in sklearn.feature_extraction.text. In that context, it is known as latent semantic analysis (LSA)." Further down, the documentation describes the n_components parameter like this: "Desired dimensionality of output data. Must be strictly less than the number of features. For LSA, a value of 100 is recommended."

Most NLP practitioners agree that passing n_components=100 reduces a TFIDF matrix to an efficient size while maintaining useful column information. Next, we'll follow this recommendation by running `TruncatedSVD(n_components=100).fit_transform(tfidf_matrix)`. The method call will return a 100-column `shrunk_matrix` result that will be a 2D NumPy array even if we pass the SciPy-based `tfidf_matrix` as our input.

Listing 15.33 Dimensionally reducing `tfidf_matrix` using SVD

The final SVD output depends on the orientation of the computed eigenvectors. As we saw in the previous section, that orientation is determined randomly. Thus, we run np.random.seed(0) to ensure consistent results.

```
np.random.seed(0)    ⟵
from sklearn.decomposition import TruncatedSVD

shrunk_matrix = TruncatedSVD(n_components=100).fit_transform(tfidf_matrix)
print(f"We've dimensionally reduced a {tfidf_matrix.shape[1]}-column "
      f"{type(tfidf_matrix)} matrix.")
```

```
print(f"Our output is a {shrunk_matrix.shape[1]}-column "
      f"{type(shrunk_matrix)} matrix.")
```

```
We've dimensionally reduced a 114441-column
<class 'scipy.sparse.csr.csr_matrix'> matrix.
Our output is a 100-column <class 'numpy.ndarray'> matrix.
```

Our shrunk matrix contains just 100 columns. We can now efficiently compute the cosine similarities by running shrunk_matrix @ shrunk_matrix.T. However, first we need to confirm that the matrix rows remain normalized. Let's check the magnitude of shrunk_matrix[0].

Listing 15.34 Checking the magnitude of shrunk_matrix[0]

```
magnitude = norm(shrunk_matrix[0])
print(f"The magnitude of the first row is {magnitude:.2f}")
```

```
The magnitude of the first row is 0.49
```

The magnitude of the row is less than 1. Scikit-learn's SVD output has not been automatically normalized. We need to manually normalize the matrix before computing the similarities. Scikit-learn's built-in normalize function will assist us in that process. We import normalize from sklearn.preprocessing and then run normalize (shrunk_matrix). The magnitude of the rows in the resulting normalized matrix will subsequently equal 1.

Listing 15.35 Normalizing the SVD output

```
from sklearn.preprocessing import normalize
shrunk_norm_matrix = normalize(shrunk_matrix)
magnitude = norm(shrunk_norm_matrix[0])
print(f"The magnitude of the first row is {magnitude:.2f}")
```

```
The magnitude of the first row is 1.00
```

The shrunken matrix has been normalized. Now, running shrunk_norm_matrix @ shrunk_norm_matrix.T should produce a matrix of all-by-all cosine similarities.

Listing 15.36 Computing all-by-all cosine similarities

```
cosine_similarity_matrix = shrunk_norm_matrix @ shrunk_norm_matrix.T
```

We have our similarity matrix. Let's use it to choose a random pair of very similar texts. We start by randomly selecting a post at some index1. We next select an index of cosine_similarities[index1] that has the second-highest cosine similarity. Then, we print both the indices and their similarity before displaying the texts.

Listing 15.37 Choosing a random pair of similar posts

```
np.random.seed(1)
index1 = np.random.randint(dataset_size)
```

```
index2 = np.argsort(cosine_similarity_matrix[index1])[-2]
similarity = cosine_similarity_matrix[index1][index2]
print(f"The posts at indices {index1} and {index2} share a cosine "
      f"similarity of {similarity:.2f}")
```

```
The posts at indices 235 and 7805 share a cosine similarity of 0.91
```

Listing 15.38   Printing a randomly chosen post

```
print(newsgroups.data[index2].replace('\n\n', '\n'))
```

> This post contains blank lines. We filter out these lines to conserve space.

```
Hello,
    Who can tell me   Where can I find the PD or ShareWare
Which can CAPTURE windows 3.1's output of printer mananger?
    I want to capture the output of HP Laser Jet III.
    Though the PostScript can setup to print to file,but HP can't.
    I try DOS's redirect program,but they can't work in Windows 3.1
        Thankx for any help....
--
 Internet Address: u7911093@cc.nctu.edu.tw
    English Name: Erik Wang
    Chinese Name: Wang Jyh-Shyang
```

Once again, the printed post is a question. It's safe to assume that the post at `index1` is an answer to that question.

Listing 15.39   Printing the most similar post response

```
print(newsgroups.data[index1].replace('\n\n', '\n'))
```

```
u7911093@cc.nctu.edu.tw ("By SWH ) writes:
>Who can tell me which program (PD or ShareWare) can redirect windows 3.1's
>output of printer manager to file?
>     I want to capture HP Laser Jet III's print output.
>     Though PostScript can setup print to file,but HP can't.
>     I use DOS's redirect program,but they can't work in windows.
>       Thankx for any help...
>--
> Internet Address: u7911093@cc.nctu.edu.tw
>     English Name: Erik Wang
>     Chinese Name: Wang Jyh-Shyang
> National Chiao-Tung University,Taiwan,R.O.C.
Try setting up another HPIII printer but when choosing what port to connect
it to choose FILE instead of like :LPT1.  This will prompt you for a file
name everytime you print with that "HPIII on FILE" printer. Good Luck.
```

Thus far, we have examined two pairs of similar posts. Each post pair was composed of a question and a reply, where the question was included in the reply. Such boring pairs of overlapping texts are trivial to extract. Let's challenge ourselves to find something more interesting. We'll search for clusters of similar texts where posts in a cluster share some text without perfectly overlapping.

15.5 *Clustering texts by topic*

In section 10, we introduced two clustering algorithms: K-means and DBSCAN. K-means can only cluster on Euclidean distance. Conversely, DBSCAN can cluster based on any distance metric. One possible metric is cosine distance, which equals 1 minus cosine similarity.

> **NOTE** Why use cosine distance instead of cosine similarity? Well, all clustering algorithms assume that two identical data points share a distance of 0. Meanwhile, the cosine similarity equals 0 if two data points have nothing in common. It also equals 1 when two data points are perfectly identical. We can fix this discrepancy by running `1 - cosine_similarity_matrix`, thus converting our result to cosine distance. After the conversion, two identical texts will share a cosine distance of 0.

Cosine distance is commonly used in conjunction with DBSCAN. That is why scikit-learn's `DBSCAN` implementation permits us to specify cosine distance directly during object initialization. We simply need to pass `metric='cosine'` into the class constructor. Doing so will initialize a `cluster_model` object that's set to cluster based on cosine distance.

> **NOTE** Scikit-learn's `DBSCAN` implementation computes cosine distance by first recomputing `cosine_similarity_matrix`. Alternatively, we can avoid the recomputation by passing `metric='precomputed'` into the constructor. Doing so initializes a `cluster_model` object that's set to cluster on a matrix of precomputed distances. Next, running `cluster_model.fit_transform(1 - cosine_similarity_matrix)` should theoretically return the clustering results. However, practically speaking, negative values in the distance matrix (which can arise from floating-point errors) could cause issues during clustering. All negative values in the distance matrix must be replaced with zero before clustering. This operation would need to be run manually in NumPy by executing `x[x < 0] = 0`, where `x = 1 - cosine_similarity_matrix`.

Let's cluster `shrunk_matrix` with DBSCAN based on cosine distance. During clustering, we will make the following reasonable assumptions:

- Two newsgroup posts fall in a cluster if they share a cosine similarity of at least 0.6 (which corresponds to a cosine distance of no greater than 0.4).
- A cluster contains at least 50 newsgroup posts.

Based on these assumptions, the algorithm's `eps` and `min_samples` parameters should equal 0.4 and 50, respectively. Thus, we initialize DBSCAN by running `DBSCAN(eps=0.4, min_samples=50, metric='cosine')`. Then we use the initialized `cluster_model` object to cluster `shrunk_matrix`.

Listing 15.40   Clustering newsgroup posts with DBSCAN

```
from sklearn.cluster import DBSCAN
cluster_model = DBSCAN(eps=0.4, min_samples=50, metric='cosine')
clusters = cluster_model.fit_predict(shrunk_matrix)
```

We've generated an array of clusters. Let's quickly estimate the clustering quality. We already know that the newsgroups dataset covers 20 newsgroup categories. Some of the category names are very similar to each other; other topics are incredibly broad. Thus, it's reasonable to assume that the dataset covers 10 to 25 truly diverging topics. Consequently, we can expect our `clusters` array to contain somewhere between 10 and 25 clusters—otherwise, there's something wrong with our input clustering parameters. We now count the number of clusters.

Listing 15.41   Counting the number of DBSCAN clusters

```
cluster_count = clusters.max() + 1
print(f"We've generated {cluster_count} DBSCAN clusters")
```

```
We've generated 3 DBSCAN clusters
```

We've generated just three clusters, which is way lower than our expected cluster count. Clearly, our DBSCAN parameters were wrong. Is there some algorithmic method to adjust these parameters accordingly? Or are there perhaps well-known DBSCAN settings in the literature that yield acceptable text clusters? Sadly, no. As it happens, DBSCAN clustering of text is highly sensitive to the inputted document data. DBSCAN parameters for clustering specific types of texts (such as newsgroup posts) are unlikely to transfer well to other document categories (such as news articles or emails). Consequently, unlike with SVD, the DBSCAN algorithm lacks consistent NLP parameters. This does not mean DBSCAN cannot be applied to our text data, but the appropriate `eps` and `min_samples` inputs must be determined by trial and error. Unfortunately, DBSCAN lacks a well-established algorithm for optimizing these two crucial parameters.

K-means, on the other hand, takes as input a single *K* parameter. We can estimate *K* using the elbow plot technique, which we introduced in section 10. However, the K-means algorithm can only cluster based on Euclidean distance: it cannot process cosine distance. Is this a problem? Not necessarily. As it happens, we're in luck! All rows in `shrunk_norm_matrix` are normalized unit vectors. In section 13, we showed how the Euclidean distance of two normalized vectors v1 and v2 equals `(2 - 2 * v1 @ v2) ** 0.5`. Furthermore, the cosine distance between the vectors equals `1 - v1 @ v2`. With basic algebra, we can easily show that the Euclidean distance of two normalized vectors is proportional to the square root of the cosine distance. The two distance metrics are very closely related! This relationship provides us with mathematical justification for clustering `shrunk_norm_matrix` using K-means.

WARNING If two vectors are normalized, their Euclidean distance is an adequate substitute for cosine similarity. However, this is not the case for non-normalized vectors. Thus, we should never apply K-means to text-derived matrices if these matrices have not been normalized.

Research has shown that K-means clustering provides a reasonable segmentation of text data. This may seem confusing, since in previous sections, DBSCAN gave us superior results. Regrettably, in data science, the right choice of algorithm varies by domain. Rarely can one algorithm solve every type of problem. By analogy, not every task requires a hammer—sometimes we need a screwdriver or a wrench. Data scientists must remain flexible when choosing the appropriate tool for a given task.

NOTE Sometimes we may not know which algorithm to use on a given problem. When we are stuck, it helps to read known solutions online. The scikit-learn website in particular provides insightful solutions to common problems. For instance, the scikit-learn site offers example code for clustering text at http://mng.bz/wQ9q. Notably, the documented code illustrates how K-means can cluster text vectors (after SVD processing). The documentation also specifies that the vectors must be normalized "for better results."

Let's utilize K-means to cluster `shrunk_norm_matrix` into *K* different groups. We first need to assign a value for *K*. Supposedly, our texts belong to 20 different newsgroup categories. But as mentioned earlier, the actual cluster count may not equal 20. We want to estimate the true value of *K* by generating an elbow plot. To this end, we'll execute K-means across *K* values of 1 through 60 and then plot the inertia results.

However, we face a problem. Our dataset is large, containing over 10,000 points. The scikit-learn `KMeans` implementation will take a second or two to cluster the data. That lag time is acceptable for a single clustering run, but it's not acceptable for 60 different runs, where the execution time may add up to multiple minutes. How can we speed up the K-means running time? Well, one approach is to sample randomly from our hefty dataset. We can choose 1,000 random newsgroup posts during the K-means centroid calculation, then select another random 1,000 posts, and then update the cluster centers based on post content. In this manner, we can iteratively estimate the centers through sampling. At no point will we need to analyze the full dataset all at once. This modified version of the K-means algorithm is known as *mini-batch K-means*. Scikit-learn offers a mini-batch implementation with its `MiniBatchKMeans` class. `MiniBatchKMeans` is nearly identical in its methods to the standard `KMeans` class. Next, we import both implementations and compare their running times.

NOTE We should emphasize that even with `MiniBatchKMeans`, efficient computation time is possible only because we have dimensionally reduced our data.

Listing 15.42   Comparing `KMeans` to `MiniBatchKMeans`

```
np.random.seed(0)
import time
from sklearn.cluster import KMeans, MiniBatchKMeans

k=20
times = []
for KMeans_class in [KMeans, MiniBatchKMeans]:
    start_time = time.time()
    KMeans_class(k).fit(shrunk_norm_matrix)
    times.append(time.time() - start_time)

running_time_ratio = times[0] / times[1]
print(f"Mini Batch K-means ran {running_time_ratio:.2f} times faster "
      "than regular K-means")
```

Computes the running time of each clustering algorithm implementation

Running time.time() returns the current time, in seconds.

```
Mini Batch K-means ran 10.53 times faster than regular K-means
```

`MiniBatchKMeans` runs approximately 10 times faster than regular `KMeans`. That decrease in running time carries a minor cost: it has been shown that `MiniBatchK-Means` produces clusters of slightly lower quality than `KMeans`. However, our immediate concern isn't cluster quality; rather, we are interested in estimating *K* using an elbow plot across `range(1, 61)`. The speedy `MiniBatchKMeans` implementation should serve us just fine as an estimation tool.

We now generate the plot using mini-batch K-means. We also add grid lines to the plot, to better isolate potential elbow coordinates. As seen in section 10, we can visualize such grid lines by calling `plt.grid(True)`. Finally, we want to compare the elbow with the official newsgroup category count. For this purpose, we will plot a vertical line at a *K* value of 20 (figure 15.1).

Listing 15.43   Plotting an elbow curve using `MiniBatchKMeans`

```
np.random.seed(0)
import matplotlib.pyplot as plt

k_values = range(1, 61)
inertia_values = [MiniBatchKMeans(k).fit(shrunk_norm_matrix).inertia_
                  for k in k_values]
plt.plot(k_values, inertia_values)
plt.xlabel('K')
plt.ylabel('Inertia')
plt.axvline(20, c='k')
plt.grid(True)
plt.show()
```

Our plotted curve decreases smoothly. The precise location of a bent elbow–shaped transition is difficult to spot. We do see that the curve is noticeably steeper when *K* is less than 20. Somewhere after 20 clusters, the curve begins to flatten out, but there is

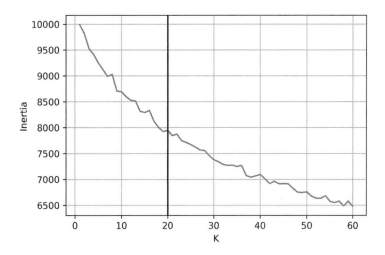

Figure 15.1 An elbow plot generated using mini-batch K-means across *K* values ranging from 1 to 61. The precise location of an elbow is difficult to determine. However, the plotted curve is noticeably steeper before a *K* of 20. Also, it begins to flatten after a *K* of 20. We thus infer that a value of approximately 20 is an appropriate input for *K*.

no singular location at which the elbow suddenly bends. The dataset lacks a perfect *K* at which the texts fall into natural clusters. Why? For one thing, real-world text is messy and nuanced. Categorical boundaries are not always obvious. For instance, we can engage in a conversation about technology or a conversation about politics. In addition, we can openly discuss how politics is influenced by technology. Seemingly distinct discussion topics can meld together, forming novel topics of their own. Due to such complexities, there rarely exists a single, smooth transition between text clusters. Consequently, figuring out an ideal *K* is hard. But we can make certain useful inferences: based on the elbow plot, we can infer that 20 is a reasonable estimate of the *K* parameter. Yes, the curve is fuzzy, and perhaps an input of 18 or 22 would also do. However, we need to start somewhere, and a *K* of 20 makes more sense than a *K* of 3 or 50. Our solution isn't perfect, but it's feasible. Sometimes, when we deal with real-world data, a feasible solution is the best that we can expect.

> **NOTE** If you are uncomfortable choosing the elbow qualitatively by staring at the plot, consider using the external Yellowbrick library. The library contains a `KElbowVisualizer` class (http://mng.bz/7lV9) that uses both Matplotlib and scikit-learn's mini-batch K-means implementation to highlight the elbow location in an automated manner. If we initialize `KElbowVisualizer` and apply it to our data, the corresponding object returns a *K* of 23. Additionally, Yellowbrick offers more powerful *K*-selection methodologies, such as the silhouette score (which we alluded to in section 10.) The library can be installed by running `pip install yellowbrick`.

We will now divide `shrunk_norm_matrix` into 20 clusters. We run the origin KMeans implementation for maximum accuracy and then store the text indices and cluster IDs in a Pandas table for easier analysis.

Listing 15.44   Clustering newsgroup posts into 20 clusters

```
np.random.seed(0)
cluster_model = KMeans(n_clusters=20)
clusters = cluster_model.fit_predict(shrunk_norm_matrix)
df = pd.DataFrame({'Index': range(clusters.size), 'Cluster': clusters})
```

We have clustered our texts and are ready to explore the cluster contents. However, first we must briefly discuss one important consequence of executing K-means on large matrix inputs: the resulting clusters may vary slightly across different computers, even if we run `np.random.seed(0)`. This divergence is driven by how different machines round floating-point numbers. Some computers round small numbers up, while others round these numbers down. Normally, these differences are not noticeable. Unfortunately, in a 10,000-by-100 element matrix, small differences can impact the clustering results. K-means is not deterministic, as we've discussed in section 10— it can converge in multiple ways to multiple sets of equally valid clusters. Thus, your locally run text clusters may differ from outputs in this book, but your observations and conclusions should be similar.

With this in mind, let's proceed with the analysis. We begin by analyzing a single cluster. Later, we analyze all the clusters simultaneously

15.5.1 *Exploring a single text cluster*

One of our 20 clusters contains the car post at index 0 of `newsgroups.data`. Let's isolate and count the number of texts that group together with that car-themed message.

Listing 15.45   Isolating the car cluster

```
df_car = df[df.Cluster == clusters[0]]
cluster_size = df_car.shape[0]
print(f"{cluster_size} posts cluster together with the car-themed post "
      "at index 0")
```

```
393 posts cluster together with the car-themed post at index 0
```

> **WARNING** As we've just discussed, the contents of the cluster may differ slightly on your local machine. The total cluster size may minimally diverge from 393. If this happens, the subsequent sequence of code listings may produce different results. Regardless of these differences, you should still be able to draw similar conclusions from your locally generated outputs.

393 posts cluster with the car-themed texts at index 0. Presumably, these posts are also about cars. If so, then a randomly chosen post should mention an automobile. Let's verify if this is the case.

Listing 15.46 Printing a random post in the car cluster

```
np.random.seed(1)
def get_post_category(index):          ◁──────────────
    target_index = newsgroups.target[index]
    return newsgroups.target_names[target_index]

random_index = np.random.choice(df_car.Index.values)
post_category = get_post_category(random_index)

print(f"This post appeared in the {post_category} discussion group:\n")
print(newsgroups.data[random_index].replace('\n\n', '\n'))
```

> Returns the post category of the newsgroup post found at index "index". We will reuse the function elsewhere in the section.

```
This post appeared in the rec.autos discussion group:

My wife and I looked at, and drove one last fall. This was a 1992 model.
It was WAYYYYYYYYY underpowered. I could not imagine driving it in the
mountains here in Colorado at anything approaching highway speeds. I
have read that the new 1993 models have a newer, improved hp engine.
I'm quite serious that I laughed in the salesman face when he said "once
it's broken in it will feel more powerful". I had been used to driving a
Jeep 4.0L 190hp engine. I believe the 92's Land Cruisers (Land Yachts)
were 3.0L, the sames as the 4Runner, which is also underpowered (in my
own personal opinion).
They are big cars, very roomy, but nothing spectacular.
```

The random post discusses a model of Jeep. It was posted in the *rec.autos* discussion group. How many of the nearly 400 posts in the cluster belong to *rec.autos*? Let's find out.

Listing 15.47 Checking cluster membership to *rec.autos*

```
rec_autos_count = 0
for index in df_car.Index.values:
    if get_post_category(index) == 'rec.autos':
        rec_autos_count += 1

rec_autos_percent = 100 * rec_autos_count / cluster_size
print(f"{rec_autos_percent:.2f}% of posts within the cluster appeared "
      "in the rec.autos discussion group")
```

```
84.73% of posts within the cluster appeared in the rec.autos discussion
group
```

In this cluster, 84% of the posts appeared in *rec.autos*. The cluster is thus dominated by that car discussion group. What about the remaining 16% of the clustered posts? Did they fall erroneously into the cluster? Or are they relevant to the topic of automobiles? We'll soon find out. Let's isolate the indices of posts in df_car that do not belong to *rec.autos*. Then we'll choose a random index and print the associated post.

Listing 15.48   Examining a post that did not appear in *rec.autos*

```
np.random.seed(1)
not_autos_indices = [index for index in df_car.Index.values
                     if get_post_category(index) != 'rec.autos']

random_index = np.random.choice(not_autos_indices)
post_category = get_post_category(random_index)

print(f"This post appeared in the {post_category} discussion group:\n")
print(newsgroups.data[random_index].replace('\n\n', '\n'))

This post appeared in the sci.electronics discussion group:

>The father of a friend of mine is a police officer in West Virginia.  Not
>only is his word as a skilled observer good in court, but his skill as an
>observer has been tested to be more accurate than the radar gun in some
>cases . . ..  No foolin!  He can guess a car's speed to within 2-3mph just
>by watching it blow by - whether he's standing still or moving too!  (Yes,
1) How was this testing done, and how many times?  (Calibrated
speedometer?)
2) It's not the "some cases" that worry me, it's the "other cases" :-)


They are big cars, very roomy, but nothing spectacular.
```

The random post appeared in an electronics discussion group. The post describes the use of radar to measure car speed. Thematically, it's about automobiles, so it appears to have clustered correctly. What about the other 60 or so posts represented by the not_autos_indices list? How do we evaluate their relevance? We could read each post, one by one, but that is not a scalable solution. Instead, we can aggregate their content by displaying the top-ranking words across all posts. We rank each word by summing its TFIDF across each index in not_autos_indices. Then we'll sort the words based on their aggregated TFIDF. Printing out the top 10 words will help us determine if our content is relevant to cars.

Next, we define a rank_words_by_tfidf function. The function takes as input a list of indices and ranks the words across these indices using the approach described previously. The ranked words are stored in a Pandas table for easier display. The summed TFIDF values used to rank the words are also stored in that table. Once our function is defined, we will run rank_words_by_tfidf(not_autos_indices) and output the top 10 ranked results.

NOTE   Given an indices array, we want to aggregate the rows of tfidf_np_matrix[indices]. As discussed earlier, we can sum over rows by running tfidf_np_matrix[indices].sum(axis=0). Additionally, we can generate that sum by running tfidf_matrix[indices].sum(axis=0), where tfidf_matrix is a SciPy CSR object. Summing over the rows of a sparse CSR matrix is computationally much faster, but that summation returns a 1-by-*n* shaped matrix that is not a NumPy object. We need to convert the output to a NumPy array by running np.asarray(tfidf_matrix[indices].sum(axis=0))[0].

Listing 15.49 Ranking the top 10 words with TFIDF

```
def rank_words_by_tfidf(indices, word_list=words):
    summed_tfidf = np.asarray(tfidf_matrix[indices].sum(axis=0))[0]    ⟵
    data = {'Word': word_list,
            'Summed TFIDF': summed_tfidf}
    return pd.DataFrame(data).sort_values('Summed TFIDF', ascending=False)

df_ranked_words = rank_words_by_tfidf(not_autos_indices)
print(df_ranked_words[:10].to_string(index=False))
```

Word	Summed TFIDF
car	8.026003
cars	1.842831
radar	1.408331
radio	1.365664
ham	1.273830
com	1.164511
odometer	1.162576
speed	1.145510
just	1.144489
writes	1.070528

> This summation is equivalent to running tfidf_np_matrix[indices].sum(axis=0). The simpler NumPy array aggregation takes approximately 1 second to compute. A single second may not seem like much, but once we repeat the computation over 20 clusters, the running time will add up to 20 seconds. The summation over the rows of the sparse matrix is noticeably faster.

The first two top-ranking words are *car* and *cars*.

NOTE The word *cars* is the plural of *car*. We can aggregate these words together based on the *s* at the end of *cars*. This process of reducing a plural to its root word is called *stemming*. The external Natural Language Toolkit library (https://www.nltk.org) provides useful functions for efficient stemming.

Elsewhere on the ranked list, we see mentions of *radar*, *odometer*, and *speed*. Some of these terms also appeared in our randomly chosen *sci.electronics* post. The use of radar technology to measure car speed appears to be a common theme in the texts represented by not_autos_indices. How do these speed-themed keywords compare with the rest of the posts in the car cluster? We can check by inputting df_car.Index.values into rank_words_by_tfidf.

Listing 15.50 Ranking the top 10 words in the car cluster

```
df_ranked_words = rank_words_by_tfidf(df_car.Index.values)
print(df_ranked_words[:10].to_string(index=False))
```

Word	Summed TFIDF
car	47.824319
cars	17.875903
engine	10.947385
dealer	8.416367
com	7.902425
just	7.303276
writes	7.272754
edu	7.216044
article	6.768039
good	6.685494

Generally, the posts in the `df_car` cluster focus on car engines and car dealers. However, a minority of the posts discuss radar measurements of car speed. These radar posts are more likely to appear in the *sci.electronics* newsgroup. Nonetheless, these posts legitimately discuss cars (as opposed to discussing politics, software, or medicine). Thus, our `df_car` cluster appears to be genuine. By examining the top keywords, we were able to validate the cluster without having to read each clustered post manually.

In this same manner, we can utilize `rank_words_by_tfidf` to get the top keywords for each of the 20 clusters. The keywords will allow us to understand the topic of each cluster. Unfortunately, printing 20 different word tables isn't very visually efficient— the printed tables will take up too much space, adding redundant pages to this book. Alternatively, we can visualize these cluster keywords as images in a single coherent plot. Let's learn how to visualize the contents of multiple text clusters.

15.6   *Visualizing text clusters*

Our aim is to visualize ranked keywords across multiple text clusters. First we need to solve a simpler problem: how do we visualize the important keywords in a single cluster? One approach is just to print the keywords in their order of importance. Unfortunately, this sorting lacks any sense of relative significance. For instance, in our `df_ranked_words` table, the word *cars* is immediately followed by *engine*. However, *cars* has a summed TFIDF score of 17.8, while *engine* has a score of 10.9. Thus, *cars* is approximately 1.6 times more significant than *engine*, relative to the car cluster. How do we incorporate relative significance into our visualization? Well, we could signify importance using font size: we could display *cars* with a font size of 17.8 and *engine* with a font size of 10.9. In the display, *cars* would be 1.6 times bigger and thus 1.6 times more important. Of course, a font size of 10.9 may be too small to comfortably read. We can make the font size bigger by doubling the summed TFIDF significance scores.

Python does not let us modify font size directly during printing. However, we can modify font size using Matplotlib's `plt.text` function. Running `plt.text(x, y, word, fontsize=z)` displays a word at coordinates (x, y) and sets the font size to equal z. The function allows us to visualize the words in a 2D grid where word size is proportional to significance. This type of visualization is called a *word cloud*. Let's utilize `plt.text` to generate a word cloud of the top words in `df_ranked_words`. We plot the word cloud as a five-word by five-word grid (figure 15.2). Each word's font size equals double its significance score.

Listing 15.51   **Plotting a word cloud with Matplotlib**

```
i = 0
for x_coord in np.arange(0, 1, .2):
    for y_coord in np.arange(0, 1, .2):
        word, significance = df_ranked_words.iloc[i].values
        plt.text(y_coord, x_coord, word, fontsize=2*significance)
        i += 1

plt.show()
```

Figure 15.2 A word cloud generated using Matplotlib. The word cloud is a mess because of word overlap.

Our visualization is a mess! Large words like *car* take up too much space. They overlap with other words, making the image indecipherable. We need to plot our words much more intelligently. No two words should ever overlap. Eliminating the overlap of 2D plotted words is not a trivial task. Fortunately, the hard work has been done for us by the creators of the external Wordcloud library. The library is able to generate word clouds in a manner that's visually appealing. We now install Wordcloud and then import and initialize the library's `WordCloud` class.

> **NOTE** Call `pip install wordcloud` from the command line terminal to install the Wordcloud library.

Listing 15.52 Initializing the `WordCloud` class

> The positions of the words in the word cloud are generated randomly. To maintain output consistency, we must pass the random seed directly using the random_state parameter.

```
from wordcloud import WordCloud
cloud_generator = WordCloud(random_state=1)
```

Running `WordCloud()` returns a `cloud_generator` object. We'll use the object's `fit_words` method to generate a word cloud. Running `cloud_generator.fit_words(words_to_score)` will create an image from `words_to_score`, which is a dictionary mapping of words to their significance scores.

> **NOTE** Please note that running `cloud_generator.generate_from_frequencies(word_to_score)` will achieve the same results.

Let's create an image from the most significant words in `df_ranked_words`. We'll store that image in a `wordcloud_image` variable, but we won't plot the image just yet.

Listing 15.53   Generating a word cloud image

```
words_to_score = {word: score
                  for word, score in df_ranked_words[:10].values}
wordcloud_image = cloud_generator.fit_words(words_to_score)
```

Now we're ready to visualize `wordcloud_image`. Matplotlib's `plt.imshow` function is able to plot images based on a variety of inputted image formats. Running `plt.imshow` `(wordcloud_image)` will display our generated word cloud (figure 15.3).

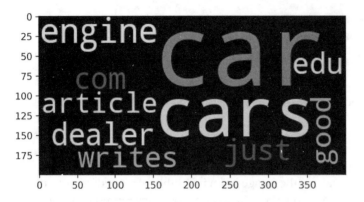

Figure 15.3   A word cloud generated using the `WordCloud` class. The words no longer overlap. However, the background is too dark. Also, some letters appear rough around the edges.

NOTE   There are multiple ways of representing images in Python. One approach is to store an image as a 2D NumPy array. Alternatively, we can store the image using a special class from the Python Imaging Library (PIL). The `plt.imshow` function can display images stored as NumPy objects or as PIL `Image` objects. It can also display custom image objects that include a `to_image` method, but that method's output must return a NumPy array or a PIL `Image` object.

Listing 15.54   Plotting an image using `plt.imshow`

```
plt.imshow(wordcloud_image)
plt.show()
```

We've visualized the word cloud. Our visualization is not ideal: the dark background makes it hard to read the words. We can change the background from black to white by running `WordCloud(background_color='white')` during initialization. Also, the edges of the individual letters are pixelated and blocky: we can smooth all the edges in our image plot by passing `interpolation="bilinear"` into `plt.imshow`. Let's regenerate the word cloud with a lighter background while also smoothing out the visualized letters (figure 15.4).

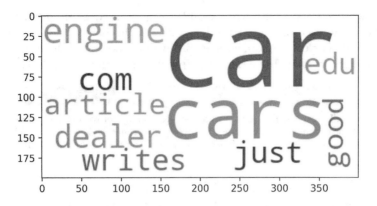

Figure 15.4 A word cloud generated using the `WordCloud` class. The background is set to white, for better visibility, and the letters are smoothed out at the edges.

Listing 15.55 Improving the word cloud image quality

```
cloud_generator = WordCloud(background_color='white',
                            random_state=1)
wordcloud_image = cloud_generator.fit_words(words_to_score)
plt.imshow(wordcloud_image, interpolation="bilinear")
plt.show()
```

The top words in the car cluster have been successfully visualized. The words *car* and *cars* clearly dominate over lesser terms, such as *engine* and *dealer*. We can interpret the contents of the cluster merely by glancing at the word cloud. Of course, we have already examined the car cluster in great detail, and we aren't gleaming anything new from this visualization. Let's instead apply word cloud visualization to a randomly chosen cluster (figure 15.5). The word cloud will display the cluster's 15 most significant words, and we'll use the display to figure out the main topic of the cluster.

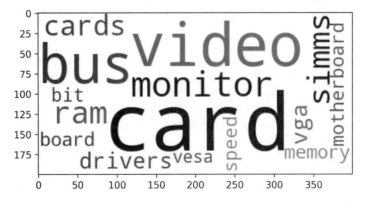

Figure 15.5 A random cluster's word cloud. The topic of the cluster appears to be technology and computer hardware.

> **NOTE** The word colors in the word cloud are generated at random, and some of the random colors would render poorly in the black-and-white version of this book. For this reason, we specifically limit the color selection to a small subset of colors using the `color_func` parameter in the `WordCloud` class.

Listing 15.56   Plotting a word cloud for a random cluster

Takes as input a df_cluster table and returns a word cloud image for the top max_words words corresponding to the cluster. The previously defined rank_words_by_tfidf function is used to rank the words in the cluster.

```
np.random.seed(1)

def cluster_to_image(df_cluster, max_words=15):    <—
    indices = df_cluster.Index.values
    df_ranked_words = rank_words_by_tfidf(indices)[:max_words]
    words_to_score = {word: score
                      for word, score in df_ranked_words[:max_words].values}
    cloud_generator = WordCloud(background_color='white',
                                color_func=_color_func,    <—
                                random_state=1)
    wordcloud_image = cloud_generator.fit_words(words_to_score)
    return wordcloud_image

def _color_func(*args, **kwargs):
    return np.random.choice(['black', 'blue', 'teal', 'purple', 'brown'])

cluster_id = np.random.randint(0, 20)
df_random_cluster = df[df.Cluster == cluster_id]
wordcloud_image = cluster_to_image(df_random_cluster)
plt.imshow(wordcloud_image, interpolation="bilinear")
plt.show()
```

Helper function to randomly assign one of five acceptable colors to each word

The WordCloud class includes an optional color_func parameter. The parameter expects a color-selection function that assigns a color to each word. Here, we define a custom function to control the color settings.

Our randomly chosen cluster includes top words such as *monitor, video, memory, card, motherboard, bit,* and *ram.* The cluster seems to focus on technology and computer hardware. We can verify by printing the most common newsgroup category in the cluster.

> **NOTE** By observing the words *card, video,* and *memory,* we can infer that *card* refers to either *video card* or a *memory card.* In NLP, such sequences of two consecutive words are called *bigrams.* Generally, a sequence of *n* consecutive words is called an *n-gram.* `TfidfVectorizer` is able to vectorize across n-grams of arbitrary length. We simply need to pass in an `ngram_range` parameter during initialization. Running `TfidfVectorizer(ngram_range(1, 3))` creates a vectorizer that tracks all 1-grams (single words), 2-grams (such as *video card*), and 3-grams (such as *natural language processing*). Of course, these n-grams cause the vocabulary size to rise into the millions. However, we can limit the vocabulary to the top 100,000 n-grams by passing `max_features=100000` into the vectorizer's initialization method.

Listing 15.57 Checking the most common cluster category

```
from collections import Counter

def get_top_category(df_cluster):
    categories = [get_post_category(index)
                    for index in df_cluster.Index.values]
    top_category, _ = Counter(categories).most_common()[0]
    return top_category

top_category = get_top_category(df_random_cluster)
print("The posts within the cluster commonly appear in the "
      f"'{top_category}' newsgroup")

The posts within the cluster commonly appear in the
'comp.sys.ibm.pc.hardware' newsgroup
```

Many of the posts in the cluster appeared in the *comp.sys.ibm.pc.hardware* newsgroup. We've thus successfully identified the cluster's topic of hardware. We did this simply by looking at the word cloud.

So far, we've generated two separate word clouds for two distinct clusters. However, our end goal is to display multiple word clouds simultaneously. We'll now visualize all word clouds in a single figure using a Matplotlib concept called a *subplot*.

Common methods for visualizing words

- `plt.text(word, x, y, fontsize=z)`—Plots a word positioned at coordinates `(x, y)` with a font size of `z`.
- `cloud_generator = WordCloud()`—Initializes an object that can generate a word cloud. The background of that word cloud is black.
- `cloud_generator = WordCloud(background_color='white')`—Initializes an object that can generate a word cloud. The background of that word cloud is white.
- `wordcloud_image = cloud_generator.fit_words(words_to_score)`—Generates a word cloud image from the `words_to_score` dictionary, which maps words to their significance scores. The size of every word in `wordcloud_image` is computed relative to its significance.
- `plt.imshow(wordcloud_image)`—Plots the computed `wordcloud_image`.
- `plt.imshow(wordcloud_image, interpolation="bilinear")`—Plots the computed `wordcloud_image` while smoothing out the visualized letters.

15.6.1 *Using subplots to display multiple word clouds*

Matplotlib allows us to include multiple plots in a single figure. Each distinct plot is called a *subplot*. Subplots can be organized in any number of ways, but they're most commonly arranged in a grid-like pattern. We can create a subplot grid containing `r` rows and `c` columns by running `plt.subplots(r, c)`. The `plt.subplots` function generates the grid while also returning a tuple: (figure, axes). The figure variable is a special class that tracks the main figure, which encompasses the grid. Meanwhile, the axes variable is a 2D list containing r rows and c columns. Each element of axes is a Matplotlib AxesSubplot object. Every subplot object can be used to output a unique visualization: running axes[i][j].plot(x, y) plots x versus y in the subplot positioned in the *i*th row and *j*th column of the grid.

> **WARNING**   Running subplots(1, z) or subplots(z, 1) returns a 1D axes list where len(axes) == z rather than a 2D grid.

Let's demonstrate the use of plt.subplots. We generate a two-by-two grid of subplots by running plt.subplots(2, 2). Then we iterate over each row r and column c in the grid. For every unique subplot positioned at (r, c), we plot a quadratic curve in which y = r * x*x + c * x. By linking curve parameters to the grid position, we generate four distinct curves, all of which appear in the bounds of a single figure (figure 15.6).

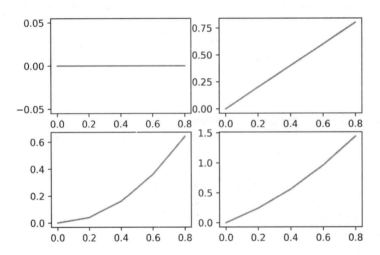

Figure 15.6   Four different curves plotted across four subplots in a single figure

Listing 15.58   Generating four subplots using Matplotlib

```
figure, axes = plt.subplots(2, 2)
for r in range(2):
    for c in range(2):
        x = np.arange(0, 1, .2)
        y = r * x * x + c * x
        axes[r][c].plot(x, y)

plt.show()
```

Four different curves appear in the subplots of our grid. We can replace any of these curves with a word cloud. Let's visualize wordcloud_image in the lower-left quadrant of the grid by running `axes[1][0].imshow(wordcloud_image)` (figure 15.7). Let's also assign a title to that subplot: the title equals `top_category`, which is *comp.sys.ibm.pc .hardware*. We set the subplot title by running `axes[r][c].set_title(top_category)`.

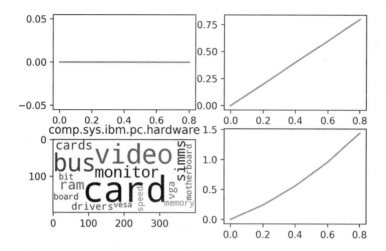

Figure 15.7   **Three curves and a word cloud plotted in four subplots. There are issues with word cloud readability due to formatting problems and figure size.**

Listing 15.59   Plotting a word cloud within a subplot

```
figure, axes = plt.subplots(2, 2)
for r in range(2):
    for c in range(2):
        if (r, c) == (1, 0):
            axes[r][c].set_title(top_category)
            axes[r][c].imshow(wordcloud_image,
                              interpolation="bilinear")
        else:
            x = np.arange(0, 1, .2)
            y = r * x * x + c * x
        axes[r][c].plot(x, y)

plt.show()
```

We've visualized a word cloud in the subplot grid, but there are some issues with the visualization. The words in the cloud are hard to read because the subplot is so small. We need to make the subplot bigger, which requires us to alter the figure size. We can do so using the `figsize` parameter. Passing `figsize=(width, height)` into `plt.sub-plots` creates a figure that is `width` inches wide and `height` inches high. Each subplot in the figure is also adjusted to fit the updated size.

In addition, we can make other minor changes to improve the plot. Reducing the visualized word count from 15 to 10 will make the smaller word cloud easier to read.

We should also remove the axis tick marks from the plot—they take up too much space and provide no useful information. We can delete the x-axis and y-axis tick marks from `axis[r][c]` by calling `axis[r][c].set_xticks([])` and `axis[r][c].set_yticks([])`, respectively. With this in mind, let's generate a figure that's 20 inches wide and 15 inches high (listing 15.60).

NOTE   The actual dimensions of the figure in the book are not 20 by 15 inches, due to image formatting.

The large figure has 20 subplots aligned in a five-by-four grid. Each subplot contains a word cloud corresponding to one of our clusters, and every subplot title is set to the dominant newsgroup category in a cluster. We also include the cluster index in each title for later reference. Finally, we remove the axis tick marks from all plots. The final visualization gives us a bird's-eye-view of all the dominant word patterns across all 20 clusters (figure 15.8).

Figure 15.8   20 word clouds visualized across 20 subplots. Each word cloud corresponds to one of 20 clusters. The title of each subplot equals the top newsgroup category in each cluster. In most of the word clouds, the title corresponds with the displayed word content; but certain word clouds (such as those of clusters 1 and 7) do not offer informative displays.

Common subplot methods

- `figure, axes = plt.subplots(x, y)`—Creates a figure containing an x-by-y grid of subplots. If `x > 1` and `y > 1`, then `axes[r][c]` corresponds to the subplot in row `r` and column `c` of the subplot grid.
- `figure, axes = plt.subplots(x, y, figsize=(width, height))`—Creates a figure containing an x-by-y grid of subplots. The figure is `width` inches wide and `height` inches high.
- `axes[r][c].plot(x_values, y_values)`—Plots data in the subplot positioned at row `r` and column `c`.
- `axes[r][c].set_title(title)`—Adds a title to the subplot positioned at row `r` and column `c`.

Listing 15.60 Visualizing all clusters using 20 subplots

```
np.random.seed(0)

def get_title(df_cluster):                ⟵  Generates a subplot title by combining
    top_category = get_top_category(df_cluster)   the cluster ID with the most common
    cluster_id = df_cluster.Cluster.values[0]     newsgroup category in a cluster
    return f"{cluster_id}: {top_category}"

figure, axes = plt.subplots(5, 4, figsize=(20, 15))
cluster_groups = list(df.groupby('Cluster'))
for r in range(5):
    for c in range(4):
        _, df_cluster = cluster_groups.pop(0)
        wordcloud_image = cluster_to_image(df_cluster, max_words=10)
        ax = axes[r][c]
        ax.imshow(wordcloud_image,
                interpolation="bilinear")                      Increases the title
        ax.set_title(get_title(df_cluster), fontsize=20)  ⟵   font to 20 for better
        ax.set_xticks([])                                      readability
        ax.set_yticks([])

plt.show()
```

We've visualized the top words across all 20 clusters. For the most part, the visualized words make sense! The main topic of cluster 0 is cryptography: its top words include *encryption*, *secure*, *keys*, and *nsa*. The main topic of cluster 2 is space: its top words include *space*, *nasa*, *shuttle*, *moon*, and *orbit*. Cluster 4 is centered on shopping, with top words like *sale*, *offer*, *shipping*, and *condition*. Clusters 9 and 18 are sports clusters: their main topics are *baseball* and *hockey*, respectively. Posts in cluster 9 frequently mention *games*, *runs*, *baseball*, *pitching*, and *team*. Posts in cluster 18 frequently mention *game*, *team*, *players*, *hockey*, and *nhl*. A majority of the clusters are easy to interpret, based on their word clouds. Arguably, 75% of the clusters contain top words corresponding with their dominant category titles.

Of course, there are issues with our output. Several of the word clouds do not make sense: for instance, cluster 1 has a subplot title of `sci.electronics`, yet its word cloud is composed of general words like *just*, *like*, *does*, and *know*. Meanwhile, cluster 7 has a subplot title of `sci.med`, yet its word cloud is composed of words like *pitt*, *msg*, and *gordon*. Unfortunately, word cloud visualization isn't always perfect. Sometimes the underlying clusters are malformed, or the dominant language in the clusters is biased toward unexpected text patterns.

> **NOTE**   Reading some sampled posts in the clusters can help reveal these biases. For instance, many of the electronics questions in cluster 1 include the question, "does anyone know?" Also, many of the posts in cluster 7 were written by a student named Gordon, who studied at the University of Pittsburgh (*pitt*).

Fortunately, there are steps we can take to salvage the indecipherable word clouds. For instance, we can filter out obviously useless words and then regenerate the cloud. Or we can simply disregard the top *x* words in the cluster and visualize the cloud using the next top-ranking words. Let's remove the top 10 words from cluster 7 and recompute its word cloud (figure 15.9).

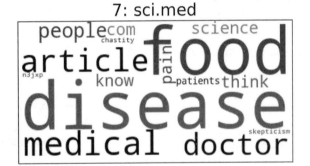

Figure 15.9   Cluster 7's word cloud, recomputed after filtering. It is now clear that medicine is the main topic of the cluster.

Listing 15.61   Recomputing a word cloud after filtering

```
np.random.seed(3)
df_cluster= df[df.Cluster == 7]
df_ranked_words = rank_words_by_tfidf(df_cluster.Index.values)

words_to_score = {word: score
                  for word, score in df_ranked_words[10:25].values}
cloud_generator = WordCloud(background_color='white',
                            color_func=_color_func,
                            random_state=1)
wordcloud_image = cloud_generator.fit_words(words_to_score)
plt.imshow(wordcloud_image, interpolation="bilinear")
plt.title(get_title(df_cluster), fontsize=20)
plt.xticks([])
plt.yticks([])
plt.show()
```

We visualize the top 15 words since we're not spatially restricted by a subplot.

Note that plt lacks a subplot's set_title, set_xticks, and set_yticks methods. Instead, we must call plt.title, plt.xticks, and plt.yticks to achieve the same results.

Cluster 7 is dominated by words like *disease, medical, doctor, food, pain,* and *patients.* Its medicinal topic is now clear; by disregarding the useless keywords, we've managed to elucidate the cluster's true contents. Of course, this simple approach will not always work. NLP is messy, and there is no silver bullet that will slay all of our problems. Nonetheless, there's still much we can accomplish, despite the unstructured nature of complex texts. Consider what we have achieved: we've taken 10,000 diverse real-world texts and clustered them into multiple meaningful topics. Furthermore, we've visualized these topics in a single image, and most of the topics in that image are interpretable. We've attained these results using a straightforward series of steps, which can be applied to any large text dataset. Effectively, we've developed a pipeline for clustering and visualizing unstructured text data. That pipeline works as follows:

1. Transform our text into a normalized TFIDF matrix using the `TfidfVectorizer` class.
2. Reduce the matrix to 100 dimensions using the SVD algorithm.
3. Normalize the dimensionally reduced output for clustering purposes.
4. Cluster the normalized output using K-means. We can estimate *K* by generating an elbow plot using mini-batch K-means, which is optimized for speed.
5. Visualize the top words in each cluster using a word cloud. All word clouds are displayed as subplots in a single figure. Words are ranked based on their summed TFIDF values across all the texts in a cluster.
6. Interpret the topic of each cluster using the word cloud visualization. Any uninterpretable clusters are examined in more detail.

Given our text-analysis pipeline, we can effectively cluster and interpret almost any real-world text dataset.

Summary

- Scikit-learn's newsgroup dataset contains over 10,000 newsgroup posts spread out across 20 newsgroup categories.
- We can convert the posts into a TF matrix using scikit-learn's `CountVectorizer` class. The generated matrix is stored in the *CSR* format. This format is used to efficiently analyze sparse matrices, which are composed mostly of zeros.
- Generally, TF matrices are sparse; a single row may only reference a few dozen words from the entire dataset vocabulary. We can access these nonzero words with the help of the `np.flatnonzero` function.
- The most frequently occurring words in a text tend to be *stop words,* which are common English words like *the* or *this.* Stop words should be filtered from text datasets before vectorization.
- Even after stop-word filtering, certain overly common words will remain. We can minimize the impact of these words using their document frequencies. A word's *document frequency* equals the total fraction of texts in which that word

appears. Words that are more common are less significant. Hence, less significant words have higher document frequencies.

- We can combine term frequencies and document frequencies into a single significance score called *TFIDF*. Generally, TFIDF vectors are more informative than TF vectors. We can convert texts to TFIDF vectors using scikit-learn's `TfidfVectorizer` class. That vectorizer returns a TFIDF matrix whose rows are automatically normalized for easier similarity computation.

- Large TFIDF matrices should be dimensionally reduced before clustering. The recommended number of dimensions is 100. Scikit-learn's dimensionally reduced SVD output needs to be normalized before subsequent analysis.

- We can cluster normalized, dimensionally reduced text data using either K-means or DBSCAN. Unfortunately, it's hard to optimize DBSCAN's parameters during text clustering. Thus, K-means remains the preferable clustering algorithm. We can estimate *K* using an elbow plot. If our dataset is large, we should generate the plot using `MiniBatchKMeans` for a faster runtime.

- For any given text cluster, we want to view the words that are most relevant to the cluster. We can rank each word by summing its TFIDF values across all matrix rows represented by the cluster. Furthermore, we can visualize the ranked words in a *word cloud*: a 2D image composed of words, where word size is proportional to significance.

- We can plot multiple word clouds in a single figure using the `plt.subplots` function. This visualization gives us a bird's-eye view of all the dominant word patterns across all clusters.

Extracting text
from web pages

16

This section covers

- Rendering web pages with HTML
- The basic structure of HTML files
- Extracting text from HTML files with the Beautiful Soup library
- Downloading HTML files from online sources

The internet is a great resource for text data. Millions of web pages offer limitless text content in the form of news articles, encyclopedia pages, scientific papers, restaurant reviews, political discussions, patents, corporate financial statements, job postings, etc. All these pages can be analyzed if we download their Hypertext Markup Language (HTML) files. A *markup language* is a system for annotating documents that distinguishes the annotations from the document text. In the case of HTML, these annotations are instructions on how to visualize a web page.

Web page visualization is usually carried out using a web browser. First, the browser downloads the page's HTML based on its web address, the URL. Next, the browser parses the HTML document for layout instructions. Finally, the browser's rendering engine formats and displays all images and text per the markup specifications. The rendered page can easily be read by a human being.

Of course, during large-scale data analysis, we don't need to render every page. Computers can process document texts without requiring any visualization. Thus, when analyzing HTML documents, we can focus on the text while skipping over the display instructions. Nonetheless, we shouldn't totally ignore the annotations—they can provide us with valuable information. For example, the annotated title of a document can summarize the document's contents concisely. Therefore, we can benefit by discerning that title from an annotated paragraph in the document. If we can distinguish between various document parts, we can run a more informed investigation. Consequently, a basic knowledge of HTML structure is imperative for online text analysis. With this in mind, we begin this section by reviewing the HTML structure. Then we learn how to parse that structure using Python libraries.

NOTE   If you are already familiar with basic HTML, feel free to skip ahead to subsection 16.2.

16.1   *The structure of HTML documents*

An HTML document is composed of HTML elements. Each element corresponds to a document component. For instance, the document's title is an element; every single paragraph in the document is also an element. The starting location of an element is demarcated by a start tag: for instance, the start tag of a title is `<title>`, and the start tag of a paragraph is `<p>`. Every start tag begins and ends with angled brackets, `<>`. Adding a forward slash to the tag transforms it into an end tag. The endpoints of most elements are demarcated by end tags: thus the immediate text of a title is followed by `</title>`, and the text of a paragraph is followed by `</p>`.

Shortly, we explore many common HTML tags. But first we must introduce the most important HTML tag: `<html>`, which specifies the start of the entire HTML document. Let's utilize that tag to create a document composed of just a single word: *Hello*. We generate the contents of the document by coding `html_contents = "<html>Hello</html>"`

Listing 16.1   Defining a simple HTML string

```
html_contents = "<html>Hello</html>"
```

HTML contents are intended to be rendered in a web browser. Thus, we can visualize `html_contents` by saving it to a file and then loading it in a browser of our choice. Alternatively, we can render `html_contents` directly in an IPython Jupyter Notebook. We simply need to import `HTML` and `display` from `IPython.core.display`. Then, executing `display(HTML(html_contents))` will display the rendered output (figure 16.1).

Listing 16.2   Rendering an HTML string

```
from IPython.core.display import display, HTML
def render(html_contents): display(HTML(html_contents))   ◁——
render(html_contents)
```

Defines a single-line render function to repeatedly visualize our HTML using less code

**Figure 16.1   A rendered HTML document.
It contains a single word: *Hello*.**

We've rendered our HTML document. It's not very impressive—the body is composed of a single word. Furthermore, the document lacks a title. Let's assign the document a title using the `<title>` tag. We'll set the title to something simple, like *Data Science is Fun*. To do so, we begin by creating a title string that is equal to `"<title>Data Science is Fun</title>"`.

Listing 16.3   Defining a title in HTML

```
title = "<title>Data Science is Fun</title>"
```

Now we nest the title in `<html>` and `</html>` by running `html_contents = f"<html>{title}Hello</html>"` and then render the updated contents (figure 16.2).

**Figure 16.2   A rendered HTML document. The
document's title does not appear in the rendered
output—only the word *Hello* is visible.**

Listing 16.4   Adding a title to the HTML string

```
html_contents = f"<html>{title}Hello</html>"
render(html_contents)
```

Our output is identical to what we saw before! The title does not appear in the body of the rendered HTML; it only appears in the title bar of the web browser (figure 16.3).

**Figure 16.3   A web
browser rendering of the
HTML document. The
document's title appears
in the browser's title bar.**

Despite its partial invisibility, the title provides us with very important information: it summarizes the contents of the document. For instance, in a job listing, the title directly summarizes the nature of the job. Thus, the title reflects vital information despite its absence from the body of the document. This critical distinction is commonly emphasized using `<head>` and `<body>` tags. The content delimited by the HTML

<body> tag will appear in the body of the output. Meanwhile, <head> delimits vital information that is not rendered in the body. Let's emphasize this distinction by nesting title in the *head* element of the HTML. We also nest the visible *Hello* in the *body* element of the contents.

Listing 16.5   Adding a head and body to the HTML string

```
head = f"<head>{title}</head>"
body = "<body>Hello</body>"
html_contents = f"<html> {title} {body}</html>"
```

Occasionally, we want to display a document's title in the body of a page. For instance, in a job posting, the employer will likely want to show the title of the job. This visualized title is referred to as the page *header* and is demarcated with the <h1> tag. Of course, that tag is nested in <body>, where all visualized content is found. Let's add a header to the body of our HTML (figure 16.4).

Listing 16.6   Adding a header to the HTML string

> HTML elements can be nested like Russian nesting dolls. Here we nest the header element inside the body element, and we nest both the body and title elements in the <html> and </html> tags.

```
header = "<h1>Data Science is Fun</h1>"
body = f"<body>{header}Hello</body>"
html_contents = f"<html> {title} {body}</html>"
render(html_contents)
```

Data Science is Fun
Hello

Figure 16.4   A rendered HTML document. A large header appears in the rendered output.

Our single word looks awkward relative to the large header. Generally, HTML documents are intended to have more than one word in the body—they usually contain multiple sentences in multiple paragraphs. As previously mentioned, such paragraphs are marked with a <p> tag.

Let's add two consecutive paragraphs to our HTML (figure 16.5). We compose these dummy paragraphs from sequences of repeating words: the first paragraph features the phrase *Paragraph 0* repeating 40 times; in the subsequent paragraph, we replace 0 with 1.

Listing 16.7   Adding paragraphs to the HTML string

```
paragraphs = ''
for i in range(2):
```

```
    paragraph_string = f"Paragraph {i} " * 40
    paragraphs += f"<p>{paragraph_string}</p>"

body = f"<body>{header}{paragraphs}</body>"
html_contents = f"<html> {title} {body}</html>"
render(html_contents)
```

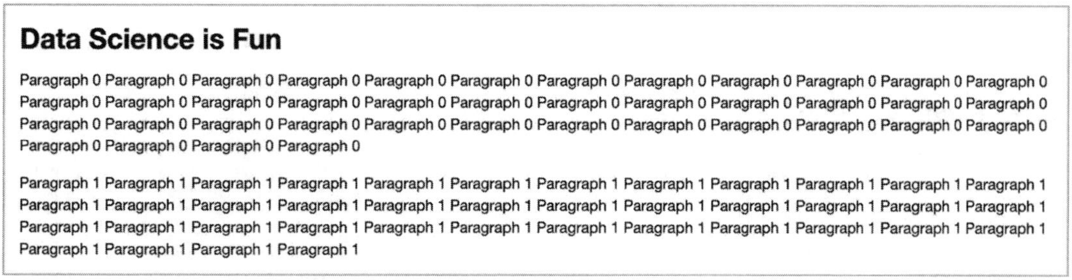

Data Science is Fun

Paragraph 0 Paragraph 0 Paragraph 0 Paragraph 0 Paragraph 0 Paragraph 0 Paragraph 0 Paragraph 0 Paragraph 0 Paragraph 0 Paragraph 0 Paragraph 0
Paragraph 0 Paragraph 0 Paragraph 0 Paragraph 0 Paragraph 0 Paragraph 0 Paragraph 0 Paragraph 0 Paragraph 0 Paragraph 0 Paragraph 0 Paragraph 0
Paragraph 0 Paragraph 0 Paragraph 0 Paragraph 0 Paragraph 0 Paragraph 0 Paragraph 0 Paragraph 0 Paragraph 0 Paragraph 0 Paragraph 0 Paragraph 0
Paragraph 0 Paragraph 0 Paragraph 0 Paragraph 0

Paragraph 1 Paragraph 1 Paragraph 1 Paragraph 1 Paragraph 1 Paragraph 1 Paragraph 1 Paragraph 1 Paragraph 1 Paragraph 1 Paragraph 1 Paragraph 1
Paragraph 1 Paragraph 1 Paragraph 1 Paragraph 1 Paragraph 1 Paragraph 1 Paragraph 1 Paragraph 1 Paragraph 1 Paragraph 1 Paragraph 1 Paragraph 1
Paragraph 1 Paragraph 1 Paragraph 1 Paragraph 1 Paragraph 1 Paragraph 1 Paragraph 1 Paragraph 1 Paragraph 1 Paragraph 1 Paragraph 1 Paragraph 1
Paragraph 1 Paragraph 1 Paragraph 1 Paragraph 1

Figure 16.5   A rendered HTML document. Two paragraphs appear in the rendered output.

We've inserted paragraph elements into our HTML. These elements are distinguishable by their internal text. However, their <p> tags are both identical; an HTML parser cannot easily distinguish between the first and second tags. Occasionally, it's worth making the difference between tags much more pronounced (particularly if each paragraph is formatted uniquely). We can discriminate between <p> tags by assigning each tag a unique ID, which can be inserted directly into the tag brackets. For example, we identify the first paragraph as *paragraph 0* by writing <p id="paragraph 0">. The added id is referred to as an *attribute* of the paragraph element. Attributes are inserted into element start tags to track useful tag information.

We now add id attributes to our paragraph tags. Later, we utilize these attributes to distinguish between the paragraphs.

Listing 16.8   Adding id attributes to the paragraphs

```
paragraphs = ''
for i in range(2):
    paragraph_string = f"Paragraph {i} " * 40
    attribute = f"id='paragraph {i}'"
    paragraphs += f"<p {attribute}>{paragraph_string}</p>"

body = f"<body>{header}{paragraphs}</body>"
html_contents = f"<html> {title} {body}</html>"
```

HTML attributes play many critical roles. They are especially necessary when linking between documents. The internet is built on top of *hyperlinks*, which are clickable texts that connect web pages. Clicking a hyperlink takes you to a new HTML document. Each hyperlink is marked by an anchor tag, <a>, which makes the text clickable.

However, additional information is required to specify the address of the linked document. We can provide that information using the `href` attribute, where *href* stands for *hypertext reference*. For instance, demarcating text with `<a href="https://www.manning.com">` links that text to the Manning website.

Next, we create a hyperlink that reads *Data Science Bookcamp* and link that clickable text to the website for this book. Then we insert the hyperlink into a new paragraph and assign that paragraph an ID of `paragraph 3` (figure 16.6).

Data Science is Fun

Paragraph 0 Paragraph 0

Paragraph 1 Paragraph 1

Here is a link to Data Science Bookcamp

Figure 16.6   A rendered HTML document. One more paragraph has been added to the rendered output, containing a clickable link to *Data Science Bookcamp*.

Listing 16.9   Adding a hyperlink to the HTML string

> **Creates a clickable hyperlink. Clicking the words Data Science Bookcamp will take a user to the book's online URL.**

```
link_text = "Data Science Bookcamp"
url = "https://www.manning.com/books/data-science-bookcamp"
hyperlink = f"<a href='{url}'>{link_text}</a>"
new_paragraph = f"<p id='paragraph 2'>Here is a link to {hyperlink}</p>"
paragraphs += new_paragraph
body = f"<body>{header}{paragraphs}</body>"
html_contents = f"<html> {title} {body}</html>"
render(html_contents)
```

HTML text elements can vary in complexity. Beyond just headers and paragraphs, we can also visualize lists of texts in an HTML document. Suppose, for instance, that we wish to display a list of popular data science libraries. We start by defining that list in Python.

Listing 16.10   Defining a list of data science libraries

```
libraries = ['NumPy', 'SciPy', 'Pandas', 'Scikit-Learn']
```

Now we demarcate every item in our list with an `<li>` tag, which stands for *list item*. We store these items in an `items` string.

Listing 16.11 Demarcating list items with an `<li>` tag.

```
items = ''
for library in libraries:
    items += f"<li>{library}</li>"
```

Finally, we nest the `items` string in a `<ul>` tag, where `ul` stands for *unstructured list*. Then we append the unstructured list to the body of our HTML. We also insert a second header between the paragraphs and the list: *Common Data Science Libraries*. We use the `<h2>` tag to differentiate between the second header and the first (figure 16.7).

Listing 16.12 Adding an unstructured list to the HTML string

```
unstructured_list = f"<ul>{items}</ul>"
header2 = '<h2>Common Data Science Libraries</h2>'
body = f"<body>{header}{paragraphs}{header2}{unstructured_list}</body>"
html_contents = f"<html> {title} {body}</html>"
render(html_contents)
```

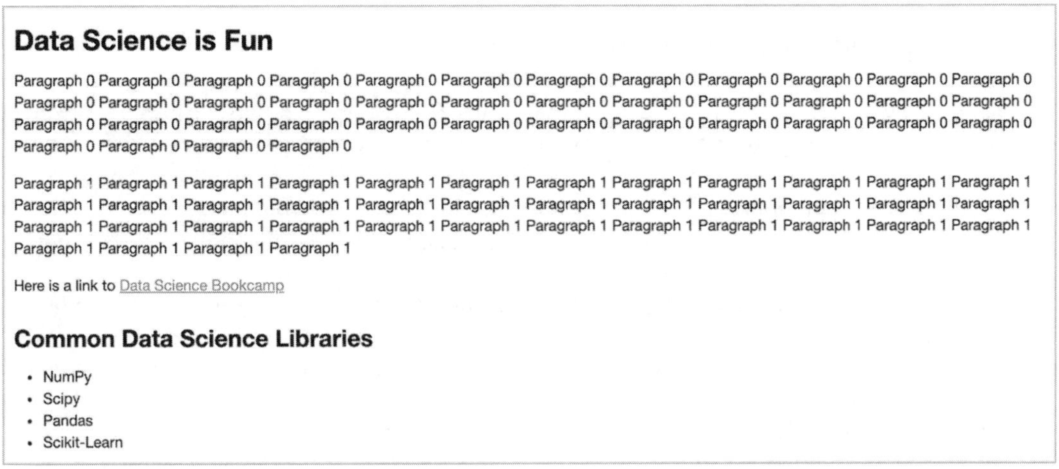

Data Science is Fun

Paragraph 0 Paragraph 0

Paragraph 1 Paragraph 1

Here is a link to Data Science Bookcamp

Common Data Science Libraries

- NumPy
- Scipy
- Pandas
- Scikit-Learn

Figure 16.7 A rendered HTML document. The updated document contains a bulleted list of common data science libraries.

The data science libraries have been rendered as a list of bulleted points. Each bullet occupies a separate line. Traditionally, such bullet points are used to signify diverse conceptual categories, ranging from data science libraries to breakfast foods to required skills in a job posting.

At this point, it's worth noting that our HTML body is divided into two distinct parts: the first part corresponds to a sequence of three paragraphs, and the second part corresponds to the bulleted list. Typically, such divisions are captured using special `<div>` tags that allow frontend engineers to track the divided elements and customize their formatting accordingly. Usually, each `<div>` tag is distinguished by some attribute. If the attribute is unique to a division, then that attribute is an `id`; if the attribute is shared by more than one division, a special `class` signifier is used.

For consistency's sake, we divide our two sections by nesting them in two different divisions. The first division is assigned a `paragraph` ID, and the second is assigned a `list` ID. Additionally, since both divisions only contain text, we assign a `text` class attribute to each one. We also add a third empty division to the body; we'll update it later. The ID and class of this empty division are both set to `empty`.

Listing 16.13   Adding divisions to the HTML string

```
div1 = f"<div id='paragraphs' class='text'>{paragraphs}</div>"
div2 = f"<div id='list' class='text'>{header2}{unstructured_list}</div>"
div3 = "<div id='empty' class='empty'></div>"        ◁───
body = f"<body>{header}{div1}{div2}{div3}</body>"
html_contents = f"<html> {title}{body}</html>"
```

> The third division is empty, but it can still be accessed by both class and ID. Later, we will access this division to insert additional text.

Common HTML elements and attributes

- `<html>..</html>`—Demarcates the entire HTML document.
- `<title>..</title>`—The title of the document. This title appears in a web browser's title bar but not in the browser's rendered contents.
- `<head>..</head>`—The head of the document. The information in the head is not intended to appear in the browser's rendered contents.
- `<body>..</body>`—The body of the document. The information in the body is intended to appear in a browser's rendered contents.
- `<h1>..</h1>`—A header in the document. It is generally rendered in large, bold letters.
- `<h2>..</h2>`—A header in the document whose formatting slightly differs from `<h1>`.
- `<p>..</p>`—A single paragraph in the document.
- `<p id="unique_id">..</p>`—A single paragraph in the document containing a unique `id` attribute that is not shared by any other document elements.
- `<a href="http://www.manning.com">..</a>`—A clickable text hyperlink. Clicking the text sends a user to the URL specified in the `href` attribute.
- `<ul>..</ul>`—An unstructured list composed of individual list items that appear as bullet points in a browser's rendered contents.
- `<li>..</li>`—An individual list item in an unstructured list.
- `<div>..</div>`—A division demarcating a specific subsection of the document.
- `<div class="category_class">..</div>`—A division demarcating a specific subsection of the document. The division is assigned a category class by way of the `class` attribute. Unlike a unique ID, this class can be shared across other divisions in the HTML.

We've made many changes to our `html_contents` string. Let's review its altered contents.

Listing 16.14   Printing the altered HTML string

```
print(html_contents)
```

```
<html> <title>Data Science is Fun</title><body><h1>Data Science is Fun</h1>
<div id='paragraphs' class='text'><p id='paragraph 0'>Paragraph 0
Paragraph 0 Paragraph 0 Paragraph 0 Paragraph 0 Paragraph 0 Paragraph 0
Paragraph 0 Paragraph 0 Paragraph 0 Paragraph 0 Paragraph 0 Paragraph 0
Paragraph 0 Paragraph 0 Paragraph 0 Paragraph 0 Paragraph 0 Paragraph 0
Paragraph 0 Paragraph 0 Paragraph 0 Paragraph 0 Paragraph 0 Paragraph 0
Paragraph 0 Paragraph 0 Paragraph 0 Paragraph 0 Paragraph 0 Paragraph 0
Paragraph 0 Paragraph 0 Paragraph 0 Paragraph 0 Paragraph 0 Paragraph 0
Paragraph 0 Paragraph 0 Paragraph 0 </p><p id='paragraph 1'>Paragraph 1
Paragraph 1 Paragraph 1 Paragraph 1 Paragraph 1 Paragraph 1 Paragraph 1
Paragraph 1 Paragraph 1 Paragraph 1 Paragraph 1 Paragraph 1 Paragraph 1
Paragraph 1 Paragraph 1 Paragraph 1 Paragraph 1 Paragraph 1 Paragraph 1
Paragraph 1 Paragraph 1 Paragraph 1 Paragraph 1 Paragraph 1 Paragraph 1
Paragraph 1 Paragraph 1 Paragraph 1 Paragraph 1 Paragraph 1 Paragraph 1
Paragraph 1 Paragraph 1 Paragraph 1 Paragraph 1 Paragraph 1 Paragraph 1
Paragraph 1 Paragraph 1 Paragraph 1 </p><p id='paragraph 2'>
Here is a link to <a href='https://www.manning.com/books/data-science-bookcamp'>
Data Science Bookcamp</a></p></div><div id='list' class='text'>
<h2>Common Data Science Libraries</h2><ul><li>NumPy</li>
<li>SciPy</li><li>Pandas</li><li>Scikit-Learn</li>
</ul></div><div id='empty' class='empty'></div></body></html>
```

The printed output is a mess! The HTML contents are nearly unreadable. Also, extracting individual elements from `html_contents` is exceedingly difficult. Imagine if we wanted to extract the title of the HTML document: we'd need to first split `html_contents` on the > bracket. Then we'd have to iterate over the split results, stopping at the string that's equal to `<title`. Next, we'd need to go one index over and extract the string containing the title's text. Finally, we'd have to clean the title string by splitting on the remaining < bracket. This convoluted title-extraction process is illustrated next.

Listing 16.15   Extracting the HTML title using basic Python

```
split_contents = html_contents.split('>')
for i, substring in enumerate(split_contents):        ⟵ Iterates over each
    if substring.endswith('<title'):          ⟵       substring that follows >
        next_string = split_contents[i + 1]
        title = next_string.split('<')[0]             The substring ends on the title
        print(title)                                  start tag. Thus, the next
        break                                         substring equals the title.
```

```
Data Science is Fun
```

Is there a cleaner way to extract elements from HTML documents? Yes! We don't need to manually parse the documents. Instead, we can use the external Beautiful Soup library.

16.2   *Parsing HTML using Beautiful Soup*

We start by installing the Beautiful Soup library. Then we import the `BeautifulSoup` class from bs4. Following a common convention, we import `BeautifulSoup` as simply bs.

NOTE   Call `pip install bs4` from the command line terminal to install the Beautiful Soup library.

Listing 16.16   Importing the `BeautifulSoup` class

```
from bs4 import BeautifulSoup as bs
```

We now initialize the `BeautifulSoup` class by running bs(`html_contents`). In keeping with convention, we assign the initialized object to a soup variable (listing 16.17).

NOTE   By default, the bs class uses Python's built-in HTML parser to extract the HTML contents. However, more efficient parsers are available through external libraries. One popular library is called lxml, which can be installed by running `pip install lxml`. After installation, the lxml parser can be used during bs initialization. We simply need to execute bs(`html_contents`, `'lxml'`).

Listing 16.17   Initializing `BeautifulSoup` using an HTML string

```
soup = bs(html_contents)
```

Our soup object tracks all elements in the parsed HTML. We can output these elements in a clean, readable format by running the `soup.prettify()` method.

Listing 16.18   Printing readable HTML with Beautiful Soup

```
print(soup.prettify())

<html>
 <title>
  Data Science is Fun
 </title>
 <body>
  <h1>
   Data Science is Fun
  </h1>
  <div class="text" id="paragraphs">
   <p id="paragraph 0">
    Paragraph 0 Paragraph 0 Paragraph 0 Paragraph 0 Paragraph 0 Paragraph 0
Paragraph 0 Paragraph 0 Paragraph 0 Paragraph 0 Paragraph 0 Paragraph 0
Paragraph 0 Paragraph 0 Paragraph 0 Paragraph 0 Paragraph 0 Paragraph 0
Paragraph 0 Paragraph 0 Paragraph 0 Paragraph 0 Paragraph 0 Paragraph 0
Paragraph 0 Paragraph 0 Paragraph 0 Paragraph 0 Paragraph 0 Paragraph 0
Paragraph 0 Paragraph 0 Paragraph 0 Paragraph 0 Paragraph 0 Paragraph 0
Paragraph 0 Paragraph 0 Paragraph 0 Paragraph 0
   </p>
   <p id="paragraph 1">
```

```
      Paragraph 1 Paragraph 1 Paragraph 1 Paragraph 1 Paragraph 1 Paragraph 1
Paragraph 1 Paragraph 1 Paragraph 1 Paragraph 1 Paragraph 1 Paragraph 1
Paragraph 1 Paragraph 1 Paragraph 1 Paragraph 1 Paragraph 1 Paragraph 1
Paragraph 1 Paragraph 1 Paragraph 1 Paragraph 1 Paragraph 1 Paragraph 1
Paragraph 1 Paragraph 1 Paragraph 1 Paragraph 1 Paragraph 1 Paragraph 1
Paragraph 1 Paragraph 1 Paragraph 1 Paragraph 1 Paragraph 1 Paragraph 1
Paragraph 1 Paragraph 1 Paragraph 1 Paragraph 1
     </p>
     <p id="paragraph 2">
     Here is a link to
     <a href="https://www.manning.com/books/data-science-bookcamp">
      Data Science Bookcamp
     </a>
     </p>
    </div>
    <div class="text" id="list">
     <h2>
     Common Data Science Libraries
     </h2>
     <ul>
      <li>
       NumPy
      </li>
      <li>
       SciPy
      </li>
      <li>
       Pandas
      </li>
      <li>
       Scikit-Learn
      </li>
     </ul>
    </div>
    <div class="empty" id="empty">
    </div>
   </body>
</html>
```

Suppose we want to access an individual element, such as the title. The soup object provides that access through its `find` method. Running `soup.find('title')` returns all content enclosed in the title's start and end tags.

Listing 16.19 Extracting the title with Beautiful Soup

```
title = soup.find('title')
print(title)

<title>Data Science is Fun</title>
```

The outputted `title` appears to be an HTML string demarcated by the title tags. However, our `title` variable is not a string: it's an initialized Beautiful Soup `Tag` class. We can verify by printing `type(title)`.

Listing 16.20   Outputting the title's data type

```
print(type(title))

<class 'bs4.element.Tag'>
```

Each Tag object contains a text attribute, which maps to the text in the tag. Thus, printing title.text returns *Data Science is Fun.*

Listing 16.21   Outputting the title's text attribute

```
print(title.text)

Data Science is Fun
```

We've accessed our title tag by running soup.find('title'). We can also access that same tag simply by running soup.title. Therefore, running soup.title.text returns a string equal to title.text.

Listing 16.22   Accessing the title's text attribute from soup

```
assert soup.title.text == title.text
```

In this same manner, we can access the body of our document by running soup.body. Next, we output all the text in the body of our HTML.

Listing 16.23   Accessing the body's text attribute from soup

```
body = soup.body
print(body.text)

Data Science is FunParagraph 0 Paragraph 0 Paragraph 0 Paragraph 0
Paragraph 0 Paragraph 0 Paragraph 0 Paragraph 0 Paragraph 0 Paragraph 0
Paragraph 0 Paragraph 0 Paragraph 0 Paragraph 0 Paragraph 0 Paragraph 0
Paragraph 0 Paragraph 0 Paragraph 0 Paragraph 0 Paragraph 0 Paragraph 0
Paragraph 0 Paragraph 0 Paragraph 0 Paragraph 0 Paragraph 0 Paragraph 0
Paragraph 0 Paragraph 0 Paragraph 0 Paragraph 0 Paragraph 0 Paragraph 0
Paragraph 0 Paragraph 0 Paragraph 0 Paragraph 0 Paragraph 0 Paragraph 0
Paragraph 1 Paragraph 1 Paragraph 1 Paragraph 1 Paragraph 1 Paragraph 1
Paragraph 1 Paragraph 1 Paragraph 1 Paragraph 1 Paragraph 1 Paragraph 1
Paragraph 1 Paragraph 1 Paragraph 1 Paragraph 1 Paragraph 1 Paragraph 1
Paragraph 1 Paragraph 1 Paragraph 1 Paragraph 1 Paragraph 1 Paragraph 1
Paragraph 1 Paragraph 1 Paragraph 1 Paragraph 1 Paragraph 1 Paragraph 1
Paragraph 1 Paragraph 1 Paragraph 1 Paragraph 1
Here is a link to Data Science BookcampCommon Data Science
    LibrariesNumPySciPyPandasScikit-Learn
```

Our output is an aggregation of all the text in the body. This text blob includes all headers, bullet points, and paragraphs. It is virtually unreadable. Rather than outputting all the text, we should instead narrow the scope of our output. Let's print the text of just the first paragraph by printing `body.p.text`. Alternatively, printing `soup.p.text` generates the same output.

Listing 16.24   Accessing the text of the first paragraph

```
assert body.p.text == soup.p.text
print(soup.p.text)
```

```
Paragraph 0 Paragraph 0 Paragraph 0 Paragraph 0 Paragraph 0 Paragraph 0
Paragraph 0 Paragraph 0 Paragraph 0 Paragraph 0 Paragraph 0 Paragraph 0
Paragraph 0 Paragraph 0 Paragraph 0 Paragraph 0 Paragraph 0 Paragraph 0
Paragraph 0 Paragraph 0 Paragraph 0 Paragraph 0 Paragraph 0 Paragraph 0
Paragraph 0 Paragraph 0 Paragraph 0 Paragraph 0 Paragraph 0 Paragraph 0
Paragraph 0 Paragraph 0 Paragraph 0 Paragraph 0 Paragraph 0 Paragraph 0
Paragraph 0 Paragraph 0 Paragraph 0 Paragraph 0
```

Accessing `body.p` returns the first paragraph in body. How do we access the remaining two paragraphs? Well, we can utilize the `find_all` method. Running `body.find_all('p')` returns a list of all the paragraph tags in the body.

Listing 16.25   Accessing all paragraphs in the body

```
paragraphs = body.find_all('p')
for i, paragraph in enumerate(paragraphs):
    print(f"\nPARAGRAPH {i}:")
    print(paragraph.text)
```

```
PARAGRAPH 0:
Paragraph 0 Paragraph 0 Paragraph 0 Paragraph 0 Paragraph 0 Paragraph 0
Paragraph 0 Paragraph 0 Paragraph 0 Paragraph 0 Paragraph 0 Paragraph 0
Paragraph 0 Paragraph 0 Paragraph 0 Paragraph 0 Paragraph 0 Paragraph 0
Paragraph 0 Paragraph 0 Paragraph 0 Paragraph 0 Paragraph 0 Paragraph 0
Paragraph 0 Paragraph 0 Paragraph 0 Paragraph 0 Paragraph 0 Paragraph 0
Paragraph 0 Paragraph 0 Paragraph 0 Paragraph 0 Paragraph 0 Paragraph 0
Paragraph 0 Paragraph 0 Paragraph 0 Paragraph 0

PARAGRAPH 1:
Paragraph 1 Paragraph 1 Paragraph 1 Paragraph 1 Paragraph 1 Paragraph 1
Paragraph 1 Paragraph 1 Paragraph 1 Paragraph 1 Paragraph 1 Paragraph 1
Paragraph 1 Paragraph 1 Paragraph 1 Paragraph 1 Paragraph 1 Paragraph 1
Paragraph 1 Paragraph 1 Paragraph 1 Paragraph 1 Paragraph 1 Paragraph 1
Paragraph 1 Paragraph 1 Paragraph 1 Paragraph 1 Paragraph 1 Paragraph 1
Paragraph 1 Paragraph 1 Paragraph 1 Paragraph 1 Paragraph 1 Paragraph 1
Paragraph 1 Paragraph 1 Paragraph 1 Paragraph 1

PARAGRAPH 2:
Here is a link to Data Science Bookcamp
```

Similarly, we access our list of bullet points by running `body.find_all('li')`. Let's utilize `find_all` to print all the bulleted libraries in the body.

Listing 16.26   Accessing all bullet points in the body

```
print([bullet.text for bullet
       in  body.find_all('li')])
```

```
['NumPy', 'Scipy', 'Pandas', 'Scikit-Learn']
```

The find and find_all methods allow us to search the elements by tag type and attribute. Suppose we wish to access an element with a unique ID of x. To search on that attribute ID, we simply need to execute find(id='x'). With this in mind, let's output the text of the final paragraph whose assigned ID is paragraph_2.

Listing 16.27   Accessing a paragraph by ID

```
paragraph_2 = soup.find(id='paragraph 2')
print(paragraph_2.text)
```

```
Here is a link to Data Science Bookcamp
```

The contents of paragraph_2 include a web link to *Data Science Bookcamp*. The actual URL is stored in the href attribute. Beautiful Soup permits us to access any attribute using the get method. Thus, running paragraph_2.get('id') returns *paragraph 2*. Running paragraph_2.a.get('href') returns the URL; let's print it.

Listing 16.28   Accessing an attribute in a tag

```
assert paragraph_2.get('id') == 'paragraph 2'
print(paragraph_2.a.get('href'))
```

```
https://www.manning.com/books/data-science-bookcamp
```

All attribute IDs have unique values assigned to them in our HTML. However, not all of our attributes are unique. For instance, two of our three division elements share the class attribute of text. Meanwhile, the third division element contains a unique class that's set to empty. Running body.find_all('div') returns all three division elements. How do we obtain just those two divisions where the class is set to text? We just need to run body.find_all('div', class_='text'). The added class_ parameter limits our results to those divisions where the class is set appropriately. Listing 16.29 searches for these divisions and outputs their text contents.

> **NOTE**   Why do we run find_all on class_ rather than class? Well, in Python, the class keyword is a restricted identifier, which is used to define novel classes. Beautiful Soup allows for a special class_ parameter to get around this keyword restriction.

Listing 16.29   Accessing divisions by their shared class attribute

```
for division in soup.find_all('div', class_='text'):
    id_ = division.get('id')
```

```
    print(f"\nDivision with id '{id_}':")
    print(division.text)
```

```
Division with id 'paragraphs':
Paragraph 0 Paragraph 0 Paragraph 0 Paragraph 0 Paragraph 0 Paragraph 0
Paragraph 0 Paragraph 0 Paragraph 0 Paragraph 0 Paragraph 0 Paragraph 0
Paragraph 0 Paragraph 0 Paragraph 0 Paragraph 0 Paragraph 0 Paragraph 0
Paragraph 0 Paragraph 0 Paragraph 0 Paragraph 0 Paragraph 0 Paragraph 0
Paragraph 0 Paragraph 0 Paragraph 0 Paragraph 0 Paragraph 0 Paragraph 0
Paragraph 0 Paragraph 0 Paragraph 0 Paragraph 0 Paragraph 0 Paragraph 0
Paragraph 0 Paragraph 0 Paragraph 0 Paragraph 0 Paragraph 1 Paragraph 1
Paragraph 1 Paragraph 1 Paragraph 1 Paragraph 1 Paragraph 1 Paragraph 1
Paragraph 1 Paragraph 1 Paragraph 1 Paragraph 1 Paragraph 1 Paragraph 1
Paragraph 1 Paragraph 1 Paragraph 1 Paragraph 1 Paragraph 1 Paragraph 1
Paragraph 1 Paragraph 1 Paragraph 1 Paragraph 1 Paragraph 1 Paragraph 1
Paragraph 1 Paragraph 1 Paragraph 1 Paragraph 1 Paragraph 1 Paragraph 1
Paragraph 1 Paragraph 1 Paragraph 1 Paragraph 1 Paragraph 1 Paragraph 1
Paragraph 1 Paragraph 1 Here is a link to Data Science Bookcamp
```

```
Division with id 'list':
Common Data Science LibrariesNumPyScipyPandasScikit-Learn
```

So far, we've used Beautiful Soup to access elements in the HTML. However, the library also allows us to edit individual elements. For example, given a tag object, we can delete that object by running tag.decompose(). The decompose method removes that element from all our data structures, including soup. Thus, calling body.find (id='paragraph 0').decompose() will remove all traces of the first paragraph. Also, calling soup.find(id='paragraph 1').decompose() will delete the second paragraph from both the soup and body objects. After these deletions, only the third paragraph will remain. Let's confirm.

Listing 16.30 Paragraph deletion with Beautiful Soup

```
body.find(id='paragraph 0').decompose()
soup.find(id='paragraph 1').decompose()
print(body.find(id='paragraphs').text)
```

⊲ **The decompose method deletes the paragraph from all nested tag objects. Deleting the paragraph from soup also deletes it from body, and vice versa.**

```
Here is a link to Data Science Bookcamp
```

Additionally, we're able to insert new tags into the HTML. Suppose we wish to insert a new paragraph into our final empty division. To do so, we must first create a new paragraph element. Running soup.new_tag('p') returns an empty paragraph Tag object.

Listing 16.31 Initializing an empty paragraph Tag

```
new_paragraph = soup.new_tag('p')
print(new_paragraph)
```

```
<p></p>
```

Next, we must update the initialized paragraph's text by assigning it to new_para-graph.string. Running new_paragraph.string = x sets the paragraph's text to equal x.

Listing 16.32   Updating the text of an empty paragraph

```
new_paragraph.string = "This paragraph is new"
print(new_paragraph)
```

```
<p>This paragraph is new</p>
```

Finally, we append the updated new_paragraph to an existing Tag object. Given two Tag objects, tag1 and tag2, we can insert tag1 into tag2 by running tag2.append (tag1). Thus, running soup.find(id='empty').append(new_paragraph) should append the paragraph to the empty division. Let's update our HTML and then confirm the changes by rendering the updated results (figure 16.8).

Figure 16.8   A rendered HTML document. The document has been edited, two of the three original paragraphs have been removed, and a new paragraph has been inserted.

Listing 16.33   Paragraph insertion with Beautiful Soup

```
soup.find(id='empty').append(new_paragraph)
render(soup.prettify())
```

Common Beautiful Soup methods

- soup = bs(html_contents)—Initializes a BeautifulSoup object from the HTML elements in the parsed html_contents.
- soup.prettify()—Returns the parsed HTML document in a clean, easily readable format.
- title = soup.title—Returns a Tag object associated with the title element of a parsed document.
- title = soup.find('title')—Returns a Tag object associated with the title element of a parsed document.
- tag_object = soup.find('element_tag')—Returns a Tag object associated with the first HTML element demarcated by the specified element_tag tag.

- `tag_objects = soup.find_all('element_tag')`—Returns a list of all `Tag` objects demarcated by the specified `element_tag` tag.
- `tag_object = soup.find(id='unique_id')`—Returns a `Tag` object that contains the specified unique `id` attribute.
- `tag_objects = soup.find_all('element_tag', class_='category_class')`—Returns a list of `Tag` objects that are demarcated by the specified `element_tag` tag and that contain the specified class attribute.
- `tag_object = soup.new_tag('element_tag')`—Creates a new `Tag` object whose HTML element type is specified by the `element` tag.
- `tag_object.decompose()`—Deletes the `Tag` object from `soup`.
- `tab_object.append(tag_object2)`—Given two `Tag` objects, `tag_object` and `tag_object2`, inserts `tag_object2` into `tag_object`.
- `tag_object.text`—Returns all visible text in a `Tag` object.
- `tag_object.get('attribute')`—Returns an HTML attribute that has been assigned to the `Tag` object.

16.3 Downloading and parsing online data

The Beautiful Soup library allows us to easily parse, analyze, and edit HTML documents. In most cases, these documents must be downloaded directly from the web. Let's briefly review the procedure for downloading HTML files using Python's built-in `urllib` module. We start by importing the `urlopen` function from `urllib.request`.

> **NOTE** The `urlopen` function is sufficient when downloading a single HTML document from a single, unsecured online page. However, for more complicated downloads, you should consider using the external Requests library (https://requests.readthedocs.io).

Listing 16.34   Importing the `urlopen` function

```
from urllib.request import urlopen
```

Given the URL of an online document, we can download the associated HTML contents by running `urlopen(url).read()`. Next, we use `urlopen` to download the Manning website for this book. Then we print the first 1,000 characters of the downloaded HTML.

> **WARNING** The following code will only run with a valid internet connection. Also, the downloaded HTML may change with alterations to the website.

Listing 16.35   Downloading an HTML document

```
url = "https://www.manning.com/books/data-science-bookcamp"
html_contents = urlopen(url).read()
print(html_contents[:1000])
```

The `urlopen` function establishes a network connection with the specified URL. That connection is tracked using a special URLopener object. Calling the object's read method downloads text from the established connection.

```
b'\n<!DOCTYPE html>\n<!--[if lt IE 7 ]> <html lang="en" class="no-js ie6
ie"> <![endif]-->\n<!--[if IE 7 ]>     <html lang="en" class="no-js ie7
ie"> <![endif]-->\n<!--[if IE 8 ]>     <html lang="en" class="no-js ie8
ie"> <![endif]-->\n<!--[if IE 9 ]>     <html lang="en" class="no-js ie9
ie"> <![endif]-->\n<!--[if (gt IE 9)|!(IE)]><!--> <html lang="en"
class="no-js"><!--<![endif]-->\n<head>\n
<title>Manning | Data Science Bookcamp</title>\n\n
<meta name="msapplication-TileColor" content=" #343434"/>\n
<meta name="msapplication-square70x70logo" content="/assets/favicon/windows-
    small-tile-6f6b7c9200a7af9169e488a11d13a7d3.png"/>\n
<meta name="msapplication-square150x150logo"
    content="/assets/favicon/windows-medium-tile-
    8fae4270fe3f1a6398f15015221501fb.png"/>\n
<meta name="msapplication-wide310x150logo" content="/assets/favicon/windows-
    wide-tile-a856d33fb5e508f52f09495e2f412453.png"/>\n
<meta name="msapplication-square310x310logo"
content="/assets/favicon/windows-large-tile-072d5381c2c83afa'
```

Let's extract the title from our messy HTML using Beautiful Soup.

Listing 16.36   Accessing the title with Beautiful Soup

```
soup = bs(html_contents)
print(soup.title.text)
```

```
Manning | Data Science Bookcamp
```

Using our `soup` object, we can further analyze the page. For instance, we can extract the division that contains an *about the book* header to print a description of this book.

> **WARNING** Online HTML is continually updated. Future updates to the Manning site may cause the following code to malfunction. Readers who encounter differences between expected and actual outputs are encouraged to manually explore the HTML to extract the book description.

Listing 16.37   Accessing a description of this book

```
for division in soup.find_all('div'):          ◁──     Iterates over the
    header = division.h2      ◁──                       divisions in the page
    if header is None:            Checks if a division
        continue                 header is present

    if header.text.lower() == 'about the book':
        print(division.text)          ◁──     Prints the book's description
                                               once the "about" section has
about the book                                 been identified
```

```
Data Science Bookcamp is a comprehensive set of challenging projects
carefully designed to grow your data science skills from novice to master.
Veteran data scientist Leonard Apeltsin sets five increasingly difficult
exercises that test your abilities against the kind of problems you'd
encounter in the real world. As you solve each challenge, you'll acquire
and expand the data science and Python skills you'll use as a professional
```

data scientist. Ranging from text processing to machine learning, each
project comes complete with a unique, downloadable data set and a fully
explained step-by-step solution. Because these projects come from Dr.
Apeltsin's vast experience, each solution highlights the most likely
failure points along with practical advice for getting past unexpected
pitfalls. When you wrap up these five awesome exercises, you'll have a
diverse, relevant skill set that's transferable to working in industry.

We are now ready to use Beautiful Soup to parse job postings as part of our case
study solution.

Summary

- HTML documents are composed of nested elements that provide auxiliary information about the text. Most elements are defined by a start tag and an end tag.
- The text in some elements is intended to be rendered in a browser. Traditionally, this rendered information is nested in the *body* element of the document. Other non-rendered texts (such as the document's title) are nested in the document's *head* element.
- Attributes can be inserted into HTML start tags to track additional tag information. Unique id attributes can help distinguish tags of the same type. Furthermore, class attributes can be used to track elements by category. Unlike the unique id, the class attribute can be shared by multiple elements in the same category.
- Manually extracting text from HTML is difficult to do in basic Python. Fortunately, the Beautiful Soup library simplifies the text-extraction process. Beautiful Soup allows us to query elements by tag type and assigned attribute values. Furthermore, the library permits us to edit the underlying HTML.
- Using Python's built-in urlopen function, we can download HTML files directly from the web. Then we can analyze the text in these files using Beautiful Soup.

Case study 4 solution

This section covers
- Parsing text from HTML
- Computing text similarities
- Clustering and exploring large text datasets

We have downloaded thousands of job postings by searching on this book's table of contents for case studies 1 through 4 (see the problem statement for details). Besides the downloaded postings, we also have at our disposal two text files: resume.txt and table_of_contents.txt. The first file contains a resume draft, and the second contains the truncated table of contents used to query for job listing results. Our goal is to extract common data science skills from the downloaded job postings. Then we'll compare these skills to our resume to determine which skills are missing. We will do so as follows:

1. Parse all text from the downloaded HTML files.
2. Explore the parsed output to learn how job skills are described in online postings. We'll pay particular attention to whether certain HTML tags are more associated with skill descriptions.
3. Attempt to filter any irrelevant job postings from our dataset.
4. Cluster job skills based on text similarity.

5 Visualize the clusters using word clouds.

6 Adjust clustering parameters, if necessary, to improve the visualized output.

7 Compare the clustered skills to our resume to uncover missing skills.

WARNING Spoiler alert! The solution to case study 4 is about to be revealed. We strongly encourage you to try to solve the problem before reading the solution. The original problem statement is available for reference at the beginning of the case study.

17.1 Extracting skill requirements from job posting data

We begin by loading all the HTML files in the job_postings directory. We store the contents of these files in an `html_contents` list.

WARNING Be sure to manually unzip the compressed job_postings.zip directory before executing the following code.

Listing 17.1 Loading HTML files

```
import glob
html_contents = []
```

> We use the Python 3 glob module to obtain filenames with HTML extensions in the job_postings directory. These filenames are sorted to maintain output consistency across readers' personal machines. This ensures that the first two sampled files remain the same for all the readers.

```
for file_name in sorted(glob.glob('job_postings/*.html')):   ◁
    with open(file_name, 'r') as f:
        html_contents.append(f.read())

print(f"We've loaded {len(html_contents)} HTML files.")

We've loaded 1458 HTML files.
```

Each of our 1,458 HTML files can be parsed using Beautiful Soup. Let's execute the parsing and store the parsed results in a `soup_objects` list. We also confirm that each parsed HTML file contains a title and a body.

Listing 17.2 Parsing HTML files

```
from bs4 import BeautifulSoup as bs

soup_objects = []
for html in html_contents:
    soup = bs(html)
    assert soup.title is not None
    assert soup.body is not None
    soup_objects.append(soup)
```

Each parsed HTML file contains a title and a body. Are there any duplicates across the titles or bodies of these files? We can find out by storing all title text and body text in two columns in a Pandas table. Calling the Pandas `describe` method will reveal the presence of any duplicates in the text.

Listing 17.3   Checking title and body texts for duplicates

```
import pandas as pd
html_dict = {'Title': [], 'Body': []}

for soup in soup_objects:
    title = soup.find('title').text
    body = soup.find('body').text
    html_dict['Title'].append(title)
    html_dict['Body'].append(body)

df_jobs = pd.DataFrame(html_dict)
summary = df_jobs.describe()
print(summary)

Title   \
count                            1458
unique                           1364
top      Data Scientist - New York, NY
freq                               13

                                             Body
count                                        1458
unique                                       1458
top      Data Scientist - New York, NY 10011\nAbout the...
freq                                            1
```

1,364 of the 1,458 titles are unique. The remaining 94 titles are duplicates. The most common title is repeated 13 times: it is for a data scientist position in New York. We can easily verify that all the duplicate titles correspond to unique body text. All 1,458 bodies are unique, so none of the job postings occur more than once, even if some postings share a common generic title.

We've confirmed that no duplicates are present in the HTML. Now, let's explore the HTML content in more detail. The goal of our exploration is to determine how job skills are described in the HTML.

17.1.1 *Exploring the HTML for skill descriptions*

We start our exploration by rendering the HTML at index 0 of `html_contents` (figure 17.1).

Listing 17.4   Rendering the HTML of the first job posting

```
from IPython.core.display import display, HTML
assert len(set(html_contents)) == len(html_contents)
display(HTML(html_contents[0]))
```

The rendered job posting is for a data science position. The posting starts with a brief position overview, from which we learn that the job entails drawing insights from government data. The various required skills include model building, statistics, and

Data Scientist - Beavercreek, OH

Data Scientist

Position Overview:

Centauri is looking for a detail oriented, motivated, and organized Data Scientist to work as part of a team to clean, analyze, and produce insightful reporting on government data. The ideal candidate is adept at using large data sets to find trends for intelligence reporting and will be proficient in process optimization and using models to test the effectiveness of different courses of action. They must have strong experience using a variety of data mining/data analysis methods, using a variety of data tools, building and implementing models, using/creating algorithms and producing easily understood visuals to represent findings. Candidate will work closely with Data Managers and stakeholders to tailor their analysis to answer key questions. The candidate must have a strong understanding of Geographic Information Systems (GIS) and statistical analysis.

Responsibilities:

- Use statistical research methods to analyze datasets produced through multiple sources of intelligence production
- Mine and analyze data from databases to answer key intelligence questions
- Assess the effectiveness and accuracy of new data sources and data gathering techniques
- Develop custom data models and algorithms to apply to data sets
- Use predictive modeling to produce reporting about future trends based on historical data
- Spatially analyze geographic data using GIS tools
- Visualize findings in easily understood graphics and aesthetically appealing finished reports

Qualifications for Data Scientist:

- Experience using statistical computer languages (R, Python, SLQ, etc.) to manipulate data and draw insights from large data sets
- Experience in basic visualization methods, especially using tools such as Tableau, ggplot, and matplotlib
- Knowledge of a variety of machine learning techniques (clustering, decision tree learning, artificial neural networks, etc.) and their real-world advantages/drawbacks
- Knowledge of advanced statistical techniques and concepts (regression, properties of distributions, statistical tests and proper usage, etc.) and experience with applications

Figure 17.1   The rendered HTML for the first job posting. The initial paragraph summarizes the data science job. The paragraph is followed by lists of bullet points, each containing a skill that is required to get the job.

visualization. These skills are further elaborated in the two bolded subsections: Responsibilities and Qualifications. Each subsection is composed of multiple single-sentence bullet points. The bullets are varied in their content: responsibilities include statistical method usage (bullet 1), future trend discovery (bullet 5), spatial analysis of geographic data (bullet 6), and aesthetically appealing visualization (bullet 7). Additionally, the bulleted qualifications cover computer languages such as R or Python (bullet 1), visualization tools such as Matplotlib (bullet 2), machine learning techniques including clustering (bullet 3), and knowledge of advanced statistical concepts (bullet 4).

It's worth noting that the qualifications are not that different from the responsibilities. Yes, the qualifications focus on tools and concepts, while the responsibilities are more attuned to actions on the jobs; but in a way, their bullet points are interchangeable. Each bullet describes a skill that an applicant must have to perform well at the job. Thus, we can subdivide `html_contents[0]` into two conceptually different parts:

- An initial job summary
- A list of bulleted skills required to get the job

Is the next job posting structured in a similar manner? Let's find out by rendering `html_contents[1]` (figure 17.2).

Data Scientist - Seattle, WA 98101

Are you interested in being a part of an Artificial Intelligence Marketing (AIM) company that is transforming how B2C enterprises engage with their customers; improving customer experience, marketing throughput and for the first time directly optimizing key business KPIs? Do you want to join a startup company backed by the top firms in the venture capital and SaaS industries? Would you like to be part of a company that prides itself on being a meritocracy, where passion, innovation, integrity, and our customers are at the heart of all that we do? Then, consider joining us at Amplero, an Artificial Intelligence Marketing company that leverages machine learning and multi-armed bandit experimentation to dynamically test thousands of permutations to adaptively optimize every customer interaction and maximize customer lifetime value and loyalty. We are growing our customer base and are looking for Data Scientists to join our innovative and energetic team! This is a unique opportunity to both drive innovations for our technology and to realize their impact as you work closely with our client engagement teams to best leverage our scientific capabilities within the Amplero product for marketing optimization and customer insights.

As an Amplero Data Scientist you would:

- Interface with our internal engagement teams and clients to understand business questions, and perform analytical "deep dives" to develop relevant and interpretive insights in support of our client engagements
- Smartly leverage appropriate technologies to answer tough questions or understand root causes of unexpected outcomes and statistical anomalies
- Develop analysis tools which will influence both our products and clients; including python pipelines focused on the productization of data science and insights tools for marketing performance and optimization
- Feature generation and selection from a wide variety of raw data types including time series and graphs
- Work with the Amplero Product Team to provide ongoing feedback to the features and priorities most aligned with our clients' current and future needs to inform the product roadmap, test product hypotheses as well as to help plan the product lifecycle

We'd love to hear from you if:

- You're an expert with data analysis and visualization tools including Python (including NumPy, SciPy, Pandas, scikit-learn) and other packages that enable data mining and machine learning
- You have a proven track record of applying data science to solve difficult real-world business problems
- You're familiar with areas of marketing data science where beyond-human scale, advanced experimentation and machine learning capabilities are used for achieving marketing performance, for example, DMP's in display advertising, Multivariate Testing, Statistical Significance Evaluation
- You've got excellent written and verbal communication skills for team and customer interactions - specifically, you're a genius at communicating results and the value of complex technical solutions to a non-technical audience

Figure 17.2   The rendered HTML for the second job posting. As in the first posting, the initial paragraph summarizes the data science job, and a list of bullet points describes the skills required to get the job.

Listing 17.5   Rendering the HTML of the second job posting

```
display(HTML(html_contents[1]))
```

The job posting is for a data science position in an AI marketing company. The structure of the posting is similar to that of `html_contents[0]`: the job is summarized in the post's initial paragraph, and then the required skills are presented in bullet points. These bulleted skills are varied in terms of technical requirements and details. For example, the fourth bullet from the bottom calls for expertise in the Python data science stack (NumPy, SciPy, Pandas, scikit-learn), the next bullet requires a track record of solving difficult real-world business problems, and the final bullet calls for excellent written and verbal communication skills. These three bulleted skills are very different. The difference is intentional—the author of the posting is emphasizing the diverse requirements needed to obtain the job. Thus, the bullet points in `html_contents[0]` and `html_contents[1]` serve a singular purpose: they offer us brief, sentence-length descriptions of unique skills required for each position.

Do these types of bulleted skill descriptions appear in other job posts? Let's find out. First we'll extract the bullets from each of our parsed HTML files. As a reminder, a bullet point is represented by the HTML tag `<li>`. Any bulleted file contains multiple such tags; thus, we can extract a list of bullet points from a soup object by calling `soup.find_all('li')`. Next, we'll iterate over our `soup_objects` list and extract all bullets from each element of that list. We store these results in a `Bullets` column in our existing `df_jobs` table.

Listing 17.6 Extracting bullets from the HTML

```
df_jobs['Bullets'] = [[bullet.text.strip()          ◁──────────┐   Strips the line break from each
                       for bullet in soup.find_all('li')]           bullet to avoid printing the line
                       for soup in soup_objects]                    breaks in our later investigations
```

The bullets in each job posting are stored in `df_jobs.Bullets`. However, it is possible that some (or most) of the postings don't include any bullets. What percentage of job postings actually contain bulleted text? We need to find out! If that percentage is too low, further bullet analysis is not worth our time. Let's measure the percentage.

Listing 17.7 Measuring the percent of bulleted postings

```
bulleted_post_count = 0
for bullet_list in df_jobs.Bullets:
    if bullet_list:
        bulleted_post_count += 1

percent_bulleted = 100 * bulleted_post_count / df_jobs.shape[0]
print(f"{percent_bulleted:.2f}% of the postings contain bullets")
```

```
90.53% of the postings contain bullets
```

90% of the job postings contain bullets. Do all (or most) of these bullets focus on skills? We currently don't know. However, we can better gauge the contents of the bullet points by printing the top-ranked words in their text. We can rank these words by occurrence count; alternatively, we can carry out the ranking using term frequency-inverse document frequency (TFIDF) values rather than raw counts. As discussed in section 15, such TFIDF rankings are less likely to contain irrelevant words.

Next, we rank the words using summed TFIDF values. First we compute a TFIDF matrix in which rows correspond to individual bullets. Then we sum across the rows of the matrix: these sums are used to rank the words, which correspond to matrix columns. Finally, we check the top five ranked words for skill-related terminology.

Listing 17.8 Examining the top-ranked words in the HTML bullets

```
import pandas as pd                                                Returns a sorted
from sklearn.feature_extraction.text import TfidfVectorizer        Pandas table of
                                                                   top-ranked
def rank_words(text_list):              ◁──────────┘               words
    vectorizer = TfidfVectorizer(stop_words='english')
    tfidf_matrix = vectorizer.fit_transform(text_list).toarray()
    df = pd.DataFrame({'Words': vectorizer.get_feature_names(),
```

```
                 'Summed TFIDF': tfidf_matrix.sum(axis=0)})
    sorted_df = df.sort_values('Summed TFIDF', ascending=False)
    return sorted_df
```

Words are sorted based on the summed TFIDF values across rows in tfidf_matrix.

```
all_bullets = []
for bullet_list in df_jobs.Bullets:
    all_bullets.extend(bullet_list)

sorted_df = rank_words(all_bullets)
print(sorted_df[:5].to_string(index=False))
```

```
     Words  Summed TFIDF
experience    878.030398
      data    842.978780
    skills    440.780236
      work    371.684232
   ability    370.969638
```

Terms such as *skills* and *ability* appear among the top five bulleted words. There's reasonable evidence that the bullets correspond to individual job skills. How do these bulleted words compare to the remaining words in each job posting? Let's find out. We iterate over the body of each posting and delete any bulleted lists using Beautiful Soup's decompose method. Then we extract the remaining body text and store it in a non_bullets list. Finally, we apply our rank_words function to that list and display the top five non-bullet words.

Listing 17.9   Examining the top-ranked words in the HTML bodies

```
non_bullets = []
for soup in soup_objects:
    body = soup.body
    for tag in body.find_all('li'):
        tag.decompose()

    non_bullets.append(body.text)

sorted_df = rank_words(non_bullets)
print(sorted_df[:5].to_string(index=False))
```

Alternatively, calling body.find_all('ul') will achieve the same result.

```
     Words  Summed TFIDF
      data     99.111312
      team     39.175041
      work     38.928948
experience     36.820836
  business     36.140488
```

The words *skills* and *ability* are no longer present in the ranked output. They have been replaced by the words *business* and *team*. Thus, the non-bulleted text appears to be less skill oriented than the bullet contents. However, it's still interesting to note that certain top-ranked words are shared between bullets and non_bullets: these words are *data, experience,* and *work.* Strangely, the words *scientist* and *science* are missing from the list. Do some posts pertain to data-driven jobs that aren't directly data sci-ence jobs? Let's actively explore this possibility. We start by iterating over all the titles across all jobs and checking if each title mentions a data science position. Then we measure the percentage of jobs where the terms *data science* and *data scientist* are miss-ing from the titles. Finally, we print a sample of 10 such titles for evaluation purposes.

> **NOTE** As discussed in section 11, we match our terms to the title text using regular expressions.

Listing 17.10 Checking titles for references to data science positions

```
regex = r'Data Scien(ce|tist)'
df_non_ds_jobs = df_jobs[~df_jobs.Title.str.contains(regex, case=False)]    ◁─┐

percent_non_ds = 100 * df_non_ds_jobs.shape[0] / df_jobs.shape[0]
print(f"{percent_non_ds:.2f}% of the job posting titles do not mention a "
      "data science position. Below is a sample of such titles:\n")

for title in df_non_ds_jobs.Title[:10]:
    print(title)
```

> The Pandas str.contains methods can match a regular expression to column text. Passing case=False ensures that the match is not case sensitive.

```
64.81% of the job posting titles do not mention a data science position. Below
is a sample of such titles:

Patient Care Assistant / PCA - Med/Surg (Fayette, AL) - Fayette, AL
Data Manager / Analyst - Oakland, CA
Scientific Programmer - Berkeley, CA
JD Digits - AI Lab Research Intern - Mountain View, CA
Operations and Technology Summer 2020 Internship-West Coast - Universal City, CA
Data and Reporting Analyst - Olympia, WA 98501
Senior Manager Advanced Analytics - Walmart Media Group - San Bruno, CA
Data Specialist, Product Support Operations - Sunnyvale, CA
Deep Learning Engineer - Westlake, TX
Research Intern, 2020 - San Francisco, CA 94105
```

Nearly 65% of the posting titles do not mention a data science position. However, from our sampled output, we can glean the alternative language that can be used to describe a data science job. A posting may call for a *data specialist*, a *data analyst*, or a *scientific programmer*. Furthermore, certain job postings are for research internships, which we can assume are data-centric. But not all sampled jobs are fully relevant: mul-tiple postings are for management positions, which don't align with our immediate career goals. Management is a separate career track that requires its own unique set of skills. We should consider excluding management positions from our analysis.

More troublingly, the first posting on the list is for a *Patient Care Assistant* or *PCA*. Clearly, this posting has been crawled erroneously. Perhaps the crawling algorithm confused the job title with the PCA data-reduction technique. The erroneous posting contains skills that we lack and also have no interest in obtaining. These irrelevant skills pose a danger to our analysis and will serve as a source of noise if not removed. We can illustrate this danger by printing the first five bullets of df_non_ds_jobs[0].

Listing 17.11 Sampling bullets from a non-data science job

```
bullets = df_non_ds_jobs.Bullets.iloc[0]
for i, bullet in enumerate(bullets[:5]):
    print(f"{i}: {bullet.strip()}")
```

```
0: Provides all personal care services in accordance with the plan of
treatment assigned by the registered nurse
1: Accurately documents care provided
2: Applies safety principles and proper body mechanics to the performance
of specific techniques of personal and supportive care, such as ambulation
of patients, transferring patients, assisting with normal range of motions
and positioning
3: Participates in economical utilization of supplies and ensures that
equipment and nursing units are maintained in a clean, safe manner
4: Routinely follows and adheres to all policies and procedures
```

We are data scientists; our primary objective isn't patient care (index 0) or nursing equipment maintenance (index 4). We need to delete these skills from our dataset, but how? One approach is to use text similarity. We could compare the postings to our resume and delete the jobs that don't align with our resume content. Also, we should consider comparing the postings with this book's table of contents for added signal. Basically, we should evaluate the relevance of each job relative to both the resume and book material; this would allow us to filter the extraneous postings and retain only the most relevant jobs.

Alternatively, we could consider filtering the individual skills contained in the bullet points. Basically, we'd rank the individual bullet points rather than individual jobs. But there's a problem with this second approach. Imagine if we filter out all bullets that don't align with our resume or book material: the bullets that remain will cover skills that we already possess. This is counter to our goal of uncovering our missing skills using relevant data science postings. Instead, we should accomplish our goal as follows:

1 Obtain relevant job postings that partially match our existing skill set.
2 Examine which bullet points in these postings are missing from our existing skill set.

With this strategy in mind, we'll now filter the jobs by relevance.

17.2 *Filtering jobs by relevance*

Our goal is to evaluate job relevance using text similarity. We want to compare the text in each posting to our resume and/or the book's table of contents. In preparation, let's store our resume in a resume string.

Listing 17.12 Loading the resume

```
resume = open('resume.txt', 'r').read()
print(resume)
```

```
Experience

1. Developed probability simulations using NumPy.
2. Assessed online ad-clicks for statistical significance using Permutation
   testing.
3. Analyzed disease outbreaks using common clustering algorithms.

Additional Skills

1. Data visualization using Matplotlib.
2. Statistical analysis using SciPy.
3. Processing structured tables using Pandas.
4. Executing K-Means clustering and DBSCAN clustering using Scikit-Learn.
5. Extracting locations from text using GeonamesCache.
6. Location analysis and visualization using GeonamesCache and Cartopy.
7. Dimensionality reduction with PCA and SVD, using Scikit-Learn.
8. NLP analysis and text topic detection using Scikit-Learn.
```

In this same manner, we can store the table of contents in a `table_of_contents` string.

Listing 17.13   Loading the table of contents

```
table_of_contents = open('table_of_contents.txt', 'r').read()
```

Together, `resume` and `table_of_contents` summarize our existing skill set. Let's concatenate these skills into a single `existing_skills` string.

Listing 17.14   Combining skills into a single string

```
existing_skills = resume + table_of_contents
```

Our task is to compute the text similarity between each job posting and our existing skills. In other words, we want to compute all similarities between `df_jobs.Body` and `existing_skills`. This computation first requires that we vectorize all texts. We need to vectorize `df_jobs.Body` together with `existing_skills` to ensure that all vectors share the same vocabulary. Next, we combine our job posts and our skill string into a single list of texts and vectorize these texts using scikit-learn's `Tfidf-Vectorizer` implementation.

Listing 17.15   Vectorizing our skills and the job-posting data

```
text_list = df_jobs.Body.values.tolist() + [existing_skills]
vectorizer = TfidfVectorizer(stop_words='english')
tfidf_matrix = vectorizer.fit_transform(text_list).toarray()
```

Our vectorized texts are stored in a matrix format in `tfidf_matrix`. The final matrix row (`tfidf_matrix[-1]`) corresponds to our existing skill set, and all the other rows in (`tfidf_matrix[:-1]`) correspond to the job postings. Thus, we can easily compute the cosine similarities between the job postings and `existing_skills`. We simply need to execute `tfdf_matrix[:-1] @ tfidf_matrix[-1]`: this matrix-vector product returns an array of cosine similarities. Listing 17.16 computes that `cosine_similarities` array.

> **NOTE** You may wonder if it's worthwhile to visualize the distribution of rankings. The answer is yes! We will plot this distribution shortly to obtain valuable insights, but first we want to carry out a simple sanity check by printing the top-ranking job titles. Doing so will confirm that our hypothesis is correct and all the printed jobs are relevant.

Listing 17.16   Computing skill-based cosine similarities

```
cosine_similarities = tfidf_matrix[:-1] @ tfidf_matrix[-1]
```

The cosine similarities capture the text overlap between our existing skills and the posted jobs. Jobs with greater overlap are more relevant, and jobs with lesser overlap are less relevant. Thus, we can use cosine similarities to rank jobs by relevance. Let's carry out the ranking. First, we need to store the cosine similarities in a `Relevance` column of `df_jobs`. Then, we sort the table by `df_jobs.Relevance` in descending order. Finally, we print the 20 least relevant job titles in the sorted table and confirm whether these low-ranking jobs have anything to do with data science.

Listing 17.17   Printing the 20 least relevant jobs

```
df_jobs['Relevance'] = cosine_similarities
sorted_df_jobs = df_jobs.sort_values('Relevance', ascending=False)
for title in sorted_df_jobs[-20:].Title:
    print(title)


Data Analyst Internship (8 month minimum) - San Francisco, CA
Leadership and Advocacy Coordinator - Oakland, CA 94607
Finance Consultant - Audi Palo Alto - Palo Alto, CA
RN - Hattiesburg, MS
Configuration Management Specialist - Dahlgren, VA
Deal Desk Analyst - Mountain View, CA
Dev Ops Engineer AWS - Rockville, MD
Web Development Teaching Assistant - UC Berkeley (Berkeley) - Berkeley, CA
Scorekeeper - Oakland, CA 94612
Direct Care - All Experience Levels (CNA, HHA, PCA Welcome) - Norwell, MA 02061
Director of Marketing - Cambridge, MA
Certified Strength and Conditioning Specialist - United States
PCA - PCU Full Time - Festus, MO 63028
Performance Improvement Consultant - Los Angeles, CA
Patient Services Rep II - Oakland, CA
Lab Researcher I - Richmond, CA
Part-time instructor of Statistics for Data Science and Machine Learning - San
    Francisco, CA 94105
Plant Engineering Specialist - San Pablo, CA
Page Not Found - Indeed Mobile
Director of Econometric Modeling - External Careers
```

Most of the printed jobs are completely irrelevant. Various extraneous employment opportunities include *Leadership and Advocacy Coordinator, Financial Consultant, RN* (registered nurse), and *Scorekeeper*. One of the job titles even reads *Page Not Found*, which indicates that the web page was not downloaded correctly. However, a few of the jobs are related to data science: for instance, one calls for a *Part-time instructor of Statistics and Data Science and Machine Learning*. Still, this job is not exactly what we're looking for. After all, our immediate goal is to practice data science, not teach it. We can discard the 20 lowest-ranking jobs in the sorted table. Now, for comparison's sake, let's print the 20 most relevant job titles in sorted_ds_jobs.

Listing 17.18 Printing the 20 most relevant jobs

```
for title in sorted_df_jobs[:20].Title:
    print(title)
```

```
Chief Data Officer - Culver City, CA 90230
Data Scientist - Beavercreek, OH
Data Scientist Population Health - Los Angeles, CA 90059
Data Scientist - San Diego, CA
Data Scientist - Beavercreek, OH
Senior Data Scientist - New York, NY 10018
Data Architect - Raleigh, NC 27609
Data Scientist (PhD) - Spring, TX
Data Science Analyst - Chicago, IL 60612
Associate Data Scientist (BS / MS) - Spring, TX
Data Scientist - Streetsboro, OH 44241
Data Scientist - Los Angeles, CA
Sr Director of Data Science - Elkridge, MD
2019-57 Sr. Data Scientist - Reston, VA 20191
Data Scientist (PhD) - Intern - Spring, TX
Sr Data Scientist. - Alpharetta, GA 30004
Data Scientist GS 13/14 - Clarksburg, WV 26301
Data Science Intern (BS / MS) - Intern - Spring, TX
Senior Data Scientist - New York, NY 10038
Data Scientist - United States
```

Almost all of the printed job titles are for data science jobs. Some jobs, such as *Chief Data Officer*, probably lie beyond our existing level of expertise, but the top-ranking jobs appear to be quite relevant to our data science career.

> **NOTE** Based on its title, the position of *Chief Data Officer* appears to be a management position. As we stated earlier, a management position requires its own separate set of skills. However, if we output the job posting's body (sorted_df_jobs.iloc[0].Body), we immediately discover that the job isn't a management job at all! The company is simply searching for a highly experienced data scientist to cover all its data science needs. Sometimes job titles can be deceiving; glancing briefly over a title cannot fully substitute for carefully reading the body text.

Clearly, when df_jobs.Relevance is high, the associated job postings are relevant. As df_jobs.Relevance decreases, the associated jobs become less relevant. Thus, we can presume that there exists some df_jobs.Relevance cutoff that separates the relevant jobs from the non-relevant jobs. Let's try to identify that cutoff. We start by visualizing the shape of the sorted relevance distribution relative to rank. In other words, we plot range(df_jobs.shape[0]) versus sorted_df_jobs.Relevance (figure 17.3). In the plot, we expect to see a relevance curve that's continuously decreasing; any sudden decreases of relevance in the curve indicate a separation between relevant and non-relevant jobs.

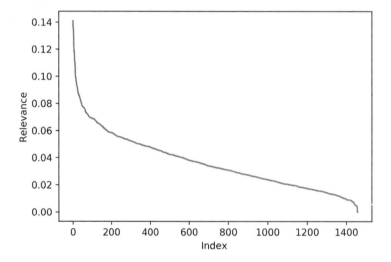

Figure 17.3   Ranked job posting indices plotted vs. relevance. Lower indices indicate higher relevance. The relevance is equal to the cosine similarity between each job and existing_skills. This relevance drops rapidly at an index of approximately 60.

Listing 17.19   Plotting job ranking vs. relevance

```
import matplotlib.pyplot as plt
plt.plot(range(df_jobs.shape[0]), sorted_df_jobs.Relevance.values)
plt.xlabel('Index')
plt.ylabel('Relevance')
plt.show()
```

Our relevance curve resembles a K-means elbow plot. Initially, the relevance drops rapidly. Then, at an x-value of approximately 60, the curve begins to level off. Let's emphasize this transition by drawing a vertical line through the x-position of 60 in our plot (figure 17.4).

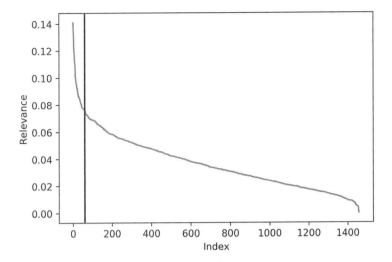

Figure 17.4 Ranked job posting indices are plotted vs. relevance. A vertical cutoff of 60 is also included in the plot. Indices below 60 correspond to much higher relevance values.

Listing 17.20 Adding a cutoff to the relevance plot

```
plt.plot(range(df_jobs.shape[0]), sorted_df_jobs.Relevance.values)
plt.xlabel('Index')
plt.ylabel('Relevance')
plt.axvline(60, c='k')
plt.show()
```

Our plot implies that the first 60 jobs are noticeably more relevant than all subsequent jobs. We'll now probe this implication. As we've already seen, the first 20 jobs are highly relevant. Based on our hypothesis, jobs 40 through 60 should be highly relevant as well. Next, we print `sorted_ds_jobs[40: 60].Title` for evaluation purposes.

Listing 17.21 Printing jobs below the relevance cutoff

```
for title in sorted_df_jobs[40: 60].Title.values:
    print(title)

Data Scientist III - Pasadena, CA 91101
Global Data Engineer - Boston, MA
Data Analyst and Data Scientist - Summit, NJ
Data Scientist - Generalist - Glendale, CA
Data Scientist - Seattle, WA
IT Data Scientist - Contract - Riverton, UT
Data Scientist (Analytic Consultant 4) - San Francisco, CA
Data Scientist - Seattle, WA
Data Science & Tagging Analyst - Bethesda, MD 20814
Data Scientist - New York, NY
```

```
Senior Data Scientist - Los Angeles, CA
Principal Statistician - Los Angeles, CA
Senior Data Analyst - Los Angeles, CA
Data Scientist - Aliso Viejo, CA 92656
Data Engineer - Seattle, WA
Data Scientist - Digital Factory - Tampa, FL 33607
Data Scientist - Grapevine, TX 76051
Data Scientist - Bioinformatics - Denver, CO 80221
EPIDEMIOLOGIST - Los Angeles, CA
Data Scientist - Bellevue, WA
```

Almost all of the printed jobs are for data scientist/analyst positions. The only outlier is a posting for an epidemiologist, which probably appeared due to our stated experience of tracking disease epidemics. The outlier notwithstanding, the remaining jobs are highly relevant. Implicitly, the relevance should decrease when we print the next 20 job titles since they lie beyond the bounds of index 60. Let's verify if this is the case.

Listing 17.22   Printing jobs beyond the relevance cutoff

```python
for title in sorted_df_jobs[60: 80].Title.values:
    print(title)
```

```
Data Scientist - Aliso Viejo, CA
Data Scientist and Visualization Specialist - Santa Clara Valley, CA 95014
Data Scientist - Los Angeles, CA
Data Scientist Manager - NEW YORK LOCATION! - New York, NY 10036
Data Science Intern - San Francisco, CA 94105
Research Data Analyst - San Francisco, CA
Sr Data Scientist (Analytic Consultant 5) - San Francisco, CA
Data Scientist, Media Manipulation - Cambridge, MA
Manager, Data Science, Programming and Visualization - Boston, MA
Data Scientist in Broomfield, CO - Broomfield, CO
Senior Data Scientist - Executive Projects and New Solutions - Foster City, CA
Manager of Data Science - Burbank California - Burbank, CA
Data Scientist Manager - Hiring in Burbank! - Burbank, CA
Data Scientists needed in NY - Senior Consultants and Managers! - New York, NY
    10036
Data Scientist - Menlo Park, CA
Data Engineer - Santa Clara, CA
Data Scientist - Remote
Data Scientist I-III - Phoenix, AZ 85021
SWE Data Scientist - Santa Clara Valley, CA 95014
Health Science Specialist - San Francisco, CA 94102
```

A few of the job titles for postings 60 through 80 are noticeably less relevant. Some jobs are management positions, and one is a health science specialist position. Nonetheless, a majority of the jobs refer to data science/analyst roles outside the scope of health science or management. We can quickly quantify this observation using regular expressions. We define a `percent_relevant_titles` function, which returns the percent of non-management data science and analysis jobs in a data frame slice. Then we apply that function to `sorted_df_jobs[60: 80]`. The output gives us a very simple alternative measure of relevance based on job post titles.

Listing 17.23   Measuring title relevance in a subset of jobs

```
import re
def percent_relevant_titles(df):
    regex_relevant = re.compile(r'Data (Scien|Analy)',
                                flags=re.IGNORECASE)
    regex_irrelevant = re.compile(r'\b(Manage)',
                                  flags=re.IGNORECASE)
    match_count = len([title for title in df.Title
                       if regex_relevant.search(title)
                       and not regex_irrelevant.search(title)])
    percent = 100 * match_count / df.shape[0]
    return percent

percent = percent_relevant_titles(sorted_df_jobs[60: 80])
print(f"Approximately {percent:.2f}% of job titles between indices "
      "60 - 80 are relevant")
```

> **Matches relevant job titles that mention data science/analyst positions**

> **Matches irrelevant job titles that mention management positions**

> **Counts the number of non-management data science/analyst title matches**

```
Approximately 65.00% of job titles between indices 60 - 80 are relevant
```

Approximately two-thirds of the job titles in `sorted_df_jobs[60: 80]` are relevant. Although the job relevance has decreased beyond index 60, more than 50% of the titles still refer to data science jobs. Perhaps that percentage will drop if we sample the next 20 jobs across an index range of 80 to 100. Let's check.

Listing 17.24   Measuring title relevance in the next subset of jobs

```
percent = percent_relevant_titles(sorted_df_jobs[80: 100])
print(f"Approximately {percent:.2f}% of job titles between indices "
      "80 - 100 are relevant")
```

```
Approximately 80.00% of job titles between indices 80 - 100 are relevant
```

Nope! The data science title percentage rose to 80%. At what point will the percentage drop below 50%? We can easily find out! Let's iterate over `sorted_df_jobs[i: i + 20]` for all values of `i`. At every iteration, we compute the relevance percentage. Then we plot all the percentages (figure 17.5). We also plot a horizontal line at 50% to allow us to determine the index at which relevant job titles fall into the minority.

Listing 17.25   Plotting percent relevance across all title samples

```
def relevant_title_plot(index_range=20):
    percentages = []
```

> **The function runs percent_relevant_titles across each consecutive slice of index_range jobs. Next, all the percentages are plotted. The index_range parameter is preset to 20. Later, we adjust that parameter value.**

```
        start_indices = range(df_jobs.shape[0] - index_range)
        for i in start_indices:
            df_slice = sorted_df_jobs[i: i + index_range]
            percent = percent_relevant_titles(df_slice)
            percentages.append(percent)

        plt.plot(start_indices, percentages)
        plt.axhline(50, c='k')
        plt.xlabel('Index')
        plt.ylabel('% Relevant Titles')

relevant_title_plot()
plt.show()
```

> **Analyzes
> sorted_df_jobs[i: i +
> index_range], where i
> ranges from 0 to the
> total posting count
> minus the index range**

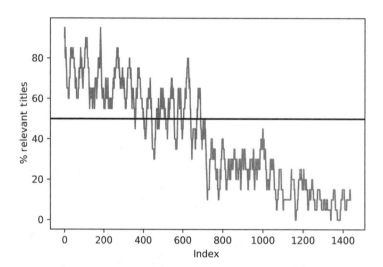

**Figure 17.5   Ranked job posting indices plotted vs. title relevance. Title
relevance is equal to the percent of data science titles across 20 consecutive
job postings (starting at some index). A horizontal line demarcates 50%
relevance. The relevance drops below 50% at an index of approximately 700.**

The plot fluctuates with a high degree of variance. But despite the fluctuations, we
can observe that the relevant data science titles drop below 50% at an index of
around 700. Of course, it's possible that the cutoff of 700 is merely an artifact of
our chosen index range. Will the cutoff still be present if we double our index range?
We'll find out by running relevant_title_plot(index_range=40) (figure 17.6). We
also plot a vertical line at index 700 to confirm that the percentage drops below
50% beyond that line.

Listing 17.26   Plotting percent relevance across an increased index range

```
relevant_title_plot(index_range=40)
plt.axvline(700, c='k')
plt.show()
```

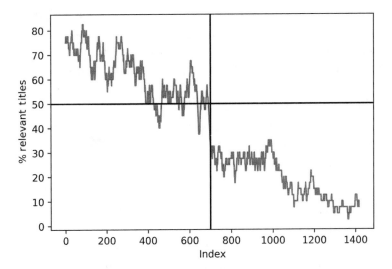

Figure 17.6   Ranked job-posting indices plotted vs. title relevance. Title relevance is equal to the percent of data science titles across 40 consecutive job postings (starting at some index). A horizontal line demarcates 50% relevance, and a vertical line demarcates an index of 700. Below that line, relevance drops to less than 50%.

Our updated plot continues to drop below 50% at an index cutoff of 700.

> **NOTE**   There's more than one way to approximate that cutoff. Suppose, for instance, that we simplify our regex to `r'Data (Science|Scientist)'`. We thus ignore all mentions of analysts or managers. Also, suppose we eliminate the use of index ranges and instead count the total number of data science titles appearing below each index. If we plot these simple results, we see a curve that levels off at an index of 700. Despite our simplifications, we achieve very similar results. In data science, there's frequently more than one path toward an insightful observation.

At this point, we face a choice between two relevance cutoffs. Our first cutoff, at index 60, is highly precise: most jobs below that cutoff are data science positions. However, the cutoff has limited recall: hundreds of data science jobs appear beyond an index of 60. Meanwhile, our second cutoff of 700 captures many more data science positions, but some irrelevant jobs also appear below the cutoff range. There's almost a 12-fold difference between the two relevance cutoffs. So, which cutoff do we choose? Do we prefer higher precision or higher recall? If we choose higher recall, will the noise hurt our analysis? If we choose higher precision, will the limited diversity of seen skills render our analysis incomplete? These are all important questions. Unfortunately, there's no immediate right answer. Higher precision at the expense of recall could potentially hurt us, and vice versa. What should we do?

How about trying both cutoffs? That way, we can compare the trade-offs and benefits of each! First, we'll cluster the skill sets from job postings below an index of 60. Then, we'll repeat our analysis for job postings below an index of 700. Finally, we'll integrate these two different analyses into a single, coherent conclusion.

17.3   *Clustering skills in relevant job postings*

Our aim is to cluster the skills in the 60 most relevant job postings. The skills in each posting are diverse and partially represented by bullet points. Thus we face a choice:

- Cluster the 60 texts in `sorted_df_jobs[:60].Body`.
- Cluster the hundreds of individual bullet points in `sorted_df_jobs[:60]` `.Bullets`.

The second option is preferable for the following reasons:

- Our stated aim is to identify missing skills. The bullet points focus more on individual skills than the heterogeneous body of each posting.
- The short bullet points are easy to print and read. This is not the case for the larger postings. Thus, clustering by bullets allows us to examine each cluster by outputting a sample of the clustered bullet text.

We'll cluster the scraped bullets. We start by storing `sorted_df_jobs[:60].Bullets` in a single list.

Listing 17.27   Obtaining bullets from the 60 most relevant jobs

```
total_bullets = []
for bullets in sorted_df_jobs[:60].Bullets:
    total_bullets.extend(bullets)
```

How many bullets are in the list? Are any of the bullets duplicated? We can check by loading `total_bullets` into a Pandas table and then applying the `describe` method.

Listing 17.28   Summarizing basic bullet statistics

```
df_bullets = pd.DataFrame({'Bullet': total_bullets})
print(df_bullets.describe())

Bullet
count                                              1091
unique                                              900
top      Knowledge of advanced statistical techniques a...
freq                                                  9
```

The list contains 1,091 bullets. However, only 900 are unique—the remaining 91 bullets are duplicates. The most frequent duplicate is mentioned nine times. If we don't deal with this issue, it could affect our clustering. We should remove all duplicate texts before proceeding with our analysis.

NOTE Where do the duplicates originate? We can find out by tracing back a few duplicates to their original job posts. For brevity's sake, this analysis is not included in the book. However, you're encouraged to try it yourself. The output shows how certain companies reuse job templates for different jobs. Each template is modified for each position, but certain repeated bullet points remain. These repeated bullet points could bias our clusters toward company-specific skills and thus should be removed from `total_bullets`.

Next, we filter empty strings and duplicates from our bullet list. Then we vectorize the list using a TFIDF vectorizer.

Listing 17.29 Removing duplicates and vectorizing the bullets

```
total_bullets = sorted(set(total_bullets))
vectorizer = TfidfVectorizer(stop_words='english')
tfidf_matrix = vectorizer.fit_transform(total_bullets)
num_rows, num_columns = tfidf_matrix.shape
print(f"Our matrix has {num_rows} rows and {num_columns} columns")
```

Converts total_bullets into a set to remove the 91 duplicates. We sort that set to ensure consistent ordering (and thus consistent output). Alternatively, we can drop the duplicates directly from our Pandas table by running df_bullets.drop_duplicates(inplace=True).

We've vectorized our deduplicated bullet list. The resulting TFIDF matrix has 900 rows and over 2,000 columns; it thus contains over 1.8 million elements. This matrix is too large for efficient clustering. Let's dimensionally reduce the matrix using the procedure described in section 15: we'll shrink the matrix to 100 dimensions with SVD, and then we'll normalize the matrix.

Listing 17.30 Dimensionally reducing the TFIDF matrix

```
import numpy as np
from sklearn.decomposition import TruncatedSVD
from sklearn.preprocessing import normalize
np.random.seed(0)

def shrink_matrix(tfidf_matrix):
    svd_object = TruncatedSVD(n_components=100)
    shrunk_matrix = svd_object.fit_transform(tfidf_matrix)
    return normalize(shrunk_matrix)

shrunk_norm_matrix = shrink_matrix(tfidf_matrix)
```

Applies SVD to an inputted TFIDF matrix. The matrix is reduced to I00 dimensions, normalized, and returned.

We are nearly ready to cluster our normalized matrix using K-means. However, first we need to estimate *K*. Let's generate an elbow plot using mini-batch K-means, which is optimized for speed (figure 17.7).

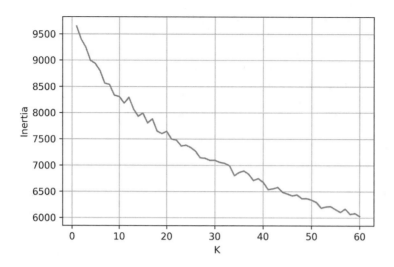

Figure 17.7   An elbow plot generated using mini-batch K-means, across *K* values ranging from 1 to 60. The precise location of the elbow is difficult to determine.

Listing 17.31   Plotting an elbow curve using mini-batch K-means

```
np.random.seed(0)
from sklearn.cluster import MiniBatchKMeans
def generate_elbow_plot(matrix):        ◁────┐   Generates an elbow plot
    k_values = range(1, 61)                       across an inputted data matrix
    inertia_values = [MiniBatchKMeans(k).fit(matrix).inertia_    using mini-batch K-means
                      for k in k_values]
    plt.plot(k_values, inertia_values)                  The number of
    plt.xlabel('K')                                     clusters ranges
    plt.ylabel('Inertia')                               from 1 to 60.
    plt.grid(True)     ◁───────┐ Plots grid lines to help us
    plt.show()                   identify where the elbow
                                 lies on the x-axis

generate_elbow_plot(shrunk_norm_matrix)
```

Our plotted curve decreases smoothly. The precise location of a bent elbow–shaped transition is difficult to spot: that curve drops rapidly at a *K* of 10 and then gradually bends into an elbow somewhere between a *K* of 10 and a *K* of 25. Which *K* value should we choose? 10, 25, or some value in between, such as 15 or 20? The right answer is not immediately clear. So why not try multiple values of *K*? Let's cluster our data multiple times using *K* values of 10, 15, 20, and 25. Then we'll compare and contrast the results. If necessary, we'll consider choosing a different *K* for clustering. We'll start by grouping our job skills into 15 clusters.

NOTE   Our aim is to investigate outputs for four different values of *K*. The order in which we generate the outputs is completely arbitrary. In this book, we start with a *K* value of 15 because the resulting cluster count is not too large and not too small. This sets a nice baseline for the subsequent discussion of the outputs.

17.3.1 Grouping the job skills into 15 clusters

We execute K-means using a *K* of 15. Then we store the text indices and cluster IDs in a Pandas table. We also store the actual bullet text for easier accessibility. Finally, we utilize the Pandas `groupby` method to split the table by cluster.

Listing 17.32   Clustering bullets into 15 clusters

Tracks each clustered bullet's index in clusters, cluster ID, and text

Executes K-means clustering on the input shrunk_norm_matrix. The K parameter is preset to 15. The function returns a list of Pandas tables, where each table represents a cluster. Clustered bullets are included in these tables; the bullets were passed in through an optional bullets parameter.

```
np.random.seed(0)
from sklearn.cluster import KMeans

def compute_cluster_groups(shrunk_norm_matrix, k=15,          ◁
                           bullets=total_bullets):
    cluster_model = KMeans(n_clusters=k)
    clusters = cluster_model.fit_predict(shrunk_norm_matrix)
    df = pd.DataFrame({'Index': range(clusters.size), 'Cluster': clusters,
                       'Bullet': bullets})
    return [df_cluster for _, df_cluster in df.groupby('Cluster')]

cluster_groups = compute_cluster_groups(shrunk_norm_matrix)
```

Each of our text clusters is stored as a Pandas table in the `cluster_groups` list. We can visualize the clusters using word clouds. In section 15, we defined a custom `cluster_to_image` function for word cloud visualization. The function took as input a cluster-specific Pandas table and returned a word cloud image. Listing 17.33 redefines that function and applies it to `cluster_groups[0]` (figure 17.8).

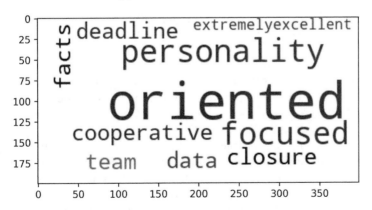

Figure 17.8   A word cloud generated for the cluster at index 0. The language in the word cloud is a little vague. It appears to be describing a focused, data-oriented personality.

NOTE Why should we redefine the function? Well, in section 15, cluster_to_image depended on a fixed TFIDF matrix and vocabulary list. In our current analysis, these parameters are not fixed—both the matrix and vocabulary will shift as we adjust our relevancy index. Thus, we need to update the function to allow for more dynamic input.

Listing 17.33   Visualizing the first cluster

Takes as input a df_cluster table and returns a word cloud image for the top max_words words corresponding to the cluster. The words are obtained from the inputted vectorizer class. They are ranked by summing over the rows of the inputted tfidf_matrix. When we extend our job threshold from 60 to 700, both vectorizer and tfidf_matrix must be adjusted accordingly.

```
from wordcloud import WordCloud
np.random.seed(0)

def cluster_to_image(df_cluster, max_words=10, tfidf_matrix=tfidf_matrix,
                     vectorizer=vectorizer):
    indices = df_cluster.Index.values
    summed_tfidf = np.asarray(tfidf_matrix[indices].sum(axis=0))[0]
    data = {'Word': vectorizer.get_feature_names(),'Summed TFIDF':
     summed_tfidf}
    df_ranked_words = pd.DataFrame(data).sort_values('Summed TFIDF',
     ascending=False)
    words_to_score = {word: score
                      for word, score in df_ranked_words[:max_words].values
                      if score != 0}
    cloud_generator = WordCloud(background_color='white',
                                color_func=_color_func,
                                random_state=1)
    wordcloud_image = cloud_generator.fit_words(words_to_score)
    return wordcloud_image

def _color_func(*args, **kwargs):
    return np.random.choice(['black', 'blue', 'teal', 'purple', 'brown'])

wordcloud_image = cluster_to_image(cluster_groups[0])
plt.imshow(wordcloud_image, interpolation="bilinear")
plt.show()
```

Helper function to randomly assign one of five acceptable colors to each word

---

The language in the word cloud seems to be describing someone focused and data oriented, but it's a little vague. Perhaps we can learn more about the cluster by printing some sample bullets from cluster_group[0].

NOTE We'll print a random sample of bullets. This should be sufficiently informative to understand the cluster. However, it's worth emphasizing that not all bullets are equal: some bullets are closer to their K-means cluster centroid and therefore more representative of the cluster. Thus, we can optionally sort the bullets based on their distance to the cluster mean. In this book, we bypass bullet ranking for brevity's sake, but you're encouraged to try ranking the bullets on your own.

Listing 17.34 Printing sample bullets from cluster 0

```
np.random.seed(1)
def print_cluster_sample(cluster_id):          Prints five random bullets from
    df_cluster = cluster_groups[cluster_id]     cluster_groups[cluster_id]
    for bullet in np.random.choice(df_cluster.Bullet.values, 5,
                                    replace=False):
        print(bullet)

print_cluster_sample(0)

Data-oriented personality
Detail-oriented
Detail-oriented — quality and precision-focused
Should be extremelyExcellent facts and data oriented
Data oriented personality
```

The printed bullets all use very similar language: they call for an employee who is detail oriented and data oriented. Linguistically, this cluster is legitimate. Unfortunately, it represents a skill that is difficult to grasp. Being detail oriented is a very general skill—it's hard to quantify, demonstrate, and learn. Ideally, the other clusters will contain more concrete technical skills.

Let's examine all 15 clusters simultaneously using word clouds. These word clouds are displayed across 15 subplots in a five-row-by-three-column grid (figure 17.9).

Listing 17.35 Visualizing all 15 clusters

```
def plot_wordcloud_grid(cluster_groups, num_rows=5, num_columns=3,
                        **kwargs):
    figure, axes = plt.subplots(num_rows, num_columns, figsize=(20, 15))
    cluster_groups_copy = cluster_groups[:]        The **kwargs syntax allows us to
    for r in range(num_rows):                      pass additional parameters into the
        for c in range(num_columns):               utilized cluster_to_image function.
            if not cluster_groups_copy:            This way, we can modify both
                break                              vectorizer and tfidf_matrix
                                                   with ease.
            df_cluster = cluster_groups_copy.pop(0)
            wordcloud_image = cluster_to_image(df_cluster, **kwargs)
            ax = axes[r][c]
            ax.imshow(wordcloud_image,
            interpolation="bilinear")
            ax.set_title(f"Cluster {df_cluster.Cluster.iloc[0]}")
            ax.set_xticks([])
            ax.set_yticks([])

plot_wordcloud_grid(cluster_groups)
plt.show()
```

Plots the word clouds for each cluster in cluster_groups. The word clouds are plotted in a num_rows by num_columns grid.

Our 15 skill clusters show a diverse collection of topics. Some of the clusters are highly technical. For instance, cluster 7 fixates on external data science libraries such as scikit-learn, Pandas, NumPy, Matplotlib, and SciPy. The scikit-learn library clearly

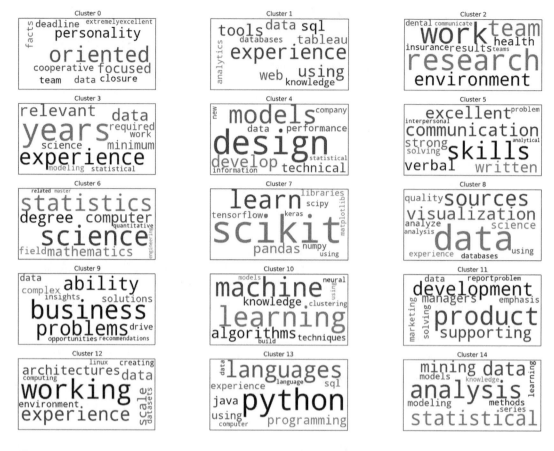

Figure 17.9   15 word clouds visualized across 15 subplots. Each word cloud corresponds to one of 15 clusters. The subplot titles correspond to cluster IDs. Some clusters, like cluster 7, describe technical skills; others, like cluster 0, are less technical.

dominates. Most of these libraries appear in our resume and have been discussed in this book. Let's print a sample of bullets from cluster 7 and confirm their focus on data science libraries.

Listing 17.36   Printing sample bullets from cluster 7

```
np.random.seed(1)
print_cluster_sample(7)

Experience using one or more of the following software packages:
scikit-learn, numpy, pandas, jupyter, matplotlib, scipy, nltk, spacy, keras,
tensorflow
Using one or more of the following software packages: scikit-learn, numpy,
pandas, jupyter, matplotlib, scipy, nltk, spacy, keras, tensorflow
Experience with machine learning libraries and platforms, like Scikit-learn
and Tensorflow
```

```
Proficiency in incorporating the use of external proprietary and open-source
libraries such as, but not limited to, Pandas, Scikit- learn, Matplotlib,
Seaborn, GDAL, GeoPandas, and ArcPy
Experience using ML libraries, such as scikit-learn, caret, mlr, mllib
```

Meanwhile, other clusters, like cluster 0, focus on nontechnical skills. These soft skills, covering business acumen, focus, strategy, communication, and collaboration, are clearly missing from our resume. Thus, on average, the nontechnical clusters should have a lower resume similarity. This line of thought leads to an interesting possibility: perhaps we can separate the technical clusters and soft-skill clusters using text similarity. The separation would allow us to more systematically examine each skill type. Let's give this a shot! We'll start by computing the cosine similarity between each bullet in total_bullets and our resume.

> **NOTE** Why utilize just the resume rather than the combined resume and table of contents sorted in the existing_skills variable? Well, our end goal is to determine which skill clusters are missing from the resume. The direct similarity between the resume and each cluster could be useful in that regard. If the similarity is low, then clustered skills are not appropriately represented in the resume's text.

Listing 17.37 Computing similarities between the bullets and our resume

```
def compute_bullet_similarity(bullet_texts):     ◁───────────────────────────────
    bullet_vectorizer = TfidfVectorizer(stop_words='english')
    matrix = bullet_vectorizer.fit_transform(bullet_texts + [resume])
    matrix = matrix.toarray()                   Computes the cosine similarities between the
    return matrix[:-1] @ matrix[-1]             inputted bullet_texts and the resume variable

bullet_cosine_similarities = compute_bullet_similarity(total_bullets)
```

Our bullet_cosine_similarities array contains the text similarities across all clustered bullets. For any given cluster, we can combine these cosine similarities into a score by taking their mean. According to our hypothesis, a technical cluster should have a higher mean similarity than a soft-skill similarity cluster. Let's confirm if this is the case for the technical cluster 7 and the soft-skill cluster 0.

Listing 17.38 Comparing mean resume similarities

```
def compute_mean_similarity(df_cluster):
    indices = df_cluster.Index.values
    return bullet_cosine_similarities[indices].mean()

tech_mean = compute_mean_similarity(cluster_groups[7])
soft_mean =  compute_mean_similarity(cluster_groups[0])
print(f"Technical cluster 7 has a mean similarity of {tech_mean:.3f}")
print(f"Soft-skill cluster 3 has a mean similarity of {soft_mean:.3f}")

Technical cluster 7 has a mean similarity of 0.203
Soft-skill cluster 3 has a mean similarity of 0.002
```

The technical cluster is 100 times more proximate to our resume than the soft-skill cluster. It appears that we're on the right track! Let's compute the average similarity for all 15 clusters. Then we'll sort the clusters by their similarity score, in descending order. If our hypothesis is correct, technical clusters will appear first in the sorted results. We'll be able to confirm by replotting the word cloud subplot grid. Listing 17.39 carries out the sorting and visualizes the sorted clusters (figure 17.10).

Figure 17.10   15 word clouds visualized across 15 subplots. Each word cloud corresponds to one of 15 clusters. The clusters are sorted by average resume similarity. The first two rows in the subplot grid correspond to more technical clusters.

NOTE   We are about to sort the clusters by technical relevance. This isn't necessarily required to complete the case study—it's possible to examine each cluster individually, in unsorted order. However, by reordering the clusters, we can extract insights at a faster rate. Thus, sorting is a preferable way of simplifying our workflow.

Listing 17.39　Sorting subplots by resume similarity

```
def sort_cluster_groups(cluster_groups):
    mean_similarities = [compute_mean_similarity(df_cluster)
                         for df_cluster in cluster_groups]

    sorted_indices = sorted(range(len(cluster_groups)),
                            key=lambda i: mean_similarities[i],
                            reverse=True)
    return [cluster_groups[i] for i in sorted_indices]

sorted_cluster_groups = sort_cluster_groups(cluster_groups)
plot_wordcloud_grid(sorted_cluster_groups)
plt.show()
```

Sorts the inputted cluster_groups array by their mean cosine similarity to the resume

Our hypothesis was right! The first two rows in the updated subplot clearly correspond to technical skills. Furthermore, these technical skills are now conveniently sorted based on their similarity to our resume. This allows us to systematically rank the skills from most similar (and thus represented by our resume) to least similar (and thus likely to be missing from our resume).

17.3.2　*Investigating the technical skill clusters*

Let's turn our attention to the six technical-skill clusters in the first two rows of the subplot grid. Next, we replot their associated word clouds in a two-row-by-three-column grid (figure 17.11). This technically focused visualization will allow us to expand the size of the word cloud. Later, we return to the remaining soft-skill word clouds in figure 17.10.

Listing 17.40　Plotting just the first six technical clusters

```
plot_wordcloud_gri(sorted_cluster_groups[:6], num_rows=3, num_columns=2)
plt.show()
```

The first four technical-skill clusters in the grid plot are very informative. We'll now examine these clusters one by one, starting with the grid's upper-left quadrant. For brevity's sake, we rely solely on the word clouds; their contents should be sufficient to grasp the skills represented by each cluster. However, if you wish to dive deeper into any cluster, feel free to sample the cluster's bullet points.

The first four technical clusters can be described as follows:

- *Cluster 7 (row 0, column 0)*—This data science library cluster has already been discussed. Libraries such as scikit-learn, NumPy, SciPy, and Pandas have been covered in this book.

  The following two libraries have not been covered: TensorFlow and Keras. These are deep learning libraries used by AI practitioners to train complex, predictive models on high-powered hardware. The boundary between data science positions and AI positions is not always clear. Although deep learning

Figure 17.11   Six word clouds associated with six technical-skill clusters. They are sorted by average resume similarity. The first four word clouds are informative: they focus on data science libraries, statistical analysis, Python programming, and machine learning. The remaining two word clouds are vague and uninformative.

knowledge is not usually a prerequisite, sometimes it will help you get a job. With this in mind, if you wish to study these libraries in more detail, check out *Machine Learning with TensorFlow* by Nishant Shukla (Manning, 2018, www .manning.com/books/machine-learning-with-tensorflow) or *Deep Learning with Python, Second Edition,* by François Chollet (Manning, 2021, www.manning.com/ books/deep-learning-with-python-second-edition).

- *Cluster 14 (row 0, column 1)*—This cluster discusses statistical analysis, which is represented in our resume. Statistical methods were covered in case study 2 of this book.

- *Cluster 13 (row 1, column 0)*—This cluster focuses on programming language proficiency. Among the languages, Python clearly dominates. Given our experience with Python, why doesn't this programming cluster rank higher? Well, it turns out Python is not mentioned anywhere in our resume! Yes, we refer to plenty of Python libraries, implying our familiarity with the language, but the Python skills that we've honed over the course of this book are not explicitly referenced. Perhaps we should update our resume by mentioning our Python skills.

- *Cluster 10 (row 1, column 2)*—This cluster focuses on machine learning. The machine learning field encompasses a variety of data-driven prediction algorithms. Many of these algorithms are presented in the subsequent case study in this book; but until this case study has been completed, we cannot reference machine learning in our resume.

  As a side note, we should mention that clustering techniques are sometimes referred to as *unsupervised* machine learning algorithms. Thus, a reference to unsupervised techniques is permissible. But any reference to more general machine learning will give a false impression of our skills.

The final two technical-skill clusters are vague and uninformative. They mention numerous unrelated tools and analysis techniques. Listing 17.41 samples bullets from these clusters (8 and 1) to confirm a lack of pattern.

NOTE Both clusters mention databases. Database usage is a useful skill to have but not a major topic in either cluster. Later in this section, we encounter a database cluster, which arises when we increase the value of *K*.

Listing 17.41 Printing sample bullets from clusters 8 and 1

```
np.random.seed(1)
for cluster_id in [8, 1]:
    print(f'\nCluster {cluster_id}:')
    print_cluster_sample(cluster_id)
```

```
Cluster 8:
Use data to inform and label customer outcomes and processes
Perform exploratory data analysis for quality control and improved
understanding
Champion a data-driven culture and help develop best-in-class data science
capabilities
Work with data engineers to plan, implement, and automate integration of
external data sources across a variety of architectures, including local
databases, web APIs, CRM systems, etc
Design, implement, and maintain a cutting-edge cloud-based
data-infrastructure for large data-sets

Cluster 1:
Have good knowledge on Project management tools JIRA, Redmine, and Bugzilla
Using common cloud computing platforms including AWS and GCP in addition to
their respective utilities for managing and manipulating large data sources,
model, development, and deployment
Experience in project deployment using Heroku/Jenkins and using web Services
like Amazon Web Services (AWS)
Expert level data analytics experience with T-SQL and Tableau
Experience reviewing and assessing military ground technologies
```

We've finished our analysis of the technical-skill clusters. Four of these clusters were relevant, and two were not. Now, let's turn our attention to the remaining soft-skill clusters. We want to see if any relevant soft-skill clusters are present in the data.

17.3.3 Investigating the soft-skill clusters

We start by visualizing the remaining nine soft-skill clusters in a three-row-by-three-column grid (figure 17.12).

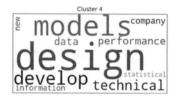

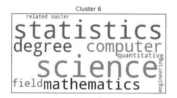
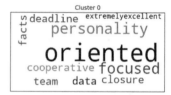

Figure 17.12   Nine word clouds associated with nine soft-skill clusters. They are sorted by average resume similarity. Most of the clusters are vague and uninformative, but the communication skills clusters in the first row are worth noting.

Listing 17.42   Plotting the remaining nine soft-skill clusters

```
plot_wordcloud_grid(sorted_cluster_groups[:6], num_rows=3, num_columns=3)
plt.show()
```

The remaining clusters appear much more ambiguous than the first four technical clusters. They are harder to interpret. For example, cluster 2 (row 2, column 0) uses vague terms such as *work, team, research,* and *environment.* Cluster 12 (row 1, column 0)

is equally enigmatic, composed of terms such as *environment, working,* and *experience.* Furthermore, the output is made more complicated by clusters that do not represent true skills! For instance, cluster 3 (row 0, column 0) is composed not of skills but of temporal experience: it consists of bullets requiring a minimum number of years working in industry. Similarly, cluster 6 (row 2, column 1) is not composed of skills; it represents educational constraints, requiring a quantitative degree to land an interview. We were slightly wrong in our assumptions—not all bullets represent true skills. We can confirm our error by sampling bullet points from clusters 6 and 3.

Listing 17.43 Printing sample bullets from clusters 6 and 3

```
np.random.seed(1)
for cluster_id in [6, 3]:
    print(f'\nCluster {cluster_id}:')
    print_cluster_sample(cluster_id)


Cluster 6:
MS in a quantitative research discipline (e.g., Artificial Intelligence,
Computer Science, Machine Learning, Statistics, Applied Math, Operations
Research)
Master's degree in data science, applied mathematics, or bioinformatics
preferred.
PhD degree preferred
Ph.D. in a quantitative discipline (e.g., statistics, computer science,
economics, mathematics, physics, electrical engineering, industrial
engineering or other STEM fields)
7+ years of experience manipulating data sets and building statistical
models, has advanced education in Statistics, Mathematics, Computer Science
or another quantitative field, and is familiar with the following
    software/tools:

Cluster 3:
Minimum 6 years relevant work experience (if Bachelor's degree) or minimum 3
years relevant work experience (if Master's degree) with a proven track
record in driving value in a commercial setting using data science skills.
Minimum five (5) years of experience manipulating data sets and building
statistical models, and familiarity with:
5+ years of relevant work experience in data analysis or related field.
(e.g., as a statistician / data scientist / scientific researcher)
3+ years of statistical modeling experience
Data Science: 2 years (Required)
```

One of our soft-skill clusters is very easy to interpret: cluster 5 (row 0, column 1) focuses on interpersonal communication skills, both written and verbal. Good communication skills are crucial in a data science career. The insights we extract from complex data must be carefully communicated to all stakeholders. The stakeholders will then take consequential actions based on the persuasiveness of our argument. If we are unable to communicate our results, all our hard work will come to nothing.

Unfortunately, communication skills are not easy to learn. Simply reading a book is insufficient; practiced collaboration with other individuals is required. If you would like to broaden your communication abilities, you should consider interacting with other budding data scientists, either locally or remotely. Choose a data-driven project, and complete that project as part of a team. Then be sure to emphasize your honed communication skills in your resume.

17.3.4 *Exploring clusters at alternative values of K*

K-means clustering gave us decent results when we set *K* to 15. However, that parameter input was partially arbitrary since we couldn't determine a perfectly optimal *K*. The arbitrary nature of our insights is a bit troubling: perhaps we just got lucky, and a different *K* would have yielded no insights at all. Or maybe we've missed critical clusters by choosing *K* incorrectly. The issue we need to probe is cluster consistency. How many of our insight-driving clusters will remain if we modify *K*? To find out, we'll regenerate the clusters using alternative values of *K*. We begin by setting *K* to 25 and plotting the results in a five-row-by-five-column grid (figure 17.13). The subplots will be sorted based on cluster similarity to our resume.

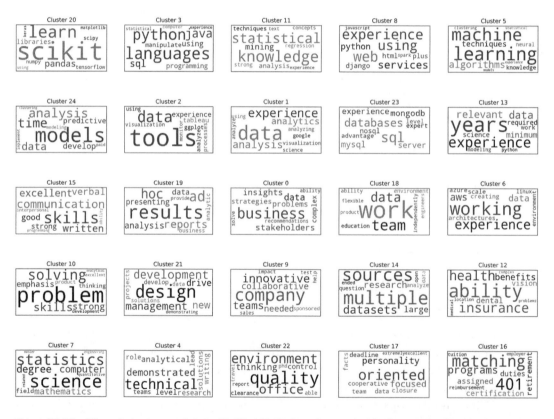

Figure 17.13   25 word clouds associated with 25 skill clusters. Our previously discussed skills remain present even after we've increased the value *K*. Additionally, we see new technical skills that are worth noting, including web service usage and familiarity with databases.

Listing 17.44 Visualizing 25 sorted clusters

```
np.random.seed(0)
cluster_groups = compute_cluster_groups(shrunk_norm_matrix, k=25)
sorted_cluster_groups = sort_cluster_groups(cluster_groups)
plot_wordcloud_grid(sorted_cluster_groups, num_rows=5, num_columns=5)
plt.show()
```

Most of the previously observed clusters remain in the updated output. These include data science library usage (row 0, column 0), statistical analysis (row 0, column 2), Python programming (row 0, column 1), machine learning (row 1, column 2), and communication skills (row 2, column 0). Additionally, we gain three insightful technical skill clusters, which appear among the first two rows of the grid:

- *Cluster 8 (row 0, column 4)*—This cluster focuses on web services. These are tools that propagate communication between a client and a remote server. In most industrial data science settings, data is stored remotely on a server and can be transferred using custom APIs. In Python, these API protocols are commonly coded using the Django framework. For budding data scientists, some familiarity with these tools is preferable but not necessarily required. To learn more about web services and API transfers, see *Amazon Web Services in Action* by Michael Wittig and Andreas Wittig (Manning, 2018, https://www.manning.com /books/amazon-web-services-in-action-second-edition) and *The Design of Web APIs* by Arnaud Lauret (Manning, 2019, https://www.manning.com/books/the-design-of-web-apis).

- *Cluster 23 (row 1, column 3)*—This cluster focuses on various types of databases. Large-scale structured data is commonly stored in relational databases and can be queried using Structured Query Language (SQL). However, not all databases are relational. Sometimes data is stored in alternative, unstructured databases, such as MongoDB. Data in an unstructured database can be queried using a NoSQL query language. Knowledge of the various database types can be quite useful in a data science career. If you would like to learn more about the subject, check out *Understanding Databases* (Manning, 2019, www.manning.com/ books/understanding-databases); and to learn more about MongoDB, see *MongoDB in Action, Second Edition* by Kyle Banker et al. (Manning, 2016, www.manning .com/books/mongodb-in-action-second-edition).

- *Cluster 2 (row 1, column 1)*—This cluster focuses on non-Python visualization tools, such as Tableau and ggplot. Tableau is paid software provided by Salesforce and is commonly used by businesses that can afford the Salesforce contract; you can read more about it in *Practical Tableau* by Ryan Sleeper ((O'Reilly, 2018, http://mng.bz/Xrdv). ggplot is a data-visualization package for the statistical programming language R. Generally, Python data scientists are not expected to know R; but if you would like to familiarize yourself with the subject, see *Practical Data Science with R, Second Edition* by Nina Zumel and

John Mount (Manning, 2019, www.manning.com/books/practical-data-science-with-r-second-edition).

Our plot also contains seven newly added clusters. These clusters contain mostly generic skills like problem solving (row 3, column 0) and teamwork (row 2, column 3). Also, at least one of the new skill clusters doesn't correspond to an actual skill (like the health insurance benefits cluster in row 3, column 4).

Increasing *K* from 15 to 25 retained all the previously observed insightful clusters and introduced several interesting new clusters. Will the stability of these clusters persist if we shift *K* to an intermediate value of 20? We find out next by plotting 20 sorted clusters in a four-row-by-five-column grid (figure 17.14).

Listing 17.45 Visualizing 20 sorted clusters

```
np.random.seed(0)
cluster_groups = compute_cluster_groups(shrunk_norm_matrix, k=20)
sorted_cluster_groups = sort_cluster_groups(cluster_groups)
plot_wordcloud_grid(sorted_cluster_groups, num_rows=4, num_columns=5)
plt.show()
```

Figure 17.14 20 word clouds associated with 20 skill clusters. Most of our previously discussed skills remain, but the statistical analysis cluster is now missing from the output.

Most of our observed insightful clusters remain at k=20, including data science library usage (row 0, column 0), Python programming (row 0, column 3), machine learning (row 1, column 0), communication skills (row 1, column 4), web services (row 0, column 1), and database usage (row 0, column 4). However, the non-Python visualization cluster is gone. More troublingly, the statistical analysis cluster observed at K values of 15 and 25 is missing.

> **NOTE** This statistical analysis cluster appears to have been replaced by a statistical algorithm cluster, which is positioned at row 0, column 2 of the grid. It is dominated by three terms: *algorithms*, *clustering*, and *regression*. Of course, by now, we're intimately familiar with clustering. However, regression techniques are missing from our resume because we haven't learned them yet. We will learn these techniques in case study 5 and can then add them to our resume.

A seemingly stable cluster has been eliminated. Unfortunately, such fluctuations are quite common. Text clustering is sensitive to parameter changes due to the complex nature of human language. Language topics can be interpreted in a multitude of ways, making it hard to find consistently perfect parameters. Clusters that appear under one set of parameters may disappear if these parameters are tweaked. If we cluster over just a single value of K, we risk missing out on useful insights. Thus, it's preferable to visualize results over a range of K values during text analysis. With this in mind, let's see what happens when we reduce K to 10 (figure 17.15).

Listing 17.46   Visualizing 10 sorted clusters

```
np.random.seed(0)
cluster_groups = compute_cluster_groups(shrunk_norm_matrix, k=10)
sorted_cluster_groups = sort_cluster_groups(cluster_groups)
plot_wordcloud_grid(sorted_cluster_groups, num_rows=5, num_columns=2)
plt.show()
```

The 10 visualized clusters are quite limited. Nonetheless, 4 of the 10 clusters contain critical skills we've observed previously: Python programming (row 0, column 0), machine learning (row 0, column 1), and communication skills (row 2, column 1). The statistical analysis cluster has also reappeared (row 1, column 0). Surprisingly, some of our skill clusters are versatile and appear even when the K value is radically adjusted. Despite some stochasticity in our clustering, a level of consistency remains. Thus, the insights we observe aren't just random outputs—they are tangible patterns that we've captured across complex, messy, real-world texts.

So far, our observations have been limited to the 60 most relevant job postings. However, as we've seen, there is some noise in that data subset. What will happen if we extend our analysis to the top 700 postings? Will our observations change or stay the same? Let's find out.

Figure 17.15   10 word clouds associated with 10 skill clusters. Four of our previously discussed skills remain, despite the low value of K.

17.3.5 Analyzing the 700 most relevant postings

We start by preparing `sorted_df_jobs[:700].Bullets` for clustering by doing the following:

1   Extract all the bullets while removing duplicates.
2   Vectorize the bullet texts.
3   Dimensionally reduce the vectorized texts, and normalize the resulting matrix.

Listing 17.47   Preparing `sorted_df_jobs[:700]` for clustering analysis

```
np.random.seed(0)
total_bullets_700 = set()
for bullets in sorted_df_jobs[:700].Bullets:
```

```
total_bullets_700.update([bullet.strip()
                                    for bullet in bullets])

total_bullets_700 = sorted(total_bullets_700)
vectorizer_700 = TfidfVectorizer(stop_words='english')
tfidf_matrix_700 = vectorizer_700.fit_transform(total_bullets_700)
shrunk_norm_matrix_700 = shrink_matrix(tfidf_matrix_700)
print(f"We've vectorized {shrunk_norm_matrix_700.shape[0]} bullets")

We've vectorized 10194 bullets
```

We've vectorized 10,194 bullet points. Now, we generate an elbow plot across the vectorized results. Based on previous observations, we don't expect the elbow plot to be particularly informative, but we create the plot to stay consistent with our previous analyses (figure 17.16).

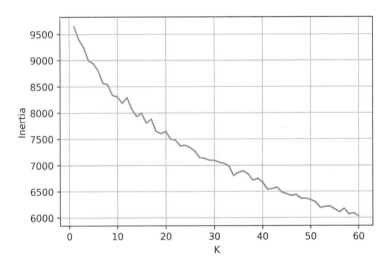

Figure 17.16 An elbow plot generated using bullets from the top 700 most relevant postings. The precise location of the elbow is difficult to determine.

Listing 17.48 Plotting an elbow curve for 10,194 bullets

```
np.random.seed(0)
generate_elbow_plot(shrunk_norm_matrix_700)
plt.show()
```

As expected, the precise location of the elbow is not clear in the plot. The elbow is spread out between a *K* of 10 and 25. We'll deal with ambiguity by arbitrarily setting *K* to 20. Let's generate and visualize 20 clusters; if necessary, we'll adjust *K* for comparative clustering (figure 17.17).

Figure 17.17   20 word clouds generated by clustering over 10,000 bullets. Despite the 10-fold increase in bullets, the observed skill clusters mostly remain the same.

WARNING   As we discussed in section 15, the K-means output can vary across computers for large matrices containing 10,000-by-100 elements. Your local clustering results may differ from the output shown here, but you should be able to draw conclusions similar to those presented in this book.

Listing 17.49   Visualizing 20 sorted clusters for 10,194 bullets

```
np.random.seed(0)
cluster_groups_700 = compute_cluster_groups(shrunk_norm_matrix_700, k=20,
                                            bullets=total_bullets_700)
bullet_cosine_similarities = compute_bullet_similarity(total_bullets_700)
sorted_cluster_groups_700 = sort_cluster_groups(cluster_groups_700)
plot_wordcloud_grid(sorted_cluster_groups_700, num_rows=4, num_columns=5,
                    vectorizer=vectorizer_700,
                    tfidf_matrix=tfidf_matrix_700)
```

Recomputes bullet_cosine_similarities for sorting purposes

We need to pass the updated TFIDF matrix and vectorizer into our plotting function.

Our clustering output looks very similar to what we've seen before. The key insightful clusters we observed at 60 postings remain, including data science library usage (row 0, column 0), statistical analysis (row 0, column 1), Python programming (row 0, column 4), machine learning (row 0, column 3), and communication skills (row 1, column 3). Some subtle changes are present, but for the most part, the output is the same.

> **NOTE** One interesting change is the appearance of a generalized visualization cluster (row 0, column 2). This cluster encompasses a variety of visualization tools, including Matplotlib. Additionally, the freely available JavaScript library D3.js is mentioned in the cluster's word cloud. The D3.js library is used by some data scientists to make interactive web visualizations. To learn more about the library, see *D3.js in Action, Second Edition* by Elijah Meeks (Manning, 2017, www.manning.com/books/d3js-in-action-second-edition).

Certain skills consistently appear in the job postings. These skills are not very sensitive to our selected relevance threshold, so we can elucidate them even if our threshold remains uncertain.

17.4 Conclusion

We're ready to update the draft of our resume. First and foremost, we should emphasize our Python skills. A single line saying that we're *proficient in Python* should be sufficient. Additionally, we want to assert our communication skills. How do we show that we're good communicators? It's tricky; simply stating that we can *clearly communicate complex results to different audiences* is not enough. Instead, we should describe a personal project in which we did the following:

- Collaborated with teammates on a difficult data problem
- Conveyed complex results, in oral or written form, to a nontechnical audience

> **NOTE** If you've experienced working on this type of project, you should definitely add it to your resume. Otherwise, you're encouraged to pursue this type of project voluntarily. The skills you'll gain will prove invaluable while also bettering your employment prospects.

Furthermore, before we complete our resume, we need to address our remaining skill deficiencies. Machine learning experience is crucial to a successful data science career. We haven't yet studied machine learning, but in the subsequent case study, we expand our machine learning skills. Then we'll be able to proudly describe our machine learning abilities in our resume.

Finally, it's worthwhile to demonstrate some experience with tools to fetch and store remote data. These tools include databases and hosted web services. Their use is beyond the scope of this book, but they can be learned through independent study. Database and web services experience isn't always required to get the job; nevertheless, some limited experience is always welcomed by potential employers.

Summary

- Text data should not be analyzed blindly. We should always sample and read some of the text before running any algorithms. This is especially true of HTML files, where tags can demarcate unique signals in the text. By rendering sampled job postings, we discovered that unique job skills are marked by bullet points in each HTML file. If we had blindly clustered the body of each file, our final results wouldn't have been as informative.

- Text clustering is hard. An ideal cluster count rarely exists because language is fluid, and so are boundaries between topics. But despite the uncertainty, certain topics consistently appear across multiple cluster counts. So, even if our elbow plot does not reveal the exact number of clusters, the situation is salvageable: sampling over multiple clustering parameters can reveal stable topics in the text.

- Choosing parameter values is not always easy. This issue extends well beyond mere clustering. When selecting our relevance cutoff, we were torn between two values: 60 and 700. Neither value seemed much superior to the other, so we tried both! In data science, some problems don't have an ideal threshold or parameter. However, we shouldn't give up and ignore such problems. On the contrary, we should experiment. Scientists learn by exploring outputs across a range of parameter inputs. As data scientists, we can gain invaluable insights by tweaking and adjusting our parameters.

Predicting future friendships from social network data

Problem statement

Welcome to FriendHook, Silicon Valley's hottest new startup. FriendHook is a social networking app for college undergrads. To join, an undergrad must scan their college ID to prove their affiliation. After approval, undergrads can create a FriendHook profile, which lists their dorm name and scholastic interests. Once a profile is created, an undergrad can send *friend requests* to other students at their college. A student who receives a friend request can either approve or reject it. When a friend request is approved, the pair of students are officially *FriendHook friends*. Using their new digital connection, FriendHook friends can share photographs, collaborate on coursework, and keep each other up to date on the latest campus gossip.

The FriendHook app is a hit. It's utilized on hundreds of college campuses worldwide. The user base is growing, and so is the company. You are Friend-Hook's first data science hire! Your first challenging task will be to work on FriendHook's friend recommendation algorithm.

Introducing the friend-of-a-friend recommendation algorithm

Sometimes FriendHook users have trouble finding their real-life friends on the digital app. To facilitate more connections, the engineering team has implemented a simple friend-recommendation engine. Once a week, all users receive an email recommending a new friend who is not yet in their network. The users can ignore the email, or they can send a friend request. That request is then either accepted or rejected/ignored.

Currently, the recommendation engine follows a simple algorithm called the *friend-of-a-friend recommendation algorithm*. The algorithm works like this. Suppose we want to recommend a new friend for student A. We pick a random student B who is already friends with student A. We then pick a random student C who is friends with student B but not student A. Student C is then selected as the recommended friend for student A, as shown in figure CS5.1.

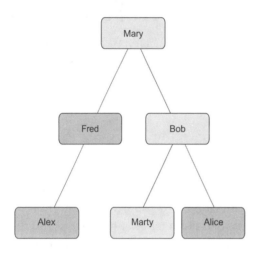

Figure CS5.1   The friend-of-a-friend recommendation algorithm in action. Mary has two friends: Fred and Bob. One of these friends (Bob) is randomly selected. Bob has two additional friends: Marty and Alice. Neither Alice nor Marty are friends with Mary. A friend of a friend (Marty) is randomly selected. Mary receives an email suggesting that she should send a friend request to Marty.

Essentially, the algorithm assumes that a friend of your friend is also likely to be your friend. This assumption is reasonable but also a bit simplistic. How well does this assumption hold? Nobody knows! However, as the company's first data scientist, it's your job to find out. You have been tasked with building a model that predicts student behavior in response to the recommendation algorithm.

Predicting user behavior

The friend-of-a-friend recommendation engine can elicit three types of behaviors:

- A user reads the emailed friend recommendation and either rejects or ignores that recommendation.
- A user sends a friend request based on the recommendation. That request is rejected or ignored.
- A user sends a friend request based on the recommendation. The friend request is accepted, and a new FriendHook connection is established.

Is it possible to predict these three behaviors? The FriendHook CTO would like you to find out. The CTO has provided you with FriendHook data from a randomly selected university. That data covers all FriendHook users at the university, including observed behaviors for all users in response to the weekly friend recommendations. The data also includes profile information for each user covering things like student major and residential dormitory name. This personal profile information has been encrypted to protect each user's privacy (more on that later). Finally, the data includes a network of existing FriendHook connections at the university, compiled right before friendship recommendations were emailed.

Your task is to build a model that predicts user behavior based on user profiles and social network data. The model must generalize to other colleges and universities. This generalizability is very important—a model that cannot be utilized at other colleges is worthless to the product team. Consider, for example, a model that accurately predicts behavior in one or two of the dorms at the sampled university. In other words, it requires specific dorm names to make accurate predictions. Such a model is not useful because other universities will have different dormitory names. Ideally, the model should generalize to all dormitories across all universities worldwide.

Once you've built the generalized model, you should explore its inner workings. Your goal is to gain insights into how university life facilitates new FriendHook connections.

The project goals are ambitious but also very doable. You can complete them by carrying out the following tasks:

1 Load the three datasets pertaining to user behavior, user profiles, and the user friendship network. Explore each dataset, and clean it as required.

2 Build and evaluate a model that predicts user behavior based on user profiles and established friendship connections. You can optionally split this task into two subtasks: build a model using just the friendship network, and then add the profile information and test whether this improves the model's performance.

3 Determine whether the model generalizes well to other universities.

4 Explore the inner workings of the model to gain better insights into student behavior.

Dataset description

Our data contains three files stored in a friendhook directory. These files are CSV tables and are named Profiles.csv, Observations.csv, and Friendships.csv. Let's discuss each table individually.

The Profiles table

Profiles.csv contains profile information for all the students at the chosen university. This information is distributed across six columns: Profile_ID, Sex, Relationship_ Status, Major, Dorm, and Year. Maintaining student privacy is very important to the FriendHook team, so all the profile information has been carefully encrypted.

FriendHook's encryption algorithm takes in descriptive text and returns a unique, scrambled 12-character code known as a *hash code*. Suppose, for example, that a student lists their major as physics. The word *physics* is then scrambled and replaced with a hash code such as *b90a1221d2bc*. If another student lists their major as art history, a different hash code is returned (for example, *983a9b1dc2ef*). In this manner, we can check whether two students share the same major without necessarily knowing the identity of that major. All six profile columns have been encrypted as a precautionary measure. Let's discuss the separate columns in detail:

- Profile_ID—A unique identifier used to track each student. The identifier can be linked to the user behaviors in the Observations table. It can also be linked to FriendHook connections in the Friendships table.

- Sex—This optional field describes the sex of a student as Male or Female. Students who don't wish to specify a gender can leave the Sex field blank. Blank inputs are stored as empty values in the table.

- Relationship_Status—This optional field specifies the relationship status of the student. Each student has three relationship categories to choose from: Single, In a Relationship, or It's Complicated. All students have a fourth option of leaving this field blank. Blank inputs are stored as empty values in the table.

- Major—The chosen area of study for the student, such as physics, history, economics, etc. This field is required to activate a FriendHook account. Students who have not yet picked their major can select Undecided from among the options.

- Dorm—The name of the dormitory where the student resides. This field is required to activate a FriendHook account. Students who reside in off-campus housing can select Off-Campus Housing from among the options.

- Year—The undergraduate student's year. This field must be set to one of four options: Freshman, Sophomore, Junior, or Senior.

The Observations table

Observations.csv contains the observed user behavior in response to the emailed friend recommendation. It includes the following five fields:

- Profile_ID—The ID of the user who received a friend recommendation. The ID corresponds to the profile ID in the Profiles table.

- Selected_Friend—An existing friend of the user in the Profile_ID column.

- Selected_Friend_of_Friend—A randomly chosen friend of Selected_Friend who is not yet a friend of Profile_ID. This random friend of a friend is emailed as a friend recommendation for the user.

- Friend_Request_Sent—A Boolean column that is True if a user sends a friend request to the suggested friend of a friend or False otherwise.

- Friend_Request_Accepted—A Boolean column that is True only if a user sends a friend request and that request is accepted.

This table stores all the observed user behaviors in response to the weekly recommendation email. Our goal is to predict the Boolean outputs of the final two table columns based on the profile and social networking data.

The Friendships table

Friendships.csv contains the FriendHook friendship network corresponding to the selected university. This network was used as input into the friend-of-a-friend recommendation algorithm. The Friendships table has just two columns: Friend A and Friend B. These columns contain profile IDs that map to the Profile_ID columns of the Profiles and Observations tables. Each row corresponds to a pair of FriendHook friends. For instance, the first row contains IDs b8bc075e54b9 and 49194b3720b6. From these IDs, we can infer that the associated students have an established FriendHook connection. Using the IDs, we can look up the profile of each student. The profiles then allow us to explore whether the friends share the same major or reside together in the same dorm.

Overview

To address the problem at hand, we need to know how to do the following:

- Analyze network data using Python
- Discover friendship clusters in social networks
- Train and evaluate supervised machine learning models
- Probe the inner workings of trained models to draw insights from our data

An introduction to graph theory and network analysis

This section covers

- Representing diverse datasets as networks
- Network analysis with the NetworkX library
- Optimizing travel paths in a network

The study of connections can potentially yield billions of dollars. In the 1990s, two graduate students analyzed the properties of interconnected web pages. Their insights led them to found Google. In the early 2000s, an undergraduate began to digitally track connections between people. He went on to launch Facebook. Connection analysis can lead to untold riches, but it can also save countless lives. Tracking the connections between proteins in cancer cells can generate drug targets that will wipe out that cancer. Analyzing connections between suspected terrorists can uncover and prevent devious plots. These seemingly disparate scenarios have one thing in common: they can be studied using a branch of mathematics called *network theory* by some and *graph theory* by others.

Network theory is the study of connections between objects. These objects can be anything: people connected by relationships, web pages connected by web links, or cities connected by roads. A collection of objects and their dispersed connections is called either a *network* or a *graph*, depending on whom you ask. Engineers prefer to use the term *network*, while mathematicians prefer *graph*. For our intents and purposes, we'll use the two terms interchangeably. Graphs are simple abstractions that capture the complexity of our entangled, interconnected world. Properties of graphs remain surprisingly consistent across systems in society and nature. Graph theory is a framework for mathematically tracking these consistencies. It combines ideas from diverse branches of mathematics, including probability theory and matrix analysis. These ideas can be used to gain useful real-world insights ranging from search engine page rankings to social circle clustering, so some knowledge of graph theory is indispensable to doing good data science.

In the next two sections, we learn the fundamentals of graph theory by building on previously studied data science concepts and libraries. We start slowly by addressing basic problems while exploring graphs of web page links and roads. Later, in section 19, we utilize more advanced techniques to detect clusters of friends in social graphs. However, we begin with a much simpler data science task of ranking websites by popularity.

18.1 Using basic graph theory to rank websites by popularity

There are many data science websites on the internet. Some sites are more popular than others. Suppose you wish to estimate the most popular data science website using data that is publicly available. This precludes privately tracked traffic data. What should you do? Network theory offers us a simple way of ranking websites based on their public links. To see how, let's build a simple network composed of two data science websites: a NumPy tutorial and a SciPy tutorial. In graph theory, these websites are referred to as the *nodes* in the graph. Nodes are network points that can form connections with each other; these connections are called *edges*. Our two website nodes will form an edge if one site links to the other or vice versa.

We begin by storing our two nodes in a two-element list. These elements equal `'NumPy'` and `'SciPy'`, respectively.

Listing 18.1   Defining a node list

```
nodes = ['NumPy', 'SciPy']
```

Suppose the SciPy website is discussing NumPy dependencies. This discussion includes a web link to the NumPy page. Clicking that link will take the reader from the website represented by `nodes[1]` to the website represented by `nodes[0]`. We treat this connection as an edge that goes from index 1 to index 0, as shown in figure 18.1. The edge can be expressed as the tuple `(1, 0)`. Here, we form an edge by storing `(1, 0)` in an `edges` list.

Listing 18.2   Defining an edge list

```
edges = [(1, 0)]
```

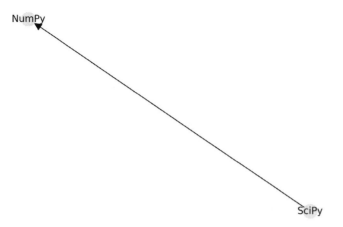

Figure 18.1 Two websites, NumPy and SciPy, are represented as circular nodes. A directed edge points from SciPy to NumPy, indicating a directed link between the sites. If NumPy and SciPy are stored as node indices 0 and 1, we can represent the edge as tuple `(1, 0)`. Later in this section, we learn how to generate the network diagram in this figure.

Our single edge `(1, 0)` represents a link that directs a user from `nodes[1]` to `nodes[0]`. This edge has a specific direction and is referred to as a *directed edge*. Graphs containing directed edges are referred to as *directed graphs*. In a directed graph, edge `(i, j)` is treated differently from edge `(j, i)`. The presence of `(i, j)` in an `edges` list does not imply the presence of `(j, i)`. For instance, in our network, the NumPy page does not yet link to the SciPy page, so edge tuple `(0, 1)` is not present in the `edges` list.

Given our directed `edges` list, we can easily check if a web page at index `i` links to a web page at index `j`. That connection exists if `(i, j) in edges` equals `True`. Thus, we can define a one-line `edge_exists` function, which checks for edges between indices `i` and `j`.

Listing 18.3 Checking for the existence of an edge

```
def edge_exists(i, j): return (i, j) in edges

assert edge_exists(1, 0)
assert not edge_exists(0, 1)
```

Our `edge_exists` function works, but it's not efficient. The function must traverse a list to check the presence of an edge. This traversal is not an issue for an edge list of size 1. However, if we were to increase our network size to 1,000 web pages, then our edge list size might increase to as many as 1 million edges. Traversing a million-edge list is not computationally justifiable. We need an alternative solution.

One alternative approach is to store the presence or absence of each edge (i, j) in the *i*th row and *j*th column of a table. Essentially, we can construct a table t in which t[i][j] = edge_exists(i, j), so edge lookup will become instantaneous. Furthermore, we can represent this table as a 2D binary array if we store not edge_exists(i, j) as 0 and edge_exists(i, j) as 1, so we can represent our graph as a binary matrix M, where M[i][j] = 1 if an edge exists between node i and node j. This matrix representation of a network is known as an *adjacency matrix*. We now compute and print an adjacency matrix for our two-node single-edge directed graph. Initially, that matrix contains just 0s. Then we iterate each edge (i, j) in edges and set adjacency_matrix[i][j] to 1.

Listing 18.4 Tracking nodes and edges using a matrix

```
import numpy as np
adjacency_matrix = np.zeros((len(nodes), len(nodes)))
for i, j in edges:
    adjacency_matrix[i][j] = 1

assert adjacency_matrix[1][0]
assert not adjacency_matrix[0][1]

print(adjacency_matrix)
```

```
[[0. 0.]
 [1. 0.]]
```

Our matrix printout permits us to view the edges present in the network. Additionally, we can observe potential edges that are missing from the network. For instance, we can clearly see an edge from Node 1 to Node 0. Meanwhile, possible edges (0, 0), (0, 1), and (1, 1) are not present in the graph. Neither is there a link going from Node 0 to Node 0. The NumPy page does not link to itself, although theoretically, it could! We can imagine a poorly designed web page in which a hyperlink points to itself—the link would be useless since clicking it would take you right back where you started, but this type of self-linkage is possible. In graph theory, such self-referential edges are called *self-loops* or *buckles*. In the next section, we encounter an algorithm that is improved if we incorporate self-loops. However, for the time being, we limit our analysis to edges between different pairs of nodes.

Let's add the missing edge from Node 0 to Node 1. This will imply that the NumPy page now links to the SciPy page.

Listing 18.5 Adding an edge to the adjacency matrix

```
adjacency_matrix[0][1] = 1
print(adjacency_matrix)
```

```
[[0. 1.]
 [1. 0.]]
```

Suppose we wish to expand our website network by adding two more data science sites that discuss Pandas and Matplotlib. Adding them will increase our node count from two to four, so we need to expand the adjacency matrix dimensions from two-by-two to four-by-four. During that expansion, we'll also maintain all existing relationships between Node 0 and Node 1. Unfortunately, in NumPy, it's hard to resize a matrix while maintaining all existing matrix values—NumPy is not designed to easily handle growing arrays whose shape is constantly expanding. This conflicts with the expanding nature of the internet, where new websites are constantly being added. Therefore, NumPy is not the best tool for analyzing expanding networks. What should we do?

> **NOTE** NumPy is inconvenient for tracking newly added nodes and edges. However, as we previously discussed, it is indispensable for efficiently executing matrix multiplication. In the next section, we multiply the adjacency matrix to analyze social graphs. Thus, our use of NumPy will prove essential for advanced network analysis. But for the time being, we rely on an alternative Python library to more easily construct our networks.

We need to switch to a different Python library. NetworkX is an external library that allows for easy network modification. It also provides additional useful features, including network visualization. Let's proceed with our website analysis using NetworkX.

18.1.1 *Analyzing web networks using NetworkX*

We begin by installing NetworkX. Then we import `networkx` as `nx`, per the common NetworkX usage convention.

> **NOTE** Call `pip install networkx` from the command line terminal to install the NetworkX library.

Listing 18.6 Importing the NetworkX library

```
import networkx as nx
```

Now we will utilize `nx` to generate a directed graph. In NetworkX, directed graphs are tracked using the `nx.DiGraph` class. Calling `nx.DiGraph()` initializes a new directed graph object containing zero nodes and zero edges. The following code initializes that directed graph; per NetworkX convention, we refer to the initialized graph as `G`.

Listing 18.7 Initializing a directed graph object

```
G = nx.DiGraph()
```

Let's slowly expand the directed graph. To start, we add a single node. Nodes can be added to a NetworkX graph object using the `add_node` method. Calling `G.add_node(0)` creates a single node whose adjacency matrix index is 0. We can view this adjacency matrix by running `nx.to_numpy_array(G)`.

WARNING The add_node method always expands the graph's adjacency matrix by a single node. This expansion happens regardless of the method input. Hence, G.add_node(1000) also creates a node whose adjacency matrix index is 0. However, that node will also be tracked using a secondary index of 1000, which of course can lead to confusion. It's a good practice to ensure that numeric inputs into add_node correspond to added adjacency matrix indices.

Listing 18.8 Adding a single node to a graph object

```
G.add_node(0)
print(nx.to_numpy_array(G))

[[0.]]
```

Our single node is associated with a NumPy web page. We can explicitly record this association by executing G.nodes[0]['webpage'] = 'NumPy'. The G.nodes datatype is a special class intended to track all the nodes in G. It is structured like a list. Running G[i] returns a dictionary of attributes associated with the node at i. These attributes are intended to help us track the identity of the node. In our case, we wish to assign a web page to the node, so we map a value to G.nodes[i]['webpage'].

The following code iterates across G.nodes and prints the attribute dictionary at G.nodes[i]. Our initial output represents a single node whose attribute dictionary is empty: we assign a web page to that node and print its dictionary again.

Listing 18.9 Adding an attribute to an existing node

```
def print_node_attributes():
    for i in G.nodes:
        print(f"The attribute dictionary at node {i} is {G.nodes[i]}")

print_node_attributes()
G.nodes[0]['webpage'] = 'NumPy'
print("\nWe've added a webpage to node 0")
print_node_attributes()

The attribute dictionary at node 0 is {}

We've added a webpage to node 0
The attribute dictionary at node 0 is {'webpage': 'NumPy'}
```

We can assign attributes directly while inserting a node into the graph. We just need to pass attribute=some_value into the G.add_node method. For instance, we are about to insert a node with an index of 1, which is associated with a SciPy web page. Executing G.add_node(1, webpage='SciPy') adds the node and its attribute.

Listing 18.10 Adding a node with an attribute

```
G.add_node(1, webpage='SciPy')
print_node_attributes()
```

```
The attribute dictionary at node 0 is {'webpage': 'NumPy'}
The attribute dictionary at node 1 is {'webpage': 'SciPy'}
```

Note that we can output all the nodes together with their attributes simply by running G.nodes(data=True).

Listing 18.11 Outputting nodes together with their attributes

```
print(G.nodes(data=True))

[(0, {'webpage': 'NumPy'}), (1, {'webpage': 'SciPy'})]
```

Now, let's add a web link from Node 1 (SciPy) to Node 0 (NumPy). Given a directed graph, we can insert an edge from i to j by running G.add_edge(i, j).

Listing 18.12 Adding a single edge to a graph object

```
G.add_edge(1, 0)
print(nx.to_numpy_array(G))

[[0. 0.]
 [1. 0.]]
```

From the printed adjacency matrix, we can observe an edge going from Node 1 to Node 0. Unfortunately, our matrix printouts will grow cumbersome as other nodes are added. Tracking 1s and 0s in a 2D table is not the most intuitive way to display a network. What if, instead, we plotted the network directly? Our two nodes could be plotted as two points in 2D space, and our single edge could be plotted as a line segment connecting these points. Such a plot can easily be generated using Matplotlib. That is why our G object has a built-in draw() method for plotting the graph with the Matplotlib library. We call G.draw() to visualize our graph (figure 18.2).

Listing 18.13 Plotting a graph object

```
import matplotlib.pyplot as plt
np.random.seed(0)   ◄────
nx.draw(G)
plt.show()   ◄──────┐
```

The locations of the nodes are determined using a randomized algorithm. We seed that randomization to ensure consistent visualization.

Per Matplotlib requirements, we must call plt.show() to display the plotted results.

Our plotted graph could clearly use some improvement. First, we need to make our arrow bigger. This can be accomplished using the arrowsize parameter: passing arrowsize=20 into G.draw will double the length and width of the plotted arrow. We should also add labels to the nodes; labels can be plotted with the labels parameter, which takes as input a dictionary mapping between node IDs and the intended labels. Listing 18.14 generates the mapping by running {i: G.nodes[i]['webpage']

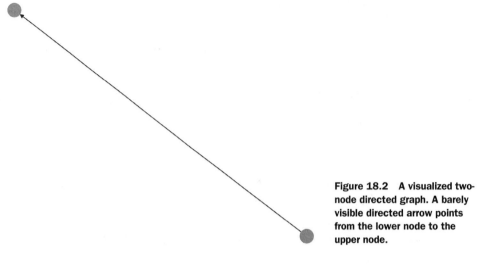

Figure 18.2 A visualized two-node directed graph. A barely visible directed arrow points from the lower node to the upper node.

for i in G.nodes} and then replots our network with the node labels and larger arrow (figure 18.3).

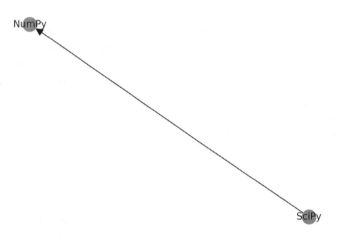

Figure 18.3 A visualized two-node directed graph. A directed arrow points from the lower node to the upper node. Both nodes are labeled, but the labels are hard to see.

NOTE Additionally, we can modify the node size by passing a node_size parameter into nx.draw. But for the time being, our nodes are appropriately sized at their default value of 300.

Listing 18.14 Tweaking the graph visualization

```
np.random.seed(0)
labels = {i: G.nodes[i]['webpage'] for i in G.nodes}
nx.draw(G, labels=labels, arrowsize=20)
plt.show()
```

The arrow is now bigger, and the node labels are partially visible. Unfortunately, these labels are obscured by the dark node color. We can make the labels more visible by changing the node color to something lighter, like cyan. We adjust the node color by passing `node_color="cyan"` into `G.draw` (figure 18.4).

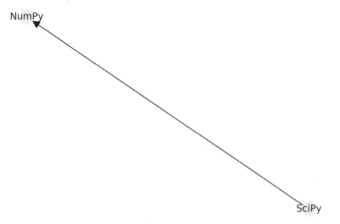

Figure 18.4 **A visualized two-node directed graph. Both nodes are labeled. The color of the nodes has been adjusted so that the labels are clearly visible.**

Listing 18.15 **Altering the node color**

```
np.random.seed(0)
nx.draw(G, labels=labels, node_color="cyan", arrowsize=20)
plt.show()
```

In our latest plot, the labels are much more visible. We see the directed link from SciPy to NumPy. Now, let's add a reverse web link from NumPy to SciPy (figure 18.5).

Listing 18.16 **Adding a back-link between web pages**

```
np.random.seed(0)
G.add_edge(0, 1)
nx.draw(G, labels=labels, node_color="cyan", arrowsize=20)
plt.show()
```

We are now ready to expand our network by adding two more web pages: Pandas and Matplotlib. These web pages will correspond to nodes with IDs 2 and 3, respectively. We can insert the two nodes individually by calling `G.add_node(2)` and then `G.add_node(3)`. Alternatively, we can insert the nodes simultaneously using the `G.add_nodes_from` method, which takes a list of nodes to be inserted into a graph. Thus, running `G.add_nodes_from([2, 3])` will add the proper node IDs to our network. However, these new nodes will lack any web page attribute assignments. Fortunately, the

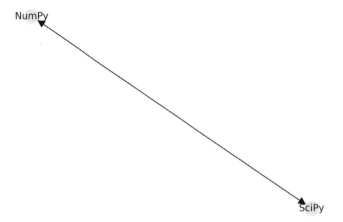

Figure 18.5 **A visualized two-node directed graph. Pointed arrows are present at both ends of the edge between the nodes, indicating that the edge is bidirectional.**

`G.add_nodes_from` method allows us to pass attribute values along with the node IDs. We simply need to pass `[(2, attributes_2), [(3, attributes_3)]` into the method. Essentially, we must pass a list of tuples corresponding to both node IDs and attributes. The attributes are stored in a dictionary that maps attribute names with attribute values. For instance, the Pandas `attributes_2` dictionary will equal `{'webpage': 'Pandas')`. Let's insert these nodes, together with their attributes, and output `G.nodes(data=True)` to verify that the new nodes are present.

Listing 18.17 **Adding multiple nodes to a graph object**

```
webpages = ['Pandas', 'Matplotlib']
new_nodes = [(i, {'webpage': webpage})
             for i, webpage in enumerate(webpages, 2)]
G.add_nodes_from(new_nodes)

print(f"We've added these nodes to our graph:\n{new_nodes}")
print('\nOur updated list of nodes is:')
print(G.nodes(data=True))

We've added these nodes to our graph:
[(2, {'webpage': 'Pandas'}), (3, {'webpage': 'Matplotlib'})]

Our updated list of nodes is:
[(0, {'webpage': 'NumPy'}), (1, {'webpage': 'SciPy'}), (2, {'webpage':
    'Pandas'}), (3, {'webpage': 'Matplotlib'})]
```

We've added two more nodes. Let's visualize the updated graph (figure 18.6)

Matplotlib

NumPy

Pandas

SciPy

Figure 18.6   A visualized web-page directed graph. The Pandas and Matplotlib pages remain disconnected.

Listing 18.18   Plotting the updated four-node graph

```
np.random.seed(0)
labels = {i: G.nodes[i]['webpage'] for i in G.nodes}
nx.draw(G, labels=labels, node_color="cyan", arrowsize=20)
plt.show()
```

Our current web link network is disconnected. We add two more web links: a link from Matplotlib (Node 3) to NumPy (Node 0), and a link from NumPy (Node 0) to Pandas (Node 2). These links can be added by calling G.add_edge(3, 0) and then G.add_edge(0, 2). Alternatively, we can add the edges simultaneously using the G.add_edges_from method: this method takes as input a list of edges, where each edge is a tuple of the form (i, j). Hence, running G.add_edges_from([(0, 2), (3, 0)]) should insert the two new edges into our graph. The following code inserts these edges and regenerates our plot (figure 18.7).

Listing 18.19   Adding multiple edges to a graph object

```
np.random.seed(1)
G.add_edges_from([(0, 2), (3, 0)])
nx.draw(G, labels=labels, node_color="cyan", arrowsize=20)
plt.show()
```

NOTE   In our graph visualization, the nodes have been spread apart to emphasize the connectivity of their respective edges. This effect was achieved using a technique known as a *force-directed layout* visualization. A force-directed layout is based on physics. The nodes are modeled as negatively charged particles that are repelled by one another, and the edges are modeled as springs connecting the particles. As the connected nodes move apart, the springs

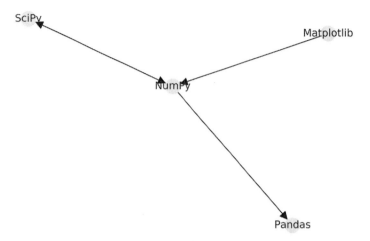

Figure 18.7   A visualized web page directed graph. Two inbound links point at the NumPy page. All the other pages have at most one inbound link.

begin to pull them back together. Modeling the physics equations in this system produces our graph visualization.

The NumPy web page appears in the center of our updated graph. Two web pages, SciPy and Matplotlib, have links that point to NumPy. All the other web pages have at most a single inbound link. More web content creators took the effort to reference the NumPy page than any other website: we can infer that NumPy is our most popular site since it has more inbound links than any other page. We've basically developed a simple metric for ranking websites on the internet. That metric equals the number of inbound edges pointing toward the site, also known as the *in-degree*. This is the opposite of the *out-degree*, which equals the number of edges pointing away from a site. By looking at our plotted graph, we can infer each website's in-degree automatically. However, we can also compute the in-degree directly from the graph's adjacency matrix. To demonstrate how, we first print our updated adjacency matrix.

Listing 18.20   Printing the updated adjacency matrix

```
adjacency_matrix = nx.to_numpy_array(G)
print(adjacency_matrix)

[[0. 1. 1. 0.]
 [1. 0. 0. 0.]
 [0. 0. 0. 0.]
 [1. 0. 0. 0.]]
```

As a reminder, the ith column in the matrix tracks the inbound edges of node i. The total number of inbound edges equals the number of ones in that column. Therefore, the sum of values in the column is equal to the node's in-degree. For instance, Column 0 of our matrix equals `[0, 1, 0, 1]`. The sum of these values reveals an in-degree of 2, corresponding to the NumPy page. In general, executing `adjacency_matrix.sum(axis=0)` returns a vector of in-degrees. That vector's largest element corresponds to the most popular page in our internet graph.

> **NOTE** Our simple ranking system assumes that all inbound links have equal weight, but this is not the case. An inbound link from a very popular website carries more weight since it drives more traffic to the site. In the next section, we present a more sophisticated ranking algorithm called PageRank that incorporates the popularity of traffic-directing websites.

Listing 18.21 Computing in-degrees using the adjacency matrix

```
in_degrees = adjacency_matrix.sum(axis=0)
for i, in_degree in enumerate(in_degrees):
    page = G.nodes[i]['webpage']
    print(f"{page} has an in-degree of {in_degree}")

top_page = G.nodes[in_degrees.argmax()]['webpage']
print(f"\n{top_page} is the most popular page.")

NumPy has an in-degree of 2.0
SciPy has an in-degree of 1.0
Pandas has an in-degree of 1.0
Matplotlib has an in-degree of 0.0

NumPy is the most popular page.
```

Alternatively, we can compute all in-degrees using the NetworkX `in_degree` method. Calling `G.in_degree(i)` returns the in-degree of node i, so we expect `G.in_degree(0)` to equal 2. Let's confirm.

Listing 18.22 Computing in-degrees using NetworkX

```
assert G.in_degree(0) == 2
```

In this code, we had to remember that `G.nodes[0]` corresponds to the NumPy page. Tracking the mapping between node IDs and page names can be slightly inconvenient, but we can bypass that inconvenience by assigning string IDs to individual nodes. For instance, given an empty graph G2, we insert our node IDs as strings by running `G2.add_nodes_from(['NumPy', 'SciPy', 'Matplotlib', 'Pandas'])`. Then calling `G2.in_degree('NumPy')` returns the in-degree of the NumPy page.

> **NOTE** Storing node IDs as strings makes it more convenient to access certain nodes in the graph. However, the price of that convenience is a lack of correspondence between node IDs and indices in the adjacency matrix. As we'll learn, the adjacency matrix is indispensable for certain network tasks, so it is usually good practice to store the node IDs as indices and not strings.

Listing 18.23 Using strings as node IDs in a graph

```
G2 = nx.DiGraph()
G2.add_nodes_from(['NumPy', 'SciPy', 'Matplotlib', 'Pandas'])
G2.add_edges_from([('SciPy', 'NumPy'), ('SciPy', 'NumPy'),
                   ('NumPy', 'Pandas'), ('Matplotlib', 'NumPy')])
assert G2.in_degree('NumPy') == 2
```

Given a set of node attributes and a set of edges, we can generate the graph in just three lines of code. This pattern proves useful in many network problems. Commonly, when dealing with graph data, data scientists are provided with two files: one containing all the node attributes and another containing the linkage information. For instance, in this case study, we are provided with a table of FriendHook profiles as well as a table of existing friendships. These friendships serve as edges, which can be loaded by calling add_edges_from. Meanwhile, the profile information depicts attributes of each user in the friendship graph. After proper preparation, the profiles can be mapped back to the nodes by calling add_nodes_from. Thus, it's very straightforward to load the FriendHook graph into NetworkX for further analysis.

Introductory NetworkX graph methods

- G = nx.DiGraph()—Initializes a new directed graph.
- G.add_node(i)—Creates a new node with index i.
- G.nodes[i]['attribute'] = x—Assigns an attribute x to node i.
- G.add_node(i, attribute=x)—Creates a new node i with attribute x.
- G.add_nodes_from([i, j])—Creates new nodes with indices i and j.
- G.add_nodes_from([(i, {'a': x}), (j, {'a': y})])—Creates new nodes with indices i and j. The attribute a of each new node is set to x and y, respectively.
- G.add_edge(i, j)—Creates an edge going from node i to node j.
- G.add_edges_from([(i, j), (k, m)])—Creates new edges going from i to j and from k to m.
- nx.draw(G)—Plots graph G.

So far, we've focused on directed graphs, in which traversal between nodes is limited. Each directed edge is like a one-way street that forbids travel in a certain direction. What if, instead, we treated every edge as though it were a two-way street? Our edges would be *undirected*, and we'd obtain an *undirected graph*. In an undirected graph, we can traverse connected nodes in either direction. This paradigm doesn't apply to the directed network underlying the internet, but it applies to the undirected network of roads connecting cities throughout the world. In the next subsection, we analyze road travel using undirected graphs. Later, we'll utilize these graphs to optimize the travel time between towns.

18.2 Utilizing undirected graphs to optimize the travel time between towns

In business logistics, product delivery time can impact certain critical decisions. Consider the following scenario, in which you've opened your own kombucha brewery. Your plan is to deliver batches of the delicious fermented tea to all the towns within a reasonable driving radius. More specifically, you'll only deliver to a town if it's within a two-hour driving distance of the brewery; otherwise, the gas costs won't justify the revenue from that delivery. A grocery store in a neighboring county is interested in regular deliveries. What is the fastest driving time between your brewery and that store?

Normally, you could obtain the answer by searching for directions on a smartphone, but we'll assume that existing tech solutions are not available (perhaps the area is remote and the local maps have not been scanned into an online database). In other words, you need to replicate the travel time computations carried out by existing smartphone tools. To do this, you consult a printed map of the local area. On the map, roads zigzag between towns, and some towns connect directly via a road. Conveniently, the travel times between connected towns are illustrated clearly on the map. We can model these connections using undirected graphs.

Suppose that a road connects two towns, Town 0 and Town 1. The driving time between the towns is 20 minutes. Let's record this information in an undirected graph. First, we generate the graph in NetworkX by running `nx.Graph()`. Next we add an undirected edge to that graph by executing `G.add_edge(0, 1)`. Finally, we add the drive time as an attribute of the inserted edge by running `G[0][1]['travel_time'] = 20`.

Listing 18.24 Creating a two-node undirected graph

```
G = nx.Graph()
G.add_edge(0, 1)
G[0][1]['travel_time'] = 20
```

Our travel time is an attribute of the edge `(0, 1)`. Given an attribute k of edge `(i, j)`, we can access that attribute by running `G[i][j][k]`, so we can access the travel time by running `G[0][1]['travel_time']`. In our undirected graph, the travel time between towns is not dependent on direction, so `G[1][0]['travel_time']` also equals 20.

Listing 18.25 Checking the edge attribute of a graph

```
for i, j in [(0, 1), (1, 0)]:
    travel_time = G[i][j]['travel_time']
    print(f"It takes {travel_time} minutes to drive from Town {i} to Town {j}.")
```

```
It takes 20 minutes to drive from Town 0 to Town 1.
It takes 20 minutes to drive from Town 1 to Town 0.
```

Towns 1 and 0 are connected on our map. However, not all towns are directly connected. Imagine an additional Town 2 that is connected to Town 1 but not Town 0. There is no road between Town 0 and Town 2, but there *is* a road between Town 1 and Town 2. The travel time on that road is 15 minutes. Let's add this new connection to our graph. We add the edge and travel time in a single line of code by executing G.add_edge(1, 2, travel_time=15), and then we visualize the graph using nx.draw. We set the visualized node labels to equal the node IDs by passing with_labels=True into the draw function (figure 18.8).

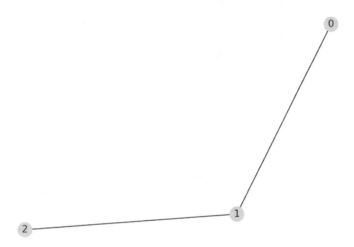

Figure 18.8   A visualized travel path from Town 0 to Town 2 by way of Town 1

Listing 18.26   Visualizing a path between multiple towns

```
np.random.seed(0)
G.add_edge(1, 2, travel_time=15)
nx.draw(G, with_labels=True, node_color='khaki')
plt.show()
```

Traveling from Town 0 to Town 2 requires us to first traverse Town 1. Hence, the total travel time is equal to the sum of G[0][1]['travel_time'] and G[1][2]['travel_time']. Let's compute that travel time.

Listing 18.27   Computing the travel time between towns

```
travel_time = sum(G[i][1]['travel_time'] for i in [0, 2])
print(f"It takes {travel_time} minutes to drive from Town 0 to Town 2.")
```

```
It takes 35 minutes to drive from Town 0 to Town 2.
```

We've computed the fastest travel time between the two towns. Our computation was trivial since there is just one route between Town 0 and Town 2. However, in real life, many routes can exist between localized towns. Optimizing driving times between multiple towns is not so simple. To illustrate this point, let's build a graph containing more than a dozen towns spread across multiple counties. In our graph model, the travel time between towns will increase when towns are in different counties. We'll assume the following:

- Our towns are located in six different counties.
- Each county contains 3 to 10 towns.
- 90% of the towns in a single county are directly connected by roads. The average travel time on a county road is 20 minutes.
- 5% of the towns across different counties are directly connected by a road. The average travel time on an intra-county road is 45 minutes.

We'll now model this scenario. Then we'll devise an algorithm to compute the fastest travel time between any two towns in our complex network.

Common NetworkX methods and attribute assignments

- `G = nx.Graph()`—Initializes a new undirected graph
- `G.nodes[i]['attribute'] = x`—Assigns an attribute x to node i
- `G[i][j]['attribute'] = x`—Assigns an attribute x to edge (i, j)

18.2.1 Modeling a complex network of towns and counties

Let's start by modeling a single county that contains five towns. First, we insert five nodes into an empty graph. Each node is assigned a `county_id` attribute of 0, indicating that all nodes belong to the same county.

Listing 18.28 Modeling five towns in the same county

```
G = nx.Graph()
G.add_nodes_from((i, {'county_id': 0}) for i in range(5))
```

Next, we assign random roads to our five towns (figure 18.9). We iterate over each combination of node pairs and flip a biased coin. The coin lands on heads 90% of the time: whenever we see heads, we add an edge between the pair of nodes. Each edge's `travel_time` parameter is chosen at random by sampling from a normal distribution whose mean is 20.

> **NOTE** As a reminder, the normal distribution is a bell-shaped curve commonly used to analyze random processes in probability and statistics. Refer back to section 6 for a more detailed discussion of that curve.

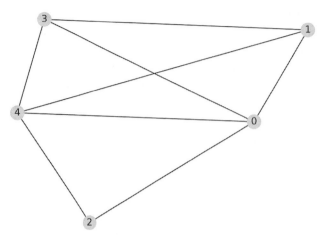

Figure 18.9   A randomly generated road network in a five-town county

Listing 18.29   Modeling random intra-county roads

```
import numpy as np
np.random.seed(0)

def add_random_edge(G, node1, node2, prob_road=0.9,
                    mean_drive_time=20):
    if np.random.binomial(1, prob_road):
        drive_time = np.random.normal(mean_drive_time)
        G.add_edge(node1, node2, travel_time=round(drive_time, 2))

nodes = list(G.nodes())
for node1 in nodes[:-1]:
    for node2 in nodes[node1 + 1:]:
        add_random_edge(G, node1, node2)

nx.draw(G, with_labels=True, node_color='khaki')
plt.show()
```

The function attempts to generate a random edge between node1 and node2 in graph G. The probability of edge insertion is equal to prob_road. If an edge is inserted, a randomized travel time attribute is assigned. The travel time is chosen from a normal distribution with a mean of mean_travel_time.

Flips a coin to determine whether an edge is inserted

Chooses the travel time from a normal distribution

We've connected most of the towns in County 0. In this same manner, we can randomly generate roads and towns for a second county: County 1. Here, we generate County 1 and store that output in a separate graph (figure 18.10). The number of towns in County 1 is a randomly chosen value between 3 and 10.

Listing 18.30   Modeling a second random county

```
np.random.seed(0)
def random_county(county_id):
    numTowns = np.random.randint(3, 10)
    G = nx.Graph()
    nodes = [(node_id, {'county_id': county_id})
             for node_id in range(numTowns)]
```

Generates a random county graph

Chooses the number of towns in the county at random from an integer range of 3 to 10

```
        G.add_nodes_from(nodes)
        for node1, _ in nodes[:-1]:
            for node2, _ in nodes[node1 + 1:]:           Randomly adds
                add_random_edge(G, node1, node2)  <──┘   intra-county roads

        return G

G2 = random_county(1)
nx.draw(G2, with_labels=True, node_color='khaki')
plt.show()
```

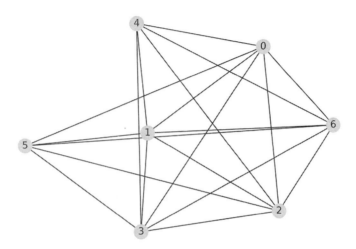

Figure 18.10 **A randomly generated road network in a second county. The number of towns in the county has also been chosen at random.**

Currently, County 1 and County 2 are stored in two separate graphs: G and G2. We need to somehow combine these graphs. Merging the graphs is made more difficult by the shared IDs of nodes in G and G2. Fortunately, our task is simplified by the nx.disjoint_union function, which takes as input two graphs: G and G2. It then resets each node ID to a unique value between 0 and the total node count. Finally, it merges the two graphs. Here, we execute nx.disjoint_union(G, G2) and then plot the results (figure 18.11).

Listing 18.31 Merging two separate graphs

```
np.random.seed(0)
G = nx.disjoint_union(G, G2)
nx.draw(G, with_labels=True, node_color='khaki')
plt.show()
```

Our two counties appear in the same graph. Each town in the graph is assigned a unique ID. Now it's time to generate random roads between the counties (figure 18.12).

Figure 18.11   Two county networks merged together

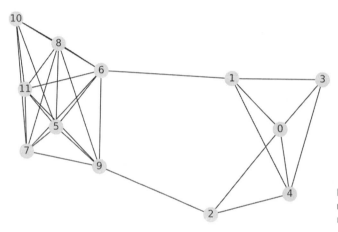

Figure 18.12   Two county networks connected by random roads

We iterate over all the pairs of inter-county nodes (in which G[n1]['county_id'] != G[n2]['county_id']). For each node pair, we apply add_random_edge. The probability of the edge is set low to 0.05, and the average travel time is set high to 90 minutes.

Listing 18.32   Adding random inter-county roads

```
np.random.seed(0)
def add_intercounty_edges(G):            ◁──    Adds random edges between
    nodes = list(G.nodes(data=True))            nodes in graph G whose
    for node1, attributes1 in nodes[:-1]:   ◁── county IDs do not match
        county1 = attributes1['county_id']          Iterates over every node and
        for node2, attributes2 in nodes[node1:]:  ◁── its associated attributes
            if county1 != attributes2['county_id']:  ◁──
                                                         Iterates over node
                                                         pairs that we have
                                                         not yet compared
```

```
                    add_random_edge(G, node1, node2,
                                prob_road=0.05, mean_drive_time=45)     ◁──┐
        return G
```
**Attempts to add a
random inter-
county edge**

```
G = add_intercounty_edges(G)
np.random.seed(0)
nx.draw(G, with_labels=True, node_color='khaki')
```

We've successfully simulated two interconnected counties. Now we simulate six inter-connected counties (figure 18.13).

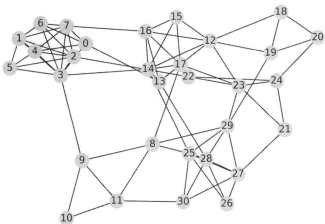

Figure 18.13   Six county networks connected by random roads

Listing 18.33   Simulating six interconnected counties

```
np.random.seed(1)
G = random_county(0)
for county_id in range(1, 6):
    G2 = random_county(county_id)
    G = nx.disjoint_union(G, G2)

G = add_intercounty_edges(G)
np.random.seed(1)
nx.draw(G, with_labels=True, node_color='khaki')
plt.show()
```

We've visualized our six-county graph, but individual counties are tricky to decipher in the visualization. Fortunately, we can improve our plot by coloring each node based on county ID. Doing so requires that we modify our input into the node_color parameter: rather than passing a single color string, we'll pass a list of color strings. The *i*th color in the list will correspond to the assigned color of the node at index i. The following code ensures that nodes in different counties receive different color assignments, while nodes that share a county are assigned the same color (figure 18.14).

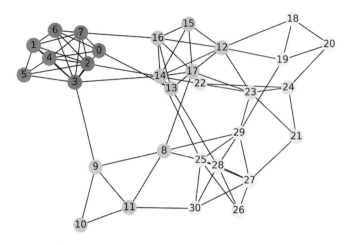

Figure 18.14   Six county networks connected by random roads. The individual towns have been colored based on county ID.

Listing 18.34   Coloring nodes by county

```
np.random.seed(1)
county_colors = ['salmon', 'khaki', 'pink', 'beige', 'cyan', 'lavender']
county_ids = [G.nodes[n]['county_id']
              for n in G.nodes]
node_colors = [county_colors[id_]
               for id_ in county_ids]
nx.draw(G, with_labels=True, node_color=node_colors)
plt.show()
```

The individual counties are now visible. Most counties form tight clumps in the network. Later, we extract these clumps automatically using network clustering. For now, we focus our attention on computing the fastest travel time between nodes.

Common NetworkX graph visualization functions

- `nx.draw(G)`—Plots graph G.
- `nx.draw(G, labels=True)`—Plots graph G with node labels. The labels equal the node IDs.
- `nx.draw(G, labels=ids_to_labels)`—Plots graph G with node labels. The nodes are labeled using a mapping between nodes IDs and labels. That mapping is specified by the `ids_to_labels` dictionary.
- `nx.draw(G, node_color=c)`—Plots graph G. All nodes are colored using color c.
- `nx.draw(G, node_color=ids_to_colors)`—Plots graph G. All nodes are colored using a mapping between node IDs and colors. That mapping is specified by the `ids_to_colors` dictionary.
- `nx.draw(G, arrowsize=20)`—Plots directed graph G while increasing the arrow size of the graph's directed edges.
- `nx.draw(G, node_size=20)`—Plots graph G while decreasing the node size from a default value of 300 to 20.

18.2.2 *Computing the fastest travel time between nodes*

Suppose our brewery is located in Town 0 and our potential client is located in Town 30. We want to determine the fastest travel time between Town 0 and Town 30. In the process, we need to compute the fastest travel time between Town 0 and every other town. How do we do this? Initially, all we know is the trivial travel time between Town 0 and itself: 0 minutes. Let's record this travel time in a `fastest_times` dictionary. Later, we populate this dictionary with the travel times to every town.

Listing 18.35 Tracking the fastest-known travel times

```
fastest_times = {0: 0}
```

Next, we can answer a simple question: what is the known travel distance between Town 0 and its neighboring towns? Neighbors, in this context, are towns with roads connecting to Town 0. In NetworkX, we can access the neighbors of Town 0 by executing `G.neighbors(0)`. That method call returns an iterable over the IDs of nodes connecting to node 0. Alternatively, we can access the neighbors by running `G[0]`. Here, we output the IDs of all the neighboring towns.

Listing 18.36 Accessing the neighbors of Town 0

```
neighbors = list(G.neighbors(0))
assert list(neighbors) == list(G[0])
print(f"The following towns connect directly with Town 0:\n{neighbors}")

The following towns connect directly with Town 0:
[3, 4, 6, 7, 13]
```

Now, we record the travel times between Town 0 and each of its five neighbors and use these times to update `fastest_times`. Additionally, we output the travel times in sorted order for further analysis.

Listing 18.37 Tracking the travel times to neighboring towns

```
time_to_neighbor = {n: G[0][n]['travel_time'] for n in neighbors}
fastest_times.update(time_to_neighbor)
for neighbor, travel_time in sorted(time_to_neighbor.items(),
                                    key=lambda x: x[1]):
    print(f"It takes {travel_time} minutes to drive from Town 0 to Town "
          f"{neighbor}.")

It takes 18.04 minutes to drive from Town 0 to Town 7.
It takes 18.4 minutes to drive from Town 0 to Town 3.
It takes 18.52 minutes to drive from Town 0 to Town 4.
It takes 20.26 minutes to drive from Town 0 to Town 6.
It takes 44.75 minutes to drive from Town 0 to Town 13.
```

It takes approximately 45 minutes to drive from Town 0 to Town 13. Is this the fastest travel time between these two towns? Not necessarily! A detour through another town may speed up travel, as shown in figure 18.15.

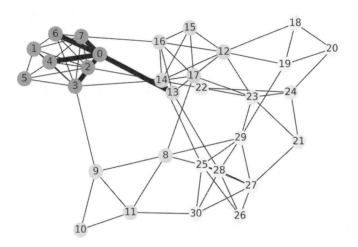

Figure 18.15   The roads connecting Town 0 to its neighbors are highlighted with thick, dark edges. The travel times across these five roads are known. It is possible that faster travel routes exist, but these routes would require additional detours.

Consider, for instance, a detour through Town 7. It's our most proximate town, with a drive time of only 18 minutes. What if there's a road between Town 7 and Town 13? If that road exists, and its travel time is under 27 minutes, then a faster route to Town 13 is possible! The same logic applies to Towns 3, 4, and 6. We can potentially shave minutes off our travel time if we examine the neighbors of Town 7. Let's carry out that examination like this:

1 Obtain the neighbors of Town 7.
2 Obtain the travel time between Town 7 and every neighboring Town N.
3 Add 18.04 minutes to the travel time obtained in the previous step. This represents the travel time between Town 0 and Town N when we take a detour through Town 7.
4 If N is present in `fastest_times`, check whether the detour is faster than `fastest_times[N]`. If an improvement is discovered, update `fastest_times` and print the faster travel time.
5 If N is not present in `fastest_times`, update that dictionary with the travel time computed in step 3. This represents the travel time between Town 0 and Town N when a direct road does not link the two towns.

The following code executes these steps.

Listing 18.38 Searching for faster detours through Town 7

The travel time between Town 0 and town_id

Checks whether a detour through town_id alters the fastest known travel times from Town 0 to other towns

The detour time from Town 0 to a neighbor of town_id

```
def examine_detour(town_id):
    detour_found = False

    travel_time = fastest_times[town_id]
    for n in G[town_id]:
        detour_time = travel_time + G[town_id][n]['travel_time']
        if n in fastest_times:
            if detour_time < fastest_times[n]:
                detour_found = True
                print(f"A detour through Town {town_id} reduces "
                    f"travel-time to Town {n} from "
                    f"{fastest_times[n]:.2f} to "
                    f"{detour_time:.2f} minutes.")
                fastest_times[n] = detour_time

        else:
            fastest_times[n] = detour_time

    return detour_found

if not examine_detour(7):
    print("No detours were found.")

addedTowns = len(fastest_times) - 6
print(f"We've computed travel-times to {addedTowns} additional towns.")
```

Checks if the detour improved the fastest known travel time from Town 0 to n

Records the fastest known travel time from Town 0 to n

Checks how many new towns have been added to fastest_times in addition to the six towns that were initially present in the dictionary

```
No detours were found.
We've computed travel-times to 3 additional towns.
```

We've uncovered travel times to three additional towns, but we have not found any faster detours for travel to neighbors of Town 0. Still, those detours might exist. Let's choose another viable detour candidate. We'll select a town that's proximate to Town 0, whose neighbors we have not examined. Doing so requires that we do the following:

1 Combine the neighbors of Town 0 and Town 7 into a pool of detour candidates. Note that both Town 0 and Town 7 will be present in that pool, thus necessitating the next step.

2 Remove Town 0 and Town 7 from the pool of candidates, leaving behind a set of unexamined towns.

3 Select an unexamined town with the fastest known travel time to Town 0.

Let's run these steps to choose our next detour candidate, using the logic visualized in figure 18.16.

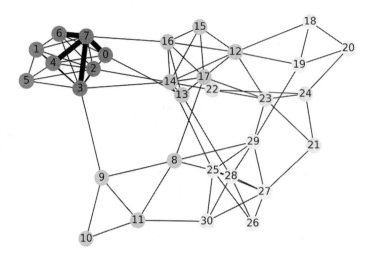

Figure 18.16 Direct detours taken through Town 7 to reach the neighbors of Town 0 are highlighted with thick, dark edges. The detours did not improve our driving times. Perhaps an additional detour through Town 3 will yield improved results.

Listing 18.39   Selecting an alternative detour candidate

Removes all previously examined towns from the candidate set

The pool of detour candidates combines the neighbors of Town 0 and Town 7. Note that both of these towns are neighbors of each other. Thus, they need to be removed from the candidate set.

```
candidate_pool = set(G[0]) | set(G[7])
examinedTowns = {0, 7}
unexaminedTowns = candidate_pool - examinedTowns
detour_candidate = min(unexaminedTowns,
                key=lambda x: fastest_times[x])
travel_time = fastest_times[detour_candidate]
print(f"Our next detour candidate is Town {detour_candidate}, "
      f"which is located {travel_time} minutes from Town 0.")
```

Selects a detour candidate with the fastest known travel time to Town 0

```
Our next detour candidate is Town 3, which is located 18.4 minutes from Town 0.
```

Our next detour candidate is Town 3. We check Town 3 for detours: examining this town's neighbors may reveal new, unexamined towns. We insert all such towns into unexaminedTowns, which will allow us to track the remaining detour candidates for further analysis. Note that candidate tracking requires us to shift Town 3 from unexaminedTowns to examinedTowns after examination.

Listing 18.40   Searching for faster detours through Town 3

```
if not examine_detour(detour_candidate):
    print("No detours were found.")
```

Examines Town 3 for possible detours

```
def new_neighbors(town_id):                ◄──────────┐
    return set(G[town_id]) - examinedTowns             │

def shift_to_examined(town_id):      ◄─────┐
    unexaminedTowns.remove(town_id)        │
    examinedTowns.add(town_id)             │
```

> This helper function obtains the
> neighbors of Town 3 that are not yet
> included in our set of detour candidates.

> This helper shifts Town 3 to
> examinedTowns after examination.

```
unexaminedTowns.update(new_neighbors(detour_candidate))
shift_to_examined(detour_candidate)
num_candidates = len(unexaminedTowns)
print(f"{num_candidates} detour candidates remain.")
```

```
No detours were found.
9 detour candidates remain.
```

Once again, no detours were discovered. However, nine detour candidates remain in
our unexaminedTowns set. Let's examine the remaining candidates. Listing 18.41 iteratively does the following:

1. Select an unexamined town with the fastest known travel time to Town 0.
2. Check that town for detours using examine_detour.
3. Shift the town's ID from unexaminedTowns to examinedTowns.
4. Repeat step 1 if any unexamined towns remain. Terminate otherwise.

> **Listing 18.41   Examining every town for faster detours**

**The iteration continues
until every possible town
has been examined.**

**Selects a new detour
candidate based on the
fastest travel time to Town 0**

**Examines the
candidate for detours**

**Removes the
candidate from
unexamined-
Towns**

**Adds previously
unseen neighbors
of the candidate to
unexaminedTowns**

```
while unexaminedTowns:
    detour_candidate = min(unexaminedTowns,
                    key=lambda x: fastest_times[x])    ◄───
    examine_detour(detour_candidate)                   ◄───
    shift_to_examined(detour_candidate)
    unexaminedTowns.update(new_neighbors(detour_candidate))  ◄───
```

```
A detour through Town 14 reduces travel-time to Town 15 from 83.25 to 82.27
    minutes.
A detour through Town 22 reduces travel-time to Town 23 from 111.21 to 102.38
    minutes.
A detour through Town 28 reduces travel-time to Town 29 from 127.60 to 108.46
    minutes.
A detour through Town 28 reduces travel-time to Town 30 from 126.46 to 109.61
    minutes.
A detour through Town 19 reduces travel-time to Town 20 from 148.03 to 131.23
    minutes.
```

We've examined the travel time to every single town and discovered five possible
detours. Two of the detours are directed through Town 28: they reduce the travel
times to Towns 29 and 30 from 2.1 hours to 1.8 hours, so both towns fall in a viable
driving range for our kombucha brewery.

How many other towns are within two hours of Town 0? Let's find out.

Listing 18.42   Counting all the towns within a two-hour driving range

```
closeTowns = {town for town, drive_time in fastest_times.items()
              if drive_time <= 2 * 60}

num_closeTowns = len(closeTowns)
totalTowns = len(G.nodes)
print(f"{num_closeTowns} of our {totalTowns} towns are within two "
      "hours of our brewery.")
```

```
29 of our 31 towns are within two hours of our brewery.
```

All but two of our towns are within two hours of the brewery. We've figured this out by solving the *shortest path length problem*. The problem applies to graphs whose edges contain numeric attributes, which are called *edge weights*. Additionally, a sequence of node transitions in the graph is called a *path*. Each path traverses a sequence of edges. The sum of edge weights in that sequence is called the *path length*. The problem asks us to compute the shortest path lengths between a node N and every node in the graph. If all the edge weights are positive, we can compute these path lengths like this:

1 Create a dictionary of shortest path lengths. Initially, that dictionary equals $\{N: 0\}$.
2 Create a set of examined nodes. Initially, it is empty.
3 Create a set of nodes we wish to examine. Initially, it contains just N.
4 Remove an unexamined node U from our set of unexamined nodes. We pick a U whose path length to N is minimized.
5 Obtain all neighbors of U.
6 Compute the path length between each neighbor and N. Update the dictionary of shortest path lengths accordingly.
7 Add every neighbor that has not yet been examined to our set of unexamined nodes.
8 Add U to our set of examined nodes.
9 Repeat step 4 if any unexamined nodes remain. Terminate otherwise.

This shortest path length algorithm is included in NetworkX. Given graph G with an edge weight attribute of `weight`, we can compute all shortest path lengths from node N by running `nx.shortest_path_length(G, weight='weight', source=N)`. Here, we utilize the `shortest_path_length` function to compute `fastest_times` in a single line of code.

Listing 18.43   Computing shortest path lengths with NetworkX

```
shortest_lengths = nx.shortest_path_length(G, weight='travel_time',
                                           source=0)
for town, path_length in shortest_lengths.items():
    assert fastest_times[town] == path_length
```

Our shortest path length algorithm doesn't actually return the shortest path. However, in real-world circumstances, we want to know the path that minimizes the distance between nodes. For instance, simply knowing the fastest travel time between Town 0 and Town 30 is insufficient: we also need the driving directions that will get us there in under two hours. Fortunately, the shortest path length algorithm can be easily modified to track the shortest path. All we need to do is add a dictionary structure that tracks the transition between nodes. The actual sequence of traversed nodes can be represented by a list. For brevity's sake, we forgo defining a shortest path tracker from scratch; however, you are encouraged to code a shortest path function and compare its outputs to the built-in NetworkX `shortest_path` function. Calling `nx.shortest_path_length(G, weight='weight', source=N)` computes all shortest paths from node N to every node in G. Hence, executing `nx.shortest_path(G, weight='travel_time', source=0)[30]` should return the fastest travel route between Town 0 and Town 30. We'll now print that route, which is also displayed in figure 18.17.

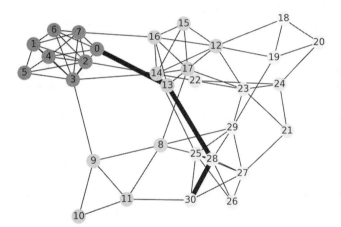

Figure 18.17 The shortest path between Town 0 and Town 30 is highlighted on the graph with thick, dark edges. The path goes from Town 0 to Town 13, followed by Towns 28 and 30. It's worth noting that alternative paths exist in the graph: for example, we can travel from Town 13 to Town 25 and then to Town 30. However, our highlighted path is guaranteed to have the shortest possible path length.

Listing 18.44 Computing shortest paths with NetworkX

```
shortest_path = nx.shortest_path(G, weight='travel_time', source=0)[30]
print(shortest_path)
```

```
[0, 13, 28, 30]
```

Driving time is minimized if we travel from Town 0 to Town 13 to Town 28 and finally to Town 30. We expect that travel time to equal `fastest_times[30]`. Let's confirm.

Listing 18.45 Verifying the length of a shortest path

```
travel_time = 0
for i, town_a in enumerate(shortest_path[:-1]):
    town_b = shortest_path[i + 1]
    travel_time += G[town_a][town_b]['travel_time']
```

```
print("The fastest travel time between Town 0 and Town 30 is "
      f"{travel_time} minutes.")
assert travel_time == fastest_times[30]
```

```
The fastest travel time between Town 0 and Town 30 is 109.61 minutes.
```

Basic network theory allows us to optimize the travel paths between geolocations. In the following section, we build on that theory to develop more advanced techniques. More precisely, we simulate the traffic flow across the network of towns. The simulation will allow us to uncover the most central towns in the graph. Later, we use these traffic simulations to cluster the towns into distinct counties and illustrate how this clustering technique can be used to identify friend groups in a social graph.

> ### Common NetworkX path-related techniques
> - `G.neighbors(i)`—Returns all neighbors of node `i`.
> - `G[i]`—Returns all neighbors of node `i`.
> - `G[i][j]['weight']`—Returns the length of a single transition path between neighboring nodes `i` and `j`.
> - `nx.shortest_path_length(G, weight='weight', source=N)`—Returns the dictionary of shortest path lengths from node `N` to all accessible nodes in the graph. The `weight` attribute is used to measure the path length.
> - `nx.shortest_path(G, weight='weight', source=N)`—Returns the dictionary of shortest paths from node `N` to all accessible nodes in the graph.

Summary

- *Network theory* is the study of connections between objects. A collection of objects and their dispersed connections is called either a *network* or a *graph*. The objects are called *nodes*, and the connections are called *edges*.
- If an edge has a specific direction, it is called a *directed edge*. Graphs with directed edges are called *directed graphs*. If a graph is not directed, it is called an *undirected graph*.
- We can represent a graph as a binary matrix M, where M[i][j] = 1 if an edge exists between node `i` and node `j`. This matrix representation of a graph is known as an *adjacency matrix*.
- In a directed graph, we can count the inbound and outbound edges for each node. The number of inbound edges is called the *in-degree*, and the number of outbound edges is called the *out-degree*. In certain graphs, the in-degree serves as a measure of a node's popularity. We can compute the in-degree by summing over the rows in the adjacency matrix.
- We can use graph theory to optimize travel between nodes. A sequence of node transitions is called a *path*. A length can be associated with that path if each

edge has a numeric attribute assigned. That numeric attribute is called an *edge weight*. The sum of edge weights across the node sequence in a path is called the *path length*. The *shortest path length* problem attempts to minimize the path lengths from node N to all other nodes in the graph. If the edge weights are positive, the path lengths can be minimized algorithmically.

Dynamic graph theory techniques for node ranking and social network analysis

19

This section covers

- Finding the most central network locations
- Clustering the connections in a network
- Understanding social graph analysis

In the previous section, we investigated several types of graphs. We examined web pages connected by directed links and also a network of roads spanning multiple counties. In our analysis, we've mostly treated the network as frozen, static objects—we've counted neighboring nodes as though they were frozen clouds in a photograph. In real life, clouds are constantly in motion, and so are many networks. Most networks worth studying are perpetually buzzing with dynamic activity. Cars race across networks of roads, causing traffic congestion near popular towns. In that same vein, web traffic flows across the internet as billions of users explore the many web links. Our social networks are also flowing with activity as gossip, rumors, and cultural memes spread across tight circles of close friends. Understanding this dynamic flow can help uncover friend groups in an automated manner. Understanding the flow can also help us identify the most heavily trafficked web pages on the internet. Such modeling of dynamic network activity is critical to the function of many large tech organizations. In fact, one of the modeling methods presented in this section led to the founding of a trillion-dollar company.

The dynamic flow (of people, cars, etc.) across a graph is an inherently random process, so it can be studied using random simulations similar to those presented in section 3. In the early part of this section, we utilize random simulations to study the traffic flow of cars. Then we attempt to compute the traffic probabilities more efficiently using matrix multiplication. Later, we use our matrix analysis to uncover clusters of communities with heavy traffic. We then apply our clustering technique to uncover groups of friends in social networks.

Let's get started. We begin with the straightforward problem of uncovering heavily trafficked towns based on traffic simulations.

19.1 Uncovering central nodes based on expected traffic in a network

In the previous section, we simulated a road network connecting 31 towns in 6 different counties (figure 19.1). We stored that network in a graph called G. Our goal was to optimize business delivery travel times across the 31 towns. Let's explore this scenario further.

Suppose our business is growing at an impressive rate. We wish to expand our customer base by putting up a billboard advertisement in one of the local towns represented by G.nodes. To maximize billboard views, we'll choose the town with the heaviest traffic. Intuitively, traffic is determined by the number of cars that pass through town every day. Can we rank the 31 towns in G.nodes based on the expected daily traffic? Yes, we can! Using simple modeling, we can predict traffic flow from the network of roads between the towns. Later, we'll expand on these traffic-flow techniques to identify local counties in an automated manner.

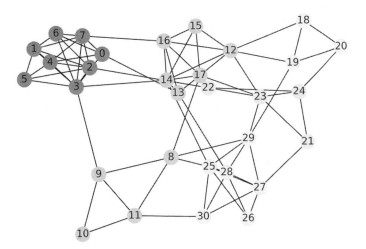

Figure 19.1 A simulated node network from section 18, which is stored in graph G. The roads connect 31 towns that are spread across six counties. Each town is colored based on its county ID.

We need a way of ranking the towns based on expected traffic. Naively, we could simply count the inbound roads into each town: a town with five roads can receive traffic from five different directions, while a town with just one road is more limited in its traffic flow. The road count is analogous to our in-degree ranking of websites introduced in section 18. As a reminder, the in-degree of a node is the number of directed edges pointing at a node. However, unlike the website graph, our network of roads is undirected: there's no distinction between inbound edges and outbound edges. Thus, there's no distinction between a node's in-degree and out-degree; both values are equal, so the edge count of a node in an undirected graph is simply called the node's *degree*. We can compute the degree of any node i by summing over the *i*th column of the graph's adjacency matrix, or we can measure the degree by running `len(G.nodes[i])`. Alternatively, we can utilize the NetworkX `degree` method by calling `G.degree(i)`. Here, we use all these techniques to count the roads passing through Town 0.

> **Listing 19.1   Computing the degree of a single node**

```
adjacency_matrix = nx.to_numpy_array(G)
degree_town_0 = adjacency_matrix[:,0].sum()
assert degree_town_0 == len(G[0])
assert degree_town_0 == G.degree(0)
print(f"Town 0 is connected by {degree_town_0:.0f} roads.")

Town 0 is connected by 5 roads.
```

Using their degrees, we rank our nodes based on importance. In graph theory, any measure of a node's importance is commonly called *node centrality*, and ranked importance based on a node's degree is called the *degree of centrality*. We now select the node with the highest degree of centrality in G: this central node will serve as our initial choice for the billboard's location (figure 19.2).

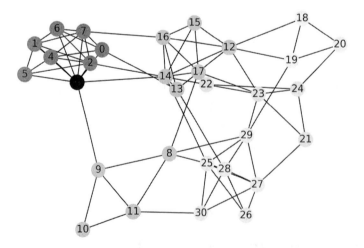

Figure 19.2   A network of roads between different towns. Town 3 has the highest degree of centrality and is colored black.

Listing 19.2   Selecting a central node using degree of centrality

```
np.random.seed(1)
central_town = adjacency_matrix.sum(axis=0).argmax()
degree = G.degree(central_town)
print(f"Town {central_town} is our most central town. It has {degree} "
      "connecting roads.")
node_colors[central_town] = 'k'
nx.draw(G, with_labels=True, node_color=node_colors)
plt.show()
```

```
Town 3 is our most central town. It has 9 connecting roads.
```

Town 3 is our most central town. Roads connect it to nine different towns and three different counties. How does Town 3 compare with the second-most-central town? We'll quickly check by outputting the second-highest degree in G.

Listing 19.3   Selecting a node with the second-highest degree of centrality

```
second_town = sorted(G.nodes, key=lambda x: G.degree(x), reverse=True)[1]
second_degree = G.degree(second_town)
print(f"Town {second_town} has {second_degree} connecting roads.")
```

```
Town 12 has 8 connecting roads.
```

Town 12 has eight connecting roads—it lags behind Town 3 by just one road. What would we do if these two towns had equal degrees? Let's challenge ourselves to find out. In figure 19.2, we see a road connecting Town 3 and Town 9. Suppose that road is closed due to disrepair. That closure necessitates the removal of an edge in G. Running G.remove(3, 9) removes the edge between nodes 3 and 9, so the degree of Town 3 shifts to equal the degree of Town 12. There are also other important structural changes to the network. Here, we visualize these changes (figure 19.3).

Listing 19.4   Removing an edge from the most central node

```
np.random.seed(1)
G.remove_edge(3, 9)
assert G.degree(3) == G.degree(12)      ◁──┐  After edge deletion, Towns 3
nx.draw(G, with_labels=True, node_color=node_colors)    and 12 share the same
plt.show()                                              degree of centrality.
```

Removal of the road has partially isolated Town 3 as well as its neighboring towns. Town 3 is in County 0, which encompasses Towns 0 through 7. Previously, a single road passing through Town 3 linked County 0 to County 1; now that road has been eliminated, so Town 3 is less accessible than it was before. This is in contrast to Town 12, which continues to be the neighbor of multiple different counties.

Town 3 is now less central than Town 12, but the degrees of both towns are equal. We've exposed a significant flaw of the degree of centrality: connecting roads don't matter if they don't lead anywhere important.

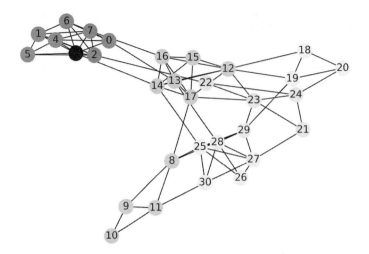

Figure 19.3   A network of roads between different towns after a road closure. Towns 3 and 12 now share the same degree of centrality. Despite their shared degree, Town 12 appears to be in a more central position in the graph. Its county borders multiple other counties. Meanwhile, the closed road has partially isolated Town 3 from the outside world.

Imagine if a town has 1,000 roads, all of which lead to dead ends. Now imagine a town with just four roads, but each road leads to a large metropolitan city. We would expect the second town to have heavier traffic than the first, despite the extreme difference in degrees. Similarly, we expect Town 12 to garner more traffic than Town 3, even though their degrees are equal. In fact, we can quantitate these differences using random simulations. In the next subsection, we measure town centrality by simulating traffic flows between towns.

19.1.1 *Measuring centrality using traffic simulations*

We'll shortly simulate traffic in our network by having 20,000 simulated cars drive randomly around our 31 towns. However, first we need to simulate the random path of a single car. The car will start its journey in a random town `i`. Then the driver will randomly select one of the `G.degree(i)` roads that cut through town and pay a visit to a random neighboring town of `i`. Next, another random road will be selected. The process will repeat until the car has driven through 10 towns. Let's define a `random_drive` function to run this simulation on graph `G`; the function returns the final location of the car.

> **NOTE**   In graph theory, this type of random traversal between nodes is called a *random walk*.

Listing 19.5 Simulating the random route of a single car

```
np.random.seed(0)
def random_drive(num_stops=10):          ◄─┐   The function simulates
    town = np.random.choice(G.nodes)      ◄┐ │ the random path of a car
    for _ in range(num_stops):             │ │ across num_paths towns.
        town = np.random.choice(G[town])  ◄┼─┘
                                           │       The car's starting
    return town                            │       location is chosen
                                           │       at random.
destination = random_drive()              ◄┘   The car drives to a random
print(f"After driving randomly, the car has reached Town {destination}.")
                                               neighboring town.
```

```
After driving randomly, the car has reached Town 24.
```

Listing 19.6 repeats this simulation with 20,000 cars and counts the number of cars in each of the 31 towns. That car count represents the traffic in each town. We print the traffic in the most heavily visited town. We also time our 20,000 iterations to get a sense of the running-time costs associated with traffic simulations.

> **NOTE** Our simulation is greatly oversimplified. In real life, people don't drive randomly from town to town: there is a lot of traffic in certain areas because they are between places people must regularly go, where they find lots of housing, employment opportunities, retailers, etc. But our simplification isn't detrimental; it's beneficial! Our model generalizes beyond just car traffic. It can be applied to web traffic and also to the flow of social interactions. Shortly, we'll expand our analysis to these other categories of graphs— and that expansion would not have been possible if our model was less simple and more concrete.

Listing 19.6 Simulating traffic using 20,000 cars

```
import time
np.random.seed(0)
car_counts = np.zeros(len(G.nodes))      ◄─┐   Stores the traffic counts
num_cars = 20000                              in an array rather than a
                                              dictionary to more easily
start_time = time.time()                      vectorize these counts in
for _ in range(num_cars):                     subsequent code
    destination = random_drive()
    car_counts[destination] += 1

central_town = car_counts.argmax()
traffic = car_counts[central_town]
running_time = time.time() - start_time
print(f"We ran a {running_time:.2f} second simulation.")
print(f"Town {central_town} has the most traffic.")
print(f"There are {traffic:.0f} cars in that town.")
```

```
We ran a 3.47 second simulation.
Town 12 has the most traffic.
There are 1015 cars in that town.
```

Town 12 has the most traffic, with over 1,000 cars. This is not surprising, given that Town 12 and Town 3 share the highest degree of centrality. Based on our previous discussion, we also expect Town 12 to have heavier traffic than Town 3. Let's confirm.

Listing 19.7   Checking the traffic in Town 3

```
print(f"There are {car_counts[3]:.0f} cars in Town 3.")
```

```
There are 934 cars in Town 3.
```

Our expectations are verified. Town 3 has fewer than 1000 cars. We should note that car counts can be cumbersome to compare, especially when num_cars is large. Hence, it's preferable to replace these direct counts with probabilities through division by the simulation count. If we execute car_counts / num_cars, we obtain a probability array: each ith probability equals the likelihood that a randomly traveling car winds up in Town i. Let's print these probabilities for Towns 12 and 3.

Listing 19.8   Converting traffic counts to probabilities

```
probabilities = car_counts / num_cars
for i in [12, 3]:
    prob = probabilities[i]
    print(f"The probability of winding up in Town {i} is {prob:.3f}.")
```

```
The probability of winding up in Town 12 is 0.051.
The probability of winding up in Town 3 is 0.047.
```

According to our random simulation, we'll wind up in Town 12 5.1% of the time and Town 3 just 4.7% of the time. Hence, we've shown that Town 12 is more central than Town 3. Unfortunately, our simulation process is slow and doesn't scale well to larger graphs.

> **NOTE**   Our simulations took 3.47 seconds to run. This seems like a reasonable running time, but larger graphs will require more simulations to estimate travel probabilities. This is due to the law of large numbers, which we introduced in section 4. A graph with 1,000 times more nodes would require 1,000 times more simulations, which would increase our running time to approximately one hour.

Can we compute these probabilities directly without simulating the flow of 20,000 cars? Yes! In the next section, we show how to compute the traffic probabilities using straightforward matrix multiplication.

19.2 Computing travel probabilities using matrix multiplication

Our traffic simulation can be modeled mathematically using matrices and vectors. We'll break this process into simple, manageable parts. Consider, for instance, a car that is about to leave Town 0 for one of the neighboring towns. There are `G.degree(0)` neighboring towns to choose from, so the probability of traveling from Town 0 to any neighboring town is `1 / G.degree(0)`. Let's compute this probability.

Listing 19.9 Computing the probability of travel to a neighboring town

```
num_neighbors = G.degree(0)
prob_travel = 1 / num_neighbors
print("The probability of traveling from Town 0 to one of its "
      f"{G.degree(0)} neighboring towns is {prob_travel}")

The probability of traveling from Town 0 to one of its
5 neighboring towns is 0.2
```

If we're in Town 0 and Town i is a neighboring town, there's a 20% chance of us traveling from Town 0 to Town i. Of course, if Town i is not a neighboring town, the probability drops to 0.0. We can track the probabilities for every possible i using a vector v. The value of `v[i]` will equal 0.2 if i is in `G[0]` and 0 otherwise. Vector v is called a *transition vector* since it tracks the probability of transitioning from Town 0 to other towns. There are multiple ways to compute the transition vector:

- Run `np.array([0.2 if i in G[0] else 0 for i in G.nodes])`. Each ith element will equal 0.2 if i is in `G[0]` and 0 otherwise.
- Run `np.array([1 if i in G[0] else 0 for i in G.nodes]) * 0.2`. Here, we are simply multiplying 0.2 by the binary vector that tracks the presence or absence of edges linking to `G[0]`.
- Run `M[:,0] * 0.2`, where M is the adjacency matrix. Each adjacency matrix column tracks the binary presence or absence of edges between nodes, so column 0 of M will equal the array in the previous example.

The third computation is the simplest. Of course, `0.2` is equal to `1 / G.degree(0)`. As we discussed at the beginning of this section, the degree can also be computed by summing across an adjacency matrix column. Thus, we can also compute the transitional vector by running `M[:,0] / M[:,0].sum()`. Listing 19.10 computes the transition vector using all the listed methodologies.

NOTE Currently, an adjacency matrix M is stored with an `adjacency_matrix` variable. However, that matrix does not take into account the deleted edge between Town 3 and Town 9, so we recompute the matrix by running `adjacency_matrix = nx.to_numpy_array(G)`.

Listing 19.10 Computing a transition vector

```
transition_vector = np.array([0.2 if i in G[0] else 0 for i in G.nodes])

adjacency_matrix = nx.to_numpy_array(G)
v2 = np.array([1 if i in G[0] else 0 for i in G.nodes]) * 0.2
v3 = adjacency_matrix[:,0] * 0.2
v4 = adjacency_matrix[:,0] / adjacency_matrix[:,0].sum()

for v in [v2, v3, v4]:
    assert np.array_equal(transition_vector, v)

print(transition_vector)
```

Recomputes the adjacency matrix to take into account our earlier edge deletion

Computes the transition vector directly from the adjacency matrix column

All four computed versions of the transition vector are identical.

```
[0.  0.  0.  0.2 0.2 0.  0.2 0.2 0.  0.  0.  0.  0.  0.2 0.  0.  0.  0.
 0.  0.  0.  0.  0.  0.  0.  0.  0.  0.  0.  0.  0. ]
```

We can compute the transition vector for any Town *i* by running `M[:,i] / M[:,i]`
`.sum()`, where `M` is the adjacency matrix. Furthermore, we can compute these vectors
all at once by running `M / M.sum(axis=0)`. The operation divides each column of the
adjacency matrix by the associated degree. The end result is a matrix whose columns
correspond to transition vectors. This matrix, which is illustrated in figure 19.4, is
referred to as a *transition matrix*. It is also commonly called the *Markov matrix*, named
after Andrey Markov, a Russian mathematician who studied random processes. We
now compute the transition matrix: based on our expectation, the output's column 0
should equal Town 0's `transition_vector`.

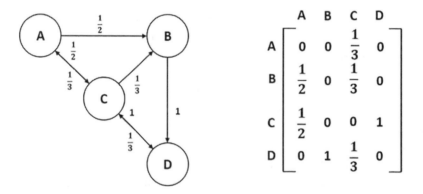

Figure 19.4 If `M` is the adjacency matrix, then `M / M.sum(axis=0)` equals the
transition matrix, even if the adjacencies are directed. This figure shows a directed
graph. Edges are marked with the transition probabilities. These probabilities are also
displayed in a matrix equal to `M / M.sum(axis=0)`. Each column in the matrix is
a transition vector whose probabilities sum to 1.0. According to the matrix, the
probability of travel from A to C is $1/2$, and the probability of travel from C to A is $1/3$.

Listing 19.11   Computing a transition matrix

```
transition_matrix = adjacency_matrix / adjacency_matrix.sum(axis=0)
assert np.array_equal(transition_vector, transition_matrix[:,0])
```

Our transition matrix has a fascinating property: it allows us to compute the traveling probability to every town in just a few lines of code! If we want to know the probability of winding up in Town *i* after 10 stops, then we simply need to do the following:

1 Initialize a vector v, where v equals `np.ones(31) / 31`.
2 Update v to equal `transition_matrix @ v` over 10 iterations.
3 Return `v[i]`.

Later, we derive this amazing property from scratch. For now, let's prove our claims by computing the travel probabilities to Towns 12 and 3 using matrix multiplication. We expect these probabilities to equal 0.051 and 0.047, based on our previous observations.

Listing 19.12   Computing travel probabilities using the transition matrix

```
v = np.ones(31) / 31
for _ in range(10):
    v = transition_matrix @ v

for i in [12, 3]:
    print(f"The probability of winding up in Town {i} is {v[i]:.3f}.")
```

```
The probability of winding up in Town 12 is 0.051.
The probability of winding up in Town 3 is 0.047.
```

Our expectations are confirmed.

We can model traffic flow using a series of matrix multiplications. These multiplications serve as the basis for *PageRank centrality*, which is the most profitable node-importance measure in history. PageRank centrality was invented by the founders of Google; they used it to rank web pages by modeling a user's online journey as a series of random clicks through the internet's graph. These page clicks are analogous to a car that drives through randomly chosen towns. More popular web pages have a higher likelihood of visits. This insight allowed Google to uncover relevant websites in a purely automated manner. Google was thus able to outperform its competition and become a trillion-dollar company. Sometimes, data science can pay off nicely.

PageRank centrality is easy to compute but not so easy to derive. Nonetheless, with basic probability theory, we can demonstrate why repeated `transition_matrix` multiplications directly yield the travel probabilities.

NOTE If you're not interested in the PageRank centrality derivation, skip ahead to the next subsection. It describes PageRank usage in NetworkX.

19.2.1 *Deriving PageRank centrality from probability theory*

We know that `transition_matrix[i][j]` equals the probability of traveling from Town *j* directly to Town *i*, but this assumes that our car is actually located in Town *j*. What if the car's location is not certain? For instance, what if there is just a 50% chance that the car is located in Town *j*? Under such circumstances, the travel probability equals `0.5 * transition_matrix[i][j]`. Generally, if the probability of our current location is `p`, then the probability of travel from the current location `j` to new location `i` equals `p * transition_matrix[i][j]`.

Suppose a car begins its journey in a random town and travels one town over. What is the probability that the car will travel from Town 3 to Town 0? Well, the car can start the journey in any of 31 different towns, so the probability of starting in Town 3 is `1 / 31`. Thus the probability of traveling from Town 3 to Town 0 is `transition_matrix[0][3] / 31`.

> **Listing 19.13   Computing a travel likelihood from a random starting location**

```
prob = transition_matrix[0][3] / 31
print("Probability of starting in Town 3 and driving to Town 0 is "
      f"{prob:.2}")

Probability of starting in Town 3 and driving to Town 0 is 0.004
```

There are multiple ways of reaching Town 0 directly from a random starting location. Let's print all nonzero instances of `transition_matrix[0][i] / 31` for every possible Town *i*.

> **Listing 19.14   Computing travel likelihoods of random routes leading to Town 0**

```
for i in range(31):
    prob = transition_matrix[0][i] / 31
    if not prob:
        continue

    print(f"Probability of starting in Town {i} and driving to Town 0 is "
          f"{prob:.2}")

print("\nAll remaining transition probabilities are 0.0")

Probability of starting in Town 3 and driving to Town 0 is 0.004
Probability of starting in Town 4 and driving to Town 0 is 0.0054
Probability of starting in Town 6 and driving to Town 0 is 0.0065
Probability of starting in Town 7 and driving to Town 0 is 0.0046
Probability of starting in Town 13 and driving to Town 0 is 0.0054

All remaining transition probabilities are 0.0
```

Five different routes take us to Town 0. Each route has a different probability, and the sum of these probabilities equals the likelihood of starting at any random town and traveling directly to Town 0 (figure 19.5). We'll now compute that likelihood. Furthermore,

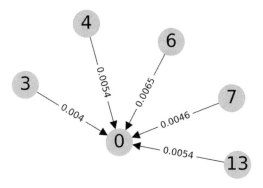

Figure 19.5 Five different routes take us from a random initial town directly to Town 0. Each route has a small probability assigned. Summing these values gives the probability of starting at a random town and traveling directly to Town 0.

we'll compare the likelihood to the result of random simulations. We run the simulations by executing random_drive(num_stops=1) 50,000 times, which yields the frequency with which Town 0 appears as the first stop on a randomized journey. We expect that frequency to approximate our probability sum.

Listing 19.15   Computing the probability that the first stop is Town 0

```
np.random.seed(0)
prob = sum(transition_matrix[0][i] / 31 for i in range(31))
frequency = np.mean([random_drive(num_stops=1) == 0
                     for _ in range(50000)])

print(f"Probability of making our first stop in Town 0: {prob:.3f}")
print(f"Frequency with which our first stop is Town 0: {frequency:.3f}")

Probability of making our first stop in Town 0: 0.026
Frequency with which our first stop is Town 0: 0.026
```

Our computed probability is consistent with the observed frequency: we will make the first stop of our journey in Town 0 approximately 2.6% of the time. It's worth noting that the probability can be computed more concisely as a vector dot-product operation—we just need to run transition_matrix[0] @ v, where v is a 31-element vector whose elements all equal 1 / 31. Let's execute this computation shortcut.

Listing 19.16   Computing a travel probability using a vector dot product

```
v = np.ones(31) / 31
assert transition_matrix[0] @ v == prob
```

Executing transition_matrix[i] @ v returns the likelihood of making our first stop in Town *i*. We can compute this likelihood for every town by running [transition_matrix[i] @ v for i in range(31). Of course, this operation is equivalent to the matrix product between transition_matrix and v, so transition_matrix @ v returns all first-stop probabilities. Listing 19.17 computes this stop_1_probabilities array and prints the probability of making our first stop in Town 12. That probability should approximate the frequency computed through random simulations.

Listing 19.17   Computing all first stop probabilities

```
np.random.seed(0)
stop_1_probabilities = transition_matrix @ v
prob = stop_1_probabilities[12]
frequency = np.mean([random_drive(num_stops=1) == 12
                     for _ in range(50000)])

print('First stop probabilities:')
print(np.round(stop_1_probabilities, 3))
print(f"\nProbability of making our first stop in Town 12: {prob:.3f}")
print(f"Frequency with which our first stop is Town 12: {frequency:.3f}")

First stop probabilities:
[0.026 0.033 0.045 0.046 0.033 0.019 0.025 0.038 0.033 0.031 0.019 0.041
 0.052 0.03  0.036 0.019 0.031 0.039 0.023 0.031 0.027 0.019 0.018 0.044
 0.038 0.046 0.015 0.045 0.04  0.035 0.023]

Probability of making our first stop in Town 12: 0.052
Frequency with which our first stop is Town 12: 0.052
```

We've established that `transition_matrix @ v` returns a vector of first-stop probabilities. Now we need to prove that iteratively repeating this operation will eventually yield a vector of tenth-stop probabilities. However, first let's answer a simpler question: what is the probability of making our second stop in Town i? Based on our previous discussions, we know the following:

- The probability of making our first stop in Town j equals `stop_1_probabilities[j]`.
- If the probability of our current location is p, then the probability of travel from the current location j to new location i equals `p * transition_matrix[i][j]`.
- Hence, the probability of first stopping in Town j and then travelling to Town i is `p * transition_matrix[i][j]`, where `p = stop_1_probabilities[j]`.
- We can compute this travel probability for every possible Town j.
- The sum of these probabilities equals the likelihood of making our first stop at a random town and then traveling directly to Town i. The sum equals `sum(p * transition_matrix[i][j] for j, p in enumerate(stop_1_probabilities))`.
- We can compute this likelihood more concisely as a vector dot-product operation. That operation equals `transition_matrix[i] @ stop_1_probabilities`.

The probability of making our second stop in Town i equals `transition_matrix[i] @ stop_1_probabilities`. We can compute this likelihood for every town using a matrix-vector product. Thus, `transition_matrix @ stop_1_probabilities` returns all second-stop probabilities. However, `stop_1_probabilities` is equal to `transition_matrix @ v`, so the second-stop probabilities are also equal to `transition_matrix @ transition_matrix @ v`.

Let's confirm our calculations by obtaining the second-stop probabilities. Then we print the probability of making our second stop in Town 12, which should approximate the frequency computed through random simulations.

Listing 19.18 Computing all second-stop probabilities

```
np.random.seed(0)
stop_2_probabilities = transition_matrix @ transition_matrix @ v
prob = stop_2_probabilities[12]
frequency = np.mean([random_drive(num_stops=2) == 12
                     for _ in range(50000)])

print('Second stop probabilities:')
print(np.round(stop_2_probabilities, 3))
print(f"\nProbability of making our second stop in Town 12: {prob:.3f}")
print(f"Frequency with which our second stop is Town 12: {frequency:.3f}")

Second stop probabilities:
[0.027 0.033 0.038 0.043 0.033 0.023 0.028 0.039 0.039 0.026 0.021 0.032
 0.048 0.034 0.039 0.023 0.032 0.041 0.023 0.029 0.025 0.024 0.023 0.04
 0.029 0.043 0.021 0.036 0.036 0.042 0.031]

Probability of making our second stop in Town 12: 0.048
Frequency with which our second stop is Town 12: 0.048
```

We were able to derive our second-stop probabilities directly from our first-stop probabilities. In a similar vein, we can derive the third-stop probabilities. If we repeat our derivation, we can easily show that `stop_3_probabilities` equals `transition_matrix @ stop_2_probabilities`. Of course, this vector also equals `M @ M @ M @ v`, where `M` is the transition matrix.

We can repeat this process to compute the fourth-stop probabilities, then the fifth-stop probabilities, and eventually the Nth-stop probabilities. To compute the Nth-stop probabilities, we simply need to execute `M @ v` across N iterations. Let's define a function that computes all Nth-stop probabilities directly from transition matrix M.

NOTE We're dealing with a random process composed of N distinct steps, in which Nth-step probabilities can be computed directly from the N − 1 step. Such processes are called *Markov chains*, after the mathematician Andrey Markov.

Listing 19.19 Computing the Nth-stop probabilities

```
def compute_stop_likelihoods(M, num_stops):
    v = np.ones(M.shape[0]) / M.shape[0]
    for _ in range(num_stops):
        v = M @ v

    return v

stop_10_probabilities = compute_stop_likelihoods(transition_matrix, 10)
prob = stop_10_probabilities[12]
```

```
print('Tenth stop probabilities:')
print(np.round(stop_10_probabilities, 3))
print(f"\nProbability of making our tenth stop in Town 12: {prob:.3f}")


Tenth stop probabilities:
[0.029 0.035 0.041 0.047 0.035 0.023 0.029 0.041 0.034 0.021 0.014 0.028
 0.051 0.038 0.044 0.025 0.037 0.045 0.02  0.026 0.02  0.02  0.019 0.039
 0.026 0.047 0.02  0.04  0.04  0.04  0.027]

Probability of making our tenth stop in Town 12: 0.051
```

As we've discussed, our iterative matrix multiplications form the basis for PageRank centrality. In the next subsection, we compare our outputs to the NetworkX Page-Rank implementation. This comparison will give us deeper insights into the PageRank algorithm.

19.2.2 Computing PageRank centrality using NetworkX

A function to compute PageRank centrality is included in NetworkX. Calling nx.pagerank(G) returns a dictionary mapping between the node IDs and their centrality values. Let's print the PageRank centrality of Town 12. Will it equal 0.051?

> **Listing 19.20   Computing PageRank centrality using NetworkX**

```
centrality = nx.pagerank(G)[12]
print(f"The PageRank centrality of Town 12 is {centrality:.3f}.")


The PageRank centrality of Town 12 is 0.048.
```

The printed PageRank value is 0.048, which is slightly lower than expected. The difference is due to a slight tweak that ensures PageRank works on all possible networks. As a reminder: PageRank was initially intended to model random clicks through a web link graph. A web link graph has directed edges, which means certain web pages might not have any outbound links. Thus, an internet user might get stuck on a dead-end page if they rely on outbound links to traverse the web (figure 19.6). To counter this, the PageRank designers assumed that a user would eventually get tired of clicking web links and would reboot their journey by going to a totally random web page—in other words, they'd teleport to one of the len(G.nodes) nodes in the internet graph. The PageRank designers programmed teleportation to occur in 15% of transversal instances. Teleportation ensures that a user will never get stranded on a node with no outbound links.

In our road network example, teleportation is analogous to calling a helicopter service. Imagine that in 15% of our town visits, we get bored with the local area. We then call for a helicopter, which swoops in and takes us to a totally random town. Once in the air, our probability of flying to any town equals 1 / 31. After we land, we rent a car and continue our journey using the existing network of roads. Hence, 15% of the time, we fly from Town i to Town j with a probability of 1 / 31. In the remaining

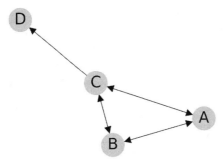

Figure 19.6   A directed graph containing four nodes. We can freely travel between interconnected nodes A, B, and C, but node D has no outbound edges. Sooner or later, a random traversal will take us from C to D. We will then be stuck forever at node D. Teleportation prevents this from happening. In 15% of our traversals, we'll teleport to a randomly chosen node. Even if we travel to node D, we can still teleport back to nodes A, B, and C.

85% of instances, we drive from Town i to Town j with a probability of transition_matrix[j][i]. Consequently, the actual travel probability equals the weighted mean of transition_matrix[j][i] and 1 / 31. The respective weights are 0.85 and 0.15. As discussed in section 5, we can compute the weighted average using the np.average function. We can also compute that mean directly by running 0.85 * transition_matrix[j][i] + 0.15 / 31.

Taking the weighted mean across all elements of the transition matrix will produce an entirely new transition matrix. Let's input that new matrix into our compute_stop_likelihoods function and print Town 12's new travel probability. We expect that probability to drop from 0.051 to 0.048.

Listing 19.21   Incorporating randomized teleportation into our model

```
new_matrix = 0.85 * transition_matrix + 0.15 / 31      ⟵────────┐
stop_10_probabilities = compute_stop_likelihoods(new_matrix, 10)

prob = stop_10_probabilities[12]
print(f"The probability of winding up in Town 12 is {prob:.3f}.")

The probability of winding up in Town 12 is 0.048.
```

> **Multiplies transition_matrix by 0.85 and then adds 0.15 / 31 to every element. See section 13 for a more in-depth discussion of arithmetic operations on 2D NumPy arrays.**

Our new output is consistent with the NetworkX result. Will that output remain consistent if we increase the number of stops from 10 to 1,000? Let's find out. We'll input 1,000 stops into compute_stop_likelihoods and check whether Town 12's PageRank is still equal to 0.048.

Listing 19.22   Computing the probability after 1,000 stops

```
prob = compute_stop_likelihoods(new_matrix, 1000)[12]
print(f"The probability of winding up in Town 12 is {prob:.3f}.")

The probability of winding up in Town 12 is 0.048.
```

The centrality is still 0.048. Ten iterations were sufficient for convergence to a stable value. Why is this the case? Well, our PageRank computation is nothing more than the repeated multiplication of a matrix and a vector. The elements of the multiplied vector are all values between 0 and 1. Perhaps this sounds familiar: our PageRank computation is nearly identical to the power iteration algorithm that we presented in section 14. Power iteration repeatedly takes the product of a matrix and a vector; eventually, the product converges to an eigenvector of the matrix. As a reminder, the eigenvector v of a matrix M is a special vector where `norm(v) == norm(M @ v)`. Usually, 10 iterations are sufficient to achieve convergence. Hence, our PageRank values converge because we're running power iteration! This proves that our centrality vector is an eigenvector of the transition matrix. Thus, PageRank centrality is inexplicably linked to the beautiful mathematics behind dimensional reduction.

Given any graph G, we compute its PageRank centralities using the following series of steps:

1 Obtain the graph's adjacency matrix M.
2 Convert the adjacency matrix into the transition matrix by running `M = M / M.sum(axis=0)`.
3 Update M to allow for random teleportation. This is done by taking the weighted mean of M and 1 / n, where n equals the number of nodes in the graph. The weights are usually set to 0.85 and 0.15, so the weighted mean equals `0.85 * M + 0.15 / n`.
4 Return the largest (and only) eigenvector of M. We can compute the eigenvector by running `v = M @ v` across approximately 10 iterations. Initially, vector v is set to `np.ones(n) / n`.

Markov matrices tie graph theory together with probability theory and matrix theory. They can also be used to cluster network data using a procedure called *Markov clustering*. In the next subsection, we utilize Markov matrices to cluster communities in graphs.

> **Common NetworkX centrality computations**
> - `G.in_degree(i)`—Returns the in-degree of node `i` in a directed graph
> - `G.degree(i)`—Returns the degree of node `i` in an undirected graph
> - `nx.pagerank(G)`—Returns a dictionary mapping between node IDs and their PageRank centralities

19.3 *Community detection using Markov clustering*

Graph G represents a network of towns, some of which fall into localized counties. Currently, we know the county IDs, but what if we didn't? How would we identify the counties? Let's ponder this question by visualizing G without any sort of color mapping (figure 19.7).

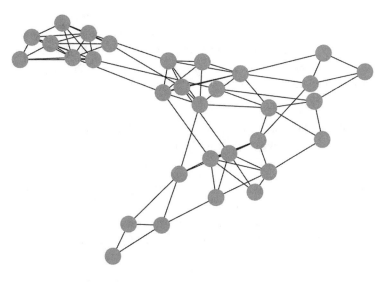

Figure 19.7   A network of roads between different towns. The towns have not been colored based on their counties. But we can still spot certain counties in our network: they appear as spatially clustered clumps.

Listing 19.23   Plotting G without county-based coloring

```
np.random.seed(1)
nx.draw(G)
plt.show()
```

Our plotted graph has neither colors nor labels. Still, we can spot potential counties: they look like tightly connected node clusters in the network. In graph theory, such clusters are formally referred to as *communities*. Graphs with clearly visible communities contain a *community structure*. Many types of graphs contain a community structure, including graphs of towns and graphs of social media friends.

> **NOTE** Some common graphs do not contain a community structure. For instance, the internet lacks tightly clustered communities of web pages.

The process of uncovering graph communities is called *community detection* or *graph clustering*. Multiple graph-clustering algorithms exist, some of which depend on simulations of traffic flow.

How can we use traffic to uncover clusters of counties in our network? Well, we know that towns in the same country are more likely to share a road than towns in different counties, so if we drive to a neighboring town, we are likely to remain in the same county. In community-structured graphs, this logic holds even if we drive two towns over. Suppose, for instance, that we drive from Town i to Town j and then to Town k. Based on our network structure, Towns i and k are more likely to be in the same county. We will confirm this statement shortly; however, first we need to compute the probability of a transition from Town i to Town k after two stops. This probability is called the *stochastic flow*, or *flow* for short. Flow is closely related to the transition probability; but unlike the transition probability, flow covers towns that aren't directly connected. We need to calculate the flow between each pair of towns and store that output in a *flow matrix*. Later, we show that the average flow is higher in towns that share the same community.

> **NOTE**   Generally, in network theory, flow is a very loosely defined concept. But in Markov clustering, that definition is constrained to the probability of eventual travel between nodes.

How do we calculate a matrix of flow values? One strategy is to simulate a two-stop journey between random towns. The simulated frequencies can then be converted into probabilities. However, it's far easier to compute these probabilities directly. With a bit of math, we can show that the flow matrix is equal to `transition_matrix @ transition_matrix`.

> **NOTE**   We can prove this statement as follows. Previously, we showed that the second-stop probabilities equal `transition_matrix @ transition_matrix @ v`. Furthermore, `transition_matrix @ transition_matrix` produces a new matrix, `M`. So, the second-stop probabilities equal `M @ v`. Essentially, `M` serves the same purpose as the `transition_matrix`, but it tracks two stops and not one; so `M` fits our definition of the flow matrix.

Basically, the random simulation approximates the product of the transition matrix with itself. Let's quickly verify before proceeding.

Listing 19.24   Comparing computed flow to random simulations

```
np.random.seed(0)
flow_matrix = transition_matrix @ transition_matrix           Tracks the frequency
                                                              with which we travel
                                                              from Town i to Town k
simulated_flow_matrix = np.zeros((31, 31))                    after two stops
num_simulations = 10000
for town_i in range(31):
    for _ in range(num_simulations):                               Ensures that
        town_j = np.random.choice(G[town_i])                   our simulated
        town_k = np.random.choice(G[town_j])           frequencies closely
        simulated_flow_matrix[town_k][town_i] += 1   ◁──   resemble the directly
                                                              computed flow
simulated_flow_matrix /= num_simulations
assert np.allclose(flow_matrix, simulated_flow_matrix, atol=1e-2)   ◁─────
```

Our `flow_matrix` is consistent with random simulations. Now, let's test our theory that flow is higher between towns in the same county. As a reminder, each town in `G.nodes` has been assigned a county ID. We believe that the average flow between Towns i and j is higher if `G.nodes[i]['county_id']` equals `G.nodes[j]['county_id']`. We can confirm by separating all flows into two lists: `county_flows` and between_county_flows. The two lists track intra-county flows and inter-county flows, respectively. We'll plot a histogram for each of the lists and compare their mean flow values (figure 19.8). If we are correct, then np.mean(county_flows) should be noticeably higher than the mean flow of the second list. We'll also check whether any inter-county flows are explicitly less than np.min(county_flows).

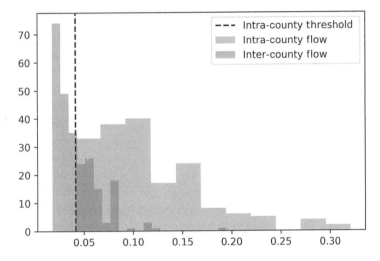

Figure 19.8 Two histograms representing all nonzero inter-county flows and intra-county flows. A separation between flow types is clearly visible. The inter-county flows skew strongly to the left: a threshold of approximately 0.042 is sufficient to separate 132 inter-county flows from the intra-county flow distribution.

Note that for a fair comparison, we should consider only the nonzero flows. So, we must skip over flow_matrix[j][i] if it has a zero value. A zero value implies that it's impossible to travel from i to j in just two stops (the probability of this occurring is zero). At least three stops are required, which indicates that the towns are far away from each other. This practically guarantees that they are in different counties. Hence, the inclusion of zero flows would unfairly skew our distribution of inter-county values toward zero. Let's challenge ourselves to examine the flows between only those towns that are in close proximity.

Listing 19.25 Comparing intra- and inter-county flow distributions

```
def compare_flow_distributions():
    county_flows = []                               Tracks nonzero
    between_county_flows = []                        intra-county flows
    for i in range(31):                              Tracks nonzero
        county = G.nodes[i]['county_id']             inter-county flows
        nonzero_indices = np.nonzero(flow_matrix[:,i])[0]
```

Tracks nonzero intra-county flows

Tracks nonzero inter-county flows

We only iterate over nonzero rows in column i.

```
        for j in nonzero_indices:
            flow = flow_matrix[j][i]

            if county == G.nodes[j]['county_id']:          ◄─┐  Checks if two
                county_flows.append(flow)                     │  towns are in the
            else:                                             │  same county
                between_county_flows.append(flow)

        mean_intra_flow = np.mean(county_flows)
        mean_inter_flow = np.mean(between_county_flows)
        print(f"Mean flow within a county: {mean_intra_flow:.3f}")
        print(f"Mean flow between different counties: {mean_inter_flow:.3f}")

        threshold = min(county_flows)
        num_below = len([flow for flow in between_county_flows
                            if flow < threshold])
        print(f"The minimum intra-county flow is approximately {threshold:.3f}")
        print(f"{num_below} inter-county flows fall below that threshold.")

        plt.hist(county_flows, bins='auto',  alpha=0.5,
                label='Intra-County Flow')
        plt.hist(between_county_flows,  bins='auto', alpha=0.5,
                label='Inter-County Flow')                   ◄─┐  A histogram plot
        plt.axvline(threshold, linestyle='--', color='k',     │  of inter-county
                label='Intra-County Threshold')               │  flows
        plt.legend()
        plt.show()

compare_flow_distributions()
```

Tracks all inter-county flows that are below the minimum intra-county flows (label for `threshold`/`num_below` block)

A histogram plot of intra-county flows (label for first `plt.hist` block)

```
Mean flow within a county: 0.116
Mean flow between different counties: 0.042
The minimum intra-county flow is approximately 0.042
132 inter-county flows fall below that threshold.
```

The mean flow between counties is three times lower than the mean flow between towns in different counties. This difference is clearly visible in the plotted distribution: flows below a threshold of approximately 0.04 are guaranteed to represent inter-county values. Thus, we can isolate inter-county towns using an explicit threshold cutoff. Of course, we're only able to observe this threshold due to our advance knowledge of county identities. In a real-world scenario, the actual county IDs would not be known, so the separation cutoff would be impossible to explicitly determine. We'd be forced to assume that the cutoff is a low value, like 0.01. Suppose we made that assumption with our data. How many nonzero inter-county flows are less than 0.01? Let's find out.

Listing 19.26   Decreasing the separation threshold

```
num_below = np.count_nonzero((flow_matrix > 0.0) & (flow_matrix < 0.01))
print(f"{num_below} inter-county flows fall below a threshold of 0.01")
```

```
0 inter-county flows fall below a threshold of 0.01
```

None of the flow values fall below the stringent threshold of 0.01. What should we do? One option is to manipulate the flow distribution to exaggerate the difference between large and small values. Ideally, we'll force small values to fall below 0.01 while ensuring that larger flows do not drop in value. This manipulation can be carried out with a simple process called *inflation*. Inflation is intended to influence the values of a vector while keeping its mean constant. Values below the mean drop, while the remaining values increase. We'll demonstrate inflation with a simple example. Suppose we're inflating some vector v, which is equal to [0.7, 0.3]. The mean of v is 0.5. We want to increase v[0] while decreasing v[1]. A partial solution is to square each element of v by running v ** 2. Doing so decreases v[1] from 0.3 to 0.09. Unfortunately, it also decreases v[0] from 0.7 to 0.49, so v[0] drops below the original vector mean. We can alleviate the drop by dividing the squared vector by its sum to produce an inflated vector v2, whose sum is 1. It follows that v2.mean() equals v.mean(). Furthermore, v2[0] is greater than v[0], and v2[1] is less than v[1]. Let's confirm.

Listing 19.27 Exaggerating value differences through vector inflation

```
v = np.array([0.7, 0.3])
v2 = v ** 2
v2 /= v2.sum()
assert v.mean() == round(v2.mean(), 10)
assert v2[0] > v[0]
assert v2[1] < v[1]
```

Like vector v, the columns of our flow matrix are vectors whose elements sum to 1. We can inflate each column by squaring its elements and then dividing by the subsequent column sum. Let's define an `inflate` function for this purpose. Then we'll inflate the flow matrix and rerun `compare_flow_distributions()` to check whether our inter-county threshold has decreased (figure 19.9).

Listing 19.28 Exaggerating flow differences through vector inflation

```
def inflate(matrix):
    matrix = matrix ** 2
    return matrix / matrix.sum(axis=0)

flow_matrix = inflate(flow_matrix)
compare_flow_distributions()

Mean flow within a county: 0.146
Mean flow between different counties: 0.020
The minimum intra-county flow is approximately 0.012
118 inter-county flows fall below that threshold.
```

After inflation, our threshold has decreased from 0.042 to 0.012, but it still remains above 0.01. How do we further exaggerate the difference between inter-county and intra-county edges? The answer is surprisingly simple, although its reasoning is not immediately obvious: all we need to do is take the product of flow_matrix with itself

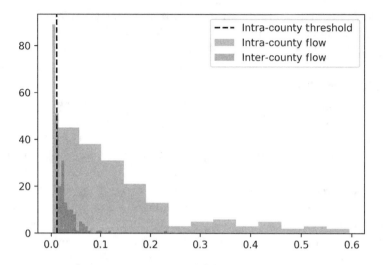

Figure 19.9 Two histograms representing all nonzero inter-county flows and intra-county flows after inflation. The separation between flows has become more visible: inflation has decreased the separation threshold from 0.042 to 0.012.

and then inflate the results. In other words, setting the flow matrix to equal `inflate` (`flow_matrix @ flow_matrix`) will cause the threshold to drastically decrease. Let's verify this claim before discussing the intuitive reasons behind the threshold drop (figure 19.10).

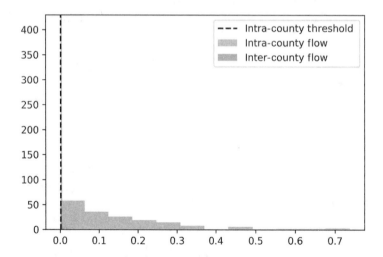

Figure 19.10 Two histograms representing all nonzero inter-county flows and intra-county flows after inflating `flow_matrix @ flow_matrix`. Most of the inter-county flows now fall below the very small separation threshold of 0.001.

Listing 19.29 Inflating the product of `flow_matrix` with itself

```
flow_matrix = inflate(flow_matrix @ flow_matrix)
compare_flow_distributions()
```

> Before this step, flow_matrix was equal to inflate(transition_matrix @ transition_matrix). We are essentially repeating a matrix product that is then coupled with inflation.

```
Mean flow within a county: 0.159
Mean flow between different counties: 0.004
The minimum intra-county flow is approximately 0.001
541 inter-county flows fall below that threshold.
```

The threshold decreased to 0.001. More than 500 inter-county roads fall below that threshold. Why was our strategy successful? We can answer with a straightforward analogy. Suppose that we can build new roads between the towns, but all built roads require some annual maintenance. A poorly maintained road will develop cracks and fissures. Drivers will be more reluctant to go down a damaged road, so periodic repairs are very important. However, in our analogy, there isn't enough money to build new roads while repairing all existing roads in G. A local transportation bureau is given the difficult task of deciding

- Which new roads are built
- Which existing roads are maintained
- Which existing roads are ignored

The bureau makes the following assumption: pairs of towns with heavy flows require a better transportation infrastructure. Hence, a road between Towns i and j will be maintained only if `flow_matrix[i][j]` or `flow_matrix[j][i]` is high. If `flow_matrix[i][j]` is high but there is no road between i and j, then resources will be allocated to connect Towns i and j directly.

> **NOTE** A pair of non-neighboring towns will still have a high flow if multiple short detours exist between them. Building a road between that pair of towns makes sense since doing so will alleviate traffic along the detours.

Regrettably, not all existing roads will be maintained. Less-traveled inter-county roads will have a lower flow and will not receive attention from the bureau. Therefore, these roads will partially decay, and drivers will be less likely to travel between counties. Instead, the drivers will prefer to take the well-maintained intra-county roads, as well as newly built roads between the towns.

> **NOTE** As a reminder, we're assuming that drivers travel randomly, without a particular destination in mind. Their aimless cruising is determined solely by the quality of road conditions.

Road construction, maintenance, and decay will inevitably alter our transition matrix. Transition probabilities between decaying low-flow roads will drop. Meanwhile, the transition probabilities between well-maintained high-flow roads will increase. We need to somehow model the alteration to our matrix while ensuring that matrix columns still sum to 1. How? With inflation, of course! Our inflation function exaggerates the differences between values in the matrix while maintaining a column sum of 1. Thus, we'll model the consequences of the bureau's decision making by updating our transition matrix M to equal `inflation(flow_matrix)`.

But the story isn't over. By changing the transition matrix, we also change the flow within the graph. Flow is equal to `M @ M`, where M is the flow matrix after inflation. Of course, the change will alter local resource allocation: after a new round of road construction and decay, the transition probabilities will come to equal `inflate(M @ M)`. We can model the impact of the iterative road work as `M = inflate(M @ M)`. Note that in the current version of our code, M is set to `flow_matrix`. Thus, running `flow_matrix = inflate(flow_matrix @ flow_matrix)` will reinforce well-traveled roads even as less popular roads wither away (figure 19.11).

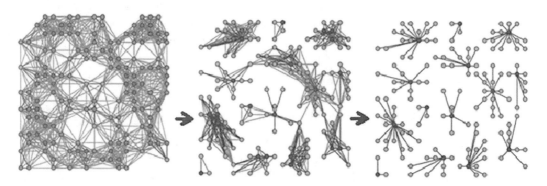

Figure 19.11   Modeling changes to a road graph using inflation. Roads between tightly connected towns are reinforced. Meanwhile, resources are diverted from less trafficked roads, which causes these roads to decay. Eventually, only the roads within the graph's communities remain.

This iterative feedback loop has unexpected ramifications: every year, the inter-county roads get worse and worse. As a result, more drivers stay within the boundaries of their county. More resources are allocated to the internal county roads, and the inter-county roads get less support and crumble further. It's a vicious cycle—eventually, the inter-county roads will crumble to dust, and it will no longer be possible to travel from county to county. Each separate county will become like an isolated island that is completely cut off from its neighbors. This isolation makes for terrible transportation policy, but it greatly simplifies the process of community detection. An isolated town cluster is easy to detect since it lacks boundaries with any other cluster. Consequently, our model of road build-up and decay serves as a basis for a network clustering algorithm: the *Markov Cluster Algorithm* (MCL), also referred to as *Markov clustering*.

MCL is executed by running `inflate(flow_matrix @ flow_matrix)` over many repeating iterations. With each iteration, the inter-county flows get smaller and smaller; eventually they drop to zero. Meanwhile, the intra-county flows maintain their positive values. This binary difference allows us to identify tightly connected county clusters. Listing 19.30 attempts to execute MCL by running `flow_matrix = inflate (flow_matrix @ flow_matrix)` across 20 iterations.

Listing 19.30 Inflating the product of `flow_matrix` repeatedly with itself

```
for _ in range(20):
    flow_matrix = inflate(flow_matrix @ flow_matrix)
```

Based on our discussion, certain edges in graph G should now have a flow of zero. We expect these edges to connect diverging counties. Let's isolate the suspected inter-county edges. We iterate over every edge (i, j) by calling the G.edges() method. Then we track each edge (i, j) for which the flow is nonexistent and sort all the tracked edges in a `suspected_inter_county` edges list.

Listing 19.31 Selecting suspected inter-county edges

```
suspected_inter_county = [(i, j) for (i, j) in G.edges()
                          if not (flow_matrix[i][j] or flow_matrix[j][i])]
num_suspected = len(suspected_inter_county)
print(f"We suspect {num_suspected} edges of appearing between counties.")
```

```
We suspect 57 edges of appearing between counties.
```

57 edges lack any flow. We suspect that these edges connect towns between diverging counties. Deleting the suspected edges from our graph should sever all cross-county connections, so only clustered counties should remain if we visualize the graph after edge deletion. Let's verify by deleting the suspected edges from a copy of our graph (figure 19.12). We utilize the NetworkX `remove_edge_from` method to delete all edges in the `suspected_inter_county` list.

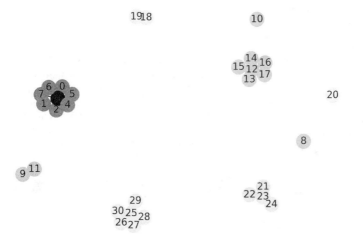

Figure 19.12 A network of towns after the deletion of all suspected inter-county edges. All counties have been fully isolated from each other. Four of the six counties have been fully preserved, but the remaining two counties are no longer fully connected.

Listing 19.32   Deleting suspected inter-county edges

```
np.random.seed(1)
G_copy = G.copy()          Running G.copy() returns a copied version of graph G. We can delete
G_copy.remove_edges_from(suspected_inter_county)   the edges in the copy while preserving edges in the original graph.
nx.draw(G_copy, with_labels=True, node_color=node_colors)
plt.show()
```

All inter-county edges have been eliminated. Unfortunately, a few key intra-county edges have also been deleted. Towns 8, 10, and 20 are no longer connected to any other towns. Our algorithm acted too aggressively. Why is this the case? The problem is due to a minor error in our model: it assumes that travelers can drive to neighboring towns, but it does not allow travelers to remain in their current location. This has unexpected consequences.

We'll illustrate with a simple two-node network. Imagine that a single road connects Towns A and B. In our current model, a driver in Town A has no choice except to travel to Town B. But the driver cannot stay: they must turn around and go back to Town A. A two-stop path does not exist between the towns, even though they are connected. Consequently, the flow between the towns will equal zero, and their connecting road will be eliminated. Of course, this situation is ridiculous—we should give the driver an option of remaining in Town B. How? One solution is to add an edge from Town B to itself. That edge is like a looping road, which takes you back to your current destination (figure 19.13). In other words, the edge is a self-loop. Adding self-loops to a graph will limit unexpected model behavior. Listing 19.33 illustrates the impact of self-loops in a simple two-node adjacency matrix.

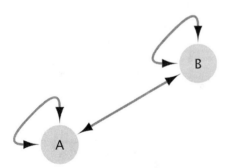

Figure 19.13   A graph indicating possible travel paths between Town A and Town B. Circular self-loops in each of the nodes allow a traveler to remain in place rather than journeying to a neighboring town. Without these loops, the traveler is forced to journey nonstop from A to B and back. If this happens, the flow between the towns will equal zero.

Listing 19.33   Improving flow by adding self-loops

```
def compute_flow(adjacency_matrix):
    transaction_matrix = adjacency_matrix / adjacency_matrix.sum(axis=0)
    return (transaction_matrix @ transaction_matrix)[1][0]

M1 = np.array([[0, 1], [1, 0]])
M2 = np.array([[1, 1], [1, 1]])
```

```
flow1, flow2 = [compute_flow(M) for M in [M1, M2]]
print(f"The flow from A to B without self-loops is {flow1}")
print(f"The flow from A to B with self-loops is {flow2}")

The flow from A to B without self-loops is 0.0
The flow from A to B with self-loops is 0.5
```

Adding self-loops to graph G should limit inappropriate edge deletions. We can add the loops by running G.add_edge(i, i) for every i in G.nodes. With this in mind, let's now define a run_mcl function that runs MCL on an inputted graph by executing the following steps:

1 Add a self-loop to each node in the graph.
2 Compute the graph's transition matrix by dividing the adjacency matrix by its column sums.
3 Calculate the flow matrix from transition_matrix @ transition_matrix.
4 Set flow_matrix to equal inflate(flow_matrix @ flow_matrix) over the course of 20 iterations.
5 Delete all edges in the graph that lack a flow.

After defining run_mcl, we execute the function on a copy of graph G. The plotted output should retain all relevant intra-county edges while also deleting all edges between the communities (figure 19.14).

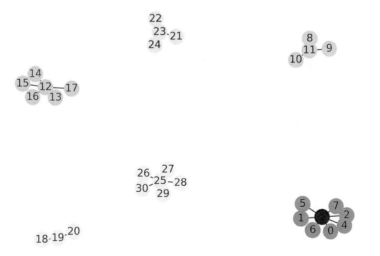

Figure 19.14 **A network of towns after MCL was used to delete all inter-county edges. All counties have been fully isolated from each other. The internal connections within each county have also been fully preserved.**

Listing 19.34   Defining an MCL function

```
def run_mcl(G):
    for i in G.nodes:
        G.add_edge(i, i)          ⟵  Adds self-loops to each
                                      node in the graph

    adjacency_matrix = nx.to_numpy_array(G)
    transition_matrix = adjacency_matrix / adjacency_matrix.sum(axis=0)
    flow_matrix = inflate(transition_matrix @ transition_matrix)

    for _ in range(20):
        flow_matrix = inflate(flow_matrix @ flow_matrix)

    G.remove_edges_from([[(i, j) for i, j in G.edges()
                         if not (flow_matrix[i][j] or flow_matrix[j][i])]])

G_copy = G.copy()
run_mcl(G_copy)
nx.draw(G_copy, with_labels=True, node_color=node_colors)
plt.show()
```

Our graph has clustered perfectly into six secluded counties. The towns in each country are accessible to each other while remaining isolated from the outside world. In graph theory, such isolated clusters are referred to as *connected components*: two nodes are in the same connected component if a path exists between them. Otherwise, the nodes exist in different components (and thus in different communities). To compute the full component of a node, it is sufficient to run nx.shortest_path_length on that node. The shortest path length algorithm returns only those nodes that are accessible within a clustered community. The following code uses nx.shortest_path_length to compute all towns that remain accessible from Town 0 and confirm that all these towns share the same county ID.

Listing 19.35   Using path lengths to uncover a county cluster

```
component = nx.shortest_path_length(G_copy, source=0).keys()
county_id = G.nodes[0]['county_id']
for i in component:
    assert G.nodes[i]['county_id'] == county_id

print(f"The following towns are found in County {county_id}:")
print(sorted(component))

The following towns are found in County 0:
[0, 1, 2, 3, 4, 5, 6, 7]
```

With minor modifications to the shortest path length algorithm, we can extract a graph's connected components. For brevity's sake, we will not discuss these modifications, but you're encouraged to try to work them out for yourself. This modified component algorithm is incorporated into NetworkX: calling nx.connected_components(G) returns an iterable over all connected components in G. Each connected component is stored as a set of node IDs. Let's utilize this function to output all the county clusters.

Listing 19.36 Extracting all the clustered connected components

```
for component in nx.connected_components(G_copy):
    county_id = G.nodes[list(component)[0]]['county_id']
    print(f"\nThe following towns are found in County {county_id}:")
    print(component)
```

```
The following towns are found in County 0:
{0, 1, 2, 3, 4, 5, 6, 7}

The following towns are found in County 1:
{8, 9, 10, 11}

The following towns are found in County 2:
{12, 13, 14, 15, 16, 17}

The following towns are found in County 3:
{18, 19, 20}

The following towns are found in County 4:
{24, 21, 22, 23}

The following towns are found in County 5:
{25, 26, 27, 28, 29, 30}
```

Common network matrix computations

- `adjaceny_matrix = nx.to_numpy_array(G)`—Returns the graph's adjacency matrix.
- `degrees = adjaceny_matrix.sum(axis=0)`—Computes the degree vector using the adjacency matrix.
- `transition_matrix = adjacency_matrix / degrees`—Computes the graph's transition matrix.
- `stop_1_probabilities = transition_matrix @ v`—Computes the probabilities of making a first stop at each node. Here, we assume that `v` is a vector of equally likely starting probabilities.
- `stop_2_probabilities = transition_matrix @ stop_1_probabilities`—Computes the probabilities of making a second stop at each node.
- `transition_matrix @ stop_n_probabilities`—Returns the probabilities of making an $N + 1$ stop at each node.
- `flow_matrix = transition_matrix @ transition_matrix`—Computes the probability matrix of transitioning between `i` and `j` in two stops.
- `(flow_matrix ** 2) / (flow_matrix ** 2).sum(axis=0)`—Inflates the flows in the flow matrix.

We've successfully uncovered the communities in our graph using very little code. Unfortunately, our MCL implementation will not scale to very large networks. Further optimizations are required for successful scaling; these optimizations have been integrated into the external Markov clustering library. Let's install the library and import two functions from the installed `markov_clustering` module: `get_clusters` and `run_mcl`.

> **NOTE** Call `pip install markov_clustering` from the command line terminal to install the Markov clustering library.

Listing 19.37 Importing from the Markov clustering library

```
from markov_clustering import get_clusters, run_mcl
```

Given an adjacency matrix `M`, we can efficiently execute Markov clustering by running `get_clusters(run_mcl(M))`. The nested function call returns a `clusters` list. Each element in `clusters` equals a tuple of nodes that form a clustered community. Let's carry out this clustering on our original graph `G`. The outputted clusters should remain consistent with the connected components in `G_copy`.

Listing 19.38 Clustering with the Markov clustering library

```
adjacency_matrix = nx.to_numpy_array(G)
clusters = get_clusters(run_mcl(adjacency_matrix))

for cluster in clusters:
    county_id = G.nodes[cluster[0]]['county_id']
    print(f"\nThe following towns are found in County {county_id}:")
    print(cluster)

The following towns are found in County 0:
(0, 1, 2, 3, 4, 5, 6, 7)

The following towns are found in County 1:
(8, 9, 10, 11)

The following towns are found in County 2:
(12, 13, 14, 15, 16, 17)

The following towns are found in County 3:
(18, 19, 20)

The following towns are found in County 4:
(21, 22, 23, 24)

The following towns are found in County 5:
(25, 26, 27, 28, 29, 30)
```

With Markov clustering, we can detect communities in community-structured graphs. This will prove useful when we search for groups of friends in social networks.

19.4   *Uncovering friend groups in social networks*

We can represent many processes as networks, including relationships between people. In these *social networks*, nodes represent individual people. An edge exists between two people if they somehow socially interact. For instance, we can connect two people by an edge if they are friends.

Many different types of social networks are possible. Some networks are digital: for example, FriendHook's service is structured around online connections. However, social networks were studied for many decades before the rise of social media. One of the most-studied social networks originated in the 1970s: *Zachery's Karate Club*, based on the social structure of a university karate club, recorded by a scientist named Wayne Zachery. Over the course of three years, Zachery tracked friendships between the 34 members of the club. Edges were assigned to track friends who frequently met up outside the club. After three years, something unexpected happened: a karate instructor named Mr. Hi left to start a new club of his own, and half of the karate club went with him. Much to Zachery's surprise, most of the departing members could be identified solely from network structure.

We'll now repeat Zachery's experiment. First we'll load his famous karate network, which is available through NetworkX. Calling `nx.karate_club_graph()` returns that graph. The following code prints the graph nodes along with their attributes. As a reminder, we can output nodes with attributes by calling `G.nodes(data=True)`.

Listing 19.39   Loading the karate club graph

```
G_karate = nx.karate_club_graph()
print(G_karate.nodes(data=True))

[(0, {'club': 'Mr. Hi'}), (1, {'club': 'Mr. Hi'}), (2, {'club': 'Mr. Hi'}),
(3, {'club': 'Mr. Hi'}), (4, {'club': 'Mr. Hi'}), (5, {'club': 'Mr. Hi'}),
(6, {'club': 'Mr. Hi'}), (7, {'club': 'Mr. Hi'}), (8, {'club': 'Mr. Hi'}),
(9, {'club': 'Officer'}), (10, {'club': 'Mr. Hi'}), (11, {'club':
'Mr. Hi'}), (12, {'club': 'Mr. Hi'}), (13, {'club': 'Mr. Hi'}), (14,
{'club': 'Officer'}), (15, {'club': 'Officer'}), (16, {'club': 'Mr. Hi'}),
(17, {'club': 'Mr. Hi'}), (18, {'club': 'Officer'}), (19, {'club':
'Mr. Hi'}), (20, {'club': 'Officer'}), (21, {'club': 'Mr. Hi'}), (22,
{'club': 'Officer'}), (23, {'club': 'Officer'}), (24, {'club':
'Officer'}), (25, {'club': 'Officer'}), (26, {'club': 'Officer'}), (27,
{'club': 'Officer'}), (28, {'club': 'Officer'}), (29, {'club': 'Officer'}),
(30, {'club': 'Officer'}), (31, {'club': 'Officer'}), (32, {'club':
'Officer'}), (33, {'club': 'Officer'})]
```

Our nodes track 34 people. Each node has a `club` attribute set to `Mr. Hi` if the person joined Mr. Hi's new club or `Officer` otherwise. Let's visualize the network: we color each node based on `club` attribute type (figure 19.15).

Listing 19.40   Visualizing the karate club graph

```
np.random.seed(2)
club_to_color = {'Mr. Hi': 'k', 'Officer': 'b'}
```

```
node_colors = [club_to_color[G_karate.nodes[i]['club']]
                for i in G_karate]

nx.draw(G_karate, node_color=node_colors)
plt.show()
```

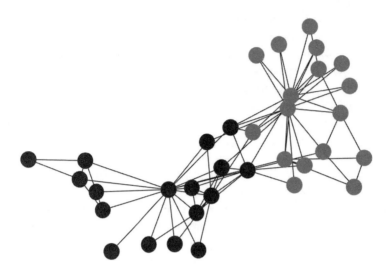

Figure 19.15   **The visualized karate club graph. The node colors correspond to the splitting of the club. These colors overlap with the graph's community structure.**

The karate club graph has a clear community structure. This is not surprising; many social networks contain detectable communities. In this case, the communities correspond to the splitting of the club: the black-colored cluster on the left side of the plot represents the club members who left to join with Mr. Hi, and the right-side cluster represents students who stayed behind. These clusters represent friend groups that formed over multiple years. When the split happened, most members simply went along with their preferred group of friends.

Can we extract these friend clusters automatically? We can try, using MCL. First we run the algorithm on the graph's adjacency matrix and print all the resulting clusters.

Listing 19.41 Clustering the karate club graph

```
adjacency_matrix = nx.to_numpy_array(G_karate)
clusters = get_clusters(run_mcl(adjacency_matrix))
for i, cluster in enumerate(clusters):
    print(f"Cluster {i}:\n{cluster}\n")

Cluster 0:
(0, 1, 3, 4, 5, 6, 7, 10, 11, 12, 13, 16, 17, 19, 21)
```

```
Cluster 1:
(2, 8, 9, 14, 15, 18, 20, 22, 23, 24, 25, 26, 27, 28, 29, 30, 31, 32, 33)
```

Two clusters have been outputted, as expected. We now replot the graph while coloring each node based on cluster ID (figure 19.16).

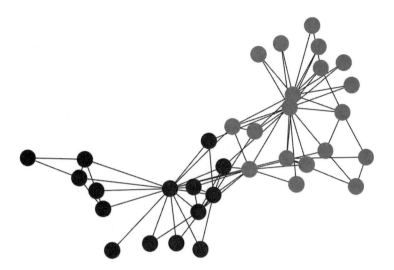

Figure 19.16   The visualized karate club graph. The node colors correspond to the community clusters. These colors overlap with the eventual splitting of the club.

Listing 19.42   Coloring the plotted graph based on cluster

```
np.random.seed(2)
cluster_0, cluster_1 = clusters
node_colors = ['k' if i in cluster_0 else 'b'
               for i in G_karate.nodes]

nx.draw(G_karate, node_color=node_colors)
plt.show()
```

Our clusters are nearly identical to the two splintered clubs. MCL has capably extracted the friend groups in the social network, so the algorithm should serve us well as we pursue our case study solution. In our case study, we're asked to analyze a digital social network. Extracting existing friend groups could prove invaluable to that analysis. Of course, in a large network, the number of groups will be greater than two—we can expect to encounter a dozen (or perhaps a few dozen) friend clusters. We'll also probably want to visualize these clusters in the graph. Manually assigning colors to a dozen clusters is a tedious task, so we'll want to generate the cluster colors automatically. In NetworkX, we can automate color assignment as follows:

1 Create a mapping between each node and its cluster ID by adding a `cluster_id` attribute to each node.

2 Set each element of `node_colors` to equal a cluster ID, rather than the color. This can be done by running `[G.nodes[n]['cluster_id'] for n in G.nodes]`, where `G` is the clustered social graph.

3 Pass `cmap=plt.cm.tab20` into `nx.draw`, along with the numeric `node_colors` list. The `cmap` parameter assigns a color mapping to each cluster ID. `plt.cm.tab20` represents the color palette used to generate that mapping; we've previously used color palette mappings to generate heatmap plots (see section 8 for details).

Let's execute these steps to color our clusters automatically (figure 19.17).

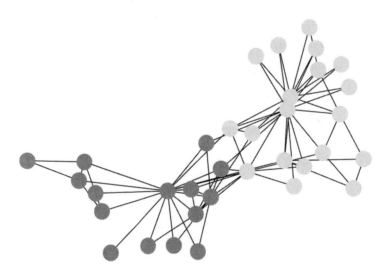

Figure 19.17   The visualized karate club graph. The node colors correspond to the community clusters. These colors were generated in an automated manner.

Listing 19.43   Coloring social graph clusters automatically

```
np.random.seed(2)
for cluster_id, node_indices in enumerate(clusters):         Assigns a
    for i in node_indices:                                   cluster ID to
        G_karate.nodes[i]['cluster_id'] = cluster_id   ◁──┘  every node

node_colors = [G_karate.nodes[n]['cluster_id'] for n in G_karate.nodes]
nx.draw(G_karate, node_color=node_colors, cmap=plt.cm.tab20)   ◁───────
plt.show()
                                                    Uses the plt.cm.tab20
Maps node colors to                               color palette to assign a color
numeric cluster IDs                                 mapping to each cluster ID
```

We've completed our deep dive into graph theory. In the next section, we use our newfound knowledge to derive a simple, graph-based prediction algorithm.

Summary

- The edge count of a node in an undirected graph is simply called the node's *degree*. We can compute the degree of every node by summing over the columns of the graph's adjacency matrix.

- In graph theory, any measure of a node's importance is commonly called *node centrality*. Ranked importance based on a node's degree is called the *degree of centrality*.

- Sometimes, the degree of centrality is an inadequate measure of node importance. We can better derive centrality by simulating random traffic in the network. The traffic can be converted into a probability of randomly winding up at a particular node.

- Traffic probability can be computed directly from the graph's *transition matrix*. The transition matrix tracks the likelihood of randomly traveling from node i to node j. Repeatedly taking the product of the transition matrix and a probability vector produces a vector of final end-point likelihoods. Higher likelihoods correspond to more central nodes. This measure of centrality is known as *PageRank centrality*; mathematically, it is equal to the eigenvector of the transition matrix.

- Certain graphs, when visualized, show tightly connected clusters. These clusters of nodes are called *communities*. Graphs with clearly visible communities are said to contain a *community structure*. The process of uncovering communities in graphs is called *community detection*.

- We can detect communities using the *Markov Cluster Algorithm* (MCL). This algorithm requires us to compute a *stochastic flow*, which is a multistop transition probability. Taking the product of the transition matrix with itself produces a flow matrix. Lower flow values are more likely to correspond with inter-community edges. This difference between low and high flow values can be further amplified via *inflation*. Iteratively repeating matrix multiplication and inflation causes inter-community flows to drop to zero. Then, deleting zero-flow edges completely isolates the graph's communities. These isolated components can be identified with a variant of the shortest path length algorithm.

- In *social networks*, edges represent relationships between people. Social networks commonly contain a community structure, so we can use MCL to detect clusters of friends in these networks.

Network-driven
supervised machine learning

This section covers

- Using classifiers in supervised machine learning
- Making simple predictions based on similarity
- Metrics for evaluating the quality of predictions
- Common supervised learning methods in scikit-learn

People can learn from real-world observations. In some respects, machines can do the same. Teaching computers to metaphorically understand the world through curated experience is referred to as *supervised machine learning*. In recent years, supervised machine learning has been all over the news: computers have been taught to predict stock prices, diagnose diseases, and even drive cars. These advancements have been rightly heralded as cutting-edge innovations. Yet, in some ways, the algorithms behind these innovations are not that novel. Variants of existing machine learning techniques have been around for many decades; but due to limited computing power, these techniques could not be adequately applied. Only now has our computing strength caught up. Hence, ideas planted many years ago are finally bearing the fruits of significant technological advancements.

In this section, we explore one of the oldest and simplest supervised learning techniques. This algorithm, called K-nearest neighbors, was first developed by the US Air Force in 1951. It is rooted in network theory and can be traced back to discoveries made by the medieval scholar Alhazen. Despite its age, the algorithm's usage has much in common with more modern techniques. Thus, the insights we'll gain will be transferable to the broader field of supervised machine learning.

20.1 The basics of supervised machine learning

Supervised machine learning is used to automate certain tasks that would otherwise be done by human beings. The machine observes a human carrying out a task and then learns to replicate the observed behavior. We'll illustrate this learning using the flower dataset introduced in section 14. As a reminder, the dataset represents three different species of the iris flower, which are displayed in figure 20.1. Visually, the three species look alike; botanists use subtle variations along the lengths and widths of the leaves to distinguish the species. That type of expert knowledge must be learned—no human or machine can distinguish between the species without training.

Iris Setosa   Iris Versicolor   Iris Virginica

Figure 20.1   Three species of iris flowers: *Setosa*, *Versicolor*, and *Virginica*. The species all look alike. Subtle differences in their leaves can be utilized to tell the species apart, but training is required to appropriately identify the different species.

Suppose a botany professor conducts an ecological analysis of a local pasture. Hundreds of iris plants are growing in the pasture, and the professor wishes to know the distribution of iris species among these plants. However, the professor is busy writing grants and doesn't have time to examine all the flowers personally. The professor thus hires an assistant to examine the flowers in the field. Unfortunately, the assistant is not a botanist and lacks the skills to tell the species apart. Instead, the assistant chooses to meticulously measure the lengths and widths of the leaves for every flower. Can these measurements be used to automatically identify all species? This question lies at the heart of supervised learning.

Essentially, we want to construct a model that maps inputted measurements to one of three species categories. In machine learning, these inputted measurements are called *features*, and the outputted categories are called *classes*. The goal of supervised learning is to construct a model that can identify classes based on features. Such a model is called a *classifier*.

> **NOTE**   By definition, classes are discrete, categorical variables such as species of flower or type of car. Alternatively, there are models called *regressors* that predict numeric variables, such as the price of a house or the speed of a car.

There are many different types of machine learning classifiers. Whole books are dedicated to demarcating the various classifier categories. But despite their diversity, most classifiers require the same common steps for construction and implementation. To implement a classifier, we need to do the following:

1 Compute the features for each data point. In our botany example, all data points are flowers, so we need to measure the leaf lengths for each flower.

2 A domain expert must assign labels to a subset of the data points. Our botanist has no choice but to manually identify the species in a subset of the flowers. Without the professor's supervision, the classifier cannot be constructed properly. The term *supervised learning* is derived from this supervised labeling phase. Labeling the subset of flowers takes time, but that effort will pay off once the classifier can make automated predictions.

3 Show the classifier the combination of features and manually labeled classes. It then attempts to learn the association between the features and the classes. This learning phase varies from classifier to classifier.

4 Show the classifier a set of features that it has not previously encountered. It then attempts to predict the associated classes based on its exposure to the labeled data.

To construct a classifier, our botanist needs a set of features for a collection of identified flowers. Each flower is assigned the following four features (previously discussed in section 14):

- The length of a colorful petal
- The width of the colorful petal
- The length of a green leaf supporting the petal
- The width of the green leaf supporting the petal

We can store these features in a feature matrix. Each matrix column corresponds to one of the four features, and each matrix row corresponds to a labeled flower. The class labels are stored in a NumPy array. Such arrays are intended to hold numbers and not text; so, in machine learning, class labels are represented as integers that range from 0 to $N-1$ (where N is the total number of classes). In our iris example, we are dealing with three species, so class labels range from 0 to 2.

As seen in section 14, we can load known iris features and class labels using scikit-learn's `load_iris` function. Let's do that now. Per existing scikit-learn convention, a feature matrix is usually assigned to a variable called X, and the class-label array is assigned to a variable called y. Following this convention, the following code loads the iris X and y by passing return_X_y=True into load_iris.

Listing 20.1 Loading iris features and class labels

```
from sklearn.datasets import load_iris
X, y = load_iris(return_X_y=True)
num_classes = len(set(y))
print(f"We have {y.size} labeled examples across the following "
      f"{num_classes} classes:\n{set(y)}\n")
print(f"First four feature rows:\n{X[:4]}")
print(f"\nFirst four labels:\n{y[:4]}")

We have 150 labeled examples across the following 3 classes:
{0, 1, 2}

First four feature rows:
[[5.1 3.5 1.4 0.2]
 [4.9 3.  1.4 0.2]
 [4.7 3.2 1.3 0.2]
 [4.6 3.1 1.5 0.2]]

First four labels:
[0 0 0 0]
```

All 150 flower measurements have been labeled as belonging to one of three flower species. Such labeling is hard work. Imagine that our botanist only has time to label one-fourth of the flowers. The professor then constructs a classifier to predict the classes of the remaining flowers. Let's simulate this scenario. We start by choosing the first one-fourth of data points in X and y. This data slice is referred to as X_train and y_train since it is used for training purposes; such datasets are called *training sets*. After sampling our training set, we investigate the contents of y_train.

Listing 20.2 Creating a training set

```
sampling_size = int(y.size / 4)
X_train, y_train = X[:sampling_size], y[:sampling_size]
print(f"Training set labels:\n{y_train}")

Training set labels:
[0 0 0 0 0 0 0 0 0 0 0 0 0 0 0 0 0 0 0 0 0 0 0 0 0 0 0 0 0 0 0 0 0 0 0 0 0]
```

Our training set contains just the labeled examples with Species 0; the remaining two flower species are not represented. To increase representation, we should sample at random from X and y. Random sampling can be achieved using scikit-learn's train_test_split function, which takes as input X and y and returns four randomly generated outputs. The first two outputs are X_train and y_train, corresponding to our training set. The next two outputs cover the features and classes outside of our training set. These outputs can be utilized to test the classifier after training, so that data is commonly called the *test set*. We'll refer to the test features and classes as X_test and y_test, respectively. Later in this section, we use the test set to evaluate our trained model.

Listing 20.3 calls the train_test_split function and passes it an optional train_size=0.25 parameter. The train_size parameter ensures that 25% of our total data winds up in the training set. Finally, we print y_train to ensure that all three labels are properly represented.

Listing 20.3 Creating a training set through random sampling

```
from sklearn.model_selection import train_test_split
import numpy as np
np.random.seed(0)
X_train, X_test, y_train, y_test = train_test_split(X, y, train_size=0.25)
print(f"Training set labels:\n{y_train}")


Training set labels:
[0 2 1 2 1 0 2 0 2 0 0 2 0 2 1 1 1 2 2 1 1 0 1 2 2 0 1 1 1 0 0 0 2 1 2 0]
```

All three label classes are present in the training data. How can we utilize both X_train and y_train to predict the classes of the remaining flowers in the test set? One simple strategy involves geometric proximity. As we saw in section 14, the features in the iris dataset can be plotted in multidimensional space. This plotted data forms spatial clusters: elements in X_test are more likely to share their class with the X_train points found in the adjacent cluster.

Let's illustrate this intuition by plotting both X_train and X_test in 2D space (figure 20.2). We use principal component analysis to shrink our data to two dimensions, and then we plot the reduced features in our training set while coloring each plotted point based on its labeled class. We also plot the elements of our test set using a

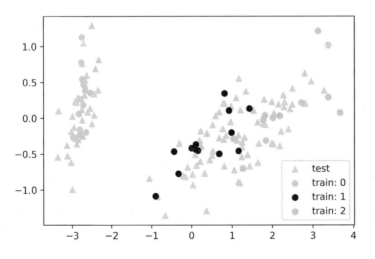

Figure 20.2 **Flower data points plotted in 2D. Each labeled flower is colored based on its species class. Unlabeled flowers are also present in the plot. Visually, we can guess the identity of the unlabeled flowers based on their proximity to labeled points.**

triangular marker to indicate the lack of a label. We then guess the identity of the unlabeled points based on their proximity to labeled data.

Listing 20.4 Plotting the training and test sets

```
import matplotlib.pyplot as plt
from sklearn.decomposition import PCA

pca_model = PCA()
transformed_data_2D = pca_model.fit_transform(X_train)

unlabeled_data = pca_model.transform(X_test)
plt.scatter(unlabeled_data[:,0], unlabeled_data[:,1],
            color='khaki', marker='^', label='test')

for label in range(3):
    data_subset = transformed_data_2D[y_train == label]
    plt.scatter(data_subset[:,0], data_subset[:,1],
            color=['r', 'k', 'b'][label], label=f'train: {label}')

plt.legend()
plt.show()
```

In the left-hand section of our plot, many unlabeled points cluster around Species 0. There is no ambiguity here: these unlabeled flowers clearly belong to the same species. Elsewhere in the plot, certain unlabeled flowers are proximate to both Species 1 and Species 2. For each such point, we need to quantify which labeled species are closer. Doing so requires us to track the Euclidean distance between each feature in X_test and each feature in X_train. Essentially, we need a distance matrix M where M[i][j] equals the Euclidean distance between X_test[i] and X_test[j]. Such a matrix can easily be generated using scikit-learn's euclidean_distances function. We simply need to execute euclidean_distances(X_test, X_train) to return the distance matrix.

Listing 20.5 Computing Euclidean distances between points

```
from sklearn.metrics.pairwise import euclidean_distances
distance_matrix = euclidean_distances(X_test, X_train)

f_train, f_test = X_test[0], X[0]
distance = distance_matrix[0][0]
print(f"Our first test set feature is {f_train}")
print(f"Our first training set feature is {f_test}")
print(f"The Euclidean distance between the features is {distance:.2f}")

Our first test set feature is [5.8 2.8 5.1 2.4]
Our first training set feature is [5.1 3.5 1.4 0.2]
The Euclidean distance between the features is 4.18
```

Given any unlabeled point in X_test, we can assign a class using the following strategy:

1 Sort all data points in the training set based on their distance to the unlabeled points.

2 Select the top *K*-nearest neighbors of the point. For now, we'll arbitrarily set *K* to equal 3.

3 Pick the most frequently occurring class across the *K* neighboring points.

Essentially, we're assuming that each unlabeled point shares a class that is common to its neighbors. This strategy forms the basis for the *K-nearest neighbors* (KNN) algorithm. Let's try this strategy on a randomly chosen point.

Listing 20.6 Labeling a point based on its nearest neighbors

```
from collections import Counter
np.random.seed(6)
random_index = np.random.randint(y_test.size)
labeled_distances = distance_matrix[random_index]
labeled_neighbors = np.argsort(labeled_distances)[:3]
labels = y_train[labeled_neighbors]

top_label, count = Counter(labels).most_common()[0]
print(f"The 3 nearest neighbors of Point {random_index} have the "
      f"following labels:\n{labels}")
print(f"\nThe most common class label is {top_label}. It occurs {count} "
      "times.")

The 3 nearest neighbors of Point 10 have the following labels:
[2 1 2]

The most common class label is 2. It occurs 2 times.
```

The most common class label among the neighbors of Point 10 is Label 2. How does this compare to the actual class of the flower?

Listing 20.7 Checking the true class of a predicted label

```
true_label = y_test[random_index]
print(f"The true class of Point {random_index} is {true_label}.")

The true class of Point 10 is 2.
```

KNN successfully identified the flower class of Point 10. All we needed to do was to check the labeled neighbors and count the most common label among them. Interestingly, this process can be reformulated as a graph theory problem. We can treat each point as a node and its label as a node attribute and then choose an unlabeled point and extend edges to its *K* closest labeled neighbors. Visualizing the neighbor graph allows us to identify the point.

NOTE This type of graph structure is called a *K-nearest neighbor graph* (k-NNG). Such graphs are used in a variety of fields, including transportation planning, image compression, and robotics. Additionally, these graphs can be used to improve the DBSCAN clustering algorithm.

Let's demonstrate the network formulation of the problem by plotting the neighbor graph of Point 10 (figure 20.3). We utilize NetworkX for the purpose of this visualization.

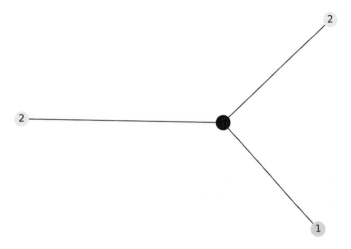

Figure 20.3   A NetworkX graph representing an unlabeled point and its three nearest labeled neighbors. Two of three neighbors are labeled Class 2. Thus, we can hypothesize that the unlabeled point also belongs to that majority class.

Listing 20.8   Visualizing nearest neighbors with NetworkX

```
import networkx as nx                              Plots and returns a NetworkX graph containing
np.random.seed(0)                                  connections between an unlabeled data point and
                                                   the labeled nearest neighbors of that point

def generate_neighbor_graph(unlabeled_index, labeled_neighbors):
    G = nx.Graph()
    nodes = [(i, {'label': y_train[i]}) for i in labeled_neighbors]
    nodes.append((unlabeled_index, {'label': 'U'}))
    G.add_nodes_from(nodes)
    G.add_edges_from([(i, unlabeled_index) for i in labeled_neighbors])
    labels = y_train[labeled_neighbors]
    label_colors = ['pink', 'khaki', 'cyan']
    colors = [label_colors[y_train[i]] for i in labeled_neighbors] + ['k']
    labels = {i: G.nodes[i]['label'] for i in G.nodes}
    nx.draw(G, node_color=colors, labels=labels, with_labels=True)
    plt.show()
    return G

G = generate_neighbor_graph(random_index, labeled_neighbors)
```

Obtains the labels of the nearest neighbors

Colors the labeled neighbors based on their labels

KNN works when there are just three neighbors. What happens if we increase the neighbor count to four? Let's find out (figure 20.4).

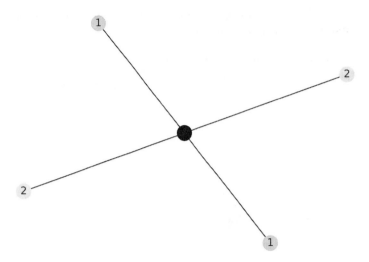

Figure 20.4   A NetworkX graph representing an unlabeled point and its four nearest labeled neighbors. Two of four neighbors are labeled Class 2, and the remaining two neighbors belong to Class 1. No majority class is present. Thus, we are unable to identify the unlabeled point

Listing 20.9   Increasing the number of nearest neighbors

```
np.random.seed(0)
labeled_neighbors = np.argsort(labeled_distances)[:4]
G = generate_neighbor_graph(random_index, labeled_neighbors)
```

There is a tie! No label dominates the majority. We can't make a decision. What should we do? One option is to break the tie at random. A better approach is to factor in the distances to the labeled points. Labeled points that are closer to Point 10 are more likely to share the correct class. Hence, we should give more weight to more proximate points, but how?

Well, in our initial KNN implementation, each labeled point received an equal vote, like in a fair democracy. Now we want to weigh each vote based on distance. One simple weighing scheme is to give each labeled point 1 / distance votes: a point that's one unit away will receive one vote, a point that's 0.5 units away will receive two votes, and a point that's two units away will receive just half a vote. This doesn't make for fair politics, but it could improve the output of our algorithm.

The following code assigns each labeled point a vote amount equal to its inverse distance from Point 10. Then we let the labeled points vote based on their class. We utilize the tallied votes to choose an elected class for our Point 10.

Listing 20.10   Weighing votes of neighbors based on distance

```
from collections import defaultdict
class_to_votes = defaultdict(int)
```

```
for node in G.neighbors(random_index):
    label = G.nodes[node]['label']
    distance = distance_matrix[random_index][node]
    num_votes = 1 / distance
    print(f"A data point with a label of {label} is {distance:.2f} units "
          f"away. It receives {num_votes:.2f} votes.")
    class_to_votes[label] += num_votes

print()
for class_label, votes in class_to_votes.items():
    print(f"We counted {votes:.2f} votes for class {class_label}.")

top_class = max(class_to_votes.items(), key=lambda x: x[1])[0]
print(f"Class {top_class} has received the plurality of the votes.")

A data point with a label of 2 is 0.54 units away. It receives 1.86 votes.
A data point with a label of 1 is 0.74 units away. It receives 1.35 votes.
A data point with a label of 2 is 0.77 units away. It receives 1.29 votes.
A data point with a label of 1 is 0.98 units away. It receives 1.02 votes.

We counted 3.15 votes for class 2.
We counted 2.36 votes for class 1.
Class 2 has received the plurality of the votes.
```

Once again, we've correctly chosen Class 2 as the true class of Point 10. The optional weighted voting can potentially improve our final prediction. Of course, this improvement is by no means guaranteed; occasionally, weighted voting can worsen the outputted results. Depending on the preset value of our *K*, weighted voting can either improve or worsen our predictions. We won't know for sure until we test prediction performance across a range of parameters. Such testing will require us to develop a robust metric for measuring performance accuracy.

20.2 *Measuring predicted label accuracy*

Thus far, we've examined class prediction for a single, randomly chosen point. Now we want to analyze predictions across all the points in X_test. We define a `predict` function for this purpose, which takes as input the index of an unlabeled point and a value of *K*, which we preset to 1.

> **NOTE** We're purposefully inputting a low value of *K* to generate a multitude of errors worth improving. Later, we measure the error across multiple *K*-values to optimize performance.

The final parameter is a `weighted_voting` Boolean, which we set to `False`. That Boolean determines whether votes should be distributed according to distance.

Listing 20.11 Parameterizing KNN predictions

Predicts the label of a point using its row index in the distance matrix based on its K-nearest neighbors. The weighted_voting Boolean determines whether voting is weighted by neighbor distance.

```
def predict(index, K=1, weighted_voting=False):        ◁————————
    labeled_distances = distance_matrix[index]
```

Returns the
class label
with the
most votes

Obtains the
K-nearest
neighbors

```
        labeled_neighbors = np.argsort(labeled_distances)[:K]
        class_to_votes = defaultdict(int)
        for neighbor in labeled_neighbors:
            label = y_train[neighbor]
            distance = distance_matrix[index][neighbor]
            num_votes = 1 / max(distance, 1e-10) if weighted_voting else 1
            class_to_votes[label] += num_votes
    return max(class_to_votes, key=lambda x: class_to_votes[x])

assert predict(random_index, K=3) == 2
assert predict(random_index, K=4, weighted_voting=True) == 2
```

Weighs votes equally if weighted_voting is False and by
inverse distance otherwise. We take precautions when
computing the inverse to avoid dividing by zero.

Let's execute `predict` across all unlabeled indices. Following a common naming convention, we store the predicted classes in an array named y_pred.

Listing 20.12   Predicting all unlabeled flower classes

```
y_pred = np.array([predict(i) for i in range(y_test.size)])
```

We want to compare the predicted classes with the actual classes in y_test. Let's start by printing out both the y_pred and the y_test arrays.

Listing 20.13   Comparing the predicted and actual classes

```
print(f"Predicted Classes:\n{y_pred}")
print(f"\nActual Classes:\n{y_test}")


Predicted Classes:
[2 1 0 2 0 2 0 1 1 1 2 1 1 1 2 0 2 1 0 0 2 1 0 0 2 0 0 1 1 0 2 1 0 2 2 1 0
 2 1 1 2 0 2 0 0 1 2 2 1 2 1 2 1 1 1 1 1 1 1 2 1 0 2 1 1 1 2 2 0 0 2 1 0 0
 1 0 2 1 0 1 2 1 0 2 2 2 2 0 0 2 2 0 2 0 2 2 0 0 2 0 0 0 1 2 2 0 0 0 1 1 0
 0 1]

Actual Classes:
[2 1 0 2 0 2 0 1 1 1 2 1 1 1 1 0 1 1 0 0 2 1 0 0 2 0 0 1 1 0 2 1 0 2 2 1 0
 1 1 1 2 0 2 0 0 1 2 2 2 2 1 2 1 1 2 2 2 2 1 2 1 0 2 1 1 1 2 0 0 2 1 0 0
 1 0 2 1 0 1 2 1 0 2 2 2 2 0 0 2 2 0 2 0 2 2 0 0 2 0 0 0 1 2 2 0 0 0 1 1 0
 0 1]
```

It's difficult to compare the two printed arrays. We can run an easier comparison if we aggregate the arrays into a single matrix M that contains three rows and three columns, corresponding to the number of classes. The rows track predicted classes, and the columns track the true class identities. Each element M[i][j] counts the co-occurrences between predicted Class *i* and actual Class *j*, as is illustrated in figure 20.5.

This type of matrix representation is known as a *confusion matrix* or an *error matrix*. As we shall see shortly, the confusion matrix can help quantify prediction errors. We

		Actual		
		Setosa	Versicolor	Virginica
Predicted	Setosa	**14**	1	1
	Versicolor	1	**11**	3
	Verginica	1	3	**10**

Figure 20.5 A hypothetical matrix representation of the predicted and actual classes. The rows correspond to predicted classes, and the columns correspond to the actual classes. Each element `M[i][j]` counts the co-occurrences between predicted Class *i* and actual Class *j*. Hence, the matrix diagonal is counting all the accurate predictions.

now compute the confusion matrix using `y_pred` and `y_test` and visualize the matrix as a heatmap using Seaborn (figure 20.6).

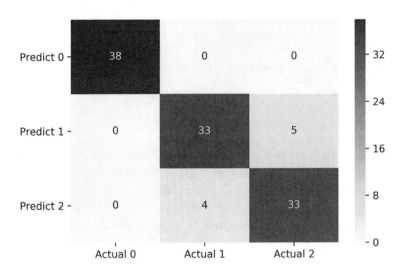

Figure 20.6 A confusion matrix comparing the predicted results to the actual results. The rows correspond to predicted classes, and the columns correspond to the actual classes. The matrix elements count all corresponding instances between the predicted and actual classes. The diagonal of the matrix counts all accurate predictions. Most of our counts lie along the matrix diagonal, indicating that our model is highly accurate.

Listing 20.14 Computing the confusion matrix

Checks for the total number of classes. This value defines the number of matrix rows and columns.

Computes the confusion matrix between y_pred and y_test

```
import seaborn as sns
def compute_confusion_matrix(y_pred, y_test):
    num_classes = len(set(y_pred) | set(y_test))
```

```
    confusion_matrix = np.zeros((num_classes, num_classes))
    for prediction, actual in zip(y_pred, y_test):
        confusion_matrix[prediction][actual] += 1     ◁

    return confusion_matrix


M = compute_confusion_matrix(y_pred, y_test)
sns.heatmap(M, annot=True, cmap='YlGnBu',
            yticklabels=[f"Predict {i}" for i in range(3)],
            xticklabels = [f"Actual {i}" for i in range(3)])
plt.yticks(rotation=0)
plt.show()
```

Each predicted class Prediction corresponds to an actual class Actual. For every such pair, we add a 1 to the row Prediction and column Actual of our matrix. Note that if Prediction == Actual, then the added value appears on the diagonal of the matrix.

Most of the values in the matrix lie along its diagonal. Each diagonal element `M[i][i]` tracks the number of accurately predicted instances of Class *i*. Such accurate predictions are commonly called *true positives*. Based on our displayed diagonal values, we know that our true positive count is very high. Let's print the total true positive count by summing across `M.diagonal()`.

Listing 20.15   Counting the number of accurate predictions

```
num_accurate_predictions = M.diagonal().sum()
print(f"Our results contain {int(num_accurate_predictions)} accurate "
      "predictions.")
```

```
Our results contain 104 accurate predictions.
```

The results include 104 accurate predictions: our accuracy is high. Of course, not all the predictions are accurate. Occasionally, our classifier gets confused and predicts the wrong class label: out of 113 total predictions, 9 predictions in the matrix lie outside the diagonal. The fraction of total accurate predictions is referred to as the *accuracy* score. Accuracy can be computed by dividing the diagonal sum across the total sum of matrix elements: in our case, dividing 104 by 113 produces a high accuracy value.

Listing 20.16   Measuring the accuracy score

```
accuracy = M.diagonal().sum() / M.sum()
assert accuracy == 104 / (104 + 9)
print(f"Our predictions are {100 * accuracy:.0f}% accurate.")
```

```
Our predictions are 92% accurate.
```

Our predictions are quite accurate, but they are not perfect. Errors are present in the output. These errors are not equally distributed: for instance, by examining the matrix, we can see that our Class 0 predictions are always right. The model never confuses Class 0 with any other class or vice versa; all 38 predictions for that class lie along the diagonal. This is not the case for the other two classes: the model periodically confuses instances of Classes 1 and 2.

Let's try to quantify the observed confusion. Consider the elements in matrix Row 1, which tracks our predictions of Class 1. Summing across this row yields the total count of elements that we've predicted as belonging to Class 1.

Listing 20.17 Counting the predicted Class 1 elements

```
row1_sum = M[1].sum()
print(f"We've predicted that {int(row1_sum)} elements belong to Class 1.")
```

```
We've predicted that 38 elements belong to Class 1.
```

We predicted that Class 1 has 38 elements. How many of these predictions are correct? Well, 33 predictions lie along the `M[1][1]` diagonal. Thus, we've correctly identified 33 true positives of Class 1. Meanwhile, the remaining 5 predictions lie in Column 2. These 5 *false positives* represent Class 2 elements that we've misidentified as belong to Class 1; they make our Class 1 predictions less reliable. Just because our model returns a Class 1 label does not mean the prediction is correct. In fact, our Class 1 label is correct in just 33 of 38 total instances. The ratio 33 / 38 produces a metric called *precision*: the true positive count divided by the sum of true positives and false positives. The precision of Class i is also equal to `M[i][i]` divided by the sum across Row i. A low precision indicates that a predicted class label is not very reliable. Let's output the precision of Class 1.

Listing 20.18 Computing the precision of Class 1

```
precision = M[1][1] / M[1].sum()
assert precision == 33 / 38
print(f"Precision of Class 1 is {precision:.2f}")
```

```
Precision of Class 1 is 0.87
```

The precision of Class 1 is 0.87, so a Class 1 label is reliable only 87% percent of the time. In the remaining 13% of instances, the prediction is a false positive. These false positives are a cause of error, but they're not the only one: additional errors can be detected across the confusion matrix columns. Consider, for example, Column 1, which tracks all elements in `y_test`, whose true label is equal to Class 1. Summing over Column 1 yields the total count of Class 1 elements.

Listing 20.19 Counting the total Class 1 elements

```
col1_sum = M[:,1].sum()
assert col1_sum == y_test[y_test == 1].size
print(f"{int(col1_sum)} elements in our test set belong to Class 1.")
```

```
37 elements in our test set belong to Class 1.
```

37 elements in our test set belong to Class 1. 33 of these elements lie along the `M[1][1]` diagonal: these true positive elements have been identified correctly. The remaining four elements lie in Row 2; these *false negatives* represent Class 1 elements that we've misidentified as belonging to Class 2. Hence, our identification of Class 1 elements is incomplete. Of the 37 possible class instances, only 33 have been identified correctly. The ratio 33 / 37 produces a metric called *recall*: the true positive count divided by the sum of true positives and false negatives. The recall of Class *i* is also equal to `M[i][i]` divided by the sum across Column *i*. A low recall indicates that our predictor commonly misses valid instances of a class. Let's output the recall of Class 1.

Listing 20.20   Computing the recall of Class 1

```
recall = M[1][1] / M[:,1].sum()
assert recall == 33 / 37
print(f"Recall of Class 1 is {recall:.2f}")
```

```
Recall of Class 1 is 0.89
```

The recall of Class 1 is 0.89, so we're able to detect 89% of valid Class 1 instances. The remaining 11% of instances are misidentified. The recall measures the fraction of identified Class 1 flowers in the pasture. By contrast, the precision measures the likelihood that a Class 1 prediction is correct.

It's worth noting that a maximum recall of 1.0 is trivial to achieve: we simply need to label each incoming data point as belonging to Class 1. We will detect all valid instances of Class 1, but this high recall will come at a cost. Precision will drop drastically, because all instances of Class 0 and Class 2 will be misidentified as belonging to Class 1. This low precision score equals `M[1][1] / M.sum()`.

Listing 20.21   Checking precision at a recall of 1.0

```
low_precision = M[1][1] / M.sum()
print(f"Precision at a trivially maximized recall is {low_precision:.2f}")
```

```
Precision at a trivially maximized recall is 0.29
```

In this same manner, a maximized precision is worthless if the recall is low. Imagine if the Class 1 precision equaled 1.0. We'd thus have 100% confidence that all Class 1 predictions are correct. However, if the corresponding recall is too low, most Class 1 instances will be misidentified as belonging to another class. Hence, high-level confidence is of little use if the classifier ignores most true instances.

A good predictive model should yield both high precision and high recall. We therefore should combine precision and recall into a single score. How can we combine the two distinct measures? One obvious solution is to take their average by running `(precision + recall) / 2`. Unfortunately, this solution has an unexpected drawback. Both precision and recall are fractions: `M[1][1] / M[1].sum()` and `M[1][1] / M[:,1].sum()`, respectively. They share the same numerator but have different denominators. This is problematic; fractions should only be added if their denominators are equal. Thus, the summation required to take the average is ill advised. What should we do? Well, we can take the inverse of both precision and recall. The inversions will swap each numerator with the denominators, so `1 / precision` and `1 / recall` will share an equal denominator of `M[1][1]`. These inverted fractions can then be summed. Let's see what happens when we take the average of the inverted metrics.

Listing 20.22 Taking the mean of the inverted metrics

```
inverse_average = (1 / precision + 1 / recall) / 2
print(f"The average of the inverted metrics is {inverse_average:.2f}")
```

```
The average of the inverted metrics is 1.14
```

The average of the inverses is greater than 1.0, but both precision and recall have a maximum ceiling of 1.0. Thus, their aggregation should fall below 1.0. We can guarantee this by inverting the computed average.

Listing 20.23 Taking the inverse of the inverted mean

```
result = 1 / inverse_average
print(f"The inverse of the average is {result:.2f}")
```

```
The inverse of the average is 0.88
```

Our final aggregated score is 0.88, which lies between the precision of 0.87 and the recall of 0.89. Hence, this aggregation is a perfect balance of precision and recall. This aggregated metric is called the *f1-measure*, *f1-score*, or, commonly, simply the *f-measure*. The f-measure can be computed more directly by running `2 * precision * recall / (precision + recall)`.

> **NOTE** This inversion of the arithmetic mean of inverse values is called the *harmonic mean*. The harmonic mean is intended to measure the central tendency of rates, such as velocities. Suppose, for instance, that an athlete runs three laps around a one-mile lake. The first lap takes 10 minutes, the next lap takes 16 minutes, and the final lap takes 20 minutes, so the athlete's velocities in miles per minute are 1 / 10 (0.1), 1 / 16 (0.0625), and 1 / 20 (0.05). The arithmetic mean is (0.1 + 0.0625 + 0.05) / 3: approximately 0.071. However, this value is erroneous since diverging denominators are summed. Instead, we should compute the harmonic mean, 3 / (10 + 16 + 20), which is approximately 0.065 miles per minute. By definition, the f-measure equals the harmonic mean of precision and recall.

Listing 20.24 Computing the f-measure of Class 1

```
f_measure = 2 * precision * recall / (precision + recall)
print(f"The f-measure of Class 1 is {f_measure:.2f}")
```

```
The f-measure of Class 1 is 0.88
```

We should note that although in this instance, the f-measure is equal to the average of the precision and recall, this is not always the case. Consider a prediction that has one true positive, one false positive, and zero false negatives. What are the precision and the recall? How does their average compare to the f-measure? Let's check.

Listing 20.25   Comparing the f-measure to the average

```
tp, fp, fn = 1, 1, 0
precision = tp / (tp + fp)
recall = tp / (tp + fn)
f_measure = 2 * precision * recall / (precision + recall)
average = (precision + recall) / 2
print(f"Precision: {precision}")
print(f"Recall: {recall}")
print(f"Average: {average}")
print(f"F-measure: {f_measure:.2f}")

Precision: 0.5
Recall: 1.0
Average: 0.75
F-measure: 0.67
```

In this theoretical example, the precision is low: 50%. Meanwhile, the recall is a perfect 100%. The average value between these two measures is a tolerable 75%. However, the f-measure is much lower than the average because the high recall cannot be justified by the exceptionally low precision value.

The f-measure provides us with a robust evaluation for an individual class. With this in mind, we'll now compute the f-measure for each class in our dataset.

Listing 20.26   Computing the f-measure for each class

```
def compute_f_measures(M):
    precisions = M.diagonal() / M.sum(axis=0)
    recalls = M.diagonal() / M.sum(axis=1)
    return 2 * precisions * recalls / (precisions + recalls)

f_measures = compute_f_measures(M)
for class_label, f_measure in enumerate(f_measures):
    print(f"The f-measure for Class {class_label} is {f_measure:.2f}")

The f-measure for Class 0 is 1.00
The f-measure for Class 1 is 0.88
The f-measure for Class 2 is 0.88
```

The f-measure for Class 0 is 1.0: that distinct class can be identified with perfect precision and perfect recall. Meanwhile, Class 1 and Class 2 share an f-measure of 0.88. The distinction between these classes is not perfect, and one is commonly mistaken for the other. These mistakes degrade the precision and recall of each class. Nonetheless, the final f-measure of 0.88 is wholly acceptable.

NOTE There's no official standard for an acceptable f-measure. Appropriate values can vary from problem to problem. But it's common to treat f-measures like exam grades: an f-measure of 0.9 to 1.0 is treated like an A; the model performs exceptionally well. An f-measure of 0.8 to 0.89 is treated like a B; there's room for improvement even though the model is acceptable. An f-measure of 0.7 to 0.79 is treated like a C; the model performs adequately but is not very impressive. An f-measure of 0.6 to 0.69 is treated like a *D*; unacceptable but still better than random. F-measure values below 0.6 are usually treated as totally unreliable.

We computed three f-measures across three different classes. These f-measures can be combined into a single score by taking their mean. Listing 20.27 outputs that unified f-measure score.

NOTE Our three f-measures are fractions with potentially different denominators. As we've discussed, it's best to combine fractions only when the denominators are equal. Unfortunately, unlike with precision and recall, there's no existing method for achieving denominator equality among f-measure outputs. Hence, we have no choice but to compute their average if we wish to obtain a unified score.

Listing 20.27 Computing a unified f-measure for all classes

```
avg_f = f_measures.mean()
print(f"Our unified f-measure equals {avg_f:.2f}")

Our unified f-measure equals 0.92
```

The f-measure of 0.92 is identical to our accuracy. This is not surprising since both f-measure and accuracy are intended to measure model performance. However, we must emphasize that f-measure and accuracy are not guaranteed to be the same. The difference between the metrics is especially noticeable when the classes are *imbalanced*. In an imbalanced dataset, there are far more instances of some Class A than of some Class B. Let's consider an example where we have 100 instances of Class A and just 1 instance of Class B. Furthermore, let's suppose our Class B predictions have a recall of 100% and a precision of 50%. We can represent this scenario with a two-by-two confusion matrix of the form `[[99, 0], [1, 1]]`. Let's compare the accuracy with the unified f-measure for this imbalanced result.

Listing 20.28 Comparing performance metrics across imbalanced data

```
M_imbalanced = np.array([[99, 0], [1, 1]])
accuracy_imb = M_imbalanced.diagonal().sum() / M_imbalanced.sum()
f_measure_imb =  compute_f_measures(M_imbalanced).mean()
print(f"The accuracy for our imbalanced dataset is {accuracy_imb:.2f}")
print(f"The f-measure for our imbalanced dataset is {f_measure_imb:.2f}")

The accuracy for our imbalanced dataset is 0.99
The f-measure for our imbalanced dataset is 0.83
```

Our accuracy is nearly 100%. That accuracy is misleading—it doesn't truly represent the terrible precision with which the model predicts the second class. Meanwhile, the lower f-measure better reflects the balance between the different class predictions. Generally, the f-measure is considered a superior prediction metric due to its sensitivity to imbalance. Going forward, we rely on the f-measure to evaluate our classifiers.

20.2.1 *Scikit-learn's prediction measurement functions*

All the prediction metrics that we've discussed thus far are available in scikit-learn. They can be imported from the `sklearn.metrics` module. Each metric function takes as input `y_pred` and `y_test` and returns the metric criteria of our choice. For instance, we can compute the confusion matrix by importing and running `confusion_matrix`.

Listing 20.29 Computing the confusion matrix using scikit-learn

```
from sklearn.metrics import confusion_matrix
new_M = confusion_matrix(y_pred, y_test)
assert np.array_equal(new_M, M)
print(new_M)

[[38  0  0]
 [ 0 33  5]
 [ 0  4 33]]
```

In that same manner, we can compute the accuracy by importing and running `accuracy_score`.

Listing 20.30 Computing the accuracy using scikit-learn

```
from sklearn.metrics import accuracy_score
assert accuracy_score(y_pred, y_test) == accuracy
```

Also, the f-measure can be computed with the `f1_score` function. Using this function is a bit more nuanced since the f-measure can be returned as a vector or unified mean. Passing `average=None` into the function returns a vector of individual f-measures for each class.

Listing 20.31 Computing all f-measures using scikit-learn

```
from sklearn.metrics import f1_score
new_f_measures = f1_score(y_pred, y_test, average=None)
assert np.array_equal(new_f_measures, f_measures)
print(new_f_measures)

[1.   0.88 0.88]
```

Meanwhile, passing `average='macro'` returns a single average score.

NOTE Passing `average='micro'` computes the mean precision and mean recall across all classes. Then, these mean values are used to compute a single f-measure score. Generally, this approach does not significantly impact the final unified f-measure result.

Listing 20.32 Computing a unified f-measure using scikit-learn

```
new_f_measure = f1_score(y_pred, y_test, average='macro')
assert new_f_measure == new_f_measures.mean()
assert new_f_measure == avg_f
```

Using the `f1_score` function, we can readily optimize our KNN classifier across its input parameters.

Common scikit-learn classifier evaluation functions

- `M = confusion_matrix(y_pred, y_test)`—Returns the confusion matrix `M` based on predicted classes in `y_pred` and the actual classes in `y_test`. Each matrix element `M[i][j]` counts the number of times that `y_pred[index] == i` while `y_test[index] == j` across every possible `index`.
- `accuracy_score(y_pred, y_test)`—Returns the accuracy score based on predicted classes in `y_pred` and the actual classes in `y_test`. Given the confusion matrix `M`, the accuracy score is equal to `M.diagonal().sum() / M.sum()`.
- `f_measure_vector = f1_score(y_pred, y_test, average=None)`—Returns a vector of f-measures for all possible `f_measure_vector.size` classes. The f-measure of Class *i* is equal to `f_measure_vector[i]`. This equals the harmonic mean of the precision and recall of Class *i*. Both precision and recall can be computed from the confusion matrix `M`. The precision of Class *i* equals `M[i][i] / M[i].sum()`, and the recall of Class *i* equals `M[i][i] / M[:,i].sum()`. The final f-measure value `f_measure_vector[i]` equals `2 * precision * recall / (precision + recall)`.
- `f1_score(y_pred, y_test, average='macro')`—Returns the average f-measure, equal to `f_measure_vector.mean()`.

20.3 *Optimizing KNN performance*

Currently, our `predict` function takes two input parameters: *K* and `weighted_voting`. These parameters must be set before training and influence the classifier's performance. Data scientists refer to such parameters as *hyperparameters*. All machine learning models have some hyperparameters that can be tweaked to enhance predictive power. Let's try to optimize our classifier's hyperparameters by iterating over all possible combinations of *K* and `weighted_voting`. Our *K* values range from 1 to `y_train.size`, and our Boolean `weighted_voting` parameter is set to `True` or `False`. For each hyperparameter combination, we train on `y_train` and compute `y_pred`. We then obtain the f-measure based on our predictions. All f-measures are plotted relative to the input *K*. We plot two separate curves: one for `weighted_voting = True` and another for `weighted_voting = False` (figure 20.7). Finally, we find the maximum f-measure in the plot and return its optimized parameters.

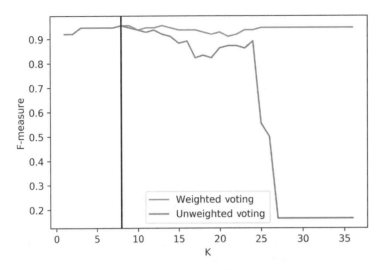

Figure 20.7   A plot of KNN weighted and unweighted voting performance measures across a range of input *K* values. F-measure is maximized when *K* is set to 8. There's no significant difference for weighted and unweighted voting for low values of *K*. However, unweighted performance starts to degrade when *K* is larger than 10.

Listing 20.33   Optimizing KNN hyperparameters

```
k_values = range(1, y_train.size)               Tracks the mapping
weighted_voting_bools = [True, False]           between each parameter
f_scores = [[], []]                             combination and the
                                                f-measure
params_to_f = {}          ◁
for k in k_values:
    for i, weighted_voting in enumerate(weighted_voting_bools):   Computes a KNN
        y_pred = np.array([predict(i, K=k,                        prediction for
                     weighted_voting=weighted_voting)             each parameter
                     for i in range(y_test.size)])   ◁           combination
        f_measure = f1_score(y_pred, y_test, average='macro')
        f_scores[i].append(f_measure)
        params_to_f[(k, weighted_voting)] = f_measure

(best_k, best_weighted), best_f = max(params_to_f.items(),
                                  key=lambda x: x[1])   ◁        Finds the
plt.plot(k_values, f_scores[0], label='Weighted Voting')         parameters
plt.plot(k_values, f_scores[1], label='Unweighted Voting')       that maximize
plt.axvline(best_k, c='k')                                       the f-measure
plt.xlabel('K')
plt.ylabel('F-measure')
plt.legend()
plt.show()

print(f"The maximum f-measure of {best_f:.2f} is achieved when K={best_k} "
      f"and weighted_voting={best_weighted}")

The maximum f-measure of 0.96 is achieved when K=8 and weighted_voting=True
```

Computes the f-measure for each parameter combination (annotation pointing to `f_scores[i].append(f_measure)`)

Performance is maximized when *K* is set to 8 and weighted voting is activated. However, there's no significant difference between the weighted and unweighted voting output for that value of *K*. Interestingly, as *K* continues to increase, the unweighted f-measure drops rapidly. Meanwhile, the weighted f-measure continues to hover at above 90%. Thus, weighted KNN appears to be more stable than the unweighted variant.

We gained these insights by exhaustively iterating over all the possible input parameters. This exhaustive approach is called a *parameter sweep* or *grid search*. A grid search is a simple but effective way to optimize hyperparameters. Though it suffers from computational complexity when the parameter count is high, a grid search is very easy to parallelize. With enough computing power, a grid search can effectively optimize many common machine learning algorithms. Generally, a grid search is conducted like this:

1 Select our hyperparameters of interest.
2 Assign a range of values to each hyperparameter.
3 Split our input data into a training set and a validation set. The validation set is used to measure the prediction quality. This approach is called *cross-validation*. Note that it is possible to split the data further into multiple training and validation sets; that way, multiple prediction metrics can be averaged out into a single score.
4 Iterate over all possible hyperparameter combinations.
5 At each iteration, train a classifier on the training data using the specified hyperparameters.
6 Measure the classifier's performance using the validation set.
7 Once all iterations are completed, return the hyperparameter combination with the highest metric output.

Scikit-learn allows us to execute a grid search on all its built-in machine learning algorithms. Let's utilize scikit-learn to run a grid search on KNN.

20.4 Running a grid search using scikit-learn

Scikit-learn has built-in logic for running KNN classification. We utilize this logic by importing the `KNeighborsClassifier` class.

> **Listing 20.34 Importing scikit-learn's KNN class**

```
from sklearn.neighbors import KNeighborsClassifier
```

Initializing the class creates a KNN classifier object. Per common convention, we store this object in a `clf` variable.

> **NOTE** The KNN algorithm can be extended beyond mere classification: it can be modified to predict continuous values. Imagine that we wish to predict the sale price of a house. We can do this by averaging the known sales prices for similar houses in the neighborhood. In that same way, we construct a

KNN regressor that predicts a data point's continuous value by averaging known values of its neighbors. Scikit-learn includes a `KNeighborsRegressor` class that is designed for this specific purpose.

Listing 20.35   Initializing scikit-learn's KNN classifier

```
clf = KNeighborsClassifier()
```

The initialized `clf` object has preset specifications for *K* and weighted voting. The *K* value is stored in the `clf.n_neighbors` attribute, and the weighted voting specifications are stored in the `clf.weights` attribute. Let's print and examine both these attributes.

Listing 20.36   Printing the preset KNN parameters

```
K = clf.n_neighbors
weighted_voting = clf.weights
print(f"K is set to {K}.")
print(f"Weighted voting is set to '{weighted_voting}'.")

K is set to 5.
Weighted voting is set to 'uniform'.
```

Our *K* is set to 5, and weighted voting is set to `uniform`, indicating that all votes are weighted equally. Passing `weights='distance'` into the initialization function ensures that votes are weighted by distance. Additionally, passing `n_neighbors=4` sets *K* to 4. Let's reinitialize `clf` with these parameters.

Listing 20.37   Setting scikit-learn's KNN parameters

```
clf = KNeighborsClassifier(n_neighbors=4, weights='distance')
assert clf.n_neighbors == 4
assert clf.weights == 'distance'
```

Now we want to train our KNN model. Any scikit-learn `clf` classifier can be trained using the `fit` method. We simply need to execute `clf.fit(X, y)`, where X is a feature matrix and y is a class-label array. Let's train the classifier using the training set defined by X_train and y_train.

Listing 20.38   Training scikit-learn's KNN classifier

```
clf.fit(X_train, y_train)
```

After training, `clf` can predict the classes of any input X_test matrix (whose dimensions match X_train). Predictions are carried out with the `clf.predict` method. Running `clf.predict(X_test)` returns a y_pred prediction array. Subsequently, y_pred together with y_test can be used to calculate the f-measure.

Listing 20.39 Predicting classes with a trained KNN classifier

```
y_pred = clf.predict(X_test)
f_measure = f1_score(y_pred, y_test, average='macro')
print(f"The predicted classes are:\n{y_pred}")
print(f"\nThe f-measure equals {f_measure:.2f}.")

The predicted classes are:
[2 1 0 2 0 2 0 1 1 1 2 1 1 1 1 0 1 1 0 0 2 1 0 0 2 0 0 1 1 0 2 1 0 2 2 1 0
 2 1 1 2 0 2 0 0 1 2 2 1 2 1 2 1 1 1 1 1 1 1 2 1 0 2 1 1 1 2 0 0 2 1 0 0
 1 0 2 1 0 1 2 1 0 2 2 2 2 0 0 2 2 0 2 0 2 2 0 0 2 0 0 0 1 2 2 0 0 0 1 1 0
 0 1]

The f-measure equals 0.95.
```

`clf` also allows us to extract more nuanced prediction outputs. For instance, we can generate the fraction of the votes received by each class for an inputted sample in `X_test`. To obtain this voting distribution, we need to run `clf.predict_proba(X_test)`. The `predict_proba` method returns a matrix whose columns correspond to vote ratios. Here we print the first four rows of this matrix, which correspond to `X_test[:5]`.

Listing 20.40 Outputting vote ratios for each class

```
vote_ratios = clf.predict_proba(X_test)
print(vote_ratios[:4])

array([[0.        , 0.21419074, 0.78580926],
       [0.        , 1.        , 0.        ],
       [1.        , 0.        , 0.        ],
       [0.        , 0.        , 1.        ]])
```

As we can see, the data point at `X_test[0]` received 78.5% of votes for Class 2. The rest of the votes were given to Class 1. Meanwhile, `X_test[4]` received a full 100% of votes for Class 2. Even though both data points are assigned a class label of 2, the second point is assigned that label with a higher degree of confidence.

It's worth noting that all scikit-learn classifiers include their own version of `predict_proba`. The method returns an estimated probability distribution of data points belonging to some class. The column index with the highest probability is equal to the class label in `y_pred`.

Relevant scikit-learn classifier methods

- `clf = KNeighborsClassifier()`—Initializes a KNN classifier where $K = 5$ and voting is uniform across the five nearest neighbors.
- `clf = KNeighborsClassifier(n_neighbors=x)`—Initializes a KNN classifier where $K = x$ and voting is uniform across the x neighbors.

(continued)

- `clf = KNeighborsClassifier(n_neighbors=x, weights='distance')`— Initializes a KNN classifier where $K = x$ and voting is weighted by distance to each of the x neighbors.
- `clf.fit(X_train, y_train)`—Fits any classifier `clf` to predict classes `y` from features `X` based on training features `X_train` and training labeled classes `y_train`.
- `y = clf.predict(X)`—Predicts an array of classes associated with the feature matrix `X`. Each predicted class `y[i]` maps the matrix feature row `X[i]`.
- `M = clf.predict_proba(X)`—Returns a matrix `M` of probability distributions. Each row `M[i]` represents the probability distribution of data point `i` belonging to some class. The class prediction of that data point equals the distribution's maximum value. More concisely, `M[i].argmax() == clf.predict(X)[i]`.

Now, let's turn our attention to running a grid search across `KNeighborsClassifier`. First we need to specify a dictionary mapping between our hyperparameters and their value ranges. The dictionary keys equal our input parameters `n_neighbors` and `weights`. The dictionary values equal the respective iterables, `range(1, 40)`, and `['uniform', 'distance']`. Let's create this `hyperparams` dictionary.

Listing 20.41 Defining a hyperparameter dictionary

```
hyperparams = {'n_neighbors': range(1, 40),      ⊲
               'weights': ['uniform', 'distance']}
```

In our manual grid search, the neighbor count ranged from 1 to y_train.size, where y_train.size equaled 37. However, that parameter range can be set to any arbitrary value. Here, we set the range cutoff to 40, which is a nice round number.

Next, we need to import scikit-learn's `GridSearchCV` class, which we'll use to execute the grid search.

Listing 20.42 Importing scikit-learn's grid search class

```
from sklearn.model_selection import GridSearchCV
```

It's time to initialize the `GridSearchCV` class. We input three parameters into the initializing method. The first parameter is `KNeighborsClassifier()`: an initialized scikit-learn object whose hyperparameters we wish to optimize. Our second input is the `hyperparams` dictionary. Our final input is `scoring='f1_macro'`, which sets the evaluation metric to the averaged f-measure value.

The following code executes `GridSearchCV(KNeighborsClassifier(), hyperparams, scoring='f1_macro')`. The initialized object can perform classification, so we assign it to the variable `clf_grid`.

Listing 20.43 Initializing scikit-learn's grid search class

```
clf_grid = GridSearchCV(KNeighborsClassifier(), hyperparams,
                        scoring='f1_macro')
```

We're ready to run grid search on our fully labeled dataset `X`, `y`. Running `clf_grid.fit(X, y)` executes this parameter sweep. Scikit-learn's internal methods automatically split `X` and `y` during the validation process.

Listing 20.44 Running a grid search using scikit-learn

```
clf_grid.fit(X, y)
```

We've executed the grid search. The optimized hyperparameters are stored in the `clf_grid.best_params_` attribute, and the f-measure associated with these parameters is stored in `clf_grid.best_score_`. Let's output these results.

Listing 20.45 Checking the optimized grid search results

```
best_f = clf_grid.best_score_
best_params = clf_grid.best_params_
print(f"A maximum f-measure of {best_f:.2f} is achieved with the "
      f"following hyperparameters:\n{best_params}")

A maximum f-measure of 0.99 is achieved with the following hyperparameters:
{'n_neighbors': 10, 'weights': 'distance'}
```

Scikit-learn's grid search achieved an f-measure of 0.99. This value is higher than our custom grid search output of 0.96. Why is it higher? Well, scikit-learn has carried out a more sophisticated version of cross-validation. Rather than splitting the dataset into two parts, it split the data into five equal parts. Each individual data partition served as a training set, and the data outside each partition was used for testing. The five f-scores across the five training sets were computed and averaged. The final mean value of 0.99 represents a more accurate estimation of classifier performance.

> **NOTE** Splitting the data into five parts for evaluation purposes is called *5-fold cross-validation.* Generally, we can split the data into *K* equal parts. In GridSearchCV, the splitting is controlled by the `cv` parameter. Passing `cv = 2` splits the data into two parts, and the final f-measure resembles our original value of 0.96.

Maximized performance is achieved when `n_neighbors` is set to 10 and weighted voting is activated. The actual KNN classifier containing these parameters is stored in the `clf_grid.best_estimator_` attribute.

> **NOTE** Multiple hyperparameter combinations lead to an f-measure of 0.99. The chosen combination may vary across different machines. Thus, your parameter outputs may be slightly different even though the optimized f-measure will remain the same.

Listing 20.46   Accessing the optimized classifier

```
clf_best = clf_grid.best_estimator_
assert clf_best.n_neighbors == best_params['n_neighbors']
assert clf_best.weights == best_params['weights']
```

By using `clf_best`, we can carry out predictions on new data. Alternatively, we can carry out predictions directly with our optimized `clf_grid` object by running `clf_grid.predict`. Both objects return identical results.

Listing 20.47   Generating predictions with `clf_grid`

```
assert np.array_equal(clf_grid.predict(X), clf_best.predict(X))
```

Relevant scikit-learn grid search methods and attributes

- `clf_grid = GridSearchCV(ClassifierClass(), hyperparams, scoring = scoring_metric)`—Creates a grid search object intended to optimize classifier prediction across all possible hyperparameters based on a scoring metric specified by `scoring`. If `ClassifierClass()` is equal to `KNeighbors-Classifier()`, then `clf_grid` serves to optimize KNN. If the `scoring_metric` is equal to `f1_macro`, the average f-measure is utilized for optimization.
- `clf_grid.fit(X, y)`—Executes a grid search to optimize classifier performance across all possible combinations of hyperparameter values.
- `clf_grid.best_score_`—Returns the optimal measure of classifier performance after a grid search has been executed.
- `clf_grid.best_params_`—Returns the combination of hyperparameters that leads to optimal performance based on the grid search.
- `clf_best = clf_grid.best_estimator_`—Returns a scikit-learn classifier object that shows optimal performance based on a grid search.
- `clf_grid.predict(X)`—A shortcut to execute `clf_grid.best_estimator_.predict(X)`.

20.5   *Limitations of the KNN algorithm*

KNN is the simplest of all supervised learning algorithms. That simplicity leads to certain flaws. Unlike other algorithms, KNN is not interpretable: we can predict the class and inputted data point, but we cannot comprehend why that data point belongs to that class. Suppose we train a KNN model that predicts whether a high school student belongs to 1 of 10 possible social cliques. Even if the model is accurate, we still can't understand why the student is classified as a jock and not as a member of the glee club. Later, we'll encounter other algorithms that can be used to better understand how data features relate to class identity.

Additionally, KNN only works well when the feature count is low. As the number of features increases, potentially redundant information begins to creep into the data.

Hence, the distance measures become less reliable, and the prediction quality suffers. Fortunately, feature redundancy can partially be alleviated by the dimension-reduction techniques introduced in section 14. But even with the proper application of these techniques, large feature sets can still lead to less accurate predictions.

Finally, the biggest problem with KNN is its speed. The algorithm can be very slow to run when the training set is large. Suppose we build a training set with a million labeled flowers. Naively, finding the nearest neighbors of an unlabeled flower would require us to scan its distance to each of the million flowers. This will take a lot of time. Of course, we can optimize for speed by organizing the training data more efficiently. The process is analogous to organizing words in a dictionary. Imagine we want to look up the word *data* in an unalphabetized dictionary. Since words are stored haphazardly, we need to scan each page. In the 6,000-page Oxford dictionary, this would take a very long time. Fortunately, all dictionaries are alphabetized, so we quickly look up the word by flipping open the dictionary at approximately its middle point. Here, at page 3,000, we encounter the letters *M* and *N*. Then we can flip the pages to the halfway point between page 3,000 and the inside cover; this takes us to page 1,500, which should contain words with the letter *D*. We're thus much closer to our goal. Repeating this process several more times will take us to the word *data*.

In a similar manner, we can quickly scan nearest neighbors if we first organize the training set by spatial distance. Scikit-learn employs a special data structure called a *K-D tree* to ensure that proximate training points are stored more closely to each other. This leads to faster scanning and quicker neighbor lookup. The details of K-D tree construction are beyond the scope of this book, but you're encouraged to read Manning's *Advanced Algorithms and Data Structures* by Marcello La Rocca to learn more about this very useful technique (2021, www.manning.com/books/algorithms-and-data-structures-in-action).

Despite the built-in lookup optimization, as we mentioned, KNN can still be slow to run when the training set is large. The reduction is especially cumbersome during hyperparameter optimization. We'll illustrate this slowdown by increasing the elements in our training set (X, y) 2,000-fold. Then we'll time the grid search for the expanded data.

WARNING   The following code will take a long time to run.

Listing 20.48   Optimizing KNN on a large training set

```
import time
X_large = np.vstack([X for _ in range(2000)])
y_large = np.hstack([y for _ in range(2000)])
clf_grid = GridSearchCV(KNeighborsClassifier(), hyperparams,
                        scoring='f1_macro')
start_time = time.time()
clf_grid.fit(X_large, y_large)
running_time = (time.time() - start_time) / 60
print(f"The grid search took {running_time:.2f} minutes to run.")

The grid search took 16.23 minutes to run.
```

Our grid search took over 16 minutes to run! This is not an acceptable running time. We need an alternative solution. In the following section, we explore new classifiers whose prediction running time is not dependent on the training set size. We develop these classifiers from commonsense first principles and then we utilize their scikit-learn implementations.

Summary

- In *supervised machine learning*, our goal is to find a mapping between inputted measurements called *features* and outputted categories called *classes*. A model that identifies classes based on features is called a *classifier*.

- To construct a classifier, we first require a dataset with both features and labeled classes. This dataset is called a *training set*.

- One very simple classifier is *K-nearest neighbors* (KNN). KNN can classify an unlabeled point based on the plurality class among the *K*-nearest labeled points in the training set. Essentially, these neighbors vote to decide the unknown classes. Optionally, the voting can be weighted based on the distance of the neighbors to the unlabeled point.

- We can evaluate the performance of a classifier by computing a *confusion matrix*, M. Each diagonal element M[i][i] tracks the number of accurately predicted instances of class i. Such accurate predictions are called the *true positive* instances of a class. The fraction of total elements along the diagonal of M is the *accuracy score*.

- Predicted Class A elements that actually belong to Class B are called the *false positives* of Class A. Dividing the true positive count by the sum of true positives and false positives produces a metric called *precision*. A low precision indicates that the predicted class label is not very reliable.

- Actual Class A elements that are predicted to belong to Class B are called the *false negatives* of Class A. Dividing the true positive count by the sum of true positives and false negatives produces a metric known as *recall*. A low recall indicates that our predictor commonly misses valid instances of a class.

- A good classifier should yield both high precision and high recall. We can combine precision and recall into a single metric called the *f-measure*. Given precision p and recall r, we can compute the f-measure by running 2 * p * r / (p + r). Multiple f-measures across multiple classes can be averaged into a single score.

- The f-measure can sometimes be superior to the accuracy, especially when data is imbalanced, so it's the preferable evaluation metric.

- To optimize KNN performance, we need to choose an optimal value for *K*. We also need to decide whether to utilize weighted voting. These two parameterized inputs are called *hyperparameters*. Such hyperparameters must be set before training. All machine learning models have hyperparameters that can be tweaked to enhance predictive power.

- The simplest hyperparameter optimization technique is called a *grid search*, which is conducted by iterating over every possible hyperparameter combination. Before the iterations, the original dataset is split into a training set and a validation set. This splitting is referred to as *cross-validation*. Then we iterate over the parameters. At each iteration, the classifier is trained and evaluated. Finally, we choose the hyperparameter values that lead to the highest metric output.

Training linear classifiers
with logistic regression

This section covers

- Separating data classes with simple linear cuts
- What is logistic regression?
- Training linear classifiers using scikit-learn
- Interpreting the relationship between class prediction and trained classifier parameters

Data classification, much like clustering, can be treated as a geometry problem. Similarly, labeled classes cluster together in an abstract space. By measuring the distance between points, we can identify which data points belong to the same cluster or class. However, as we learned in the last section, computing that distance can be costly. Fortunately, it's possible to find related classes without measuring the distance between all points. This is something we have done before: in section 14, we examined the customers of a clothing store. Each customer was represented by two features: height and weight. Plotting these features revealed a cigar-shaped plot. We flipped the cigar on its side and sliced it vertically into three segments representing three classes of customers: small, medium, and large.

It's possible to separate distinct classes of data by carving out those classes as though with a knife. The carving can be carried out with simple linear cuts. Previously, we limited ourselves to vertical downward cuts. In this section, we learn how to cut the data at an angle to maximize class separation. Through directed linear cuts, we can classify our data without relying on distance calculations. In the process, we learn how to train and interpret linear classifiers. Let's get started by revisiting the problem of separating customers by size.

21.1 Linearly separating customers by size

In section 14, we simulated customer heights (in inches) and weights (in pounds). Customers with larger inch/pound combinations fell into the Large customer class. We'll now rerun that simulation. Our heights and weights are stored in a feature matrix X, and the customer classes are stored in the class-label array of y. For the purpose of this exercise, we focus on the two classes Large and Not Large. We assume that customers in the Large class are taller than 72 inches and heavier than 160 lb. After we simulate this data, we make a scatter plot of X in which the plotted points are colored based on the class labels in y (figure 21.1). This visual representation will help us look for the spatial separation between the different customer types.

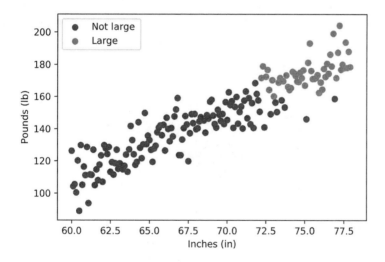

Figure 21.1 A plot of customer measurements: inches vs. lbs. Large and Not Large customers are colored differently based on their class.

Listing 21.1 Simulating categorized customer measurements

```
import matplotlib.pyplot as plt
import numpy as np
np.random.seed(1)


def plot_customers(X, y, xlabel='Inches (in)', ylabel='Pounds (lb)'):
    colors = ['g', 'y']
```

Plots customer measurements while coloring the customers based on class. Customer heights and weights are treated as two different features in the feature matrix X. Customer class type is stored with the label array y.

Customers fall into two classes, Large and Not Large.

```
labels = ['Not Large', 'Large']
for i, (color, label) in enumerate(zip(colors, labels)):
    plt.scatter(X[:,0][y == i], X[:,1][y == i], color=color, label=label)

plt.xlabel(xlabel)
plt.ylabel(ylabel)
```

```
inches = np.arange(60, 78, 0.1)
random_fluctuations = np.random.normal(scale=10, size=inches.size)
pounds = 4 * inches - 130 + random_fluctuations
X = np.array([inches, pounds]).T
y = ((X[:,0] > 72) & (X[:,1] > 160)).astype(int)
```

Follows the linear formula from section 14 to model weight as a function of height

```
plot_customers(X, y)
plt.legend()
plt.show()
```

Customers are considered Large if their height is greater than 72 inches and their weight is greater than 160 lb.

Our plot resembles a cigar with different shades of colors at both ends. We can imagine a knife slicing through the cigar to separate the colors. The knife acts like a boundary that separates the two customer classes. We can represent this boundary using a line with a slope of −3.5 and a y-intercept of 415. The formula for the line is `lbs = -3.5 * inches + 415`. Let's add this linear boundary to the plot (figure 21.2).

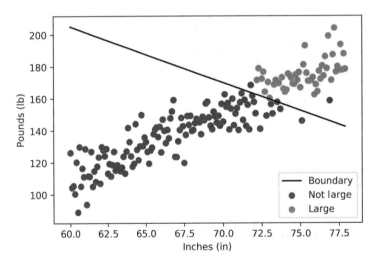

Figure 21.2   A plot of customer measurements: `inches` vs. `lbs`. A linear boundary separates the Large and Not Large customers.

NOTE   We learn how to automatically compute the linear boundary later in this section.

Listing 21.2 Plotting a boundary to separate the two customer classes

```
def boundary(inches): return  -3.5 * inches + 415
plt.plot(X[:,0], boundary(X[:,0]), color='k', label='Boundary')
plot_customers(X, y)
plt.legend()
plt.show()
```

The plotted line is called a *linear decision boundary* because it can be utilized to accurately choose a customer's class. Most of the customers in the Large class are located above that line. Given a customer with a measurement of (inches, lbs), we predict the customer's class by checking whether lbs > -3.5 * inches + 415. If the inequality is true, then the customer is Large. Let's use the inequality to predict the customer classes. We store our predictions in a y_pred array and evaluate our predictions by printing the f-measure.

> **NOTE** As we discussed in section 20, the f-measure is our preferred way of evaluating class prediction quality. As a reminder, the f-measure equals the harmonic mean of a classifier's precision and recall.

Listing 21.3 Predicting classes using a linear boundary

```
from sklearn.metrics import f1_score
y_pred = []
for inches, lbs in X:
    prediction = int(lbs > -3.5 * inches + 415)
    y_pred.append(prediction)

f_measure = f1_score(y_pred, y)
print(f'The f-measure is {f_measure:.2f}')
```

If b is a **Python Boolean**, int(b) returns 1 if the Boolean is True and 0 otherwise. Hence, we can return the class label for measurements (inches, lbs) by running int(lbs > –3.5 * inches + 415).

```
The f-measure is 0.97
```

As expected, the f-measure is high. Given the inequality lbs > -3.5 * inches + 415, we can accurately classify our data. Furthermore, we can run the classification more concisely using vector dot products. Consider the following:

1 Our inequality rearranges to 3.5 * inches + lbs - 415 > 0.
2 The dot product of two vectors [x, y, z] and [a, b, c] is equal to a * x + b * y + c * z.
3 If we take the dot product of vectors [inches, lbs, 1] and [3.5, 1, -415], the result equals 3.5 * inches + lbs - 415.
4 Thus our inequality reduces to w @ v > 0, where w and v are both vectors, and @ is the dot-product operator, as show in figure 21.3.

Note that only one of the vectors is dependent on values of lbs and inches. The second vector, [3.5, 1, -415], does not vary with customer measurements. Data scientists refer to this invariant vector as the *weight vector* or simply *weights*.

NOTE   This name is unrelated to our measured customer weights in pounds.

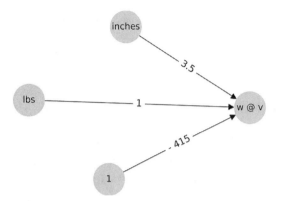

Figure 21.3   We can visualize the dot product between `weights` **and** `[inches, lbs, 1]` **as a directed graph. In the graph, the leftmost nodes represent the measurements** `[inches, lbs, 1]`**, and the edge weights represent the weights** `[3.5, 1, -415]`**. We multiply each node by its corresponding edge weight and sum the results. That sum equals the product between our two vectors v and w. Customer classification is determined by whether** `w @ v > 0`**.**

Using vector dot products, we'll re-create the contents of y_pred in two lines of code:

1   Assign a `weights` vector to equal `[3.5, 1, -415]`.

2   Classify each (inches, lbs) customer sample in X using the dot product of `weights` and `[inches, lbs, 1]`.

Listing 21.4   Predicting classes using vector dot products

```
weights = np.array([3.5, 1, -415])
predictions = [int(weights @ [inches, lbs, 1] > 0) for inches, lbs in X]
assert predictions == y_pred
```

We can further consolidate our code if we use matrix multiplication.

Consider the following:

1   Currently, we must iterate over each `[inches, lbs]` row in matrix X and append a 1 to get vector `[inches, lbs, 1]`.

2   Instead, we can concatenate a column of ones to matrix X and obtain a three-column matrix M. Each matrix row equals `[inches, lbs, 1]`. We refer to M as the *padded feature matrix.*

3   Running `[weights @ v for v in M]` returns the dot product between `weights` and every row in matrix M. Of course, this operation is equivalent to the matrix product between M and `weights`.

4   We can concisely compute the matrix product by running `M @ weights`.

5   Running `M @ weights > 0` returns a Boolean array. Each element is true only if `3.5 * inches + lbs - 415 > 0` for the corresponding customer measurements.

Essentially, `M @ weights > 0` returns a Boolean vector whose *i*th value is true if `y_pred[i] == 1` and false otherwise. We can transform the Booleans into numeric labels using NumPy's astype method. Consequently, we can generate our predictions just by running `(M @ weights > 0).astype(int)`. Let's confirm.

| Listing 21.5 | Predicting classes using matrix multiplication |

```
M = np.column_stack([X, np.ones(X.shape[0])])          ◁⎯⎯⎯┐  Concatenates a
print("First five rows of our padded feature matrix are:")    column of ones to
print(np.round(M[:5], 2))                                      feature matrix X to
                                                               create the three-
predictions = (M @ weights > 0).astype(int)                    column matrix M
assert predictions.tolist() == y_pred     ◁⎯⎯⎯┐

First five rows of our padded feature matrix are:
[[ 60.   126.24   1.  ]
 [ 60.1  104.28   1.  ]
 [ 60.2  105.52   1.  ]
 [ 60.3  100.47   1.  ]
 [ 60.4  120.25   1.  ]]
```

Checks to ensure that our predictions remain the same. Note that the matrix product returns a NumPy array, which must be converted to a list for this comparison.

We've boiled down customer classification to a simple matrix-vector product. This matrix product classifier is called a *linear classifier*. A weight vector is all that is required for a linear classifier to categorize input features. Here, we define a linear_classifier function that takes as input a feature matrix X and weight vector weights. It returns an array of class predictions.

| Listing 21.6 | Defining a linear classifier function |

```
def linear_classifier(X, weights):
    M = np.column_stack([X, np.ones(X.shape[0])])
    return (M @ weights > 0).astype(int)

predictions = linear_classifier(X, weights)
assert predictions.tolist() == y_pred
```

Linear classifiers check whether weighted features and a constant add up to a value greater than zero. The constant value, which is stored in weights[-1], is referred to as the *bias*. The remaining weights are called the *coefficients*. During classification, every coefficient is multiplied against its corresponding feature. In our case, the inches coefficient in weights[0] is multiplied against inches, and the lbs coefficient in weights[1] is multiplied against lbs. Thus, weights contains two coefficients and one bias, taking the form [inches_coef, lbs_coef, bias].

We've derived our weights vector using a known decision boundary, but weights can also be computed directly from our training set (X, y). In the following subsection, we discuss how to train a linear classifier. Training consists of finding coefficients and a bias that linearly separate our customer classes.

> **NOTE** The trained results are not equal to weights because an infinite number of weights vectors satisfy the inequality M @ weights > 0. We can prove this by multiplying both sides by a positive constant k. Of course, 0 * k equals 0. Meanwhile, weights * k produces a new vector w2. Hence, M @ w2 is greater than 0 whenever M @ weights > 0 (and vice versa). There are infinite numbers of

k constants and hence an infinite number of w2 vectors, but these vectors point in the same direction.

21.2 *Training a linear classifier*

We want to find a weight vector that optimizes class prediction on X. Let's start by setting weights to equal three random values. Then we compute the f-measure associated with this random vector. We expect the f-measure to be very low.

Listing 21.7   Classification using random weights

```
np.random.seed(0)
weights = np.random.normal(size=3)
y_pred = linear_classifier(X, weights)
f_measure = f1_score(y_pred, y)

print('We inputted the following random weights:')
print(np.round(weights, 2))
print(f'\nThe f-measure is {f_measure:.2f}')

We inputted the following random weights:
[1.76 0.4  0.98]

The f-measure is 0.43
```

As expected, our f-measure is terrible! We can gain insight into why by printing y_pred.

Listing 21.8   Outputting the predicted classes

```
print(y_pred)

[1 1 1 1 1 1 1 1 1 1 1 1 1 1 1 1 1 1 1 1 1 1 1 1 1 1 1 1 1 1 1 1 1 1 1 1 1
 1 1 1 1 1 1 1 1 1 1 1 1 1 1 1 1 1 1 1 1 1 1 1 1 1 1 1 1 1 1 1 1 1 1 1 1 1
 1 1 1 1 1 1 1 1 1 1 1 1 1 1 1 1 1 1 1 1 1 1 1 1 1 1 1 1 1 1 1 1 1 1 1 1 1
 1 1 1 1 1 1 1 1 1 1 1 1 1 1 1 1 1 1 1 1 1 1 1 1 1 1 1 1 1 1 1 1 1 1 1 1 1
 1 1 1 1 1 1 1 1 1 1 1 1 1 1 1 1 1 1 1 1 1 1 1 1 1 1 1 1 1 1 1]
```

All our data points are assigned a class label of 1! The product of our weights and each feature vector is always greater than zero, so our weights must be too high. Lowering the weights will yield more Class 0 predictions. For instance, if we set the weights to [0, 0, 0], all our class predictions equal 0.

Listing 21.9   Shifting the class predictions by lowering the weights

```
assert np.all(linear_classifier(X, [0, 0, 0]) == 0)
```

Lowering the weights yields more Class 0 predictions. Raising them yields more Class 1 predictions. Thus, we can intelligently raise and lower the weights until our predictions align with the actual class labels. Let's devise a strategy for adjusting the weights to match the labels. We start by adjusting the bias at weights[-1].

NOTE Adjusting the coefficients requires a bit more nuance, so for now, we'll focus on the bias.

Our goal is to minimize the difference between the predictions in y_pred and the actual labels in y. How do we do this? One simple strategy entails comparing each *predicted/actual* class-label pair. Based on each comparison, we can tweak the bias like this:

- If the prediction equals the actual class, then the prediction is correct. Hence, we will not modify the bias.
- If the prediction is 1 and the actual class is 0, then the weight is too high. Hence, we'll lower the bias by one unit.
- If the prediction is 0 and the actual class is 1, the weight is too low. Hence, we'll increase the bias by one unit.

Let's define a function to compute this bias shift based on predicted and actual labels.

NOTE Keep in mind that per existing conventions, the bias shift is subtracted from the weights. So, our get_bias_shift function returns a positive value when the weights are intended to decrease.

Listing 21.10 Computing the bias shift based on prediction quality

```
def get_bias_shift(predicted, actual):
    if predicted == actual:
        return 0
    if predicted > actual:
        return 1

    return -1
```

Mathematically, we can show that our get_bias_shift function is equivalent to predicted - actual. The following code definitively proves this for all four combinations of predicted and actual class labels.

Listing 21.11 Computing the bias shift using arithmetic

```
for predicted, actual in [(0, 0), (1, 0), (0, 1), (1, 1)]:
    bias_shift = get_bias_shift(predicted, actual)
    assert bias_shift == predicted - actual
```

It's worth noting that our single unit shift is an arbitrary value. Rather than shifting the bias by a single unit, we can shift it one-tenth of a unit, or 10 units, or 100 units. The value of the shift can be controlled by a parameter called the *learning rate*. The learning rate is multiplied against predicted - actual to adjust the shift size. So if we want to lower the shift to 0.1, we can easily do so by running learning_rate * (predicted - actual), where learning_rate is equal to 0.1. This adjustment can influence the quality of training. We'll therefore redefine our get_bias_shift function with a learning_rate parameter that is preset to 0.1.

Listing 21.12   Computing the bias shift with a learning rate

```
def get_bias_shift(predicted, actual, learning_rate=0.1):
    return learning_rate * (predicted - actual)
```

Now we are ready to adjust our bias. Listing 21.13 iterates over each [inches, lbs, 1] vector in M. For every *i*th vector, we predict the class label and compare it to the actual class in y[i].

> **NOTE**   As a reminder, the class prediction for every vector v is equal to int(v @ weights > 0).

Using each prediction, we compute the bias shift and subtract it from the bias stored in weights[-1]. When all the iterations are complete, we print the adjusted bias and compare it to its original value.

Listing 21.13   Iteratively shifting the bias

```
def predict(v, weights): return int(v @ weights > 0)      ⟵──┐ Predicts the class
                                                             │ label for vector v
starting_bias = weights[-1]                                  │ associated with a
for i, actual in enumerate(y):                               │ row in matrix M
    predicted = predict(M[i], weights)
    bias_shift = get_bias_shift(predicted, actual)
    weights[-1] -= bias_shift

new_bias = weights[-1]
print(f"Our starting bias equaled {starting_bias:.2f}.")
print(f"The adjusted bias equals {new_bias:.2f}.")
```

```
Our starting bias equaled 0.98.
The adjusted bias equals -12.02
```

The bias has drastically decreased. This makes sense, given that our weights were way too large. Let's check whether the shift improved our f-measure.

Listing 21.14   Checking performance after the bias shift

```
y_pred = linear_classifier(X, weights)
f_measure = f1_score(y_pred, y)
print(f'The f-measure is {f_measure:.2f}')
```

```
The f-measure is 0.43
```

Our f-measure remains the same. Simply adjusting the bias is insufficient. We need to adjust the coefficients as well, but how? Naively, we could subtract the bias shift from every coefficient. We could just iterate over each training example and run weights -= bias_shift. Unfortunately, this naive approach is flawed: it always adjusts the coefficients, but it is dangerous to adjust the coefficients when their associated features are equal to zero. We'll illustrate why with a simple example.

Imagine that a blank entry in our customer dataset is erroneously recorded as (0, 0). Our model treats this data point as a customer who weighs nothing and is 0 inches tall. Of course, such a customer is not physically possible, but that's beside the point. This theoretical customer is definitely Not Large, so their correct class label should be 0. When our linear model classifies the customer, it takes the dot product of [0, 0, 1] and [inches_coef, lbs_coef, bias]. Of course, the coefficients are multiplied by zero and cancel out, so the final dot product is equal to just bias (figure 21.4). If bias > 0, the classifier incorrectly assigns a Class 1 label. Here, we'd need to decrease the bias using bias_shift. Would we also adjust the coefficients? No! Our coefficients did not impact the prediction. Thus, we can't evaluate the coefficient quality. For all we know, the coefficients are set to their optimal values. If so, then subtracting the bias shift would make the model worse.

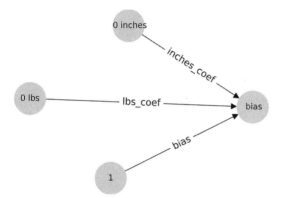

Figure 21.4   We can visualize the dot product between weights and [0, 0, 1] as a directed graph. In the graph, the leftmost nodes represent the zero-value features, and the edge weights represent the coefficients and the bias. We multiply each node by its corresponding edge weight and sum the results. That sum equals bias. Customer classification is determined by whether bias > 0. The coefficients don't impact the prediction and therefore should not be altered in any way.

We should never shift lbs_coef if the lbs features equal zero. However, for nonzero inputs, subtracting bias_shift from lbs_coef remains appropriate. We could ensure this by setting the lbs_coef shift to equal bias_shift if lbs else 0. Alternatively, we can set the shift to equal bias_shift * lbs. This product is zero when lbs is zero. Otherwise, the product shifts lbs_coef in the same direction as the bias. Similarly, we can shift inches_coef by bias_shift * inches units. In other words, we'll shift each coefficient by the product of its feature and bias_shift.

NumPy allows us to compute our weight shifts all at once by running bias_shift * [inches, lbs, 1]. Of course, the [inches, lbs, 1] vector corresponds to a row in the padded feature matrix M. Thus, we can adjust the weights based on each ith prediction by running weights -= bias_shift * M[i].

With this in mind, let's iterate over each actual label in y and adjust the weights based on the predicted values. Then we check whether the f-measure has improved.

Listing 21.15   Computing all weight shifts in one line of code

```
old_weights = weights.copy()
for i, actual in enumerate(y):
    predicted = predict(M[i], weights)
    bias_shift = get_bias_shift(predicted, actual)
    weights -= bias_shift * M[i]

y_pred = linear_classifier(X, weights)
f_measure = f1_score(y_pred, y)

print("The weights previously equaled:")
print(np.round(old_weights, 2))
print("\nThe updated weights now equal:")
print(np.round(weights, 2))
print(f'\nThe f-measure is {f_measure:.2f}')

The weights previously equaled:
[  1.76    0.4  -12.02]

The updated weights now equal:
[ -4.64    2.22 -12.12]

The f-measure is 0.78
```

During the iteration, inches_coef has decreased by 6.39 units (from 1.76 to –4.63), and the bias has decreased by just 0.1 units (from –12.02 to –12.12). This discrepancy makes sense because the coefficient shift is proportional to height. Customers are on average 64 inches tall, so the coefficient shift is 64-fold greater than the bias. As we'll soon discover, large differences in weight shifts can lead to problems. Later, we eliminate these problems through a process called *standardization*; but first let's turn to our f-measure.

Our f-measure has risen from 0.43 to 0.78. The weight-shift strategy is working! What happens if we repeat the iteration 1,000 times? Let's find out. Listing 21.16 monitors the changes in f-measure over 1,000 weight-shift iterations. Then we plot each *i*th f-measure relative to the *i*th iteration (figure 21.5). We utilize the plot to monitor how the classifier's performance improves over time.

> **NOTE**   For the purpose of this exercise, we set weights to their original seeded random values. This allows us to monitor how performance improves relative to our starting f-measure of 0.43.

Listing 21.16   Tweaking the weights over multiple iterations

```
np.random.seed(0)
weights = np.random.normal(size=3)      ⊲——┤ Sets the starting weights
                                             to random values
f_measures = []
for _ in range(1000):                   ⊲——┤ Repeats the weight-shift logic
    y_pred = linear_classifier(X, weights)    across 1,000 iterations
    f_measures.append(f1_score(y_pred, y))
```

Tracks performance for the weights at each iteration

```
for i, actual in enumerate(y):
    predicted = predict(M[i], weights)
    bias_shift = get_bias_shift(predicted, actual)
    weights -= bias_shift * M[i]
```

⟵ **Shifts the weights by iterating over each predicted/actual class-label pair**

```
print(f'The f-measure after 1000 iterations is {f_measures[-1]:.2f}')
plt.plot(range(len(f_measures)), f_measures)
plt.xlabel('Iteration')
plt.ylabel('F-measure')
plt.show()
```

The f-measure after 1000 iterations is 0.68

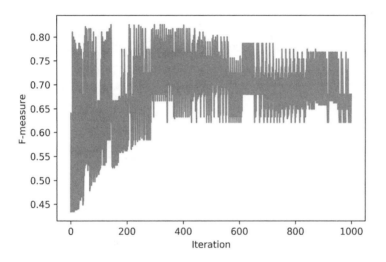

Figure 21.5   Plotted iterations vs. model f-measure. The model weights are tweaked at each iteration. The f-measure oscillates widely between low and reasonable values. These oscillations need to be eliminated.

The final f-measure is 0.68. Our classifier is very poorly trained. What happened? Well, according to our plot, the classifier performance oscillates wildly throughout the iterations. Sometimes the f-measure goes as high as 0.80; other times, it drops to approximately 0.60. After about 400 iterations, the classifier fluctuates nonstop between these two values. The rapid fluctuations are caused by a weight shift that is consistently too high. This is analogous to an airplane that is flying much too fast. Imagine an airplane flying 600 miles per hour after takeoff. The airplane maintains this rapid speed, allowing it to cover 1,500 miles in under three hours. However, as the airplane approaches its destination, the pilot refuses to slow down, so the plane overshoots its target airport and is forced to turn around. If the pilot doesn't lower the velocity, the plane will miss the landing again. This will lead to a sequence of never-ending aerial U-turns, similar to the oscillations in our plot. For the pilot, the solution is simple: reduce speed over the course of the flight.

We face an analogous solution: we should slowly lower the weight shift over each additional iteration. How do we lower the weight shift? One approach is to divide the shift by k for each *k*th iteration. Let's execute this strategy. We reset our weights to random values and iterate over k values ranging from 1 to 1,001. In each iteration, we set the weight shift equal to `bias_shift * M[i] / k`. Then we regenerate our performance plot (figure 21.6).

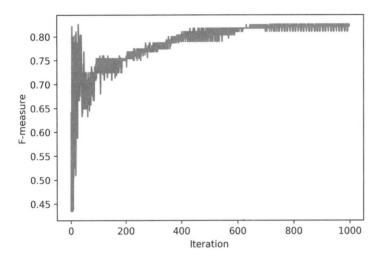

Figure 21.6   **Plotted iterations vs. model f-measure. The model weights are tweaked at each *k*th iteration, in proportion to `1/k`. Dividing the weight shifts by k limits oscillation. Thus, the f-measure converges to a reasonable value.**

Listing 21.17   Reducing weight shifts over multiple iterations

Trains a linear model from features X and labels y. The function is reused elsewhere in this section.

The predict function drives the weight shift by allowing us to compare predicted and actual class outputs. Later in this section, we modify predict to add nuance to the weight shifts.

```
np.random.seed(0)
def train(X, y,
          predict=predict):
    M = np.column_stack([X, np.ones(X.shape[0])])
    weights = np.random.normal(size=X.shape[1] + 1)
    f_measures = []
    for k in range(1, 1000):
        y_pred = linear_classifier(X, weights)
        f_measures.append(f1_score(y_pred, y))

        for i, actual in enumerate(y):
            predicted = predict(M[i], weights)
            bias_shift = get_bias_shift(predicted, actual)
            weights -= bias_shift * M[i] / k
```

A model with N features has N + 1 total weights representing N coefficients and one bias.

At each *k*th iteration, we dampen the weight shift by dividing by k. This reduces the weight-shift oscillations.

```
        return weights, f_measures
```
⟵——⎸ **Returns the optimized weights along
with tracked performance across
the 1,000 iterations**

```
weights, f_measures = train(X, y)
print(f'The f-measure after 1000 iterations is {f_measures[-1]:.2f}')
plt.plot(range(len(f_measures)), f_measures)
plt.xlabel('Iteration')
plt.ylabel('F-measure')
plt.show()
```

```
The f-measure after 1000 iterations is 0.82
```

Our gradual weight-shift reduction was successful. The f-measure converges to a steady value of 0.82. We achieved convergence using a *perceptron training algorithm*. A *perceptron* is a simple linear classifier that was invented in the 1950s. Perceptrons are very easy to train. We just need to apply the following steps to training set (X, y):

1. Append a column of ones to feature matrix X to create a padded matrix M.
2. Create a weights vector containing M.shape[1] random values.
3. Iterate over every *i*th row in M, and predict the *i*th class by running M[i] @ weights > 0.
4. Compare the *i*th prediction to the actual class label in y[i]. Then, compute the bias shift by running (predicted - actual) * lr, where lr is the learning rate.
5. Adjust the weights by running weights -= bias_shift * M[i] / k. Initially, the constant k is set to 1.
6. Repeat steps 3 through 5 over multiple iterations. At each iteration, increment k by 1 to limit oscillation.

Through repetition, the perceptron training algorithm eventually converges to a steady f-measure. However, that f-measure is not necessarily optimal. For instance, our perceptron converged to an f-measure of 0.82. This level of performance is acceptable, but it doesn't match our initial performance of 0.97. Our trained decision boundary doesn't separate the data as well as our initial decision boundary.

How do the two boundaries compare visually? We can easily find out. Using algebraic manipulation, we can transform a weight vector [inches_coef, lbs_coef, bias] into a linear decision boundary equal to lbs = -(inches_coef * inches + bias) / lbs_coef. With this in mind, we'll plot both our new and old decision boundaries, together with our customer data (figure 21.7).

Listing 21.18   Comparing new and old decision boundaries

```
inches_coef, lbs_coef, bias = weights
def new_boundary(inches):
    return -(inches_coef * inches + bias) / lbs_coef

plt.plot(X[:,0], new_boundary(X[:,0]), color='k', linestyle='--',
         label='Trained Boundary', linewidth=2)
```

```
plt.plot(X[:,0], boundary(X[:,0]), color='k', label='Initial Boundary')
plot_customers(X, y)
plt.legend()
plt.show()
```

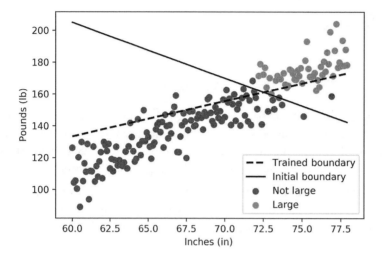

Figure 21.7   A plot of customer measurements: `inches` vs. `lbs`. Two linear boundaries separate the Large and Not Large customers. The trained boundary's separation is worse relative to the baseline boundary.

Our trained linear boundary is inferior to our initial linear boundary, but this is not the fault of the perceptron algorithm. Instead, the training is hindered by large, fluctuating features in matrix X. In the next subsection, we discuss why large X values impede performance. We'll limit that impediment through a process called *standardization*, in which X is adjusted to equal `(X - X.mean(axis=0)) / X.std(axis=0)`.

21.2.1 *Improving perceptron performance through standardization*

Perceptron training is impeded by large feature values in X. This is due to the discrepancy between the coefficient shifts and bias shifts. As we discussed, the coefficient shift is proportional to the associated feature value. Furthermore, these values can be quite high. For instance, the average customer height is greater than 60 inches: the `inches_coef` shift is more than 60-fold higher than the bias shift, so we can't tweak the bias by a little without tweaking the coefficients by a lot. Thus, by tuning the bias, we are liable to significantly shift `inches_coef` toward a less-than-optimal value.

Our training lacks all nuance because the coefficient shifts are much too high. However, we can lower these shifts by reducing column means in matrix X. Additionally, we need to lower the dispersion in the matrix. Otherwise, unusually large customer measurements could cause overly large coefficient shifts. We therefore need to decrease the column means and standard deviations. To start, let's print the current values of `X.mean(axis=0)` and `X.std(axis=0)`.

```
means = X.mean(axis=0)
stds = X.std(axis=0)
print(f"Mean values: {np.round(means, 2)}")
print(f"STD values: {np.round(stds, 2)}")

Mean values: [ 68.95 146.56]
STD values: [ 5.2  23.26]
```

The feature means and standard deviations are relatively high. How do we make them smaller? Well, as we learned in section 14, it is trivial to shift a dataset's mean toward zero: we simply need to subtract `means` from `X`. Adjusting the standard deviations is less straightforward, but mathematically we can show that `(X - means) / stds` returns a matrix whose column dispersions all equal 1.0.

> **NOTE** Here is the proof. Running `X - means` returns a matrix whose every column v has a mean of 0.0. Hence, the variance of each v equals [e * e for e in v] / N, where N is the number of column elements. Of course, this operation can be expressed as a simple dot product, `v @ v / N`. The standard deviation std equals the square root of the variance, so `std = sqrt(v @ v) / sqrt(N)`. Note that `sqrt(v @ v)` is equal to the magnitude of v, which we can express as `norm(v)`. Thus, `std = norm(v) / sqrt(N)`. Suppose we divide v by std to generate a new vector v2. Since `v2 = v / std`, we expect the magnitude of v2 to equal `norm(v) / std`. The standard deviation of v2 is equal to `norm(v2) / sqrt(N)`. By substituting out `norm(v2)`, we get `norm(v) / (sqrt(N) * std)`. However, `norm(v) / sqrt(N) = std`. So the standard deviation of v2 reduces to std / std, which equals 1.0.

This simple process is called *standardization*. Let's standardize our feature matrix by running `(X - means) / stds`. The resulting matrix has column means of 0 and column standard deviations of 1.0.

```
def standardize(X):            ◁──┐  Standardizes measurements derived from
    return (X - means) / stds         the customer distribution. We reuse the
                                       function elsewhere in this section.
X_s = standardize(X)
assert np.allclose(X_s.mean(axis=0), 0)
assert np.allclose(X_s.std(axis=0), 1)
```

We now check whether training on the standardized feature matrix improves our results. We also plot the trained decision boundary relative to the standardized data (figure 21.8).

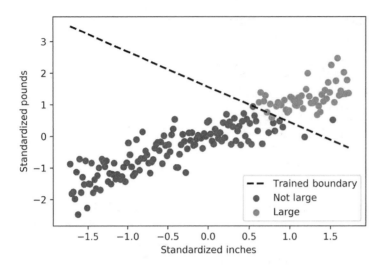

Figure 21.8 A plot of standardized customer measurements. A trained decision boundary separates Large and Not Large customers. The trained boundary's separation is on par with the baseline decision boundary in figure 21.2.

Listing 21.21   Training on the standardized feature matrix

```
np.random.seed(0)
weights, f_measures = train(X_s, y)
print(f'After standardization, the f-measure is {f_measures[-1]:.2f}')

def plot_boundary(weights):
    a, b, c = weights
    new_boundary = lambda x: -(a * x + c) / b
    plt.plot(X_s[:,0], new_boundary(X_s[:,0]), color='k', linestyle='--',
        label='Trained Boundary', linewidth=2)
    plot_customers(X_s, y, xlabel='Standardized Inches',
                   ylabel='Standardized Pounds')
    plt.legend()
    plt.show()

plot_boundary(weights)

After standardization, the f-measure is 0.98
```

Transforms the weights into a linear function → (points to `new_boundary = lambda x: -(a * x + c) / b`)

Plots the linear decision boundary derived from weights, together with the standardized data ← (points to `def plot_boundary(weights):`)

Success! Our new f-measure equals 0.98. This f-measure is higher than our baseline value of 0.97. Furthermore, the angle of our new decision boundary closely resembles the baseline boundary in figure 21.2. We achieved improvement in performance through standardization.

NOTE Standardization is similar to normalization. Both techniques lower the values in inputted data and eliminate unit differences (such as inches versus centimeters). For some tasks, such as PCA analysis, the two techniques can be used interchangeably. However, when we're training linear classifiers, standardization achieves superior results.

We should note that our trained classifier now requires all input data to be standardized before classification. Hence, given any new data d, we need to classify that data by running `linear_classifier(standardize(d), weights)`.

Listing 21.22 Standardizing new classifier inputs

```
new_data = np.array([[63, 110], [76, 199]])
predictions = linear_classifier(standardize(new_data), weights)
print(predictions)
```

```
[0 1]
```

We've standardized our data and achieved a high level of performance. Unfortunately, this optimal f-measure is still not guaranteed by the training algorithm. Perceptron training quality can fluctuate, even if the algorithm is run repeatedly on the same training set. This is due to the random weights assigned in the initial training step: certain starting weights converge to a worse decision boundary. Let's illustrate the model's inconsistency by training a perceptron five times. After each training run, we check whether the resulting f-measure falls below our initial baseline of 0.97.

Listing 21.23 Checking a perceptron's training consistency

```
np.random.seed(0)
poor_train_count = sum([train(X_s, y)[1][-1] < 0.97 for _ in range(5)])
print("The f-measure fell below our baseline of 0.97 in "
      f"{poor_train_count} out of 5 training instances")
```

```
The f-measure fell below our baseline of 0.97 in 4 out of 5
training instances
```

In 80% of instances, the trained model performance falls below the baseline. Our basic perceptron model is clearly flawed. We discuss its flaws in the subsequent subsection. In the process, we derive one of the most popular linear models in data science: logistic regression.

21.3 *Improving linear classification with logistic regression*

During class prediction, our linear boundary makes a simple binary decision. However, as we learned in section 20, not all predictions should be treated equally. Sometimes we are more confident in some predictions than others. For instance, if all neighbors in a KNN model vote unanimously for Class 1, we are 100% confident in that prediction. But if just six of nine neighbors vote for Class 1, we are 66% confident in that prediction. This measure of confidence is lacking in our perceptron model.

The model has just two outputs: 0 and 1, based on whether the data lies above or below the decision boundary.

What about a data point that lies exactly on the decision boundary? Currently, our logic will assign Class 0 to that point.

> **NOTE** If measurements in v lie on the decision boundary, then `weights @ v == 0`. Hence `int(weights @ v > 0)` returns 0.

However, that assignment is arbitrary. If the point is not positioned above or below the decision boundary, we cannot decide on either class! Thus, our confidence in either class should equal 50%. What if we shift the point 0.0001 units above the boundary? Our confidence in Class 1 should go up, but not by much. We can assume that the Class 1 likelihood increases to 50.001% while the Class 0 likelihood decreases to 49.999%. Only if the point is positioned far from the boundary should our confidence rise sharply, as illustrated in figure 21.9. For instance, if the point is 100 units above the boundary, then our confidence in Class 1 should reach 100% and our confidence in Class 0 should drop to 0%.

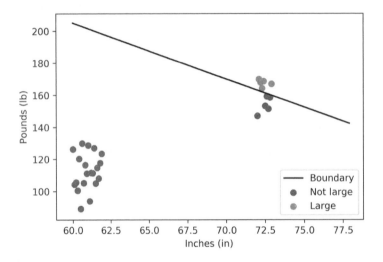

Figure 21.9 **A plot of customer measurements: `inches` vs. `lbs`. A linear boundary separates our two customer classes. Only customers who are either close to or far from the boundary are displayed. Customers who are too close to the boundary are harder to classify. We are much more confident in the class label of those customers who lie far from the decision boundary.**

Class confidence is determined by distance from the boundary and position relative to the boundary. If a point lies 100 units below the decision boundary, its Class 1 and 0 likelihoods should be flipped. We can capture both distance and position with *directed distance*. Unlike regular distance, directed distance can be negative. We'll assign each point a negative distance if it falls below the decision boundary.

NOTE Hence, if a point is 100 units below the boundary, its directed distance to the boundary equals −100.

Let's select a function to compute the Class 1 confidence based on directed distance from the boundary. The function should rise to 1.0 as the directed distance rises to infinity. Conversely, it should drop to 0.0 as the directed distance drops to negative infinity. Finally, the function should equal 0.5 when the directed distance equals zero. In this book, we have encountered a function that fits these criteria: in section 7, we introduced the cumulative distribution function of the normal curve. This S-shaped curve equals the probability of randomly drawing a value from a normal distribution that's less than or equal to some z. The function starts at 0.0 and increases to 1.0. It's also equal to 0.5 when z == 0. As a reminder, the cumulative distribution can be computed by running `scipy.stats.norm.cdf(z)`. Here, we plot the CDF for z-values ranging from −10 to 10 (figure 21.10).

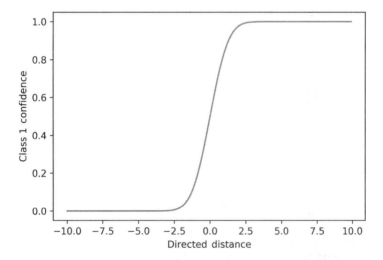

Figure 21.10 A cumulative distribution function of a normal distribution. The S-shaped curve starts at 0.0 and rises toward 1.0. It equals 0.5 when the input is 0.0. This plot fits our criteria for capturing uncertainty based on the directed distance from the decision boundary.

Listing 21.24 Measuring uncertainty using `stats.norm.cdf`

```
from scipy import stats
z = np.arange(-10, 10, 0.1)
assert stats.norm.cdf(0.0) == 0.5
plt.plot(z, stats.norm.cdf(z))
plt.xlabel('Directed Distance')
```

◁—— **Confirms the curve has equal confidence in both classes when z lies directly on the 0.0 threshold**

```
plt.ylabel('Confidence in Class 1')
plt.show()
```

The S-shaped cumulative normal distribution curve fits our stated confidence criteria. It's an adequate function for computing classifier uncertainty. But in recent decades, this curve's usage has fallen out of favor. There are several reasons. One of the most pressing concerns is that no exact formula exists for calculating `stats.norm.cdf`: instead, the area under the normal distribution is computed by approximation. Consequently, data scientists have turned to a different S-shaped curve, whose straightforward formula is easy to remember: the *logistic* curve. The logistic function of z is `1 / (1 - e ** z)` where e is a constant equal to approximately 2.72. Much like the cumulative normal distribution, the logistic function ranges from 0 to 1 and is equal to 0.5 when z `== 0`. Let's plot the logistic curve, together with `stats.norm.cdf` (figure 21.11).

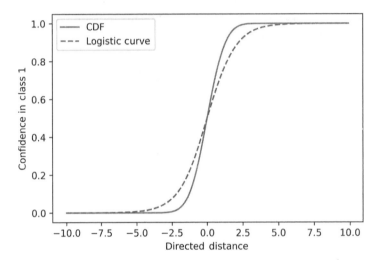

Figure 21.11   **A cumulative distribution function of a normal distribution, plotted together with the logistic curve. Both S-shaped curves start at 0.0 and rise toward 1.0. They equal 0.5 when the input is 0.0. Both curves fit our criteria for capturing uncertainty based on the directed distance from the decision boundary.**

Listing 21.25   Measuring uncertainty using the logistic curve

```
from math import e
plt.plot(z, stats.norm.cdf(z), label='CDF')
plt.plot(z, 1 / (1 + e ** -z), label='Logistic Curve', linestyle='--')
plt.xlabel('Directed Distance')
plt.ylabel('Confidence in Class 1')
plt.legend()
plt.show()
```

The two curves don't precisely overlap, but they both

- Equal approximately 1 when z > 5
- Equal approximately 0 when -z > 5
- Equal an ambiguous value between 0 and 1 when -5 < z < 5
- Equal 0.5 when z == 0

Hence, we can use the logistic curve as our measure of uncertainty. Let's utilize the curve to assign Class 1 label likelihoods for all our customers. This requires us to compute the directed distance between each customer's measurements and the boundary. Computing these distances is surprisingly simple: we just need to execute M @ weights, where M is the padded feature matrix. Essentially, we were computing these distances all along—we just weren't fully utilizing them until now!

> **NOTE** Let's quickly prove that M @ weights returns the distances to the decision boundary. For clarity's sake, we'll use our initial weights of [3.5, 1, -415], representing the decision boundary lbs = -3.5 * inches - 415. Thus, we're taking the distance between measurements (inches, lbs) and the decision boundary point (inches, -3.5 * inches + 415). Of course, the x-axis coordinates both equal inches, so we're taking the distance along the y-axis. This distance equals lbs - (-3.5* inches + 415). The formula rearranges to 3.5 * inches + lbs - 415. This equals the dot product of [3.5, 1, -415] and [inches, lbs, 1]. The first vector equals weights, and the second vector represents a row in M. Therefore, M @ weights returns an array of directed distances.

If M @ weights returns the directed distances, then 1 / (1 + e ** -(M @ weights)) returns the Class 1 likelihoods. Listing 21.26 plots distance versus likelihood. We also add our binary perceptron predictions to the plot: these correspond to M @ weights > 0 (figure 21.12).

> **NOTE** As a reminder, we computed weights by training on the standardized features in X_s. Hence, we must append a column of ones to X_s to pad the feature matrix.

Listing 21.26   Comparing logistic uncertainty to the perceptron's predictions

```
M = np.column_stack([X_s, np.ones(X_s.shape[0])])
distances = M @ weights
likelihoods = 1 / (1 + e ** -distances)
plt.scatter(distances, likelihoods, label='Class 1 Likelihood')
plt.scatter(distances, distances > 0,
            label='Perceptron Prediction', marker='x')

plt.xlabel('Directed Distance')
plt.legend()
plt.show()
```

Directed distances to the boundary equals the product of the padded feature matrix and weights.

Perceptron predictions are determined by distances > 0. Note that Python automatically converts Booleans True and False to integers 1 and 0, so we can plug distances > 0 directly into plt.scatter without an integer conversion.

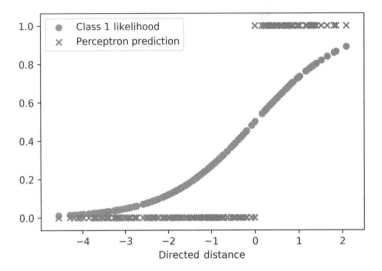

Figure 21.12   Class 1 likelihoods from the logistic curve plotted together with the perceptron predictions. The likelihoods show nuance, while the perceptron predictions are limited to either 0 or 1.

The plotted logistic likelihoods continuously increase with directed distance. In contrast, the perceptron predictions are brutishly simple: the perceptron has either 100% confidence in a Class 1 label or 0% confidence. Interestingly, both the logistic curve and the perceptron are 0% confident when the directed distance is very negative. However, as the directed distance rises, the plots begin to diverge. The logistic plot is more conservative: its confidence increases slowly and mostly falls below 85%. Meanwhile, the perceptron model's confidence jumps to 100% when `distances > 0`. This jump is unwarranted. The model is overconfident, like an inexperienced teenager—it is bound to make mistakes! Fortunately, we can teach the model caution by incorporating the uncertainty captured by the logistic curve.

We can incorporate uncertainty by updating our weight-shift computation. Currently, the weight shift is proportional to `predicted - actual`, where the variables represent predicted and actual class labels. Instead, we can make the shift proportional to `confidence(predicted) - actual`, where `confidence(predicted)` captures our confidence in the predicted class. In a perceptron model, `confidence(predicted)` always equals 0 or 1. By contrast, in the nuanced logistic model, the weight shift takes on a more granular range of values.

Consider, for example, a data point that has a class label of 1 and lies directly on the decision boundary. The perceptron computes a 0 weight shift when presented with this data during training, so the perceptron will not adjust its weights. It learns absolutely nothing from the observation. By contrast, a logistic model returns a weight shift that's proportional to 0.5 − 1 == −0.5. The model will tweak its appraisal of the class label's uncertainty and adjust the weights accordingly. Unlike the perceptron, the logistic model has a flexible capacity to learn.

Let's update our model training code to incorporate logistic uncertainty. We simply need to swap our `predict` function output from `int(weights @ v > 0)` to `1 / (1 + e ** -(weights @ v))`. Here, we make the swap using two lines of code. Then we train our improved model to generate a new vector of weights and plot the new decision boundary to validate our result (figure 21.13).

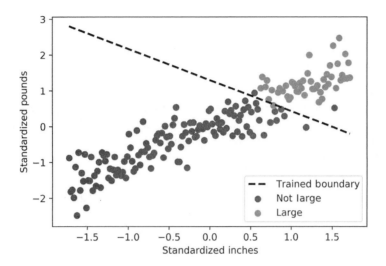

Figure 21.13 **A plot of standardized customer measurements. A logistically trained decision boundary separates Large and Not Large customers. The trained boundary's separation is on par with the baseline decision boundary in figure 21.2.**

Listing 21.27 Incorporating uncertainty into training

> **Our train function takes an optional row-level class predictor called predict. This predictor is preset to return int(weights @ v > 0). Here, we swap it out for the more nuanced logistic_predict function.**

```
np.random.seed(0)
def logistic_predict(v, weights): return 1 / (1 + e ** -(weights @ v))
def train_logistic(X, y): return train(X, y, predict=logistic_predict)
logistic_weights = train_logistic(X_s, y)[0]
plot_boundary(logistic_weights)
```

The learned decision boundary is nearly identical to that of the perceptron output. However, our `train_logistic` function is subtly different: it produces more consistent results than the perceptron. Previously, we showed that the trained perceptron model performs below our baseline in four out of five training runs. Is this the case for `train_logistic`? Let's find out.

Listing 21.28   Checking the logistic model's training consistency

```
np.random.seed(0)
poor_train_count = sum([train_logistic(X_s, y)[1][-1] < 0.97
                        for _ in range(5)])
print("The f-measure fell below our baseline of 0.97 in "
      f"{poor_train_count} out of 5 training instances")

The f-measure fell below our baseline of 0.97 in 0 out of 5
training instances
```

The trained model does not fall below the baseline in any of the runs, so it is superior to the perceptron. This superior model is called a *logistic regression classifier*. The model's training algorithm is also commonly called *logistic regression*.

> **NOTE**   Arguably, this name is not semantically correct. Classifiers predict categorical variables, while regression models predict numeric values. Technically speaking, the logistic regression classifier uses logistic regression to predict the numeric uncertainty, but it is not a regression model. But the term *logistic regression* has become ubiquitous with the term *logistic regression classifier* in the machine learning community.

A logistic regression classifier is trained just like a perceptron, but with one small difference. The weight shift is not proportional to `int(distance - y[i] > 0)`, where distance = `M[i] @ weights`. Instead, it is proportional to `1 / (1 + e ** -distance) - y[i]`. This difference leads to much more stable performance over random training runs.

> **NOTE**   What happens if the weight shift is directly proportional to `distance - y[i]`? Well, the trained model learns to minimize the distance between a line and the values in y. For classification purposes, this is not really useful; but for regression, it is invaluable. For instance, if we set y to equal `lbs` and X to equal `inches`, we could train a line to predict customer weight using customer height. With two lines of code, we utilize `train` to implement this type of linear regression algorithm. Can you figure out how?

21.3.1   *Running logistic regression on more than two features*

We've trained our logistic regression model on two customer measurements: height (inches) and weight (lbs). However, our `train_logistic` function can process any number of input features. We'll prove this by adding a third feature: customer waist circumference. On average, waist circumference is equal to 45% of an individual's height. We'll use this fact to simulate the customer waist measurements. Then we'll input all three measurements into `train_logistic` and evaluate the trained model's performance.

Listing 21.29   Training a three-feature logistic regression model

```
np.random.seed(0)
random_fluctuations = np.random.normal(size=X.shape[0], scale=0.1)
```

```
waist = 0.45 * X[:,0] + random_fluctuations
X_w_waist =  np.column_stack([X_s, (waist - waist.mean()) / waist.std()])
weights, f_measures = train_logistic(X_w_waist, y)

print("Our trained model has the following weights:")
print(np.round(weights, 2))
print(f'\nThe f-measure is {f_measures[-1]:.2f}')

Our trained model has the following weights:
[ 1.65  2.91  1.26 -4.08]

The f-measure is 0.97
```

We need to standardize waists before appending that array to other standardized customer measurements.

Each waist measurement equals 45% of a customer's height, with a random fluctuation.

The trained three-feature model continues to perform exceptionally, with an f-measure of 0.97. The main difference is that the model now contains four weights. The first three weights are coefficients corresponding to the three customer measurements, and the final weight is the bias. Geometrically, the four weights represent a higher-dimensional linear boundary that takes the form of a three-dimensional line called a *plane*. The plane separates our two customer classes in 3D space, as illustrated in figure 21.14.

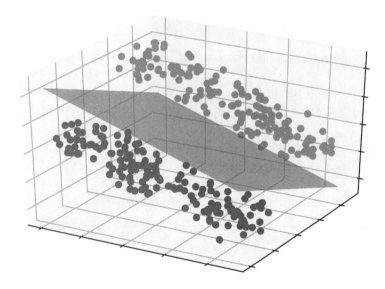

Figure 21.14 Linear classification in 3D space. A linear plane slices through the data like a cleaver and separates that data into two distinct classes.

Similarly, we can optimize for linear separation in any arbitrary number of dimensions. The resulting weights represent a multidimensional linear decision boundary. Shortly, we will run logistic regression on a dataset with 13 features. Scikit-learn's implementation of the logistic regression classifier will prove useful for this purpose.

21.4   *Training linear classifiers using scikit-learn*

Scikit-learn has a built-in class for logistic regression classification. We start by importing this `logisticRegression` class.

> **NOTE** Scikit-learn also includes a `perceptron` class, which can be imported from `sklearn.linear_model`.

Listing 21.30   Importing scikit-learn's `LogisticRegression` class

```
from sklearn.linear_model import LogisticRegression
```

Next, we initialize the classifier object `clf`.

Listing 21.31   Initializing scikit-learn's `LogisticRegression` classifier

```
clf = LogisticRegression()
```

As discussed in section 20, we can train any `clf` by running `clf.fit(X, y)`. Let's train our logistic classifier using the two-feature standardized matrix X_s.

Listing 21.32   Training scikit-learn's `LogisticRegression` classifier

```
clf.fit(X_s, y)
```

The classifier has learned the weight vector `[inches_coef, lbs_coef, bias]`. The vector's coefficients are stored in the `clf.coef_` attribute. Meanwhile, the bias must be accessed separately using the `clf.intercept_` attribute. Combining these attributes gives us the full vector, which can be visualized as a decision boundary (figure 21.15).

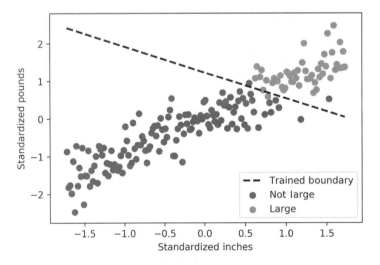

Figure 21.15   A plot of standardized customer measurements. A logistically trained decision boundary derived with scikit-learn separates Large and Not Large customers.

Listing 21.33 Accessing the trained decision boundary

```
coefficients = clf.coef_
bias = clf.intercept_
print(f"The coefficients equal {np.round(coefficients, 2)}")
print(f"The bias equals {np.round(bias, 2)}")
plot_boundary(np.hstack([clf.coef_[0], clf.intercept_]))

The coefficients equal [[2.22 3.22]]
The bias equals [-3.96]
```

We can make predictions on new data by executing `clf.predict`. As a reminder, the inputted data must be standardized for our predictions to make sense.

Listing 21.34 Predicting classes with the linear classifier

```
new_data = np.array([[63, 110], [76, 199]])
predictions = clf.predict(standardize(new_data))
print(predictions)

[0 1]
```

Additionally, we can output the class-label probabilities by running `clf.predict_proba`. These probabilities represent the class-label uncertainties generated by the logistic curve.

Listing 21.35 Outputting the uncertainty associated with each class

```
probabilities = clf.predict_proba(standardize(new_data))
print(probabilities)

[[9.99990471e-01 9.52928118e-06]
 [1.80480919e-03 9.98195191e-01]]
```

In the previous two code listings, we've relied on a custom `standardize` function to standardize our input data. Scikit-learn includes its own standardization class called `StandardScaler`. Here, we import and initialize that class.

Listing 21.36 Initializing scikit-learn's standardization class

```
from sklearn.preprocessing import StandardScaler
standard_scaler = StandardScaler()
```

Running `standard_scaler.fit_transform(X)` returns a standardized matrix. The means of the matrix columns equal 0, and the standard deviations equal 1. Of course, the matrix is identical to our existing standardized matrix, `X_s`.

Listing 21.37 Standardizing training data using scikit-learn

```
X_transformed = standard_scaler.fit_transform(X)
assert np.allclose(X_transformed.mean(axis=0), 0)
```

```
assert np.allclose(X_transformed.std(axis=0), 1)
assert np.allclose(X_transformed, X_s)
```

The `standard_scaler` object has learned the means and standard deviations associated with our feature matrix, so it can now standardize data based on these statistics. Listing 21.38 standardizes our `new_data` matrix by running `standard_scaler.transform(new_data)`. We pass the standardized data into our classifier. The predicted output should equal our previously seen `predictions` array.

Listing 21.38 Standardizing new data using scikit-learn

```
data_transformed = standard_scaler.transform(new_data)
assert np.array_equal(clf.predict(data_transformed), predictions)
```

By combining the `LogisticRegression` and `StandardScaler` classes, we can train logistic models on complex inputs. In the next subsection, we train a model that can process more than two features and predict more than two class labels.

Relevant scikit-learn linear classifier methods

- `clf = LogisticRegression()`—Initializes a logistic regression classifier
- `scaler = StandardScaler()`—Initializes a standard scaler
- `clf.fit(scalar.fit_transform(X))`—Trains the classifier on standardized data
- `clf.predict(scalar.transform(new_data))`—Predicts classes from the standardized data
- `clf.predict_proba(scalar.transform(new_data))`—Predicts class probabilities from the standardized data

---

21.4.1 *Training multiclass linear models*

We've shown how linear classifiers can find decision boundaries that separate two classes of data. However, many problems require us to differentiate between more than two classes. Consider, for example, the centuries-old practice of wine tasting. Some experts are renowned for being able to distinguish between many classes of wine using sensory input. Suppose we try to build a wine-tasting machine. Using sensors, the machine will detect chemical patterns in a glass of wine. These measurements will be fed into a linear classifier as features. The classifier will then identify the wine (impressing us with its refinement and sophistication). To train the linear classifier, we need a training set. Fortunately, such a dataset is provided via scikit-learn. Let's load this dataset by importing and running the `load_wine` function and then print the feature names and class labels from the data.

Listing 21.39 Importing scikit-learn's wine dataset

```
from sklearn.datasets import load_wine
data = load_wine()
```

```
num_classes = len(data.target_names)
num_features = len(data.feature_names)
print(f"The wine dataset contains {num_classes} classes of wine:")
print(data.target_names)
print(f"\nIt contains the {num_features} features:")
print(data.feature_names)
```

```
The wine dataset contains 3 classes of wine:
['class_0' 'class_1' 'class_2']

It contains the 13 features:
['alcohol', 'malic_acid', 'ash', 'alcalinity_of_ash', 'magnesium',
'total_phenols', 'flavanoids', 'nonflavanoid_phenols', 'proanthocyanins',
'color_intensity', 'hue', 'od280/od315_of_diluted_wines', 'proline']
```

The dataset has "flavonoids" misspelled as "flavanoids."

The dataset contains 13 measured features, including alcohol content (Feature 0), magnesium level (Feature 4), and hue (Feature 10). It also contains three classes of wine.

> **NOTE** The actual identities of these wines are lost to time, although they probably correspond to different types of red wines such as Cabernet, Merlot, and Pinot Noir.

How do we train a logistic regression model to distinguish between the three wine types? Well, we could initially train a simple binary classifier to check whether a wine belongs to Class 0. Alternatively, we could train a different classifier that predicts whether a wine belongs to Class 1. Finally, a third classifier would determine whether the wine is a Class 2 wine. This is essentially scikit-learn's built-in logic for multiclass linear classification. Given three class categories, scikit-learn learns three decision boundaries, one for each class. Then the model computes three different predictions on inputted data and chooses the prediction with the highest confidence level.

> **NOTE** This is another reason computed confidence is critical to carrying out linear classification.

If we train our logistic regression pipeline on the three-class wine data, we'll obtain three decision boundaries corresponding to Classes 0, 1, and 2. Each decision boundary will have its own weight vector. Every weight vector will have a bias, so the trained model will have three biases. These three biases will be stored in a three-element clf.intercept_ array. Accessing clf.intercept_[i] will provide us with the bias for Class *i*. Let's train the wine model and print the resulting three biases.

Listing 21.40 Training a multiclass wine predictor

```
X, y = load_wine(return_X_y=True)
clf.fit(standard_scaler.fit_transform(X), y)
biases = clf.intercept_

print(f"We trained {biases.size} decision boundaries, corresponding to "
      f"the {num_classes} classes of wine.\n")
```

```
for i, bias in enumerate(biases):
    label = data.target_names[i]
    print(f"The {label} decision boundary has a bias of {bias:0.2f}")
```

We trained 3 decision boundaries, corresponding to the 3 classes of wine.

```
The class_0 decision boundary has a bias of 0.41
The class_1 decision boundary has a bias of 0.70
The class_2 decision boundary has a bias of -1.12
```

Along with the bias, each decision boundary must have coefficients. The coefficients are used to weigh the inputted features during classification, so there is a one-to-one correspondence between coefficients and features. Our dataset contains 13 features representing various properties of wine, so each decision boundary must have 13 corresponding coefficients. The coefficients for the three different boundaries can be stored in a 3-by-13 matrix. In scikit-learn, that matrix is contained in `clf.coef_`. Each *i*th row of the matrix corresponds to the boundary of Class *i*, and each *j*th column corresponds to the *j*th feature coefficient. For example, we know that Feature 0 equals the alcohol content of a wine, so `clf_coeff_[2][0]` equals the Class 2 boundary's alcohol coefficient.

Let's visualize the coefficient matrix as a heatmap (figure 21.16). This will allow us to display the feature names and class labels corresponding to the rows and columns. Note that the lengthy feature names are easier to read if we display a transpose of the matrix. Thus, we input `clf.coeff_.T` into `sns.heatmap`.

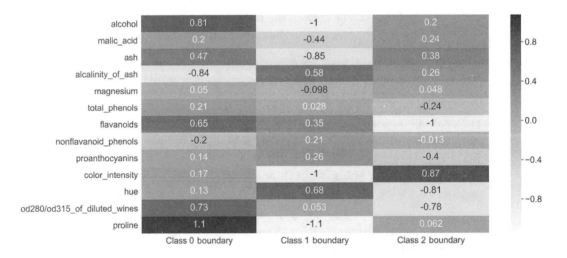

Figure 21.16   A heatmap representing 13 feature coefficients across the three decision boundaries

Listing 21.41 Displaying a transpose of the coefficient matrix

```
import seaborn as sns
plt.figure(figsize = (20, 10))
coefficients = clf.coef_
```
Adjusts the width and height of the plotted heatmap to 20 inches and 10 inches, respectively

```
sns.heatmap(coefficients.T, cmap='YlGnBu', annot=True,
            xticklabels=[f"Class {i} Boundary" for i in range(3)],
            yticklabels=data.feature_names)
plt.yticks(rotation=0)
sns.set(font_scale=2)
plt.show()
```
Transposes the coefficient matrix for easier display of the coefficient names

Adjusts the label font for readability

In the heatmap, the coefficients vary from boundary to boundary. For example, the alcohol coefficients equal –0.81, –1, and 0.2 for class boundaries 0, 1, and 2, respectively. Such differences in coefficients can be very useful; they allow us to better understand how the inputted features drive prediction.

Relevant scikit-learn linear classifier attributes

- `clf.coef_`—Accesses the coefficient matrix of a trained linear classifier
- `clf.intercept_`—Accesses all bias values in a trained linear classifier

---

21.5 Measuring feature importance with coefficients

In section 20, we discussed how the KNN classifier is not interpretable. Using KNN, we can predict the class associated with the inputted features, but we cannot comprehend why these features belong to that class. Fortunately, the logistic regression classifier is easier to interpret. We can gain insights into how the model's features drive the prediction by examining their corresponding coefficients.

Linear classification is driven by the weighted sum of the features and the coefficients. So if a model takes three features A, B, and C and relies on three coefficients [1, 0, 0.25], then the prediction is partially determined by the value A + 0.25 * C. Note that in this example, feature B is zeroed out. Multiplying a zero coefficient by a feature always produces a zero value, so that feature never impacts the model's predicted output.

Now, let's consider a feature whose coefficient is very close to zero. The feature influences predictions, but its impact is minimal. Alternatively, if a coefficient is far from zero, the associated feature will impact the model's prediction much more heavily. Basically, coefficients with higher absolute values have more impact on the model, so their associated features are more important when assessing model performance. For instance, in our example, feature A is the most impactful because its coefficient is furthest from zero (figure 21.17).

Features can be rated by their coefficients to assess their *feature importance*: a score that ranks the usefulness of features during classification. Different classifier models

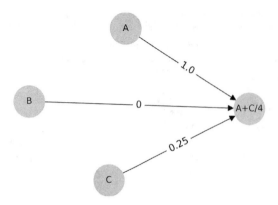

Figure 21.17 We can visualize the weighted sum of features [A, B, C] and coefficients [1, 0, 0.25] as a directed graph. In the graph, the leftmost nodes represent the features, and the edge weights represent the coefficients. We multiply each node by its corresponding edge weight and sum the results. That sum equals A + C / 4, so A is four times more impactful than C. Meanwhile, B is zeroed out and has no impact on the final results.

yield different feature importance scores. In linear classifiers, the absolute values of the coefficients serve as crude measures of importance.

NOTE The models presented in section 22 have more nuanced feature importance scores.

What feature is most useful for correctly detecting a Class 0 wine? We can check by sorting the features based on the absolute values of the Class 0 coefficients in `clf.coef_[0]`.

Listing 21.42   Ranking Class 0 features by importance

```
def rank_features(class_label):
    absolute_values = np.abs(clf.coef_[class_label])
    for i in np.argsort(absolute_values)[::-1]:
        name = data.feature_names[i]
        coef = clf.coef_[class_label][i]
        print(f"{name}: {coef:.2f}")

rank_features(0)

proline: 1.08
alcalinity_of_ash: -0.84
alcohol: 0.81
od280/od315_of_diluted_wines: 0.73
flavanoids: 0.65
ash: 0.47
total_phenols: 0.21
malic_acid: 0.20
nonflavanoid_phenols: -0.20
color_intensity: 0.17
proanthocyanins: 0.14
hue: 0.13
magnesium: 0.05
```

Ranks the features based on the absolute value of the coefficients in clf.coef_[class_label]

Computes the absolute values

Sorts feature indices by absolute values in descending order

Proline appears at the top of the ranked list; it is a chemical commonly found in wine whose concentration is dependent on grape type. Proline concentration is the most important feature for identifying Class 0 wines. Now, let's check which feature drives Class 1 wine identification.

Listing 21.43 Ranking Class 1 features by importance

```
rank_features(1)

proline: -1.14
color_intensity: -1.04
alcohol: -1.01
ash: -0.85
hue: 0.68
alcalinity_of_ash: 0.58
malic_acid: -0.44
flavanoids: 0.35
proanthocyanins: 0.26
nonflavanoid_phenols: 0.21
magnesium: -0.10
od280/od315_of_diluted_wines: 0.05
total_phenols: 0.03
```

Proline concentration is the most important feature for both Class 0 and Class 1 wines. However, that feature influences the two class predictions in different ways: the Class 0 proline coefficient is positive (1.08), while the Class 1 coefficient is negative (–1.14). The coefficient signs are very important. Positive coefficients increase the weighted sum of linear values, and negative values decrease that sum. Therefore, proline decreases the weighted sum during Class 1 classification. That decrease leads to a negative directed distance from the decision boundary, so the Class 1 likelihood drops to zero. Meanwhile, the positive Class 0 coefficient has a completely opposite effect. Thus a high proline concentration implies the following:

- A wine is less likely to be a Class 1 wine.
- A wine is more likely to be a Class 0 wine.

We can check our hypothesis by plotting histograms of proline concentration for the two classes of wine (figure 21.18).

Listing 21.44 Plotting proline histograms across Classes 0 and 1 wines

```
index = data.feature_names.index('proline')
plt.hist(X[y == 0][:, index], label='Class 0')
plt.hist(X[y == 1][:, index], label='Class 1', color='y')
plt.xlabel('Proline concentration')
plt.legend()
plt.show()
```

On average, proline concentration is higher in Class 0 than in Class 1. This difference serves as a signal for distinguishing between the two wines. Our classifier has successfully learned this signal. By probing the classifier's coefficients, we have also learned something about the chemical makeup of different wines.

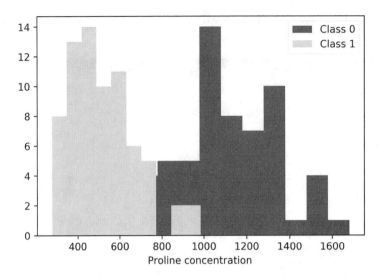

Figure 21.18   A histogram of proline concentrations across Class 0 and Class 1 wines. The Class 0 concentrations are noticeably greater than those of Class 1. Our classifier has picked up on this signal by making proline the top-ranking coefficient for both Class 0 and Class 1.

Unlike KNN models, logistic regression classifiers are interpretable. They're also easy to train and fast to run, so linear classifiers are an improvement over KNN models. Unfortunately, linear classifiers still suffer from some very serious flaws that limit their practical use in certain circumstances.

21.6   *Linear classifier limitations*

Linear classifiers work poorly on raw data. As we've observed, standardization is required to achieve the best results. Similarly, linear models cannot handle categorical features without data preprocessing. Suppose we're building a model to predict whether a pet will be adopted from a shelter. Our model can predict on three pet categories: cat, dog, and bunny. The simplest way to represent these categories is with numbers: 0 for cat, 1 for dog, and 2 for bunny. However, this representation will cause a linear model to fail. The model gives bunnies twice the attention that it gives dogs, and it entirely ignores cats. For the model to treat each pet with equal attention, we must transform the categories into a three-element binary vector v. If a pet belongs to category i, v[i] is set to 1. Otherwise, v[i] equals 0. Thus, we represent a cat as v = [1, 0, 0], a dog as v = [0, 1, 0], and a bunny as v = [0, 0, 1]. This vectorization is similar to the text vectorization seen in section 13. We can carry it using scikit-learn. Still, such transformations can be cumbersome. The models covered in the subsequent section can analyze raw data without additional preprocessing.

NOTE Categorical variable vectorization is often called *one-hot encoding*. Scikit-learn includes a `OneHotEncoder` transformer, which can be imported from `sklearn.preprocessing`. The `OneHotEncoder` class can automatically detect and vectorize all categorical features in your training set.

The most serious limitation of linear classifiers is right there in the name: linear classifiers learn *linear* decision boundaries. More precisely, a line (or plane in higher dimensions) is required to separate the classes of data. However, there are countless classification problems that are not linearly separable. Consider, for example, the problem of classifying urban and non-urban households. Let's assume prediction is driven by the distance to the city center. All households less than two distance units from the center are classified as urban; all other households are considered suburban. The following code simulates these households with a 2D normal distribution. We also train a logistic regression classifier to distinguish between household classes. Finally, we visualize the model's linear boundary and the actual households in 2D space (figure 21.19).

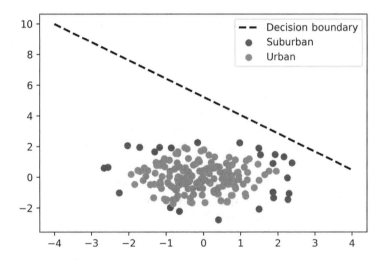

Figure 21.19 Simulated households plotted relative to the city center at (0, 0). Households that are closer to the center are considered urban. No linear separation exists between the urban and suburban households, so the trained linear boundary is unable to distinguish between them.

Listing 21.45 Simulating a nonlinearly separable scenario

The x and y coordinates of each household are drawn from two standard normal distributions.

The city center is located at a coordinate (0, 0). A household's spatial distance from the center is therefore equal to its norm. Households within two units of the center are labeled urban.

```
np.random.seed(0)
X = np.array([[np.random.normal(), np.random.normal()]
              for _ in range(200)])
y = (np.linalg.norm(X, axis=1) < 2).astype(int)
```

```
clf = LogisticRegression()
clf.fit(X, y)
weights = np.hstack([clf.coef_[0], clf.intercept_])

a, b, c = weights
boundary = lambda x: -(a * x + c) / b
plt.plot(range(-4, 5), boundary(range(-4, 5)),  color='k', linestyle='--',
                             linewidth=2, label='Decision Boundary')
for i in [0, 1]:
    plt.scatter(X[y == i][:, 0], X[y == i][:, 1],
             label= ['Suburban', 'Urban'][i],
             color=['b', 'y'][i])

plt.legend()
plt.show()
```

Our data was drawn from a distribution with a mean of 0 and an std of 1. Standardization is therefore not required to train the linear model.

Plots the trained decision boundary alongside the household coordinates

The linear boundary fails to separate the classes. The dataset's geometry does not allow for such a separation. In data science terms, the data is *not linearly separable*. Hence, a linear classifier cannot be adequately trained. We need to run a nonlinear approach. In the subsequent section, we learn about decision tree techniques that can overcome this limitation.

Summary

- In certain instances, we can separate data classes using *linear decision boundaries*. All data points below the linear boundary are classified as belonging to Class 0, and all data points above the linear boundary are classified as belonging to Class 1. Effectively, the linear boundary checks whether the weighted features and a constant add to a value greater than zero. The constant value is called the *bias*, and the remaining weights are called the *coefficients*.

- Through algebraic manipulation, we can transform linear classification into the matrix product inequality defined by `M @ weights > 0`. Such multiplication-driven classification defines a *linear classifier*. The matrix `M` is a *padded feature matrix* with an appended column of ones, `weights` is a vector, and the final vector element is the bias. The remaining weights are coefficients.

- To obtain a good decision boundary, we start by randomly initializing `weights`. We then iteratively adjust the weights based on the difference between predicted and actual classes. In the simplest possible linear classifier, this weight shift is proportional to the difference between the predicted and actual classes. Hence, the weight shift is proportional to one of three values: –1, 0, or 1.

- We should never tweak a coefficient if the associated feature equals zero. We can ensure this constraint if we multiply the weight shift by the corresponding feature value in matrix `M`.

- Iteratively tweaking the weights can cause the classifier to fluctuate between good and subpar performance. To limit oscillation, we need to lower the weight shift with every subsequent iteration. This can be done by dividing the weight shift by k over each *k*th iteration.

- Iterative weight adjustment can converge on a decent decision boundary, but it is not guaranteed to locate the optimal decision boundary. We can improve the boundary by decreasing the data's mean and standard deviation. Such *standardization* can be achieved if we subtract the means and then divide by the standard deviations. The resulting dataset has a mean of 0 and a standard deviation of 1.

- The simplest linear classifier is known as a *perceptron*. Perceptrons perform well, but their results can be inconsistent. The failure of the perceptrons are partially caused by a lack of nuance. Points closer to the decision boundary are more ambiguous with regard to their classification. We can capture this uncertainty using an S-shaped curve that ranges between values of 0 and 1. The cumulative normal distribution function serves as a decent measure of uncertainty, but the simpler *logistic curve* is easier to compute. The logistic curve is equal to `1 / (1 + e ** -z)`.

- We can incorporate uncertainty into model training by setting the weight shift proportionally to `actual - 1 / (1 + e ** -distance)`. Here, `distance` represents the directed distance to the decision boundary. We can compute all directed distances by running `M @ weights`.

- A classifier trained using logistic uncertainty is called a *logistic regression classifier*. This classifier yields more consistent results than a simple perceptron.

- Linear classifiers can be extended to *N* classes by training *N* different linear decision boundaries.

- The coefficients in a linear classifier serve as a measure of *feature importance*. Coefficients with the largest absolute values map to features that have a significant impact on a model's predictions. The coefficient's sign determines whether the presence of a feature indicates the presence or absence of a class.

- Linear classification models fail whenever the data is not *linearly separable* and a good linear decision boundary does not exist.

Training nonlinear classifiers with decision tree techniques

This section covers

- Classifying datasets that are not linearly separable
- Automatically generating `if/else` logical rules from training data
- What is a decision tree?
- What is a random forest?
- Training tree-based models using scikit-learn

Thus far, we have investigated supervised learning techniques that rely on the geometry of data. This association between learning and geometry does not align with our everyday experiences. On a cognitive level, people do not learn through abstract spatial analysis; they learn by making logical inferences about the world. These inferences can then be shared with others. A toddler realizes that by throwing a fake tantrum, they can sometimes get an extra cookie. A parent realizes that indulging the toddler inadvertently leads to even more bad behavior. A student realizes that through preparation and study, they will usually do well on their exam. Such realizations are not particularly new; they are part of our collective social wisdom. Once a useful logical inference has been made, it can be shared with others for broader use. Such sharing is the basis of modern science. A scientist realizes that certain viral proteins make good targets for a drug. They publish their inferences in a journal, and that knowledge propagates across the entire scientific community. Eventually, a new antiviral drug is developed based on the scientific findings.

In this section, we learn how to algorithmically derive logical inferences from our training data. These simple, logical rules will provide us with predictive models that are not constrained by the data's geometry.

22.1 Automated learning of logical rules

Let's analyze a seemingly trivial problem. Suppose a lightbulb hangs above a stairwell. The bulb is connected to two switches at the top and bottom of the stairs. When both switches are off, the bulb stays off. If either switch is turned on, the bulb shines. However, if both switches are flipped on, the bulb turns off. This arrangement allows us to activate the light when we are at the bottom of the stairs and then deactivate it after we ascend.

We can represent the off and on states of the switches and the bulb as binary digits 0 and 1. Given two switch variables `switch0` and `switch1`, we can trivially show that the bulb is on whenever `switch0 + switch1 == 1`. Using the material from the previous two sections, can we train a classifier to learn this trivial relationship? We'll find out by storing every possible light switch combination in a two-column feature matrix `X`. Then we'll plot the matrix rows in 2D space while marking each point based on the corresponding on/off state of the bulb (figure 22.1). The plot will give us insight into how KNN and linear classifiers can handle this classification problem.

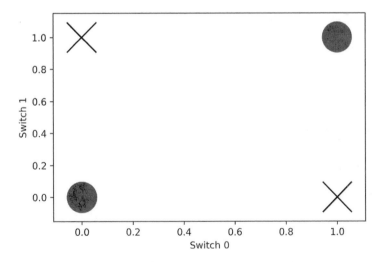

Figure 22.1 Plotting all the states of the light switch system. An activated lightbulb is represented by an X, and a deactivated bulb is represented by an O. The nearest neighbors of each O are X markers (and vice versa). Thus, KNN cannot be used for classification. Also, there's no linear separation between the X markers and O markers, so linear classification cannot be applied.

Listing 22.1   Plotting the two-switch problem in 2D space

```
import numpy as np
import matplotlib.pyplot as plt
X = np.array([[0, 0], [1, 0], [0, 1], [1, 1]])
y = (X[:,0] + X[:,1] == 1).astype(int)

for i in [0, 1]:
    plt.scatter(X[y == i][:,0], X[y == i][:,1],
                marker=['o', 'x'][i], color=['b', 'k'][i],
                s=1000)
plt.xlabel('Switch 0')
plt.ylabel('Switch 1')
plt.show()
```

The four plotted points lie on the four corners of a square. Each pair of points in the same class is positioned diagonally on that square, and all adjacent points belong to different classes. The two nearest neighbors of each on-switch combination are members of the off class (and vice versa). Therefore, KNN will fail to properly classify the data. There also is no linear separation between the labeled classes, so we cannot draw a linear boundary without cutting through a diagonal that connects two identically classified points. Consequently, training a linear classifier is also out of the question. What should we do? One approach is to define two nested if/else statements as our prediction model. Let's code and test this if/else classifier.

Listing 22.2   Classifying data using nested if/else statements

```
def classify(features):
    switch0, switch1 = features

    if switch0 == 0:
        if switch1 == 0:
            prediction = 0
        else:
            prediction = 1
    else:
        if switch1 == 0:
            prediction = 1
        else:
            prediction = 0

    return prediction

for i in range(X.shape[0]):
    assert classify(X[i]) == y[i]
```

Our if/else classifier is 100% accurate, but we didn't train it. Instead, we programmed the classifier ourselves. Manual model construction does not count as supervised machine learning, so we need to find a way to automatically derive accurate if/else statements from the training data. Let's figure out how.

We start with a simple training example. Our training set represents a series of recorded observations between a single light switch and a single bulb. Whenever the switch is on, the bulb is on, and vice versa. We randomly flip the lightbulb on and off and record what we see. The state of the bulb is recorded in a y_simple array. Our single feature, corresponding to the switch, is recorded in a single-column X_simple matrix. Of course, X_simple[i][0] will always equal y[i]. Let's generate this basic training set.

Listing 22.3   Generating a single-switch training set

```
np.random.seed(0)
y_simple = np.random.binomial(1, 0.5, size=10)
X_simple = np.array([[e] for e in y_simple])
print(f"features: {X_simple}")
print(f"\nlabels: {y_simple}")

features: [[1]
 [1]
 [1]
 [1]
 [0]
 [1]
 [0]
 [1]
 [1]
 [0]]

labels: [1 1 1 0 1 0 1 1 0]
```

The state of the bulb is simulated using a random coin flip.

The state of the switch is always equal to the state of the bulb.

Next, we count all observations in which the switch is off and the light is off.

Listing 22.4   Counting the off-state co-occurrences

```
count = (X_simple[:,0][y_simple == 0] == 0).sum()
print(f"In {count} instances, both the switch and the light are off")

In 3 instances, both the switch and the light are off
```

Now, let's count the instances in which both the switch and the lightbulb are turned on.

Listing 22.5   Counting the on-state co-occurrences

```
count = (X_simple[:,0][y_simple == 1] == 1).sum()
print(f"In {count} instances, both the switch and the light are on")

In 7 instances, both the switch and the light are on
```

These co-occurrences will prove useful during classifier training. Let's track the counts more systematically in a co-occurrence matrix M. The matrix rows track the off/on state of the switch, and the matrix columns track the state of the bulb. Each element `M[i][j]` counts the number of examples where the switch is in state `i` and the bulb is in state `j`. Hence, `M[0][0]` should equal 7, and `M[1][1]` should equal 3.

We now define a `get_co_occurrence` function to compute the co-occurrence matrix. The function takes as input a training set `(X, y)`, as well as a column index `col`. It returns the co-occurrences between all classes in `y` and all feature states in `X[:,col]`.

Listing 22.6   Computing a co-occurrence matrix

```
def get_co_occurrence(X, y, col=0):
    co_occurrence = []
    for i in [0, 1]:
        counts = [(X[:,col][y == i] == j).sum()
                  for j in [0, 1]]
        co_occurrence.append(counts)

    return np.array(co_occurrence)

M = get_co_occurrence(X_simple, y_simple)
assert M[0][0] == 3
assert M[1][1] == 7
print(M)

[[3 0]
 [0 7]]
```

Using `get_co_occurrence`, we've computed matrix `M`. All co-occurrences lie along the diagonal of the matrix. The bulb is never on when the switch is flipped off, and vice versa. However, let's suppose that there's a flaw in the switch toggle. We flip the switch off, but the bulb stays on! Let's add this anomalous observation to our data and then recompute matrix `M`.

Listing 22.7   Adding a flawed mismatch to the data

```
X_simple = np.vstack([X_simple, [1]])
y_simple = np.hstack([y_simple, [0]])
M = get_co_occurrence(X_simple, y_simple)
print(M)

[[3 1]
 [0 7]]
```

When we shut off the switch, the lightbulb turns off most of the time, but it doesn't turn off every time. How accurately can we predict the state of the lightbulb if we know that the switch is off? To find out, we must divide `M[0]` by `M[0].sum()`. Doing so produces a probability distribution over possible lightbulb states whenever the switch state is set to `0`.

Listing 22.8   Computing bulb probabilities when the switch is off

```
bulb_probs = M[0] / M[0].sum()
print("When the switch is set to 0, the bulb state probabilities are:")
print(bulb_probs)
```

```
prob_on, prob_off = bulb_probs
print(f"\nThere is a {100 * prob_on:.0f}% chance that the bulb is off.")
print(f"There is a {100 * prob_off:.0f}% chance that the bulb is on.")
```

```
When the switch is set to 0, the bulb state probabilities are:
[0.75 0.25]
```

```
There is a 75% chance that the bulb is off.
There is a 25% chance that the bulb is on.
```

When the switch is off, we should assume that the bulb is off. Our guess will be correct 75% of the time. This fraction of correction fits our definition of accuracy from section 20, so when the switch is off, we can predict the state of the bulb with 75% accuracy.

Now let's optimize the accuracy for the scenario in which the switch is on. We start by computing bulb_probs over M[1]. Next, we choose the switch state corresponding to the maximum probability. Basically, we infer that the bulb state is equal to bulb_probs.argmax() with an accuracy score of bulb_probs.max().

Listing 22.9 Predicting the state of the bulb when the switch is on

```
bulb_probs = M[1] / M[1].sum()
print("When the switch is set to 1, the bulb state probabilities are:")
print(bulb_probs)

prediction = ['off', 'on'][bulb_probs.argmax()]
accuracy = bulb_probs.max()
print(f"\nWe assume the bulb is {prediction} with "
      f"{100 * accuracy:.0f}% accuracy")
```

```
When the switch is set to 1, the bulb state probabilities are:
[0. 1.]
```

```
We assume the bulb is on with 100% accuracy
```

When the switch is off, we assume that the bulb is off with 75% accuracy. When the switch is on, we assume the bulb is on with 100% accuracy. How do we combine these values into a single accuracy score? Naively, we could simply average 0.75 and 1.0, but that approach would be erroneous. The two accuracies should not be weighted evenly since the switch is on nearly twice as often as it is off. We can confirm by summing over the columns of our co-occurrence matrix M. Running M.sum(axis=1) returns the count of off states and on states for the switch.

Listing 22.10 Counting the on and off states of the switch

```
for i, count in enumerate(M.sum(axis=1)):
    state = ['off', 'on'][i]
    print(f"The switch is {state} in {count} observations.")
```

```
The switch is off in 4 observations.
The switch is on in 7 observations.
```

The switch is on more frequently than it is off. Hence, to get a meaningful accuracy score, we need to take the weighted average of 0.75 and 1.0. The weights should correspond to the on/off switch counts obtained from M.

Listing 22.11   Computing total accuracy

```
accuracies = [0.75, 1.0]
total_accuracy = np.average(accuracies, weights=M.sum(axis=1))
print(f"Our total accuracy is {100 * total_accuracy:.0f}%")
```

```
Our total accuracy is 91%
```

If the switch is off, we predict that the bulb is off; otherwise, we predict that the bulb is on. This model is 91% accurate. Furthermore, the model can be represented as a simple if/else statement in Python. Most importantly, we are able to train the model from scratch using the following steps:

1 Choose a feature in our feature matrix X.
2 Count the co-occurrences between the two possible feature states and the two class types. These co-occurrence counts are stored in a two-by-two matrix M.
3 For row i in M, compute the probability distribution of classes whenever the feature is in state i. This probability distribution is equal to M[i] / M[i].sum(). There are just two rows in M, so we can store distributions in two variables: probs0 and probs1.
4 Define the if portion of our conditional model. If the feature equals 0, we return a label of probs0.argmax(). This maximizes the accuracy of the if statement. That accuracy is equal to probs0.max().
5 Define the else portion of our conditional model. When the feature does not equal 0, we return a label of probs1.argmax(). This maximizes the accuracy of the else statement. That accuracy is equal to probs1.max().
6 Combine the if and else statements into a single conditional if/else statement. Occasionally, probs0.argmax() will equal probs1.argmax(). In such circumstances, using an if/else statement is redundant. Instead, we can return the trivial rule f"prediction = {probs0.argmax()}".
7 The accuracy of the combined if/else statement equals the weighted average of probs0.max() and probs1.max(). The weights correspond to the count of feature states obtained by summing up the columns of M.

Let's define a train_if_else function to carry out these seven steps. The function returns a trained if/else statement along with the corresponding accuracy.

Listing 22.12 Training a simple `if/else` model

Creates the written if/else statement

If both parts of the conditional statement return the same prediction, we simplify the statement to just that prediction.

```
def train_if_else(X, y, feature_col=0, feature_name='feature'):
    M = get_co_occurrence(X, y, col=feature_col)
    probs0, probs1 = [M[i] / M[i].sum() for i in [0, 1]]

    if_else = f"""if {feature_name} == 0:
    prediction = {probs0.argmax()}
else:
    prediction = {probs1.argmax()}
""".strip()

    if probs0.argmax() == probs1.argmax():
        if_else = f"prediction = {probs0.argmax()}"

    accuracies = [probs0.max(), probs1.max()]
    total_accuracy = np.average(accuracies, weights=M.sum(axis=1))
    return if_else, total_accuracy
```

Trains an if/else statement on the training set (X, y) and returns the written statement along with the corresponding accuracy. The statement is trained on the feature in X[:,feature_col]. The corresponding feature name is stored in feature_name.

```
if_else, accuracy = train_if_else(X_simple, y_simple, feature_name='switch')
print(if_else)
print(f"\nThis statement is {100 * accuracy:.0f}% accurate.")

if switch == 0:
    prediction = 0
else:
    prediction = 1

This statement is 91% accurate.
```

We're able to train a simple `if/else` model using a single feature. Now, let's figure out how to train a nested `if/else` model using two features. Later, we'll expand that logic to more than two features.

22.1.1 Training a nested if/else model using two features

Let's return to our system of two light switches connecting to a single staircase bulb. As a reminder, all states of this system are represented by dataset (X, y), generated in listing 22.1. Our two features, `switch0` and `switch1`, correspond to columns 0 and 1 of matrix X. However, the `train_if_else` function can only train on one column at a time. Let's train two separate models: one on `switch0` and another on `switch1`. How well will each of the models perform? We'll find out by outputting their accuracies.

Listing 22.13 Training models on the two-switch system

```
feature_names = [f"switch{i}" for i in range(2)]
for i, name in enumerate(feature_names):
    _, accuracy = train_if_else(X, y, feature_col=i, feature_name=name)
    print(f"The model trained on {name} is {100 * accuracy:.0f}% "
          "accurate.")

The model trained on switch0 is 50% accurate.
The model trained on switch1 is 50% accurate.
```

Both models perform terribly! A single `if`/`else` statement is insufficient to capture the complexity of the problem. What should we do? One approach is to break the problem into parts by training two separate models: Model A considers only those scenarios in which `switch0` is off, and Model B considers all remaining scenarios in which `switch0` is on. Later, we'll combine Model A and Model B into a single coherent classifier.

Let's investigate the first scenario, where `switch0` is off. When it is off, `X[:,0] == 0`. Hence, we start by isolating a training subset that satisfies this Boolean requirement. We store this training subset in variables `X_switch0_off` and `y_switch0_off`.

Listing 22.14   Isolating a training subset where `switch0` is off

```
is_off = X[:,0] == 0
X_switch0_off = X[is_off]
y_switch0_off = y[is_off]
print(f"Feature matrix when switch0 is off:\n{X_switch0_off}")
print(f"\nClass labels when switch0 is off:\n{y_switch0_off}")
```

```
Feature matrix when switch0 is off:
[[0 0]          ⟵⎤  All elements of column 0
 [0 1]]          ⎦  now equal 0.

Class labels when switch0 is off:
[0 1]
```

In the training subset, `switch0` is always off. Hence, `X_switch0_off[:,0]` always equals zero. This zero column is now redundant, and we can delete the useless column using NumPy's `np.delete` function.

Listing 22.15   Deleting a redundant feature column

```
X_switch0_off = np.delete(X_switch0_off, 0, axis=1)    ⟵────────────────
print(X_switch0_off)
                                        Running np.delete(X, r) returns a copy of X with
[[0]      ⟵⎤  The 0 element column      row r deleted, and running np.delete(X, c, axis=1)
 [1]]      ⎦  has been deleted.         returns a copy of X with column c deleted. Here,
                                        we delete the redundant column 0.
```

Next, we train an `if`/`else` model on the training subset. The model predicts bulb activation based on the `switch1` state. These predictions are valid only if `switch0` is off. We store the model in a `switch0_off_model` variable, and we store the model's accuracy in a corresponding `switch0_off_accuracy` variable.

Listing 22.16   Training a model when `switch0` is off

```
results = train_if_else(X_switch0_off, y_switch0_off,
                        feature_name='switch1')
switch0_off_model, off_accuracy = results
print("If switch 0 is off, then the following if/else model is "
      f"{100 * off_accuracy:.0f}% accurate.\n\n{switch0_off_model}")
```

```
If switch 0 is off, then the following if/else model is 100% accurate.

if switch1 == 0:
    prediction = 0
else:
    prediction = 1
```

If switch0 is off, then our trained if/else model can predict the bulb state with 100% accuracy. Now, let's train a corresponding model to cover all the cases where switch0 is on. We start by filtering our training data based on the condition X[:,0] == 1.

Listing 22.17 Isolating a training subset where switch0 is on

Filters the training data based on the feature in the feature_col column of matrix X. Returns a subset of the training data where the feature equals a specified condition value.

A Boolean array where the *i*th element is True if X[i][feature_col] equals condition

```
def filter_X_y(X, y, feature_col=0, condition=0):
    inclusion_criteria = X[:,feature_col] == condition
    y_filtered = y[inclusion_criteria]
    X_filtered = X[inclusion_criteria]
    X_filtered = np.delete(X_filtered, feature_col, axis=1)
    return X_filtered, y_filtered

X_switch0_on, y_switch0_on = filter_X_y(X, y, condition=1)
```

The column feature_col becomes redundant since all the filtered values equal condition. Hence, this column is filtered from the training data.

Next, we train switch0_on_model using the filtered training set.

Listing 22.18 Training a model when switch0 is on

```
results = train_if_else(X_switch0_on, y_switch0_on,
                        feature_name='switch1')
switch0_on_model, on_accuracy = results
print("If switch 0 is on, then the following if/else model is "
      f"{100 * on_accuracy:.0f}% accurate.\n\n{switch0_on_model}")

If switch 0 is on, then the following if/else model is 100% accurate.

if switch1 == 0:
    prediction = 1
else:
    prediction = 0
```

If switch == 0, then switch0_off_model performs with 100% accuracy. In all other cases, the switch1_on_model performs with 100% accuracy. Together, the two models can easily be combined into a single nested if/else statement. Here, we define a combine_if_else function that merges two separate if/else statements; we then apply that function to our two models.

Listing 22.19 Combining separate `if`/`else` models

```
def combine_if_else(if_else_a, if_else_b, feature_name='feature'):
    return f"""
if {feature_name} == 0:
{add_indent(if_else_a)}
else:
{add_indent(if_else_b)}
""".strip()

def add_indent(if_else):
    return '\n'.join([4 * ' ' + line for line in if_else.split('\n')])

nested_model = combine_if_else(switch0_off_model, switch0_on_model,
                               feature_name='switch0')
print(nested_model)
```

Combines two if/else statements if_else_a and if_else_b into a single nested statement

The standard four-space Python indent is added to each statement during nesting.

This helper function helps indent all statements during nesting.

```
if switch0 == 0:
    if switch1 == 0:
        prediction = 0
    else:
        prediction = 1
else:
    if switch1 == 0:
        prediction = 1
    else:
        prediction = 0
```

We've reproduced the nested `if`/`else` model from listing 22.2. This model is 100% accurate. We can confirm by taking the weighted average of `off_accuracy` and `on_accuracy`. These accuracies correspond to the `off`/`on` states of `switch0`, so their weights should correspond to the `off`/`on` counts associated with `switch0`. The counts equal the lengths of the `y_switch0_off` and `y_switch0_on` arrays. Let's take the weighted average and confirm that the total accuracy equals 1.0.

Listing 22.20 Computing total nested accuracy

```
accuracies = [off_accuracy, on_accuracy]
weights = [y_switch0_off.size, y_switch0_on.size]
total_accuracy = np.average(accuracies, weights=weights)
print(f"Our total accuracy is {100 * total_accuracy:.0f}%")

Our total accuracy is 100%
```

We're able to generate a nested two-feature model in an automated manner. Our strategy hinges on the creation of separate training sets. That separation is determined by the on/off states of one of the features. This type of separation is called a *binary split*. Typically, we split training set (`X`, `y`) using two parameters:

- Feature `i` corresponding to column `i` of `X`. For example, `switch0` in column 0 of `X`.
- Condition `c`, where `X[:,i] == c` is True for some but not all of the data points. For example, condition 0 corresponding to the `off` state.

A split on feature i and condition c can be carried out as follows:

1 Obtain a training subset (X_a, y_a) in which X_a[:,i] == c.
2 Obtain a training subset (X_b, y_b) in which X_b[:,i] != c.
3 Delete column i from both X_a and X_b.
4 Return the separated subsets (X_a, y_a) and (X_b, y_b).

NOTE These steps are not intended to run on a continuous feature. Later in this section, we discuss how to transform a continuous feature into a binary variable to carry out the split.

Let's define a split function to execute these steps. Then we'll incorporate this function into a systematic training pipeline.

Listing 22.21 Defining a binary split function

Carries out a binary split across the feature in column feature_col of feature matrix X

The split creates two training sets (X_a, y_a) and (X_b, y_b). In the first training set, X_a[:,feature_col] always equals condition.

In the second training set, X_a[:,feature_col] never equals condition.

```
def split(X, y, feature_col=0, condition=0):
    has_condition = X[:,feature_col] == condition
    X_a, y_a = [e[has_condition] for e in [X, y]]
    X_b, y_b = [e[~has_condition] for e in [X, y]
    X_a, X_b = [np.delete(e, feature_col, axis=1) for e in [X_a, X_b]]
    return [X_a, X_b, y_a, y_b]

X_a, X_b, y_a, y_b = split(X, y)
assert np.array_equal(X_a, X_switch0_off)
assert np.array_equal(X_b, X_switch0_on)
```

By splitting on switch0, we were able to train a nested model. Before that split, we first tried training simple if/else models. These models performed terribly—we had no choice but to split the training data. But trained nested models should still be compared with simpler models returned by train_if_else. If a simpler model shows comparable performance, it should be returned instead.

NOTE A nested two-feature model will never perform worse than a simple model based on a single feature. However, it is possible for the two models to perform equally well. Under these circumstances, it's best to follow Occam's razor: when two competing theories make exactly the same predictions, the simpler one is the better theory.

Let's formalize our process for training two-feature nested models. Given training set (X, y), we carry out these steps:

1 Choose a feature i to split on. Initially, that feature is specified using a parameter. Later, we learn how to choose that feature in an automated manner.
2 Attempt to train a simple, single feature model on feature i. If that model performs with 100% accuracy, return it as our output.

    Theoretically, we could train two single-feature models on columns 0 and 1 using train_if_else. Then we could compare all single-feature models systematically. However, this approach won't scale when we increase the feature count from two to *N*.

3 Split on feature i using `split`. The function returns two training sets (`X_a, y_a`) and (`X_b, y_b`).

4 Train two simple models `if_else_a` and `if_else_b` using the training sets returned by `split`. The corresponding accuracies equal `accuracy_a` and `accuracy_b`.

5 Combine `if_else_a` and `if_else_b` into a nested `if/else` conditional model.

6 Compute the nested model's accuracy using the weighted mean of `accuracy_a` and `accuracy_b`. The weights equal `y_a.size` and `y_b.size`.

7 Return the nested model if it outperforms the simple model computed in step 2. Otherwise, return the simple model.

Let's define a `train_nested_if_else` function to execute these steps. The function returns the trained model and that model's accuracy.

Listing 22.22   Training a nested `if/else` model

Trains a nested if/else statement on the two-feature training set (X, y) and returns the written statement along with the corresponding accuracy. The statement is trained by splitting on the feature in X[:,split_col]. The feature names in the statement are stored in the feature_names array.

```
def train_nested_if_else(X, y, split_col=0,
                         feature_names=['feature1', 'feature1']):    ←
    split_name = feature_names[split_col]
    simple_model, simple_accuracy = train_if_else(X, y, split_col,
                                                  split_name)    ←
    if simple_accuracy == 1.0:
        return (simple_model, simple_accuracy)

    X_a, X_b, y_a, y_b = split(X, y, feature_col=split_col)
    in_name = feature_names[1 - split_col]
    if_else_a, accuracy_a = train_if_else(X_a, y_a, feature_name=in_name)    ←
    if_else_b, accuracy_b = train_if_else(X_b, y_b, feature_name=in_name)
    nested_model = combine_if_else(if_else_a, if_else_b, split_name)
    accuracies = [accuracy_a, accuracy_b]
    nested_accuracy = np.average(accuracies, weights=[y_a.size, y_b.size])
    if nested_accuracy > simple_accuracy:
        return (nested_model, nested_accuracy)

    return (simple_model, simple_accuracy)


feature_names = ['switch0', 'switch1']
model, accuracy = train_nested_if_else(X, y, feature_names=feature_names)
print(model)
print(f"\nThis statement is {100 * accuracy:.0f}% accurate.")


if switch0 == 0:
    if switch1 == 0:
        prediction = 0
```

The name of the feature located in the inner portion of the nested statement

The feature names in the statement are stored in the feature_names array.

Combines the simple models

Trains two simple models

```
    else:
        prediction = 1
else:
    if switch1 == 0:
        prediction = 1
    else:
        prediction = 0

This statement is 100% accurate.
```

Our function trained a model that's 100% accurate. Given our current training set, that accuracy should hold even if we split on `switch1` instead of `switch0`. Let's verify.

Listing 22.23 Splitting on `switch1` instead of `switch0`

```
model, accuracy = train_nested_if_else(X, y, split_col=1,
                                       feature_names=feature_names)
print(model)
print(f"\nThis statement is {100 * accuracy:.0f}% accurate.")

if switch1 == 0:
    if switch0 == 0:
        prediction = 0
    else:
        prediction = 1
else:
    if switch0 == 0:
        prediction = 1
    else:
        prediction = 0

This statement is 100% accurate.
```

Splitting on either feature yields the same result. This is true of our two-switch system, but it is not the case for many real-world training sets. It's common for one split to outperform another. In the next subsection, we explore how to prioritize the features during splitting.

22.1.2 Deciding which feature to split on

Suppose we wish to train an `if/else` model that predicts whether it's raining outside. The model returns `1` if it is raining and `0` otherwise. The model relies on the following two features:

- Is the current season autumn? Yes or No?

    We'll assume that fall/autumn is the local rainy season and that the feature predicts rain 60% of the time.

- Is it currently wet outside? Yes or No?

    Usually it's raining when it's wet. Occasionally, wetness is caused by a sprinkler system on a sunny day; and conditions might appear dry during a drizzly morning in the forest, if the trees impede the raindrops. We'll assume this feature predicts rain 95% of the time.

Let's simulate the features and class labels through random sampling. We sample across 100 weather observations and store the outputs in training set (X_rain, y_rain).

Listing 22.24   Simulating a rainy-day training set

```
np.random.seed(1)
y_rain = np.random.binomial(1, 0.6, size=100)          ◁──┐   It rains 60% of the time.
is_wet = [e if np.random.binomial(1, 0.95) else 1 - e for e in y_rain]
is_fall = [e if np.random.binomial(1, 0.6) else 1 - e for e in y_rain]  ◁──
X_rain = np.array([is_fall, is_wet]).T
```

95% of the time, the state of wetness equals the state of rain.

60% of the time, the state of autumn equals the state of rain.

Now, let's train a model by splitting on the autumn feature.

Listing 22.25   Training a model with an autumn split

```
feature_names = ['is_autumn', 'is_wet']
model, accuracy = train_nested_if_else(X_rain, y_rain,
                                       feature_names=feature_names)
print(model)
print(f"\nThis statement is {100 * accuracy:.0f}% accurate.")

if is_autumn == 0:
    if is_wet == 0:
        prediction = 0
    else:
        prediction = 1
else:
    if is_wet == 0:
        prediction = 0
    else:
        prediction = 1

This statement is 95% accurate.
```

We trained a nested model that is 95% accurate. What if we split on the wetness feature instead?

Listing 22.26   Training a model with a wetness split

```
model, accuracy = train_nested_if_else(X_rain, y_rain, split_col=1,
                                       feature_names=feature_names)
print(model)
print(f"\nThis statement is {100 * accuracy:.0f}% accurate.")

if is_wet == 0:
    prediction = 0
```

```
else:
    prediction = 1
```

```
This statement is 95% accurate.
```

Splitting on wetness yields a simpler (and hence better) model while retaining the previously seen accuracy. Not all splits are equal: splitting on some features leads to preferable results. How should we select the best feature for the split? Naively, we could iterate over all features in X, train models by splitting on each feature, and return the simplest model with the highest accuracy. This brute-force approach works when X.size[1] == 2, but it won't scale as the feature count increases. Our goal is to develop a technique that can scale to thousands of features, so we need an alternate approach.

One solution requires us to examine the distribution of classes in the training set. Currently, our y_rain array contains two binary classes: 0 and 1. The label 1 corresponds to a rainy observation. Therefore, the array sum equals the number of rainy observations. Meanwhile, the array size equals the total number of observations, so y_rain.sum() / y_rain.size equals the overall probability of rain. Let's print that probability.

```
prob_rain = y_rain.sum() / y_rain.size
print(f"It rains in {100 * prob_rain:.0f}% of our observations.")
```

```
It rains in 61% of our observations
```

It rains in 61% of total observations. How is that probability altered when we split on autumn? Well, the split returns two training sets with two class-label arrays. We'll call these arrays y_fall_a and y_fall_b. Dividing y_fall_b.sum() by the array size returns the likelihood of rain during autumn. Let's print that likelihood and the probability of rain during the other seasons.

```
y_fall_a, y_fall_b = split(X_rain, y_rain, feature_col=0)[-2:]
for i, y_fall in enumerate([y_fall_a, y_fall_b]):
    prob_rain = y_fall.sum() / y_fall.size
    state = ['not autumn', 'autumn'][i]
    print(f"It rains {100 * prob_rain:.0f}% of the time when it is "
          f"{state}")
```

```
It rains 55% of the time when it is not autumn
It rains 66% of the time when it is autumn
```

As expected, we're more likely to see rain during the autumn season, but that likelihood difference is not very large. It rains 66% of the time during autumn, and 55% of the time during the other seasons. It's worth noting that these two probabilities are close to our overall rain likelihood of 61%. If we know that it is autumn, we are slightly more confident about rain. Still, our confidence increase is not very substantial relative to the original training set, so the split on autumn is not very informative. What if instead we split on wetness? Let's check if that split shifts the observed probabilities.

Listing 22.29 Computing the probability of rain based on wetness

```
y_wet_a, y_wet_b = split(X_rain, y_rain, feature_col=1)[-2:]
for i, y_wet in enumerate([y_wet_a, y_wet_b]):
    prob_rain = y_wet.sum() / y_wet.size
    state = ['not wet', 'wet'][i]
    print(f"It rains {100 * prob_rain:.0f}% of the time when it is "
          f"{state}")
```

```
It rains 10% of the time when it is not wet
It rains 98% of the time when it is wet
```

If we know it's wet outside, then we have nearly perfect confidence in rain. Whenever it is dry, the chance of rain remains at 10%. This percentage is low but very significant to our classifier. We know that dry conditions predict a lack of rain with 90% accuracy.

Intuitively, wetness is a more informative feature than autumn. How should we quantify our intuition? Well, the wetness split returns two class-label arrays whose corresponding rain probabilities are either very low or very high. These extreme probabilities are an indication of class imbalance. As we learned in section 20, an imbalanced dataset has far more of some Class A relative to another Class B. This makes it easier for a model to isolate Class A in the data. By comparison, the autumn split returns two arrays whose likelihoods are in the moderate range of 55 to 66%. The classes in y_fall_a and y_fall_b are more balanced. Thus, it's not as easy to tell the rain/not-rain classes apart.

When choosing between two splits, we should select the split that yields more imbalanced class labels. Let's figure out how to quantify class imbalance. Generally, imbalance is associated with the shape of the class probability distribution. We can treat this distribution as a vector v, where v[i] equals the probability of observing Class *i*. A higher value of v.max() indicates a greater class imbalance. In our two-class dataset, we can compute v as [1 - prob_rain, prob_rain], where prob_rain is the probability of rain. This two-element vector can be visualized as a line segment in 2D space, per our discussion in section 12 (figure 22.2).

Such visualizations can prove insightful. We'll now do the following:

1 Compute the class distribution vectors for the autumn split using arrays y_fall_a and y_fall_b.
2 Compute the class distribution vectors for the wetness split using arrays y_wet_a and y_wet_b.
3 Visualize all four arrays as line segments in 2D space.

That visualization will reveal how to effectively measure class imbalance (figure 22.3).

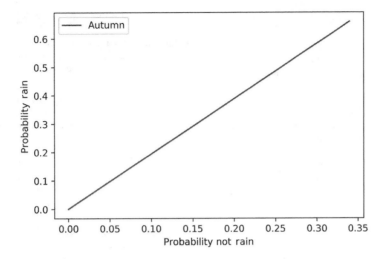

Figure 22.2 The probability distribution over class labels in `y_fall_a`
(is autumn) visualized as a 2D line segment. The y-axis represents the
probability of rain (`0.66`), and the x-axis represents the probability of no
rain (`1 - 0.66 = 0.36`).

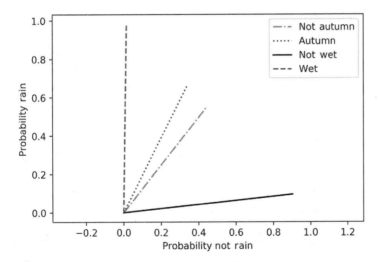

Figure 22.3 A plot of the four vector distributions across each feature
split. The wetness vectors are much more imbalanced and thus are
positioned closer to the axes. More importantly, the wetness vectors
appear longer than the autumn vectors.

Listing 22.30   Plotting the class distribution vectors

```
def get_class_distribution(y):
    prob_rain = y.sum() / y.size
    return np.array([1 - prob_rain, prob_rain])
```
←── Returns the probability distribution across class labels in a binary, two-class system. The distribution can be treated as a 2D vector.

```
def plot_vector(v, label, linestyle='-', color='b'):
    plt.plot([0, v[0]], [0, v[1]], label=label,
             linestyle=linestyle, c=color)
```
←── Plots a 2D vector v as a line segment that stretches from the origin to v

```
classes = [y_fall_a, y_fall_b, y_wet_a, y_wet_b]
distributions = [get_class_distribution(y) for y in classes]
labels = ['Not Autumn', 'Autumn', 'Not Wet', 'Wet']
colors = ['y', 'g', 'k', 'b']
linestyles = ['-.', ':', '-', '--']
for tup in zip(distributions, labels, colors, linestyles):
    vector, label, color, linestyle = tup
    plot_vector(vector, label, linestyle=linestyle, color=color)
```
←── Iterates over the four unique distribution vectors that result from every possible split and then plots these four vectors

```
plt.legend()
plt.xlabel('Probability Not Rain')
plt.ylabel('Probability Rain')
plt.axis('equal')
plt.show()
```

In our plot, the two imbalanced wetness vectors skew heavily toward the x- and y-axes. Meanwhile, the two balanced autumn vectors are approximately equidistant from both axes. However, what really stands out is not vector direction but vector length: the balanced autumn vectors are much shorter than the vectors associated with wetness. This isn't a coincidence. Imbalanced distributions are proven to have greater vector magnitudes. Also, as we showed in section 13, the magnitude is equal to the square root of v @ v. Hence, the dot product of a distribution vector with itself is greater if that vector is more imbalanced!

Let's demonstrate this property for every 2D vector v = [1 - p, p], where p is the probability of rain. Listing 22.31 plots the magnitude of v across rain likelihoods ranging from 0 to 1. We also plot the square of the magnitude, which is equal to v @ v. The plotted values should be maximized when p is very low or very high and minimized when v is perfectly balanced at p = 0.5 (figure 22.4).

Listing 22.31   Plotting the distribution vector magnitudes

Computes the squares of vector magnitudes as a simple dot product

The probability of rain ranges from 0 to 1.0 (inclusive).

Vectors represent all possible two-class distributions, where the classes are rain and not rain.

```
prob_rain = np.arange(0, 1.001, 0.01)          ←──
vectors = [np.array([1 - p, p]) for p in prob_rain]    ←──
magnitudes = [np.linalg.norm(v) for v in vectors]      ←──
square_magnitudes = [v @ v for v in vectors]
plt.plot(prob_rain, magnitudes, label='Magnitude')
```

Vector magnitudes computed using NumPy

```
plt.plot(prob_rain, square_magnitudes, label='Squared Magnitude',
        linestyle='--')
plt.xlabel('Probability of Rain')
plt.axvline(0.5, color='k', label='Perfect Balance', linestyle=':')
plt.legend()
plt.show()
```

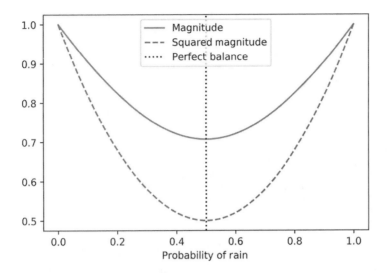

Figure 22.4   A plot of distribution vector magnitudes and squared magnitudes across each distribution vector [1 - p, p]. The plotted values are minimized when the vector is perfectly balanced at p = 0.5.

The squared magnitude is maximized at 1.0 when v is fully imbalanced at p = 0.0 and p = 1.0. It's also minimized at 0.5 when v is balanced. Thus, v @ v serves as an excellent metric for class-label imbalance, but data scientists prefer the slightly different metric of 1 - v @ v. This metric, called the *Gini impurity*, essentially flips the plotted curve: it is minimized at 0 and maximized at 0.5. Let's confirm by plotting the Gini impurity across all values of p (figure 22.5).

> **NOTE**   The Gini impurity has a concrete interpretation in probability theory. Suppose that for any data point, we randomly assign a class of i with probability v[i], where v is the vectorized distribution. The probability of choosing a point belonging to Class *i* is also equal to v[i]. Hence, the probability of choosing a point belonging to Class *i* and correctly labeling that point is equal to v[i] * v[i]. It follows that the probability of correctly labeling any point is equal to sum(v[i] * v[i] for i in range(len(v)). This simplifies to v @ v. Thus, 1 - v @ v equals the probability of incorrectly labeling our data. The Gini impurity is equal to the probability of error, which decreases as the data grows more imbalanced.

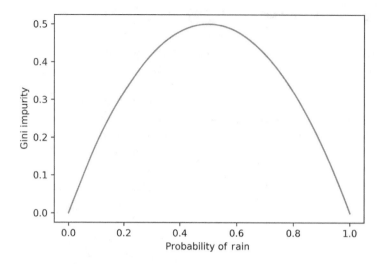

**Figure 22.5   A plot of Gini impurities across each distribution vector
[1 - p, p]. The Gini impurity is maximized when the vector is perfectly
balanced at p = 0.5.**

Listing 22.32   Plotting the Gini impurity

```
gini_impurities = [1 - (v @ v) for v in vectors]
plt.plot(prob_rain, gini_impurities)
plt.xlabel('Probability of Rain')
plt.ylabel('Gini Impurity')
plt.show()
```

Gini impurity is a standard measure of class imbalance. Highly imbalanced datasets are considered more "pure" since labels lean heavily toward one class over any other. When training a nested model, we should split on the feature that minimizes overall impurity. For any split with class labels y_a and y_b, we can compute the impurity like this:

1 Compute the impurity of y_a.
  – It's equal to 1 - v_a @ v_a, where v_a is the class distribution over y_a.
2 Next, we compute the impurity of y_b.
  – It's equal to 1 - v_b @ v_b, where v_b is the class distribution over y_b.
3 Finally, we take the weighted mean of the two impurities.
  – The weights will equal y_a.size and y_b.size, just like in our total accuracy computation.

Let's compute the impurities associated with autumn and wetness.

Listing 22.33   Computing each feature's Gini impurity

**The class distribution
vector of y_b**

**Returns the weighted Gini
impurity associated with class
labels stored in arrays y_a and y_b**

```
def compute_impurity(y_a, y_b):
    v_a = get_class_distribution(y_a)
    v_b = get_class_distribution(y_b)
    impurities = [1 - v @ v for v in [v_a, v_b]]
    weights = [y.size, y_b.size]
    return np.average(impurities, weights=weights)

fall_impurity = compute_impurity(y_fall_a, y_fall_b)
wet_impurity = compute_impurity(y_wet_a, y_wet_b)
print(f"When we split on Autumn, the Impurity is {fall_impurity:0.2f}.")
print(f"When we split on Wetness, the Impurity is {wet_impurity:0.2f}.")
```

**The class distribution
vector of y_a**

**The Gini impurities across
the two class distributions**

**Returns the weighted mean
of the two Gini impurities**

```
When we split on Autumn, the Impurity is 0.45.
When we split on Wetness, the Impurity is 0.04.
```

As expected, the impurity is minimized when we split on wetness. This split leads to more imbalanced training data, which simplifies the training of the classifier. Going forward, we will split on features whose Gini impurity is minimized. With this in mind, let's define a `sort_feature_indices` function. The function takes as input a training set (`X`, `y`) and returns a list of sorted feature indices based on the impurity associated with each feature split.

Listing 22.34   Sorting features by Gini impurity

```
def sort_feature_indices(X, y):
    feature_indices = range(X.shape[1])
    impurities = []

    for i in feature_indices:
        y_a, y_b = split(X, y, feature_col=i)[-2:]
        impurities.append(compute_impurity(y_a, y_b))

    return sorted(feature_indices, key=lambda i: impurities[i])

indices = sort_feature_indices(X_rain, y_rain)
top_feature = feature_names[indices[0]]
print(f"The feature with the minimal impurity is: '{top_feature}'")

The feature with the minimal impurity is: 'is_wet'
```

**Sorts the feature indices in X by
their associated Gini impurities,
from smallest to largest**

**Splits on the feature in
column i and computes
the impurity of the split**

**Returns the sorted column indices of
X. The first column corresponds to the
smallest impurity.**

The `sort_feature_indices` function will prove invaluable as we train nested `if`/`else` models with more than two features.

22.1.3 *Training if/else models with more than two features*

Training a model to predict the current weather is a relatively trivial task. We'll now train a more complicated model that predicts whether it will rain tomorrow. The model relies on the following three features:

- Has it rained at any point today?

    If it rained today, then it is very likely to rain tomorrow.

- Is today a cloudy day? Yes or No?

    It's more likely to rain on a cloudy day. This increases the chance that it will rain tomorrow.

- Is today an autumn day? Yes or No?

    We assume that it's both rainier and cloudier in autumn.

We further assume a complex but realistic interrelationship between the three features, to make the problem much more interesting:

- There's a 25% chance that today is autumn.
- During autumn, it is cloudy 70% of the time. Otherwise, it's cloudy 30% of the time.
- If today is cloudy, there's a 40% of rain at some point in the day. Otherwise, the chance of rain is 5%.
- If it rains today, there's a 50% chance it will rain tomorrow.
- If today is a dry and sunny autumn day, there's a 15% chance it will rain tomorrow. Otherwise, on dry and sunny spring, summer, and winter days, the chance of rain tomorrow falls to 5%.

The following code simulates a training set (X_rain, y_rain) based on the probabilistic relationships between the features.

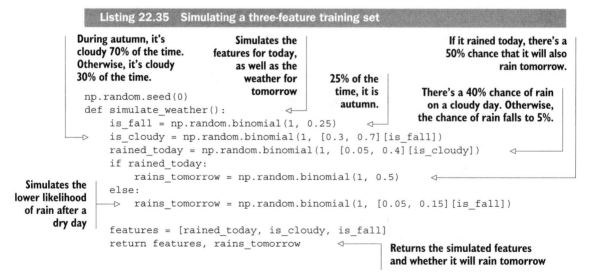

Listing 22.35 Simulating a three-feature training set

During autumn, it's cloudy 70% of the time. Otherwise, it's cloudy 30% of the time.

Simulates the features for today, as well as the weather for tomorrow

25% of the time, it is autumn.

If it rained today, there's a 50% chance that it will also rain tomorrow.

There's a 40% chance of rain on a cloudy day. Otherwise, the chance of rain falls to 5%.

Simulates the lower likelihood of rain after a dry day

```
np.random.seed(0)
def simulate_weather():
    is_fall = np.random.binomial(1, 0.25)
    is_cloudy = np.random.binomial(1, [0.3, 0.7][is_fall])
    rained_today = np.random.binomial(1, [0.05, 0.4][is_cloudy])
    if rained_today:
        rains_tomorrow = np.random.binomial(1, 0.5)
    else:
        rains_tomorrow = np.random.binomial(1, [0.05, 0.15][is_fall])

    features = [rained_today, is_cloudy, is_fall]
    return features, rains_tomorrow
```

Returns the simulated features and whether it will rain tomorrow

```
X_rain, y_rain = [], []
for _ in range(1000):                         ◁──────────────────┐   Simulates a dataset with
    features, rains_tomorrow = simulate_weather()               │   1,000 training examples
    X_rain.append(features)
    y_rain.append(rains_tomorrow)

X_rain, y_rain = np.array(X_rain), np.array(y_rain)
```

The columns in X_rain correspond to features 'is_fall', 'is_cloudy', and 'rained_today'. We can sort these features by Gini impurity to measure how well they split the data.

Listing 22.36 Sorting three features by Gini impurity

```
feature_names = ['rained_today', 'is_cloudy', 'is_fall']
indices = sort_feature_indices(X_rain, y_rain)
print(f"Features sorted by Gini Impurity:")
print([feature_names[i] for i in indices])


Features sorted by Gini Impurity:
['is_fall', 'is_cloudy', 'rained_today']
```

Splitting on the autumn feature yields the lowest Gini impurity, and cloudiness ranks second. The rainy feature has the highest Gini impurity: it yields the most balanced datasets and is not a good candidate for splitting.

> **NOTE** The high Gini impurity of the rainy feature may seem surprising. After all, if it rained today, we know it's much more likely to rain tomorrow. Hence, when X_rain[:,0] == 1, the Gini impurity is low. But on a dry day, we have little indication of tomorrow's weather; so when X_rain[:,0] == 0, the Gini impurity is high. There are more dry days than there are rainy days during the year, so the mean Gini impurity is high. In contrast, the autumn feature is much more informative. It provides us with insight into tomorrow's weather on both autumn and non-autumn days.

Given our ranked feature list, how should we train our model? After all, trained_nested_if_else is intended to process two features, not three. One intuitive solution is to train the model on just the two top-ranked features. These features lead to a greater training set imbalance, making it easier to decipher between rainy and non-rainy class labels.

Here, we train a two-feature model on just the autumn and cloudiness features. We also set the split column to autumn since autumn has the lowest Gini impurity.

Listing 22.37 Training a model on the two best features

```
                                           │   Ignores the final feature, which
                                           │   has the worst Gini impurity
skip_index = indices[-1]            ◁──────┘
X_subset = np.delete(X_rain, skip_index, axis=1)   ◁──┐   The feature subset with
name_subset = np.delete(feature_names, skip_index)    │   the two best features
```

```
split_col = indices[0] if indices[0] < skip_index else indices[0] - 1    ◁────┐
model, accuracy = train_nested_if_else(X_subset, y_rain,
                                       split_col=split_col,           ┌─ Trains a
                                       feature_names=name_subset) ◁──┤ nested model
print(model)                                                         │ on the two
print(f"\nThis statement is {100 * accuracy:.0f}% accurate.")        │ best features

prediction = 0                                    Adjusts the column of the best
                                                  split feature relative to the filtered
This statement is 74% accurate.                   index of the worst, deleted feature
```

Our trained model is a frivolously simple. It always predicts no rain, no matter what! This trivial model is only 74% accurate—that accuracy is not disastrous, but we can definitely do better. Ignoring the rainy feature has limited our predictive capacity. We must incorporate all three features to raise the accuracy score. We can incorporate all three features like this:

1. Split on the feature with the lowest Gini impurity. This, of course, is autumn.
2. Train two nested models using the `train_nested_if_else` function. Model A will consider only those scenarios in which the season is not autumn, and Model B will consider all remaining scenarios in which the season is autumn.
3. Combine Model A and Model B into a single coherent classifier.

NOTE These steps are nearly identical to the logic behind the `nested_if_else` function. The main difference is that now we're expanding that logic to more than two features.

Let's start by splitting on the autumn feature, whose index is stored in `indices[0]`.

Listing 22.38   Splitting on the feature with the lowest impurity

```
X_a, X_b, y_a, y_b = split(X_rain, y_rain, feature_col=indices[0])
```

Next, let's train a nested model on `(X_a, y_a)`. This training set contains all of our non-autumn observations.

Listing 22.39   Training a model when the season is not autumn

```
name_subset = np.delete(feature_names, indices[0])           Splits on the feature in
split_col = sort_feature_indices(X_a, y_a)[0]        ◁──┐    X_a that yields the best
model_a, accuracy_a = train_nested_if_else(X_a, y_a,       │    (lowest) Gini impurity
                             split_col=split_col,
                             feature_names=name_subset)  ◁──┐
print("If it is not autumn, then the following nested model is "   │
      f"{100 * accuracy_a:.0f}% accurate.\n\n{model_a}")           │

If it is not autumn, then the following nested model is 88% accurate.

if is_cloudy == 0:                              Trains a nested two-feature
    prediction = 0                                 model on (X_a, y_a)
```

```
else:
    if rained_today == 0:
        prediction = 0
    else:
        prediction = 1
```

Our trained `model_a` is highly accurate. Now we will train a second `model_b` based on the autumn observations stored in `(X_b, y_b)`.

Listing 22.40 Training a model when the season is autumn

```
split_col = sort_feature_indices(X_b, y_b)[0]
model_b, accuracy_b = train_nested_if_else(X_b, y_b,
                                    split_col=split_col,
                                    feature_names=name_subset)
print("If it is autumn, then the following nested model is "
      f"{100 * accuracy_b:.0f}% accurate.\n\n{model_b}")

If it is autumn, then the following nested model is 79% accurate.

if is_cloudy == 0:
    prediction = 0
else:
    if rained_today == 0:
        prediction = 0
    else:
        prediction = 1
```

> Splits on the feature in **X_b** that yields the best (lowest) Gini impurity

> **Trains a nested two-feature model on (X_b, y_b)**

When it is autumn, `model_b` performs with 79% accuracy. Otherwise, `model_a` performs with 88% accuracy. Let's combine these models into a single nested statement. We use our `combine_if_else` function, which we previously defined for this exact purpose. We also compute the total accuracy, which equals the weighted mean of `accuracy_a` and `accuracy_b`.

Listing 22.41 Combining the models into a nested statement

```
nested_model = combine_if_else(model_a, model_b,
                               feature_names[indices[0]])
print(nested_model)
accuracies = [accuracy_a, accuracy_b]
accuracy = np.average(accuracies, weights=[y_a.size, y_b.size])
print(f"\nThis statement is {100 * accuracy:.0f}% accurate.")

if is_fall == 0:
    if is_cloudy == 0:
        prediction = 0
    else:
        if rained_today == 0:
            prediction = 0
        else:
            prediction = 1
```

```
else:
    if is_cloudy == 0:
        prediction = 0
    else:
        if rained_today == 0:
            prediction = 0
        else:
            prediction = 1
```

```
This statement is 85% accurate.
```

We were able to generate a nested 3-feature model. The process was very similar to how we trained a nested 2-feature model. In this manner, we can extend our logic to train a 4-feature model, or a 10-feature model, or a 100-feature model. In fact, our logic can generalize to training any nested N-feature model. Suppose we're given a training set (X, y), where X contains N columns. We should be able to easily train a model by executing the following steps:

1 If N equals 1, return the simple, non-nested `train_if_else(X, y)` output. Otherwise, go to the next step.

2 Sort our N features based on the Gini impurity, from lowest to highest.

3 Attempt to train a simpler, $N-1$ feature model (using the top-ranked features from step 2). If that model performs with 100% accuracy, return it as our output. Otherwise, go to the next step.

4 Split on the feature with the smallest Gini impurity. That split returns two training sets (X_a, y_a) and (X_b, y_b). Each training set contains $N-1$ features.

5 Train two $N-1$ feature models: `model_a` and `model_b`, using the training sets from the previous step. The corresponding accuracies equal `accuracy_a` and `accuracy_b`.

6 Combine `model_a` and `model_b` into a nested `if/else` conditional model.

7 Compute the nested model's accuracy using the weighted mean of `accuracy_a` and `accuracy_b`. The weights equal `y_a.size` and `y_b.size`.

8 Return the nested model if it outperforms the simpler model computed in step 3. Otherwise, return the simpler model.

Here, we define a recursive `train` function that carries out these steps.

Listing 22.42   Training a nested model with N features

> Trains a nested if/else statement on the N feature training set (X, y) and returns the written statement along with the corresponding accuracy. The feature names in the statement are stored in the feature_names array.

```
def train(X, y, feature_names):     ◁────────────────────────
    if X.shape[1] == 1:
        return train_if_else(X, y, feature_name=feature_names[0])

    indices = sort_feature_indices(X, y)     ◁────┐  Sorts the feature
    X_subset = np.delete(X, indices[-1], axis=1)   │  indices by Gini impurity
```

```
                name_subset = np.delete(feature_names, indices[-1])
                simple_model, simple_accuracy = train(X_subset, y, name_subset)
                if simple_accuracy == 1.0:
                    return (simple_model, simple_accuracy)

                split_col = indices[0]
                name_subset = np.delete(feature_names, split_col)
                X_a, X_b, y_a, y_b = split(X, y, feature_col=split_col)
                model_a, accuracy_a = train(X_a, y_a, name_subset)
                model_b, accuracy_b = train(X_b, y_b, name_subset)
                accuracies = [accuracy_a, accuracy_b]
                total_accuracy = np.average(accuracies, weights=[y_a.size, y_b.size])
                nested_model = combine_if_else(model_a, model_b, feature_names[split_col])
                if total_accuracy > simple_accuracy:
                    return (nested_model, total_accuracy)

                return (simple_model, simple_accuracy)


        model, accuracy = train(X_rain, y_rain, feature_names)
        print(model)
        print(f"\nThis statement is {100 * accuracy:.0f}% accurate.")


        if is_fall == 0:
            if is_cloudy == 0:
                prediction = 0
            else:
                if rained_today == 0:
                    prediction = 0
                else:
                    prediction = 1
        else:
            if is_cloudy == 0:
                prediction = 0
            else:
                if rained_today == 0:
                    prediction = 0
                else:
                    prediction = 1
```

Splits on the feature with the lowest Gini impurity → (marks `split_col = indices[0]`)

Combines the simpler models → (marks `nested_model = combine_if_else(...)`)

Tries to train a simpler N – 1 feature model to see if it performs with 100% accuracy → (marks `simple_model, simple_accuracy = train(X_subset, y, name_subset)`)

Trains two simpler N – 1 feature models on the two training sets returned after the split → (marks `model_a, accuracy_a = train(X_a, y_a, name_subset)`)

```
This statement is 85% accurate.
```

The branching `if/else` statements in our trained output resemble the branches of a tree. We can make the resemblance more explicit by visualizing the output as a *decision tree diagram*. Decision trees are special network structures used to symbolize `if/else` decisions. Features are nodes in the network, and conditions are edges. The `if` condition branches to the right of the feature nodes, and the `else` condition branches to the left. Figure 22.6 represents our rain-prediction model using a decision tree diagram.

Any nested `if/else` statement can be visualized as a decision tree, so trained `if/else` conditional classifiers are referred to as *decision tree classifiers*. Trained decision tree classifiers have been in common use since the 1980s. Numerous strategies exist for training these classifiers effectively, all of which have the following properties in common:

- The *N* feature training problem is simplified down to multiple *N* − 1 feature subproblems by splitting on one of the features.
- The split is carried out by choosing the feature that yields the highest class imbalance. This is commonly done using the Gini impurity, although alternative metrics do exist.
- Caution is taken to avoid needlessly complex if/else statements if simpler statements work equally well. This process is called *pruning*, since excessive if/else branches are pruned out.

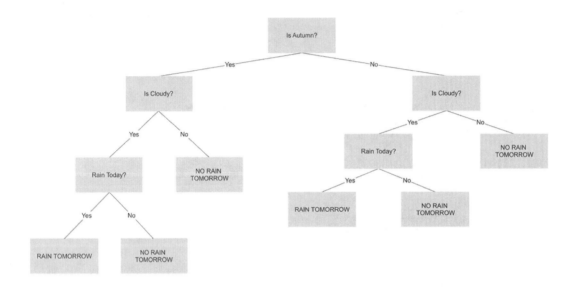

Figure 22.6 Visualizing the rain-prediction model using a decision tree diagram. The diagram is a network. The network nodes represent the model's features, such as "Is Autumn?". The edges represent the conditional if/else statements. For instance, if it's autumn, the diagram's Yes edge branches left; otherwise, the No edge branches right.

Scikit-learn includes a highly optimized decision tree implementation. We explore it in the next subsection.

22.2 *Training decision tree classifiers using scikit-learn*

In scikit-learn, decision tree classification is carried out by the DecisionTreeClassifier class. Let's import that class from sklearn.tree.

Listing 22.43 Importing scikit-learn's DecisionTreeClassifier class

```
from sklearn.tree import DecisionTreeClassifier
```

Next, we initialize the class as clf. Then we train clf on the two-switch system introduced at the beginning of the section. That training set is stored in parameters (X, y).

Listing 22.44 Initializing and training a decision tree classifier

```
clf = DecisionTreeClassifier()
clf.fit(X, y)
```

We can visualize the trained classifier using a decision tree diagram. Scikit-learn includes a plot_tree function, which uses Matplotlib to carry out that visualization. Calling plot_tree(clf) plots the trained decision tree diagram. The feature names and class names in that plot can be controlled using the feature_names and class_names parameters.

Let's import plot_tree from sklearn.tree and visualize clf (figure 22.7). In the plot, the feature names equal Switch0 and Switch1, and the class labels equal the two bulb states: Off and On.

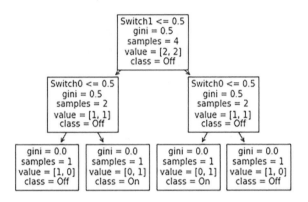

Figure 22.7 A plot of the two-switch system's decision tree diagram. Each top node contains a feature name along with additional statistics such as the Gini impurity and the dominant class. The bottom nodes contain the final predicted bulb classifications.

Listing 22.45 Displaying a trained decision tree classifier

```
from sklearn.tree import plot_tree
feature_names = ['Switch0', 'Switch1']
class_names = ['Off', 'On']
plot_tree(clf, feature_names=feature_names, class_names=class_names)
plt.show()
```

The visualized diagram tracks the class distribution at each conditional position in the tree. It also tracks the associated Gini impurity, as well as the dominant class. Such visualizations can be useful, but these tree plots can get unwieldy when the total feature count is large. That is why scikit-learn provides an alternative visualization function: export_text allows us to display the tree using a simplified text-based diagram. Calling export_text(clf) returns a string. Printing that string reveals a tree composed of | and - characters. The feature names in that text tree can be specified with the feature_names parameter; but due to the limited nature of the output, we can't print the class names. Let's import export_text from sklearn.tree and then visualize our tree as a simple string.

Listing 22.46   Displaying a decision tree classifier as a string

```
from sklearn.tree import export_text
text_tree = export_text(clf, feature_names=feature_names)
print(text_tree)
```

```
|--- Switch0 <= 0.50
|   |--- Switch1 <= 0.50
|   |   |--- class: 0
|   |--- Switch1 >  0.50
|   |   |--- class: 1
|--- Switch0 >  0.50
|   |--- Switch1 <= 0.50
|   |   |--- class: 1
|   |--- Switch1 >  0.50
|   |   |--- class: 0
```

In the text, we clearly see the branching logic. Initially, the data is split using Switch0. The branch selection depends on whether Switch0 <= 0.50. Of course, because Switch0 is either 0 or 1, that logic is identical to Switch0 == 0. Why does the tree use an inequality when the simple Switch0 == 0 statement should suffice? The answer has to do with how DecisionTreeClassifier handles continuous features. Thus far, all of our features have been Booleans; but in most real-world problems, the features are numeric. Fortunately, any numerical feature can be transformed into a Boolean feature. We simply need to run feature >= thresh, where thresh is some numeric threshold. In scikit-learn, decision trees scan for this threshold automatically.

How should we select the optimal threshold for splitting a numeric feature? It's easy; we just need to choose the threshold that minimizes the Gini impurity. Suppose that we're examining a dataset that's driven by a single numeric feature. In that data, the class always equals 0 when the feature is less than 0.7, or 1 otherwise. Hence, y = (v >= 0.7).astype(int), where v is the feature vector. By applying a threshold of 0.7, we can perfectly separate our class labels. Splitting on that threshold leads to a Gini impurity of 0.0, so we can isolate the threshold by computing the Gini impurity across a range of possible threshold values. Then we can select the value at which the impurity is minimized. Listing 22.47 samples a feature vector from a normal distribution, sets y to equal (feature >= 0.7).astype(int), computes the impurity across a range of thresholds, and plots the results (figure 22.8). The minimal impurity appears at the threshold of 0.7.

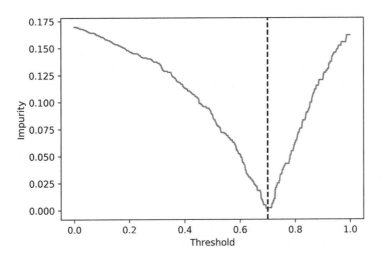

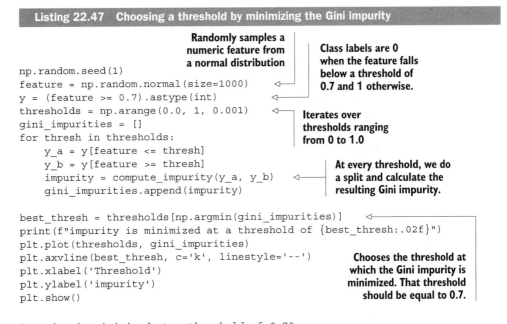

Figure 22.8 **A plot of Gini impurities across each possible threshold of a feature. The Gini impurity is minimized at a threshold of 0.7. Thus, we can convert the numeric feature f into a binary feature f >= 0.7.**

Listing 22.47 Choosing a threshold by minimizing the Gini impurity

Randomly samples a numeric feature from a normal distribution

Class labels are 0 when the feature falls below a threshold of 0.7 and 1 otherwise.

```
np.random.seed(1)
feature = np.random.normal(size=1000)
y = (feature >= 0.7).astype(int)
thresholds = np.arange(0.0, 1, 0.001)
gini_impurities = []
for thresh in thresholds:
    y_a = y[feature <= thresh]
    y_b = y[feature >= thresh]
    impurity = compute_impurity(y_a, y_b)
    gini_impurities.append(impurity)
```

Iterates over thresholds ranging from 0 to 1.0

At every threshold, we do a split and calculate the resulting Gini impurity.

```
best_thresh = thresholds[np.argmin(gini_impurities)]
print(f"impurity is minimized at a threshold of {best_thresh:.02f}")
plt.plot(thresholds, gini_impurities)
plt.axvline(best_thresh, c='k', linestyle='--')
plt.xlabel('Threshold')
plt.ylabel('impurity')
plt.show()
```

Chooses the threshold at which the Gini impurity is minimized. That threshold should be equal to 0.7.

```
Impurity is minimized at a threshold of 0.70
```

In this manner, scikit-learn obtains inequality thresholds for all features used to train `DecisionTreeClassifier`, so the classifier can derive conditional logic from numeric data. Let's now train `clf` on the numeric wine data introduced in the previous section. After training, we visualize the tree.

NOTE   As a reminder, the wine dataset contains three classes of wine. Thus far, we've only trained decision trees on two-class systems. However, our branching if/else logic can easily be extended to predict more than two classes. Consider, for instance, the statement 0 if x == 0 else 1 if y == 0 else 2. The statement returns 0 if x == 0. Otherwise, the statement returns 1 if y == 0 and 2 if y != 0. It's straightforward to incorporate this added conditional logic into our classifier.

Listing 22.48   Training a decision tree on numeric data

```
np.random.seed(0)
from sklearn.datasets import load_wine
X, y = load_wine(return_X_y=True)
clf.fit(X, y)
feature_names = load_wine().feature_names
text_tree = export_text(clf, feature_names=feature_names)
print(text_tree)
```

```
|--- proline <= 755.00
|   |--- od280/od315_of_diluted_wines <= 2.11
|   |   |--- hue <= 0.94
|   |   |   |--- flavanoids <= 1.58
|   |   |   |   |--- class: 2
|   |   |   |--- flavanoids >  1.58
|   |   |   |   |--- class: 1
|   |   |--- hue >  0.94
|   |   |   |--- color_intensity <= 5.82
|   |   |   |   |--- class: 1
|   |   |   |--- color_intensity >  5.82
|   |   |   |   |--- class: 2
|   |--- od280/od315_of_diluted_wines >  2.11
|   |   |--- flavanoids <= 0.80
|   |   |   |--- class: 2
|   |   |--- flavanoids >  0.80
|   |   |   |--- alcohol <= 13.17
|   |   |   |   |--- class: 1
|   |   |   |--- alcohol >  13.17
|   |   |   |   |--- color_intensity <= 4.06
|   |   |   |   |   |--- class: 1
|   |   |   |   |--- color_intensity >  4.06
|   |   |   |   |   |--- class: 0
|--- proline >  755.00
|   |--- flavanoids <= 2.17
|   |   |--- malic_acid <= 2.08
|   |   |   |--- class: 1
|   |   |--- malic_acid >  2.08
|   |   |   |--- class: 2
|   |--- flavanoids >  2.17
|   |   |--- magnesium <= 135.50
|   |   |   |--- class: 0
|   |   |--- magnesium >  135.50
|   |   |   |--- class: 1
```

The printed tree is larger than any tree or conditional statement seen thus far. The tree is large because it is deep. In machine learning, tree depth equals the number of nested `if/else` statements required to capture the logic within the tree. For instance, our single switch example required a single `if/else` statement. It therefore had a depth of 1. Meanwhile, our two-switch system had a depth of 2. Also, our three-feature weather predictor had a depth of 3. Our wine predictor is even deeper, making it more difficult to follow the logic. In scikit-learn, we can limit the depth of a trained tree using the `max_depth` hyperparameter. For example, running `DecisionTreeClassifier(max_depth=2)` will create a classifier whose depth cannot exceed two nested statements. Let's demonstrate by training a limited depth classifier on our wine data.

Listing 22.49 Training a tree with limited depth

```
clf = DecisionTreeClassifier(max_depth=2)
clf.fit(X, y)
text_tree = tree.export_text(clf, feature_names=feature_names)
print(text_tree)

|--- proline <= 755.00
|   |--- od280/od315_of_diluted_wines <= 2.11
|   |   |--- class: 2
|   |--- od280/od315_of_diluted_wines >  2.11
|   |   |--- class: 1
|--- proline >  755.00
|   |--- flavanoids <= 2.17
|   |   |--- class: 2
|   |--- flavanoids >  2.17
|   |   |--- class: 0
```

The printed tree is two `if/else` statements deep. The outer statement is determined by the proline concentration: if the proline concentration is greater than 755, flavonoids are used to identify the wine.

NOTE The dataset has *flavonoids* misspelled as *flavanoids*.

Otherwise, the `OD280 / OD315` of diluted wines is utilized for class determination. Based on the output, we can fully comprehend the working logic in the model. Furthermore, we can infer the relative importance of features that are driving class prediction:

- Proline is the most important feature. It appears at the top of the tree and therefore has the lowest Gini impurity. Splitting on that feature must thus lead to the most imbalanced data. In an imbalanced dataset, it is much easier to isolate one class over another, so knowing the proline concentration allows us to more easily separate the different classes of wine.

  This is consistent with our linear model trained in section 21, where proline coefficients yielded the most noticeable signal.

- Flavonoids and OD280 / OD315 are also important drivers of prediction (although not as important as proline).
- The remaining 10 features are less relevant.

The depth at which a feature appears in the tree is an indicator of its relative importance. That depth is determined by the Gini impurity. Hence, the Gini impurity can be used to compute an importance score. The importance scores across all features are stored in the feature_importances_ attribute of clf. Listing 22.50 prints clf.feature_importances_.

> **NOTE**   More precisely, scikit-learn computes feature importance by subtracting the Gini impurity of the feature split from the Gini impurity of the previous split. For instance, in the wine tree, the impurity of the flavonoids at depth 2 is subtracted from the impurity of proline at depth 1. After the subtraction, the importance is weighted by the fraction of training samples represented during the split.

Listing 22.50   Printing the feature importances

```
print(clf.feature_importances_)

[0.          0.          0.          0.          0.          0.
 0.117799   0.          0.          0.          0.          0.39637021
 0.48583079]
```

In the printed array, the importance of feature i is equal to feature_importances_[i]. Most of the features receive a score of 0 because they are not represented in the trained tree. Let's rank the remaining features based on their importance score.

Listing 22.51   Ranking relevant features by importance

```
for i in np.argsort(clf.feature_importances_)[::-1]:
    feature = feature_names[i]
    importance = clf.feature_importances_[i]
    if importance == 0:
        break

    print(f"'{feature}' has an importance score of {importance:0.2f}")

'proline' has an importance score of 0.49
'od280/od315_of_diluted_wines' has an importance score of 0.40
'flavanoids' has an importance score of 0.12
```

Among our features, proline is ranked as most important. It's followed by OD280 / OD315 and the flavonoids.

Tree-based feature ranking can help draw meaningful insights from our data. We'll emphasize this point by exploring the serious problem of cancer diagnosis.

22.2.1 *Studying cancerous cells using feature importance*

An identified tumor could be cancerous. The tumor needs to be examined under a microscope to determine if it is malignant (cancerous) or benign (noncancerous). Zooming in on the tumor reveals individual cells. Each cell has a multitude of measurable features, including these:

- Area
- Perimeter
- Compactness (the ratio of the squared perimeter to the area)
- Radius (a cell is not perfectly round, so the radius is computed as the mean distance from the center to the perimeter)
- Smoothness (variations in the distance from the cell center to the perimeter)
- Concave points (the number of inward curves on the perimeter)
- Concavity (the average inward angle of the concave points)
- Symmetry (if one side of the cell resembles the other)
- Texture (he standard deviation of color shades in the cell image)
- Fractal dimension (the "wriggliness" of the perimeter, based on the number of separate straight-ruler measurements required to measure the wriggly border)

Imaging technology allows us to compute these features for each individual cell. However, the tumor biopsy will reveal dozens of cells beneath the microscope (figure 22.9), so the individual features must somehow be aggregated together. The simplest way to aggregate the features is to compute their mean and standard deviation. We can also store the most extreme value computed across each cell: for instance, we can record the largest concavity measured across the cells. Informally, we'll refer to this statistic as the *worst concavity*.

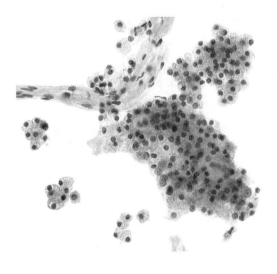

Figure 22.9 **Dozens of tumor cells seen through a microscope. Each cell has 10 different measurable features. We can aggregate these features across cells using three different statistics, so we obtain 30 features total for determining whether the tumor is malignant or benign.**

NOTE   Usually, these features are not computed on the cell itself. Instead, they are computed on the nucleus of the cell. The nucleus is an enclosed, circular structure in the center of the cell that is easily visible through a microscope.

The three different aggregations across 10 measured features lead to 30 features total. Which features are most important for determining cancer-cell malignancy?. We can find out. Scikit-learn includes a cancer-cell dataset: let's import it from `sklearn.datasets` and print the feature names and class names.

Listing 22.52   Importing scikit-learn's cancer-cell dataset

```
from sklearn.datasets import load_breast_cancer

data = load_breast_cancer()
feature_names = data.feature_names
num_features = len(feature_names)
num_classes = len(data.target_names)
print(f"The cancer dataset contains the following {num_classes} classes:")
print(data.target_names)
print(f"\nIt contains these {num_features} features:")
print(feature_names)


The cancer dataset contains the following 2 classes:
['malignant' 'benign']

It contains these 30 features:
['mean radius' 'mean texture' 'mean perimeter' 'mean area'
 'mean smoothness' 'mean compactness' 'mean concavity'
 'mean concave points' 'mean symmetry' 'mean fractal dimension'
 'radius error' 'texture error' 'perimeter error' 'area error'
 'smoothness error' 'compactness error' 'concavity error'
 'concave points error' 'symmetry error' 'fractal dimension error'
 'worst radius' 'worst texture' 'worst perimeter' 'worst area'
 'worst smoothness' 'worst compactness' 'worst concavity'
 'worst concave points' 'worst symmetry' 'worst fractal dimension']
```

The dataset contains 30 different features. Let's rank them by importance and output the ranked features along with their importance scores. We ignore features whose importance scores are close to zero.

Listing 22.53   Ranking tumor features by importance

```
X, y = load_breast_cancer(return_X_y=True)
clf = DecisionTreeClassifier()
clf.fit(X, y)
for i in np.argsort(clf.feature_importances_)[::-1]:
    feature = feature_names[i]
    importance = clf.feature_importances_[i]
    if round(importance, 2) == 0:
        break
    print(f"'{feature}' has an importance score of {importance:0.2f}")
```

```
'worst radius' has an importance score of 0.70
'worst concave points' has an importance score of 0.14
'worst texture' has an importance score of 0.08
'worst smoothness' has an importance score of 0.01
'worst concavity' has an importance score of 0.01
'mean texture' has an importance score of 0.01
'worst area' has an importance score of 0.01
'mean concave points' has an importance score of 0.01
'worst fractal dimension' has an importance score of 0.01
'radius error' has an importance score of 0.01
'smoothness error' has an importance score of 0.01
'worst compactness' has an importance score of 0.01
```

The three top-ranking features are *worst radius, worst concave points,* and *worst texture.* Neither the mean nor the standard deviation drives the malignancy of the tumor; instead, it is the presence of a few extreme outliers that determines the cancer diagnosis. Even one or two irregularly shaped cells can indicate malignancy. Among the top-ranking features, worst radius particularly stands out: it has an importance score of 0.70. The next-highest importance score is 0.14. This difference suggests that the radius of the largest cell is an extremely important indicator of cancer. We an check this hypothesis by plotting histograms of the worst-radius measurements across the two classes (figure 22.10).

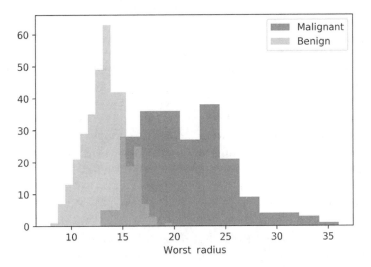

Figure 22.10 **A histogram of worst-radius measurements across cancerous and noncancerous tumors. That radius is noticeably greater when the tumor is malignant and not benign.**

Listing 22.54 **Plotting two worst radius histograms**

```
index = clf.feature_importances_.argmax()
plt.hist(X[y == 0][:, index], label='Malignant', bins='auto')
plt.hist(X[y == 1][:, index], label='Benign', color='y', bins='auto',
        alpha=0.5)
```

```
plt.xlabel('Worst Radius')
plt.legend()
plt.show()
```

The histogram reveals an enormous separation between malignant and benign worst-radius measurements. In fact, the presence of any cell radius greater than 20 units is a sure-fire indication of malignancy.

By training a decision tree, we gained insights into medicine and biology. Generally, decision trees are very useful tools for comprehending signals in complex datasets. The trees are very interpretable; their learned logical statements can easily be probed by data science. Furthermore, decision trees offer additional benefits:

- Decision tree classifiers are very quick to train. They are orders of magnitude faster than KNN classifiers. Also, unlike linear classifiers, they are not dependent on repeated training iterations.
- Decision tree classifiers don't depend on data manipulation before training. Logistic regression requires us to standardize the data before training; decision trees do not require standardization. Also, linear classifiers cannot handle categorical features without pretraining transformations, but a decision tree can handle these features directly.
- Decision trees are not limited by the geometric shape of the training data. In contrast, as shown in figure 22.1, KNN and linear classifiers cannot handle certain geometric configurations.

All these benefits come at a price: trained decision tree classifiers sometimes perform poorly on real-world data.

22.3   *Decision tree classifier limitations*

Decision trees learn the training data well—sometimes too well. Certain trees simply memorize the data without yielding any useful real-world insights. There are serious limits to rote memorization. Imagine a college student who is studying for a physics final. The previous year's exam is available online and includes written answers to all the questions. The student memorizes last year's exam. Given last year's questions, the student can easily recite the answers. The student is feeling confident—but on the day of the final, disaster strikes! The questions on the final are slightly different. Last year's exam asked for the velocity of a tennis ball dropped from 20 feet, but this exam asks for the velocity of a billiard ball dropped from 50 feet. The student is at a loss. They learned the answers but not the general patterns driving those answers; they can't do well on the exam because their knowledge does not generalize.

Overmemorization limits the usefulness of our trained models. In supervised machine learning, this phenomenon is referred to as *overfitting*. An overfitted model corresponds too closely to the training data, so it may fail to predict accurately on new observations. Decision tree classifiers are particularly prone to overfitting since they can memorize the training data. For instance, our cancer detector `clf` has perfectly memorized the training set (`X`, `y`). We can confirm by outputting the accuracy with which `clf.predict(X)` corresponds to `y`.

Listing 22.55 Checking the accuracy of the cancer-cell model

```
from sklearn.metrics import accuracy_score
accuracy = accuracy_score(clf.predict(X), y)
print("Our classifier has memorized the training data with "
     f"{100 * accuracy:.0f}% accuracy.")
```

```
Our classifier has memorized the training data with 100% accuracy.
```

The classifier can identify any training example with 100% accuracy, but this does not mean it can generalize as well to real-world data. We can better gauge the classifier's true accuracy using cross-validation. Listing 22.56 splits (`X`, `y`) into training set (`X_train`, `y_train`) and validation set (`X_test`, `y_test`). We train `clf` to perfectly memorize (`X_train`, `y_train`) and then check how well the model can generalize to data that it has not encountered before. We do this by computing the model's accuracy on the validation set.

Listing 22.56 Checking model accuracy with cross-validation

```
np.random.seed(0)
from sklearn.model_selection import train_test_split
X_train, X_test, y_train, y_test = train_test_split(X, y, )
clf = DecisionTreeClassifier()
clf.fit(X_train, y_train)
accuracy = accuracy_score(clf.predict(X_test), y_test)
print(f"The classifier performs with {100 * accuracy:.0f}% accuracy on "
     "the validation set.")
```

```
The classifier performs with 90% accuracy on the validation set.
```

The classifier's true accuracy is at 90%. That accuracy is decent, but we can definitely do better. We need a way to improve the performance by limiting overfitting in the tree. This can be done by training multiple decision trees at once using a technique called *random forest classification.*

Relevant scikit-learn decision tree classifier methods

- `clf = DecisionTreeClassifier()`—Initializes a decision tree classifier
- `clf = DecisionTreeClassifier(max_depth=x)`—Initializes a decision tree classifier with a maximum depth of `x`
- `clf.feature_importances_`—Accesses the feature importance scores of a trained decision tree classifier
- `plot_tree(clf)`—Plots a decision tree diagram associated with tree `clf`

(continued)

- `plot_tree(clf, feature_names=x, class_names=y)`—Plots a decision tree diagram with customized feature names and class labels
- `export_text(clf)`—Represents the decision tree diagram as a simple string
- `export_text(clf, feature_names=x)`—Represents the decision tree diagram as a simple string with customized feature names

22.4   *Improving performance using random forest classification*

Sometimes, in human affairs, the aggregated viewpoint of a crowd outperforms all individual predictions. In 1906, a crowd gathered at the Plymouth country fair to guess the weight of a 1,198-pound ox. Each person present wrote down their best guess, and the median of these guesses was tallied. The final median estimate of 1,207 pounds was within 1% of the actual weight. This aggregated triumph of collective intelligence is called the *wisdom of the crowd.*

Modern democratic institutions are built on the wisdom of the crowd. In democratic nations, the people come together and vote on the future of their country. Usually, the voters have incredibly diverse political views, opinions, and life experiences. But somehow, their accumulated choices average out into a decision that can benefit their country in the long run. This democratic process is partially dependent on the diversity of the populace. If everyone has the exact same opinion, everyone is prone to the same errors—but a diversity of views helps limit those errors. The crowd tends to make its best decisions when its members think in different ways.

The wisdom of the crowd is a natural phenomenon. It's seen not just in people but also in animals. Bats, fish, birds, and even flies can optimize their behavior when surrounded by other members of their species. The phenomenon can also be observed in machine learning. A crowd of decision trees can sometimes outperform a single tree; however, for this to happen, the inputs into each tree must be diverse.

Let's explore the wisdom of the crowd by initializing 100 decision trees. A large collection of trees is (not surprisingly) referred to as a *forest.* Hence, we store our trees in a `forest` list.

Listing 22.57   Initializing a 100-tree forest

```
forest = [DecisionTreeClassifier() for _ in range(100)]
```

How should we train the trees in the forest? Naively, we could train each individual tree on our cancer training set (`X_train`, `y_train`). However, we would end up with 100 trees that memorized the exact same data. The trees would therefore make identical predictions, so the key element of diversity would be missing from the forest. Without diversity, the wisdom of the crowd cannot be applied. What should we do?

One solution is to randomize our training data. In section 7, we studied a technique called bootstrapping with replacement. In this technique, the contents of an *N*-element dataset are sampled repeatedly. The elements are sampled with replacement, which means duplicate elements are allowed. Through sampling, we can generate a new *N*-element dataset whose contents differ from the original data. Let's bootstrap our training data to randomly generate a new training set (X_train_new, y_train_new).

Listing 22.58   Randomly sampling a new training set

Applies bootstrapping to training set (**X, y**) to generate a brand-new training set

Samples random indices of data points in (**X, y**). The sampling is carried out with replacement, so certain indices may be sampled twice.

```
np.random.seed(1)
def bootstrap(X, y):
    num_rows = X.shape[0]
    indices = np.random.choice(range(num_rows), size=num_rows,
                               replace=True)
    X_new, y_new = X[indices], y[indices]
    return X_new, y_new
```

Returns a random training set based on the sampled indices

```
X_train_new, y_train_new = bootstrap(X_train, y_train)
assert X_train.shape == X_train_new.shape
assert y_train.size == y_train_new.size
assert not np.array_equal(X_train, X_train_new)
assert not np.array_equal(y_train, y_train_new)
```

The bootstrapped training set is as large as the original training set.

The bootstrapped training set is not equal to the original set.

Now, let's run our bootstrap function 100 times to generate 100 different training sets.

Listing 22.59   Randomly sampling 100 new training sets

```
np.random.seed(1)
features_train, classes_train = [], []
for _ in range(100):
    X_train_new, y_train_new = bootstrap(X_train, y_train)
    features_train.append(X_train_new)
    classes_train.append(y_train_new)
```

Across our 100 training sets, the data may be different, but all the features are the same. However, we can increase the overall diversity by randomizing the features in features_train. In general, the wisdom of the crowd works best when different individuals pay attention to diverging features. For instance, in a democratic election, the top priorities of urban voters might not overlap with those of rural voters. Urban voters might focus on housing policies and crime, and rural voters might focus on crop tariffs and property taxes. These diverging priorities can lead to a consensus that benefits both urban and rural voters in the long run.

More concretely, in supervised machine learning, feature diversity can limit overfitting. Consider, for example, our cancer dataset. As we have seen, "worst radius" is an incredibly impactful feature. Thus, all trained models where that feature is included will rely on the radius as a crutch. But on certain rare occasions, a tumor might be cancerous even if the radius is low. Conformist models will mislabel that tumor if they all rely on the same features. Imagine, however, if we train some models without including the radius in their feature sets: these models will be forced to search for alternate, subtle patterns of cell malignancy and will be more resilient to fluctuating real-world observations. Individually, each model might not perform as well because its feature set is limited. Collectively, models should perform better than each individual tree.

We'll aim to train the trees in the forest on random samples of features in `features_train`. Currently, each feature matrix holds 30 cancer-related measurements. We need to lower the feature count in each random sample from 30 to a smaller number. What is an appropriate sample count? Well, it has been shown that the square root of the total feature count is usually a good choice for the sample size. The square root of 30 equals approximately 5, so we'll set our sample size to 5.

Let's iterate over `features_train` and filter each feature matrix to five random columns. We also track the indices of the randomly chosen features for later use during validation.

Listing 22.60   Randomly sampling the training features

We randomly sample 5 of 30 feature columns for each tree. Sampling is carried out without replacement because a duplicate feature will not yield novel signals during training.

The feature sample size is equal to approximately the square root of the total feature count.

```
np.random.seed(1)
sample_size = int(X.shape[1] ** 0.5)
assert sample_size == 5
feature_indices = [np.random.choice(range(30), 5, replace=False)
                   for _ in range(100)]
```

Given 30 features total, we expect the sample size to equal 5.

```
for i, index_subset in enumerate(feature_indices):
    features_train[i] = features_train[i][:, index_subset]
```

```
for index in [0, 99]:
    index_subset = feature_indices[index]
    names = feature_names[index_subset]
    print(f"\nRandom features utilized by Tree {index}:")
    print(names)
```

Prints the randomly sampled feature names in the very first and very last feature subsets

```
Random features utilized by Tree 0:
['concave points error' 'worst texture' 'radius error'
 'fractal dimension error' 'smoothness error']
```

Five randomly sampled features do not include the worst-radius measurement.

```
Random features utilized by Tree 99:
['mean smoothness' 'worst radius' 'fractal dimension error'
 'worst concave points' 'mean concavity']
```

Five randomly sampled features include the impactful worst-radius measurement.

We've randomized each of our 100 feature matrices by both row (data point) and column (feature). The training data for every tree is very diverse. Let's train each *i*th tree in `forest` on training set (`features_train[i]`, `classes_train[i]`).

Listing 22.61   Training the trees in the forest

```
for i, clf_tree in enumerate(forest):
    clf_tree.fit(features_train[i], classes_train[i])
```

We've trained every tree in the forest. Now, let's put the trained trees to a vote. What is the class label of the data point at X_test[0]? We can check using the wisdom of the crowd. Here, we iterate across every trained clf_tree in the forest. For every *i*th iteration, we do the following:

1   Utilize the tree to predict the class label at X_test[0]. As a reminder, each *i*th tree in forest depends on a random subset of features. The chosen feature indices are stored in feature_indices[i]. Hence, we need to filter the X_test[0] by the chosen indices before making the prediction.

2   Record the prediction as the *vote* of the tree at index i.

Once all the trees have voted, we tally the 100 votes and select the class label that has received the plurality of the votes.

> **NOTE**   This process is very similar to the KNN plurality voting that we utilized in section 20.

Listing 22.62   Using tree voting to classify a data point

```
from collections import Counter        Iterates over 100      Adjusts the columns
feature_vector = X_test[0]             trained trees          in feature_vector to
votes = []                                                    correspond with the five
for i, clf_tree in enumerate(forest):  ◁                      random feature indices
    index_subset = feature_indices[i]                         associated with each tree
    vector_subset = feature_vector[index_subset]     ◁
    prediction = clf_tree.predict([vector_subset])[0]   ◁    Each tree casts a vote
    votes.append(prediction)                                  by returning a class-
                                                              label prediction.
class_to_votes = Counter(votes)
for class_label, votes in class_to_votes.items():
    print(f"We counted {votes} votes for class {class_label}.")

top_class = max(class_to_votes.items(), key=lambda x: x[1])[0]
print(f"\nClass {top_class} has received the plurality of the votes.")
```

Counts all votes → (points to `class_to_votes = Counter(votes)`)

```
We counted 93 votes for class 0.
We counted 7 votes for class 1.

Class 0 has received the plurality of the votes.
```

93% of the trees voted for Class 0. Let's check if this majority vote is correct.

Listing 22.63   Checking the true class of the predicted label

```
true_label = y_test[0]
print(f"The true class of the data-point is {true_label}.")
```

```
The true class of the data-point is 0.
```

The forest has successfully identified the point at X_test[0]. Now, we will use voting to identify all points in the X_test validation set and utilize y_test to measure our prediction accuracy.

Listing 22.64   Measuring the accuracy of the forest model

```
predictions = []
for i, clf_tree in enumerate(forest):
    index_subset = feature_indices[i]
    prediction = clf_tree.predict(X_test[:,index_subset])
    predictions.append(prediction)

predictions = np.array(predictions)
y_pred = [Counter(predictions[:,i]).most_common()[0][0]
         for i in range(y_test.size)]
accuracy = accuracy_score(y_pred, y_test)
print("The forest has predicted the validation outputs with "
     f"{100 * accuracy:.0f}% accuracy")
```

```
The forest has predicted the validation outputs with 96% accuracy
```

Our randomly generated forest has predicted the validation outputs with 96% accuracy. It outperformed our single trained decision tree, whose accuracy hovered at 90%. By using the wisdom of the crowd, we have managed to improve performance. In the process, we have also trained a *random forest classifier*: a collection of trees whose training inputs are randomized to maximize diversity. Random forest classifiers are trained in the following manner:

1 Initialize *N* decision trees. The number of trees is a hyperparameter. Generally, more trees lead to higher accuracy, but using too many trees increasess the classifier's running time.

2 Generate *N* random training sets by sampling with replacement.

3 Choose N ** 0.5 feature columns at random for each of our *N* training sets.

4 Train all the decision trees across the *N* random training sets.

After training, each tree in the forest casts a vote on how to label inputed data. These votes are tallied, and the class with the most votes is outputted by the classifier.

Random forest classifiers are very versatile and are not prone to overfitting. Scikit-learn, of course, includes a random forest implementation.

22.5   *Training random forest classifiers using scikit-learn*

In scikit-learn, random forest classification is carried out by the RandomForest-Classifier class. Let's import that class from sklearn.ensemble, initialize the class, and train it using (X_train, y_train). Finally, we check the classifier's performance using the validation set (X_test, y_test).

Listing 22.65   Training a random forest classifier

```
np.random.seed(1)
from sklearn.ensemble import RandomForestClassifier
clf_forest = RandomForestClassifier()
clf_forest.fit(X_train, y_train)
y_pred = clf_forest.predict(X_test)
accuracy = accuracy_score(y_pred, y_test)
print("The forest has predicted the validation outputs with "
      f"{100 * accuracy:.0f}% accuracy")
```

> **This result is slightly higher than our earlier result of 96% due to random fluctuations as well as additional optimizations provided by scikit-learn.**

```
The forest has predicted the validation outputs with 97% accuracy
```

By default, scikit-learn's random forest classifier utilizes 100 decision trees. However, we can specify a lower or higher count using the n_estimators parameter. The following code reduces the number of trees to 10 by running RandomForestClassifier (n_estimators=10). Then we recompute the accuracy.

Listing 22.66   Training a 10-tree random forest classifier

```
np.random.seed(1)
clf_forest = RandomForestClassifier(n_estimators=10)
clf_forest.fit(X_train, y_train)
y_pred = clf_forest.predict(X_test)
accuracy = accuracy_score(y_pred, y_test)
print("The 10-tree forest has predicted the validation outputs with "
      f"{100 * accuracy:.0f}% accuracy")
```

```
The 10-tree forest has predicted the validation outputs with 97% accuracy
```

Even with the lower tree count, the total accuracy remains very high. Sometimes, 10 trees are more than sufficient to train a very accurate classifier.

Each of the 10 trees in clf_forest is assigned a random subset of five features. Every feature in the subset contains its own feature importance score. Scikit-learn can average all these scores across all the trees, and the aggregated averages can be accessed by calling clf_forest.feature_importances_. Let's utilize the feature_importances_ attribute to print the top three features in the forest.

Listing 22.67   Ranking the random forest features

```
for i in np.argsort(clf_forest.feature_importances_)[::-1][:3]:
    feature = feature_names[i]
    importance = clf_forest.feature_importances_[i]
    print(f"'{feature}' has an importance score of {importance:0.2f}")
```

```
'worst perimeter' has an importance score of 0.20
'worst radius' has an importance score of 0.16
'worst area' has an importance score of 0.16
```

The worst-radius feature continues to rank high, but its ranking is now on par with worst area and worst perimeter. Unlike our decision tree, the random forest does not over-rely on any individual inputted feature. This gives the random forest more flexibility in handling fluctuating signals in new data. The classifier's versatile nature makes it a popular choice when training on medium-sized datasets.

NOTE Random forest classifiers function very well on multifeature datasets with hundreds or thousands of points. However, once the dataset size enters the millions, the algorithm can no longer scale. When processing exceedingly large datasets, more powerful deep learning techniques are required. None of the problems in this book fall in the scope of that requirement.

Relevant scikit-learn random forest classifier methods
- `clf = RandomForestClassifier()`—Initializes a random forest classifier
- `clf = RandomForestClassifier(n_estimators=x)`—Initializes a random forest classifier in which the number of trees is set to x
- `clf.feature_importances_`—Accesses the feature importance scores of a trained random forest classifier

Summary

- Certain classification problems can be handled with nested `if/else` statements but not with KNN or logistic regression classifiers.
- We can train a single-feature `if/else` model by maximizing accuracy across the co-occurrence counts between each feature state and each class label.
- We can train a two-feature nested `if/else` model by doing a *binary split* on one of the features. Splitting on the feature returns two different training sets. Each training set is associated with a unique split-feature state. The training sets can be used to compute two single-feature models, and then we can combine the models into a nested `if/else` statement. The nested model's accuracy is equal to the weighted mean of the simpler model accuracies.
- The choice of feature for the binary split can impact the quality of the model. Generally, the split leads to superior results if it generates imbalanced training data. A training set's imbalance can be captured using its class-label distribution. More imbalanced training sets have a higher distribution vector magnitude. Hence, imbalanced datasets yield a higher value for v @ v, where v is the distribution vector. Additionally, the value 1 - v @ v is referred to as the *Gini impurity*. Minimizing the Gini impurity minimizes the training set imbalance, so we should always split on the feature that yields the minimal Gini impurity.
- We can extend two-feature model training to handle *N* features. We train an *N*-feature model by splitting on the feature with the minimum Gini impurity. Then we train two simpler models, each of which handles *N* – 1 features. The two simpler models are then combined into a more complex nested model whose accuracy is equal to the weighted mean of the simpler model accuracies.

- The branching `if`/`else` statements in the trained conditional models resemble the branches of a tree. We can make the resemblance more explicit by visualizing the output as a *decision tree diagram*. Decision trees are special network structures used to symbolize `if`/`else` decisions. Any nested `if`/`else` statement can be visualized as a decision tree, so trained `if`/`else` conditional classifiers are referred to as *decision tree classifiers*.

- Decision tree *depth* equals the number of nested `if`/`else` statements required to capture the logic in the tree. Limiting the depth can yield more interpretable diagrams.

- The depth at which a feature appears in the tree is an indicator of its relative importance. That depth is determined by the Gini impurity, so the Gini impurity can be used to compute an importance score.

- Overmemorization limits the usefulness of our trained models. In supervised machine learning, this phenomenon is referred to as *overfitting*. An overfitted model corresponds too closely to the training data, so it may fail to accurately predict on new observations. Decision tree classifiers are particularly prone to overfitting since they can memorize the training data.

- We can limit overfitting by training multiple decision trees in parallel. This collection of trees is called a *forest*. The collective wisdom of the forest can outperform an individual tree, but this requires us to introduce diversity to the forest. We can add diversity by generating random training sets with randomly chosen features. Then every tree in the forest is trained on a diverging training set. After training, each tree in the forest casts a vote on how to label inputted data. This voting-based ensemble model is referred to as a *random forest classifier*.

Case study 5 solution

FriendHook is a popular social networking app designed for college campuses. Students can connect as friends in the FriendHook network. A recommendation engine emails users weekly with new friend suggestions based on their existing connections; students can ignore these recommendations, or they can send out friend requests. We have been provided with one week's worth of data pertaining to friend recommendations and student responses. That data is stored in the friendhook/Observations.csv file. We're provided with two additional files: friendhook/Profiles.csv and friendhook/Friendships.csv, containing user profile information and the friendship graph, respectively. The user profiles have been encrypted to protect student privacy. Our goal is to build a model that predicts user behavior in response to the friend recommendations. We will do so by following these steps:

1 Load the three datasets containing the observations, user profiles, and friendship connections.

2 Train and evaluate a supervised model that predicts behavior based on network features and profile features. We can optionally split this task into two subtasks: training a model using network features, and then adding profile features and evaluating the shift in model performance.

3 Check to ensure that the model generalizes well to other universities.

4 Explore the inner workings of our model to gain better insights into student behavior.

> **WARNING** Spoiler alert! The solution to case study 5 is about to be revealed. We strongly encourage you to try to solve the problem before reading the solution. The original problem statement is available for reference at the beginning of the case study.

23.1 Exploring the data

Let's separately explore the Profiles, Observations, and Friendships tables. We will clean and adjust the data in these tables if required.

23.1.1 Examining the profiles

We start by loading the Profiles table into Pandas and summarizing the table's contents.

Listing 23.1 Loading the Profiles table

```
import pandas as pd

def summarize_table(df):          ◁—  We'll reuse this summarize
    n_rows, n_columns = df.shape       function on the other two
    summary = df.describe()            tables in our dataset.
    print(f"The table contains {n_rows} rows and {n_columns} columns.")
    print("Table Summary:\n")
    print(summary.to_string())

df_profile = pd.read_csv('friendhook/Profiles.csv')
summarize_table(df_profile)
```

```
The table contains 4039 rows and 6 columns.
Table Summary:
```

	Profile_ID	Sex	Relationship_Status	Dorm	Major	Year
count	4039	4039	3631	4039	4039	4039
unique	4039	2	3	15	30	4
top	b90a1222d2b2	e807eb960650	ac0b88e46e20	a8e6e404d1b3	141d4cdd5aaf	c1a648750a4b
freq	1	2020	1963	2739	1366	1796

The table contains 4,039 distinct profiles distributed across two different sexes. The most frequent sex is mentioned in 2,020 of 4,039 profiles, so we can infer that the profiles represent an equal distribution between males and females. Furthermore, the profiles capture a student body distribution that's spread across 30 majors and 15 dormitories. Suspiciously, the most frequently mentioned dorm contains over 2,700 students. This number seems large, but a quick Google search reveals that large on-campus student complexes are not uncommon. For instance, the 17-story Sandburg Residence Hall at the University of Wisconsin-Milwaukee can house 2,700 students. These numbers may also represent students in the *Off-Campus Housing* category. The count can be explained by a multitude of hypotheses—but going forward, we should consider the various driving factors behind the numbers we observe. Rather than blindly crunching numbers, we should keep in mind that our data is derived from real-world behaviors and physical constraints of university students.

There is one anomaly in the table summary, in the *Relationship Status* column. Pandas has detected three *Relationship Status* categories across 3,631 of 4,039 table rows. The remaining 400 or so rows are null—they don't contain any assigned relationship status. Let's count the number of empty rows.

```
is_null = df_profile.Relationship_Status.isnull()
num_null = df_profile[is_null].shape[0]
print(f"{num_null} profiles are missing the Relationship Status field.")
```

```
408 profiles are missing the Relationship Status field.
```

408 profiles are missing a value in the `Relationship_Status` field. This makes sense: as stated in the problem statement, the `Relationship_Status` field is optional. It appears that one-tenth of the students refused to specify that field. But we cannot continue our analysis with empty values in our data; we need to either delete the empty rows or replace the empty fields with some other value. Deleting the empty rows is not a good option—we'd be throwing out potentially valuable information in the other columns. Instead, we can treat the lack of status as a fourth *unspecified* relationship status category. To do so, we should assign these rows a category ID. What ID value should we choose? Before we answer the question, let's examine all unique IDs in the *Relationship Status* column.

```
unique_ids = set(df_profile.Relationship_Status.values)
print(unique_ids)
```

```
{'9cea719429e9', nan, '188f9a32c360', 'ac0b88e46e20'}
```

As expected, the *Relationship Status* values are composed of three hash codes and an empty nan. The hash codes are encrypted versions of the three possible status categories:

Single, In a Relationship, and *It's Complicated.* Of course, we cannot know which category is which. All we can determine is whether two profiles fall in the same status category. Our aim is to eventually use this information in a trained machine learning model. However, the scikit-learn library is unable to process hash codes or null values: it can only process numbers, so we need to convert the categories to numeric values. The simplest solution would be to assign each category a number between 0 and 4. Let's execute this assignment. We start by generating a dictionary mapping between each category and number.

Listing 23.4   **Mapping *Relationship Status* values to numbers**

```
import numpy as np
category_map = {'9cea719429e9': 0, np.nan: 1, '188f9a32c360': 2,
                'ac0b88e46e20': 3}        ◁

{'9cea719429e9': 0, nan: 1, '188f9a32c360': 2, 'ac0b88e46e20': 3}
```

Normally, we would generate this map automatically by executing category_map = {id_: i for i, id_ in enumerate(unique_ids)}, but the order of numeric assignments could vary based on Python versioning. So, we manually set the mappings to ensure consistent outputs for all readers of this section.

Next, we replace the contents of the *Relationship Status* column with the appropriate numeric values.

Listing 23.5   **Updating the *Relationship Status* column**

```
nums = [category_map[hash_code]
        for hash_code in df_profile.Relationship_Status.values]
df_profile['Relationship_Status'] = nums
print(df_profile.Relationship_Status)

0        0
1        3
2        3
3        3
4        0
        ..
4034     3
4035     0
4036     3
4037     3
4038     0
Name: Relationship_Status, Length: 4039, dtype: int64
```

We've transformed *Relationship Status* into a numeric variable, but the remaining five columns in the table still contain hash codes. Should we also replace these hash codes with numbers? Yes! Here's why:

- As previously mentioned, scikit-learn cannot process strings or hashes. It only takes numeric values as input.

- For humans, reading hash codes is more mentally taxing than reading numbers. Thus, replacing the multicharacter codes with shorter numbers will make it easier for us to explore the data.

With this in mind, let's create a category mapping between hash codes and numbers in each column. We track the category mappings in each column with a col_to_mapping dictionary. We also use the mappings to replace all hash codes with numbers in df_profile.

Listing 23.6 Replacing all *Profile* hash codes with numeric values

```
col_to_mapping = {'Relationship_Status': category_map}

for column in df_profile.columns:
    if column in col_to_mapping:
        continue

    unique_ids = sorted(set(df_profile[column].values))      ◁──────┐
    category_map = {id_: i for i, id_ in enumerate(unique_ids)}
    col_to_mapping[column] = category_map
    nums = [category_map[hash_code]
            for hash_code in df_profile[column].values]
    df_profile[column] = nums

head = df_profile.head()
print(head.to_string(index=False))
```

Sorting the IDs helps ensure consistent outputs for all readers, independent of their Python versioning. Note that we can only sort the hash code IDs if no nan values are present among the hash codes; otherwise, the sorting will cause an error.

```
Profile_ID  Sex  Relationship_Status  Dorm  Major  Year
      2899    0                    0     5     13     2
      1125    0                    3    12      6     1
      3799    0                    3    12     29     2
      3338    0                    3     4     25     0
      2007    1                    0    12      2     0
```

We've finished tweaking df_profile. Now let's turn our attention to the table of experimental observations.

23.1.2 *Exploring the experimental observations*

We start by loading the Observations table into Pandas and summarizing the table's contents.

Listing 23.7 Loading the Observations table

```
df_obs = pd.read_csv('friendhook/Observations.csv')
summarize_table(df_obs)
```

```
The table contains 4039 rows and 5 columns.
Table Summary:
```

	Profile_ID	Selected_ Friend	Selected_Friend_ of_Friend	Friend_Request_ Sent	Friend_Request_ Accepted
count	4039	4039	4039	4039	4039
unique	4039	2219	2327	2	2
top	b90a1222d2b2	89581f99fa1e	6caa597f13cc	True	True
freq	1	77	27	2519	2460

The five table columns all consistently show 4,039 filled rows. There are no empty values in the table. This is good—but the column names are hard to read. The names are very descriptive but also very long. We should consider shortening some of the names to ease our cognitive load. Let's briefly discuss the various columns and whether some renaming would be appropriate:

- *Profile_ID*—The ID of the user who received the friend recommendation. This name is short and straightforward. It also corresponds to the *Profile_ID* column in df_profile. We should keep this name as is.
- *Selected_Friend*—An existing friend of the user in the *Profile_ID* column. We can simplify this column name to just *Friend*.
- *Selected_Friend_of_Friend*—A randomly chosen friend of *Selected_Friend* who was not yet a friend of *Profile_ID*. In our analysis, this random friend-of-a-friend was emailed as a *friend recommendation* for the user. We can rename this column *Recommended_Friend* or possibly *FoF*. Let's call the column *FoF*, because this acronym is memorable and short.
- *Friend_Request_Sent*—This Boolean column is True if a user sent a friend request to the suggested friend of a friend or False otherwise. Let's shorten the column name to just *Sent*.
- *Friend_Request_Accepted*—This Boolean column is only True if a user sent a friend request and that request was accepted. We can shorten the column name to *Accepted*.

Based on our discussion, we need to rename four of the five columns. Let's rename the columns and regenerate the summary.

Listing 23.8   Renaming the observation columns

```
new_names = {'Selected_Friend': 'Friend',
             'Selected_Friend_of_Friend': 'FoF',
             'Friend_Request_Sent': 'Sent',
             'Friend_Request_Accepted': 'Accepted'}
df_obs = df_obs.rename(columns=new_names)
summarize_table(df_obs)
```

```
The table contains 4039 rows and 5 columns.
Table Summary:
```

	Profile_ID	Friend	FoF	Sent	Accepted
count	4039	4039	4039	4039	4039
unique	4039	2219	2327	2	2
top	b90a1222d2b2	89581f99fa1e	6caa597f13cc	True	True
freq	1	77	27	2519	2460

In the updated table, the statistics are clearer. The observations contain 2,219 unique *Friend* IDs and 2,327 unique *FoF* IDs out of 4,039 samples total. This means, on average, each *Friend* and *FoF* ID is utilized approximately twice. No single profile ID dominates our data, which is reassuring. This will allow us to more easily design a robust predictive model, as opposed to a model that is driven by a single profile signal and thus more susceptible to overtraining.

Further examination reveals that approximately 62% (2,519) of the friend suggestions led to a friend request being sent. This is very promising; the friend-of-a-friend suggestions are quite effective. Furthermore, approximately 60% (2,460) of sampled instances led to a friend request being accepted; the sent friend requests are ignored or rejected just 2% (2519 – 2460 = 50) of the time. Of course, our numbers assume that there are no observations where *Sent* is False and *Accepted* is True. This scenario is not possible because a friend request cannot be accepted if it has not yet been sent. Still, as a sanity check, let's test the integrity of the data by confirming that the scenario does not take place.

Listing 23.9   Ensuring that *Sent* is `True` for all accepted requests

```
condition = (df_obs.Sent == False) & (df_obs.Accepted == True)
assert not df_obs[condition].shape[0]
```

Based on our observations, user behavior follows three possible scenarios:

- A user rejects or ignores the friend recommendation listed in the *FoF* column. This occurs in 38% of instances.
- A user sends a friend request based on the recommendation, and the friend request is accepted. This occurs in 62% of instances.
- A user sends a friend request based on the recommendation, and the friend request is rejected or ignored. This scenario is rare, occurring in just 1.2% of total instances.

Each of these three scenarios represents three categories of user behavior. Hence, we can encode this categorical behavior by assigning numbers 0, 1, and 2 to behavior patterns *a*, *b*, and *c*. Here, we carry out the categorical assignments and store them in a *Behavior* column.

Listing 23.10 Assigning classes of behavior to the user observations

```
behaviors = []
for sent, accepted in df_obs[['Sent', 'Accepted']].values:
    behavior = 2 if (sent and not accepted) else int(sent) * int(accepted)   ◁──┐
    behaviors.append(behavior)                                                   │
df_obs['Behavior'] = behaviors                                                   │
```

> Python treats Boolean values True and False as simple integer values 1 and 0, respectively. So, this arithmetic operation returns either 0, 1, or 2 based on our behavior definitions.

Additionally, we must transform the profile IDs in the first three columns from hash codes to numeric IDs consistent with `df_profile.Profile_ID`. The following code utilizes the mapping stored in `col_to_mapping['Profile_ID']` for this purpose.

Listing 23.11 Replacing all *Observation* hash codes with numeric values

```
for col in ['Profile_ID', 'Friend', 'FoF']:
    nums = [col_to_mapping['Profile_ID'][hash_code]
            for hash_code in df_obs[col]]
    df_obs[col] = nums

head = df_obs.head()
print(head.to_string(index=False))
```

```
Profile_ID  Friend   FoF   Sent  Accepted  Behavior
      2485    2899  2847  False     False         0
      2690    2899  3528  False     False         0
      3904    2899  3528  False     False         0
       709    2899  3403  False     False         0
       502    2899   345   True      True         1
```

`df_obs` now aligns with `df_profile`. Only a single data table remains unanalyzed. Let's explore the friendship linkages in the `Friendships` table.

23.1.3 *Exploring the Friendships linkage table*

We start by loading the `Friendships` table into Pandas and summarizing the table's contents.

Listing 23.12 Loading the `Friendships` table

```
df_friends = pd.read_csv('friendhook/Friendships.csv')
summarize_table(df_friends)
```

The table contains 88234 rows and 2 columns.
Table Summary:

	Friend_A	Friend_B
count	88234	88234
unique	3646	4037

	Friend_A	Friend_B
top	89581f99fa1e	97ba93d9b169
freq	1043	251

There are over 88,000 friendship links in this social network. The social network is quite dense, with an average of approximately 22 friends per FriendHook profile. One social butterfly in the network (*89581f99fa1e*) has more than 1,000 friends. However, an exact friend count cannot be gauged because the two columns in the network are not symmetric. In fact, we cannot even validate whether all 4,039 profiles are appropriately represented in the table.

To carry out a more detailed analysis, we should load the friendship data into a NetworkX graph. Listing 23.13 computes the social graph. We represent the node IDs with the numeric values mapped from the hash codes in the columns. After we compute the graph, we count the number of nodes in G.nodes.

Listing 23.13   Loading the social graph into NetworkX

```
import networkx as nx
G = nx.Graph()
for id1, id2 in df_friends.values:
    node1 = col_to_mapping['Profile_ID'][id1]
    node2 = col_to_mapping['Profile_ID'][id2]
    G.add_edge(node1, node2)

nodes = list(G.nodes)
num_nodes = len(nodes)
print(f"The social graph contains {num_nodes} nodes.")

The social graph contains 4039 nodes.
```

Let's try to gain more insights into the graph structure by visualizing it with nx.draw (figure 23.1). Note that the graph is rather large, so visualization might take 10 to 30 seconds of running time to complete.

Listing 23.14   Visualizing the social graph

```
import matplotlib.pyplot as plt
np.random.seed(0)
nx.draw(G, node_size=5)
plt.show()
```

Tightly clustered social groups are clearly visible in the network. Let's extract these groups using Markov clustering and then count the number of clusters.

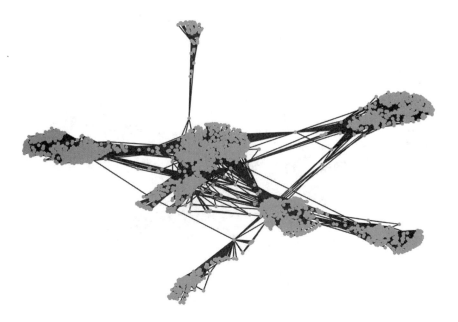

Figure 23.1 The university's visualized social graph. Tight social-group clusters are clearly visible; these can be extracted using Markov clustering.

Listing 23.15 Finding social groups using Markov clustering

```
import markov_clustering as mc
matrix = nx.toSciPysparse_matrix(G)
result = mc.run_mcl(matrix)
clusters = mc.get_clusters(result)
num_clusters = len(clusters)
print(f"{num_clusters} clusters were found in the social graph.")

10 clusters were found in the social graph.
```

Ten clusters were found in the social graph. Let's visualize these clusters by coloring each node based on cluster ID. To start, we need to iterate over clusters and assign a cluster_id attribute to every node.

Listing 23.16 Assigning cluster attributes to nodes

```
for cluster_id, node_indices in enumerate(clusters):
    for i in node_indices:
        node = nodes[i]
        G.nodes[node]['cluster_id'] = cluster_id
```

Next, we color the nodes based on their cluster attribute assignment (figure 23.2).

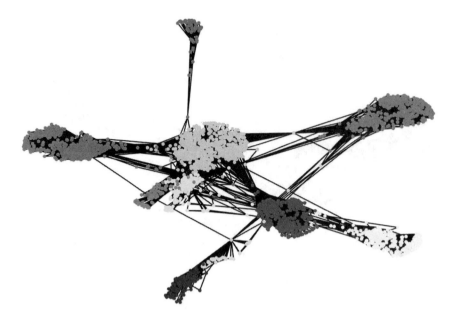

Figure 23.2   The university's visualized social graph. Tight social-group clusters have been identified using Markov clustering. The nodes in the graph are colored based on their cluster ID.

Listing 23.17   Coloring the nodes by cluster assignment

```
np.random.seed(0)
colors = [G.nodes[n]['cluster_id'] for n in G.nodes]
nx.draw(G, node_size=5, node_color=colors, cmap=plt.cm.tab20)
plt.show()
```

The cluster colors clearly correspond to tight social groups. Our clustering has been effective, so the assigned `cluster_id` attributes should be helpful during the model-building process. Similarly, it might be useful to store all five profile features as attributes in the student nodes. Let's iterate over the rows in `df_profile` and store each column value in its corresponding node.

Listing 23.18   Assigning profile attributes to nodes

```
attribute_names = df_profile.columns
for attributes in df_profile.values:
    profile_id = attributes[0]
    for name, att in zip(attribute_names[1:], attributes[1:]):
        G.nodes[profile_id][name] = att

first_node = nodes[0]
print(f"Attributes of node {first_node}:")
print(G.nodes[first_node])
```

```
Attributes of node 2899:
{'cluster_id': 0, 'Sex': 0, 'Relationship_Status': 0, 'Dorm': 5,
 'Major': 13, 'Year': 2}
```

We have finished exploring our input data. Now we'll train a model that predicts user behavior. We'll start by constructing a simple model that only utilizes network features.

23.2 Training a predictive model using network features

Our goal is to train a supervised machine learning model on our dataset to predict user behavior. Currently, all possible classes of behavior are stored in the *Behavior* columns of df_obs. Our three behavior class labels are 0, 1, and 2. As a reminder, the Class 2 label occurs in just 50 of the 4,039 sampled instances: Class 2 is very imbalanced relative to the other class labels. There is a case to be made for removing these 50 labeled examples from our training data. For the time being, let's leave in these examples to see what happens; later, we will remove them if necessary. For now, we assign our training class label array to equal the df_obs.Behavior column.

> **Listing 23.19 Assigning the class-label array y**

```
y = df_obs.Behavior.values
print(y)
```

```
[0 0 0 ... 1 1 1]
```

Now that we have class labels, we need to create a feature matrix X. Our goal is to populate this matrix with features arising from the social graph structure. Later, we'll add additional features from the student profiles, so we don't need to assemble the feature matrix all at once. We will build up the matrix slowly, adding new features in batches to better understand the impact of these features on model performance. With this in mind, let's create an initial version of X and populate it with some very basic features. The simplest question we can ask about any FriendHook user is this: how many friends does the user have? That value equals the edge count associated with the user's node in the social graph. In other words, the friend count of user n is equal to G.degree(n). Let's make this count the very first feature in the matrix. We'll iterate over all the rows in df_obs and assign an edge count to each profile referenced in each row. As a reminder, every row contains three profiles: *Profile_ID*, *Friend*, and *FoF*. We'll calculate the friend count for each profile, creating features *Profile_ID_ Edge_Count*, *Friend_Edge_Count*, and *FoF_Edge_Count*.

> **NOTE** It's not always easy to come up with a good, consistent feature name. Rather than choosing *FoF_Edge_Count*, we could have chosen *FoF_Friend_ Count* as our name. However, maintaining consistency would have forced us to include a *Friend_Friend_Count* feature as well, leading to a very awkward feature name. Alternatively, we could have named our three features *Profile_Degree*, *Friend_Degree*, and *FoF_Degree*. These names would be short and informative, but

it's worth remembering that one of our profile features pertains to college majors. In the context of college, both degrees and majors have a nearly identical definition, so a degree-based naming convention could cause confusion down the line. That is why we're sticking with an *Edge_Count* suffix.

Let's generate a matrix of 3-by-4,039 edge count features. We need a way to track these features along with the associated feature names. We also need a way to easily update features and their names with additional inputs. One straightforward solution is to store the features in a df_features Pandas table. That table will allow us to access the feature matrix via df_features.values. Let's compute df_features to create an initial version of our feature matrix.

Listing 23.20   Creating a feature matrix from edge counts

```
cols = ['Profile_ID', 'Friend', 'FoF']
features = {f'{col}_Edge_Count': [] for col in cols}
for node_ids in df_obs[cols].values:
    for node, feature_name in zip(node_ids, features.keys()):
        degree = G.degree(node)
        features[feature_name].append(degree)

df_features = pd.DataFrame(features)
X = df_features.values
```

As a reminder, the node's degree equals the edge count of that node. Hence, G.degree(n) returns the friend count associated with user n.

We have an initial training set in place. Let's check the quality of the signal in that set by training and testing a simple model. We have multiple possible models to choose from. One sensible choice is a decision tree classifier; decision trees can handle nonlinear decision boundaries and are easily interpretable. On the downside, they are prone to overtraining, so cross-validation will be required to measure model performance appropriately. Listing 23.21 trains a decision tree on a subset of (X, y) and evaluates the results on the remaining data. During the evaluation, we should keep in mind that our Class 2 labels are highly imbalanced. Thus, the f-measure metric will provide a more reasonable assessment of performance than simple accuracy.

> **NOTE**   Through the remainder of this section, we repeatedly train and test our classifier models. Listing 23.21 defines an evaluate function for this purpose that takes as input a training set (X, y) and a model type preset to DecisionTreeClassifier. The function then splits X, y into training and test sets, trains the classifier, and computes an f-measure using the test set. Finally, it returns both the f-measure and the classifier for evaluation.

Listing 23.21   Training and evaluating a decision tree classifier

```
from sklearn.tree import DecisionTreeClassifier
from sklearn.model_selection import train_test_split
from sklearn.metrics import f1_score
```

```
def evaluate(X, y, model_type=DecisionTreeClassifier, **kwargs):
    np.random.seed(0)
    X_train, X_test, y_train, y_test = train_test_split(X, y)
    clf = model_type(**kwargs)
    clf.fit(X_train, y_train)
    pred = clf.predict(X_test)
    f_measure = f1_score(pred, y_test, average='macro')
    return f_measure, clf

f_measure, clf = evaluate(X, y)
print(f"The f-measure is {f_measure:0.2f}")
```

```
The f-measure is 0.37
```

This random seed value ensures that (X, y) is split consistently from run to run.

Trains the model

Splits (X, y) into training and test sets

Computes an f-measure. The average='macro' parameter is required because three class labels are present in the training data.

We'll repeatedly utilize this function over the remainder of this section. It trains a classifier on a subsample of data in (X, y). The classifier type is specified using the model_type parameter: here, the parameter is preset to a decision tree classifier. Additional classifier hyperparameters can be specified using **kwargs. After training, the classifier's performance is evaluated using a retained subset of the data.

Our f-measure is terrible! Clearly, the edge count by itself is not sufficient for predicting user behavior. Perhaps a more sophisticated measure of node centrality is required. Earlier, we learned how the PageRank centrality measure can be more informative than edge count. Would adding PageRank values to our training set improve model performance? Let's find out.

Listing 23.22 Adding PageRank features

```
node_to_pagerank = nx.pagerank(G)
features = {f'{col}_PageRank': [] for col in cols}
for node_ids in df_obs[cols].values:
    for node, feature_name in zip(node_ids, features.keys()):
        pagerank = node_to_pagerank[node]
        features[feature_name].append(pagerank)

def update_features(new_features):
    for feature_name, values in new_features.items():
        df_features[feature_name] = values
    return df_features.values

X = update_features(features)
f_measure, clf = evaluate(X, y)

print(f"The f-measure is {f_measure:0.2f}")
```

This function is utilized repeatedly. It updates the df_features Pandas table with novel features in the new_features dictionary.

Returns the altered feature matrix

```
The f-measure is 0.38
```

The f-measure remains approximately the same. Basic centrality measures are insufficient. We need to expand X to include the social groups uncovered by Markov clustering. After all, two people in the same social group are more likely to be friends. How do we incorporate these social groups into the feature matrix? Well, naively, we could assign the `cluster_id` attribute of each referenced node as our social group feature. However, this approach has a serious downside: our current cluster IDs are only relevant to the specific social graph in `G`. They are not at all relevant to any other college network. In other words, a model trained on the cluster IDs in `G` is not applicable to some other college graph in `G_other`. This won't do! One of our goals is to construct a model that is generalizable across other colleges. Thus, we need a more nuanced solution.

One alternate approach is just to consider the following binary question: are two people in the same social group? If they are, then perhaps they are more likely to eventually become friends on FriendHook. We can make this binary comparison between each pair of profile IDs in a single row of observations. More precisely, we can ask the following:

- Does the user in the *Profile_ID* column fall in the same social group as the friend in the *Friend* column? We'll name this feature *Shared_Cluster_id_f*.
- Does the user in the *Profile_ID* column fall in the same social group as the friend of a friend in the *FoF* column? We'll name this feature *Shared_Cluster_id_fof*.
- Does the friend in the *Friend* column fall in the same social group as the friend of a friend in the *FoF* column? We'll name this feature *Shared_Cluster_f_fof*.

Let's answer these three questions by adding the three additional features. Then we test whether these features yield improved model performance.

Listing 23.23   Adding social group features

```
features = {f'Shared_Cluster_{e}': []
            for e in ['id_f', 'id_fof', 'f_fof']}

i = 0
for node_ids in df_obs[cols].values:
    c_id, c_f, c_fof = [G.nodes[n]['cluster_id']
                        for n in node_ids]
    features['Shared_Cluster_id_f'].append(int(c_id == c_f))
    features['Shared_Cluster_id_fof'].append(int(c_id == c_fof))
    features['Shared_Cluster_f_fof'].append(int(c_f == c_fof))

X = update_features(features)
f_measure, clf = evaluate(X, y)
print(f"The f-measure is {f_measure:0.2f}")

The f-measure is 0.43
```

Our f-measure has improved from 0.38 to 0.43. Performance is still poor, but the social group inclusion has led to a slight enhancement of our model. How important are the new social group features relative to the model's current performance? We can check using the `feature_importance_` attribute of our trained classifier.

Listing 23.24   **Ranking features by their importance score**

```
def view_top_features(clf, feature_names):
    for i in np.argsort(clf.feature_importances_)[::-1]:
        feature_name = feature_names[i]
        importance = clf.feature_importances_[i]
        if not round(importance, 2):
            break

        print(f"{feature_name}: {importance:0.2f}")
feature_names = df_features.columns
view_top_features(clf, feature_names)
```

Sorts the features based on importance score →

← **Prints the top features along with their importance scores in the classifier based on order of importance**

← **Features with an importance score of less than 0.01 are not displayed.**

```
Shared_Cluster_id_fof: 0.18
FoF_PageRank: 0.17
Profile_ID_PageRank: 0.17
Friend_PageRank: 0.15
FoF_Edge_Count: 0.12
Profile_ID_Edge_Count: 0.11
Friend_Edge_Count: 0.10
```

The *Shared_Cluster_id_fof* feature is the most important feature in the model. In other words, the social group overlap between the user and the friend of a friend is the most important predictor of a future online friendship. However, the PageRank features also rank highly on the list, which indicates that social graph centrality plays some role in friendship determination. Of course, our model's performance is still poor, so we should be cautious with our inferences about how the features drive predictions. Instead, we should focus on improving model performance. What other graph-based features could we utilize? Perhaps the network cluster size can impact the predictions. We can find out, but we should be careful about trying to keep our model generalizable. Cluster size can inexplicably take the place of a cluster ID, making the model very specific to the university. Let's explore how this could occur.

Suppose our dataset has two social clusters, A and B. The clusters contain 110 and 115 students, respectively. Thus, their sizes are nearly identical and should not drive prediction. Now, let's further suppose the students in Cluster A are more likely to become FriendHook friends than students in Cluster B. Our model would pick up on this during training and associate a size of 110 with a propensity for friendship. Essentially, it would treat the size like a cluster ID! This could cause trouble in the future if the model encountered a brand-new cluster with size 110.

So should we ignore cluster size altogether? Not necessarily. We are scientists, and we wish to honestly explore how cluster size impacts model prediction. But we should be very cautious: if cluster size has minimal impact on model quality, we should delete it from our features. However, if the size drastically improves model prediction, we will cautiously reevaluate our options. Let's test what happens when we add cluster size to our list of features.

Listing 23.25   Adding cluster-size features

```
cluster_sizes = [len(cluster) for cluster in clusters]
features = {f'{col}_Cluster_Size': [] for col in cols}
for node_ids in df_obs[cols].values:
    for node, feature_name in zip(node_ids, features.keys()):
        c_id = G.nodes[node]['cluster_id']
        features[feature_name].append(cluster_sizes[c_id])

X = update_features(features)
f_measure, clf = evaluate(X, y)
print(f"The f-measure is {f_measure:0.2f}")


The f-measure is 0.43
```

The cluster size did not improve the model. As a precaution, let's delete it from our feature set.

Listing 23.26   Deleting cluster-size features

Deletes all feature names in df_features that match the regex
regular expression. It is utilized elsewhere in this section.

```
import re
def delete_features(df_features, regex=r'Cluster_Size'):      ◁

    df_features.drop(columns=[name for name in df_features.columns
                              if re.search(regex, name)], inplace=True)
    return df_features.values      ◁          Returns the
                                              altered feature
X = delete_features(df_features)              matrix
```

The f-measure remains at 0.43. What else can we do? Perhaps we should try thinking outside the box. In what ways can social connections drive real-world behavior? Are there additional, problem-specific signals we can harness? Yes! Consider the following scenario. Suppose we analyze a student named Alex, whose node ID in network G is n. Alex has 50 FriendHook friends, who are accessible through G[n]. We randomly sample two of the friends in G[n]. Their node IDs are a and b. We then check if a and b are friends. They are! It seems that a is in list(G[n]). We then repeat this 100 times. In 95% of sampled instances, a is a friend of b. Basically, there's a 95% likelihood that any pair of Alex's friends are also friends with each other. We'll refer to this probability as the *friend-sharing likelihood*. Now, Mary is new to FriendHook. She just joined and added Alex as her friend. We can be fairly confident that Mary will also connect with Alex's friends—though of course this is not guaranteed. But a friend-sharing likelihood of 0.95 gives us more confidence than a likelihood of 0.10.

Let's try incorporating this likelihood into our features. We start by computing the likelihood for every node in G. We store the node-to-likelihood mapping in a friend_sharing_likelihood dictionary.

Listing 23.27 Computing friend-sharing likelihoods

```
friend_sharing_likelihood = {}
for node in nodes:
    neighbors = list(G[node])
    friendship_count = 0
    total_possible = 0
    for i, node1 in enumerate(neighbors[:-1]):
        for node2 in neighbors[i + 1:]:
            if node1 in G[node2]:
                friendship_count += 1

            total_possible += 1

    prob = friendship_count / total_possible if total_possible else 0
    friend_sharing_likelihood[node] = prob
```

- **Tracks the count of shared friendships across neighbors**
- **Tracks the total possible shared friendships. Note that with a bit of graph theory, we could prove this value always equals len(neighbors) * (len(neighbors - 1)).**
- **Checks if two neighbors are friends**

Next, we generate a friend-sharing likelihood feature for each of our three profile IDs. After adding the features, we reevaluate the trained model's performance.

Listing 23.28 Adding friend-sharing likelihood features

```
features = {f'{col}_Friend_Sharing_Likelihood': [] for col in cols}
for node_ids in df_obs[cols].values:
    for node, feature_name in zip(node_ids, features.keys()):
        sharing_likelihood = friend_sharing_likelihood[node]
        features[feature_name].append(sharing_likelihood)

X = update_features(features)
f_measure, clf = evaluate(X, y)
print(f"The f-measure is {f_measure:0.2f}")

The f-measure is 0.49
```

Performance has increased from 0.43 to 0.49! It's still not great, but it's progressively getting better. How does the friend-sharing likelihood compare to other features in the model? Let's find out.

Listing 23.29 Ranking features by their importance score

```
feature_names = df_features.columns
view_top_features(clf, feature_names)

Shared_Cluster_id_fof: 0.18
Friend_Friend_Sharing_Likelihood: 0.13
FoF_PageRank: 0.11
Profile_ID_PageRank: 0.11
Profile_ID_Friend_Sharing_Likelihood: 0.10
FoF_Friend_Sharing_Likelihood: 0.10
FoF_Edge_Count: 0.08
Friend_PageRank: 0.07
Profile_ID_Edge_Count: 0.07
Friend_Edge_Count: 0.06
```

One of our new friend-sharing features ranks quite highly: it's in second place, between `Shared_Cluster_id_fof` and `FoF_PageRank`. Our outside-the-box thinking has improved the model. But the model is incomplete. An f-measure of 0.49 is not acceptable; we need to do better. It's time to move beyond network structure. We need to incorporate features from the profiles stored in `df_profiles`.

23.3   *Adding profile features to the model*

Our aim is to incorporate the profile attributes `Sex`, `Relationship_Status`, `Major`, `Dorm`, and `Year` into our feature matrix. Based on our experience with the network data, there are three ways in which we can do this:

- *Exact value extraction*—We can store the exact value of the profile feature associated with each of the three profile ID columns in `df_obs`. This is analogous to how we utilized the exact values of edge counts and PageRank outputs from the network.

  Example feature: The relationship status of the friend of a friend in `df_obs`.

- *Equivalence comparison*—Given a profile attribute, we can carry out a pairwise comparison of the attribute across all three profile ID columns in `df_obs`. For each comparison, we return a Boolean feature demarcating whether the attribute is equal in the two columns. This is analogous to how we checked whether a profile pair belonged to the same social group.

  Example feature: Do a particular user and a friend of a friend live in the same dorm? Yes or no?

- *Size*—Given a profile attribute, we can return the number of profiles that share that attribute. This is analogous to the attempted inclusion of social group size in our model.

  Example feature: The number of students residing in a particular dorm.

Let's utilize exact value extraction to expand our feature matrix. Which of our five attributes are good candidates for this technique? Well, the categorical values of `Sex`, `Relationship_Status`, and `Year` are not college-dependent; they should remain consistent across all colleges and universities. This is not the case for `Dorm`—dormitory names will change in other college networks. Our goal is to train a model that can be applied to other social graphs, so the `Dorm` attribute is not a valid feature for exact value extraction.

What about the `Major` attribute? Here, the situation is trickier. Certain majors like biology and economics are shared by most colleges and universities. Other majors, like civil engineering, might appear at more technically oriented schools but not on a liberal arts college curriculum. And certain rare majors like bagpiping or astrobiology are specific to a few niche schools. Thus, we can expect some consistency across majors but not total consistency. A model harnessing the exact values of the majors will therefore be partially reusable; potentially, that partial signal could boost predictive power at some schools, but this would happen at the expense of other schools. Is the trade-off worth it? Perhaps. The answer is not immediately clear. For the time being, let's see how well we can train our model without relying on the added crutch of Major values. If we find ourselves unable to train an adequate model, we will revisit our decision.

Let's now apply exact value extraction to Sex, Relationship_Status, and Year and then check for improvements in our model.

Listing 23.30 Adding exact value profile features

```
attributes = ['Sex', 'Relationship_Status', 'Year']
for attribute in attributes:
    features = {f'{col}_{attribute}_Value': [] for col in cols}
    for node_ids in df_obs[cols].values:
        for node, feature_name in zip(node_ids, features.keys()):
            att_value = G.nodes[node][attribute]
            features[feature_name].append(att_value)

    X = update_features(features)

f_measure, clf = evaluate(X, y)
print(f"The f-measure is {f_measure:0.2f}")

The f-measure is 0.74
```

Wow! The f-measure dramatically increased from 0.49 to 0.74! The profile features have provided a very valuable signal, but we can still do better. We need to incorporate information from the Major and Dorm attributes. Equivalence comparison is an excellent way to do this. The question of whether two students share the same major or dorm is independent of their university. Let's apply the equivalence comparison to the Major and Dorm attributes and then recompute the f-measure.

Listing 23.31 Adding equivalence comparison profile features

```
attributes = ['Major', 'Dorm']
for attribute in attributes:
    features = {f'Shared_{attribute}_{e}': []
                for e in ['id_f', 'id_fof', 'f_fof']}

    for node_ids in df_obs[cols].values:
        att_id, att_f, att_fof = [G.nodes[n][attribute]
                                    for n in node_ids]
        features[f'Shared_{attribute}_id_f'].append(int(att_id == att_f))
        features[f'Shared_{attribute}_id_fof'].append(int(att_id == att_fof))
        features[f'Shared_{attribute}_f_fof'].append(int(att_f == att_fof))

    X = update_features(features)

f_measure, clf = evaluate(X, y)
print(f"The f-measure is {f_measure:0.2f}")

The f-measure is 0.82
```

The f-measure has risen to 0.82. Incorporating the `Major` and `Dorm` attributes has improved model performance. Now let's consider adding `Major` and `Dorm` size into the mix: we can count the number of students associated with each major and dorm and include this count as one of our features. But we need to be careful; as we previously discussed, our trained model can cheat by utilizing size as a substitute for a category ID. For instance, as we've previously seen, our largest dormitory holds over 2,700 students. Thus, we can easily identify that dorm based on its size alone. We must be cautious going forward. Let's see what happens when we incorporate `Major` and `Dorm` size into our features. If there's little impact on performance, we'll delete the features from our model. Otherwise, we'll reevaluate our options.

> **Listing 23.32 Adding size-related profile features**

```
from collections import Counter

for attribute in ['Major', 'Dorm']:
    counter = Counter(df_profile[attribute].values)
    att_to_size = {k: v
                   for k, v in counter.items()}
    features = {f'{col}_{attribute}_Size': [] for col in cols}
    for node_ids in df_obs[cols].values:
        for node, feature_name in zip(node_ids, features.keys()):
            size = att_to_size[G.nodes[node][attribute]]
            features[feature_name].append(size)



    X = update_features(features)

f_measure, clf = evaluate(X, y)
print(f"The f-measure is {f_measure:0.2f}")


The f-measure is 0.85
```

Tracks the number of times each attribute appears in our dataset

Performance has increased from 0.82 to 0.85. The introduction of size has impacted our model. Let's dive deeper into that impact. We start by printing out the feature importance scores.

> **Listing 23.33 Ranking features by their importance score**

```
feature_names = df_features.columns.values
view_top_features(clf, feature_names)


FoF_Dorm_Size: 0.25
Shared_Cluster_id_fof: 0.16
Shared_Dorm_id_fof: 0.05
FoF_PageRank: 0.04
Profile_ID_Major_Size: 0.04
FoF_Major_Size: 0.04
FoF_Edge_Count: 0.04
Profile_ID_PageRank: 0.03
Profile_ID_Friend_Sharing_Likelihood: 0.03
```

```
Friend_Friend_Sharing_Likelihood: 0.03
Friend_Edge_Count: 0.03
Shared_Major_id_fof: 0.03
FoF_Friend_Sharing_Likelihood: 0.02
Friend_PageRank: 0.02
Profile_ID_Dorm_Size: 0.02
Profile_ID_Edge_Count: 0.02
Profile_ID_Sex_Value: 0.02
Friend_Major_Size: 0.02
Profile_ID_Relationship_Status_Value: 0.02
FoF_Sex_Value: 0.01
Friend_Dorm_Size: 0.01
Profile_ID_Year_Value: 0.01
Friend_Sex_Value: 0.01
Shared_Major_id_f: 0.01
Friend_Relationship_Status_Value: 0.01
Friend_Year_Value: 0.01
```

The feature importance scores are dominated by two features: *FoF_Dorm_Size* and *Shared_Cluster_id_fof*. These two features have importance scores of 0.25 and 0.16, respectively. All other feature scores fall below 0.01.

The presence of *FoF_Dorm_Size* is a bit concerning. As we've discussed, a single dorm dominates 50% of the network data. Is our model simply memorizing that dorm based on its size? We can find out by visualizing a trained decision tree. For simplicity's sake, we limit the tree to a depth of 2, to limit our output to just those decisions driven by the two most dominant features.

Listing 23.34 Displaying the top branches of the tree

```
from sklearn.tree import export_text

clf_depth2 = DecisionTreeClassifier(max_depth=2)
clf_depth2.fit(X, y)
text_tree = export_text(clf_depth2, feature_names=list(feature_names))
print(text_tree)
```

The export_text function has trouble taking NumPy arrays as input, so we convert feature_names to a list.

```
|--- FoF_Dorm_Size <= 278.50
|   |--- Shared_Cluster_id_fof <= 0.50
|   |   |--- class: 0
|   |--- Shared_Cluster_id_fof >  0.50
|   |   |--- class: 0
|--- FoF_Dorm_Size >  278.50
|   |--- Shared_Cluster_id_fof <= 0.50
|   |   |--- class: 0
|   |--- Shared_Cluster_id_fof >  0.50
|   |   |--- class: 1
```

Friend-of-a-friend dorm size is less than 279. Under these circumstances, the most likely class label is 0 (friend suggestion ignored).

Friend-of-a-friend dorm size is >= 279.

Friend of a friend and user are not in the same social group. The most likely class label is 0.

Friend of a friend and user share the same social group. The most likely class label is 1 (FriendHook connection established).

According to the tree, the most important signal is whether *FoF_Dorm_Size* is less than 279. If the friend of a friend's dormitory holds fewer than 279 students, then the FoF and the user are unlikely to become FriendHook friends. Otherwise, they are more likely to connect if they already share the same social group (`Shared_Cluster_id_fof > 0.50`). This begs the question, how many dorms contain at least 279 students? Let's check.

Listing 23.35   Checking dorms with at least 279 students

```
counter = Counter(df_profile.Dorm.values)
for dorm, count in counter.items():
    if count < 279:
        continue

    print(f"Dorm {dorm} holds {count} students.")

Dorm 12 holds 2739 students.
Dorm 1 holds 413 students.
```

Just two of the 15 dorms contain more than 279 FriendHook-registered students. Essentially, our model relies on the two most populous dorms to make its decisions. This puts us in a bind: on the one hand, the observed signal is very interesting; Friend-Hook connections are more likely to occur in some dorms than others. Dorm size plays a factor in these connections. This insight could allow FriendHook developers to better understand user behavior, and perhaps this understanding will lead to better user engagement. We are better off having gained this knowledge. However, our current model has a serious downside.

Our model focuses mostly on the two largest dorms in the data. This focus may not generalize to other college campuses. For instance, consider a campus whose dormitories are smaller and hold 200 students at most. The model will completely fail to predict user behavior in this instance.

> **NOTE**   Theoretically, this situation can be avoided if we divide the dorm size by the total student count. This will ensure that the dorm-size feature always lies between 0 and 1.

More worryingly, we're dealing with the very real possibility that our model simply picked up on behavior that's unique to just these two specific dorms. This is exactly the type of scenario we were asked to avoid in the problem statement. What should we do?

Unfortunately, there is no explicit correct answer. Sometimes data scientists are forced to make difficult decisions, where each decision carries risks and trade-offs. We can keep our feature list as is to maintain high model performance, but we run the risk of not being able to generalize to other schools. Alternatively, we can remove size-related features and keep our model generalizable at the expense of overall performance.

Perhaps there's a third option: we can try deleting the size-related features while also adjusting our choice of classifier. There is a slight chance that we'll achieve comparable performance without relying on dorm size. This is unlikely but still worth trying. Let's assign a copy of the current feature matrix to variable X_with_sizes (in case we need it later) and then delete all size-related features from matrix X. We'll then look for other ways to boost our f-measure beyond 0.82.

Listing 23.36 Deleting all size-related features

```
X_with_sizes = X.copy()
X = delete_features(df_features, regex=r'_Size')
```

23.4 *Optimizing performance across a steady set of features*

In section 22, we learned how random forest models tend to outperform decision trees. Will switching the model type from a decision tree to a random forest improve performance? Let's find out.

Listing 23.37 Training and evaluating a random forest classifier

```
from sklearn.ensemble import RandomForestClassifier
f_measure, clf = evaluate(X, y, model_type=RandomForestClassifier)
print(f"The f-measure is {f_measure:0.2f}")

The f-measure is 0.75
```

Oh no! The performance has actually gotten worse! How can this be? Well, it's an established fact that random forests usually outperform decision trees, but this does not guarantee that random forests will always perform better. In certain training instances, decision trees are superior to random forests. This appears to be one such instance. For our particular dataset, we cannot improve predictive performance by switching to a random forest model.

> **NOTE** In supervised machine learning, there's a well-established theorem known as the *No Free Lunch Theorem*. In layman's terms, the theorem states the following: it is impossible for a certain training algorithm to always outperform all other algorithms. In other words, we cannot rely on a single algorithm for every type of training problem. An algorithm that works great most of the time will not work great all of the time. Random forests perform well on most problems but not on all problems. In particular, random forests perform poorly when prediction depends on just one or two inputted features. Random feature sampling can dilute that signal and worsen the quality of predictions.

Switching the type of model has not helped. Perhaps instead we can boost performance by optimizing on the hyperparameters. In this book, we've focused on a single decision tree hyperparameter: maximum depth. Currently, maximum depth is set to None. This means the tree's depth is not restricted. Will limiting the depth improve our predictions? Let's quickly check using a simple grid search. We scan across the `max_depth` parameter values that range from 1 to 100 and settle on the depth that optimizes performance.

Listing 23.38   Optimizing maximum depth using a grid search

```
from sklearn.model_selection import GridSearchCV
np.random.seed(0)

hyperparams = {'max_depth': list(range(1, 100)) + [None]}
clf_grid = GridSearchCV(DecisionTreeClassifier(), hyperparams,
                        scoring='f1_macro', cv=2)        ◁
clf_grid.fit(X, y)
best_f = clf_grid.best_score_
best_depth = clf_grid.best_params_['max_depth']
print(f"A maximized f-measure of {best_f:.2f} is achieved when "
      f"max_depth equals {best_depth}")


A maximized f-measure of 0.84 is achieved when max_depth equals 5
```

> **By passing cv=2, we carry out two-fold cross-validation to be more consistent with our current random splitting of (X, y) into training and test datasets. Note that the grid search could split our data slightly differently, leading to fluctuations in the f-measure value.**

Setting `max_depth` to 5 improves the f-measure from 0.82 to 0.84. This level of performance is comparable with our dorm-size-dependent model. Thus, we have achieved performance parity without relying on dorm size. Of course, the story is not over: we cannot make a fair comparison without first running a grid search on the size-inclusive `X_with_sizes` feature matrix. Will optimizing on `X_with_sizes` yield an even better classifier? Let's find out.

NOTE A curious reader may wonder whether our random forest output could be improved by running a grid search on the number of trees. In this particular instance, the answer is no. Altering the tree count from 100 to some other number will not significantly improve performance.

Listing 23.39   Applying a grid search to size-dependent training data

```
np.random.seed(0)
clf_grid.fit(X_with_sizes, y)
best_f = clf_grid.best_score_
best_depth = clf_grid.best_params_['max_depth']
print(f"A maximized f-measure of {best_f:.2f} is achieved when "
      f"max_depth equals {best_depth}")


A maximized f-measure of 0.85 is achieved when max_depth equals 6
```

The grid search did not improve performance on `X_with_sizes`. Thus, we can conclude that with the right choice of maximum depth, the size-dependent and size-independent models perform with approximately equal quality, and we can train a generalizable, size-independent model without sacrificing performance. That's great news! Let's train a decision tree on X using a `max_depth` of 5 and then explore the real-world implications of our model.

Listing 23.40   Training a decision tree with `max_depth` set to 5

```
clf = DecisionTreeClassifier(max_depth=5)
clf.fit(X, y)
```

23.5   *Interpreting the trained model*

Let's print our model's feature importance scores.

Listing 23.41   Ranking features by their importance score

```
feature_names = df_features.columns
view_top_features(clf, feature_names)

Shared_Dorm_id_fof: 0.42
Shared_Cluster_id_fof: 0.29
Shared_Major_id_fof: 0.10
Shared_Dorm_f_fof: 0.06
Profile_ID_Relationship_Status_Value: 0.04
Profile_ID_Sex_Value: 0.04
Friend_Edge_Count: 0.02
Friend_PageRank: 0.01
Shared_Dorm_id_f: 0.01
```

Only nine important features remain. The top four features pertain to shared dorms, social groups, and majors. They are followed by features demarcating the category of a user's *Sex* and *Relationship Status*. Simple network features like edge count and PageRank appear at the very bottom of the list. Interestingly enough, our friend-sharing likelihood feature doesn't even make the list! This abandoned feature required effort and imagination to implement. It was satisfying to see the f-measure rise by 0.06 units once the friend-sharing likelihood was added. But in the end, that effort did not matter. With enough additional features, the friend-sharing likelihood was rendered irrelevant. Such experiences can sometimes feel frustrating. Unfortunately, feature selection is still less of a science and more of an art; it is difficult to know in advance which features to use and which features to avoid. We cannot know how a feature will integrate holistically into a model until we actually train the model. This does not mean we shouldn't get creative—creativity usually pays off. As scientists, we should experiment! We should try to use every possible signal at our disposal until adequate performance is achieved.

Let's return to our top features. Only three features have an importance score at or above 0.10: *Shared_Dorm_id_fof*, *Shared_Cluster_id_fof*, and *Shared_Major_id_fof*. Thus, the model is primarily driven by the following three questions:

- Do the user and the friend of a friend share a dormitory? Yes or no?
- Do the user and the friend of a friend share a social group? Yes or no?
- Do the user and the friend of a friend share a major? Yes or no?

Intuitively, if the answers to all three questions are yes, then the user and the friend of a friend are more likely to connect on FriendHook. Let's test this intuition by displaying the tree. We'll limit the tree's depth to 3 to simplify our output while ensuring that the top three features are represented appropriately.

Listing 23.42   Displaying the top branches of the tree

```
clf_depth3 = DecisionTreeClassifier(max_depth=3)
clf_depth3.fit(X, y)
text_tree = export_text(clf_depth3,
                        feature_names=list(feature_names))
print(text_tree)
```

```
|--- Shared_Dorm_id_fof <= 0.50
|   |--- Shared_Cluster_id_fof <= 0.50
|   |   |--- Shared_Major_id_fof <= 0.50
|   |   |   |--- class: 0
|   |   |--- Shared_Major_id_fof >  0.50
|   |   |   |--- class: 0
|   |--- Shared_Cluster_id_fof >  0.50
|   |   |--- Shared_Major_id_fof <= 0.50
|   |   |   |--- class: 0
|   |   |--- Shared_Major_id_fof >  0.50
|   |   |   |--- class: 1
|--- Shared_Dorm_id_fof >  0.50
|   |--- Shared_Cluster_id_fof <= 0.50
|   |   |--- Profile_ID_Sex_Value <= 0.50
|   |   |   |--- class: 0
|   |   |--- Profile_ID_Sex_Value >  0.50
|   |   |   |--- class: 2
|   |--- Shared_Cluster_id_fof >  0.50
|   |   |--- Shared_Dorm_f_fof <= 0.50
|   |   |   |--- class: 1
|   |   |--- Shared_Dorm_f_fof >  0.50
|   |   |   |--- class: 1
```

The user and the friend of a friend do not share a dormitory.

The user and the friend of a friend do not share a social group. Under these circumstances, the friend suggestion is ignored (Class 0 dominates).

The user and the friend of a friend share a dormitory.

In this branch, Class 2 dominates, and the Sex feature drives Class 2 prediction. We'll soon investigate this unexpected result.

The user and the friend of a friend share a social group. Under these circumstances, the FriendHook connection is likely (Class 1 dominates).

As expected, dorm and social-group sharing primarily drive the model's predictions. If the user and friend of a friend share both a dorm and a social group, they are more likely to connect. If they share neither a dorm nor a social group, they are less likely to connect. Additionally, individuals can connect if they fall in the same social group and share the same major, even if not the same dorm.

NOTE   The text representation of the tree lacks the exact count of class labels at each tree branch. As we discussed in section 22, we can produce these counts by calling `plot_tree(clf_depth3, feature_names=list(feature_names))`. For brevity's sake, we don't generate the tree plot, but you're encouraged to try this visualization. In the visualized tree statistics, you should see that the user and the *FoF* share both a cluster and a dorm in 1,635 instances; 93% of these instances represent Class 1 labels. Also, you'll observe that the user and the *FoF* share neither cluster nor dorm in 356 instances; 97%

of these instances represent Class 0 labels. Thus, social group and dorm sharing are strong predictors of user behavior.

We are nearly ready to deliver to our employer a model based on social groups, dorms, and majors. The model's logic is very straightforward: users who share social groups and living spaces or study schedules are more likely to connect. There's nothing surprising about that. What is surprising is how the *Sex* feature drives Class 2 label prediction. As a reminder, the Class 2 label corresponds to a rejected FriendHook request. According to our tree, rejection is more likely when

- The users share a dorm but are not in the same social group.
- The request sender is of a certain specific sex.

Of course, we know that Class 2 labels are fairly sparse in our data. They occur just 1.2% of the time. Perhaps the model's predictions are caused by random noise arising from the sparse sampling. We can find out. Let's quickly check how well we predict rejection. We'll execute evaluate on (X, y_reject) where y_reject[i] equals 2 if y[i] equals 2, and equals 0 otherwise. In other words, we'll evaluate a model that only predicts rejection. If that model's f-measure is low, then our predictions are driven primarily by random noise.

Listing 23.43   Evaluating a rejection classifier

```
y_reject = y * (y == 2)
f_measure, clf_reject = evaluate(X, y_reject, max_depth=5)
print(f"The f-measure is {f_measure:0.2f}")

The f-measure is 0.97
```

Wow, the f-measure is actually very high! We can predict rejection very well, despite the sparsity of data. What features drive rejection? Let's check by printing the new feature importance scores.

Listing 23.44   Ranking features by their importance score

```
view_top_features(clf_reject, feature_names)

Profile_ID_Sex_Value: 0.40
Profile_ID_Relationship_Status_Value: 0.24
Shared_Major_id_fof: 0.21
Shared_Cluster_id_fof: 0.10
Shared_Dorm_id_fof: 0.05
```

Interesting! Rejection is primarily driven by the user's Sex and Relationship_Status attributes. Let's visualize the trained tree to learn more.

Listing 23.45   Displaying the rejection-predicting tree

```
text_tree = export_text(clf_reject,
                        feature_names=list(feature_names))
print(text_tree)
```

```
|--- Shared_Cluster_id_fof <= 0.50              ◁───┐ The user and the friend
|    |--- Shared_Major_id_fof <= 0.50                │ of a friend do not share
|    |    |--- Shared_Dorm_id_fof <= 0.50            │ a social group.
|    |    |    |--- class: 0
|    |    |    |--- Shared_Dorm_id_fof >  0.50
|    |    |    |    |--- Profile_ID_Relationship_Status_Value <= 2.50
|    |    |    |    |    |--- class: 0
|    |    |    |    |--- Profile_ID_Relationship_Status_Value >  2.50   ◁──────┐
|    |    |    |    |    |--- Profile_ID_Sex_Value <= 0.50
|    |    |    |    |    |    |--- class: 0
|    |    |    |    |    |--- Profile_ID_Sex_Value >  0.50
|    |    |    |    |    |    |--- class: 2
|    |--- Shared_Major_id_fof >  0.50
|    |    |--- Profile_ID_Sex_Value <= 0.50
|    |    |    |--- class: 0
|    |    |--- Profile_ID_Sex_Value >  0.50
|    |    |    |--- Profile_ID_Relationship_Status_Value <= 2.50
|    |    |    |    |--- class: 0
|    |    |    |--- Profile_ID_Relationship_Status_Value >  2.50
|    |    |    |    |--- class: 2
|--- Shared_Cluster_id_fof >  0.50              ◁───┐
|    |--- class: 0
```

The user's relationship status is equal to 3. If the user's sex is equal to 1, rejection (Class 2) is likely, so rejection is dependent on a user's sex and relationship status.

The user and the friend of a friend share a social group. Under such circumstances, rejection is unlikely.

According to the tree, rejection is likely to occur under the following circumstances:

- The users do not belong to the same social group.
- The users share either a dorm or a major.
- The sender's sex is Category 1.
- The sender's relationship status is Category 3. According to the tree, the status category must be greater than 2.5. However, the maximum value of df_Profile .Relationship_Status is 3.

Essentially, individuals with *Sex* Category 1 and *Relationship Status* Category 3 are sending friend requests to people outside their social group. These friend requests are likely to get rejected. Of course, we cannot precisely identify the categories that lead to rejection, but as scientists, we can still speculate. Given what we know about human nature, it wouldn't be surprising if this behavior is driven by single men. Perhaps men are trying to connect with women outside their social group to get a date; if so, their requests are likely to be rejected. Again, all this is speculation, but this hypothesis is worth discussing with the product managers at FriendHook. If our hypothesis is correct, then certain changes should be introduced to the product. More steps could be taken to limit unwanted dating requests. Alternatively, new product changes could be added that make it easier for single people to connect.

23.5.1   *Why are generalizable models so important?*

In this case study, we have agonized over keeping our model generalizable. A model that does not generalize beyond the training set is worthless, even if the performance score seems high. Unfortunately, it's hard to know whether a model can generalize until it's tested on external data. But we can try to remain aware of hidden biases that won't generalize well to other datasets. Failure to do so can yield serious consequences. Consider the following true story.

For many years, machine learning researchers have tried to automate the field of radiology. In radiology, trained doctors examine medical images (such as X-rays) to diagnose disease. This can be treated as a supervised learning problem in which the images are features and the diagnoses are class labels. By the year 2016, multiple radiology models were published in the scientific literature. Each published model was supposed to be highly accurate based on internal evaluation. That year, leading machine learning researchers publicly declared that "we should stop training radiologists" and that "radiologists should be worried about their jobs." Four years later, the negative publicity had led to a worldwide radiologist shortage—medical students were reluctant to enter a field that seemed destined for full automation. But by 2020, the promise of automation had failed to materialize. Most of the published models performed very poorly on new data. Why? Well, it turns out that imaging outputs differ from hospital to hospital. Different hospitals use slightly different lighting and different settings on their imaging machines. Thus, a model trained at Hospital A could not generalize well to Hospital B. Despite their seemingly high performance scores, the models were not fit for generalized use. The machine learning researchers had been too optimistic; they failed to take into account the biases inherent in their data. These failures inadvertently led to a crisis in the medical community. A more thoughtful evaluation of generalizability could have prevented this from happening.

Summary

- Superior machine learning algorithms do not necessarily work in every situation. Our decision tree model outperformed our random forest model, even though random forests are considered superior in the literature. We should never blindly assume that a model will always work well in every possible scenario. Instead, we should intelligently calibrate our model choice based on the specifics of the problem.

- Proper feature selection is less of a science and more of an art. We cannot always know in advance which features will boost a model's performance. However, the commonsense integration of diverse and interesting features into our model should eventually improve prediction quality.

- We should pay careful attention to the features we feed into our model. Otherwise, the model may not generalize to other datasets.

- Proper hyperparameter optimization can sometimes significantly boost a model's performance.

- Occasionally, it seems like nothing is working and our data is simply insufficient. However, with grit and perseverance, we can eventually yield meaningful resources. Remember, a good data scientist should never give up until they have exhausted every possible avenue of analysis.

index